Statistics for Management

ANAND SHARMA
B.E. (Mech.), Osmania Univ.
M.Tech. (Industrial Engg.) - IIT Delhi
Fellow, Indian Institution of Industrial Engineering

Himalaya Publishing House
ISO 9001:2015 CERTIFIED

First Edition : 2006
Second Revised Edition : 2008
Edition : 2009, 2015, 2017
Edition : 2019

Published by : Mrs. Meena Pandey for **Himalaya Publishing House Pvt. Ltd.,**
"Ramdoot", Dr. Bhalerao Marg, Girgaon, **Mumbai - 400 004.**
Phone: 022-23860170/23863863, Fax: 022-23877178
E-mail: himpub@vsnl.com; Website: www.himpub.com

Branch Offices :

New Delhi : "Pooja Apartments", 4-B, Murari Lal Street, Ansari Road, Darya Ganj, New Delhi - 110 002. Phone: 011-23270392, 23278631; Fax: 011-23256286

Nagpur : Kundanlal Chandak Industrial Estate, Ghat Road, Nagpur - 440 018. Phone: 0712-2738731, 3296733; Telefax: 0712-2721216

Bengaluru : Plot No. 91-33, 2nd Main Road, Seshadripuram, Behind Nataraja Theatre, Bengaluru - 560 020. Phone: 080-41138821; Mobile: 09379847017, 09379847005

Hyderabad : No. 3-4-184, Lingampally, Besides Raghavendra Swamy Matham, Kachiguda, Hyderabad - 500 027. Phone: 040-27560041, 27550139

Chennai : New No. 48/2, Old No. 28/2, Ground Floor, Sarangapani Street, T. Nagar, Chennai-600 012. Mobile: 09380460419

Pune : First Floor, "Laksha" Apartment, No. 527, Mehunpura, Shaniwarpeth (Near Prabhat Theatre), Pune - 411 030. Phone: 020-24496323/24496333; Mobile: 09370579333

Lucknow : House No 731, Shekhupura Colony, Near B.D. Convent School, Aliganj, Lucknow - 226 022. Phone: 0522-4012353; Mobile: 09307501549

Ahmedabad : 114, "SHAIL", 1st Floor, Opp. Madhu Sudan House, C.G. Road, Navrang Pura, Ahmedabad - 380 009. Phone: 079-26560126; Mobile: 09377088847

Ernakulam : 39/176 (New No: 60/251) 1st Floor, Karikkamuri Road, Ernakulam, Kochi – 682011. Phone: 0484-2378012, 2378016; Mobile: 09387122121

Bhubaneswar : Plot No. 214/1342, Budheswari Colony, Behind Durga Mandap, Bhubaneswar - 751 006. Phone: 0674-2575129; Mobile: 09338746007

Kolkata : 108/4, Beliaghata Main Road, Near ID Hospital, Opp. SBI Bank, Kolkata - 700 010, Phone: 033-32449649, Mobile: 7439040301

Printed at : Geetanjali Press Pvt. Ltd., Nagpur. On behalf of HPH.

PREFACE

Decision Making is a constant process as the life goes. At all times of the day, each living being makes the decision of one type or the other. Decision making cuts across the areas of utilisation. It is not required only for Business, but in all walks of life at all times. The art and science of collecting, analysing and using the information (can be called data) is utilised for identifying and solving life problems. The use of data for decision making is the body of statistical thinking.

Business environment is becoming more and more competitive. Operating in this environment is very challenging and data has a very important role in meeting such a challenge. The author himself has been a practicing manager and understands the rigors of Business Decisions. It is from this experience, arose the need to put the data to use in the form of this book. The book has, therefore, been written in the most lucid, easy to understand language and the concepts have been amply clarified so as to make at easier to use in daily business improvement exercises.

The utilisation of statistical concepts is better understood, when these make the job of the decision maker easy. As he is faced with complex situations with large data, he has various alternatives and business interests uppermost in his mind. The use of statistical methods, coupled with a structured approach to solve any problem with greater case helps a manager in day-to-day function. Basing decisions on data can, therefore, be viewed as an effective management strategy formulated through a scientific approach to quality of decisions. For various purposes, lot many comprehensive statistical softwares are now available and are being improved day by day. These are of further help for the purpose.

In the book, the learning objectives, the chapter summary and many solved problems in a very systematic manner have been made available so as to make it easily comprehensible.

I am very thankful to large number of my students, collegues and friends, who have offered many critical but useful reviews. I am also thankful to my publisher who has taken immense pains in making this book very focussed based on courses run by many universitiers at the level of under- graduates as well as post graduates.

— Author

BOOK LAYOUT

Chapters

CHAPTER CONTENTS

CHAPTER 1

DECISION-MAKING AND HUMAN INVOLVEMENT

1.1 INTRODUCTION

All living beings decide on things they do, want to do or not to do, at all times of the day and night. While taking these decisions, number of factors help in the process. If a human being wants to eat, he has to decide what to eat, depending on how hungry he is, what he has eaten the previous day or during the previous meal, what time he needs the food etc. These are only few but obvious factors for this decision-making process. For decisions of importance either for business or for the nation, a very comprehensive list of factors has to be prepared and their data collected and analysed before being put to use for a deliberate decision.

In todays environment, the quote below is very valid.

"In this brain-based economy, education is economics and economics is education." Also, **"Decision-Making depends on the quantity and quality of information and information sharing."**

Thus today's decision-making process is not only the problem at the level of human beings, it is also sharing of information through human interaction as well as through non-human involvement. There is tremendous advancement in the area of computing technology and hence with the help of Internet, a vast pool of information can be made use of. Today this sharing of information is possible through interaction of intelligent machines. Thus in this age of brain based economy, the education of decision-makers enhances the economic achievements and so also the economics of the business provides a helpful and cost effective platform for educating the decision-makers, thereby improving the quality of decisions. Time is not far when today's brain power will be replaced by the computing power to a very large extent and therefore a large proportion of decision-making can be possible through these 'so called' intelligent machines. Thus we have a wide scope of research opened up in this area and in due course, we should be able to design artificial intelligence process for much faster, accurate and reliable decision making.

Business Decision-making is dependent on the amount and the quality of the information used by the business manager. Intelligent machines are a great help to enhance decision-making capability.

1.2 MANAGERIAL DECISION-MAKING

Today's managers have a large number of machine based quantitative tools (softwares for various purposes) available to them in order to enable them to make intelligent and superior decisions, because a large number of interacting factors can have fast interactions through the machines and thus time of decision-making has been considerably reduced. The complexity of the business situations due to varied, ever-changing and highly customised demands, a large competition in all the areas due to globalisation and provisions of WTO (world Trade Organisation), has placed an intense pressure on managers at all levels in all the fields for very quick decision-making, also for innovations at 24 × 7 level (*i.e.*, all twenty four hours a day, all seven days a week). Quantitative as well as qualitative human decision-making, thus, is a highly intellectual process.

Human decision-making process involves consideration of tangible as well as non-tangible parameters as both the conscious as well as the sub-conscious mind of the decision-maker interacts constantly during the process. Thus, it is a combination of quantitatives as well as judgemental outcomes. We can identify the following stages of decision-making process :

A stepped and methodical approach to decision-making ensures consideration of all relevant factors and associated information. It results in the optimal solution to any business problem on day-to-day basis.

Cognition Stage : It is the starting point for the human mind to locate the facts in the environment around the decision-maker in order to make the decision on natural or otherwise accidental factors. This can be termed as the scientific research.

Assembly Stage : Accidental information of the cognition stage is then put into a coherent information system. This is called 'Assembly' of thoughts or information needed. The assembly of recognised facts into useful and useable information system makes the information comprehensible and is the second stage of decision-making.

Testing Stage : When mind puts these comprehensible data into a useful form, there may be some convergent and some divergent data combined into this assembly process. At the stage of testing, the decision-maker has to evaluate the relevancy of collected information for the purpose of specific decision he has to make. The testing, therefore, means segregating information data into relevant and irrelevant groups for the specific problem faced by the decision-maker. Any missing or irrevalent data or unreliable information may influence the decision. Hence quality and quantity of information for the decision is important at this stage.

This discussion brings home the very important issue of indentifying the problem being faced, in the absence of which, the testing of data will be irrevalent. Due to incorrectly identified problem, some erroneous data may be used leading to incorrect decision. In fact, there is really nothing like correct or incorrect or even good and bad decision. It is the decision made for a problem based on available information at that point of time. Thus faulty, unnecassary or unreliable information may play a very destructive role in the decision-making process. Use of quantitative tools as per reliable and relevant information utilisation will be a great help in reducing the inaccuracy of the decision. Intagible or unconscious parameters superimposed by the decision-maker can be shifting the decision to one end or the other, based on the environmental background of the decision-maker (optimistic, pessimistic or mediocre type of decision-makers as per experience.)

1.3 HUMAN ASSETS MANAGEMENT

The quality of decision-making largely depends on the decision-maker due to the influence of sub-conscious mind. The optimistic, pessimistic or a moderate thinking individual can largely vary the outcome of the decision process analysis inspite of the very best tools available to him indicating, possibly, very clear cut direction of the decision. Various individuals are the outcome of the surrounding environment, in which these people are born and brought up, the type of friends and education they have and the type of circumstantial behaviour of the society towards them. Environmental factors can play a major role in developing healthy and positive thinking mind. The influence of these factors can be greatly reduced, (if not totally eliminated, which is difficult) by systematic approach to train the mind of various personnel for the type of job they perform or are expected to perform. This systematic approach through proper selection, training, motivation and job description can help converting a human being into an asset for the organisation. In business, it is all the more important because one decision by any individual in the system can either make or mar the business altogether. Identifying the needs of the organisational work and creating human wealth to perform at optimal level, therefore, is the first step towards effective, useful and coherent decisions.

The conversion into human assets can be done through
- Appropriate recruitment process.
- Effective training-cultural and job specific.
- Motivation assessment and provision.
- Job description, enlargement and job ownership.

Two most common enemies of Decision-Making are inertia and impatience, both the characteristics generating out of the influence of the operating environment. This is, possibly, more prominent in our society, though these situations exist anywhere across the globe in different proportions. Inertia is due to our work culture, called "Chalta Hai" and it is often due to fear of change or fear of redicule during the implementations of change. Due to the effort required to implement a change, we often tend to avoid the situation and want to live happily with the present status. On the other hand, the impatience is generally opposite to inertia. It means finding quick-fix solutions to our problems, when we face an odd situation, out of which we have to pull ourselves out. When there is no other go, we quickly think to find an immediate solution, rather than thinking deeply and deliberately to evolve long term solution.

When an individual is unwilling to engage in proper collection and processing necessary and sufficient information for a specific problem, impatience disturbs the balance of decision-making process. In fact, if we look at it closely, the impatience also may be due to inertia on a long-term basis, when an individual is not willing to dwell into the root cause of the problem, trying to evolve a solution that can set things right temporarily. This is impatience coupled with inertia. :

Few other possible major contaminants of the decision-making process either rest in the individual decision-maker or represent drawbacks in the applied logic, be it a consistent or persistent. These contaminants become visible and more pronounced in unstructured or ambiguous decisions-making situations. The problem of being power-centric further agravates the situation, where decisions can be very biased due to vested interests of the decision-maker.

All these uncertainties in decision-making can be greatly minimised by appropriate design of mathematical models, their simple analysis methods and creating a robust mind of the decision-making through the process of conversion of human resources into Human Assests.

Human resources are to be optimally used for business growth and hence the concept of "conversion of human resources into human assets" becomes the datum of any growth process. All managers to be self-created assets and produce the same effects in their fellow workers.

1.4 DECISION-MAKING SYSTEM

This can be compared to any Production System, which can be applied for any problem in any walk of life. The inputs in case of decision-making can be labour, capital or the technologies in force along with the entrepreneurship capability of the decision-maker, with a managerial control system in the form of deterministic, heuristic or stochastic models helping in controlling the decision-making capability. The adoption of this model in a business situation can optimise the results through minimisation of costs and maximisation of profits in the area through legal, social or ideological constraints.

1.5 DECISION-MAKING ENVIRONMENT

At the individual level of decision-making, the characteristics and their possible utilisation for a good decision have been described in the above paragraphs. For an organisation to be effectively operating, another method used is Organisational heirarchy, *i.e.*, lower, middle and top management. By this process, various decisions can be filtered through to avoid a possible bias to a very large extent. We operate under industry based and market-based decisions to cater for the business necessity of consumers demand. Generally, these decisions embed large domestic considerations. In addition, the globalisation has necessitated incorporation of international requirements into our work. For a broad-based decision such as mission and customer satisfaction level, top management is involved to set direction for the organisation to move. These are complex, probabilistic and generally non-repeatitive situations. The middle management level personnel usually think of company-based problems. These are the people to ensure that policies and objectives set out by the top management are properly implemented. The operational decision-making level lies with these managers, so as to achieve optimisation in all company operations. Large number of constraints on these managers may affect the optimisation levels, but that is where innovative capability of the middle level or operations managers comes in to achieve the organisational objectives. Economic and technological constraints along with world-wide competition are few of the major pull-back factors.

Decision-making is becoming increasingly complex due to globalisation. Hence the system of decision-making has to cater for available environment and competitive situation for the type of business operated.

Lower management is involved in actual conduct of the operations, the method of which has been defined by the middle management. The important areas in business could be marketing, production, finance or any other important function like personnel or research. The job of lower management is generally well-defined and repetitive, but it does not bar the lower management being innovative in their own sphere of working. This innovation will ensure cost effective utilisation of resources and the achievement of quality standards to the best possible level.

The study analysis and identification of various parameters for operational areas is very important to the management system designing. It is in the form of establishing levels of information (quantity and quality), the interaction of various parameters and their thorough analysis by effective processing methods and proper utilisation of the results so obtained through appropriate quantitative tools.

Thus the working environments for the three levels of management can be summarised as under :

- Top Management : Domestic and International market and competiture situation (Industry based).
- Middle Management : Objectives, planning and method design for all the operations (Company based).
- Lower Management : Specialised specified, norrowly defined area of operation. (Department based.)

If we have been able to create the workforce totally committed to work at all levels of operations and integrate their energies into a desired direction, there is no reason to go wrong in decision making, through the process of fine-tuning the decisions by proper filtering. Various tools for Decision Making are described in chapters to follow.

●●●

CHAPTER 2

DATA ANALYSIS AND MEASURE OF CENTRAL TENDENCY

2.1 INTRODUCTION

The business environment of today being very complex and complicated, the decision making for business is a very difficult job. The experience or personal evaluation based on some known observations, therefore, is not enough in today's business scene. We need the help of some established methods, techniques and mathematical tools to structure our decision making process. These techniques would show some relationships, trends or basis of changes in the business performance parameters. For this purpose statistics plays an important role, because it provides certain concepts and methods for collection, sifting, structuring, presenting, analysing and useful interpretation of the data relevant to the business in question.

Decision-making capability of the business managers enhances with the help of authentic and sufficient data, which can be analysed to produce its coherent interpretation and its effective use while solving a business problem.

The statistical data constitutes the basic raw material, for its useful gain in decision making. Past history of business may offer relevant data or else it needs to be collected by the analyst, so that it could be grouped into useful form and can be used by the manager, i.e. the decision maker, to derive benefit for a coherent interpretation. There may be generally four types of situations available to a decision maker.

1. When data is available from the analyst in the form of tables, charts, etc.
2. When some vague hypotheses or assumptions exist, based on which some deductions or inferences can be drawn.
3. When some observed data is available, and some unknown quantities are to be estimated.
4. When decision maker has to base his decision under uncertain environment or conditions, regarding an alternative to be adopted for a business action.

The above situations give rise to the following areas of use of statistics.

1. Data collection and presentation.
2. Statistical inference and estimation.

3. Statistical theories for decision alternatives, along with their level of uncertainties and consequent.

Since decisions are made based on available information, its quality would depend on the relevance authenticity and reliability of information. It is not humanly possible to study the entire population in most of the cases, and hence we have to adopt the 'Sampling' concept for collection of data and it is here that the representativeness of information about the population becomes important. The values or observations in the sample are called statistic and the values in the population as parameters. Thus sample statistics are utilised to estimate the population parameters. Sample, thus, is an important concept of any statistical inference about a system (Universe or population). Thus statistics has its utility in planning, mathematics, economics, business, management, accountancy, industry, astronomy, social sciences, psychology and education etc.

2.2 HISTORY OF STATISTICS

Statistical theory has been and will remain a very useful tool for quality decision-making. Statistics has been used for various branches and in fact, now, it is useful in all fields of life. Both descriptive and inferential data are effective inputs in Decision Theory.

"Statistik" has been adopted from an Italian word 'statista', which means "statesman". Gottfried Achenwall, a professor at Marlborough and Göttingen and later Dr EAW Zimmerman used the word way back in 1750's. Though use of technique *i.e.* data collection, recording and effective utilization had been in use for quite a while before, last it became popular when it was extensively used by Sir John Sinclair in his book "Statistical Account of Scotland (1791 — 1799).

The word and the concept had been in use for census work in the form of records of population and resources by Egyptians and Romans. Later in the middle age, it was used for land documentations. In early Ninth Century, Charlemagne completed statistical enumeration of serfs attached to the land. Later the extensive use of data was made to prepare England's First statistical work in the form of records of ownership, extent and value of the lands of England, as ordered by the conqueror William.

In 1532, England started recording the dead in England, due to King's fear of plague. At around the same time, French made it mandatory to record baptism, deaths and marriages. By 1632, detailed recordings called Bills of Mortality listing births and deaths by sex were completed and in 1662, captain John Graunt used about 3 years of these bills to predict the death of number of people through various diseases and proportion of male and female births expected. Such live instances and usages are large since then and now it is in great demand due to complex decisions requirements based on past data. Hence quite a large number of refinements of these techniques have been evolved and many laws and methods have been developed.

Now virtually all branches of life use these techniques, broadly of two categories: Descriptive and inferential data used for one decision based on a particular parameter, without any reference to any other case, can be called a descriptive technique, such as performance of one company of a big industrial house, whereas if the performance of one unit can throw some referential light on the performance of the other units due to same business policy, the technique used is called referential.

When such references are drawn, these are called statistical references. The generalization of such references would involve probability of their validity and hence these techniques can be and are being used for Managerial Decision Making under the concept of Decision Theory.

2.3 STATISTICAL DATA

Data are collection of any number of observations pertaining to a happening. When we say that there are 60 students in a class and 25 of them belong to Delhi, it is collection of data for the purpose of knowing how many students in a particular class belong to the city of Delhi. Similarly, we may collect data about males, females (adults and children) staying in a particular locality.

The statistical data can be broadly classified into two categories.

1. Published data
2. Unpublished data

Published data are the set of information which have been collected already and are available in the form of book or any other published form, whereas unpublished data needs to he collected by the analyst for a specific purpose.

Data collection has the following preliminary requirements:

(*i*) Objectives and the scope of data collection
(*ii*) Source of information
(*iii*) Method of data collection and
(*iv*) Degree of accuracy required for the final result.

Thus the published data has to be evaluated for the purpose it serves. It may or may not suit the requirement of the purpose for which it is intended to be used. Whereas unpublished data can be more useful because it can be collected specifically knowing the purpose of its collection. Thus the reliability of the data so obtained can be checked or ascertained by the analyst while obtaining the information. The suitability and adequacy of data also requires to be established for the purpose.

Published data can be in the form of monthly publication on monetary and banking parameters, which can become the indicators of economic health of the business or country, such as those published by the Reserve Bank of India. Economic Surveys brought out by the Ministry of Economic Affairs also speak of the economy indicator. Annual survey reports on industries and census of India provides population and industrial growth. Commerce Ministry brings monthly statistics of foreign trade. Information about certain social indicators of the country, GDP, GNP and other relevant information can be made use of in future planning. Similarly, there are large number of international data published by various organisation such as ILO, World Bank, Asian Development Bank etc.

Statistical data, i.e., primary as well as secondary or published and unpublished data are very helpful for analysis and future business forecasting. There are large number of sources available for secondary data, but at times, (for latest inference), primary data becomes necessary and relevant.

Collection of primary or secondary data. even to help utilisation of published data is necessary in large number of cases. For business usage, a large quantity of data are generated by the internal systems of the organisation itself, such as cash flow data, sales data, labour utilisation statistics, production schedules or budget data. This data can be effectively used for future planning of the organisation in various areas of working.

The sources of some of the published data are described below:

1. Official publications from the Central Government such as
   (a) Monthly abstract of Statistics, Monthly Statistics of production of selected industries in India, National Income Statistics etc.
   (b) Reports on social, economic and demographic conditions, prices, area and yield of various crops etc published by National Sample Survey Organisation (NSSO),
   (c) Reports by various departments such as Income Tax, Railways, Central Excise, Central Board of Revenues, Post and Telegraphs, Directorate General of Supplies and Disposals and Textile Commissioner office etc.
2. Publications from Semi-Government Statistical Organisations, such as Reserve Bank of India monthly bulletin and annual report. Institute of Economic Growth, Delhi, The Institute of Foreign Trade, New Delhi etc.
3. Publications from Commercial institutions like FICCI, Institute of Chartered Accountants of India, Stock Exchanges, Bank Bodies and Cooperative Societies etc.

4. Publications from Research Institutions, from organisations like Indian Statistical Institute (ISI), Indian Council of Agricultural Research (ICAR), Indian Agricultural Statistics Research Institute (IASRI), National Council of Educational Research and Training (NCERT), Institute of Labour Research, Institute of Applied Manpower Research, Indian Standards Institute etc.
5. Newspapers and Periodicals : large useful data is collected on Socio-economic problems and published in various newspapers and periodicals such as Economic Times, The Financial Express, Eastern Economist, Indian Journal of Economics, Business India, India Today, Business World and Times of India Year Book etc.
6. International Publications : from organisations such as UNO, WHO, ILO, IMF, IFC (International Finance Corporation), WEF (World Economic Forum), ESCAP (Economic and Social Commission for Asia Pacific), World Bank and International Statistical Education Institute etc.

The usefulness of any data collected, whether primary or secondary, lies only in its relevance for the Specific problem solving. Hence source of data, its fullness and authenticity must be ensured by the decision maker before making its use for business decisions failing which the decision can be faulty or unrelated.

2.4 TESTS FOR DATA

Before making any worthwhile use of the collected data, it should be ensured that the data is authentic and reliable and can be used to advantage. For this purpose, we should obtain satisfactory answers to the following questions :

1. What is the source of data? Is it likely to be biased for a specific purpose?
2. Is data supporting the other evidence available for the same purpose?
3. In evidence missing as to lead us to a different or biased conclusion?
4. Do we have sufficient number of observations so as to make a worthwhile inference? Do the data represent all the groups under study?
5. Is the conclusion logical? Do we obtain a logical sense of data for specific purpose?

This test is very relevant to avoid hurry in decision making and also to avoid erroneous decisions leading to problems in business.

2.5 SAMPLES AND POPULATIONS

When it is not possible or economically viable to study the whole group of system called population, then we use certain number of observations (part of the population or the whole) to infer the behaviour of the while. These representative observations are called sample for the population under study.

Taking a total census of a country i.e. population is done through total survey whereas selecting some people to study salary levels, or the education levels of various communities can be done through samples representing the population.

Though study and use of samples is easier and less time and effort consuming, care has to be taken so as to make the sample observations representing all the sub-elements of the population. Hence sample should be a representative of the population, which means that it should contain all the relevant characteristics of the population in the same proportion as contained or included in the population.

2.6 PRESENTATION AND ANALYSIS OF DATA

Since raw data does not speak full volume of information for effective utilisation, the presentation of it in the concise, coherent and structured form becomes imperative. The incomprehensibility of raw data can be overcome by putting these into meaningful form so that it can be analysed to be of use. We now describe some of these ways of classification and presentation of the data,

The data array is the simplest method of arranging the data. The given data can either he arranged in ascending order or in descending order. By arranging the data as above, we can quickly notice the trend and spread of the data *i.e.* the highest and lowest value and steps of variation. We, then, can easily organise it into relevant sections. Also we can notice any repetitions of values so that a general pattern can be known.

When data is large and it may not be useful as Data arrays, we can arrange it in various forms as given below.

Data obtained in its raw form is not generally useful. Hence its structuring is required to be done to obtain the message conveyed through the data array. Various tables and graphs are useful forms of data structuring enhancing its usefulness.

Tables

The statistical data can be arranged either in the form of a table or can be drawn into a graphical form to summarise the utility of the data. The table indicates the logical presentation of data with reference to some other variable or in terms of its relation to time. Table can be drawn to list out relationship of parameters such as following:

TABLE 2.1. Budget Allocations to Projects

Project No	*Budget Allocations in Lakhs (Rs.)*					
	1996	*1997*	*1998*	*1999*	*2000*	*2001*
401	360	419	500	610	650	306
402	250	300	310	365	255	110
403	135	230	415	460	475	480
404	55	75	210	265	135	210
405	35	50	60	70	80	100

The above table describes the relationship of project execution with reference to the money allotted to these projects (in Rs. Lakhs). It has a number, a title indicating the information displayed, various parameters with their units and values in the form of rows and columns. The project allocations here have been defined for various years during the execution of the projects.

Data also can be presented with reference to time such as profits earned by an organisation during the last 10 years.

TABLE 2.2 Profits Earned (in Rs. Lakhs) By ABC Company

Year	*Profits (Rs. in Lakhs)*
1991	10.63
1992	12.55
1993	13.60
1994	13.75
1995	12.50
1996	12.35
1997	13.50
1998	15.50
1999	11.63
2000	18.75

Table can be arranged if the data represents the relationships of more than two parameters, such as the following :

TABLE 2.3 Sales (in Units) of Refrigerators 165 Ltr. 230 Ltr. And 310 Ltr.

Product	*Sales regionwise (2000)*											
	North			*East*			*South*			*West*		
Refrigerators	*April*	*May*	*June*	*April*	*May*	*June*	*April*	*May*	*June*	*April*	*May*	*June*
165 litres	3,505	3,010	3,210	4,310	4,510	3,005	4,010	4,650	4,700	2,000	1,500	1,710
230 litres	7,500	8,900	9,540	3,505	3,360	3,500	4560	3.310	3,300	4,500	6,000	7,680
310 litres	6,505	7,910	8,770	1,500	1,610	1,755	2,500	2,670	4,620	6,100	7,800	8,950

Diagrams

Though tabulated form of the data can speak volumes in terms of information conveyed, its presentation in the shape of various relevant diagrams can produce better understanding of the situation. Line diagrams, bar charts, pictograms, scatter diagrams or pie charts are useful with their own importance and relevance.

In a similar manner, the data can be represented in the form of diagrams. There are following types of diagrams used to present statistical data.

(i) Line Diagrams. (ii) Bar Charts. (iii) Pictograms.

(iv) Scatter Diagrams. (v) Pie Charts.

Line Diagram : In this graphical presentation, only two parameters or variables can be shown to indicate relationships, such as sales of an organisation for a particular time horizon. It can be shown as follows:

TABLE 2.4 Sales (Rs. in Lakhs)

Year (x)	*Sales (y)*
1991	350
1992	370
1993	390
1994	420
1995	450
1996	470
1997	400
1998	410
1999	460
2000	480

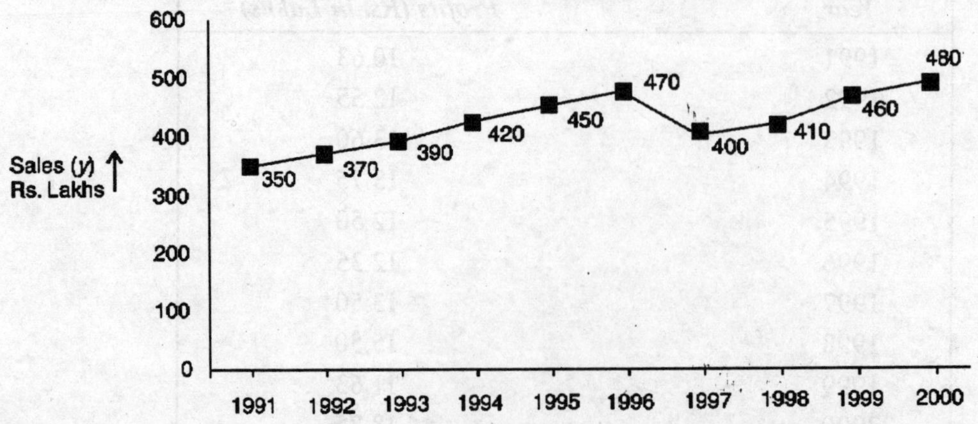

Fig. 2.1 Sales information for the last 10 years (Line diagram)

The diagram can be shown to have more utility by drawing more than one variable against a particular related variable on the other axis, such as sales can be broken into various products and shown on the same variable (time), as follows:

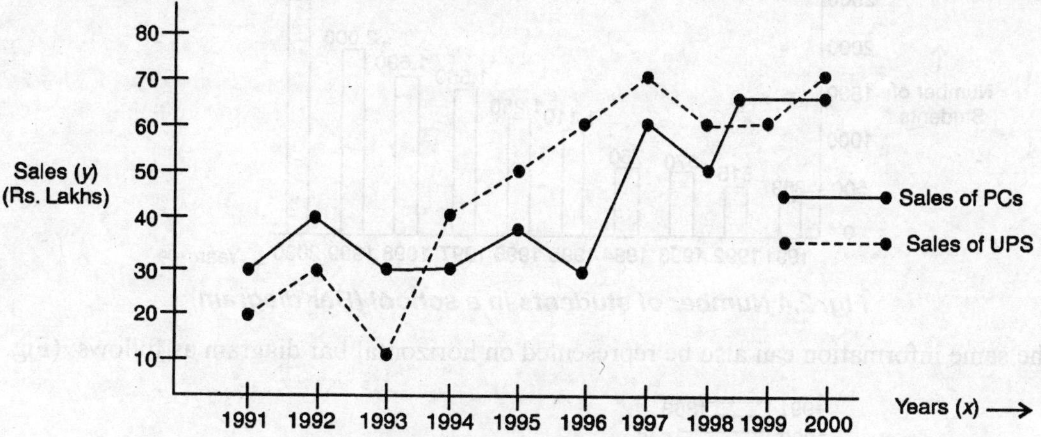

Fig. 2.2. Sales of PCs and UPS (Line diagram)

Line diagrams can be difficult to read at times. When information is produced in the form of bar-charts, may be horizonal, vertical, broken, combination or composite bars, these convey much structured information for decision-making.

Bar Diagrams/Charts : These are the easiest and most commonly used presentation diagrams, which are easily understood by all. These can be drawn for various business parameters in the form of rectangles, the magnitude of the parameter being depicted by its length, the width being arbitrary. To ensure easy comparison of data, the width of all rectangles on a Bar diagram should be maintained uniform. The magnitude written on top of each bar or in front of the bar (if bar is horizontal) would be better understood rather than using the scale for each interpretation. Bar diagrams as can be seen in Fig. 2.3 drawn for Table 2.4.

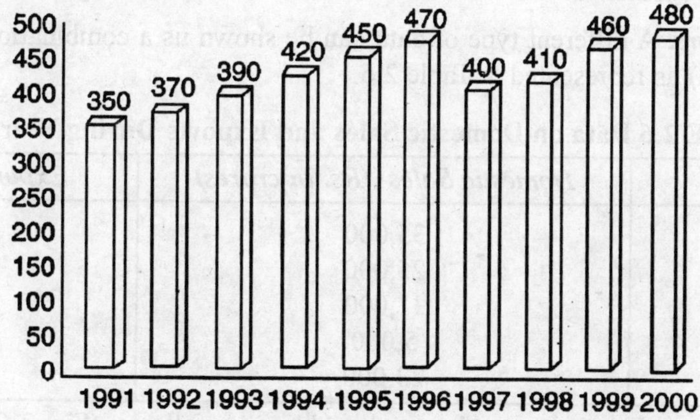

Fig. 2.3 Sales for the last 10 years (Bar diagram)

Let us lake another case of number of students admitted to a school during (say) last 10 years as given in table 2.5.

TABLE 2.5 Number of Students Admitted to a School

Year	*Number of students*	*Year*	*Number of students*
1991	363	1996	1.250
1992	515	1997	1,560
1993	670	1998	1,690
1994	750	1999	2,000
1995	1,110	2000	2,500

This can be represented by a Bar diagram as follows:

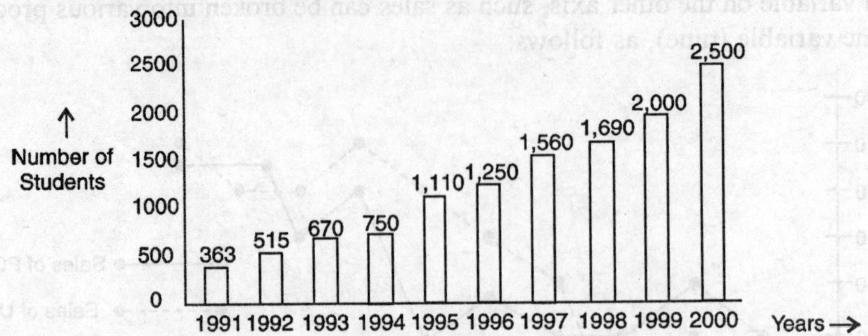

Fig. 2.4 Number of students in a school (Bar diagram)

The same information can also be represented on horizontal bar diagram as follows: (Fig. 2.5)

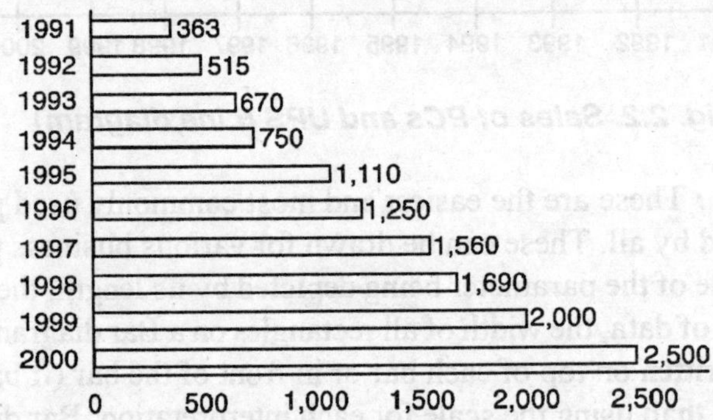

Fig. 2.5 Number of students in a school (Bar diagram)

The vertical and horizontal bars depict the information in the same form but in different directions. Both are easy to read and comprehend. The combination bar shows the cummulation of information for a particular important parameter.

Combination Bars. A different type of data can be shown us a combination of bars (either in vertical or horizontal) as represented in Table 2.6.

TABLE 2.6 Data on Domestic Sales and Exports During Year 2000

Item	*Domestic Sales (Rs. in crores)*	*Exports (Rs. in crores)*
Steel	35,000	15,000
Cotton	25,000	10,000
Electric Pumps	11,000	5,000
Motor Cars	5,000	1,500
Jewellery Items	23,000	5,500

The information can be represented by combined bars as follows: (Fig. 2.6)

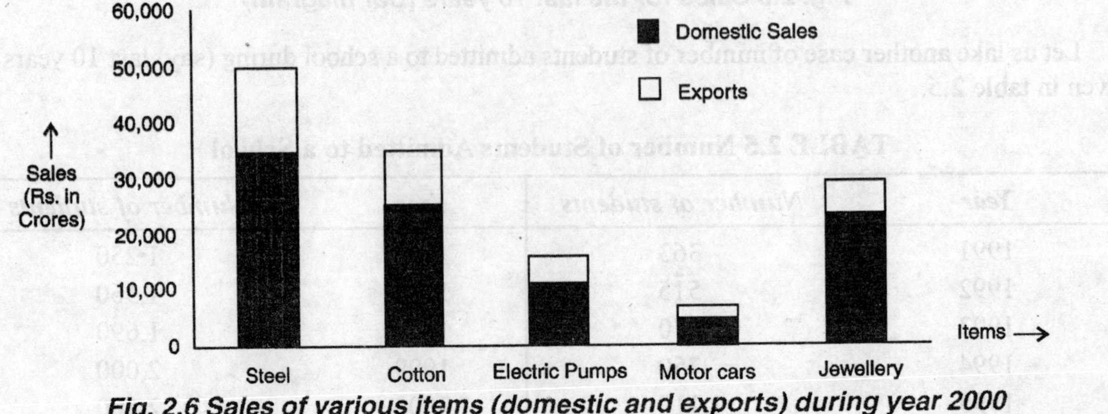

Fig. 2.6 Sales of various items (domestic and exports) during year 2000

Composite bars: The data given in Table 2.7 can be represented as bars (composite) based an the percentage contribution of its constituents.

TABLE 2.7 Monthly Family Expenditure

Item	*Expenditure*
Food	Rs. 3,500
Education	Rs. 2,000
Clothing	Rs. 1,500
Entertainment	Rs. 500
Rent	Rs. 5,000
Telephone and Electricity	Rs. 2,000
Miscellaneous	Rs. 1,500

While calculating the percentage expenditure under various heads, we get the approximate values as follows :

Food	22%
Education	12%
Clothing	9%
Entertainment	3%
Rent	31%
Telephone and Electricity	12%
Miscellaneous	11%

This information can now be represented as a bar chart as follows : (Refer Fig. 2.7.)

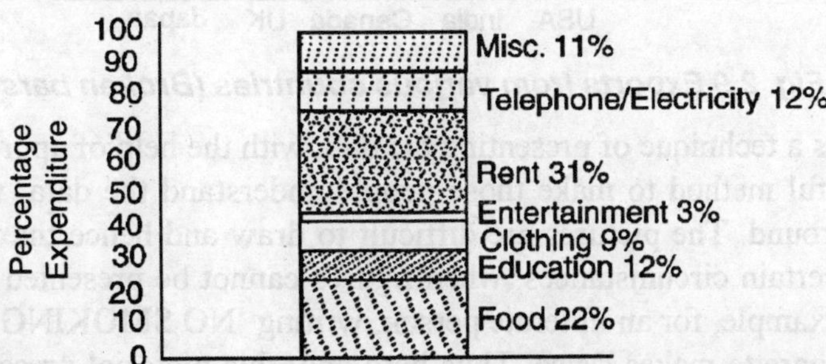

Fig. 2.7 Monthly expenditure of a family (Composite bars)

The composite bars represent the data on a percentage weightage basis, from where the totality of information can be obtained for a given parameter. The usefulness lies in representation of a peculiar problem.

Single Bar diagram can be used for representing only one characteristic or category of items whereas if inter-related data is to be compared, the use of multi-bar diagram is useful.

TABLE 2.8 Yearly Profits of Two Companies

Year	*Yearly Profits (in Rs. Crores)*	
	Company P	*Company Q*
1996	215	160
1997	305	245
1998	380	300
1999	410	365
2000	455	400

This data can be depicted by a multi-bar diagram as given in Fig. 2.8.

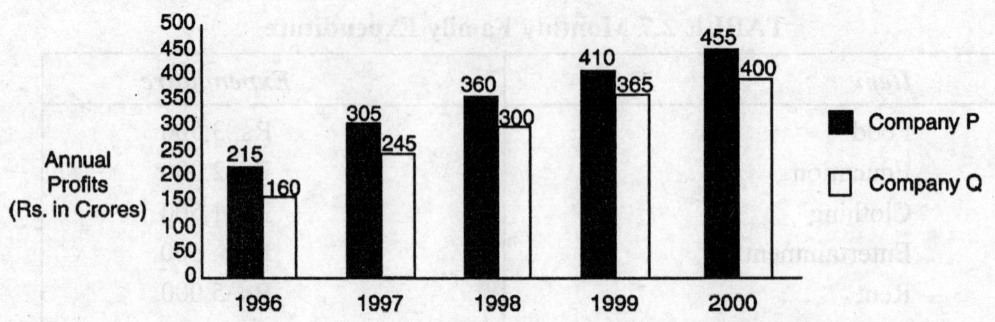

Fig. 2.8 Profits of two competiting companies (Multi bars)

When figures to be represented show wide variation *i.e.*, wide range (difference between lowest observation and the highest observation), then to depict the information on a comfortable and understandable scale may become difficult. In that case, we can take the help of broken or discontinuous bars as follows:

Broken bars are the representation of a large data with much variance, where the given scale of graph is difficult to depict. Lengthy data, thus, can be shown with broken bars. Pictogram, on the other hand, shows the data for the person, who, possibly, can not fathom the numerical figures.

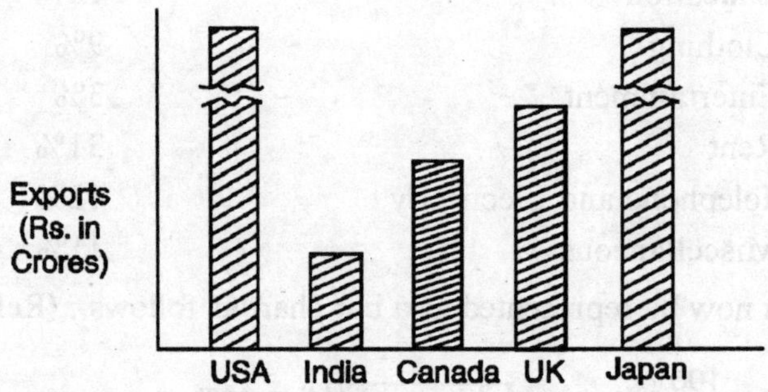

Fig. 2.9 Exports from various countries (Broken bars)

Pictograms : It is a technique of presenting the data with the help of appropriate pictures. This is a particularly useful method to make those people understand the data, who do not have any mathematical background. The pictures are difficult to draw and hence the technique is not very popular. But under certain circumstances, when figures cannot be presented otherwise, this is the best technique. For example, for an illiterate person, writing 'NO SMOKING' has no meaning, but a crossed burning cigarette makes sense. Thus here only this pictorial presentation can make the language understood. In picture form, proportions are not easy to depict and understand. Hence scaling is not normally adopted. One example of pictogram can make the presentation clear.

TABLE 2.9 The Number of Workers is an Organisations

Plants	***No. of workers (in hundreds)***
Plant A	25
Plant B	63
Plant C	45
Plant D	17
Plant E	20

This can be presented in the pictogram form as follows:

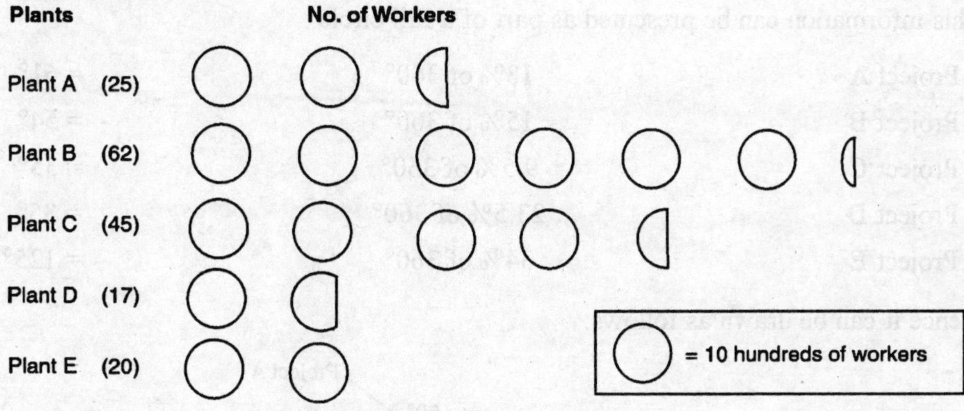

Fig. 2.10 Number of workers in 5 plants (Pictogram)

Scatter Diagram : Scatter Diagrams can be used to analyse the co-relation between two set of variables. When we represent the profit levels of an organisation for different sales volume, it can be shown as follows:

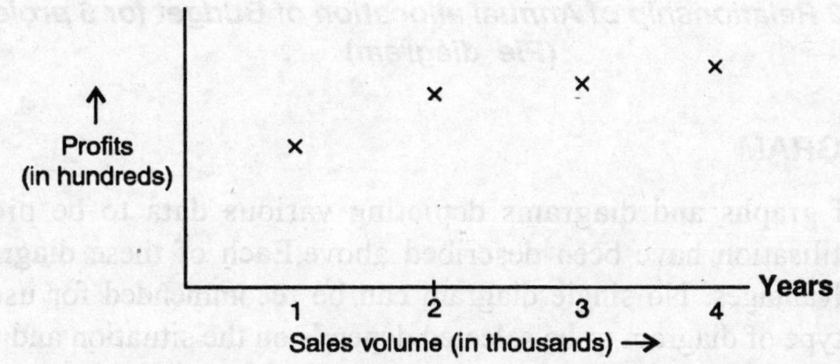

Fig. 2.11 Relationship between Sales and Profits (Scatter diagram)

It gives a clear idea that there is a high degree of relationship (*i.e.* generally profit increasing with increase in sales volume). This information can be used for future predictions as it can be anticipated that if sales are increased, the profits are likely to increase and hence future strategies for sales can indicate cash flow of the organisation.

The scatter diagram shows the spread of the data, possibly indicating a trend or otherwise. The pie diagram, on the other hand, can be useful to show the components of a problem parameters where a judicious view is necessary for larger decision.

Pie diagrams : In Pie-diagrams, the different segments of a circle show percentage contribution of various constituents to its total picture. This is a similar method of divided bars or percentage bars to indicate the information. This sub-divided circle diagram is called an angular or pie-diagram.

Lei us take an example of Budget allocations for various projects running under an organisation.

TABLE 2.10 Annual Budget Allocation to 5 Projects

Plants	*Annual Allocation (Rs. in lakhs)*	*Percentage of total Allocation*
Project A	300	18%
Project B	250	15%
Project C	160	9.5%
Project D	400	23.5%
Project E	590	34%

This information can be presented as part of a full circle.

Project A	18% of 360°	= 61°
Project B	15% of 360°	= 54°
Project C	9.5% of 360°	= 35°
Project D	23.5% of 360°	= 85°
Project E	34% of 360°	= 125°

Hence it can be drawn as follows:

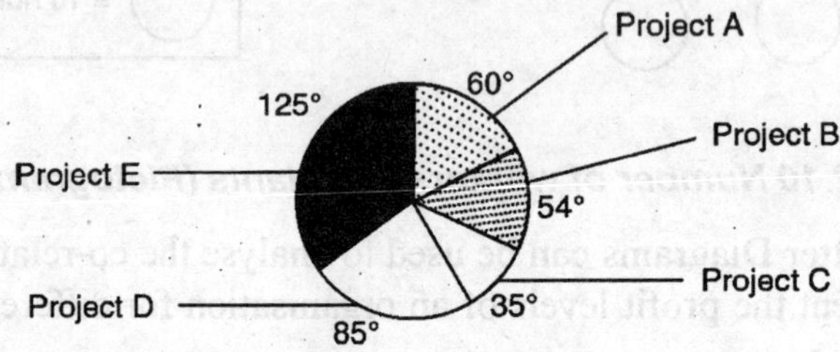

Fig. 2.12 Relationship of Annual allocation of Budget for 5 projects (Pie diagram)

The diagrams and graphs can be very useful tool for easy comprehension of the data information, but these indicate only general idea about the information and may not be very accurate figuratively. The diagrams, being subjective in nature, can be misleading at times. Hence due caution should be exercised by the decision maker for their use.

CHOICE OF A DIAGRAM

Various types of graphs and diagrams depicting various data to be presented for easy understanding and utilisation have been described above.Each of these diagrams has its own advantages and disadvantages. No single diagram can be recommended for use under a certain condition. Hence the type of diagram to be selected depends on the situation and the choice of best illustration lies with the presenter to make a mark on his audience or the customer to ensure its full benefit.

2.7. LIMITATION OF DIAGRAMS AND GRAPHS

Diagrams and graphs are very useful tools for visual display of information, but they have certain limitations as enumerated below:

1. Graphs and Diagrams should not be treated as substitutes for other forms of presentation. These may not he the ideal choice under all circumstances.
2. These depict only general idea of data and only limited and approximate information. They are more appealing to the layman, but may not be so for the analyst.
3. These are subjective in nature and hence interpretations are different.
4. For large number of observations, it is not an easy and clear presentation.

2.8. STRUCTURING OF DATA

Raw data is the information prior to the proper arrangement of the observations or the data in a required form to make it useful for some analysis. A manager will not be able to arrive at any worthwhile conclusion unless and until he has the sales or payment data of a particular day. In case the invoices collected are over a number of days, it becomes all the more difficult to find where he is heading. Let us take an example of various payment invoices during last 2 days to find out how much money has been paid under these invoices and how much delay occured in the payment process.

TABLE 2.11 Number of Days Invoice Delayed for Payment

20	45	27	38	40	42	22	20	32	40
13	25	28	37	41	40	25	22	28	41
15	40	20	21	25	37	30	27	29	28
16	27	45	25	40	37	32	35	41	35
22	35	37	26	35	25	27	34	25	27

This is a table indicating raw data for delayed payments. Now let us organise this table into an orderly way listing out delays in the descending or ascending order. The table would he modified as follows:

TABLE 2.12 Data Rearrangement (Delayed Payment) in ascending order

15	25	27	35	40
16	25	27	35	40
20	25	28	35	40
20	25	28	35	40
20	25	28	37	41
21	25	29	37	41
22	26	30	37	41
22	27	32	37	42
22	27	32	38	45
23	27	34	40	45

The same table can be rearranged in the structured manner combining similar happenings together. which are called **frequency** of occurrence. Hence Table 2.13 would indicate the number of times delay has occurred by a specific number of days.

TABLE 2.13 Frequency Table for Delayed Payment

No. of days	*Frequency*	*No. of days*	*Frequency*	*No. of days*	*Frequency*	*No. of days*	*Frequency*
15	1	23	1	29	1	37	4
16	1	25	6	30	1	38	1
20	3	26	1	32	2	40	5
21	1	27	5	34	1	41	3
22	3	28	3	35	4	42	1
						45	2

This table accounts for all the 50 observations from Table 2.11 and has now become the frequency table.

The same table can be further structured to indicate group collection of data, because some numerical numbers do not occur in the table and the frequency or the number of times an observation falls under a group of observations can be a better presentation.

Data in the individual spread form is generally not very useful. Their structuring in the form of ordinary tables or frequency tables can be very useful for analysis in quick time.

TABLE 2.14 Frequency Distribution for Delayed Payment

Class or group interval	*Frequency of occurrence*
15–19	2
20–24	8
25–29	16
30–34	4
35–39	9
40–44	9
45-49	2

The number of classes or group interval can be adjusted according to the quantum of available data. The same information can be rearranged with large class interval, as follows: (Table 2.15)

TABLE 2.15 Modified Frequency Table for Dlayed Payment

Class Interval	*Frequency of occurrence*
11–20	5
21–30	22
31–40	17
41–50	6

The frequency tables are to be used as per the specific problem. Their modifications in the form of mutually exclusive class, open ended or continuous class are helpful for understanding the distribution of the data.

It can be seen that some identical data have been grouped together, but due to two methods of grouping (Table 2.14 and 2.15), some data have been lost. Now we donot gather information about value 20 occurring 3 times, 25 occurring 6 times or 27 occurring 5 times. It also does not speak any more that the value 17, 18, 19, 24, 31 etc. donot figure in the observations list at all. Hence we know about the pattern of observations rather than individual observations.

2.9 RELATIVE FREQUENCY DISTRIBUTION

Frequency can be defined as the total number of observations or data that are grouped under a class interval or group of data. A frequency distribution is a table structuring the data into classes of suitable intervals and it shows the number of observations (called frequency) falling into a certain class interval. When frequencies are listed out as fraction or percentages of the total observations, it is called Relative Frequency Distribution.

Mutually exclusive classes : Class intervals are mutually exclusive, *i.e.* when no data falls into more than one category or class, the class intervals are non-overlapping. Some class-intervals can be overlapping such as 11-20, 15-25, 20-30 etc.

Open-ended classes : When we write a class interval as under 10 or above 50 etc. it is called Open-ended class.

Discrete class : Discrete classes are those separate classes which donot move from one class to another without a break, such as 5-10, 11-15 16-20 etc.

Continuous class : Continuous data donot progress from one class to the other without a break, such as 5-15, 15-25, 25-35 etc. This is amplified in the Tables 2.12 to 2.15 given above under different methods of counting. Now the frequency table can express the fraction /percentage of each class out of the total number of observations. Table 2.15 can now be written as follows:

TABLE 2.16 Relative Frequency Distribution for Delayed Payment

Class Interval	*Frequency*	*Relative Frequency*
11–20	5	0.10
21–30	22	0.44
31–40	17	0.34
41–50	6	0.12
Total	50	1.00

It can be seen from the above explanation that repetitive data can be clubbed together and presented in the frequency distribution table. Such a table can now be converted into a graph of frequency distribution. These graphs have the same method of presentation as that for the normal graphs and diagrams described in paras 2.3 above, but are called so because these reveal the characteristics of a frequency data and not always an individual data. The graphs are more appealing and understandable than the data in the tabular form. The graphs showing the relationships of various parameters or variables are easily perceptible to the mind of the analyser or decision maker. The graphs can be gainfully used to chart the frequency distribution information under the details of the data in a concise manner. There are following types of graphs for presenting the frequency distribution :

After drawing the frequency tables, it is better to represent them in the shape of an appropriate histogram, depending on the type of class-presentation adopted.

1. Histograms
2. Frequency Polygon
3. Frequency Curves
4. Ogives, also commonly called Cumulative Frequency Curves.

Histograms

It is easily understood, most popular and commonly used diagram for plotting continuous frequency distribution. It is drawn as a series of vertical rectangles on the *x*-axis (horizontal) with class interval depicted as the width of the rectangle and height indicating the frequency of that class interval. It can be drawn based on equal or unequal class intervals. If class intervals are the same or equal, then equal-based rectangles can be drawn, whereas if the class-intervals are different, the width of the rectangle can be proportionately drawn. Frequency distribution presentation can be done under following conditions :

Grouped Frequency Distribution: Histograms can be drawn only for continuous frequency distribution. If the classes are not continuous, then class-intervals need to be changed into Class-boundaries and then the rectangles can be drawn on the continuous classes so obtained.

Mid Points Values: Instead of the class intervals, when only mid-points of different classes are given, then the distribution has to be converted into continuous frequency distribution by ascertaining the upper and lower limits of the classes, assuming that the class frequencies are uniformly distributed over the class range.

Discrete Frequency Distribution: Discrete frequency distribution can also be drawn by regarding the values of the variables as the mid-points of the continuous classes and then drawing the histograms as per mid-point value, as explained above.

Open-ended Classes : Histograms cannot be drawn for open-end class frequency distribution unless we assume that the magnitude of the first open class is the same as that of the succeeding class and that the magnitude of the last open class is the same as that of the preceeding class.

Frequency Polygon

Frequency polygon is another graphical presentation of the frequency distribution of data. In case of discrete frequency distribution, the frequency polygon is drawn by plotting the variable values on the horizontal x-axis and the frequencies on the vertical y-axis and joining the points so obtained by straight lines connecting these points. In case of grouped or continuous frequency distribution, the curve *i.e.*, Frequency Polygon can be drawn by connecting the mid-points of class intervals by a straight line either after drawing the histogram or without the help of a histogram, simply by joining the points obtained as mid-point of class interval versus the corresponding frequency. Hence it can be seen that whereas histogram is a two-dimension representation of data of frequency distribution, a frequency polygon is only a line diagram. Polygon can be effectively used for comparison of two statistic or two distributions, whereas in case of histograms, either two histograms have to be drawn separately or the rectangles have to be drawn in two different colours on the same class-intervals, which is not easy to comprehend.

Frequency Curves

Frequency curves are the modified form of the Frequency Polygon. If we join the vertices of the Frequency Polygon through a free hand smooth curve, it becomes a frequency curve. The basic purpose of drawing the frequency curve is to eliminate any random or erratic fluctuation in the data. Though a frequency polygon and therefore a frequency curve can be drawn without a histogram, but it is easy to draw a histogram, first obtain vertices for the frequency polygon and then draw a smooth curve through these vertices to get a very regular smooth shape.

In cases where data is likely to fluctuate, the frequency curve should normally not he tried out. It gives a better representation when data is fairly regular.

Since frequency tables show the data in its general form, the oppropriate representation is done through frequency curve (to show the continuity of the assembled and structured data). In the same direction, even the cumulative frequency curves can be made use of.

Cumulative Frequency Curves (Ogives)

Cumulative Frequency Curves as the name suggests, are the graphic representation of the cumulative frequency. Hence instead of plotting frequencies on the y-axis against the class boundaries or class intervals on the x-axis, if we plot cumulative frequencies on the y-axis, the curve would indicate a gradually increasing graph.

There are two types of cumulative frequency distributions *i.e.*, 'less than' type or 'more than' type. Hence Ogives as these cumulative frequency curves are called can be drawn in these two forms, *i.e.* 'less than Ogive' and 'more than Ogive'.

Less than Ogive : This curve is obtained by plotting the cumulative frequencies of 'less than' type against the upper boundary of the class interval. The points so obtained are then joined by smooth curves to give 'less than Ogive'. It is going to be an increasing curve from left to right and would take the shape of an elongated S.

More than Ogive : In this case, we have to plot the 'More than' frequencies against the lower boundaries of the class interval. A similarly obtained curve by joining all these points would result in gradually decreasing curve sloping downwards from right to the left. It would be an elongated S shape upside down.

These curves or Ogives are generally useful for finding out the number of observations below or above a given value of the variable. These can be used for comparisons of two or more distributions by constructing curves on the same graph. If there are large number of observations, these can be represented as percentage of total frequency and curve, then, is known as Percentile Curve. These curves are now illustrated in Problems 2.9 to 2.12.

2.10 USE OF COMPUTER FOR FREQUENCY DISTRIBUTION

Though we will be using simple techniques for solution of decision problems, the calculations at times can be large and manually unmanageable. In such cases, use of computers is very helpful. Various softwares have been listed out at the end of the book under "Annexure A".

In case of frequency distributions, softwares like SAS, SPSS, SYSTAT or Minitab can be used. We are not including the details of their usage. These can be effectively employed for faster work on calculations.

2.11 MEASURE OF CENTRAL TENDENCY AND LOCATION

In the discussion so far we elaborated as to how the statistical data can be tabulated and presented in a form to draw a meaningful inference at a glance. The analysis of the data, therefore, becomes easier and can be made use of in decision making process. The objective of the statistical analysis is to determine various numerical measures and summarising the values of a variable by representing the number of values of one single variable. Two of these characteristics are "Central Tendency" and "Dispersion". Whereas central tendency is the central or middle value of the distribution, the dispersion is the spread of the data in the distribution. It can be clearly seen from fig. 2.13 that central location of curve A and B are same whereas for curve C, it is different and to the right of curve A and B.

The data presented in the form of tables, diagrams, histograms, frequency curves can further be improved to draw business decision inferences, when the spread or the dispersion of data serves the purpose. Measure of central tendency and location is a step in the direction of such an analysis.

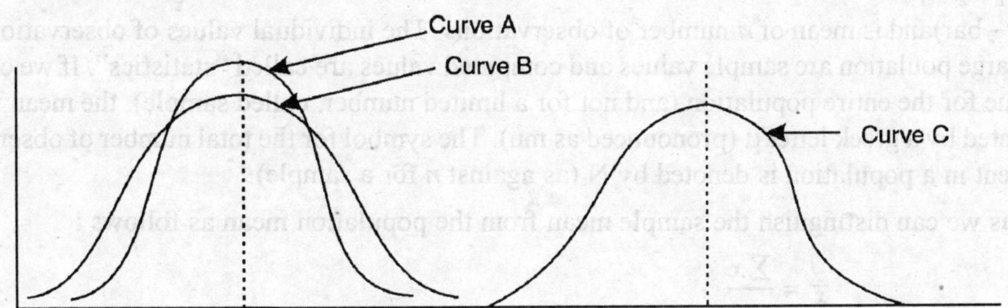

Fig. 2.13 Comparison of central location

The measure for curve A and B having the same central location is called average *i.e.* the average value of the statistic for curve A and B are the same. This measure reduces a large group of data into a single value that can be used in decision making. Averages are the values lying between the largest and the smallest value of the observations and denote the central part of the distribution of the data. These are called 'Measure of Central Tendency'. Averages are also sometimes called as 'Measure of Location' as they enable us to locate the position or place of the distribution in question. There are five measures of average — Arithmetic, Geometric and Harmonic means, median and mode.

Requisites of a Good Average

In general, the averages should satisfy following conditions :

1. It should be rigidly defined.
2. It should be based on all the relevant observations
3. It should be easily understandable.
4. It should be suitable for further mathematical treatment
5. It should not be affected much by extreme observations.
6. It should be least affected by data fluctuations.

2.12. MATHEMATICAL MEANS

Calculation of Arithmetic Mean

The arithmetic mean of a given set of data is their sum divided by the number of observations. Thus the arithmetic mean of 5. 10, 12, 18, 22, 25, 28, 30, 31, 35 can be calculated as under.

$$\text{Mean or Average} = \frac{5+10+12+18+22+25+28+30+31+35}{10}$$

$$= \frac{216}{10} = 21.6$$

Calculation of Mean for ungrouped data

The measure of central tendency can be done in the following manner —

- Average or Arithmetic mean
- Geometric mean
- Harmonic mean
- Median
- Mode
- The Arithmetic mean can be calculated through ungrouped or grouped data.

We can see that if the daily wages of 10 workers are given as Rs. 5, 10, 12, 18, 22, 25, 28, 30, 31, 35, then on the average, a worker gets Rs. 21.60 per day. The manager of this group would have a reasonable single value for a meaningful usage for his work force.

Writing the same relationship in general.

$$\text{Arthmetic mean or Average} = \bar{x} = \frac{x_1 + x_2 + x_3 + ... x_n}{n}$$

where x_1, x_2, x_3 etc are the individual values of n observations and the average value is represented by $\bar{x}$ (x - bar)and is mean of n number of observations. The individual values of observations used from a large poulation are sample values and computed values are called "statistics". If we compute this value for the entire population (and not for a limited number, called sample), the mean value is represented by a greek letter μ (pronounced as mu). The symbol for the total number of observations or element in a population is denoted by N (as against n for a sample).

Thus we can distinguish the sample mean from the population mean as follows :

$$\bar{x} = \frac{\Sigma x}{n}$$

and

$$\mu = \frac{\Sigma x}{N}$$

The greek letter Σ (sigma) is used for summation of all the values of x together, The method is called "calculation of Mean or Average value of ungrouped data".

Measurement of Mean from Grouped data

If the value of the observation is repeated, then these are called frequencies of the value and are denoted by f

$$\text{Thus} \quad \bar{x} = \frac{(x_1 + x_1 + ... f_1 \, times) + (x_2 + x_2 + ... f_2 \, times) + ...(x_n + x_n + ... f_n \, times)}{f_1 + f_2 + ... f_n}$$

$$= \frac{f_1 x_1 + f_2 x_2 + ... f_n x_n}{f_1 + f_2 + ... f_n}$$

$$= \frac{\Sigma fx}{\Sigma f}$$

$$= \frac{\Sigma fx}{n}$$

Thus sample arithmetic mean of a grouped data of n-observations can be written as

$$\bar{x} = \frac{\sum fx}{n}$$

where x = Mean value of the sample observation

f = frequency of various values

x = values of observations

n = total number of observations

Σ = symbol for the summation

The same relationship can be extended to a grouped data arranged as class intervals and their relative frequency. In this case

f = frequency of observations in each class

x = mid point of each class

Step Deviation Method for Arithmetic Mean

When values of x and f are large, then the mean calculations become very cumbersome. Hence we can use the step-deviation method for the purpose by using deviations of the given observations from any arbitrary value say A.

An important and short-cut method of Calculating Arithmetic mean is 'Step Deviation Method', wherein through a common assumed mean, we can calculate the average of the whole data base in a convenient calculation form.

Then $$d = X - A$$

and
$$\Sigma fd = \Sigma f(X - A)$$
$$= \Sigma fX - A\Sigma f \qquad \text{(A being constant)}$$
$$= \Sigma fX - n.A$$

or
$$\frac{\sum fd}{n} = \frac{\sum fX}{n} - A$$
$$= \bar{x} - A$$

$\therefore$
$$\bar{x} = A + \frac{\sum fd}{n}$$

If class intervals are of equal magnitude, the computation can be further simplified by using

$$d = \frac{X - A}{h} \qquad (h = \text{common magnitude of the class interval})$$

Hence $$hd = X - A$$

and $$hfd = fX - A.f$$

or $$h\,\Sigma fd = \Sigma fX - n.A$$

or
$$\frac{h\sum fd}{n} = \frac{\sum fX}{n} - \text{A}$$
$$= \bar{x} - A$$
$$\bar{x} = A + \frac{h\sum fd}{n}$$

Weighted Average

When all the observations in a data bank do not have the same importance, such as sal es of airconditioners in the month of March can have better bearing as the forecast sales of April (being seasonal variation), then for average computation, more importance can be attached to the sales of March than that for February and January. If these importance levels (called weightages for the observations) are taken into account, the average so obtained is termed as Weighted Average. This can be calculated as follows.

Let $w_1, w_2, w_3 .... w_n$ be the weights attached to observations $x_1, x_2, x_3....x_n$. Then weighted average of the observations can be calculated as under.

$$\overline{x}_w = \frac{w_1x_1 + w_2x_2 + ...w_nx_n}{w_1 + w_2 + ...w_n}$$

In case of frequency distribution, the relationship undergoes the change as follows :

$$\overline{x}_w = \frac{w_1(f_1x_1) + w_2(f_2x_2) + ...w_n(f_nx_n)}{w_1 + w_2 + ...w_n}$$

$$= \frac{\Sigma w(fx)}{\Sigma w}$$

The concept of weighted average is very handy when all the observations or a set of observations donot play the same part in the overall analysis. In certain specific business situation, the 'weighted average' can produce coherent and problem related solution.

Advantages of Arithmetic Mean

1. It is well known and established measure
2. It can be easily calculated
3. It is useful for many statistical procedures such as comparison of many sets of data
4. Every set of data has a mean value

Disadvantages

1. It reflects all the values of the set of observations, but can be affected by extreme values, where may not be representing the set as best.
2. It is lengthy method for large number of observations.
3. For open ended data, it is difficult to compute

CALCULATION OF GEOMETRIC MEAN

The Geometric Mean of a set of n observations is the nth root of their product. If the observations are $x_1, x_2, x_3, ... x_n$.

Then Geometric Mean (GM)= $\sqrt[n]{x_1.x_2.x_3.....x_n}$

$$= (x_1, x_2, x_3, ... x_n)^{1/n}$$

It is easy to calculate only if $n = 2$. If n is larger, then we have to use the logarithmic concept as follows

$$\text{Log (GM)} = \frac{1}{n} \log\ (x_1.x_2.x_3....x_n)$$

$$= \frac{1}{n} (\log x_1 + \log x_2 + ...\log x_n)$$

$$= \frac{1}{n} \Sigma \log x$$

Hence $$\text{GM} = \text{Anti log} \left(\frac{1}{n} \Sigma \log x\right)$$

CALCULATION OF HARMONIC MEAN

If $x_1, x_2, x_3....x_n$ is a set of n observations, their Harmonic Mean (HM) is given by

$$HM = \frac{1}{\frac{1}{n}\left[\frac{1}{x_1}+\frac{1}{x_2}+....\frac{1}{x_n}\right]}$$

$$= \frac{1}{\frac{1}{n}\sum\left[\frac{1}{x_1}\right]} = \frac{n}{\sum\left[\frac{1}{X}\right]}$$

Thus the Harmonic Mean is the reciprocal of the arithmetic mean of the reciprocals of the given observations.

RELATIONS BETWEEN ARITHMETIC MEAN, GEOMETRIC MEAN AND HARMONIC MEAN

The relationship of the three means is as follows :

$$AM \geq GM \geq HM$$

The sign of equality holds good only if all the observations are equal. This can easily be proved for two numbers. There is yet another relationship of AM, GM and HM for two numbers only *i.e.*,

$$G^2 = A \times H$$

where G = Geometic Mean

A = Arithmetic Mean

and H = Harmonic Mean

The geometric and harmonic means have very special significance for a very specific business problem. At the same time, the concept of Median can be applied to show the divide of the data group in a specific manner. It can be used for grouped or ungrouped data as per actual situation.

2.13. MEDIAN

The median is that value of the variable, which divides the group in two equal parts, one part comprising all the values greater and the other, all values less than the median. Thus median is only a positional average *i.e.* its value depends on the position occupied by a value in the frequency distribution.

Calculation of Median

Ungrouped Data : If the number of observations is odd, then the median is the middle value of the rearranged form of the observations either in the ascending or in the descending order. Thus for the observations 5, 10, 25, 15, 50, 40, 35, the arranged order is 5, 10, 15, 25, 35, 40, 50 and the median is the middle value *i.e.* 25 (3 observations are lower than 25 *i.e.* 5, 10, 15 and other 3 observations are higher than the median *i.e.* 35, 40 and 50)

If the ungrouped data contains even number of observations, then the median is calculated as the arithmetic mean of the two middle numbers, provided the data is arranged either in ascending or descending order. Thus in a list of observations 5, 10, 25, 15, 50, 40, 35, 17 the rearranged data in the descending order becomes 50, 40, 35, 25, 17, 15, 10 and 5, and the two middle values are 25 and 17. By taking the average of the two *i.e.* $\frac{25+17}{2} = 21$, we have obtained Median as 21.

Grouped Data or Frequency Distribution : In case of frequency distribution, the values of the variables are given as x_1, x_2, x_3, etc. and their related frequencies as f_1, f_2, f_3 etc. Where $\Sigma f = N$, *i.e.* the sum total of frequencies. Then the median is calculated in the following manner :

1. Rearrange the data in terms of 'less than' cumulative frequency distribution
2. Find $N/2$.
3. Check where the cumulative frequency just exceeds the value of $N/2$
4. The value of the variable corresponding to the cumulative frequency in step (3) is the Median.

Continuous Frequency Distribution : In a continuous frequency distribution data, we obtain the value of the median in the same manner as above, but here the value of the variable will be a class interval and not a specified value. This is called the Median class. For obtaining median, we use the following formula.

$$\text{Median} = l + \frac{h}{f}\left(\frac{N}{2} - c\right)$$

Where l = lower limit of the median class

h = magnitude or the width of the median class

f = frequency of the median class

c = cumulative frequency of the class preceeding the median class.

and $N = \Sigma f$ *i.e.* the total cumulative frequency .

Mode is the concept used where the occurance frequency is large. Thus the data is divided on the basis of frequency density, for which various methods are used. Frequency distribution of the data is an easy approach to work out the Mode of the data.

2.14. MODE

Mode is the value, which occurs most frequently in a set of observations. In simple language "Mode is the value which has the greatest frequency density in its immediate neighbourhood".

Computation of Mode

As per the simple definition given above, the mode is the value of the variable corresponding to the maximum frequency in a frequency distribution. Hence in a table of frequency distribution given below, the mode is the variable value for the maximum frequency.

Thus taking a case of Data array arranged in the ascending order

TABLE 2.17 Data Array in Ascending Order

Value	Count	Value	Count	Value	Count	Value	Count	Value	Count
0	2	2	4	4		8			
0		2		5	2	12		18	
1	3	2		5		15		19	3
1		2		6		16	5	19	
1		3	2	7	2	16		19	
		3		7		16		20	2
						16		20	
						16			

We observe that value 16 has occured maximum number of times (5 times) i.e. the maximum frequency is that for the value 16, the Mode, therefore for this data is 16.

Using the same data and arranging it as frequency distribution, we get

TABLE 2.18 Data Arranged as Frequency Distribution

Class	*Frequency*
0–2	9
3–5	5
6–8	4
9–11	0
12–14	1
15–17	6
18–20	6

Here the maximum frequency occurs for class-interval 0 - 2 (9 times). Thus 0 - 2 is the modal class. This is called the Grouping Method.

Multimodal Distributions : We can encounter cases, where there can be more than one observation indicating modal value or in a frequency distribution pattern, more than one class as modal class. This happens when the frequency of the value or a class interval is the same. These cases are called multimodal cases or multimodal distributions.

Taking a case of values given in the table 2.19. There are two modal values 4 and 7. This is called Bimodal case.

TABLE 2.19. Data Arranged in Ascending Order

1	4	6	9
2	4	7	9
2 } 3	4 } 4	7 } 2	9 } 4
2	4	8 } 2	9
3 } 2	5	8	10
3			

Since values 2 are occuring 3 times which are higher than the neighboring values, this is also a modal value, though not of same frequency. But values 4 and 9 are multimodal values.

Since the mode calculation indicates the "most frequent data", it can have more than one such 'most frequency' data. It this case, a multimodel distribution method of calculation of mode can be adopted.

Mode of continuous frequency distribution : In case of continuous frequency distribution, the class pertaining to the maximum frequency is called the modal class. The mode interpolation formula is given below :

$$\text{Mode} = l + \frac{h(f_1 - f_0)}{(f_1 - f_0) - (f_2 - f_1)}$$

$$= l + \frac{h(f_1 - f_0)}{2f_1 - f_0 - f_2}$$

Where l = lower limit of the class

h = magnitude or width of the modal class

f_0 = frequency of the class preceeding the modal class

f_1 = frequency of the modal class

f_2 = frequency of the class succeeding the modal class.

An alternate formula can be used for calculation of mode as under.

$$\text{Mode} = l + \left[\frac{f_2}{f_1 + f_2}\right] \times h$$

where the notations have the same meaning as given above.

Mode by method of grouping (distribution irregular) : Calculation of mode can be done as above if the frequency table is regular. If it is not, as is the case below, the method of grouping is to be applied.

Let us take the frequency distribution as follows

x	10	11	12	13	14	15	16	17	18	19
y	5	6	9	8	7	2	5	3	2	1

Here frequency is first increasing upto 9, then decreasing to 2, increasing again to 5 and then decreasing to 1, thus irregular. In such cases, various frequencies can be grouped together, initially in a group of 2 and then moving leaving the first and so on. These groupings can be done for 3 frequencies and so on. At the end of this computation, we work out the maximum number of times a particular frequency occurs. It will then be called the modal class and mode can be worked out accordingly as given in problem 2.28.

Various means have their inter-relationships, such as $G^2 = A \times H$ where G = Geometric Mean A = Arithmetic mean and H = Harmonic Mean Similarly, there is a relationship of Arithmetic mean, mode and median, i.e., Mode = 3 Median – 2 Mean.

2.15. EMPIRICAL RELATION BETWEEN MEAN, MODE AND MEDIAN

The following empirical relationship has been developed by Prof. Karl Pearson to connect Mean, Mode and Median.

$$\text{Mode} = \text{Mean} - 3\,(\text{Mean} - \text{Median}) \qquad (i)$$

or $$\text{Mean} - \text{Median} = \frac{1}{3}\,(\text{Mean} - \text{Mode}) \qquad (ii)$$

or $$\text{Mode} = 3\ \text{Median} - 2\ \text{Mean} \qquad (iii)$$

CHAPTER SUMMARY

Important terms used

- **Continuous Data -** Data which progresses from one class to another without a break and can be expressed as either whole number or a fraction.
- **Cumulative Frequency Distribution -** Table of values or observations indicating how many values are either above or below that class.
- **Data -** Data are collection of any number of observations pertaining to a happening, of either one or more variables.
- **Data Array -** An arrangement of data either in the ascending or descending order.
- **Discrete Class -** when data class does not progress from one class to another without a break.
- **Frequency Curve -** A frequency polygon modification by smoothing classes and data points for a data set.
- **Frequency Distribution -** A table structuring the data into classes of suitable intervals showing number of observations falling into a certain class interval.
- **Frequency Polygon -** A line graph connecting the midpoints of each class in a Data set at the frequency height of a class.

- **Histogram** - A graph of a data set, in the form of series of rectangles, width indicating the class interval and height as its frequency.
- **Ogive** - It is a cumulative frequency curve.
- **Open-Ended Class** - A class permitting either the upper or lower end of the quantitative class to be limit less.
- **Population** - A collection of all the elements of the system under study.
- **Raw Data** - Information or observations as collected from the system before these are arranged in any logical form.
- **Relative Frequency Distribution** - The presentation of data showing fraction or percentage of the total data under a particular class.
- **Representative sample** - A sample containing all the relevant characteristics of the population it represents, in all its proportions the same as in original population.
- **Sample** - A collection of data of some elements of a population representing all its elements in right proportion.
- **Bimodal Distribution** – A distribution of 2 observations occurring more frequently than the others in a set of values.
- **Geometric Mean** – A measure of central tendency for multiplicative effects of the set of observations.
- **Mean** – A measure of central tendency representing the arithmetic average of the given set of observations.
- **Measure of Central Tendency** – The measure of values of observations indicating their position between the highest and the lowest values of observation denoting the central part of the observations.
- **Median** – Middle point of a set of observations dividing the set into two halves.
- **Median Class** – A frequency distribution class interval denoting the median value of observations,
- **Mode** – The value most often occurring or being repeated in a set of observations
- **Statistics** – Numerical measures describing the characteristics of a sample.
- **Weighted Average** – A mean or average value calculated to take into account the importance of each value to the overall total.

Important Relationships used

- $\mu = \frac{\Sigma x}{N}$
- $\bar{x} = \frac{\Sigma x}{n}$
- $\bar{x} = \frac{\Sigma fx}{\Sigma f}$
- $\bar{x} = A + h\frac{\Sigma fd}{\Sigma f}$
- $\bar{x} = \frac{\Sigma wx}{\Sigma w}$
- $\text{GM} = \sqrt[n]{x_1, x_2, x_3 \ldots\ldots. x_n}$
- $\text{HM} = \frac{n}{\Sigma\left(\frac{1}{x}\right)}$

- $G^2 = A \times H$
- Median $= \left[\dfrac{n+1}{2}\right]$th item in a data array

  $= l + \dfrac{h}{f}\left(\dfrac{N}{2} - c\right)$
- Mode = value of most repeated observations

  $= l + \dfrac{h(f_1 - f_0)}{2f_1 - f_0 - f_2}$
- Mode $= l + h\left[\dfrac{f_2}{f_1 + f_2}\right]$

SOLVED PROBLEMS

Problem 2.1

Draw the histogram for the following frequency distribution:

Statistic Value	*Frequency*
0 – 10	10
10 – 20	5
20 – 30	12
30 – 40	35
40 – 50	17
50 – 60	15
60 – 70	8
70 – 80	62
80 – 90	37
90 – 100	25

Solution :

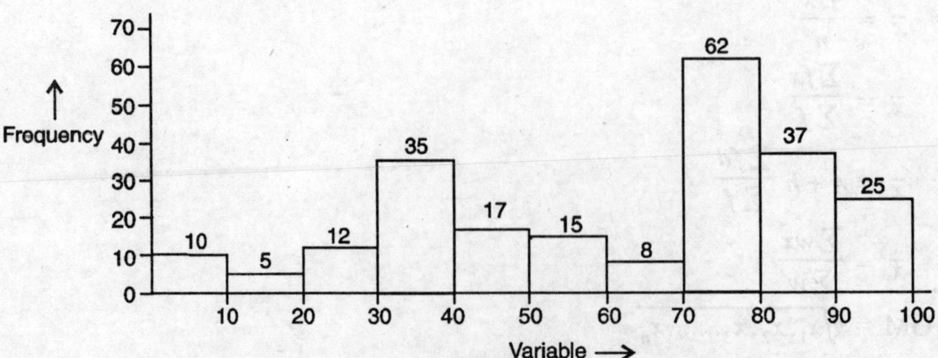

Fig. 2.13 Histogram of frequency distribution

Problem 2.2

Draw the histogram for the frequency distribution given in Table 2.14.

Solution :

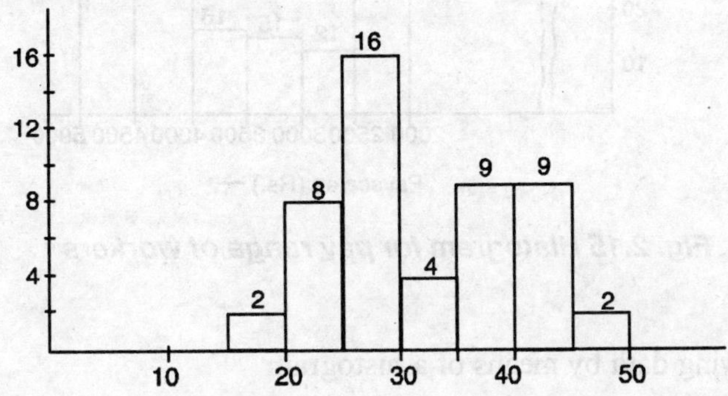

Fig. 2.14 Histogram of delayed payment

Problem 2.3

Draw the histogram for the following data distribution for pay scales of 200 workers in a factory.

Pay level (Rs.)	*No. of workers*
Less than 2,000	35
Less than 2,500	59
Less than 3.000	71
Less than 3,500	86
Less than 4,000	102
Less than 4,500	159
Less than 5,000	200

Solution :

This table indicates the number of workers in various categories as cumulative frequency under each category. We, therefore, first convert it into the frequency distribution table as follows:

Table 2.17 Payscales of Factory workers

Pay level (Rs.)	*No. of workers*
0–2,000	35
2,000–2,500	59 – 35 = 24
2,500–3,000	71 – 59 =12,
3,000–3,500	86 – 71=15
3,500–4,000	102 – 86 = 16
4,000–4,500	159 – 102 = 57
4,500–5,000	200 – 159 = 41

Now the histogram can be drawn as follows (Fig. 2.15)

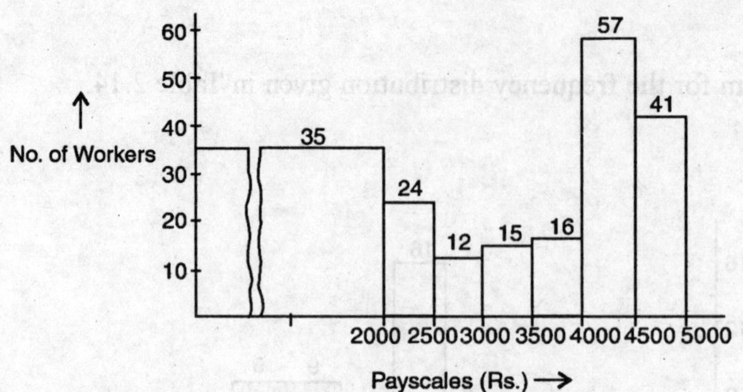

Fig. 2.15 Histogram for pay range of workers

Problem 2.4

Represent the following data by means of a histogram

Weekly wages :	10-15	15-20	20-25	25-30	30-45	40-60	60-80
No. of workers :	7	19	27	15	12	12	8

[*Delhi University. B.Com. (Hons.) 1977*]

Solution :

In this question, all class-intervals are not the same. Hence there is a necessity of adjusting the relative heights of the rectangles in the following manner:

TABLE 2.18 Frequency Distribution of Workers

Weekly Wages	*No. of Workers*	*Class Interval*	*Height of the Rectangle*
10-15	7	5	7
15-20	19	5	19
20-25	27	5	27
25 - 30	15	5	15
30-40	12	10	12/2=6
40-60	12	20	12/4=3
60-80	8	20	8/4 = 2

Now the corresponding histogram can be drawn as follows

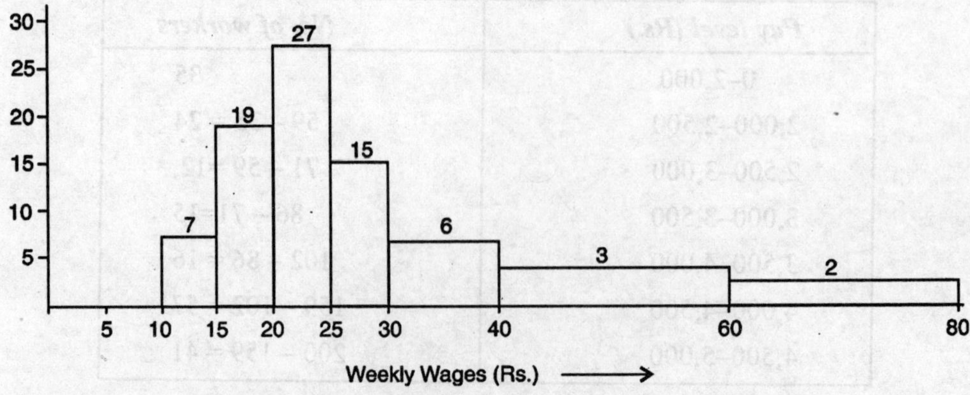

Fig. 2.16 Histogram for worker's wages distribution

Problem 2.5

Given below are the marks obtained by 35 students in a class. Make a frequency table, draw a histogram and a frequency polygon from the frequency distribution.

70, 60, 39, 65, 45, 63, 57, 42, 51, 71, 26, 63, 64, 69, 59, 54, 42, 33, 75, 65, 55, 41, 52, 64, 53, 82, 67, 61, 47, 41, 25, 36, 59, 63, 39.

Solution :

With 35 students strength, let us divide the data into class-intervals of 10. The frequency tuble is given below :

TABLE 2.19 Frequency Distribution of Marks

Class-interval (x)	*Tally marks*	*Frequency* (f)
0-10	–	0
10-20	–	0
20-30	II	2
30-40	IIII	4
40-50	IIII I	6
50-60	IIII III	8
60-70	IIII III	11
70-80	IIII IIII I	3
80-90	III	1
90-100	–	0
		Total 35

Since all the classes are of equal magnitude, we construct rectangles of proportional heights.

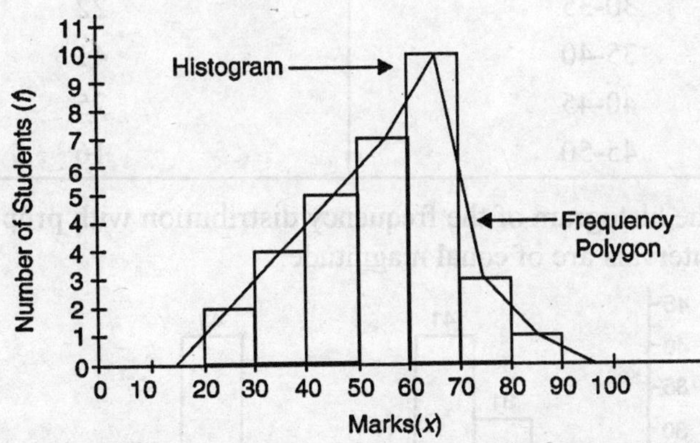

Fig. 2.17 Histogram and Polygon for marks obtained by students

The histogram as drawn above from the frequency table has now been converted into a Frequency Polygon by joining the mid-points on top of these rectangles through straight lines and Frequency Polygon obtained is marked so in Fig. 2.17.

Problem 2.6

Draw the histogram and frequency polygon for the data given below :

Mid value of the class	*Frequency*
25	5
7.5	7
12.5	31
17.5	41
22.5	20
27.5	11
32.5	22
37.5	41
42.5	25
47.5	16

Solution :

Since the mid-points of the classes have been given and the difference is uniformly 5, we can construct the frequency table as follows:

TABLE 2.20 Frequency Distribution

Class Interval	*Frequency*
0-5	5
5-10	7
10-15	31
15-20	41
20-25	20
25-30	11
30-35	22
35-40	41
40-45	25
45-50	16

Now we can draw the histogram of the frequency distribution with proportional heights of the rectangles, since class intervals are of equal magnitude.

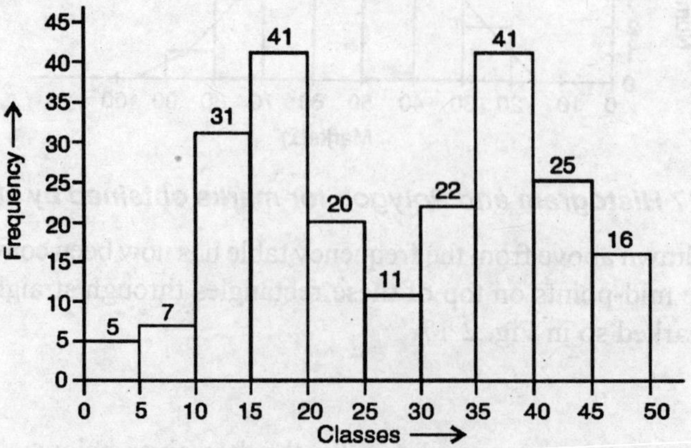

Fig.2.18 Histogram and Frequency Polygon

Problem 2.7

Draw a frequency curve for the following data :

Amount of Pocket Money (Rs.) :	0–20	20–40	40–60	60–80	80–100
Number of Children :	17	15	33	20	15

Solution :

Since the problem has classes of equal magnitude and continuous, the histogram can be drawn as follows: (Fig. 2.19).

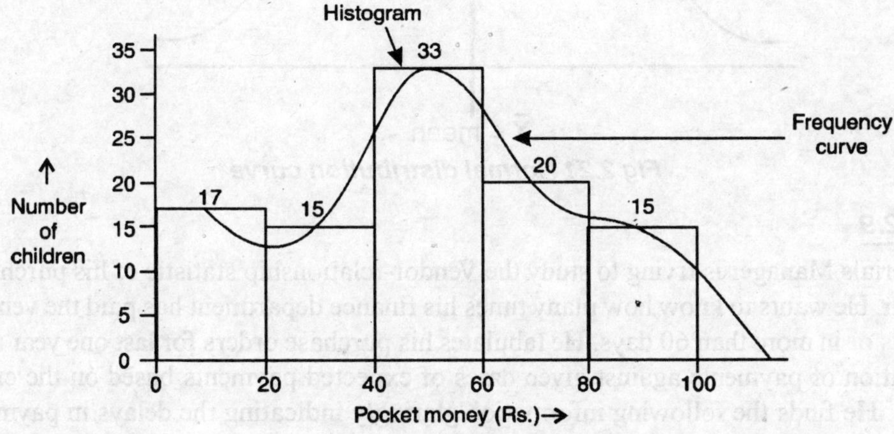

Fig. 2.19 Pocket money for children

Problem 2.8

Draw a frequency distribution curve for the following data:

Marks :	0-10	10-20	20-30	30-40	40-50	50-60	60-70	70-80	80-90
Number of Students :	40	70	120	160	180	160	120	70	40

Solution :

Based on equal magnitude class intervals, the histogram and the resultant frequency curve can be drawn as follow :

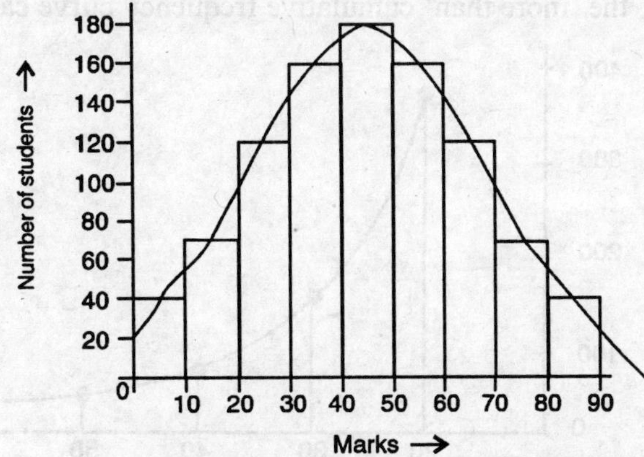

Fig. 2.20 Frequency distribution curve

The shape of the frequency curve is symmetrical and can be compared with the most commonly used symmetrical frequency distribution (normal frequency curve) given below:

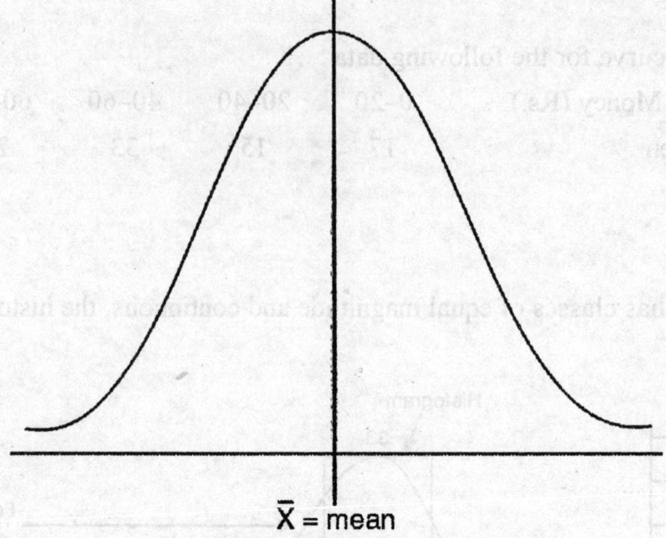

Fig 2.21 Normal distribution curve

Problem 2.9

A Materials Manager is trying to study the Vendor-relationship statistic of his purchases for the last one year. He wants to know how many times his finance department has paid the vendors in less than 30 days or in more than 60 days. He tabulates his purchase orders for last one year and collects the information of payments against given dates of expected payments based on the credit period agreements. He finds the following information glaringly indicating the delays in payments.

TABLE 2.21 Cumulative Frequency of Data on Payment System

Class	*Cumulative Frequency*
More than 20 days	357
More than 30 days	168
More than 40 days	75
More than 50 days	42
More than 60 days	15

Solution :

From the above data, the 'more than' cumulative frequency curve can be drawn.

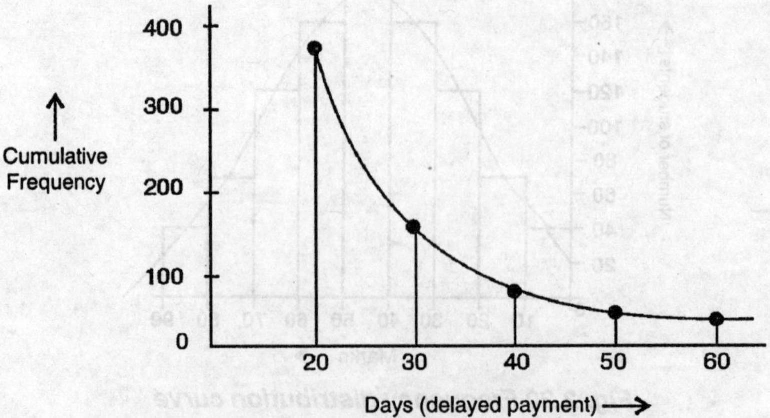

Fig. 2.22 'More than' cumulative frequency curve

Thus he can infer that in case of payments, the finance department has delayed payments for more than 60 days for 15 purchases, which can be further analysed and future corrective action initiated to avoid any disgruntlement of the vendors for late payments.

Similar analysis can be drawn by drawing 'less than' cumulative frequency curves to establish the number of purchase orders paid in less than 30 days delay, which can be explained to the vendors to indicate good payment schedules by the company.

Problem 2.10

From the given data, draw the 'less than' ogive.

Class	*Cumulative Frequency*
Less than 30 days	0
Less than 40 days	7
Less than 50 days	15
Less than 60 days	27
Less than 70 days	32
Less than 80 days	38
Less than 90 days	45

Solution :

From the above given data we can draw the 'less than' Ogive as follows: (Fig. 2.23)

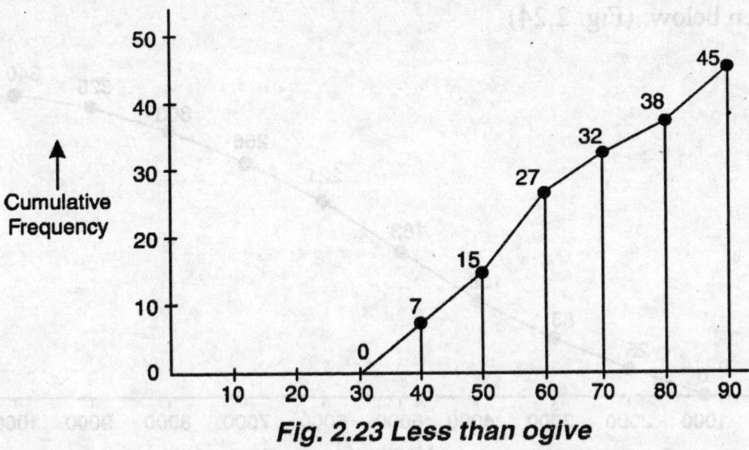

Fig. 2.23 Less than ogive

Problem 2.11

Draw a less 'than cumulative' frequency curve from the following data :

Monthly Income	*Number of Workers*
0 – 1,000	0
1,000 – 2,000	25
2,000 – 3,000	38
3,000 – 4,000	45
4,000 – 5,000	55
5,000 – 6,000	58
6,000 – 7,000	45
7,000 – 8,000	37
8,000 – 9,000	22
9,000 – 10,000	15

Solution :

The table given above has to be converted into 'less than' cumulative frequency table, as given below.

TABLE 2.22 'Less than' Cumulative Frequency Table

Monthly Income	*No. of Workers*	*Less than Cumulative Frequency*
0 – 1,000	0	0
1,000 – 2,000	25	25
2,000 – 3,000	38	63
3,000 – 4,000	45	108
4,000 – 5,000	55	163
5,000 – 6,000	58	221
6,000 – 7,000	45	266
7,000 – 8,000	37	303
8,000 – 9,000	22	325
9,000 – 10,000	15	340

Now the 'less than' cumulative frequency curve is drawn by plotting the 'less than' cumulative frequency against the upper limit of the corresponding class and joining these points through a smooth curve, as given below: (Fig. 2.24)

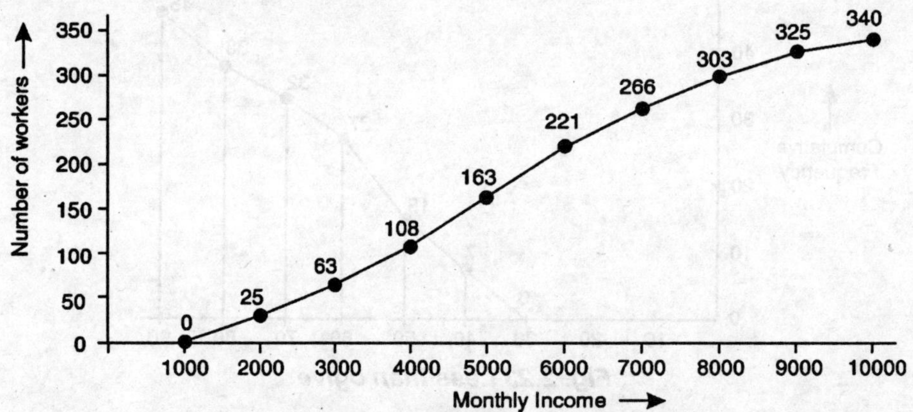

Fig. 2.24 Less than CF curve

Problem 2.12

The following table gives the distribution of monthly income of 600 families in a certain city.

Monthly Income (Rs.)	*No. of Families*
Below 75	60
75-150	170
150-225	200
225-300	60
300-375	50
375-450	40
450 and more	20

Draw a 'less than' and a 'more than' ogive curve for the above data on the same graph and from these read the median income. *[Delhi University, B.Com., (Hons.). 1974]*

Solution :

In order to draw the two curves *i.e.*, 'less than' Ogive and 'more than' Ogive, 'we convert the above table into the corresponding cumulative frequencies as follows:

TABLE 2.23 'Less than' and 'More than' Cumulative Frequency Table

Monthly Income (Rs.)	*No. of families*	*Less than cf*	*More than cf*
below 75	60	60	600
75- 150	170	230	540
150-225	200	430	370
225 - 300	60	490	170
300-375	50	540	110
375-450	40	580	60
450 and more	20	600	20

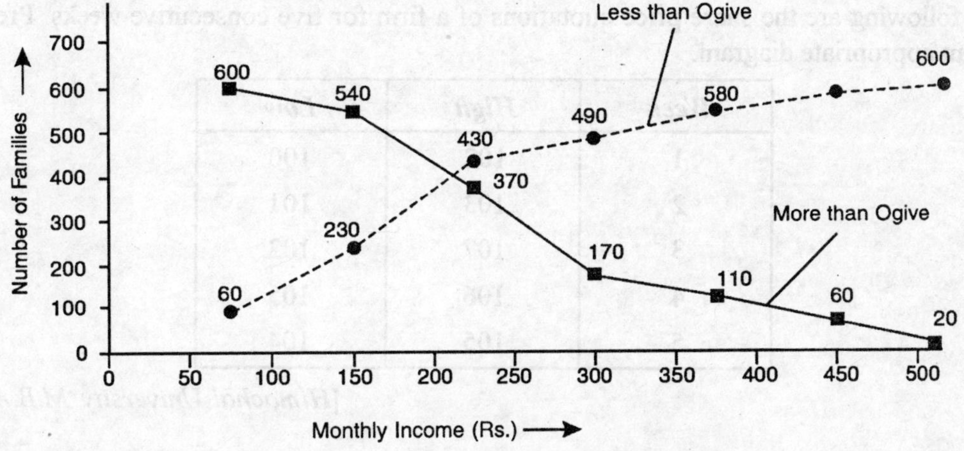

Fig. 2.25. Less than and More than Ogive

For drawing a 'less than' Ogive, we plot the less than of ' against the upper limit of the corresponging class interval, whereas for a 'more than' Ogive, we'plot 'more than' of against the lower boundary of the corresponding class and then obtain the curves by joining these points by a smooth curve respectively.

Problem 2.13

Plot the line graph for the following data :

Year	:	1991	1992	1993	1994	1995	1996	1997	1998	1999	2000
Imports	:	450	510	560	600	640	620	540	500	450	400
Exports	:	200	230	285	320	350	380	410	450	400	350

The values of imports and exports are given in Rs. in millions.

Solution :

The line graphs are drawn as follows:

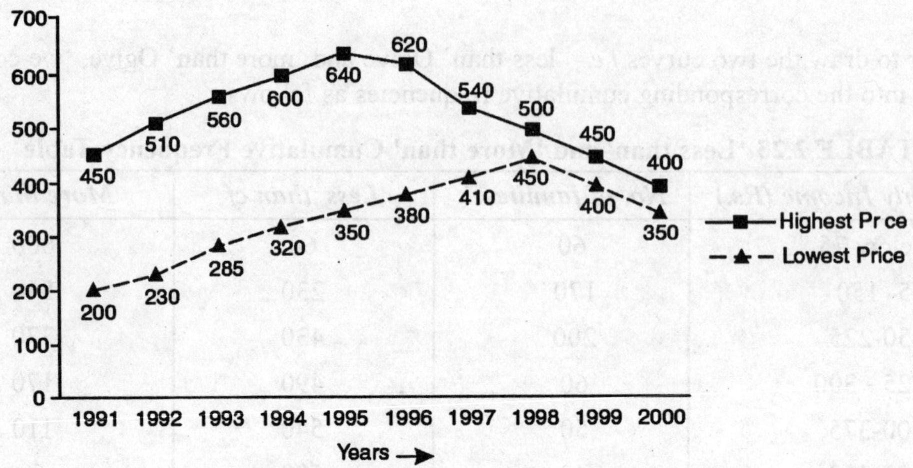

Fig. 2.26. Imports/Exports (1991-2000)

Problem 2.14

The following are the share price quotations of a firm for five consecutive weeks. Present the data by an appropriate diagram.

Week	*High*	*Low*
1	102	100
2	103	101
3	107	103
4	106	105
5	105	104

[*Himachal University, M.B.A., 1979*]

Solution :

Since two prices are indicated for each week, a graph representing the high and low prices will be drawn separately. This would indicate the range in which share prices have moved during the period under consideration.

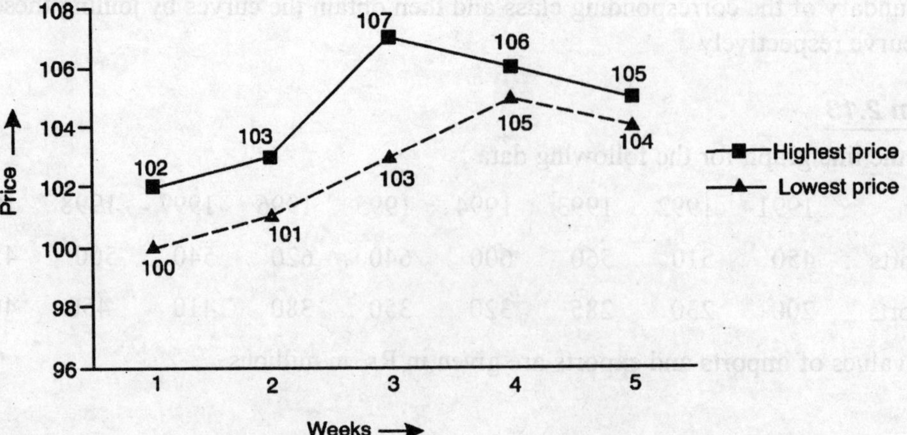

Fig. 2.27. Imports/Exports (1991-2000)

Problem 2.15

Calculate the average value of age for a class of 10 students with their ages as under : 11, 12, 13, 13, 10, 13, 12, 11, 10, 12 years.

Solution :

$$\text{Average age} = \bar{x} = \frac{11+12+13+13+10+13+12+11+10+12}{10}$$

$$= \frac{117}{10}$$

$$= 11.7 \text{ years}$$

Problem 2.16

The following table indicates the marks obtained by students in a class test. Calculate the average level of marks of the class.

Marks obtained :	0	2	3	4	5	6	7	8	9
Number of students :	11	10	9	21	12	17	8	22	15

Solution :

$$\Sigma f = 11 + 10 + 9 + 21 + 12 + 17 + 8 + 22 + 15 = 125$$

$$\Sigma fx = 11 \times 0 + 10 \times 2 + 9 \times 3 + 21 \times 4 + 12 \times 5 + 17 \times 6 + 8 \times 7 + 22 \times 8 + 15 \times 9 = 660$$

$$= \frac{\Sigma fx}{\Sigma f}$$

$$= \frac{660}{125}$$

$$= 5.3 \text{ marks}$$

The same data can be tabulated as follows and then used to calculate the average of the observations.

Number of marks (x)	*Number of students (f)*	*Product (f.x)*
0	11	0
2	10	20
3	9	27
4	21	84
5	12	60
6	17	102
7	8	56
8	22	176
9	15	135
	$N = \Sigma f = 125$	$(\Sigma fx) = 660$

$$\therefore \text{ Mean marks or class average} = \bar{x} = \frac{660}{125} = 5.3 \text{ marks.}$$

Problem 2.17

Computing Arithmetic mean using mid-values of class intervals, given below is the table for service time on a work station; calculate the average service time for the place.

Class Interval (minutes) :	0-10	10-20	20-30	30-40	40-50	50-60
Frequency (No. of Cars) :	6	5	8	12	5	15

Solution :

The data can be put into the tabulated form as follows:

Class intervals	*Mid. values (x)*	*Frequency (f)*	*fx*
0 – 10	5	6	30
10 – 20	15	5	75
20 – 30	25	8	200
30 – 40	35	12	420
40 – 50	45	5	225
50 – 60	55	15	825
		$N = \Sigma f = 51$	$\Sigma fx = 1775$

Hence average Service time $= \dfrac{\Sigma fx}{\Sigma f}$

or, $= \dfrac{1775}{51}$

= 34.8 minutes

Problem 2.18

The data in respect of daily sales of refrigerators for a company are given below (in thousands). Calculate the average sales per day for the company.

14, 23, 8, 26, 5, 27, 46, 45, 32, 30, 42, 7, 6, 32, 15, 28, 12, 16, 22, 36, 26, 15, 40, 31, 29

Solution :

The raw data can first be tabulated in the following manner :

Daily Sales (in thousands)	*Mid-values (x)*	*Frequency (f)*	*f. (x)*
1 – 10	5.5	4	22.0
11 – 20	15.5	5	77.5
21 – 30	25.5	7	178.5
31 – 40	35.5	6	213.0
41 – 50	45.5	3	136.5
		$\Sigma f = 25$	$\Sigma fx = 627.5$

Hence Average Daily Sales $= \bar{x} = \dfrac{\Sigma fx}{\Sigma f}$

$= \dfrac{627.5}{25} = 25.1$ Say 25 thousand refrigerators.

If we calculate the average daily sales by using raw data or ungrouped data, we get

$$\bar{x} = \frac{\sum x}{\sum f}$$

$$= \frac{14+23+8+26+5+27+46+45+32+30+42+7+6+32+15+28+12+16+22+36+26+15+40+31+29}{25}$$

$$= \frac{613}{25}$$

= 24.5 refrigerators

Thus there is only a marginal difference in the calculations using the raw data and the grouped frequency distribution data.

Problem 2.19

Calculate the Arithmetic Mean by Step Deviation Method for following data :

Values	:	0 – 10	10 – 20	20 – 30	30 – 40	40 – 50	50 – 60	60 – 70
Frequency	:	7	9	15	11	27	18	5

Solution :

Class interval	*Mid point (x)*	*Frequency (f)*	$d = \frac{x-35}{10}$	*f.d*
0 – 10	5	7	– 3	– 21
10 – 20	15	9	– 2	– 18
20 – 30	25	15	–1	–15
30 – 40	35	11	0	0
40 – 50	45	27	1	27
50 – 60	55	18	2	36
60 – 70	65	5	3	15
		$\Sigma f = 92 = n$		$\Sigma fd = 24$

Taking $A = 35, h = 10, d = \frac{x-35}{10}$

$$\bar{x} = A + \frac{h\Sigma fd}{n}$$

$$= 35 + \frac{10 \times 24}{92}$$

$$= 35 + 2.33$$

$$= 37.33$$

Problem 2.20

Let the table of observations be as under :

Subject	*Marks Obtained (%) (X)*	*Weightage for Admissions (W)*	*W.X*
Hindi	67	1	67
English	85	1	85
Physics	87	2	174
Chemistry	79	2	158
Maths	95	3	285

Find the Weighted Average.

Solution :

$$\bar{x}_w = \text{Weighted Average} = \frac{\Sigma WX}{\Sigma W} = \frac{769}{9}$$

$$= 85.5$$

Problem 2.21

Find the Geometric Mean of 2, 4, 8, 12, 16 and 24.

Solution :

X	2	4	8	12	16	24
Log *X*	0.3010	0.6021	0.9031	1.0792	1.2041	1.3802

Since $\log(\text{GM}) = \frac{1}{n}(\Sigma \log X)$

$= \frac{1}{6} \times 5.4697$

$= 0.9116$

Hence GM = anti log (0.9116)

$= 8.158$

Problem 2.22

Find the Geometric Mean of the following distribution.

Marks :	0 – 10	10 – 20	20 – 30	30 – 40	40 – 50	50 – 60	60 – 70
No. of students :	4	7	13	21	15	25	20

Solution :

Marks	*Mid point (x)*	*No. of student (f)*	*log X*	*f.log X*
0 – 10	5	4	0.6021	2.4084
10 – 20	15	7	0.8451	5.9157
20 – 30	25	13	1.1139	14.4807
30 – 40	35	21	1.3222	22.7662
40 – 50	45	15	1.1761	12.9415
50 – 60	55	25	1.3979	34.8475
60 – 70	65	20	1.3010	26.0200
		$\Sigma f = 105$		$\Sigma f(\log X) = 129.3800$

Hence $\quad GM = \text{Anti log}\left(\dfrac{\Sigma f(\log X)}{\Sigma f}\right)$

$$= \text{Anti log}\left(\frac{129.38}{105}\right)$$

$$= \text{Anti log } (1.2938)$$

$$= 19.88$$

Problem 2.23

The following table gives the weights of 31 persons in a sample enquiry. Calculate the mean weight using (*i*) Geometric Mean (*ii*) Harmonic Mean.

x:	130	135	140	145	146	148	149	150	157
f:	3	4	6	6	3	5	2	1	1

Solution :

Weights (*x*)	*Number of Persons* (*f*)	*log x*	*f. log x*	$\frac{1}{x}$	$\frac{f}{x}$
130	3	2.1139	6.3417	0.00769	0.02307
135	4	2.1303	8.5212	0.00741	0.02964
140	6	2.1461	12.8766	0.00714	0.04284
145	6	2.1614	12.9684	0.00690	0.04140
146	3	2.1644	6.4932	0.00685	0.02055
148	5	2.1703	10.8515	0.00676	0.03380
149	2	2.1732	4.3464	0.00671	0.01342
150	1	2.1761	2.1761	0.0067	0.00667
157	1	2.1959	2.1959	0.00637	0.00637
	$n = 31$		$\Sigma f \log x = 66.7710$		$\Sigma\frac{f}{x} = 0.21776$

Now $\quad GM = \text{Anti log}\left[\dfrac{1}{n}(\Sigma f \log x)\right]$

$$= \text{Anti log}\left[\frac{66.7710}{31}\right]$$

$$= \text{Anti log } (2.1539) = 142.5$$

$$HM = \frac{n}{\sum(f/x)}$$

$$= \frac{31}{0.21776} = 142.36$$

Problem 2.24

For the frequency table given below, calculate Median.

x:	0	1	2	3	4	5	6	7	8	9
f:	3	5	12	45	61	22	29	51	23	3

Solution :

Variable (x)	*Frequency (f)*	*Less than cf*
0	3	3
1	5	8
2	12	20
3	45	65
4	61	126
5	22	148
6	29	177
7	51	228
8	23	251
9	3	254

After obtaining less than *cf* as given above,

Let us calculate median stepwise.

(*i*) Less than *cf* has been obtained

(*ii*) $N/2 = \frac{254}{2} = 127$

(*iii*) The value of variable just above the figure of 127 is 5 (against 148 i.e. just higher than 127)

(*iv*) Hence Median of the observations is 5.

Problem 2.25

Considering the following table, obtain the median value :

Pay Scales (Rs.)	*Number of employees in that pay scale (Nos. in hundreds)*
Less than 2,000	14
Less than 3,000	19
Less than 4,000	26
Less than 5,000	35
5,000 and above	42

Solution :

We first prepare the continuous frequency distribution table as given below.

Pay Scales (Rs.)	*Number of employees in that pay scale (Nos. in hundreds)*	*Less than cf*
0 – 2,000	14	14
2,000 – 3,000	19 – 14 = 5	19
3,000 – 4,000	26 – 19 = 7	26
4,000 – 5,000	35 – 26 = 9	35
5,000 and above	42 – 35 = 7	42

Here $N = \Sigma f = 42$

Hence $\frac{N}{2} = \frac{42}{2} = 21$

Cumulative frequency just higher than this number is for class Rs. 3,000 – 4,000. Thus the class 3,000 – 4,000 is the median class, where

$l = 3{,}000;\ h = 1{,}000$

$f = 7;\ C = 19$

Hence Median $= 3{,}000 + \frac{1{,}000}{7}(21 - 19)$

$= 3{,}285.7$ (Median pay scale)

or Rs. 3,286

Problem 2.26

Given the following distribution, calculate 'Mode'.

Variable (x) :	1	2	3	4	5	6
Frequency (f) :	5	15	25	15	20	6

Solution :

The maximum frequency in this distribution is 25 and the value of the variable corresponding to this frequency is 3. Thus 3 is the Mode for the given distribution.

Poblem 2.27

Given the following data, calculate Mode.

Variable (x)	0 – 10	10 – 20	20 – 30	30 – 40	40 – 50	50 – 60	60 – 70
Frequency (f)	5	6	8	12	15	5	3

Solution :

In this case, the maximum frequency occurred is 15 and this pertains to the class 40 – 50 Hence class 40-50 is the model class.

Hence $\text{Mode} = l + \frac{h(f_1 - f_0)}{2f_1 - f_0 - f_2}$

$$= 40 + \frac{10(15-12)}{(2\times15)-(12+5)}$$

$= 42.3$

An alternate formula also can be used for calculation of Mode as follows

$$\text{Mode} = l + \left(\frac{f_2}{f_1+f_2}\right) \times h$$

$$= 40 + \left(\frac{5}{15+5}\right) \times 10$$

$= 42.5$

Since the second formula is only approximate, there is slight variation in the calculated value.

Problem 2.28

Calculate mode for the following data :

Marks	*No. of Students*	*Marks*	*No. of Students*
Below 10	4	Below 60	86
Below 20	6	Below 70	96
Below 30	24	Below 80	99
Below 40	46	Below 90	100
Below 50	67		

[*Delhi University B.Com., 1977*]

Solution :

Working out the class frequencies and writing the frequency distribution table, we obtain

Marks	*Frequency*	*Marks*	*Frequency*
0 –10	4	50 – 60	86 – 67 = 19
10 –20	6 – 4 =12	60 – 70	96 – 86 = 10
20 –30	24 – 6 = 18	70 – 80	99 – 96 = 13
30 – 40	46 – 24 = 22	80 – 90	100 – 99 = 1
40 – 50	67 – 46 = 21		

It is observed that frequencies are increasing first and then decreasing, the distribution is irregular and hence Method of grouping is used to locate modal class.

Marks	*Grouped Frequencies*					
	1	*2*	*3*	*4*	*5*	*6*
0 – 10	4	6				
10 – 20	2		20	24		
20 – 30	18	40				
30 – 40	22		43		42	61
40 – 50	21	40		62		
50 – 60	19		29			
60 – 70	10	13			50	32
70 – 80	3		4	14		
80 – 90	1					

In order to compute modal class, we prepare frequency of maximum occurance of a class interval

Column No.	*Max Frequency*	*Class interval involved*				
1	22		30 – 40			
2	40	20 – 30	3 0 – 40	40 – 50	50 – 60	
3	43		30 – 40	40 – 50		
4	62		30 – 40	40 – 50	50 – 60	
5	50			40 – 50	50 – 60	60 – 70
6	61	20 – 30	30 – 40			
Frequency of classes		2	5	5	3	1

From the frequency of occurance of various class intervals, we observe that the class 30 – 40 as well as 40 – 50 are occuring 5 times each. Hence this method does not clearly define the modal class. If maximum frequency had occured only once *i.e.* either only class 30 – 40 or class 40 – 50 it could have been declared as the modal class.

Now, we can use the relationship given in paragraph 2.15 for calculation of mode i.e.

Mode = 3 Median – 2 Mean

For calculation of mean, we can use step – deviations method by taking.

$$d = \frac{x-45}{10}$$

$$\text{Then, Mean} = A + \frac{h\sum fd}{N}$$

$$= 45 + \frac{10(-28)}{100}$$

$$= 42.2$$

Calculating Median, we have $\frac{N}{2} = 50$. Since cummulative frequency more than 50 is 67, the median class will be class 40 – 50.

$$\text{Hence Median} = 40 + \frac{h}{f}\left(\frac{N}{2} - 46\right)$$

$$= 40 + \frac{10}{21}(50 - 46)$$

$$= 41.9$$

$$\text{Now mode} = 3 \text{ Median} - 2 \text{ Mean}$$

$$= 3 \times 41.9 - 2 \times 42.2$$

$$= 41.3$$

PRACTICE PROBLEMS

2.29 Distinguish between (*i*) Primary and secondary data (*ii*) Sampling and census
[Delhi University. B.A. (Eco.). 1982]

2.30 What are the various methods of collecting statistical data? Which of these are most reliable and Why? *[Punjab University, M.A. (Eco.). 1979 ; Kurukshetra University. B.Com.. 1980]*

2.31 Distinguish between primary and secondary data. What precautions should be taken in the use of secondary data?
[Nagarjuna University B.Com., 1981; Allahabad University, B.Com., 1982; Lucknow University, B.Com., 1982]

2.32 What are the objectives of classification? Discuss different methods of classification.
[Osmania University. B.Com. (Hons.). April 1983]

2.33 (*a*) What are grouped and ungrouped frequency distributions? What are their uses? What are the considerations that one has to bear in mind while forming the frequency distribution?

(*b*) Briefly outline the considerations you will bear in mind while constructing a frequency distribution. *[Delhi University, B.Com. (Hons.), 1982]*

2.34 (*a*) What are various types of graphs used for presenting a frequency distribution ? Discuss briefly their (*i*) construction and (*ii*) relative merits and demerits.

(b) Explain briefly the various methods that are used for graphical representation of frequency distribution. [*Delhi University. M.B.A.. 1977*]

2.35 Discuss the utility and limitations of graphic method of presenting statistical data [*Delhi University. B.Com. (Hons.). 1976*]

2.36 Discuss the advantages and limitations of representing statistical data by diagrams (including graphs) [*Bombay University, B.Com., 1975*]

2.37 Distinguish between primary and secondary data. Give a brief account of the chief methods of collecting primary data and bring out their merits and defects. [*Delhi University. B.Com. (Hons.). 1979. 1977*]

2.38 Define a statistical unit and explain what should he the essential requirement of a good statistical unit. [*Osmania University, B.Com., April 1978*]

2.39 The following figures are income (x) and percentage expenditure on food (y) in 25 families. Construct a bivariate frequency table classifying x into intervals 200-300, 300-400 .... and y into 10-15, 15-20 etc. Write down the marginal distribution of x and y and the conditional distribution of x when y lies between 5 and 20.

x	y	x	y	x	y	x	y	x	y
550	12	225	25	680	13	202	29	689	11
623	14	310	26	300	25	255	27	523	12
310	18	640	20	425	16	492	18	317	18
420	16	512	18	555	15	587	21	384	17
600	15	690	12	325	23	643	19	400	19

[*Bombay University, B.Com., April 1981*]

2.40 Following are the marks obtained by 24 students in English (x) and Economics (y) in a test. Taking class intervals as 0-4, 5-9 etc. for x and y both; Construct (i) Bivariate frequency table (ii) .Marginal frequency tables of x and y.

(15.13), (0,1). (1,2.), (3,7). (16,8), (2,9), (18,12), (5,9), (4,17), (17,16), (6.6), (19,18), (14,11), (9,3). (8,5), (13.4). (10,10). (13,11). (11.14), (11,7). (12.18), (18,15). (9,15). (17.3).

[*Bombay University, B.A. (Eco.) April 1980*]

2.41 25 values of two variables X and Y are given,below. Form a two-way frequency table showing the relationship between the two. Take class-intervals of X as 10 to 20. 20 to 30. etc. and that of Y as 100 to 200. 200 to 300 etc.

X	12	34	33	22	44	37	26	36	55	48	27	37	21
Y	140	266	360	470	470	380	480	315	420	390	440	390	590
X	51	27	42	43	52	57	44	48	48	52	41	69	
Y	250	550	360	570	290	416	380	492	370	312	330	590	

[*C.A. (Inter), May 1980*]

2.42 A company wants to distribute bonus to its employees as per the following pattern :

Salary (Rs.)	*Bonus (Rs.)*
1,000 - 2,000	110
2,000 - 3,000	250
3,000 - 4,000	310

4,000 - 5,000	400
5,000 - 6.000	525
6,000 - 7,000	630
7,000 - 8,000	750
8,000 - 9,000	800
9,000- 10,000	900

Actual salaries of the employees (Rs.) are as under :

1750, 3750, 4500, 7500, 9300, 8500, 4710, 3450, 2250, 5150, 6500, 5700, 4510, 3820, 2800, 2250, 4650, 3 750, 2850, 6760.

Find out the total bonus paid to the employees.

2.43 Given below are the marks obtained by 150 students in Economics paper. Tabulate the data choosing an appropriate class interval.

70	53	37	43	59	27	37	29	31	22	42	45	39	69	36
45	44	43	42	57	37	62	39	51	53	79	42	52	49	75
55	60	65	58	64	50	58	52	36	64	33	45	75	30	20
47	51	61	39	59	53	49	59	41	25	48	37	45	35	24
30	33	37	35	49	29	41	38	37	49	42	40	33	23	28
46	40	32	34	44	44	45	35	54	39	31	42	74	75	76
46	50	26	43	53	43	44	38	32	37	44	32	52	48	46
59	63	27	48	29	35	40	42	72	42	32	55	43	39	41
48	53	34	40	50	27	47	59	42	42	53	29	37	50	40
53	42	39	47	42	47	34	42	36	31	48	46	39	44	50

2.44 Form a frequency distribution from the following data taking 4 as the magnitude of the class interval. The distribution needs to be the continuous type.

10, 17, 15, 22, 11, 16, 19, 24, 29, 18, 25, 26, 32, 14, 17, 20, 23, 27, 30, 12, 15, 18, 24,36, 18, 15, 21, 28, 33, 38, 34, 13, 10, 16, 20, 22, 29, 19, 23. 31. [*Delhi University, B.Com. 1977*]

2.45 Following figures relate to the weekly wages of workers in a factory.

Wages (in Rs.)

100	100	101	102	106	86	82	87	109	104	75	89
99	96	94	93	92	90	86	78	79	84	83	87
88	89	75	76	76	79	80	81	89	99	104	100
103	104	107	110	110	106	102	107	103	101	101	101
86	94	93	96	97	99	100	102	103	107	107	108
109	94	93	97	98	99	100	97	88	86	84	83
82	80	84	86	88	91	93	95	95	95	97	98
100	105	106	103	85	84	77	78	80	93	96	97
98	98	98	87								

Prepare a frequency table by taking a class-interval of 5 . [*Delhi University, B.Com., 1974*]

2.46 If the class-midpoints in a frequency distribution of age of a group of persons are 25, 32, 39, 46, 53 and 60, find

(*i*) The size of the class interval
(*ii*) the class boundaries
(*iii*) The class limits, assuming that the age quoted is the age completed last birthday.
[*Osmania University, B.Com., 1978*]

2.47 Convert the following distribution into 'more than' frequency distribution.

Weekly wages less than (Rs.)	*No. of workers*
20	41
40	92
60	156
80	194
100	201

[*Delhi University, B.Com., 1979*]

2.48 The credit office of a department store gave the following statements for payment due to 40 customers. Construct a frequency table of the balances due taking the class intervals as Rs. 50 and under Rs. 200, Rs. 200 and under Rs. 350 etc. Also find the percentage cumulative frequencies and interpret these values.

Balance due in Rs.

337	570	99	759	487	352	115	60	521	95
563	399	625	215	360	178	827	301	501	199
110	501	201	99	637	328	539	150	417	150
451	595	422	344	186	681	397	790	272	514

[*Bombay University, B.Com., Nov., 1982*]

2.49 The data given below relate to the marks obtained by 20 students in two subjects. Prepare a two way frequency table with class-intervals 62-64, 64-66 and so on for *A* and 115-125, 125-135 and so on for subject B.

Serial No.	*Marks in Subject A*	*Marks in Subject B*	*Serial No.*	*Marks in Subject A*	*Marks in Subject B*
1	152	67	11	129	62
2	170	70	12	163	70
3	135	65	13	139	67
4	136	65	14	122	63
5	137	64	15	134	68
6	148	69	16	140	67
7	124	63	17	132	69
8	117	65	18	120	66
9	128	70	19	148	88
10	143	71	20	129	67

[*Bombay University, B.Com., April 1978*]

2.50 Prepare a statistical table from the following data taking the class-width as 7 by inclusive method.

24, 26, 28, 32, 27, 5, 1, 7, 9, 11, 15, 13, 14, 18, 29, 31, 32, 6, 4, 2, 9, 18, 27, 36, 3, 9, 15, 21, 27, 33, 4, 8, 12, 16, 20. 5, 10, 3, 8, 1, 6, 4, 9, 2. 7, 12. 18, 27..23, 21, 29, 22, 15, 17, 28.

[*Delhi University, B.Com. 1978*]

2.51 What are the different types of diagrams which are used in statistics to show salient characteristic of group and series? Illustrate your answer.

[Delhi University, B.Com. (Hons.), 1976]

2.52 Discuss the usefulness of diagrammatic representation of facts.

[Delhi University. B.Com. (Hons.). 1977, 73]

2.53 Describe the advantages of diagrammatic representation of statistical data. Name the different types of diagrams commonly used and mention the situations where the use of each type of diagram would be appropriate. *[ICWA (Inter), June 1975]*

2.54 "Diagrams help us visualise the whole meaning of a numerical complex at a single glance". Comment. *[Osmania University, B.Com. (Hons.). April 1983]*

2.55 "Diagrams do not add anything to the meaning of statistics, but when drawn and studied intelligently, they bring to view the salient characteristics of the data". Explain.

[Osmania University, B.Com. (Hons.), Nov., 1981]

2.56 State the different methods used for the diagrammatic representation of statistical data and indicate briefly the advantages and disadvantages of them.

[Kurukshetra University, B.Com.. Sept., 1980]

2.57 Present the following information in a suitable tabular form, supplying the figures not direct given.

In 1965 out of total 2,000 workers in a factory, 1,550 were members of a trade union. The number of women workers employed was 250, out of which 200 did not belong to any trade union. In 1970, the number of union workers was 1,725, out of which 1.600 were men. The number) non-union workers was 380, among which 155 were women.

[ICWA (Inter), June 1975]

2.58 Criticise the following table :

Castings	*Weight of Metal*	*Foundry Hours*
Upto 5 kgs.	70	220
Upto 10 kgs.	110	650
All higher weights	120	810
Others	30	70
Total	330	2,010

[Madurai University, B.Com.. Oct., 1978]

2.59 The highlights of the Railway budget for 1983-84 are as follows :

The actual gross traffic receipts for 1981-82 was Rs.3,538.24 crores. The budget estimates for 1982-83 in regard to gross traffic receipts was Rs. 4,171.8 crores and the revised budget estimate for 1982-83 for the above item is Rs. 5.343.63 crores. The actual total working expenses and the net railways revenue for 1981-82 were Rs. 3,182.05 crores and Rs. 403.1 crores respectively. The budget estimates and the revised budget estimates for 1982-83 in respect of total working expenditure are Rs. 3,700.9 and 3,892.28 crores respectively, whereas the corresponding estimates for 1982-83 in respect of net railway revenues are Rs. 510.91 crores: and Rs. 533:4 crores respectively. The estimated budget total working expenses and the net railway revenue for 1983-84 exceeds the actuals for 1981-82 by Rs. 1,338.72 crores and Rs. 268.72 crores respectively. Regarding the dividend payable to general revenues the actuals for 1981-82 are Rs. 351.67 crores, the budget estimates for 1982-83 are Rs. 405.12 crores, the revised budget estimates for 1983-84 are Rs. 458.17 crores and budget estimates for 1982-83 are Rs. 465.17 crores. Present the above data in a table.

[ICWA (Inter,. June 1983]

2.60 (*a*) Calculate the average daily wages for the workers of two factories.

	Factory *A*	Factory *B*
No. of wage earners	350	300
Average daily wage	Rs. 2	Rs. 2.50

(*b*) The mean age of a combined group of men and women is 30 years. If the mean age of the group of men is 32 and that for the group of women is 27, find out the percentage of the men and women in the group. [*Osmania University, B.Com. III, April 1984*]

2.61 Calculate the mean of the following frequency distribution relating to the marks secured by students in statistics.

Marks	*No. of Students*	*Marks*	*No. of Students*
0–5	1	40–45	20
5–10	6	45–50	25
10–15	8	50–55	12
15–20	7	55–60	7
20–25	11	60–65	6
25–30	10	65–70	5
30–35	10	70–75	4
35–40	17	75–80	1

[*Delhi University, B.Com., 1976*]

2.62 Following are the marks (out of 100) obtained by students in a test.

70, 55, 51, 42, 57, 45, 60, 47, 63, 53, 33, 65, 39, 82, 55, 64, 50, 25, 65, 75, 30, 20, 58, 52, 36, 45, 42, 35, 40, 61,53, 59, 49, 41, 15, 52, 46, 42, 45, 39, 55, 65, 45, 63, 54, 48, 64, 35, 26, 18.

(*i*) Make a frequency distribution taking a class-interval of 10 marks (Take the first interval as 0-10)

(*ii*) Draw a histogram and a frequency polygon from the frequency distribution.

(*iii*) Find out the average marks of the students.

2.63 The mean weight of a student in a group of students is 119 lbs. The individual weights of 5 of them are 115, 109, 129, 117 and 114 lbs. What is the weight of the sixth student? [*Bangalore University, B.Com. May 1979*]

2.64 In the following grouped data. x are the mid-values of the class intervals and c is a constant. If the arithmetic mean of the original distribution is 35.84, find its class interval.

x-c	:	–21	–14	–7	0	7	14	21	Total
f	:	2	12	19	29	20	13	5	100

[*Bombay University, B.Com. 1982*]

2.65 From the following data of income distribution, calculate the arithmetic mean. It is given that (*i*) the total income of the persons in the highest group is Rs. 435 and (*ii*) none is earning less than Rs.20.

Income (Rs.) :	Below 30	Below 40	Below 50	Below 60	Below 70	Below 80	Over 80
No. of persons :	16	36	61	76	87	96	5

[*Kurukshetra University, B.Com., 1975*]

2.66 For a certain frequency table, which has only been partly reproduced here, the mean was found to be 1.46. Calculate the missing frequencies.

Number of accidents	:	0	1	2	3	4	5	
Frequency (No. of days)	:	46	?	?	25	10	5	Total 200

[Shivaji University, B.Com., 1978]

2.67 The average monthly wage of all workers in a factory is Rs. 444. If the average wages paid to male and female workers are Rs. 480 and Rs. 360 respectively, find the percentage of male and female workers employed by the factory. *[Delhi University, B.A. (Eco. Hons.). 1982]*

2.68 Twelve persons gambled on a certain night. Seven of them lost at an average rate of Rs. 10.50 while the remaining five gained at an average of Rs. 13.00. Is the information given above correct? If not why? *[ICWA (Inter). Dec. 1981]*

2.69 For two frequency distributions given below, the mean calculated from the first was 25.4 and that from the second was 32.5. Find the value of x and y.

Class	*Distribution Frequency I*	*Distribution Frequency II*
10–20	20	4
20–30	15	8
30–40	10	4
40–50	x	$2x$
50–60	y	y

[ICWA (Intermediate), June 1982]

2.70 The following data give the number of employees and the total wages paid in the three departments of a manufacturing unit.

Departments	*No. of employees*	*Total wages (Rs.)*
A	432	1,08,864
B	517	1,62,855
C	51	25,704

If a bonus amounting to Rs. 63 is given to each employee, what is the average percentage increase per employee for each department and for the total?

[Bombay University, B.Com., April 1982]

2.71 Calculate simple and weighted arithmetic averages from the following data and comment on them.

Designation	*Monthly Salary (Rs.)*	*Strength of the Cadre*
Class I officers	1,500	10
Class II officers	800	20
Subordinate Staff	500	70
Clerical Staff	250	100
Lower Staff	100	150

[Bombay University. B.Com., 1977]

2.72 The frequency distribution of weight in grams of mangoes of a given variety is given below. Calculate the arithmetic mean and the median.

Weight in grams	:	410–419	420–429	430–439	440–449	450–459	460–469	470–479
Number of mangoes	:	14	20	42	54	45	18	7

[Delhi University. B.A. (Eco. Hons.). 1981]

2.73 Find the missing frequency from the following distribution of sales of shops, given that the median sale of shops is Rs 2,400.

Sales in hundred Rs. :	0–10	10–20	20–30	30–40	40–50
No. of shops :	5	25	?	18	70

[*Bombay University, B.Com., May 1980*]

2.74 Find mean and median from the data given below :

Marks obtained :	0-10	10-20	20-30	30-40	40-50	50-60
No. of students :	12	18	27	20	17	6

[*Guru Nanak Dev University, B.Com. II, April 1983*]

2.75 Calculate the median annual income of a group of employees from the data given below:

Annual Income in Rs.	*Number of Employees*
Under 2,000	15
2,000–2,999	32
3,000–3,999	65
4,000–4,999	79
5,000–5,999	90
6,000–6,999	57
7,000–7,999	36
8,000–8,999	14

[*Osmania University, B.Com. III, April 1984*]

2.76 An incomplete frequency distribution is given as follows:

Variable	*Frequency*
10 – 20	12
20 – 30	30
30 – 40	?
40 – 50	65
50 – 60	?
60 – 70	25
70 – 80	19
	Total 230

You are given that Median value is 46.

(*a*) Using median formula, fill up the missing frequencies.

(*b*) Calculate the Arithmetic Mean of the complete table.

[*Guru Nanak Dev. University. B.Com., 1981*]

2.77 Calculate the mode for the following data :

Annual wages	*No. of workers*	*Annual wages*	*No. of workers*
Upto Rs. 1,200	12	Upto Rs. 1,600	150
Upto Rs. 1,300	30	Upto Rs. 1,700	220

Upto Rs. 1,400	80	Upto Rs. 1,800	300
Upto Rs. 1,500	100	Upto Rs. 1,900	330

[*Osmania University, B.Com. (Hons.), Nov., 1981*]

2.78 Find out the Mean, Median and Mode for the following series :

Size (below) :	5	10	15	20	25	30	35
Frequency :	1	3	13	17	27	36	38

[*Kurukshetra University, B.Com., Sept., 1980*]

2.79 Obtain the Median and Mode for the following table

No. of days absent	*No. of students*	*No. of days absent*	*No. of students*
Less than 5	29	Less than 25	634
Less than 10	239	Less than 30	644
Less than 15	469	Less than 35	650
Less than 20	584	Less than 40	655

[*ICWA (Inter), Dec., 1983*]

2.80 Calculate the arithmetic mean and the median of the frequency distribution given below. Hence calculate the mode using the empirical relation among the three.

Class limits	*Frequency*	*Class limits*	*Frequency*
130–134	5	150–154	17
135–139	15	155–159	10
140–144	28	160–164	1
145–149	24		
			Total 100

[*ICWA (Inter) Dec., 1984*]

2.81 The number of bacteria in a certain culture was found to be 4×10^4 at noon of one day. At noon the nest day, the number was found to be 9×10^4. If the number increased at constant rate per hour, how many bacteria were there at the intervening mid-night.

[*Delhi University. B.A. (Eco. Hons.). 1984*]

2.82 Find the geometric and harmonic mean from the following data

Item :	1	2	3	4	5	6	7	8	9	10
Value :	15	250	15.7	157	1.57	105.7	105	1.06	25.7	0.257

[*Punjab University, B.A. (Eco. Hons.). April 1984*]

2.83 The following table gives the weights of 31 persons in a sample enquiry. Calculate the mean weight using (*i*) Geometric Mean (*ii*) Harmonic Mean.

Weight (lbs.) :	130	135	140	145	146	148	149	150	157
No. of persons :	3	4	6	6	3	5	2	1	1

[*Mysore University. B.Com., April 1981*]

2.84 Calculate Mode from the following data :

Monthly wage (in Rs.)	*No. of workers*	*Monthly wage (in Rs.)*	*No. of workers*
200–250	4	400–450	33
250–300	6	450–500	17

300–350	20	500–550	8
350–400	12	550–600	2

Calculate Mode by graphic method also. [*Delhi University, B.Com. (Ext.), 1982*]

2.85 From an ordinary frequency table from the following cumulative distribution of marks obtained by 22 students and calculate (*i*) Arithmetic Mean, (*ii*) Median and (*iii*) Mode.

Marks	***Number of students***
Below 10	3
Below 20	8
Below 30	17
Below 40	20
Below 50	22

[*ICWA (Inter.) June. 1998*]

2.86 Calculate the Mode, Median and Arithmetic average from the following data :

Class	***f***	***Class***	***f***
0–2	8	25–30	45
2–4	12	30–40	60
4–10	20	40–50	20
10–15	10	50–60	13
15–20	16	60–80	15
20–25	25	80–100	4

[*Punjab University, B.Com. II, Sept., 1982*]

❁❁❁

CHAPTER 3

MEASURES OF DISPERSION, SKEWNESS AND KURTOSIS

3.1 INTRODUCTION

The measure of central tendency *i.e.* averages are indicative of the concentration of the observed data about the central part of the distribution system, but they do not reveal the spread of the data on either side of the central pivot. Hence inspite of having the same average value, the observations may vary widely and no concrete idea comes out of averages. The concepts of averages have their own utility, but their limitations too.

For obtaining true picture from a given data, averages are generally misleading due to the fact that the range and variation of data can indicate a totally different analysis and hence can change the decision rather dramatically.

The idea of spread about the central value of the observation is called "Dispersion". Whereas a small dispersion indicates high uniformity of the observations, the large dispersion would mean less uniformity. In any business function, the concept of dispersion is very useful so that variability of performance can be used to monitor and control this variability bringing in better product/service/sales etc.

To differentiate the concept from the averages, let us consider the following set of observations.

Set A	20 20 25 25 30 30 35 35	Total 220	Mean 27.5
Set B	15 20 25 30 35 30 25 40	Total 220	Mean 27.5
Set C	3 6 18 36 72 36 24 25	Total 220	Mean 27.5

It can be seen that in all the sets, the total sum and the average value is same, but the variation in set A is from 20 to 35. in set B, from 15 to 40. Whereas in set C, it is from 3 to 72. If these are the figures for sales, you can well understand the plight of the sales/marketing manager and that of the production manager to cope up with the types of demand. This variation of observations is called "Dispersion or spread".

This information has been represented in Figure 3.1 :

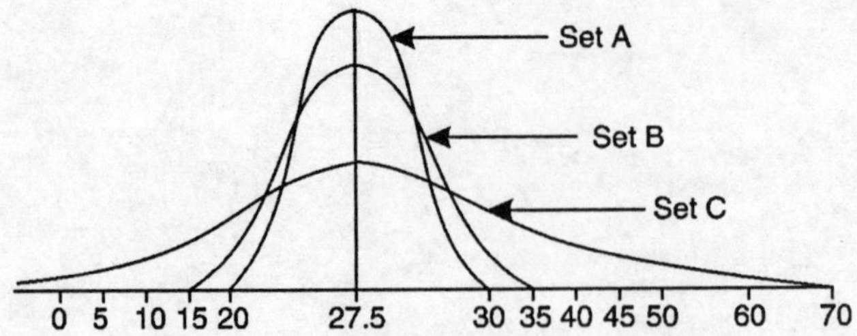

Fig. 3.1. Spread of observations

From the values of the observations given above for set A, B and C, it is observed that the data is closely centered around the mean value of 27.5, whereas for set B, the data is more spread out from the mean. For set C. the data is well spread out from 3 to 72. The concept of wide dispersion can be made use of in high risk business situations, where spread of data indicates greater level of risk due to earnings varying widely.

The spread, range or dispersion of collected data can be analysed through various measures. These measures are Range, mean and quartile deviation and more significantly the standard deviation and the variance.

3.2 MEASURES OF DISPERSION

The following measures of dispersion are commonly used

1. Range
2. Quartile Deviation
3. Mean Deviation
4. Standard Deviation and Variance
5. Lorenz Curves

Range

The difference between the highest and the lowest observation or the value of the variable is called the "Range".

$\therefore$ Range $(R) = X_{max} - X_{min}$

Where X is the variable.

Thus taking the values for set A, B and C in para 3.1 the three ranges can be writen as follows.

For set A ; $R = X_{max.} - X_{min} = 35 - 20 = 15$

For set B ; $R = X_{max} - X_{min} = 40 - 15 = 25$

For set C ; $R = X_{max} - X_{min} = 72 - 3 = 69$

The limitation of this measure is that it takes into account only the extreme values of the variable and ignores all other data. As can be seen that there can be a wide variation of its magnitude from one set of observation to the other. Inspite of this great limitation, this measure of dispersion is widely used in Industrial Quality Control for construction of quality control charts. It is also widely used in risk analysis for an investment proposal.

The expression for coefficient of range $= \dfrac{X_{max} - X_{min}}{X_{max} + X_{min}}$

Quartile Deviation

The Quartile Deviation (QD) is the difference of the third and first quartile divided by two. Thus

$$QD = \frac{Q_3 - Q_1}{2}$$

The calculation of quartiles can be done as follows :

$$Q_1 = l + \frac{h}{f}\left(\frac{N}{4} - F\right)$$

and $$Q_3 = l + \frac{h}{f}\left(3\frac{N}{4} - F\right)$$

where N = Total cumulative frequency

F = Cumulative frequency upto the lower limit of quartile

l = Lower limit of the quartile class

f = Frequency of the quartile class

h = Width of the class interval

If $Q_3 = 35, \quad Q_1 = 15$

Then $$QD = \frac{35-15}{2} = 10$$

This indicates that the dispersion on either side of mean is 10, when measured in terms of the quartile deviation. It is a better measure of dispersion than the range.

There are different names for these ranges, commonly known as interfractile range. If half the data is below or equal to this value, it is called 0.5 fractile or Median.

If 25 per cent of the data lies at or below the given value, it is called 0.25 fractile or first quartile. Thus these values are like percentages. Interfractile range is, therefore, a measure of the spread between two fracticles of the frequency distribution. This is also called Inter-quartile range, when it is spread between the first and the third quartile or 0.25 fractile and 0.75 fractile.

Hence inter quartile range = $Q_3 - Q_1$.

Based on the concept of percentage, the fractiles are named as percentiles when the data is divided into 100 equal parts. Thus decile divides the data into 10 equal parts.

As per the spread of the data, it can be divided into quartiles deciles or percentiles based on what type of categorisation of data is needed. In case of mean deviation, the analyst uses the concept of average alongwith the deviation of the mean from various values of the observations.

Mean Deviation

The Mean deviation is defined as the arithmetic average of the deviations, when the deviations are taken from the average (mean, median or mode), taking all deviations as positive. Thus, when mean is used as the average, it is called Mean deviation about the mean; while mean median is used as the average, it is termed as the Mean Deviation about the Median.

Thus Mean Deviation (MD) $= \dfrac{\sum\{x_i - \bar{x}\}}{n}$

Where $\bar{x}$ is the mean of the deviation.

In this case, we take the deviation of all observation values x_i's and the deviation of the mean is calculated from all the observations and totalled up as $\sum(x_i - \bar{x})$

$$MD = \frac{\sum(x_i - \bar{x})}{\sum f}$$

Whereas in a grouped frequency distribution, the frequency of occurence of each value of $(x_i - \bar{x})$ is available and to obtain the mean of this deviation, we have to multiply by the frequency f_i also and then summed up over the entire range for mean calculation.

If we consider a grouped frequency distribution.

$$MD = \frac{\sum f_i[x_i - \bar{x}]}{\sum f_i}$$

Since the Mean Deviation depends on all the values of the observations, it is treated as a better measure of the dispersion comparing the Range and Quartile Deviation.

Standard Deviation and Variance

Since the average value of the set of data can have individual observations on the lower as well as higher side of it, the mean deviation can be negative or positive. The concept of variance and associated standard deaviation as a measure of spread of the data, has been developed.

In case of Mean Deviation, value of $(x_i - \bar{x})$ can be negative. To avoid this situation, we use standard deviation as the measure. The best way is to square the expression $(x_i - \bar{x})$. This will always lead to a positive value. The square of the standard deviation (*i.e.* the deviation about the mean) denoted by σ^2 (σ; small sigma, a Greek alphabet, first suggested by Karl Pearson) is called the Variance.

Let us take the following data

x : 5, 10, 14, 20, 26

The average of this data $= \bar{x} = \dfrac{\sum x_i}{n}$

$$= \frac{5+10+14+20+26}{5}$$

$$= \frac{75}{5}$$

$$= 15$$

Taking the deviations about this average or mean *i.e.*, 15,

we get deviation as (5-15), (10-15), (14-15), (20-15) and (26-15)

i.e., –10, –5, –1, 5, 11

The square of these deviations are 100, 25, 1, 25, 121.

The variance is defined as the average of the square of the deviations.

$$\text{Variance} = \quad \sigma^2 = \frac{100+25+1+25+121}{5}$$

$$= \frac{272}{5} = 54.4$$

For the ungrouped data $\sigma^2 = \dfrac{\sum (x_1 - \bar{x})^2}{n}$

and for the grouped data

$$\sigma^2 = \frac{\sum f_i(x_i - \bar{x})^2}{\sum f_i}$$

Thus we can write the formula for variance (σ^2, sigma squared) as follows

$$\sigma^2 = \frac{\sum (x-\mu)^2}{N}$$

Where σ^2 = population variance

x = value of the observations

μ = population mean

N = total number of observations or items in the population

Σ = sum of all the squared values.

This can also be written as follows

$$\sigma^2 = \frac{\sum x^2}{N} - \mu^2$$

We normally use $\bar{x}$ for the mean of a sample out of the given population and μ for the population mean. Similarly n is used as the size of the sample and N as the size of the population.

Hence standard deviation is now defined as the positive square root of the variance or the square root of the means of squared deviations of the given observations from thier arithmetic means.

$$\text{Standard Deviation } \sigma = \sqrt{\frac{\Sigma(x-\bar{x})^2}{n}}$$

Where $\bar{x} = \left(\frac{\Sigma x}{n}\right)$

In terms of population mean, the population standard deviation can be written as

$$\sigma = \sqrt{\sigma^2}$$

$$= \sqrt{\frac{\Sigma(x-\mu)^2}{N}}$$

$$= \sqrt{\Sigma\frac{x^2}{N} - \mu^2}$$

From the concept of variance and standard deviation, emerges the term "standard score", which is the measure of the standard deviation for a particular given observation. It is thus the ratio of mean deviation to the standard deviation.

Standard Score

The standard deviation is found useful in specifying the deviation of the individual item in a distribution from the mean of the distribution, Standard score, is a measure of the standard deviations for a particular observation, Standard score, therefore, is the number of standard deviations a particular observation lies below or above the mean and can be written as

$$\text{Population standard score} = \frac{x-\mu}{\sigma}$$

Use of Standard Deviation (Chebyshev's Theorem)

A Russian Mathematician P.L. Chebyshev devised a theorem as "No matter what the shape of the distribution, at least 75 per cent of the value will fall within ±2 standard deviations from the mean of the distribution and at least 89 per cent of the values will be within ±3 standard deviations from the mean, It can be explained from a symmetrical bell-shaped curve as follows.

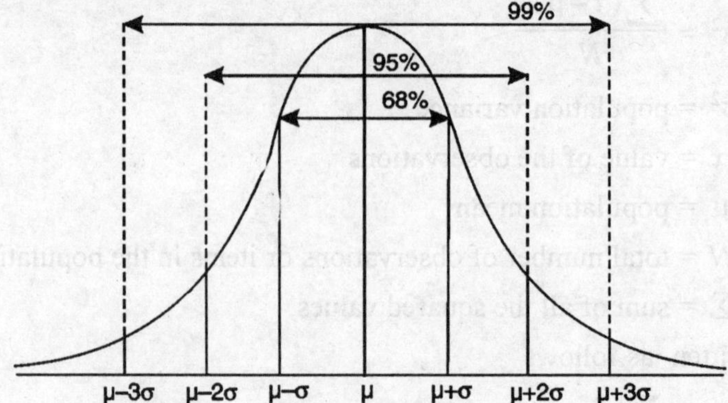

Fig 3.2. Observations around the mean

Standard deviation for samples

The relationship of standard deviation for a sample undergoes a modification as follows

$$s^2 = \frac{\sum(x-\bar{x})^2}{n-1}$$

$$= \frac{\sum x^2}{(n-1)} - \frac{n\bar{x}^2}{(n-1)}$$

and $$s = \sqrt{\frac{\sum(x-\bar{x})^2}{n-1}}$$

Where s = sample standard deviation

s^2 = sample variance

x = value of each of the observations

$\bar{x}$ = mean of the sample

n = number of observations in the sample or sample size

The standard deviation can be used through the distribution pattern of the observations and Chebyshev's theorem is very useful to show the relationship. Coefficient of variation is also a measure to show the relationship of standard deviation to the arithmetic mean of the set of observations.

Coefficient of Variation

The Standard Deviation is the measure of the dispersion of observations about their arithmetic mean and the unit of measurement of the standard deviation is the same as that of the arithmatic mean or of the variance itself. Hence the dispersion actually depends upon the measurement of the variable. In order to have the comparison of the dispersion about the arithmetic mean, we define it as the "Coefficient of Variation", which is the ratio of standard deviation to the arithmetic mean. It is calculated as

$$\text{Coefficient of Variation} = CV = \frac{\sigma_x}{\bar{x}}$$

Lorenz Curves

As against the above described measures of dispersion, the Lorenz curves are the graphic representation of the dispersion of a distribution. It was first used by Max O. Lorenz, an economic statistician for the measurement of economic inequalities such as in the distribution of income and wealth between different countries or between different periods of time. But now, Lorenz curves are used in business to study the disparities of the distribution of wages, profits, turnover, production or population etc.

In drawing these curves, we use cumulative values of the variables and the cumulative frequencies rather than their absolute values and frequencies. In a very simple manner, we draw a table of cumulative values of the data or observations and also their related cumulative frequencies. These cumulatives are then converted into percentages of the totals and both these variables (cumulative percentage values) are then plotted as x and y values of a graph.

The line joining (0, 0) and (100, 100) is called the line of equal distribution and is used for comparision of the distribution variation of the observed data. Thus curves OAP indicates a less degress of variability as compared to the data represented by OBP. Similarly curve OCP is showing greater variability than the data from curve OBP or OAP.

The disadvantage of the Lorenz curve is that it gives only the relative variability of relative dispersion as compared to the line of equal distribution. It does not provide any numerical value of the variability for the given distribution.

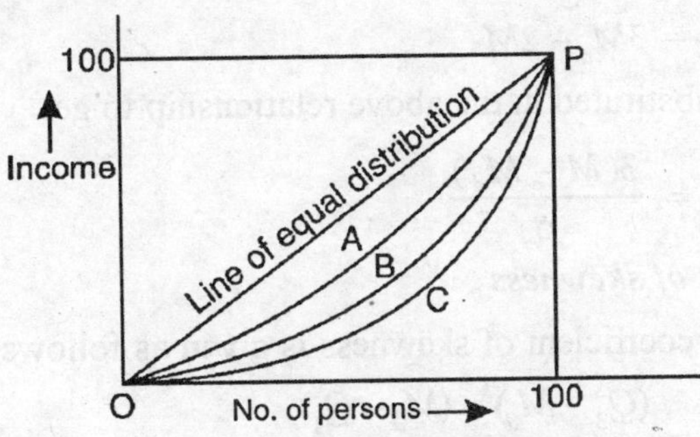

Fig. 3.3. Lorenz Curves

3.3 SKEWNESS

Skewness means "Lack of Symmetry". Thus, the study of the shape of the curve drawn with the help of frequency distribution is helpful in understanding how the observations are varying about the mean values. If the distribution curve is symmetrical about the mean value, it is a symmetric bell-shaped curve for a symmetrical distribuiton.

The nature of data is very uncertain due to variations in real-life situations. When the data is not symmetrical about the mean value, the distribution pattern changes. It can either be negatively or positively skewed. Therefore 'Skewness' has been developed as a measure of variation for such a set of data.

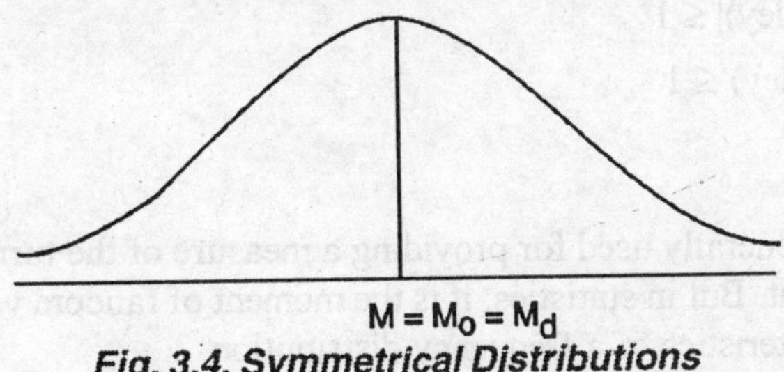

Fig. 3.4. Symmetrical Distributions

When curve is not symmetrical, the values of Mean, Mode and Median fall at different points. The curve may shift its bulk of the bell-shape either to the right or left of the Mean Value. These are called skewness to the left (positive) or right (negative) of the mean, such as

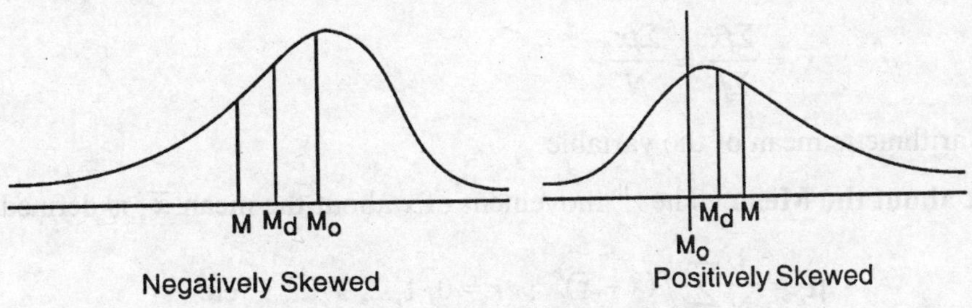

Fig. 3.5. Skewed Distribution

Measure of Skewness (SK)

1. SK $= \text{Mean} - \text{Median} = M - M_d$

   or, SK $= \text{Mean} - \text{Mode} = M - M_o$

2. SK $= (Q_3 - M_d) - (M_d - Q_1)$

   $= Q_3 + Q_1 - 2M_d$

   These are the absolute values of Skewness and not generally used :

3. ***Karl Pearson's Coefficient of Skewness***

   It is given by $\quad SK = \dfrac{Mean - Mode}{SD}$

   $$= \frac{M - M_o)}{\sigma}$$

   But $\quad M_o = 3M_d - 2M$

   Hence this can be substituted in the above relationship to get

   $$SK = \frac{3(M - M_d)}{\sigma}$$

4. ***Bowley's coefficient of skewness***

   Prof. A.L. Bowley's coefficient of skewness is given as follows

   $$SK = \frac{(Q_3 - M_d) - (M_d - Q_1)}{(Q_3 - M_d) + (M_d - Q_1)}$$

   $$= \frac{Q_3 + Q_1 - 2M_d}{Q_3 - Q_1}$$

Subject to the following limits :

$$|a - b| \le |a + b| \Rightarrow \left(\frac{a - b}{a + b}\right) \le 1 \text{ for } a, b \text{ two real positive numbers}$$

Hence | SK (Bowley)| ≤ 1

or $-1 \le$ SK (Bowley) ≤ 1

Two prominent statisticians namely Karl Pearson and Bowley have suggested the coefficient of skewness in lightly modified forms. The usage of both the coefficients is practically the same.

3.4. MOMENTS

Moment is the term generally used for providing a measure of the turning or the rotating effect of a force about some point. But in statistics, it is the moment of random variable about some point, describing various characteristics of a frequency distribution.

If we consider a distribution of a random variable x as

x	:	x_1	x_2	x_3	....	x_n
f	:	f_1	f_2	f_3	....	f_n

Then $\quad \bar{x} = \dfrac{\Sigma fx}{\Sigma f} = \dfrac{\Sigma fx}{N}$

This is the arithmetic mean of the variable.

Movement about the Mean : The rth movement of x about the mean $\bar{x}$, is defined as under :

$$\mu_r = \frac{1}{N}\sum f(x - \bar{x})^r \; ; \; r = 0, 1, 2, 3 \text{ .... etc.}$$

$$= \frac{1}{N}\left[f_1(x_1 - \bar{x})^r + f_2(x_2 - \bar{x})^r + - - - + f_n(x_n - \bar{x})^r\right]$$

It is called the central moment.

Putting $r = 0$, we obtain

$$\mu_0 = \frac{1}{N}\left[\sum f(x - \bar{x})^0\right]$$

$$= \frac{1}{N}(\Sigma f) \qquad \text{[Since } (x - \bar{x})^0 = 1\text{]}$$

$$= \frac{1}{N} . N = 1$$

Similarly $\mu_1 = \frac{1}{N}\left[\sum f(x - \bar{x})\right] = 0$

Since the algebraic sum of the deviations of a given set of observations from their mean is zero.

Thus the first moment about mean is zero.

We can now write the other measures of moments about mean as

$$\mu_1 = \frac{1}{N}\sum f(x - \bar{x})^2 = \sigma_x^2$$

$$\mu_3 = \frac{1}{N}\sum f(x - \bar{x})^3$$

$$\mu_4 = \frac{1}{N}\sum f(x - \bar{x})^4 \text{ etc.}$$

Moments about any arbitrary point A.

The rth moment of x about any point A is usually denoted by $\mu r'$ and is defined as under :

$$\mu_r' = \frac{1}{N}\sum f(x - A)^r, \; r = 0, 1, 2, 3 \ldots\ldots\ldots$$

$$= \frac{1}{N}\left[f_1(x_1 - A)^r + f_2(x_2 - A)^r + - - - - + f_n(x_n - A)^r\right]$$

Accordingly $\mu_0' = \frac{1}{N}\sum f(x - A)^0$

$$= \frac{1}{N}\Sigma f \qquad \text{[Since } (x - A)^0 = 1\text{]}$$

$$= \frac{1}{N} . N = 1$$

$$\mu_1' = \frac{1}{N}\sum f(x - A)^1$$

$$= \frac{1}{N}[\Sigma fx - \Sigma fA] \qquad \text{[Since } (x - A)^1 = 0\text{]}$$

$$= \frac{1}{N}[\Sigma fx - A\Sigma f]$$

Moment is a measure of deviation in a slightly different form. It explains the rotating effect of the force about some point. In case of statistics, it is moment of the random variable about some point, say mean or about any general observation.

$$= \frac{1}{N}[\Sigma(fx) - A.N]$$

$$= \bar{x} - A$$

$$\therefore \qquad \bar{x} = A + \mu_1'$$

Similarly $$\mu_2' = \frac{1}{N}\Sigma f(x-A)^2$$

$$\mu_3' = \frac{1}{N}\Sigma f(x-A)^3$$

and $$\mu_4' = \frac{1}{N}\Sigma f(x-A)^4$$

The rth moment about any arbitrary point A is called raw moment.

We also have $$A - \bar{x} = -\mu_1'$$

$$\mu_2 = \mu_2' - \mu_1'^2$$

and so on. And all central moments of odd order for symmetrical distribution are zero.

Yet another measure of deviation has been named as 'Kurtosis,' which describes the convexity of the data distribution. Thus it helps in identifying the shape of the distribution curve and the nature of its central portion.

3.5 KURTOSIS

Having studied the three measures the Central tendency, dispersion and skewness, we now describe Kurtosis to define a distribution in case all these measures are not in a position to define distribution completely.

Let us consider figure 3.6 in which three curves have been drawn and all three are symmetrical about the mean with the same range.

In this case, we need one more measure to define this distribution completely, which is termed as Kurtosis. Prof. Karl Pearson called it is as Convexity of the curve or Kurtosis. While skewness defines the right or left tail of the distribution curve, Kurtosis enables us to identify the shape and nature of the middle portion of the curve. It, therefore, indicates the measure of flatness of the frequency. In the Fig. 3.6, curve *B* is neither flat, nor sharply peaked. It is called the normal curve. Curve with normal type of hump is called MesoKurtic, whereas curve, which has higher peak than the normal curve is called LeptoKurtic and curves with less flatness is called Platy Kurtic.

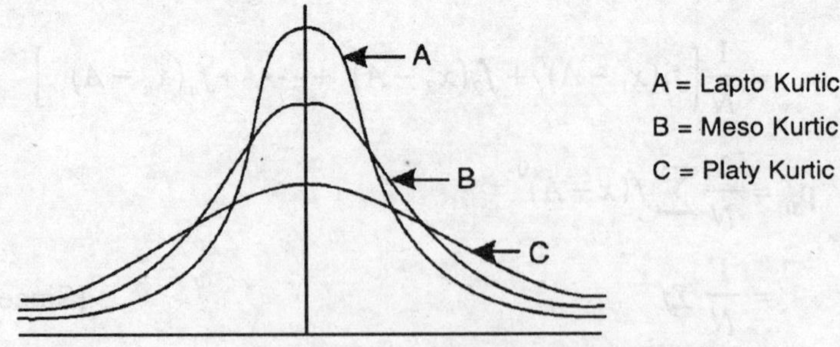

Fig. 3.6. Curves with same mean

As a measure of Kurtosis, Karl Pearson described coefficient β_2 (Beta two) or its derivative λ_2(gama two) as under

$$\beta_2 = \frac{\mu_4}{\mu_2^2} = \frac{\mu_4}{\sigma^4}$$

and $$\gamma_2 = \beta_2 - 3 = \frac{\mu_4 - 3\sigma^4}{\sigma^4}$$

For a normal curve, $\beta_2 = 3$ and $\gamma_2 = 0$

For lepto curve A, $\beta_2 > 3$ and for platy curve C, $\beta_2 < 3$. Where μ_2 and μ_4 are 2nd and 4th moment about a point menu.

CHAPTER SUMMARY

Important Terms Used

- **Bimodal Distribution.** A distribution of data in which two values occur more frequently than the rest.
- **Chebyshev's theorem.** No matter what the shape of a distribution, at least 75 per cent of the values in the population falls within 2 standard deviations of the mean and at least 89 per cent remain within 3 standard deviations.
- **Coefficient of variation.** The ratio of the standard deviation to the arithmetic mean.
- **Decile.** Fractile dividing the data into 10 equal parts.
- **Dispersion.** The spread of the data about the central value is called dispersion.
- **Fractile.** In a distribution, the location of a value at or above a given fraction is called Fractile.
- **Inter fractile range.** A measure of the spread of data between two fractiles in a distribution.
- **Inter quartile range.** The difference between the values of third and first quartiles.
- **Kurtosis.** A measure enabling to identify the shape and nature of the middle value of the distribution curve *i.e.* its peakedness.
- **Lorenz curve.** Graphic representation of the depression of a distribution.
- **Measure of dispersion.** The variation of observations or data in a given data set.
- **Mean Deviation.** Arithmetic mean of the deviations from mean.
- **Percentile.** Fractile dividing the set of data into 100 equal parts.
- **Quartile.** Fractile dividing the set of data into four equal parts.
- **Range.** The difference between the highest and the lowest observation or the value of the observation.
- **Skewness.** The lack of symmetry of the distribution, indicating the extent to which a distribution of data is concentrated at one end or the other.
- **Standard Deviation.** Positive square root of the variance or the square root of the mean of squared deviations of the given observations from the arithmetic mean.
- **Standard score.** Denoting an observation in terms of the standard deviation above or below the mean value.
- **Symmetrical.** A characterstic of a data frequency distribution in which each half is the mirror image of the other.
- **Variance.** A measure of mean squared variation or distance of the observations from their arithmetic mean.

Relationships Used

- $$\mu = \frac{\Sigma x}{N} \text{ for population}$$

- $\bar{x} = \frac{\sum x}{n}$ for ungrouped data
- $\bar{x} = \frac{\sum f_i x_i}{\sum f_i}$ for grouped data
- Range $= X_{\max} - X_{\min}$
- Interquartile range $= Q_3 - Q_1$
- First quartile $(Q_1) = l + \frac{h}{f}\left(\frac{N}{4} - F\right)$
- Third Quartile $(Q_3) = l + \frac{h}{f}\left(\frac{3N}{4} - F\right)$
- Quartile deviation $(QD) = \frac{Q_3 - Q_1}{2}$
- Mean deviation $= \left(\frac{\sum x_i - \bar{x}}{n}\right)$ for ungrouped data
- Mean deviation $(MD) = \frac{\sum f_i(x_i - \bar{x})}{\sum f_i}$ for grouped data
- Variance $(\sigma^2) = \frac{\sum(x_i - \bar{x})^2}{n-1}$ for sample
- Variance $(\sigma^2) = \frac{\sum(x_i - \mu)^2}{N}$ for population
- Standard deviation $(\sigma) = \sqrt{\frac{\sum(x_i - \mu)^2}{N}}$ for population
- Standard deviation $(s) = \sqrt{\frac{\sum(x_i - \bar{x})^2}{n-1}}$ for sample

  $= \sqrt{\frac{\sum x_i^2}{(n-1)} - \frac{n\bar{x}^2}{(n-1)}}$
- Population standard score $= \frac{x - \mu}{\sigma}$
- Sample standard score $= \frac{x_i - \bar{x}}{s}$
- Coefficient of variation $= \frac{\sigma}{\mu}$ for population

- Coefficient of variation $= \frac{\sigma_x}{\bar{x}}$ for sample
- Karl Person's coefficient of skewness (sk) $= \frac{3(\text{Mean} - \text{Median})}{\sigma}$
- Bowley's coefficient of skewness sk (bowley) $= \frac{Q_3 + Q_1 - 2\text{Median}}{\sigma}$
- Karl Person's coefficient of Kurtosis $\beta_2 = \frac{\mu_4}{\mu_2^2} = \frac{\mu_4}{\sigma_4}$ and $\gamma_2 = \beta_2 - 3 = \frac{\mu_4 - 3\sigma^2}{\sigma^4}$

SOLVED PROBLEMS

Problem 3.1

Calculate the range and coefficient of range for the following data.

Months	*Sales (in 000 units)*	*Months*	*Sales (in 000 units)*
April	145	October	180
May	151	November	180
June	161	December	182
July	164	January	184
August	165	February	185
September	170	March	190

Solution :

$$\text{Largest sales } (X_{max}) = 1{,}90{,}000 \text{ units}$$

$$\text{Smallest sales } (X_{min}) = 1{,}45{,}000 \text{ units}$$

$$\therefore \quad \text{Range} = X_{max} - X_{min}$$

$$= 1{,}90{,}000 - 1{,}45{,}000$$

$$= 45{,}000 \text{ units}$$

$$\text{Coefficient of range} = \frac{X_{max} - X_{min}}{X_{max} + X_{min}}$$

$$= \frac{1{,}90{,}000 - 1{,}45{,}000}{1{,}90{,}000 + 1{,}45{,}000}$$

$$= \frac{45{,}000}{3{,}35{,}000} = 0.134$$

Problem 3.2

Find the inter quartile range of the following data :

Class interval :	0–15	15–30	30–45	45–60	60–75	75–90	90–105
Frequency :	8	26	30	45	20	17	4

[Bombay University, Nov. 1982]

Solution :

Let us first prepare the table of cumulative frequencies

Class Interval	*Frequency (f)*	*Cumulative Frequencies (cf)*
0-15	8	8
15-30	26	34
30-45	30	64
45-60	45	109
60-75	20	129
75-90	17	146
90-105	4	150
	$N = \Sigma f = 150$	

Here $\frac{N}{4} = \frac{150}{4} = 37.5$ and $\frac{3N}{4} = 37.5 \times 3 = 112.5$

As per *cf* table, Q_1 lies in the class interval 30-45

$$Q_1 = l + \frac{h}{f}\left(\frac{N}{4} - F\right)$$

$$= 30 + \frac{15}{30}(37.5 - 34)$$

$$= 31.75$$

Similarly $$Q_3 = l + \frac{h}{f}\left(\frac{3N}{4} - F\right)$$

$$= 60 + \frac{15}{20}(112.5 - 109)$$

$$= 62.625$$

Inter quartile range $= Q_3 - Q_1$

$= 62.625 - 31.75 = 30.875$

Problem 3.3

Evaluate an appropriate measure of dispersion for the following data

Income (in Rs.)	: less than 50	50–70	70–90	90–110	110–130	130–150	above 150
Number of persons :	54	100	140	300	230	125	51

[*Calicut University, B.Com.*, 1975]

Solution :

The table below indicates the *cf*

Income (in Rs.)	*Number of persons (f)*	*Less than (cf)*
Less than 50	54	54
50–70	100	154
70–90	140	294
90–110	300	594
110–130	230	824
130–150	125	949
more than 150	51	1,000

Here $N = \Sigma f \quad = 1{,}000$

$\therefore \quad \frac{N}{4} = \frac{1{,}000}{4} = 250;$

$\frac{3N}{4} = \frac{3 \times 1{,}000}{4} = 750$

Class interval for *cf* just greater than 250 *i.e.*, 824 is 110-130

$\therefore \quad Q_1 = 70 + \frac{20}{140}(250 - 154) = 83.714$

$Q_3 = 110 + \frac{20}{230}(750 - 594) = 123.565$

$\therefore \quad QD = \frac{Q_3 - Q_1}{2} = \frac{123.565 - 83.714}{2} = 9.925$

Problem 3.4

Find the average or mean deviation from the median for the following distribution.

Mark less than :	80	70	60	50	40	30	20	10
No. of students :	100	90	80	60	32	20	13	5

[Delhi University, B.Com. (Hons.) 1973]

Solution :

Converting the above data into ordinary frequency distribution.

Marks	*cf*	*Frequency(f)*	*Mid value of class (x)*	$\lvert x-M_d \rvert$	$f\lvert x-M_d \rvert$
0–10	5	5	5	41.43	207.15
10–20	13	8	15	31.43	251.44
20–30	13	7	25	21.43	150.01
30–40	32	12	35	11.43	137.16
40–50	60	28	45	1.43	40.04
50–60	80	20	55	3.57	71.4
60–70	90	10	65	13.57	135.7
70–80	100	10	75	23.57	235.7
					$\Sigma = 1228.6$

$$\text{Median} = l + \frac{h}{f}\left(\frac{N}{2} - c\right) = 40 + \frac{10}{28}(50 - 32)$$

$$= 46.43$$

$$\therefore \quad \text{Mean deviation about median} = \frac{1}{N}\Sigma f \lvert x - M_d \rvert$$

$$= \frac{1228.6}{100}$$

$$= 12.29$$

Problem 3.5

Calculate the mean and standard deviation for the following data :

Value	:	90-99	80-89	70-79	60-69	50-59	40-49	30-39
Frequency	:	2	12	22	20	14	4	1

[*ICWA (Inter. Dec., 1981*]

Solution :

Class	*Mid Value (x)*	*Frequency (f)*	$d = \frac{x-64.5}{10}$	*fd*	fd^2
90-99	94.5	2	3	6	18
80-89	84.5	12	2	24	48
70-79	74.5	22	1	22	22
60-69	64.5	20	0	0	0
50-59	54.5	14	−1	−14	14
40-49	44.5	4	−2	−8	16
30-39	34.5	1	−3	−3	9
		$\Sigma f = N = 75$		$\Sigma fd = 27$	$\Sigma fd^2 = 127$

$$\text{Mean} = A + \frac{h\Sigma fd}{N}$$

$$= 64.5 + \frac{10 \times 27}{75} = 68.1$$

$$SD = h\sqrt{\frac{\Sigma fd^2}{N} - \left(\frac{\Sigma fd}{N}\right)^2}$$

$$= 10 \times \sqrt{\frac{127}{75} - \left(\frac{27}{75}\right)^2} = 12.5$$

Problem 3.6

The arithmetic mean and the standard deviation of a set of 9 items are 43 and 5 respectively. If an item of a value 63 is added to the set, find the mean and standard deviation of 10 items given.

Solution :

Given here

$$n = 9, \bar{x} = 43, \sigma = 5$$

Since $\bar{x} = \frac{\Sigma x}{n}$

$$\Sigma x = n\bar{x}$$

$$= 9 \times 43 = 387$$

Also $\sigma^2 = \frac{\Sigma x^2}{n} - \left(\frac{\Sigma x}{n}\right)^2$

$$= \frac{\sum x^2}{n} - (\bar{x})^2$$

$$\sum x^2 = n(\sigma^2 + \bar{x}^2)$$

$$= 9(25 + 43^2) = 16866$$

If new item 63 is added, n becomes 10

$$\text{New } \sum x = \sum x_9 + x_{10}$$

$$= 387 + 63 = 450$$

$$\text{New mean} = \frac{\sum x}{n} = \frac{450}{10} = 45$$

$$\text{New } \sum x^2 = \sum x^2 + 63^2$$

$$= 16866 + 63^2 = 20835$$

$$\text{New } SD = \sqrt{\frac{New \sum x^2}{10} - (\text{New}\bar{x})^2}$$

$$= \sqrt{\frac{20835}{10} - (45)^2}$$

$$= \sqrt{585}$$

$$= 7.65$$

Problem 3.7

The following observations have been obtained while taking a sample. Calculate the sample standard deviation and sample variance for the data given.

350, 361, 370, 373, 376, 379, 385, 387, 394 and 395.

Solution :

Arranging the observations in ascending order.

Observations (x)	*Mean* $(\bar{x})$	$(x-\bar{x})$	$(x-\bar{x})^2$	x^2
350	377	−27	729	122500
361	377	−16	256	130321
370	377	−7	49	136900
373	377	−4	16	139129
376	377	−1	1	141376
379	377	+2	4	143641
385	377	+8	64	148225
387	377	+10	100	149769
394	377	+17	289	155236
395	377	+18	324	156025
			$\sum(x-\bar{x})^2 = 1832$	$\sum(x)^2 = 1423122$

Calculating $s^2 = \frac{\Sigma(x-\bar{x})^2}{n-1}$

$$= \frac{1832}{10-1}$$

$$= \frac{1832}{9} = 203.55 \text{ (sample variance)}$$

or $s^2 = \frac{\Sigma x^2}{n-1} - \frac{n\bar{x}^2}{n-1}$

$$= \frac{1423122}{9} - \frac{10\times 142129}{9}$$

$$= 158124.66 - 157921.11$$

$$= 203.55$$

$$s = \sqrt{s^2}$$

$$= \sqrt{203.55}$$

$$= 14.267 \text{ (standard deviation of the sample)}$$

PRACTICE PROBLEMS

3.8 Find the average deviation about the median for the following distribution.

Demand :	5	15	20	25	30	35	40	45	50
Frequency :	3	2	6	8	10	5	8	7	5

3.9 From the data collected during industrial survey, as given in the table below, calculate the variance for the distribution.

Sales levels :	10	15	20	25	30
Frequency :	10	5	15	4	6

3.10 From the fluctuations given in two series x and y, find out which of the series show greater fluctuation.

Series x :	500	520	524	565	619	635	650	550
Series y :	2,100	2,150	2,340	2,350	2,400	2,300	2,100	2,500

3.11 Calculate the mean deviation about Arithmetic Mean from the following :

Values (x) :	10	11	12	13
Frequency (f) :	3	12	18	12

[ICWA (inter). Dec., 1983]

3.12 Compute the quartile deviation and mean deviation from the following data :

Height in inches :	58	59	60	61	62	63	64	65	66
No. of students :	15	20	32	35	33	22	22	10	8

(Punjab University, B.Com. II, Sept. 1981)

3.13 Compute the mean deviation from the median and from mean for the following distribution of the scores of 50 college students.

Score :	140-150	150-160	160-170	170-180	180-190	190-200
Frequency :	5	6	10	13	9	7

(Kurukshetra University, B.Com., 1980, Mysore University, B.Com., April 1981)

3.14. Calculate median and mean deviations for the following frequency distribution

Age (years) :	1-5	6-10	11-15	16-20	21-25	26-30	31-35	36-40	40-45
No. of persons :	7	10	16	32	24	18	10	5	1

(*Lucknow University, B.Com., 1972*)

3.15 Compute the coefficient of mean deviation from the following data.

Height in inches :	50-53	53-56	56-59	59-62	62-65	65-68
No. of students :	2	7	24	27	13	3

(*Punjab University, B.A.* (*Eco.*), *1983*)

3.16 Calculate the mean deviation of the following series from the mean.

Monthly wages of Workers (in Rs.)	200-250	250-300	300-350	350-400	400-450	450-500
No. of workers :	7	13	15	24	36	50
Wages :	500-550	550-600	600-650	650-700	700-750	above 750
Workers :	25	10	8	6	4	2

[*Delhi University, B.Com., 1976*]

3.17 Calculate the standard deviation of the following observations on a certain variable.
240.12, 240.13, 240.15, 240.12, 240.17, 240.15, 240.17, 240.16, 240.22, 240.21

[*ICWA* (*Inter.*), *June 1976*]

3.18 Find the standard deviation of the following distribution.

Age :	20-25	25-30	30-35	35-40	40-45	45-50
No. of persons :	170	110	80	45	40	35

(Take assumed average = 32.5) [*Delhi University, B.A.* (*Eco., Hons*), *1982*]

3.19 The mean of 5 observations is 4.4 and the variance is 3.24. If three of the five observations are *1*, 2 and 6, find the value of the other two. [*Delhi University, B.A.* (*Eco. Hons.*), *1983*]

3.20 Find the mean and standard deviation of the first *n* natural numbers.

[*Delhi University, B.A.* (*Eco. Hons.*), 1982]

3.21 Calculate the standard deviation from the following data.

Marks in Cost Accounting :	0-10	10-20	20-30	30-40	40-50	50-60	60-70
No. of students :	5	7	14	12	9	6	2

[*Osmania University, B.Com. II, April 1984*]

3.22 Find out the mean and standard deviation of the following data.

Age under :	10	20	30	40	50	60	70	80
No. of person dying :	15	30	53	75	100	110	115	125

[*Nagarjuna University, B.Com., April 1980*]

3.23 Calculate the proportion of farms in which costs of production are within the range of AM + SD in the following distribution.

Cost of production (Rs. per ltr) :	4-6	6-8	8-10	10-12	12-14	14-16
No. of dairy farms :	13	111	182	105	19	4

[*ICWA* (*Final*), *Dec., 1973*]

3.24 In the following data, two class frequencies are missing.

CI :	100-110	110-120	120-130	130-140	140-150	150-160	160-170	170-180	180-190	190-200
Frequency :	4	7	15	-	40	-	16	10	6	3

However it was possible to ascertain that the total number of frequencies was 150 and that the median has been correctly found out as 146.25. You are required to find, with the help of information given.

(*i*) The two - missing frequencies.

(*ii*) Having found the missing frequencies, calculate AM and SD

(*iii*) Without using the direct formula, find the value of mode

[*C.A.* (*Inter*). *May 1973*]

3.25 The standard deviation calculated form a set of 32 observation is 5. If the sum of the observation is 80, what is the sum of the square of these observations. [*ICWA* (*Final*), *Jan.*, *1971*]

3.26 A company paid bonus to its employees as under :

Monthly salary :	100-120	120-140	140-160	160-180	180-200	200-220	220 & over
Bonus paid (Rs.) :	500	600	700	800	900	1,000	1,100

The actual salaries of the employees were as given below :

Rs. 205, 190, 195, 218, 187, 168, 250, 168, 190, 168, 170, 175, 178, 175, 150, 125, 148, 165, 155, 145, 125, 110, 162, 130, 150, 184

Restate the data in the form of a frequency distribution and find out

(*i*) The total bonus paid,

(*ii*) The average bonus paid per emplyee, and

(*iii*) The standard deviation of the distribution. [*Meerut University, M.A.* (*Eco.*) 1976]

3.27 The following table gives the length of life of 400 radio tubes :

Length of life (hrs.)	*No. of radio tubes*	*Length of life (hrs.)*	*No. of radio tubes*
1,000-1,199	12	2,000-2,199	55
1,200-1,399	30	2,200-2,399	36
1,400-1,599	65	2,400-2,599	25
1,600-1,799	78	2,600-2,799	9
1,800-1,999	90		

Calculate (*i*) the average length of life of a radio set, (*ii*) the standard deviation of the life, (*iii*) the percentage number of tubes whose length of life falls within $\overline{X} \pm 2\sigma$.

[*Delhi University, M.B.A., 1976*]

3.28 The study of the age of 100 film stars grouped in the intervals of 10-12, 12-14... etc. revealed the mean age and standard deviation to be 32.02 and 13.18 respectively. While checking, it was discovered that the age 57 was misread as 27. Calculate the correct mean age and standard deviation. [*Punjab University, M.A.* (*Eco.*), *1973*]

3.29 The mean and standard deviation of a sample of 100 observations were calculated as 40 and 5.1 respectively by a student, who took by mistake 50 instead of 40 for one observation. Calculate the correct mean and standard deviation. [*ICWA (Inter), June 1982*]

3.30 The arithmetic mean of runs scored by three batsmen Vijay, Subhash, and Kumar in the same series of 10 innings are 50, 48 and 12 respectively. The standard deviations of their runs are respectively 15, 12, and 2. Who is the most consistent of the three ? If one of the three is to be selected, who will be selected ? [*Bombay University, B.Com. April 1978*]

3.31 Two workers on the same job show the following results over a long period of time.

	Worker *A*	Worker *B*
Mean time of completing the job (minutes) :	30	25
Standard deviation (minutes) :	6	4

(*i*) Which worker appears to be more consistent in the time he requires to complete the job?
(*ii*) Which worker appears to be faster in completing the job? Explain.

[*Osmania University, B.Com.* (*Hons.*), April 1983]

3.32 Goals scored by two teams *A* & *B* in a Football season were as under. Calculate the co-efficient of variation. Which team may be considered more consistent ?

Goals scored in a match	0	1	2	3	4
Number of matches – Team A	27	9	8	5	4
Team B	17	9	6	5	3

[*Bangalore University, B.Com. Oct., 1976*]

3.33 You are supplied the following data about heights of boys and girls in a college.

	Boys	*Girls*
Number	3,372	4,538
Average height	68″	61″
Variance	296	456

You are required to find
(*i*) Combined average of heights of boys and girls
(*ii*) Coefficient of variation for each group. [*Osmania University, B.Com. III, Oct., 1983*]

3.34 Find the standard deviation and the coefficient of variation for the following frequency distribution and clearly state the fundamental difference between these two measures of variation :

Class Interval	1-3	3-5	5-7	7-9	9-11	11-13	13-15
Frequency	3	9	25	35	17	10	1

[*Punjab University, M.A.(Eco.), Oct., 1980*]

3.35 Calculate coefficient of variation from the following data.

Income (Rs.) less than	700	800	900	1,000	1,100	1,200
No. of families	12	30	50	75	110	120

[*Himachal University, B.Com. April 1982*]

3.36 From the data given below, state which team (A or B) is more consistent.

No. of goals scored in a match	0	1	2	3	4
Number of matches - Team A	27	9	8	5	1
Team B	1	5	8	9	27

[*Kurukshetra University, B.Com. II, 1982*]

3.37 Lives of two models of refrigerators in a recent survey are :

Life (No. of years)	0-2	2-4	4-6	6-8	8-10	10-12
Number of refrigerators						
Model A	5	16	13	7	5	4
Model B	2	7	12	19	9	1

What is the average life of each model of these refrigerators?
Which model has greater uniformity?

[*Delhi University, M.B.A., 1970; Kurukshetra, M.B.A., 1975*]

3.38 A purchasing agent received samples of envelops from two suppliers. He had the sample tested for tearing weight with the following results. Find out which company's envelops are more uniform.

Tearing weight (in (lbs))	:	50-59.9	60-69.9	70-79.9	80-89.9
Samples from Company *A*	:	3	42	12	3
Company B	:	10	16	26	8

[*Karnataka University, B.Com. April 1982*]

3.39 For a group of 50 male workers, the mean and standard deviation of their weekly wages are Rs. 63 and Rs. 9 respectively. For a group of 40 female workers, these were Rs. 54 and Rs. 6 respectively. Find the standard deviation of the combined group of 90 workers.

[*Bombay University, B.Com., 1978*]

3.40 Given the following results relating to two groups containing 20 and 30 observations, calculate the coefficient of variation of all the 50 observations by combining both the groups.

	Group	
	I	***II***
Σx	45	55
Σx^2	118	132

[*Nagpur University, B.Com., 1974*]

3.41 An analysis of monthly wages paid to the workers in two firms A & B belonging to the same industry gives the following results.

	Firm A	***Firm B***
Number of workers	500	600
Average monthly wage	Rs. 186	Rs. 175
Variance of distribution of wages	81	100

(*i*) Which firm A or B has a larger wage bill?

(*ii*) In which firm A or B, is there greater variability in individual wage

[*Bangalore University, B.Com., May 1979*]

(*iii*) Calculate (*a*) the average monthly wage

(*b*) the variance of the distribution of wages of all workers in the firms A and B taken together.

[*Madurai University, B.Com., May 1978*]

3.42 Calculate the Pearson's coefficient of skewness based on Mean and Mode from the following information.

Wages (Rs.)	:	0-10	10-20	20-30	30-40	40-50
No. of workers	:	15	20	30	25	10

[*Osmania University, B.Com. III, Oct., 1983*]

❁❁❁

CHAPTER 4

CORRELATION ANALYSIS

4.1 INTRODUCTION

Business managers need the information about future trends of various parameters like demand, expenditure, cash flows, salary of workers etc. to take decisions about their future operations. In day today life also, we would like to find out whether any price increase would change our behaviour towards buying certain house hold items. For such decisions, we either use intuitive sense or a definite calculative relationship for effective and arithmetic prediction.

In this chapter, we are discussing the correlation analysis to establish such relationships.

4.2 CORRELATION

Having discussed the causes of univariates in terms of average, dispersion and skewness etc, we now wish to discuss the cases of observation sets of two or more variables. For example, the heights of individuals are generally related to weights and weights are related to the age of the individuals. When we study such cases, then we think in terms of correlation. Such distribution, in which each unit of the series assumes two values is called a bi-variate distribution and if we have more than two variables on each unit of a distribution, it is termed as multi-variate distribution.

When the effect on one variable of the data set changes the other variable, the inter-relationship of such two variables is measured in the form of correlation. It helps in understanding the forecast of one variable based on the other, provided the relationship pattern can be established.

In case of bi-variate distribution, we may be looking for the answers to the following questions;

1. Is there an association between the two variables? If so, to what extent?
2. Is there any definite relationship between the two variables? In case of an increase or decrease of one variable, any definite effect on the other variable needs be studied, if any such effect exists. Its extent also needs to be established.

This concept of relationship between two variables is denoted by Correlation. Correlation is a statistical tool which studies this relationship of two variables. Correlation Analysis involves various methods and techniques used for studying and measuring the extent of the realtionship of two variables. The cause and effect relationship *i.e.*, the extent to which variation in one variable effects the other variable is answered by "Regression technique", which will be discussed in the next chapter.

To illustrate the concept, we list out certain examples indicating the multivariate distribution.

1. In a business scenario, the sales revenue and related advertising expenditure can be cited as two interdependent variables, the effect of one may not be the result of the other always in the same proportion.
2. In an examination, the series of marks in two subjects may not have any definite relationship, but these can be compared with reference to different schools from a similar class.
3. The age details of wives and husbands in a sample of selected married couples can be a good measure of relationship of two variables.
4. The comparision of Price and its effect on demand of a particular commodity may establish relationship for future decision making.
5. The heights and weights of a selected community personnel may be good measure for designing clothes, vehicles or type of food criterion.

Various definitions of correlation have been suggested by few statisticians in different language or circumstances, but the basic theme is the source i.e. inter-relationships of specified variables.

4.3 DEFINITION OF CORRELATION

In a bi-variate distribution analysis, we would be interested in knowing whether there exists a relationship between the two variables under discussion and study.

Correlation has been defined in the following manner.

"Correlation is an analysis of the covariation between two or more variables" – *A.M. Tutle*

"When the relationship is of a quantitative nature, the appropriate statistical tool for discovering and measuring the relationship and expressing it in a brief formula is known as correlation" – *Craxton and Cowden*

"Correlation analysis contributes to the understanding of economic behaviour, aids in locating the critically important variables on which others depend, may reveal to the economist the connections by which disturbances spread and suggest to him the paths through which stabilising forces may become effective." – *W.A. Neiswanger*

"The effect of correlation is to reduce the range of uncertainty of out prediction" – *Tippett*

Thus simply putting it –

"Correlation analysis is the statistical tool we can use to describe the degree to which one variable is linearly related to another".

4.4 TYPES OF CORRELATION

Positive and Negative Correlation

While studying the realtionships of any two related variables, if we find the deviations of the values of variables in the same direction *i.e.*, if one variable increases, the corresponding values of the second variable also increase, then it is called a Positive Correlation. This is true even if decreasing values of one variable correspond to the decreasing corresponding values of the other variable. The amount of rain fall and yield of the crop may be one such example.

Some other examples of positive correlation are heights and weights of human beings, price and expenditure on luxury items etc.

On the other hand, if the variables deviation is in opposite directions such as decrease in one causes increases in the values of the other or *vice-versa*, it is called the Negative Correlation. Volume and pressure of a perfect gas or money and purchases in the market on a particular day may represent a negative correlation.

In addition, price and demand of a commodity, temperatures and sales of woollen clothes can be cited as examples of negative correlation –

The two deviations can be represented as under :

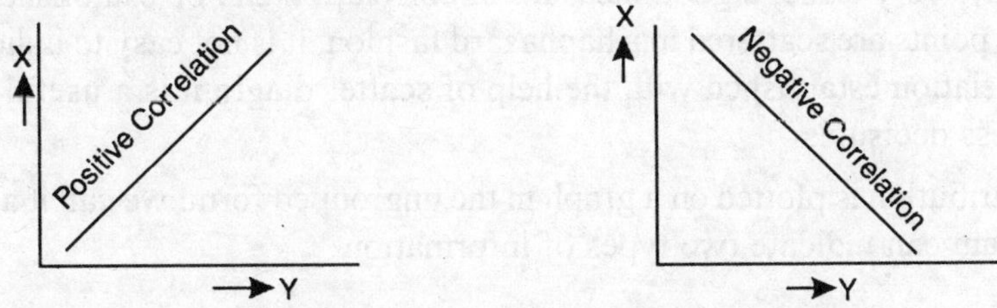

Fig. 4.1. Positive and Negative Correlation

Linear and Non-Linear Correlation

When we establish the rate of change of one variable with respect to the other and find it to be constant, it is called a Linear Correlation. When this change does not remain the same, the correlation will be termed as Non-Linear Correlation.

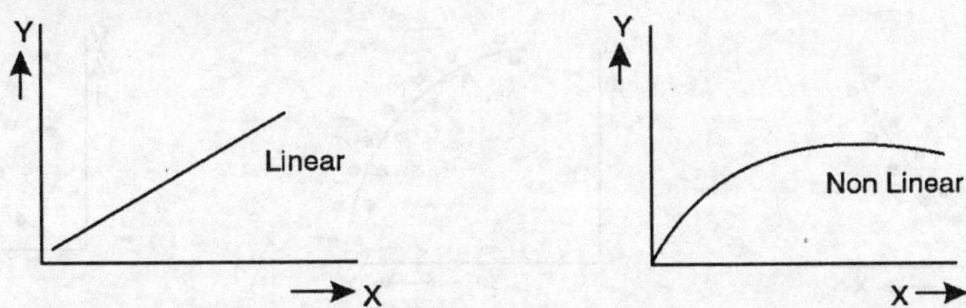

Fig. 4.2. Linear and Non-Linear Correlation

If we obtain a data for two variables x and y as follows

x	0	3	6	9	12
y	3	15	27	39	51

General relationship that can be established is $y = 4x + 3$, which is a linear trend. When this relationship does not establish a linear curve, *i.e.* a straight line passing through all the points, then it will be called a non-linear correlation. In such cases, the rate of change of one variable is not the same in all the cases.

For example of simplicity, we would like to concentrate only on linear trends because non-linear relationship analysis is complicated. Even linear relationship is not always easy specially in social and economic sciences, where formulation of mathematical models may not always be possible.

For an effective study of correlation of variables, the usefulness lies in establishing the pattern of variation with reference to the other. Thus, these can either be linear or non-linear relationships or else these can be postive or negative correlation.

4.5 CORRELATION ANALYSIS

Correlation Analysis is a statistical technique used to indicate the degree of relationship existing between one variable and the other. It is also used along with Regression Analysis (described in the next chapter) to measure how well the regression line explains the variations of the dependent variable with the independent variable.

For correlation analysis, we use the following methods

1. Scatter Diagram Method
2. Karl Pearson's Coefficient of Correlation
3. Bi-variate Correlation Method

4. Rank Correlation Method
5. Concurrent Deviations Method

Scatter Diagram Method

It is the simplest method of representation of the bi-variatc distribution. If points of relationships of two variables are very close, a good measure of correlation can be established as in case of Fig. 4.3. But when the points are scattered in a haphazard fashion, it is not easy to indicate the correlation. Straight line correlation established with the help of scatter diagram is a useful method for a large number of business decisions.

When the distribution is plotted on a graph in the ungrouped form, we call it as a scatter diagram. The scatter diagram can indicate two types of information.

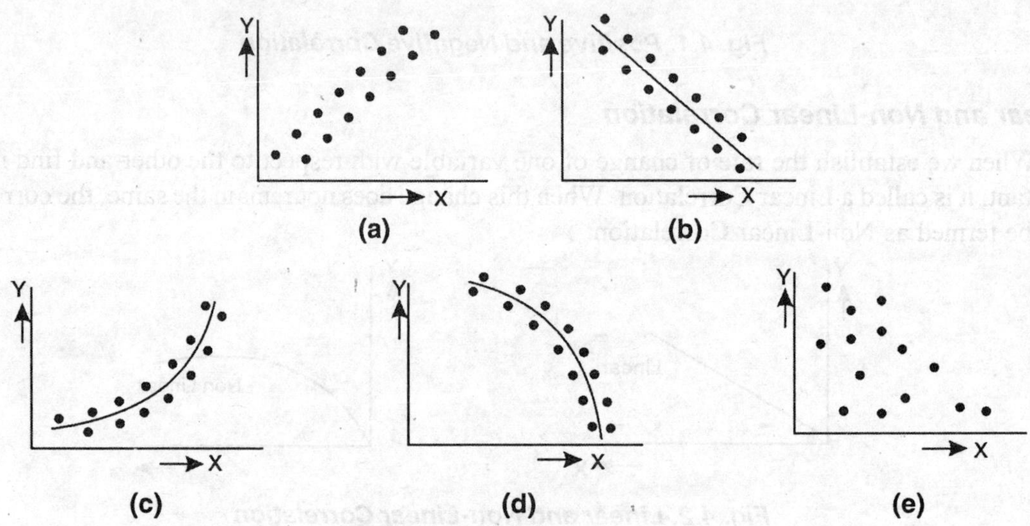

Fig. 4.3. Scatter Diagram

Few useful methods such as Karl Pearson's Coefficient of Correlation, Rank correlation or Concurrent deviation method has been suggested by statisticians and definite inferences are possible through these methods.

The scatter diagrams given above in Fig. 4.3 indicate different relationships. Fig. 4.3 (*a*) indicates a positive linear relation while Fig. 4.3 (*b*) shows a negative linear relation. Similarly, Fig. 4.3 (*c*) and (*d*) are non-linear relationships, (*c*) being positive while (*d*) as negative. When we study Fig. 4.3 (*e*), we find that no definite relationship of x and y can be established.

From the above discussion, we can easily refer that using scatter diagram is comparatively easier method to use as it is quite comprehensible and it helps us to form general opinion about the nature of relationship between the two variables only by visual inspection of the relationship graph. When number of observations are very large and don't necessarily create a trend or a pattern easily, it may not be a useful method for establishing correlation.

This method also does not indicate exact measure of relationship.

Karl Pearson's Coefficient of Correlation

The linear relationship of correlation between two variables has been suggested by Karl Pearson (1867-1936) a British Biometrician and Statistician and it is the most widely used method of correlation being practiced.

It is denoted by r or r_{xy} or $r(x, y)$ denoting the measure of correlation between two variables x and y.

It is the ratio of the co-variance between x and y written as $\text{cov}(x, y)$ to the product of the standard deviations of x and y. It can be written as :

$$r = \frac{\text{cov}(x, y)}{\sigma_x \sigma_y}$$

When $(x_1, y_1), (x_2 y_2) \ldots\ldots (x_n, y_n)$ are the n-pairs of observations of the variables x and y in a bivariate distribution.

Then $\quad \text{cov}(x, y) = \frac{1}{n}\Sigma(x - \bar{x})(y - \bar{y})$

$$\sigma_x = \sqrt{\frac{1}{n}\Sigma(x - \bar{x})^2}$$

and $\quad \sigma_y = \sqrt{\frac{1}{n}\Sigma(y - \bar{y})^2}$

Thus, we can write the Karl Pearson's coefficient of correlation as :

$$r = \frac{\frac{1}{n}\Sigma(x - \bar{x})(y - \bar{y})}{\sqrt{\frac{1}{n}\Sigma(x - \bar{x})^2 \frac{1}{n}\Sigma(y - \bar{y})^2}}$$

$$= \frac{\Sigma(x - \bar{x})(y - \bar{y})}{\sqrt{\left[\Sigma(x - \bar{x})^2 \Sigma(y - \bar{y})^2\right]}}$$

If we denote $\quad dx = x - \bar{x}$

and $\quad dy = y - \bar{y}$

Then $\quad r = \frac{\Sigma dx\, dy}{\sqrt{\Sigma dx^2 \Sigma dy^2}}$

It can also be written as

$$r = \frac{\frac{1}{n^2}[n\Sigma xy - (\Sigma x \Sigma y)]}{\sqrt{\frac{1}{n^2}\left[n\Sigma x^2 - (\Sigma x)^2\right]}\sqrt{\frac{1}{n^2}\left[n\Sigma y^2 - (\Sigma y)^2\right]}}$$

$$= \frac{n\Sigma xy - \Sigma x \Sigma y}{\sqrt{\left[n\Sigma x^2 - (\Sigma x)^2\right]}\sqrt{\left[n\Sigma y^2 - (\Sigma y)^2\right]}}$$

The most-useful method of correlation has been suggested by Karl Pearson. This method establishes relationship of mean variations and can speak the result based on linear trend of relationship.

Bivariate Correlation Method

When the data of bivariate distribution is large, this can be arranged in the form of a two way frequency table. The values of both the variables can be arranged in the steps of various class intervals and these classes of frequency may not necessarily be same. It can now become a table of $m \times n$ cells *i.e.* m classes for x - variable and n classes for y - variable. The relative frequencies for each group of class in a bivariate frequency table are written as follows.

TABLE 4.1. Bivariate Frequency Table

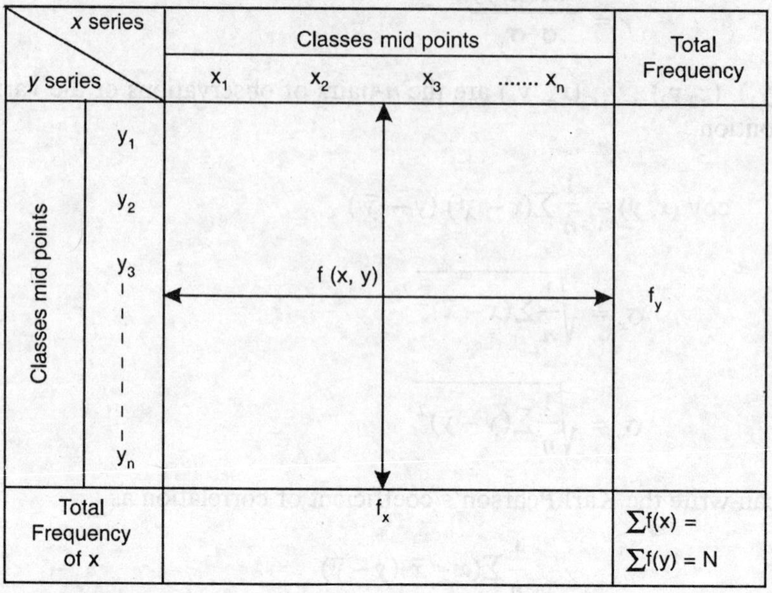

x series / y series	Classes mid points				Total Frequency
	x_1	x_2	x_3	...... x_n	
Classes mid points y_1					
y_2					
y_3		f (x, y)			f_y
|					
y_n					
Total Frequency of x		f_x			$\Sigma f(x) =$ $\Sigma f(y) = N$

A matrix method of correlating two variables is explained under 'Bivariate Correlation Method'. The change of scale and origin of variable data has also been correlated in this method.

In this case $f(x, y)$ will be the frequency of pair (x and y). For calculation of correlation coefficient, we can use the relationship,

$$r = \frac{N\sum xy\ f(x,y) - (\sum xfx)(\sum y\ fy)}{\sqrt{\left[N\sum x^2 fx(\sum x\ fx)^2\right]\left[N\sum y^2 fy - (\sum y\ fy)^2\right]}}$$

where N is the total frequency

If we change the origin and the scale in x and y, then taking

$$u = \left(\frac{x-A}{h}\right)$$

and $$v = \left(\frac{y-B}{k}\right)$$

where h and k are the class widths of series x and y and A and B as constants chosen as arbitrary origins, we can get

$$r_{xy} = r_{uv} = \frac{N\sum fuv - (\sum fu \sum fv)}{\sqrt{\left[N\sum fu^2 - \Sigma(fu)^2\right]\left[N\sum fv^2 - \Sigma(fv)^2\right]}}$$

The illustrative use of this method has been amply brought out in problems 4.5 and 4.6.

Rank Correlation Method

In addition to the Karl Pearson's Coefficient of Correlation, we use another approach for ascertaining the degree of correlation between the two variables under consideration. It is based on the ranks of the values of each variable. (The values are to be graded or ranked as per their ascending or descending sequence). The coefficient of correlation determined on this basis is called the Spearman's Rank Correlation Coefficient and is denoted by the relationship indicated below :

$$\rho = 1 - \frac{6\sum_{i=1}^{n} d_i^2}{n(n^2-1)}$$

where ρ = Spearman's Rank Correlation Coefficient

and $\qquad n$ = The difference of ranks of a value of the variables

The value of the Spearman's Rank Correlation Coefficient *i.e.* ρ(Pronounced as rho) also varies between –1 to 1.

i.e. $\qquad -1 \leq \rho \leq 1$

The ranks or gradings are alloted to the values of x and y, the two variables, according to the sequence in a particular series *i.e.*, x or y. If least value of x series is alloted rank 1, the next higher, value as 2 and so on. It is similarly done for variable y also. It can be done even in the reverse order. These ranks for each pair of variables are then subtracted to get the difference in ranks *i.e.*, di for a particular pair i of the variables.

There may arise a situation when the value of the variable is repeated in the series. In such cases, the ranks are shared at equal level by the similar values. For example, if there are two values having magnitude of say 15 each, and the normal sequential ranks come to 4, the other value 15 could be ranked 5. Actual ranks are allotted as the average value of the ranks *i.e.* $\frac{4+5}{2}$ = 4.5 each for calculation of Rank Correlation Coefficient. The modified relationship is adopted as follows :

> In Rank-correlation Method, suggested by 'Spearman', the absolute variation is not correlated, but their rank in order of ascending or descending nature. Even when a data is repeated, the correction factor has been suggested.

$$\rho = 1 - \frac{6\left[\sum d^2 + m\left(\frac{m^2-1}{12}\right)\right]}{n(n^2-1)}$$

A correction factor $\left[m\left(\frac{m^2-1}{12}\right)\right]$ has been added to compensate for the repeated ranks in this expression.

The value m = number of times an observation is repeated. Thus, if we have only the value, say 15 repeated twice, the ranks are given as 4.5 (above example) and then $m = 2$ to be incorporated in the correction factor.

For a possibility of having more than one observation repeated, the correction factor gets modified as under

$$m_1\left(\frac{m_1^2-1}{12}\right) + m_2\left(\frac{m_2^2-1}{12}\right) \text{ etc.}$$

where m_1, m_2 = Observation 1 and 2 repeated m_1 and m_2 times.

In order to show that such a relationship is valid, let us establish the proof of this relationship.

Since the method is based on ranks of x and y, we get

$$\bar{x} = \frac{\Sigma x}{n} = \frac{1+2+3+\ldots+n}{n}$$

$$= \frac{n+1}{2}$$

$$\text{similarly } \bar{y} = \frac{n+1}{2}$$

$$\sigma_x^2 = \frac{1}{n}\Sigma x^2 - (\bar{x})^2$$

$$= \frac{1}{n}[1^2 + 2^2 + \ldots\ldots n^2] - \left(\frac{n+1}{2}\right)^3$$

$$= \frac{1}{n}\left[\frac{n(n+1)(2n+1)}{6}\right] - \frac{(n+1)^2}{4}$$

$$= \frac{(n+1)}{12}[2(2n+1) - 3(n+1)]$$

$$= \frac{(n+1)}{12}[4n + 2 - 3n - 3]$$

$$= \frac{n^2 - 1}{12}$$

Same value can be obtained for σ_y^2

$$\therefore \quad \sigma_x^2 = \sigma_y^2 = \frac{n^2 - 1}{12}$$

Now $\quad d = x - y$

$$= (x - \bar{x}) - (y - \bar{y}) \text{ (linear } \bar{x} - \bar{y})$$

$$\therefore \quad d^2 = \left[(x - \bar{x}) - (y - \bar{y})\right]^2$$

$$= (x - \bar{x})^2 + (y - \bar{y})^2 - 2(x - \bar{x})(y - \bar{y})$$

$$\therefore \quad \Sigma(x - \bar{x})^2 + \Sigma(y - \bar{y})^2 - 2\Sigma(x - \bar{x})(y - \bar{y})$$

and

$$\frac{\Sigma d^2}{n} = \frac{\Sigma(x - \bar{x})^2}{n} + \frac{\Sigma(y - \bar{y})^2}{n} - 2\Sigma\frac{(x - \bar{x})(y - \bar{y})}{n}$$

$$\frac{\Sigma d^2}{n} = \sigma_x^2 + \sigma_y^2 - \frac{2\Sigma(x - \bar{x})(y - \bar{y})}{n}$$

Since Spearman's Rank correlation coefficient is given by

$$\rho = \frac{\Sigma(x - \bar{x})(y - \bar{y})}{n\sigma_x\sigma_y}$$

$$\therefore \quad \rho.\,\sigma_x\sigma_y = \frac{\Sigma(x - \bar{x})(y - \bar{y})}{n}$$

$$\therefore \quad \frac{\Sigma d^2}{n} = \sigma^2{}_x + \sigma^2{}_y - 2\rho\sigma_x\sigma_y$$

$$= \sigma_x^2 + \sigma_x^2 - 2\rho\,\sigma_x^2 \quad (\text{Since } \sigma_x = \sigma_y)$$

$$= 2\sigma_x^2\,[1 - \rho]$$

$$\therefore \quad (1 - \rho) = \frac{\Sigma d^2}{2n\sigma_x^2}$$

$$= \frac{\Sigma d^2}{2n(n^2 - 1)/12}$$

Since the Rank method is based on the ranks of the two variables, the correction factor in case of repeated data has been worked out based on its mathematically-derived expressions.

$$= \frac{6\Sigma d^2}{n(n^2-1)}$$

Thus $$\rho = 1 - \frac{6\Sigma d^2}{n(n^2-1)}$$

Spearman's limits for ρ (coefficient of Rank correlation) lies between –1 and +1, which can be establish by taking value of

$$\Sigma d^2 = n(n+1) + 4\Sigma x^2 - 4(x+1)\Sigma x$$

$$= \frac{n(n^2-1)}{3}$$

Since Σd^2 is non-negative and so is n, ρ max will be 1 – (Some non-negative) = 1

Similarly

$$\rho = 1 - \frac{6n(n^2-1)/3}{n(n^2-1)}$$

$$= 1 - 2 = -1$$

Hence $-1 \le \rho \le 1$

Concurrent Deviation Method

This is a method when precise correlation may be required. It is based on the direction of change in signs of the deviations of the variables. The non-precision values obtained are due to the fact that it does not use exact value of the variable. We use plus or minus sign or equality relationship, if the value of the variable is greater than, lesser than or equal to the preceeding value respectively. The deviation in the value of the variables is said to be concurrent, if they have the same sign. The coefficient of correlation is then calculated by the following formula.

$$r = \pm\sqrt{\pm\left(\frac{2c-n}{n}\right)}$$

Where c is the number of pairs of concurrent deviations and n is the number of pairs of deviations.

Concurrent deviation method explains the method of correlation based on the value (greater or lesser) of the variables. The method is useful for short time fluctuations of the variables.

Important :

* Since the value of r varies between –1 and 1, then quantity inside the square root should positive. Also, if we take $(2c - n)$ as positive, we use positive sign inside and outside the square root. If $(2c - n)$ is negative, we have to use negative (–) sign inside and outside the square root.
* Also, since n is number of deviations and not number of observations, it is one less than the number of observations.
* If reflects short time fluctuations only.

4.6 PROPERTIES OF CORRELATION COEFFICIENT

Property I : The value of correlation coefficient varies between –1 and 1 *i.e.*

$$-1 \le r < 1$$

also $$-1 \le \rho \le 1$$

Property II : Correlation coefficient is independent of the change of origin and scale. Thus the concept of assumed mean or the scale of observations can be used to advantage.

If $$u = \frac{x - A}{h}$$

and $$v = \frac{y - B}{h}$$

Then $$r_{xy} = \frac{\Sigma(x-\bar{x})(y-\bar{y})}{\sqrt{\Sigma(x-\bar{x})^2\,\Sigma(y-\bar{y})^2}}$$ can be transformed as

$$r_{uv} = \frac{\Sigma(u-\bar{u})(v-\bar{v})}{\sqrt{\Sigma(u-\bar{u})^2\,\Sigma(v-\bar{v})^2}} = r_{xy}$$

$\therefore$ $r_{xy} = r_{uv}$ with change of orign and scale

Property III : The independent variables are uncorrelated, but the converse is not true.

Thus $$\text{cov}(x, y) = \frac{1}{n}\sum xy - (\bar{x}\,.\bar{y})$$

and $r_{xy} = 0$ for independent variables

Correlation Coefficient has the properties of independence, of the change of origin or scale and its value varying between −1 and +1. It is also established that independent variables are un-correlated but the converse is not true. Correlation coefficient dependability is related through the concept of its Probable error.

4.7 PROBABLE ERROR

The Correlation coefficient establishes the relationship of the two variables under consideration. After ascertaining this level of relationship, we now proceed to find the extent upto which this coefficient is dependable. Probable error of the correlation coefficient is such a measure of testing the reliability of the observed value of the correlation coefficient. Probable error is denoted by PE(r).

If r is the observed value of the correlation coefficient in a sample of n pairs of observations for the two variables under consideration, then the standard error, denoted by SE(r) is expressed as

$$\text{SE}(r) = \frac{1-r^2}{\sqrt{n}}$$

The probable error of the correlation coefficient is related to standard error SE(r) in the following manner

$$\text{PE}(r) = 0.6745\ \text{SE}(r)$$

$$= 0.6745\left(\frac{1-r^2}{\sqrt{n}}\right)$$

The factor 0.6745 is used due to the fact that it is treated as the case of normal distribution of observations and that 50 per cent of the observations lie in the range of $\mu \pm 0.6745\sigma$, where μ and σ are mean and standard derivation of the data.

4.8 COEFFICIENT OF DETERMINATION

Coefficient of determination is yet another measure to indicate the extent of linear relationship between two variables.

Thus coefficient of determiation is more useful and comprehensible measure of the variation between two variables and is the ratio of the explained variance to the total variance. Mathematically coefficient of determination is the square of the coefficient of correlation. Thus coefficient of determination

$$r^2 = \frac{\text{Explained variance}}{\text{Total variance}}$$

$$= 1 - \Sigma(y - \hat{y})^2$$

It is a better measure of $\Sigma(y - \hat{y})^2$ variation because the value of r, the correlation coefficient does not necessarily indicate that for $r = 0.7$, the variation of 70% in the series of dependent variable due to the variation in the series of independent variable. But coefficient of determination *i.e.* $r^2 = 0.49$ would imply that only 49% of the variation in the dependent variable series is due to the variation in the independent variable series and the remaining 51% is due to other causes.

Similarly, the comparison of two correlation coefficients is not very effective measure to indicate that $r_1 = 0.4$ and $r_2 = 0.8$ are showing double correlation, whereas $r_1^2 = 0.16$ and $r_2^2 = 0.64$ definitely indicates that the correlation in the second case is four times as high as the correlation in the first case.

Since the measure is coefficient of determination is squared correlation coefficient, its value is always non-negative and hence it does not tell us the direction of the relationship (positive or negative of the given variables.

Coefficient of Determination is a measure of the extent of relationship between two variables. It is denoted by the square of coefficient of correlation. Due to its squared relationship, it does not indicate the direction of the relationship.

Coefficient of Non-determination

The ratio of the unexplained variation to the total variation is called the coefficient of non-determination.

∴ Coefficient of Non-determination (k^2)

∵ $k^2 = 1 -$ coefficient of determination

$= 1 - r^2$

Coefficient of Alienation

The coefficient of alienation is given by the square root of the coefficient of non-determination. This

$$k = \pm\sqrt{1 - r^2}$$

CHAPTER SUMMARY

Important terms used

- **Coefficient of correlation :** The measure of correlation between two variables.
- **Coefficient of determination :** The square of the coefficient of correlation.
- **Coefficient of non-determination :** The ratio of the unexplained variation to the total variation.
- **Coefficient of Alienation :** Square root of the coefficient of non-determination.
- **Correlation :** The association or relationship between two variables.
  A statistical tool used to describe the degree to which one variable is linearly related to another.
- **Positive correlation :** Relationship of increase/decrease in the value of one variable indicating the corresponding similar increase/decrease in another variable.

- **Negative correlation :** When values of one variable move in the direction opposite to the values of the other variable.
- **Probable Error :** Measure of testing the reliability of the observed value of the correlation coefficient.

Relationships Used

- $$r = \frac{\text{cov}(x, y)}{\sigma_x \sigma_y}$$
- $$r = \frac{\Sigma(x - \bar{x})(y - \bar{y})}{\sqrt{\left[\Sigma(x - \bar{x})^2 \Sigma(y - \bar{y})^2\right]}}$$
- $$r = \frac{n\,\Sigma xy - \Sigma x \Sigma y}{\sqrt{\left[n\Sigma x^2 - (\Sigma x)^2\right]\left[n\Sigma y^2 - (\Sigma y)^2\right]}}$$
- $$r_{xy} = x_{uv} = \frac{N\Sigma fuv - \Sigma fu \Sigma fv}{\sqrt{\left[N\Sigma fu^2 - \Sigma(fu)^2\right]\left[N\Sigma fv^2 - \Sigma(fv)^2\right]}}$$
- $$\rho = 1 - \frac{6\Sigma d^2}{n(n^2 - 1)}$$

  or $$\rho = 1 - \frac{6[\Sigma d^2 + m\left(\frac{m^2 - 1}{12}\right)}{n(n^2 - 1)}$$
- $$r = \pm\sqrt{\pm\left(\frac{2c - n}{n}\right)}$$
- $$SE_{(r)} = \frac{1 - r^2}{\sqrt{n}}$$
- $$PE_{(r)} = 0.6745\ SE_{(r)}$$
- Coefficient of determination $r^2 = 1 - \Sigma(y - \hat{y})^2$
- Coefficient of non-determination $k^2 = 1 - r^2$
- Coefficient of Alienation $k = \pm\sqrt{1 - r^2}$

SOLVED PROBLEMS

Problem 4.1

While taking the data of a certain group of employees in a company, we can establish the relationship between the length of service and corresponding level of their montly salary. The sample chosen is completely random.

One such sample is illustrated below :

Employee Code No.	*Length of Service (yrs.)* (x)	*Monthly Salary (Rs.)* (y)
92001	1	3,000
92002	2	4,000
92003	3	4,500
92004	4	5,500
92005	5	6,000
92006	5	6,500
92007	2	6,000
92008	4	7,000
92009	3	8,000
92010	5	5,000
92011	4	6,000
92012	1	4,000
92013	2	7,000
92014	6	9,000
92015	10	9,500
92016	9	9,500
92017	5	5,500
92018	6	7,500
92019	9	5,500
92020	8	9,000

For all the 20 employees, we have both the value of length of service and their monthly salary. Taking length of service as x and the monthly salary as y, draw the frequency distribution table for both the variables separately.

Solution :

LENGTH OF SERVICE OF 20 EMPLOYEES

Length of Service (x)	*Frequency (f)*
1 < 4	7
4 < 7	9
7 < 10	3
10 < 13	1

MONTHLY SALARIES OF 20 EMPLOYEES

Monthly Salary (y)	*Frequency (f)*
3,000 < 4,000	1
4,000 < 5,000	3
5,000 < 6,000	4
6,000 < 7,000	4
7,000 < 8,000	3
8,000 < 9,000	1
9,000 < 10,000	4

BIVARIATE FREQUENCY DISTRIBUTION OF 20 EMPLOYEES

y→ / ↓x	*3,000 <4,000*	*4,000 <5,000*	*5,000 <6,000*	*6,000 <7,000*	*7,000 <8,000*	*8,000 <9,000*	*9,000 <10,000*	*f(x)*
1 < 4	1	3		1	1	1		7
4 < 7			3	3	2		1	9
7<10			1				2	3
10<13							1	1
f(y)	1	3	4	4	3	1	4	20

Problem 4.2

Calculate the coefficient of correlation between x and y series from the following data.

	Series x	y
No. of pairs of observations	15	15
Arithmetic mean	25	18
Standard deviation	3.01	3.03
Sum of squares of deviations from mean	136	138

Summation of product deviations of x and y series from thier respective arithmetic mean = 122

[*Delhi University, B.Com.(Hons.)*, 1976, *ICWA (Final), June, 1981*]

Solution :

The given information can be summarised as follows

$$n = 15;\ \bar{x} = 25;\ \bar{y} = 18$$

$$\sigma_x = 3.01;\ \sigma_y = 3.03$$

$$\Sigma(x - \bar{x})^2 = 136$$

$$\Sigma(y - \bar{y})^2 = 138$$

and $$\Sigma(x - \bar{x})(y - \bar{y}) = 122$$

Karl Pearson's correlation coefficient between x and y series is given by the relationship

$$r = \frac{\Sigma(x-\bar{x})(y-\bar{y})}{n\sigma_x\sigma_y}$$

$$= \frac{122}{15 \times 3.01 \times 3.03} = 0.8917$$

The other data are found to be irrelevant.

Problem 4.3

Calculate the coeffcient from the following results:

$$n = 10;\ \Sigma x = 140;\ \Sigma y = 150$$

$$\Sigma(x - \bar{x})^2 = 180 \quad \Sigma(y - \bar{y})^2 = 215$$

$$\Sigma(x - 10)(y - 15) = 60$$ [*C.A. Inter, May 1980*]

Solution :

Substituting $u = (x-10)$ and $v = (y-15)$

We get $\Sigma u = \Sigma(x-10) = \Sigma x - 10n = 140 - 100 = 40$

Similarly $\Sigma v = \Sigma(y-15) = \Sigma y - 15n = 150 - 150 = 0$

$\Sigma u^2 = \Sigma(x-10)^2 = 180$

$\Sigma v^2 = \Sigma(y-15)^2 = 215$

and $\Sigma uv = \Sigma(x-10)(y-15) = 60$

Karl Pearson's correlation coefficient is calculated as under

$$r_{xy} = r_{uv} = \frac{n\Sigma uv - \Sigma u \Sigma v}{\sqrt{\left[n\Sigma u^2 - (\Sigma u)^2\right]\left[n\Sigma v^2 - (\Sigma v)^2\right]}}$$

$$= \frac{10 \times 60 - 40 \times 0}{\sqrt{\left[10 \times 180 - (40)^2\right]\left[10 \times 215 - 0\right]}}$$

$$= \frac{600}{\sqrt{200 \times 2150}}$$

$$= 0.91$$

Problem 4.4

A computer, while calculating correlation between two variables x and y from 25 pairs of observations, obtained the following results.

$$n = 25;\ \Sigma x = 125;\ \Sigma x^2 = 650;\ \Sigma y = 100;\ \Sigma y^2 = 460 \text{ and } \Sigma xy = 508$$

It was, however, discovered at the time of checking that two pairs of observations were incorrectly copied. They were taken as (6,14) and (8,6) while the correct values were (8, 12) and (6, 8). Prove that the correct value of the correlation should be 2/3. [*ICWA* (Final), *Dec.*, 1977]

Solution :

As per the data given above, we obtain

Correct value of $\Sigma x = 125 - 6 - 8 + 8 + 6 = 125$

Correct value of $\Sigma y = 100 - 14 - 6 + 12 + 8 = 100$

Correct value of $\Sigma x^2 = 650 - 6^2 - 8^2 + 8^2 + 6^2 = 650$

Correct value of $\Sigma y^2 = 460 - 14^2 - 6^2 + 12^2 + 8^2 = 436$

and correct vlaue of $\Sigma xy = 508 - 6 \times 14 - 8 \times 6 + 8 \times 12 + 6 \times 8 = 520$

$$r_{xy} = \frac{n\Sigma xy - (\Sigma x \Sigma y)}{\sqrt{\left[n\Sigma x^2 - \left(\Sigma x^2\right)\right]\left[n\Sigma y^2 - \left(\Sigma y\right)^2\right]}}$$

$$= \frac{25 \times 520 - 125 \times 100}{\sqrt{\left[25 \times 650 - 125^2\right]\left[25 \times 436 - 100^2\right]}}$$

$$= \frac{2}{3}$$

Problem 4.5

Find Karl Pearson's coefficient of correlation between sales and expenses of the following ten firms.

Firms	:	1	2	3	4	5	6	7	8	9	10
Sales in thousand units	:	50	50	55	60	60	65	65	60	60	50
Expenses in thousand Rs.	:	11	13	14	16	16	15	15	14	13	13

[*Madras University, B.Com., Oct., 1980, Punjab University, B.A. (Eco. Hons.), April 1980*]

Solution :

Let us substitute $u = \dfrac{x-60}{5}$ and $v = y - 14$

Then, we can build the table as follows :

Firms	x	y	u	v	u^2	v^2	uv
1	50	11	−2	−3	4	9	6
2	50	13	−2	−1	4	1	2
3	55	14	−1	0	1	0	0
4	60	16	0	2	0	4	0
5	60	16	0	2	0	4	0
6	65	15	1	1	1	1	1
7	65	15	1	1	1	1	1
8	60	14	0	0	0	0	0
9	60	13	0	−1	0	1	0
10	50	13	−2	−1	4	1	2
	$\Sigma x = 580$	$\Sigma y = 140$	$\Sigma u = -5$	$\Sigma v = 0$	$\Sigma u^2 = 15$	$\Sigma v^2 = 22$	$\Sigma uv = 12$

These values can be used for calculating coefficient of correlation as follows :

$$r_{xy} = r_{uv} = \frac{n\Sigma uv - \Sigma u \Sigma v}{\sqrt{\left[n\Sigma u^2 - (\Sigma u)^2\right]\left[n\Sigma v^2 - (\Sigma v)^2\right]}}$$

$$= \frac{10 \times 12 - (-5) \times 0}{\sqrt{\left[10 \times 15 - (-5)^2\right]\left[10 \times 22 - 0^2\right]}}$$

$$= \frac{120}{\sqrt{(150-25)(220)}}$$

$$= \frac{120}{\sqrt{125 \times 220}} = 0.73$$

Problem 4.6

(1) Compute the correlation coefficient between the corresponding values of x and y in the following table.

x	2	4	5	6	8	11
y	18	12	10	8	7	5

(2) Multiply each x value in the table by 2 and add 6. Multiply each value of y in the table by 3 and subtract 15. Find the correlation coefficient between the two new sets of values. Explain why you do or donot obtain the same result as in (1).

[ICWA (Final), June 1976]

Solution :

(1) For computation of correlation coefficient, we obtain the values from the following table.

x	y	$x - \bar{x} = x - 6$	$y - \bar{y} = y - 10$	$(x - \bar{x})^2$	$(y - \bar{y})^2$	$(x - \bar{x})(y - \bar{y})$
2	18	–4	8	16	64	–32
4	12	–2	2	4	4	–4
5	10	–1	0	1	0	0
6	8	0	–2	0	4	0
8	7	2	–3	4	9	–6
11	5	5	–5	25	25	–5
$\Sigma x = 36$	$\Sigma y = 60$	$\Sigma x - \bar{x} = 0$	$\Sigma y - \bar{y} = 0$	$\Sigma(x - \bar{x})^2 = 50$	$\Sigma(y - \bar{y})^2 = 106$	$\Sigma(x - \bar{x})(y - \bar{y}) = -67$

Because $\bar{x} = \frac{\Sigma x}{6} = \frac{36}{6} = 6$

$$\bar{y} = \frac{\Sigma y}{6} = \frac{60}{6} = 10$$

$$\therefore \quad r_{xy} = \frac{\Sigma(x-\bar{x})(y-\bar{y})}{\sqrt{\left[\Sigma(x-\bar{x})^2\right]\left[\Sigma(\bar{y}-)^2\right]}}$$

$$= \frac{-67}{\sqrt{50 \times 106}} = -0.92$$

Thus, variables x and y are having Negative high correlation.

(2) New variables can be defined as

$$u = 2x + 6 \text{ and } v = 3y - 15$$

The revised table with the new defined variables can be drawn as.

x	y	$u = 2x+6$	$v=3y-15$	u^2	v^2	uv
2	18	10	39	100	1521	390
4	12	14	21	196	441	294
5	10	16	15	256	225	240
6	8	18	9	324	81	162
8	7	22	6	484	36	132
11	5	28	0	784	0	0
		$\Sigma u = 108$	$\Sigma v = 108$	$\Sigma u^2 = 2144$	$\Sigma v^2 = 2034$	$\Sigma uv = 1218$

New coefficient of correlation is given by

$$r_{uv} = \frac{n\Sigma uv - (\Sigma u \Sigma v)}{\sqrt{\left[n\Sigma u^2 - (\Sigma u)^2\right]\left[n\Sigma v^2 - (\Sigma v)^2\right]}}$$

$$= \frac{6 \times 1218 - 108 \times 90}{\sqrt{\left[6 \times 2144 - 108^2\right]\left[6 \times 2304 - 90^2\right]}}$$

$$= \frac{-2412}{\sqrt{6868800}}$$

$$= -0.92$$

Since coefficient of correlation is independent of origin, the two values are found to be the same.

Problem 4.7

Find Karl Pearson's coefficient of correlation from the following series of marks secured by 10 students in class test in Mathematics and Statistics.

Marks in Maths :	45	70	65	30	90	40	50	75	85	60
Marks in Statistics :	35	90	70	40	95	40	60	80	80	50

Also calculate its Probable Error

Assume 60 and 65 as working means. *[Delhi University, B.Com., 1970]*

Solution :

Since the working means of two subjects are given as 60 and 65 and we can safely take a common factor of 5 for the calculations, we substitute

$$u = \frac{x - 60}{5} \text{ and } v = \frac{y - 65}{5}$$

The calculation table is now drawn as below :

x	y	$u = \frac{x-60}{5}$	$v = \frac{y-65}{5}$	u^2	v^2	uv
45	35	−3	−6	9	36	18
70	90	2	5	4	25	10
65	70	1	1	1	1	1
30	40	−6	−5	36	25	30
90	95	6	6	36	36	36
40	40	−4	−5	16	25	20
50	60	−2	1	4	1	2
75	80	3	3	9	9	9
85	80	5	3	25	9	15
60	50	0	−3	0	9	10
		$\Sigma u = 2$	$\Sigma v = -2$	$\Sigma u^2 = 140$	$\Sigma v^2 = 176$	$\Sigma uv = 141$

Hence
$$r_{xy} = r_{uv} = \frac{n\Sigma uv - (\Sigma u \Sigma v)}{\sqrt{\left[n\Sigma u^2 - (\Sigma u)^2\right]\left[n\Sigma v^2 - (\Sigma v)^2\right]}}$$

$$= \frac{10 \times 141 - 2 \times (-2)}{\sqrt{[10 \times 140 - 4][10 \times 176 - 4]}}$$

$$= \frac{1414}{\sqrt{2451376}}$$

$$= 0.9$$

Probable Error of the coefficient is given by

$$PE(r) = 0.6745 \frac{1 - r^n}{\sqrt{n}}$$

$$= 0.6745 \times \frac{1 - (0.9)^2}{\sqrt{10}} = 0.0405$$

Problem 4.8

For a given sets of 10 observations, find the Rank correlation coefficient.

x :	5	4	3	8	10	6	6	7	8	5
y :	6	2	1	5	6	3	9	8	10	7

Solution :

The data can be presented in the tabular form as follows

x	y	*Rank of x*	*Rank of y*	$d = (y–x)$	d^2
5	6	7.5	5.5	–2	4
4	2	9	9	0	0
3	1	10	10	0	0
8	5	2.5	7	4.5	20.25
10	6	1	5.5	4.5	20.25
6	3	5.5	8	2.5	6.25
6	9	5.5	2	–3.5	12.25
7	8	4	3	–1	1
8	10	2.5	1	–1.5	2.25
5	71	7.5	4	–3.5	12.25
					$\Sigma d^2 = 78.5$

∴ Rank correlation coefficient

$$\rho = 1 - \frac{6\Sigma d^2}{n(n^2-1)}$$

$$= 1 - \frac{6 \times 78.5}{10 \times 99}$$

$$= 0.525$$

Problem 4.9

Quotations of index number of security prices of a certain joint stock company and of prices of preference shares and debentures are given below :

Preference share price (x)	:	73.2	85.8	78.9	75.8	77.2	81.2	83.8
Debentures price (y)	:	97.8	99.2	98.8	98.3	98.3	96.7	97.1

Use the method of rank correlation to determine the relationship between preference prices and debenture prices. *[Madras University, B.Com., 1977]*

Solution :

For calculation of Rank Correlation Coefficient, we prepare the following table.

X	Y	*Rank of X (x)*	*Rank of Y (y)*	$d = (x - y)$	d^2
73.2	97.8	7	5	2	4
85.8	99.2	1	1	0	0
78.9	98.8	4	2	2	4
75.8	98.3	6	3.5	2.5	6.25
77.8	98.3	5	3.5	1.5	2.25
81.8	96.7	3	7	–4	16
83.8	97.1	2	6	–4	16
				$\Sigma d = 0$	$\Sigma d^2 = 48.50$

In this case, due to repeated values of y, we have to apply ranking as average to 2 ranks, which could have been alloted, if they were different values. Thus rank 3 and 4 have been allotted as 3.5 to both the values of y as 98.3. Now, we also have to apply correction factor $\frac{m(m^2-1)}{12}$ to Σd^2, where m is the number of times the value is repeated.

Here $m = 2$ (as 98.3 is repeated twice)

$$\rho = 1 - \frac{6\left[\Sigma d^2 + \frac{m(m^2-1)}{12}\right]}{n(n^2-1)}$$

$$= 1 - \frac{6\left[48.5 + \frac{2(4-1)}{12}\right]}{7(7^2-1)}$$

$$= 1 - \frac{6 \times 49}{7 \times 48}$$

$$= 0.125$$

Problem 4.10

The coefficient of rank correlation of the marks obtained by 10 students in two particular subjects are found to be 0.5. It was later discovered that the difference in ranks in two subjects obtained by one student was wrongly taken as 3 instead of 7, what should be the correct value of the coefficient of Rank correlation? *[Osmania University, B.Com. III. 1983]*

Solution :

Given here, $n = 10, \rho = 0.5$

By using the correlation Rank formula,

$$0.5 = 1 - \frac{6\Sigma d^2}{n(n^2-1)}$$

$$= 1 - \frac{6\Sigma d^2}{10(10^2-1)}$$

$$\therefore \quad \Sigma d^2 = \frac{990}{6 \times 2} = 82.5$$

Since one difference (d) was taken as 3 instead of 7, the corrected value of

$$\Sigma d^2 = 82.5 - 3^2 + 7^2$$

$$= 122.5$$

$\therefore$ Corrected value of Rank Correlation Coefficient

$$\rho = 1 - \frac{6 \times 122.5}{10 \times 99} = 0.2576.$$

Problem 4.11

Calculate the coefficient of correlation between the ages of husbands and wives from the following table :

Age of Wives	*Ages of husbands (years)*					
(Years)	*20-30*	*30-40*	*40-50*	*50-60*	*60-70*	*Total*
15-25	5	9	3	–	–	17
25-35	–	10	25	2	–	37
35-45	–	1	12	2	–	15
45-55	–	–	4	16	5	25
55-65	–	–	–	4	2	6
Total	5	20	44	24	7	100

Solution :

If we denote the ages of husbands of x and that of wives as y, we can change the origin and scale as

$$u = \frac{x-45}{10} \text{ and } v = \frac{y-40}{10}$$

Based on these substitutes, we write the bivariate frequency correlation table as follows

y \ *x*	*u*	*25*	*35*	*45*	*55*	*65*				
	v	*−2*	*−1*	*0*	*1*	*2*	*f*	*fv*	*fv*²	*fuv*
20	−2	5	9	3	–	–	17	−34	68	38
30	−1	–	10	25	2	–	37	−37	37	8
40	0	–	1	12	2	–	15	0	0	0
50	1	–	–	4	16	5	25	25	25	26
60	2	–	–	–	4	2	6	12	24	16
Total	*f*	5	20	44	24	7	100	−34	144	88
	fu	−10	−20	0	24	14	8			
	*fu*²	20	20	0	24	28	92			
	fuv	20	28	0	22	18	88			

Now using the correlation relationship

$$r_{uv} = \frac{N\Sigma fuv - (\Sigma fu)(\Sigma fv)}{\sqrt{[N\Sigma fu^2 - (\Sigma fu)^2][N\Sigma fv^2 - (\Sigma fv)^2]}}$$

$$= \frac{100 \times 88 - 8 \times -34}{\sqrt{[100 \times 92 - 8^2][100 \times 144 - (-34)^2]}}$$

$$= 0.7953$$

Problem 4.12

A psychologist wanted to compare two methods *A* and *B* of teaching. He selected a random sample of 22 students. He grouped them into 11pairs so that the students in a pair have approximately equal scores on an intelligence test. In each pair, one student was taught by method A and the other by method B and examined after the course. The marks obtained by them are tabulated below.

Pair	1	2	3	4	5	6	7	8	9	10	11
A	24	29	19	14	30	19	27	30	20	28	11
B	37	35	16	26	23	27	19	20	16	11	21

(*i*) Find the correlation coefficient between the two sets of scores.
(*ii*) Find the rank order correlation coefficient.

[*Himachal Pradesh University, MBA, 1973*]

Solution :

If we denote scores for method A by *X* and those for method B by *Y*, then we can prepare the correlation table (Karl Pearson's Method) as follows

(*i*)

X	Y	$u = X-20$	$v = Y-26$	u^2	v^2	uv
24	37	4	11	16	121	44
29	35	9	9	81	81	81
19	16	–1	–10	1	100	10
14	26	–6	0	36	0	0
30	23	10	–3	100	9	–30
19	27	–1	1	1	1	–1
27	19	7	–7	49	49	–49
30	20	10	–6	100	36	–60
20	16	0	–10	0	100	0
28	11	8	–15	64	225	–120
11	21	–9	–5	81	25	45
$\Sigma X = 251$	251	31	–35	529	747	–80

When $n = 11$

$$r_{uv} = \frac{n\Sigma uv - (\Sigma u \Sigma v)}{\sqrt{[n\Sigma u^2 - (\Sigma u)^2][n\Sigma v^2 - (\Sigma v)^2]}}$$

$$= \frac{(11)\times(-80) - (31)\times(-35)}{\sqrt{[11\times 529 - (31)^2][11\times 747 - (-35)^2]}}$$

$$= 0.0314$$

$\therefore$ $r_{xy} = 0.0314$ (Property of correlation coefficient) (*ii*) Rank correlation coefficient can be calculated by the following table.

X	*Y*	*Rank of X(x)*	*Rank of Y(y)*	$d = y - x$	d^2
24	37	6	1	–5	25
29	35	3	2	–1	1
19	16	8.5	9.5	1	1
14	26	10	4	–6	36
30	23	1.5	5	3.5	12.25
19	27	8.5	3	–5.5	30.25
27	19	5	8	3	9
30	20	1.5	7	5.5	30.25
20	16	7	9.5	2.5	6.25
28	11	4	11	7	49
11	21	11	6	–5	25
					$\Sigma d^2 = 225$

In the above table, it is observed that number of scores are repeated as follows :

score 30 twice, $m_1 = 2$

score 19 twice, $m_2 = 2$

score 16 twice, $m_3 = 2$

Hence
$$\rho = 1 - 6\left[\frac{\Sigma d^2 + m\frac{(m^2-1)}{12}}{n(n^2-1)}\right]$$

$$= 1 - 6\left[\frac{225 + \frac{3\times 2(4-1)}{12}}{11\times 120}\right]$$

$$= -0.0225$$

Problem 4.13

Ten competitors in a beauty contest are ranked by three judges in the following order

1st Judge	1	6	5	10	3	2	4	9	7	8
2nd Judge	3	5	8	4	7	10	2	1	6	9
3rd Judge	6	4	9	8	1	2	3	10	5	7

Use the rank correlation coefficient to determine which pair of judges has the nearest approach to common tastes in beauty.

Solution :

The respective ranks by three judges are already given and these can be identified as R_1, R_2, R_3 as ranks by the first, second and the third judge. The tables are worked out as under :

R_1	R_2	R_3	$d_{12} = R_1 - R_2$	$d_{13} = R_1 - R_3$	$d_{23} = R_2 - R_3$	d_{12}^2	d_{13}^2	d_{23}^2
1	3	6	–2	–5	–3	4	25	9
6	5	4	1	2	1	1	4	1
5	8	9	–3	–4	–1	9	16	1
10	4	8	6	2	–4	36	4	16
3	7	1	–4	2	6	16	4	36
2	10	2	–8	0	8	64	0	64
4	2	3	2	1	–1	4	1	1
9	1	10	8	–1	9	64	1	81
7	6	5	1	2	1	1	4	1
8	9	7	–1	1	2	1	1	4
						200	60	214

Using $n = 10$,

$$\rho_{12} = 1 - \frac{6 \times 200}{10 \times 99} = -0.2121$$

Similarly $$\rho_{13} = 1 - \frac{6 \times 60}{10 \times 99} = 0.6363$$

$$\rho_{23} = 1 - \frac{6 \times 214}{10 \times 99} = -0.2970$$

Since ρ_{13} has the maximum value, the first and third judge have shown the nearest approach to common tastes in beauty and since ρ_{12} and ρ_{23} are negative, it indicates that judges (1, 2) and (2, 3) have opposite tastes for beauty.

Problem 4.14

From the given data below for two variables X and Y, calculate the coefficient of determination.

X	1	2	3	4	5	6	7	8
Y	4	8	12	16	20	24	28	32

Solution :

Calculating the value of Mean Y

$$\bar{Y} = \frac{144}{8}$$

$$= 18$$

By drawing graph for X & Y, we can clearly see that it is a straight line passing through the origin.

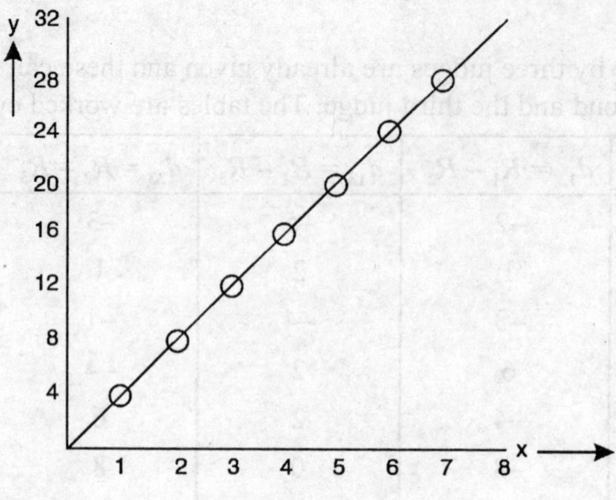

Figure 4.4

In this case, $Y = \hat{Y}$

Hence $(\Sigma Y - \hat{Y})^2 = 0$

This is variation of Y values around the relationship line.

Calculating the variation of Y values around the own mean,

$$\Sigma(Y_1 - \overline{Y})^2 = (4-18)^2 + (8-18)^2 + (12-18)^2 + (16-18)^2 + (20-18)^2 + (24-18)^2 + (32-18)^2$$

$$= 672$$

∴ Coefficient of determination

$$r^2 = 1 - \frac{\Sigma(Y - \hat{y})^2}{\Sigma(Y - \overline{Y})^2}$$

$$= 1 - \frac{0}{672} = 1$$

This shows that when coefficient of determination is unity, it is a case of perfect estimating. Similarly zero value of the coefficient of determinations would mean no correlation.

Problem 4.15

Calculate coefficient of correlation by the current deviation method.

Supply	:	112	125	126	118	118	121	125	125	131	135
Price	:	106	103	103	104	98	96	97	97	95	90

[*MD University. Rohtak, Com., Sep., 1980*]

Solution :

The following table can be prepared to calculate the correlation coefficient by concurrent deviation method.

Supply	*Sign of the deviation from preceeding value*	*Price*	*Sign of the deviation from preceeding value*	*Concurrent deviation (pairs)*
112		106		
125	+	102	–	
126	+	102	=	
118	–	104	+	
118	=	98	–	
121	+	96	–	
125	+	97	+	+
125	=	97	=	=
131	+	95	–	
135	+	90	–	

Thus there are only 9 deviations and only two equal deviations (concurrent)

$\therefore \qquad c = 2, n = 9$

$$r = \pm\sqrt{\pm\left(\frac{2\times 2-9}{9}\right)} = \pm\sqrt{\pm(0.5556)}$$

Since $(2c - n)$ is negative, we use only $(-ve)$ sign inside and outside square root

$$r = -\sqrt{-(-0.5556)} = 0.7$$

Problem 4.16

Given the following data, calculated the multiple regression line and work out the value of y when $x_1 = 10$ and $x_2 = 15$.

x_1	x_2	y
2	7	350
6	5	900
3	3	500
4	2	650
3	5	550
2	9	400

Solution :

From the given data, we can estimate values for the following

Σx_1, Σx_2, $\Sigma x_1 x_2$
Σx_1^2, Σx_2^2, $\Sigma x_1 y$ and $\Sigma x_2 y$

Tabulating the results, we obtain

x_1	x_2	y	x_1x_2	x_1^2	x_2^2	x_1y	x_2y
2	7	350	14	4	49	700	2450
6	5	900	30	36	25	5400	4500
3	3	500	9	9	9	1500	1500
4	2	650	8	16	4	2600	1300
3	5	550	15	9	25	1650	2750
2	9	400	18	4	81	800	3600
$\Sigma x_1 = 20$	$\Sigma x_2 = 31$	$\Sigma y = 3350$	$\Sigma x_1 x_2 = 94$	$\Sigma x_1^2 = 78$	$\Sigma x_2^2 = 193$	$\Sigma x_1 y = 12{,}450$	$\Sigma x_2 y = 16{,}100$

Using these values, we get the normal equations as follows

$$3{,}350 = 6a + 20b_1 + 31b_2 \qquad \ldots(i)$$
$$12{,}450 = 20a + 78b_1 + 94b_2 \qquad \ldots(ii)$$
$$16{,}100 = 31a + 94b_2 + 193b_2 \qquad \ldots(iii)$$

Solving these equations for a, b_1 and b_2 we obtain

$$a = 59.65$$
$$b_1 = 106.2$$
$$b_2 = 17.18$$

Hence multiple regression equation becomes $y = 59.65 + 106.2x_1 + 17.18b_2$

Hence estimating y for $x_1 = 10, x_2 = 15,$

$$\hat{y} = 59.65 + 106.2 \times 10 + 17.18 \times 15$$
$$= 59.65 + 106.2 + 257.7$$
$$= 1377.95$$

Problem 4.17

From the data given in problem 4.16. work out the standard error of estimation.

Solution :

We use the relationship

$$S_e = \sqrt{\frac{(y-\hat{y})^2}{n-k-1}}$$

Calculating $(y-\hat{y})$ for each value of y and obtaining its quare,

$$(y-\hat{y})^2 = 7118.80$$

$$\therefore \qquad S_e = \sqrt{\frac{7118.80}{6-3-1}}$$
$$= 596.6$$

PRACTICE PROBLEMS

4.18 Explain clearly the concept of correlation. Explain with suitable illustrations its role in dealing with business problems. *[Delhi University, M.B.A., 1975]*

4.19 Define correlation. Discuss its significance. Does correlation always signify casual relationship between two variables? Explain with illustration. *[Delhi University, B.Com., 1985]*

4.20 What is Correlation? What is a scatter Diagram? How does it help in studying correlation between two variables, in respect of both its nature and extent?

[Delhi University, M.B.A., Dec., 1981, Pune University, B.Com., 1973]

4.21 (a) Define the term correlation. Explain Ihe concept of positive and negative correlation with examples.

(b) State the nature of the following correlations (positive, negative or no correlation).

(i) Sale of woollen garments and the day temperature.

(ii) The colour of the Sari and the intelligence of the lady who wears it.

(iii) Amount of rainfall and yield of crop. *[ICWA (Final), June 1977]*

4.22 (a) "Correlation analysis attempts to determine the degree of relationship between the variables". Justify this statement with real life examples from areas in business and management.

OR

(b) To study the effectiveness of an advertisement a survey is conducted by calling people at random by asking the number of advertisements read or seen, in a week and the number of items purchased in that week

Ads. seen / read	5	10	4	0	2	7	3	6
No. of items purchased	10	12	5	2	1	3	4	8

[*Osmania University, M.B.A., April 1999*]

4.23 (a) What is correlation? Does correlation signify the existence of cause and effect relationship?

OR

(b) M/s. Voltas Ltd. gives the following information relating to the sales of refrigerators in the past 10 years.

Years :	1988	1989	1990	1991	1992	1993	1994	1995	1996	1997
Refrigerators sold in thousands :	8	10	11	11	18	15	19	19	22	24

Fit a trend line by least square method and compute trend values. Estimate sales for the year 2002. [*Osmania University, M.B.A., Sept., 1998*]

4.24 Ten competitors in a beauty contest are ranked by three judges in the following order.

1st Judge :	1	6	5	10	3	2	9	7	7
2nd Judge :	3	5	8	4	7	10	1	6	9
3rd Judge :	6	4	9	8	1	2	10	5	7

Use Rank Correlation Coefficient to determine which pair of judges has the nearest approach to common tastes in beauty. [*Osmania University, M.B.A., Sept., 1998*]

4.25 (a) Distinguish clearly between

(i) Positive and negative correlation (ii) Linear and non-linear correlation.

(b) "If the two or more quantities vary in sympathy so that the movements in one tend to be accompanied by corresponding movements in other(s), then they are said to be correlated". Discuss. [*Bombay University, B.Com., April 1972*]

4.26 While drawing a scatter diagram, if all points appear to form a straight line going downwards from left to right, then it is inferred that there is

(a) Perfect positive correlation

(b) Simple positive correlation

(c) Perfect negative correlation

(d) No correlation. [*C.A. (Inter), Nov., 1983*]

4.27 Draw a scatter diagram from the data given below and interpret it.

X :	10	20	30	40	50	60	70	80
Y :	32	20	24	36	40	28	38	44

[*Karnataka University. B.Com., Nov., 1980*]

4.28 Calculate Karl Pearson's coefficient of correlation 'between expenditure on advertising and sales, from the data given below :

Advertising expenses ('000 Rs.) :	39	65	62	90	82	75	25	98	36	78
Sales in (lakh Rs.) :	47	53	58	86	62	68	60	91	51	84

[*C.A. (Inter), Nov., 1975, Delhi University, B.Com., 1985*]

4.29 Find Karl Pearson's coefficient of correlation between sales and expenses of the following ten firms

Firms	1	2	3	4	5	6	7	8	9	10
Sales in thousand units	50	50	55	60	65	65	65	60	60	50
Expenses in thousand Rupees	11	13	14	16	16	15	15	14	13	13

[Madras University, B.Com., Oct., 1980, Punjab University. B.A. (Eco. Hons), April 1980]

4.30 Calculate the values of $Y = (X - 6)^5$ corresponding to X = 1, 2, 3, 4 & 5 and obtain the correlation coefficient between X and Y. Explain why the obtained coefficient differs from unity. *[ICWA (Final), Dec., 1974]*

4.31 Calculate coefficient of correlation between X and Y series from the following data and calculate its probable error also.

X	78	89	96	69	59	79	68	61
Y	125	137	156	112	107	136	123	108

(Take 69 as working mean for X and 112 for that for Y)

[Punjab University, B.Com., 11. Sept., 1981]

4.32 From the following data, find out the correlation coefficient between heights of fathers and sons.

Heights of fathers (inches)	65	66	67	67	68	69	70	72
Heights of sons (inches)	67	68	65	68	72	72	69	71

[Osmania University, B.Com. (Hons), 1983]

4.33 Compute Karl Pearson's coefficient of correlation in the following series relating to cost of living and wages.

Wages (Rs.)	100	101	103	102	100	99	97	98	96	95
Cost of living	98	99	99	97	95	92	95	94	90	91

[Bangalore University, B.Com.. Nov., 1981, Delhi University, B.Com., 1982]

4.34 From the following data examine whether there exists any correlation between X and Y.

X	6.9	8.5	5.8	8.6	9.6	8.0	9.7
Y	2.9	3.8	6.5	2.3	5.5	3.5	3.2

[Andhra Pradesh University, B.Com., April 1982]

4.35 Calculate Pearson's Coefficient of correlation from the following data. Take 65 and 70 as the assumed average of the variates X and Y respectively.

X	45	55	56	58	60	65	68	70	75	80	85
Y	56	50	48	60	62	64	65	70	74	82	90

[ICWA (Final), June 1980]

4.36 Calculate the coefficient of correlation (*r*) between the marks in statistics (*x*) and Accountancy (*y*) of 12 students from the following.

X	52	74	93	55	41	23	92	64	40	71	33	71
Y	45	80	63	60	35	40	70	58	43	64	51	75

Also determine the probable error of *r* *[Punjab University, B.Com., 1981]*

4.37 A student calculates the value of *r* as 0.7 when the number of items (*n*) in the sample is 25. Find the limits within which *r* lies for another sample from the same universe

[Mysore University. B.Com., 1972]

4.38 From the data given below, find the number of items (*n*).

$$r = 0.5, \Sigma xy = 120, \sigma_y = 80, \Sigma x^2 = 90$$

Where x and y are deviations from arithmetic average. [*Delhi University, M.Com., 1970*]

4.39 Ten students of BA obtained the following percentage of marks in English in the Internal Assessment Test (*X*) and University Examination (*Y*). Calculate Karl Pearson's Coefficient of correlation from actual, mean and its probable errors.

X	:	50	60	75	84	47	52	59	44	33	46
Y	:	45	52	50	65	40	65	50	60	32	51

[*Osmania University, B.Com. III, April 1984*]

4.40 Calculate Spearman's rank correlation coefficient between advertisement cost and sales from the following data.

Advertising cost ('000 Rs.)	:	39	65	62	90	82	75	25	98	36	78
Sales (Lakhs)	:	47	53	58	86	62	68	60	91	51	84

4.41 Twelve entries in painting competition were ranked by two judges as shown below.

Entry	:	A	B	C	D	E	F	G	H	I	J	K	L
Judge I	:	5	2	3	4	1	6	8	7	10	9	12	11
Judge II	:	4	5	2	1	6	7	10	9	11	12	3	8

Find the coefficient of rank correlation. [*Punjab University, B.A. (Eco. Hons.), 1977*]

4.42 An examination of eight applicants for a clerical post was taken by a firm. From the marks obtained by the applicants in the Accountancy and statistics paper, compute rank coefficient of correlation.

Applicant	:	A	B	C	D	E	F	G	H
Marks in Accountancy	:	15	20	28	12	40	60	20	80
Marks in Statistics	:	40	30	50	30	20	10	30	60

[*Delhi University, M.B.A., 1974*]

4.43 Calculate Spearman's rank correlation coefficient for the following data.

X	:	35	37	38	42	44	46	51	54	55	56
Y	:	40	32	39	42	41	31	50	52	46	55

[*Punjab University, M.A. (Eco.), Oct., 1980*]

4.44 Find the coefficient of rank correlation between the marks obtained in Mathematics (*X*) and those in statistics (*Y*) by 10 students of a certain class, out of a total of 50 marks in each subject.

Students	:	1	2	3	4	5	6	7	8	9	10
X	:	12	18	32	18	25	24	25	40	38	22
Y	:	16	15	28	16	24	22	28	36	34	19

[*Himachal University, M.A. (Eco.), July 1984*]

4.45 In two set of variables *x* and *y*, with 50 observations each, the following data are observed.

$\bar{x} = 10$, *SD* of $x = 3$

$y = 6$, *SD* of $y = 2$

Coefficient of correlation between x and y is 0.3. However, on subsequent verification, it was found that one value of *x* (=10) and one value of *y* (=6) were inaccurate and hence weeded out with the remaining 49 pairs of values, how is the original value of correlation coefficient affected? [*C.A. (Inter), May 1979*]

❁❁❁

CHAPTER 5

REGRESSION ANALYSIS

5.1 LINEAR REGRESSION ANALYSIS

> In statistics, the relationship of two variables can be understood from correlation. When these two variables have a linear relationship and the influence of one variable on the other is to be established the concept of 'Regression' can be used. Even non-linear relationships can be tackled through this concept.

The term 'Regression' was first used by Sir Francis Galton in connection with the studies on estimation of the stature of the sons of tall parents to its effect on the mean population. Now this expression is used in statistics for estimation or prediction of an unknown value of one variable from the known value of the other variable. This powerful tool is now used extensively in natural, social or physical sciences. In business, it is used to study the relationship between two or more variables that are related.

Prediction or estimation of future is an important area for the benefit of planning and looking deeper into business. Regression Analysis is one of the scientific techniques for making such a prediction. In life, we come across many inter-related events such as sales and price of the product, rainfall and yield of the crops, salary and expenditure of individuals, Rates and demand of the transport means etc.

When the estimation is related to the study of only two variables at one time, it is called Simple Regression whereas relationships of more than two variables is called Multiple Regression.

In Regression analysis, there are two types of variables, namely, dependent and independent variables. The variable which influences the value of the other variable is called Independent variable, whereas the variable, whose value is influenced by the independent variable is termed as Dependent Variable.

If the regression curve obtained by plotting the values of two variables is a straight line, it is called a linear Regression. If no such clear shape of the curve can be established or is different from that of a straight line, it is called curved or Non-linear Regression. In this book, we are restricting the discussion to linear regression most commonly used by Business Community for their future predictions or forecasting.

5.2 LINES OF REGRESSION

The line of Regression is the graphical or relationship representation of the best estimate of one variable for any given value of the other variable. The nomenclature of the line depends on the independent and dependent variables. If x and y are two variables of which relationship is to be indicated, a line which gives best estimate of y for any value of x, it is called regression line of y on x. If the dependent variable changes to x, then best estimate of x by any value of y is called regression line of x on y.

The values of the variables are to be connected with the help of best fit curve and this is based on the principle of least square. The principle of least square is that we minimise the sum of the squares of the deviations or the errors of estimates. Thus the deviations between the given observed values of the variable and their corresponding estimated values are given by the line of Best fit.

Line of Regression of y on x

Let us assume the observed values of two variables under consideration for regression analysis as (x_1, y_1); (x_2, y_2); (x_3, y_3)......(x_n, y_n). If we also assume a linear relationship between the two variables, the equation of the line of Regression can be written as $y = a + bx$.

Since the relationship of one variable (called independent variable) is to be established on the other variable (called dependent variable), for a linear correlation, this linear line is called the line of Regression of dependent variable on independent variable.

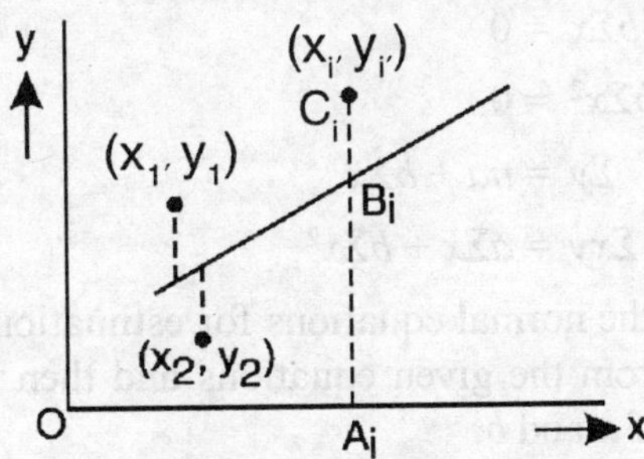

Fig. 5.1. Regression Line

For any given point (x_i, y_i), let B_i be a point indicating the x-position of x_i, on line and B_iA_i as the y position of B_i.

Then
$$C_iB_i = CiAi - BiAi$$
$$= y_i - (a + bx_i)$$

This is the error or deviation of point $C_i(x_i, y_i)$ for this *ith* point. We can, similarly, obtain the deviation of all the observed values of points from the line of best fit $y = a + bx$. These deviations will be positive for all points above the line and negative for the points below this line. Now we apply the principle of least squares to obtain the values of a and b. For finding the values of a and b, the sum of the squares of the deviations or errors should be minimum.

Hence
$$E = \sum_{i=1}^{n} (C_iB_i)^2$$
$$= \sum_{i=1}^{n} [y_i - (a + bx_i)]^2$$

To get the values of a and b, we use the concept of maxima and minima and we write partial derivatives of E with respect to a and b.

$$\frac{\partial E}{\partial a} = 0 \text{ and } \frac{\partial E}{\partial b} = 0$$

This is only a requirement for maxima or minima of E. For E to be minimum, $\frac{\partial^2 E}{\partial a^2} > 0$ and $\frac{\partial^2 E}{\partial b^2} > 0$. (Satisfied by normal equations for the values of a and b)

$$\text{or} \quad \Sigma 2(y-a-bx)\frac{\partial}{\partial a}(y-a-bx) = 0$$

$$\text{and} \quad \Sigma 2(y-a-bx)\frac{\partial}{\partial b}(y-a-bx) = 0$$

$$\text{or} \quad \Sigma 2(y-a-bx)(-1) = 0$$

$$\text{and} \quad \Sigma 2(y-a-bx)(-x) = 0$$

From where, we get the relationship as,

$$\Sigma(y-a-bx) = 0$$

$$\Sigma x\,(y-a-bx) = 0$$

$$\text{or} \quad \Sigma y - na - b\Sigma x = 0$$

$$\text{and} \quad \Sigma xy - a\Sigma x - b\Sigma x^2 = 0$$

$$\text{or} \quad \Sigma y = na + b\Sigma x \qquad \ldots(i)$$

$$\text{and} \quad \Sigma xy = a\Sigma x + b\Sigma x^2 \qquad \ldots(ii)$$

Linear line of regression has two constants, establishing the slope of the line as well as its intercept on the graph. These two constants can be evaluated based on simple simultaneous equations.

These equations are called the normal equations for estimation of a and b. The values of other expressions can be obtained from the given equations and then can be substituted in the above equations to obtain the values of a and b.

We can also write

$$a = \frac{\Sigma x^2 \Sigma y - \Sigma x \Sigma xy}{n\Sigma x^2 - (\Sigma x)^2}$$

$$\text{and} \quad b = \frac{n\Sigma xy - \Sigma x\Sigma y}{n\Sigma x^2 - (\Sigma x)^2}$$

We can extend the same relationship to other measures such as $\bar{x}$, $\bar{y}$, σ_x, σ_y and the correlation coefficient r_{xy}.

Equation (i) can be coverted as

$$\frac{1}{n}\Sigma y = a + b\frac{\Sigma x}{n}$$

$$\therefore \quad \bar{y} = a + b\bar{x} \qquad \ldots(iii)$$

This means that the regression line of y on x passes through its mean point $(\bar{x}, \bar{y})$ *i.e.* the point $(\bar{x}, \bar{y})$ lies on the regression line of y on x.

$$\text{Since} \quad \Sigma x = n\bar{x}$$

$$\text{Since} \quad \sigma_x^2 = \frac{1}{n}\Sigma x^2 - (\bar{x})^2$$

$$\therefore \quad \Sigma x^2 = n[\sigma_x^2 + (\bar{x})^2] \qquad \ldots(iv)$$

and, $\text{cov}(x, y) = \frac{1}{n}\Sigma xy - \bar{x}\,\bar{y}$

or $\Sigma xy = n[\text{cov}(x, y) + \bar{x}\,\bar{y}]$

Also, $\bar{x}\,\bar{y} = a\bar{x} + b\bar{x}^2$

Hence $\text{cov}(x, y) = b\sigma_x^2$

$$\therefore \quad b = \frac{\text{cov}(x, y)}{\sigma_x^2} \qquad \ldots(v)$$

$$\text{Now} \quad y - \bar{y} = b(x - \bar{x}) = \frac{\text{cov}(x, y)}{\sigma_x^2}(x - \bar{x})$$

$$\text{But} \quad r_{xy} = \frac{\text{cov}(x, y)}{\sigma_x \sigma_y}$$

$$\therefore \quad \text{cov}(x, y) = r.\sigma_x \sigma_y \qquad (vi)$$

$$\therefore \quad y - \bar{y} = \frac{r\sigma_x \sigma_y}{\sigma_x^2}(x - \bar{x}) = \frac{r\sigma_y}{\sigma_x}(x - \bar{x}) \qquad (vii)$$

These are important relationships for data analysis.

Similar relationship can be obtained for the regression line of x and y such as

$$\Sigma x = nA + B\Sigma y \qquad \ldots(viii)$$

$$\text{and} \quad \Sigma xy = n\Sigma y + B\Sigma y^2 \qquad \ldots(ix)$$

$$A = \frac{(\Sigma y^2)(\Sigma x) - (\Sigma y)(\Sigma xy)}{n\Sigma y^2 - (\Sigma y)^2} \qquad \ldots(x)$$

$$\text{and} \quad B = \frac{n\Sigma xy - (\Sigma x)(\Sigma y)}{n\Sigma y^2 - (\Sigma y)^2} \qquad \ldots(xi)$$

$$\text{Also} \quad B = \frac{\text{cov}(x, y)}{\sigma_y^2} = \frac{r\sigma_x}{\sigma_y} \qquad \ldots(xii)$$

$$\text{and} \quad x - \bar{x} = \frac{r\sigma_x}{\sigma_y}(y - \bar{y}) \qquad \ldots(xiv)$$

This also establishes that in case of perfect correlation ($r = \pm 1$), both the lines of regression will coincide.

When we use two regression lines based on the same two variables, the angle between the two lines establishes their inter-relationship whether two lines meet or not.

Angle between the Regression Lines

Since the regression lines can be represented as

$$(y - \bar{y}) = \frac{r\sigma_y}{\sigma_x}(x - \bar{x})$$

$$\text{and} \quad (x - \bar{x}) = \frac{r\sigma_x}{\sigma_y}(y - \bar{y})$$

$$\text{Then} \quad y - \bar{y} = \frac{\sigma_y}{r\sigma_x}(x - \bar{x})$$

Now we can write the slope of these lines as

$$m_1 = \frac{r\sigma_y}{\sigma_x} \text{ and } m_2 = \frac{\sigma_y}{r\sigma_x}$$

If θ is the angle between these lines,

$$\tan\theta = \frac{m_i - m_2}{1 + m_1 m_2} = \frac{\sigma_x \sigma_y}{\sigma_x^2 + \sigma_y^2}\left(\frac{r^2 - 1}{r}\right)$$

$$\therefore \qquad \theta = \tan^{-1}\left[\frac{\sigma_x \sigma_y}{\sigma_x^2 + \sigma_y^2}\left(\frac{r^2 - 1}{r}\right)\right] \qquad \ldots(xv)$$

5.3 COEFFICIENT OF REGRESSION

While working out the slope of the regression line, this slope is termed as the coefficient of regression. We use a simple method to find the relationship of the correlation coefficient with the coefficient of regression of the two lines.

If line of Regression is represented as $y = a + bx$, then the coefficient 'b', which is the slope of the line of Regression of y on x is called the coefficient of regression,

From equation drawn in Para 5.2, we have

$$b_{yx} = \frac{\text{cov}(x, y)}{\sigma_x^2} = \frac{r\sigma_y}{\sigma_x}$$

This represents the coefficient of Regression for line y on x.

Similarly coefficient of regression for line x on y can be written as

$$b_{xy} = \frac{r\sigma_x}{\sigma_y}$$

Thus we can establish that

$$r^2 = b_{yx} \cdot b_{xy}.$$

and $$r = \pm\sqrt{b_{yx} \cdot b_{xy}} \qquad (xvi)$$

In this relationship, if the regression coefficients are positive, we adopt positive sign for the correlation coefficient and *vice-versa.*

If one of the regresssion coefficients is greater than 1, the other must be less than unity.

Since, $$r^2 = b_{yx} \cdot b_{xy} > 1$$

It is impossible as $0 \le r^2 \le 1$

$$\therefore \qquad b_{xy} \le \frac{1}{b_{yx}} < 1 \qquad \ldots(xvii)$$

We can also establish that the arithmetic mean of the regression coefficients is greater than the correlation coefficient.

Since $$AM > GM$$

or $$\frac{a+b}{2} > \sqrt{ab}$$

Substituting $a = b_{yx}$ and $b = b_{xy}$, we have

$$\frac{1}{2}(b_{yx} + b_{xy}) > \sqrt{b_{yx} \cdot b_{xy}}$$

or, $$\frac{1}{2}(b_{yx} + b_{xy}) > r \qquad \ldots(xviii)$$

Regression coefficients are also independent of change of the origin, not of scale

Let us have

$$u = \frac{x-a}{h} \text{ and } v = \frac{y-b}{k}$$

Since correlation coefficients are independent of the origin and scale, we know

$$r_{xy} = r_{uv}$$

Here $$\sigma_x = h\sigma_u \text{ and } \sigma_y = k\sigma_v$$

Since $$b_{xy} = r_{xy} \cdot \frac{\sigma_y}{\sigma_x} = r_{uv} \cdot \frac{k\sigma_v}{h\sigma_u} = \frac{k}{h} r_{uv} \cdot \frac{\sigma_v}{\sigma_u}$$

$$= \frac{k}{h} b_{uv}$$

and $$b_{xy} = \frac{h}{k} b_{vu}$$

Thus we can say that regression coefficients are independent of origin but not of scale

Hence $$b_{yx} = b_{vu} = \frac{n\Sigma uv - (\Sigma u)(\Sigma v)}{n\Sigma u^2 - (\Sigma u)^2} \qquad \ldots(xix)$$

and $$b_{xy} = b_{uv} = \frac{n\Sigma uv - (\Sigma u)(\Sigma v)}{n\Sigma v^2 - (\Sigma v)^2} \qquad \ldots(xx)$$

5.4. THE METHOD OF LEAST SQUARES

The method of least squares is a useful approach to establish the coefficient of regression. This is also called the concept of "the line of the best fit".

We have already worked out the method of determining the equation of a straight line. This was fitting the line through various points on the scatter diagram. Now we achieve the same thing through mathematical means to establish the line of 'best fit'. The concept was used in deciding on the lines of regression under Para 5.2. It is called the line of best fit, if it minimises the error between the estimated points on the line and the actual given point used to draw the line.

Let us study the scatter diagram given below.

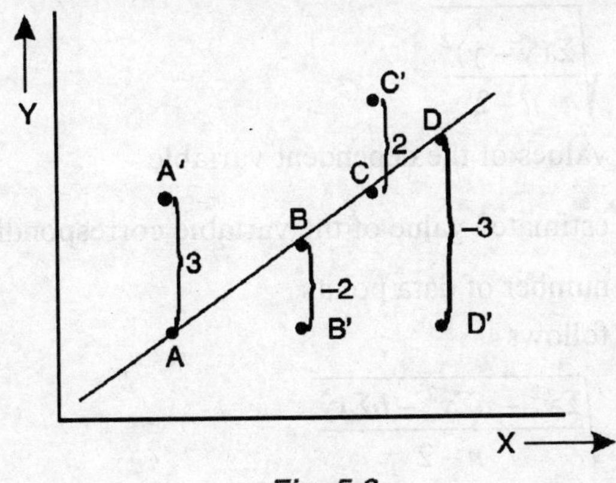

Fig. 5.2.

If we used the value of y (estimate) the value deviation from points A, B, C and D used to draw the line are taken as $AA' = 3$, $BB' = -2$, $CC' = 2$, $DD' = -3$, where A', B', C' and D' are error points with reference to the line drawn.

$$\text{Total error} = 3 - 2 + 2 - 3 = 0$$

If we use the concept of sum of the squares

$$\text{Sum of squares} = 3^2 + (-2)^2 + (2)^2 + (-3)^2$$
$$= 9 + 4 + 4 + 9 = 26$$

Now, in order to establish the straight line for minimising the sum of squares of these errors, we call the method as "Method of least squares".

Statisticians have derived the following equations for the best fit concept

$$b = \frac{\Sigma xy - n\overline{x}\overline{y}}{\Sigma x^2 - n(\overline{x})^2}$$

Where b = slope of the best fit line

x = values of the independent variables

y = values of the dependent variable

$\overline{x}$ = Mean of the values of the independent variable

and $\overline{y}$ = Mean of the values of the dependent variable

n = number of observations or data points

Another relationship obtained is

$$a = \overline{y} - b\overline{x}$$

a = y intercept of the line

b = slope of the line

$\overline{y}$ = Mean of the values of dependent variables

$\overline{x}$ = Mean of the values of independent variable

Standard error of estimate is used to establish the reliability of the estimating lines. This error measures the variability or the spread of the observed values from the given regression line.

Standard error of estimate (Linear Regression)

In order to establish the reliability of the estimating lines, we use the concept of the standard error of estimate. This measures the variability or the spread of the observed values from the given regression line.

Thus, standard error of estimate is given by

$$S_e = \sqrt{\frac{\Sigma(y - \hat{y})^2}{n-2}}$$

Where y = values of the dependent variable

$\hat{y}$ = estimated value of the variable corresponding to each value of y.

y = number of data points.

It can also be written as follows

$$S_e = \sqrt{\frac{\Sigma y^2 - a\Sigma\hat{y}^2 - b\Sigma x\hat{y}}{n-2}}$$

$$= \sigma_y \left(1 - r^2\right)^{\frac{1}{2}} \text{ or } \sigma_x \left(1 - r^2\right)^{\frac{1}{2}}$$

5.5 LINKAGE BETWEEN CORRELATION AND REGRESSION

1. Whereas the correlation is the relationship between two or more variables, when the movement of one tend to be corresponding to the other, the Regression is the return to the average value and is the mathematical average relationship between the two variables.
2. Correlation need not imply cause and effect relationship between the variables under study, whereas Regression clearly establishes this relationship. There is a definite cause and effect relationship between dependent and independent variable.
3. Correlation coefficient between two variables is the measure of direction and degree of the linear relationship between the two variables, which is mutual and symmetric *i.e.* $r_{xy} = r_{yx}$, But in case of regression, the dependent and independent variables have a definite direction. Hence there are two distinct lines of regression *i.e.*, y on x or x on y and hence $b_{yx} \neq b_{xy}$.
4. Whereas the correlation coefficient r_{xy} is a relative measure of the linear relationship of x and y and is independent of the unit of measurement, the regression coefficient b_{xy} and b_{yx} are absolute measures representing the change in the values of variable $y(x)$ for a unit change in $x(y)$.
5. There can be a non-sense correlation between the two variables; there is no such non-sense regression.
6. Correlation analysis centres around only linear relationship between the variables, whereas in regression, there can be linear and non-linear relationship.

5.6 MULTIPLE REGRESSION ANALYSIS

So far. we have discussed the estimation and analysis of one variable with reference to another variable. The independent and dependent variables are related either in the form of correlation or their estimates in the form of regression analysis. These are linear.correlation and linear regression.

We now can use more than one independent variable to estimate the dependent variable with more accuracy and this is called multiple regression analysis. The assumptions and techniques are the same as that for linear regression. Since the information available and used is more, the accuracy of estimate will be higher.

> In addition to simple linear regression, we can analyse the case of multiple regression (when we have more than one independent variable to estimate the dependent variable). This would involve the estimate of more constants depending on the number of independent variables in use.

Steps in multiple regression

We can carry out the multiple regression analysis using following steps

(*i*) Writing the multiple regression equation for identifying and crystallizing the mathematical relationships.

(*ii*) Estimating the standard error of the estimate for this relationship.

(*iii*) Using the multiple correlation analysis to establish the description of the given data, formulation of multiple regression equation.

Since there are more than one independent variables to estimate the dependent variable, the equation can be written us

$$\hat{y} = a + b_1x_1 + b_2x_2$$

Where $\hat{y}$ = estimated value of dependent variable

a = y intercept

x_1, x_2 = values of two independent variables.

b_1, b_2 = rate of change of the two independent variables respectively.

This relationship can be represented graphically a three dimensional shape as follows.

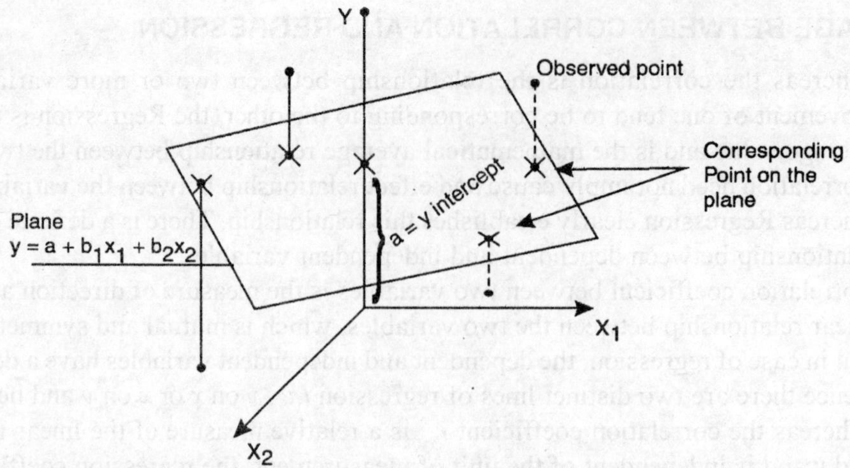

Fig.5.3. Graphical representation of multiple regresssion points

A similar measure, as in case of simple regression, can be used as the standard error concept for multiple regression also.

Normal Equations :

For the solution of the problem, we can identify the following normal equations for multiple regression analysis.

$$\Sigma y = na + b_1\Sigma x_1 + b_2\,\Sigma x_2 \quad \ldots(i)$$

$$\Sigma x_1 y = a\Sigma x_1 + b_1\Sigma x_1{}^2 + b_2\,\Sigma x_1 x_2 \quad \ldots(ii)$$

$$\Sigma x_2 y = a\Sigma x_2 + b_1\Sigma x_1 x_2 + b_2\Sigma x_2{}^2 \quad \ldots(iii)$$

By solving these three equations for the given three constants a_1, b_1 and b_2, we can obtain the multiple regression equation for further analysis.

Standard error of estimate (Multiple Regression)

As a measure of dispersion, we can use standard error of estimation for multiple regression analysis as follows

$$S_e = \sqrt{\frac{\Sigma(y-\hat{y})^2}{n-k-1}}$$

Where, S_e **= standard error of estimation**

y **= data value for dependent variable**

$\hat{y}$ **= corresponding estimated value obtained from regression equation**

n **= number of data points in the sample**

k **= number of independent variables.**

The denominator (n–k–1) indicates the reduction of degrees of freedom from n by an amount k+1, due to k+1 constant estimated.

CHAPTER SUMMARY

Important terms used

- **Coefficient of Regression : The slope of the linear line of regression.**
- **Linear Regression : Straight line relationship of dependent and independent variables.**

- **Linear Regression Analysis :** A scientific technique for making a forecast of the future.
- **Line of Regression :** Graphical or relationship representation of the best estimate of one variable for any given value of the other variable.
- **Standard Error of Estimate** : The measure of variability or the spread of the observed values from a given regression line.
- **Multiple regression :** Regression representing more than one independent variable to estimate a dependent variable.

Relationships Used

- Regression line $y = a + bx$
- $$a = \frac{\Sigma x^2 \Sigma y - \Sigma x \Sigma xy}{n\Sigma x^2 - (\Sigma x)^2}$$
  $$b = \frac{n\Sigma xy - \Sigma x \Sigma y}{n\Sigma x^2 - (\Sigma x)^2}$$
- $$\Sigma x^2 = n\,[\sigma_x^{\,2} + (\bar{x})^2]$$
- $$y - \bar{y} = \frac{r\sigma_y}{\sigma_x}(x - \bar{x})$$
- $$b_{yx} = \frac{r\sigma_y}{\sigma_x}$$
- $$b_{xy} = \frac{r\sigma_y}{\sigma_x}$$
- $$r = \pm\sqrt{by_x . by_x}$$
- $$b_{xy} = b_{vu} = \frac{n\Sigma uv - (\Sigma u)(\Sigma v)}{n\Sigma u^2 - (\Sigma u)^2}$$
- $$b_{xy} = b_{uv} = \frac{n\Sigma uv - (\Sigma u)(\Sigma v)}{n\Sigma v^2 - (\Sigma v)^2}$$
- $$b_{xy} = \frac{\Sigma xy - n\bar{x}\bar{y}}{\Sigma x^2 - n(\bar{x})^2}$$ Linear Regression
- $$SE_{(yx)} = \sigma_y\left(1 - r^2\right)^{\frac{1}{2}}$$ Linear Regression
- $$SE_{(xy)} = \sigma_x\left(1 - r^2\right)^{\frac{1}{2}}$$ Linear Regression
- $$SE = \sqrt{\frac{\Sigma(y - \hat{y})^2}{n - k - 1}}$$ Multiple Regression

SOLVED PROBLEMS

Problem 5.1

The following table shows the number of motor registrations in a certain territory for a term of 5 years and the sale of motor tyres by a firm in the territory for the same period.

Year	*Motor Registration*	*No. of Tyres Sold*
1	600	1,250
2	630	1,100
3	720	1,300
4	750	1,350
5	800	1,500

Find the regression equation to estimate the sale of tyres when the motor registration is known. Estimate sale of types when registration is 850.

[Bombay University, B.Com., April 1978]

Solution :

Here the dependent variable is number of tyres and independent variable is Motor registration. Hence we put Motor registrations as x and sales of tyres as y and we have to establish the regression line of y on x.

Calculation of values for the regression equations are given below :

x	y	$dx = x - \bar{x}$ $= x - 700$	$dy = y - \bar{y}$ $= y - 1300$	dx^2	$dx\,dy$
600	1,250	–100	–50	10,000	5,000
630	1,100	–70	–200	4,900	14,000
720	1,300	20	0	400	0
750	1,350	50	50	2,500	2,500
800	1,500	100	200	10,000	20,000
$\Sigma x = 3{,}500$	$\Sigma y = 6{,}500$	$\Sigma dx = 0$	$\Sigma dy = 0$	$\Sigma dx^2 = 27{,}800$	$\Sigma dxdy = 41{,}500$

Here,
$$\bar{x} = \frac{\Sigma x}{n} = \frac{3500}{5} = 700$$

$$\bar{y} = \frac{\Sigma y}{n} = \frac{6500}{5} = 1{,}300$$

$$b_{yx} = \frac{\Sigma(x-\bar{x})(y-\bar{y})}{\Sigma(x-\bar{x})^2} = \frac{\Sigma dxdy}{\Sigma dx^2} = \frac{41{,}500}{27{,}800} = 1.4928$$

Now we can use these values for establishing the regression line

$$y - \bar{y} = b_{yx}(x - \bar{x})$$

or
$$y - 1{,}300 = 1.4928(x - 700)$$

$$y = 1.4928x + 255.04$$

When $x = 850$, the value of y can be calculated from the above equation,

$$\therefore \quad y = 1.4928 \times 850 + 255.04$$

$$= 1{,}523.92$$

$$= 1{,}524 \text{ tyres}$$

Problem 5.2

By using the following data, find out the two lines of regression and from them, compute the Karl Pearson's coefficient of correlation.

$$\Sigma x = 250, \quad \Sigma y = 300, \quad \Sigma xy = 7{,}900$$
$$\Sigma x^2 = 6{,}500, \quad \Sigma y^2 = 10{,}000, \quad n = 10$$

[*Delhi University, B. Com.* (*Hons*.). 1984]

Solution :

From the given data

$$\bar{x} = \frac{\Sigma x}{n} = \frac{250}{10} = 25$$

$$\bar{y} = \frac{\Sigma y}{n} = \frac{300}{10} = 30$$

$\therefore$ b_{yx} = Regression coefficient of y and x.

$$= \frac{n\Sigma xy - (\Sigma x \Sigma y)}{n\Sigma x^2 - (\Sigma x)^2}$$

$$= \frac{10 \times 7{,}900 - 250 \times 300}{10 \times 6{,}500 - (250)^2} = 1.6$$

Similarly b_{xy} = Regression coefficient x on y

$$= \frac{10 \times 7{,}900 - 250 \times 300}{10 \times 10{,}000 - (300)^2} = 0.4$$

We can establish the regression lines as follows –

$$y - \bar{y} = b_{yx}(x - \bar{x})$$
$$y - 30 = 1.6(x - 25)$$

$\therefore$ $y = 1.6x - 10$ ...(i)

Similarly $x - \bar{x} = b_{xy}(y - \bar{y})$

or $x - 25 = 0.4(y - 30)$

$\therefore$ $x = 0.4y + 13$ ...(ii)

Since $r^2 = b_{yx} . b_{xy}$

$\therefore$ $r = \pm\sqrt{b_{yx} . b_{xy}}$

$$r = \pm\sqrt{1.6 \times 0.4} = \pm 0.8$$

Since regression coefficient are positive, we have to take the positive value of correlation coefficient.

$$r = +0.8$$

Problem 5.3

A panel of judges A and B graded seven debators and independently awarded the following marks.

Debator	*Marks by A*	*Marks by B*
1	40	32
2	34	39
3	28	26
4	30	30
5	44	38
6	38	34
7	31	28

An eigth debator was awarded 36 marks by Judge *A*, while Judge *B* was not present.

If Judge *B* were also present, how many marks would you expect him to award to the eight debator, assuming that the same degree of relationship exists in their judgement?

[*C.A.* (*Inter.*), *May'*82]

Solution :

Let us use marks from Judge *A* as *x* and those from Judge *B* as *y*. Now we have to work out the regression line of *y* on *x* from the calculations below :

Debator	*x*	*y*	$u = x - 35$	$v = y - 30$	u^2	v^2	uv
1	40	32	5	2	25	4	10
2	34	39	−1	9	1	81	−9
3	28	26	−7	−4	49	16	28
4	30	30	−5	0	25	0	0
5	44	38	9	8	81	64	72
6	38	34	3	4	9	16	12
7	31	28	−4	−2	16	4	8
$n = 7$			$\Sigma u = 0$	$\Sigma v = 17$	$\Sigma u^2 = 206$	$\Sigma v^2 = 185$	$\Sigma uv = 121$

Here $$\bar{x} = A + \frac{\Sigma u}{n} = 35 + \frac{0}{7} = 35$$

$$\bar{y} = B + \frac{\Sigma v}{n} = 30 + \frac{17}{7} = 32.43$$

$$b_{yx} = b_{vu} = \frac{n\Sigma uv - (\Sigma u \Sigma v)}{n\Sigma u^2 - (\Sigma u)^2}$$

$$= \frac{7 \times 121 - 0 \times 17}{7 \times 206 - 0} = 0.587$$

Hence regression equation can be written as

$$y - \bar{y} = b_{yx}(x - \bar{x})$$

or $$y - 32.34 = 0.587(x - 35)$$

or $$y = 0.587x + 11.87$$

When $x = 36$ (awarded by Judge *A*)

Then $y = 0.587 \times 36 + 11.87 = 33$

Thus if Judge *B* were present, he would have awarded 33 marks to the eigth debator.

Problem 5.4

For some bivariate data, the following results were obtained.

Mean value of variable $x = 53.2$

Mean value of variable $y = 27.9$

Regression coefficient of y on $x = -1.5$

Regression coefficient of x on $y = -0.2$

What is the most likely value of y, when $x = 60$? What is the coefficient of correlation between x and y? *[ICWA (Final), June 1984; Himachal University, M.Com., July 1980]*

Solution :

Given data indicate

$$\bar{x} = 53.2; \qquad \bar{y} = 27.9$$

$$b_{yx} = -1.5; \qquad b_{xy} = -0.2$$

To obtain value of y for $x = 60$, we establish the regression line of y on x.

$$y - \bar{y} = b_{yx}(x - \bar{x})$$

or
$$y - 27.9 = -1.5(x - 53.2)$$

or
$$y = -1.5x + 107.7$$

Putting value of $x = 60$, we obtain the corresponding value of y,

$$y = -1.5 \times 60 + 107.7$$
$$= 17.7$$

Coefficient of correlation between x and y is given by

$$r^2 = b_{yx}.b_{xy}$$
$$= -1.5 \times -0.2$$
$$= 0.3$$

$\therefore$
$$r = \pm\sqrt{0.3} = \pm 0.5477$$

Since both the regression coefficients are negative, we assign negative value to the correlation coefficient

$$r = -0.5477$$

Problem 5.5

Obtain the equations of the two lines of regressions for the following data given below :

x	:	1	2	3	4	5	6	7	8	9
y	:	9	8	10	12	11	13	14	16	15

[Bangalore University, B.Com., April 1981, ICWA (Final), Dec., 1978]

Solution :

From the given data, we get

$$\bar{x} = \frac{\Sigma x}{n}$$

$$= \frac{1+2+3+4+5+6+7+8+9}{9}$$

$$= \frac{45}{9} = 5$$

and $\bar{y} = \frac{\Sigma y}{n}$

$$= \frac{9+8+10+12+11+13+14+16+15}{9}$$

$$= \frac{108}{9} = 12$$

We can obtain the values of Σx^2, Σxy from the above data as

$$\Sigma x^2 = 225 \text{ and } \Sigma xy = 545$$

Thus, $b_{yx} = \frac{n\Sigma xy - (\Sigma x \Sigma y)}{n\Sigma x^2 - (\Sigma x)^2}$

$$= \frac{9 \times 545 - 45 \times 108}{9 \times 225 - (45)^2}$$

$$= \frac{4905 - 4860}{2025 - 2025}$$

$$= \frac{45}{0} = \infty$$

The value of b_{yx} being indeterminate, the line obtained has an infinite slope.

Problem 5.6

Write regression equations of x on y and y on x for the following data :

x :	45	48	50	55	65	70	75	72	80	85
y :	25	30	35	30	40	50	45	55	60	65

Solution :

We can prepare the table for working out the values for the regression lines.

x	y	$u = x-65$	$v = y-45$	u^2	uv	v^2
45	25	–20	–20	400	400	400
48	30	–17	–15	289	255	225
50	35	–15	–10	225	150	100
55	30	–10	–15	100	150	225
65	40	0	–5	0	0	25
70	50	5	5	25	25	25
75	45	10	0	100	0	0
72	55	7	10	49	70	100
80	60	15	15	225	225	225
85	65	20	20	400	400	400
$\Sigma x = 645$	$\Sigma y = 435$	$\Sigma u = (-5)$	$\Sigma v = -15$	$\Sigma u^2 = 1,813$	$\Sigma uv = 1,675$	$\Sigma v^2 = 1,725$

From above values, $\bar{x} = \frac{645}{10} = 64.5$

$$\bar{y} = \frac{435}{10} = 43.5$$

$$b_{yx} = b_{vu} = \frac{n\Sigma uv - (\Sigma u \Sigma v)}{n\Sigma u^2 - (\Sigma u)^2}$$

$$= \frac{10 \times 1675 - (-5 \times -15)}{10 \times 1813 - (-5)^2}$$

$$= \frac{16750 - 75}{18130 - 25}$$

$$= 0.92$$

$\therefore$ Regression of y on x is

$$y - \bar{y} = b_{yx}(x - \bar{x})$$

or $y - 43.5 = 0.92(x - 64.5)$

or $y = 0.92x - 15.84$

Similarly b_{xy} can be calculated as

$$b_{xy} = b_{uv} = \frac{n\Sigma uv - (\Sigma u \Sigma v)}{n\Sigma v^2 - (\Sigma v)^2}$$

$$= \frac{10 \times 1675 - (-5 \times -15)}{10 \times 1725 - (-15)^2}$$

$$= \frac{16750 - 75}{17250 - 225}$$

$$= 0.98$$

$\therefore$ Regression equation of x on y will be

$$x - \bar{x} = b_{xy}(y - \bar{y})$$

or $x - 64.5 = 0.98(y - 43.5)$

or $x = 0.98y + 21.87$

Problem 5.7

The lines of regression of a bivariate population are

$$8x - 10y + 66 = 0$$

$$40x - 18y = 214$$

The variance of x is 9. Find

(*i*) The mean value of x and y

(*ii*) Correlation coefficient between x and y

(*iii*) Standard deviation of y.

[*C.A. (Inter.), Nov.,1977, ICWA, June 1977, AIMA Dip. in Mgmt., July 1981*]

Solution :

The regression lines given are

$$8x - 10y + 66 = 0$$
$$40x - 18y - 214 = 0$$

(i) Since both the lines of regression pass through the mean values, the point ($\bar{x}$, $\bar{y}$) will satisfy both the equations.

Hence these equations can be written as

$$8\bar{x} - 10\bar{y} + 66 = 0$$
$$40\bar{x} - 18\bar{y} - 214 = 0$$

Solving these two equations for $\bar{x}$ and $\bar{y}$, we obtain

$$\bar{x} = 13 \text{ and } \bar{y} = 17$$

(*ii*) For correlation coefficient between *x* and *y*, we have to calculate the values of b_{yx} and b_{xy}, Rewriting the equations

$$10y = 8x + 66$$

$$\therefore \quad b_{yx} = +\frac{8}{10} = +\frac{4}{5}$$

Similarly $\quad 40x = 18y + 214$

$$\therefore \quad b_{xy} = \frac{18}{40} = \frac{9}{20}$$

By these values, we can now work out the correlation coefficient.

$$\therefore \quad r^2 = b_{yx} \cdot b_{xy}$$
$$= \frac{4}{5} \times \frac{9}{20} = \frac{9}{25}$$

$$\therefore \quad r = \pm\sqrt{\frac{9}{25}} = \pm\frac{3}{5}$$
$$= \pm 0.6$$

Both the values of the regresssion coefficients being positive, we have to consider only the positive value of the correlation coefficient, Hence $r = 0.6$.

(iii) $\quad \sigma_x^2 = 9, \sigma_x = \pm 3$

We consider $\sigma_x = 3$ as *SD* are always positive

Since $\quad b_{yx} = \frac{r\sigma_y}{\sigma_x}$

Substituting the values of b_{yx}, r and σ_x, we obtain

$$\sigma_y = \frac{4}{5} \times \frac{3}{0.6} = 4$$

Problem 5.8

If the two lines of regression are

$$4x - 5y + 30 = 0 \text{ and } 20x - 9y - 107 = 0$$

Which of these is the lines of regression of *x* on *y*? Find r_{xy} and σ_y when $\sigma_x = 3$.

[*Punjab University, M.A. Eco., 1980*]

Solution :

The given equations can be rewritten as

$$4x = 5y - 30 \text{ and } 9y = 20x + 107$$

If these lines are regression equation of x on y and y or x respectively,

We can get $$b_{xy} = \frac{5}{4} \text{ and } b_{yx} = \frac{20}{9}$$

$\therefore$ $$r^2 = b_{xy} . b_{yx}$$

$$= \frac{5}{4} \times \frac{20}{9} = 2.778$$

Since $r^2 > 1$, our presumption is wrong.

Hence line $4x - 5y + 30 = 0$ is the regression line of y on x and the other line $20x - 9y - 107 = 0$ is the regression line of x on y.

Rewriting these equations in modified form.

$$5y = 4x + 30$$

$\therefore$ $$b_{yx} = \frac{4}{5}$$

and $$20x = 9y + 107$$

$\therefore$ $$b_{xy} = \frac{9}{20}$$

Now $$r^2 = \frac{4}{5} \times \frac{9}{20} = \frac{9}{25}$$

$\therefore$ $$r_{xy} = \pm\sqrt{\frac{9}{25}} = \pm\frac{3}{5}$$

We take only positive value of r, since b_{yx} and b_{xy} are positive

$\therefore$ $$r = \frac{3}{5}$$

We have also been given $\sigma_x = 3$

Since $$b_{yx} = \frac{r\sigma_y}{\sigma_x}$$

$\therefore$ $$\sigma_y = \frac{b_{yx} . \sigma_x}{r}$$

Substituting the appropriate available values,

$$\sigma_y = \frac{\left(\frac{4}{5} \times 3\right)}{\frac{3}{5}}$$

$$= \frac{4}{5} \times 3 \times \frac{5}{3} = 4$$

Problem 5.9

Given $x = 4y + 5$ and $y = kx + 4$ are the lines of regression of x on y and y on x respectively. If k is positive, prove that it cannot exceed $\frac{1}{4}$. If $k = \frac{1}{16}$, find the means of the two variables and coefficient of correlation between them. [*ICWA (Final), June 1984*]

Solution :

Line $x = 4y + 5$ is regression line of x and y.

$$\therefore \quad b_{xy} = 4$$

Similarly from regression line of y on x as $y = kx + 4$, we get $b_{yx} = k$

$$\therefore \quad r^2 = b_{xy} \cdot b_{yx} = 4k$$

Since $0 \leq r^2 \leq 1$, we obtain $0 \leq 4k \leq 1$,

$$\text{or} \quad 0 \leq k \leq \frac{1}{4}$$

$$\text{Now for} \quad k = \frac{1}{16}, r^2 = 4 \times \frac{1}{16} = \frac{1}{4}$$

$$\therefore \quad r = \pm\frac{1}{2} = \frac{1}{2} \text{ since } b_{yx} \text{ and } b_{xy} \text{ are positive.}$$

When $k = \frac{1}{16}$, the regression line of y on x becomes

$$y = \frac{1}{16}x + 4$$

$$\text{or} \quad x - 16y + 64 = 0$$

Since line of regression passes through the mean values of the variables, we obtain revised equations as

$$\bar{x} - 4\bar{y} - 5 = 0$$

$$\text{and} \quad \bar{x} - 16\bar{y} + 64 = 0$$

Solving these two equations, we get

$$\bar{x} = 28 \text{ and } \bar{y} = 5.75$$

Problem 5.10

The height of a child increases at a rate given in the table below. Fit the straight line using the method of least squares and calculate the average increase and the standard error of estimate.

Month	:	1	2	3	4	5	6	7	8	9	10
Height	:	52.5	58.7	65.0	70.2	75.4	81.1	87.2	95.5	102.2	108.4

Solution :

For Regression calculations, we draw the following table.

Month (x)	*Height* (y)	x^2	xy
1	52.5	1	52.5
2	58.7	4	117.4
3	65.0	9	195.0
4	70.2	16	280.8
5	75.4	25	377.0
6	81.1	36	486.6
7	87.2	49	610.4
8	95.5	64	769.0
9	102.2	81	919.8
10	108.4	100	1089.0
Σx=55	Σy=796.2	Σx^2=385	Σxy = 4887.5

Considering the regression line as $y = a + bx$, we can obtain the values of a and b from the above table.

$$a = \frac{(\Sigma x^2)(\Sigma y) - (\Sigma x)(\Sigma xy)}{n\Sigma x^2 - (\Sigma x)^2}$$

$$= \frac{385 \times 769.2 - 55 \times 4887.5}{10 \times 385 - 55 \times 55}$$

$$= 45.73$$

and
$$b = \frac{n\Sigma xy - (\Sigma x \Sigma y)}{n\Sigma x^2 - (\Sigma x)^2}$$

$$= \frac{10 \times 4887.5 - 55 \times 796.2}{10 \times 385 - 55 \times 55}$$

$$= 6.16$$

Hence the regression line can be written as

$$y = 45.73 + 6.16x$$

for standard error of estimation, we note the calculated values of the variables against the observed values,

When $x = 1, y_1 = 45.73 + 6.16 = 51.89$

For $x = 2, y_2 = 45.73 + 6.16 \times 2 = 58.05$

Other values for $x = 3$ to $x = 10$ are calculated and are tabulated as follows :

x	y	y_i	$y-y_i$	$(y-y_i)^2$
1	52.5	51.89	0.61	0.372
2	58.7	58.05	0.65	0.423
3	65.0	64.21	0.79	0.624
4	70.2	70.37	–0.17	0.029
5	75.4	76.53	–1.13	1.277
6	81.1	82.69	–1.59	2.528
7	87.2	88.58	–1.65	2.723
8	95.5	95.01	0.49	0.240
9	102.2	101.17	1.03	1.061
10	108.4	107.33	1.07	1.145
				$\Sigma E^2_r = 10.421$

∴ Standard error of estimation

$$SE_{(yx)} = \sqrt{\frac{1}{n}\Sigma(y-y_i)^2}$$

$$= \sqrt{\frac{10.421}{10}}$$

$$= 1.02$$

Problem 5.11

From the following data, work out the regression line of y on x and calculate standard error of estimation.

x :	13	13	13	14	14	15	16	16	10	10	11	12	12	13	13
y :	37	40	38	40	43	44	54	55	33	34	38	43	46	46	45

Solution :

Writing the table for regression values.

n	x	y	x^2	xy	y_i	$(y-y_i)$	$(y-y_i)^2$
1	13	37	169	481	42.4	–5.4	29.16
2	13	40	169	520	42.4	–2.4	5.76
3	13	38	169	494	42.4	–9.4	19.34
4	14	40	196	560	45.15	–5.15	26.52
5	14	43	196	602	45.15	–2.15	9.62
6	15	44	225	660	47.90	–3.90	15.21
7	16	54	256	864	50.65	3.35	11.22
8	16	55	256	880	50.65	9.35	18.92
9	10	33	100	330	39.15	–1.15	1.32
10	10	34	100	340	39.15	–0.15	0.02
11	11	38	121	418	37.90	0.10	0.01
12	12	43	144	516	39.65	3.35	11.23
13	12	46	144	552	39.65	6.35	40.33
14	13	46	169	598	42.4	3.6	12.96
15	13	45	169	585	42.5	2.5	6.25
n=15	Σx=195	Σy=636	Σx^2=2,583	Σxy=8,400			$\Sigma(y-y_i)^2$=202.89

From these values from the table, we calculate the values of the constants a and b, when the regression line is

$$y = a + bx$$

By using standard formula as in problem 5.10, we get

$$a = 6.65$$

and $$b = 2.75$$

∴ The regression line becomes $y = 6.65 + 2.75x$

Now for each value of x, we calculate the values of y and write in the table as y_i against appropriate value. These are written in last three columns of the above tables.

∴ Standard error of estimation

$$SE_{(yx)} = \sqrt{\frac{1}{n}\Sigma(y - y_i)^2}$$

$$= \sqrt{\frac{1}{15} \times 202.89}$$

$$= 3.67$$

PRACTICE PROBLEMS

5.12 What is linear regression? Where are there, in general, two regression lines? When do they coincide? Explain the use of regression equations in economic enquiry.

[Punjab University. M.A. (Eco.). 1980]

5.13 Prove that the regression lines of y on x and x on y intersect at point $(\bar{x}, \bar{y})$

[Delhi University, B.A. (Eco. Hons), 1984]

5.14 Given the following values of x and y,

x :	3	5	6	8	9	11
y :	2	3	4	6	5	8

Find the equation of regression of *(i)* y on x *(ii)* x on y. Interpret the result.

[Himachal University, M.A. (Eco.), July 1983]

5.15 Obtain the equations of the two lines of regression for the data given below:

X :	1	2	3	4	5	6	7	8	9
Y :	9	8	10	12	11	13	14	16	15

[Bangalore University, B.Com., April 1981, Punjab University, M.A. (Eco.). 1978]

5.16 Fit a least square line to the following data :

(a) Using x as independent variable

(b) x as dependent variable

x :	1	3	4	8	9	11	14
y :	1	2	4	5	7	8	9

Hence obtain *(i)* The regression coefficients of y on x and x on y

(ii) x and y

(iii) Coefficient of correlation between x and y

(iv) What is the estimated value of y when $x = 10$ and of x when $y = 5$?

[Punjab University, M.A. (Eco.). 1981]

5.17 What are regression coefficients? show that $r^2 = b_{yx} \cdot b_{xy}$ where the symbols have their usual meanings (which you are to explain in course of your demonstration). What can you say about the angle between the regression lines when *(i)* $r = 0$, *(ii)* $r = \neq 1$, *(iii)* r increases from 0 to 1 ? Obtain the equations of the lines of regression of Y on X from the following data.

X :	12	18	24	30	36	42	48
Y :	5.27	5.68	6.25	7.21	8.02	8.71	8.42

Estimate the most probable value of Y, when $X = 40$ *[ICWA (Final), June 1996]*

5.18 From the following data of the age of husband and the age of wife, form two regression lines and calculate the husband's age, when the wife's age is 16

Husband's age	:	36	23	27	28	28	29	30	31	33	35
Wife's age	:	29	18	20	22	27	21	29	27	29	28

[Bangalore University, B.Com., April 1978]

5.19 The following table gives the ages and blood pressure of 10 women

Age *(X)*	:	56	42	36	47	49	42	60	72	63	55
Blood Pressure *(Y)*	:	147	125	118	128	145	140	155	160	149	150

(i) Find the correlation coefficient between X and Y *(ii)* Determine the least square regression equation of Y on X *(iii)* Estimate the blood pressure of a woman whose age is 45 years

[Delhi University, M.B.A.. 1976]

5.20 Given the following results for the height *(x)* and weight *(y)* in appropriate units of 1,000 students.

$\bar{x} = 68$, $y = 150$, $\sigma_x = 2.5$, $\sigma_y = 20$ and $r = 0.6$

Obtain the equations of the two lines of regression. Estimate the height of a student A who weights 200 units and also estimate the weight of the student B whose height is 60 units.

[ICWA (Final), Dec., 1980; Rajasthan University, M.Com., 1981]

5.21 From the following data, find out the probable yield when the rainfall is 29".

	Rainfall	***Yield***
Mean	25"	40 units per hectare
Standard Deviation	3"	6 units per hectare

Correlation Coefficient between rainfall and production = 0.8

[Osmania University, B.Com. (Hons.), April 1983]

5.22 A study of wheat prices at two cities yielded the following data.

	City A	***City B***
Average price	Rs. 2.463	Rs. 2.797
Standard Deviation	Rs. 0.326	Rs. 0.207

Coefficient of Correlation r is 0.779. Extimate from the above data the post likely .price of wheat *(i)* at City A corresponding to the price of Rs. 2.334 at City B, *(ii)* At city B corresponding to the price of Rs. 3.052 at City A. *[Punjab University, M.A. (Eco.), Oct., 1980]*

5.23 Find out the regression equation showing the regression of capacity utilisation on production from the following data.

	Average	***Standard Deviation***
Production (in lakh units)	35.6	10.5
Capacity utilisation (in percentage)	89.8	8.5

$r = 0.62$

Estimate the production, when capacity utilisation is 70%

[Allahabad University. M.B.A.. 1982, Himachal University, M.B.A., 1976 and Delhi University, M.B.A. Dec., 1980]

5.24 The following table shows the mean and standard deviation of the prices of two shares in a stock exchange.

Share	Mean (in Rs.)	Standard Deviation (in Rs.)
A Ltd.	39.5	10.8
B Ltd.	47.5	16.0

If the coefficient of correlation between the prices of two shares is 0.42, find the most likely price of share A corresponding to a price of Rs. 55 observed in the case of share B.

[*AIMA (Dip. in Mgmt.), 1977*]

5.25 Find out the regression coefficients of *Y* on X and X on *Y* on, the basis of following data.

$\Sigma X = 50$, $\overline{X} = 5$, $\Sigma Y = 60$, $\overline{Y}$ s 6, $\Sigma XY = 350$; variance of $X = 4$, variance of $Y = 9$.

[*Delhi University, B.A.(Eco. Hons), 1981*]

5.26 Find the regression equation of X on *Y* and the coefficient of correlation *from* the following data. $\Sigma X = 60$, $\Sigma Y = 40$, $\Sigma XY = 1150$, $\Sigma X^2 = 4160$, $\Sigma Y^2 = 1720$ and $N = 10$.

[*C.A. (Inter), Nov.. 1985*]

5.27 Following is the distribution of students according to their heights and weights :

Height y (in *inches)*	*Weight x (in Ibs.)* 90-100	100 -110	110 -120	120-130
50-55	4	7	5	2
55-60	6	10	7	4
60-65	6	12	10	7
65-70	3	8	6	3

Calculate *(i)* The two coefficients of regression and *(ii)* Obtain the two regression equations.

[*Nagpur University, M.Com., Oct., 1978, Delhi University, M.Com.. 1973*]

5.28 The regression equation of profits (X) on sales *(Y) of* a certain firm is $3Y - 5X + 108 = 0$. The average sales of the firm were Rs. 44,000 and the variance of profits is $\frac{9^{th}}{16}$ of the variance of sales. Find the average profits and the coefficient of correlation between the sales and profits.

[*AIMA (Dip. in Mgmt.), Jan., 1979*]

5.29 The lines of regression of *y* on *x* and *x* on *y* are $y = 0.3x + 10.0$ and $x = 1.2y + 0.8$, respectively. Determine the means of *x* and *y*, the ratio of the *SD* of *x* and *y* and the correlation between *x* and *y*. [*Delhi University, B.A. (Eco. Hons.) 1983*]

5.30 The equations of two regression lines between two variables are expressed as $2x - 3y = 0$ and $4y - 5x - 8 = 0$.

(i) Identify which of the two can be called regression of *y* on *x* and of *x* on y,

(ii) Find *x* and y and correlation coefficient (*r*) front the equations.

[*ICWA (Final), June 1983*]

5.31 Regression of savings *(S)* of a family on income *(Y)* may be expressed as $S = a + \frac{Y}{m}$, where *a* and *m* are constants. In random sample of 100 families, the variance of the savings is one-quarter of the variance of incomes and the correlation is found to be 0.9. Obtain the estimate of *m*. [*ICWA (Final), June 1974*]

5.32 Obtain the lines of regression for the following bivariate frequency distribution.

Sales revenue (Rs.'000)	Advertising expenditure (Rs.'000) 5-15	15-25	25-35	35-45	Total
75 – 125	4	1	0	0	5
125 – 175	7	6	2	1	16
175 – 225	1	3	4	2	10
225 – 275	1	1	3	4	9
Total	13	11	9	7	40

[*Delhi University MBA, 1973*]

5.33 Following is the distribution of students according to their height and weight.

Height y (in inches)	Weight x 90-100	100-100	110-120	120-130
50-55	4	7	5	2
55-60	6	10	7	4
60-65	6	12	10	7
65-70	3	8	6	3

Calculate (*i*) the two coefficients of regression and (*ii*) obtain the two regression equations.

[*Delhi University M.Com, 1973, Nagpur University Oct. 1978*]

5.34 (*a*) What is correlation? Does correlation signify the existence of cause and effect relationship ?

Or

(*b*) M/s. Voltas Ltd. gives the following information relating to the sales of refrigerators in the past 10 years.

Years :	1988	1989	1990	1991	1992	1993	1994	1995	1996	1997
Refrigerators sold in thousands :	8	10	11	11	18	15	19	19	22	24

Fit a trend line by least square method and compute trend values. Estimate sales for the year 2002. [*Osmania University, M.B.A., Sept., 1988*]

5.35 The following are the two regression equations. Find the regression equation of x on y and y on x.

$8x - 10y + 61 = 0$; $40x - 18y = 2/4$

Also find (*i*) Mean of x and y (*ii*) The regression coefficients and (*iii*) The correlation coefficient. [*Osmania University, M.B.A., July 2000*]

❁❁❁

CHAPTER 6

TIME SERIES ANALYSIS AND FORECASTING

6.1 INTRODUCTION

Time series, as the name suggests, is a series of values or data arranged in a chronological order as per time period *i.e.* description of a phenomenon over a specified period of time. When applied to business. whether for economic or commercial analysis, it can be used for forecasting future events such as price, demand, yield, sales or profits etc. In order to ensure that there is no shortage of material in a shop or for production line, we may use time series analysis to arrive at reasonably accurate estimate of demand or requirement at a particular future period of time. Time series analysis can be very helpful, thus, to estimate levels of consumptions of various consumer goods, agricultural production for next few years. national incomes increase, amount of bank deposits or rates of shares in the stock market or else in any natural or social areas.

Time Series Analysis relates to arranging the series of data in a chronological order as per the progress of time. This could be in the range of past time sequence or for future time sequence. This concept is useful for estimating the data progression with reference to time movement.

The time series, thus, can be mathematically, represented as

$$y = f(t)$$

where y is the value of the variable to be estimated and it is treated as a function of time, represented as $f(t)$

A series listed below can illustrate the time series of a variable y

Year	1991	1992	1993	1994	1995	1996
Number (y)	50	61	63	67	70	75

This shows that a statistic or number y has been specified at a definite time interval of one year. This can be the number of employees working in an organisation over a period 1991 to 1996.

In time series, the data is bivariate where one variable is time period and this time can be expressed as daily, weekly, monthly or yearly etc. The bivariate data can be plotted on a graph as a histogram with x-axis as time and the dependent variable on y-axis, as shown in Fig 6.1.

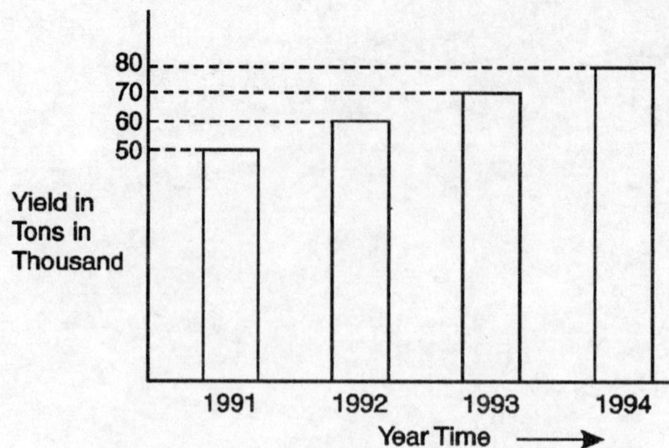

Fig. 6.1. Histogram for yield of crops.

6.2 VARIATIONS IN TIME SERIES

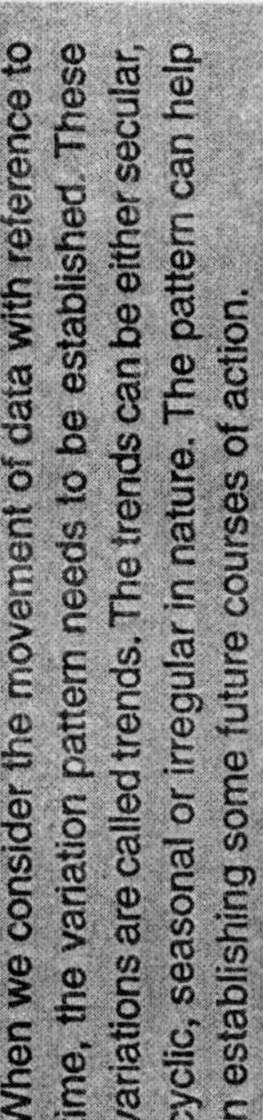

As described in the last paragraph, the time series is a group of data or observations collected over a period of time at regular intervals. There is likelihood of changes in this data as time progresses. This is termed as variation in time series. The variation may be due to either one factor or a combination of factors affecting the values of the variable over a period of time. These variations can be accounted for under four names,

1. Secular trend
2. Cyclic fluctuation *i.e.* periodic movement
3. Seasonal variation at definite time intervals
4. Irregular variation

Secular Trend

When the value of the dependent variable tends to increase or decrease over a long time horizon, this variation is called "secular trend". Increase in population, sales of products, increase in the Price Index, increase in per capita income etc. are few of such examples, where the trend is towards the increase. The death rate fall due to better health services may be called a negative trend.

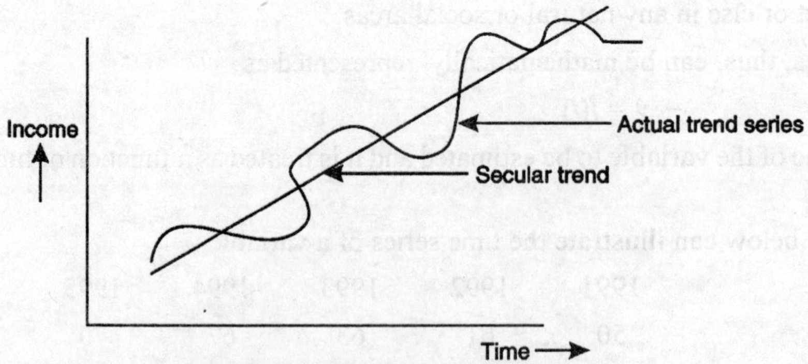

Fig. 6.2. Secular Trend (increase)

Cyclic Fluctuation

As opposed to the secular trend, there may be peaks and lows in a business trend. This can be called cyclic fluctuation. For peaks and lows, the time period may be different" for different types of business, may be one year or as long as 10 years. Cyclic phenomena donot necessity follow a uniform pattern and could be very unpredictable. (Refer fig. 6.3).

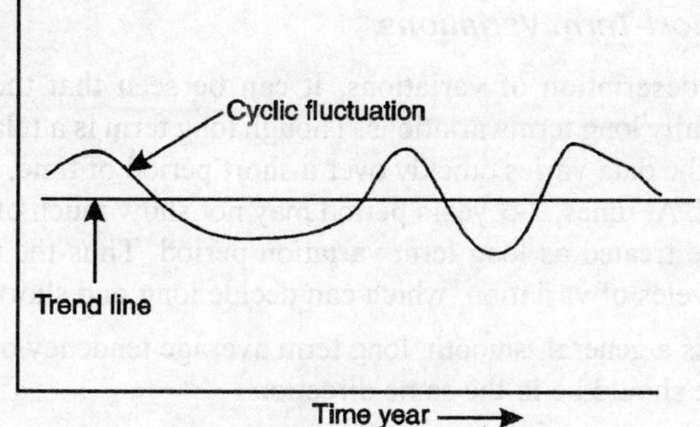

Fig. 6.3. Cyclic Fluctuation

Seasonal Variation

This kind of change occurs due to changing seasons *i.e.* the variation is pattern is observed within a year only. Sales of air-conditioners or heaters can be seen to follow seasonal variation during a specific time of the year such as airconditioners peak the sales during summer *i.e.* April-May and heaters during winter *i.e.* October - November. (Refer fig 6.4).

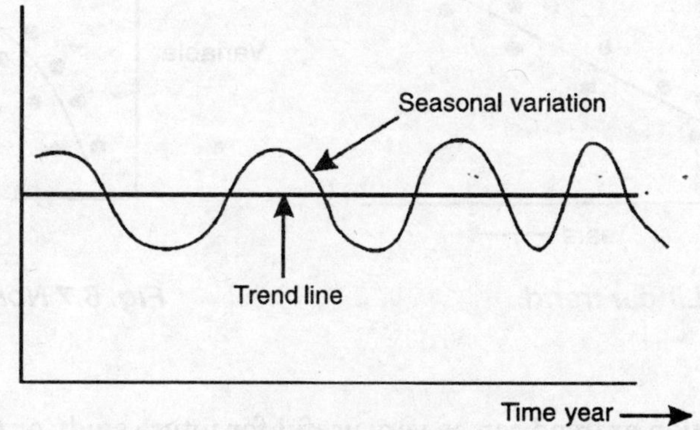

Fig. 6.4. Seasonal Variations

Regular increase and decrease of data values without any regular pattern is called irregular variation. Whereas the regular pattern can be called seasonal or cyclic variation.

Irregular Variation

It is fourth type of variation when no definite pattern of variation is observed. It is completely unpredictable and changes occur in a very random manner.

These types of variations can be shown as fig 6.5.

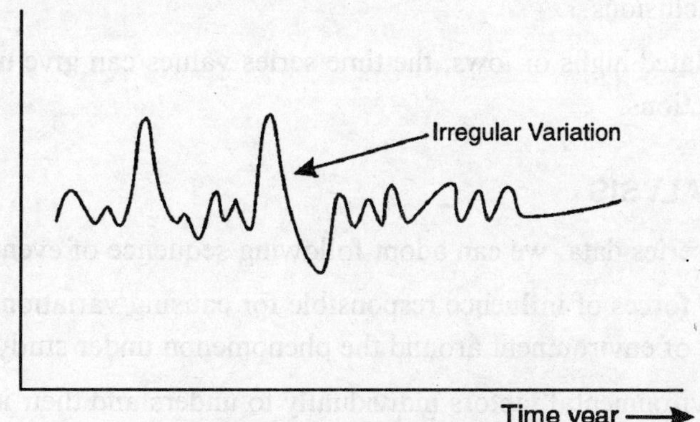

Fig. 6.5. Irregular Variations

Long-Term and Short-Term Variations

From the above description of variations, it can be seen that the secular trend and cyclic fluctuations are generally long term variations. Though long term is a relative term, it can depend on the nature of data. If the data varies quickly over a short period of time, say even hours, this can be called long term trend. At times, 2-3 years period may not show much of the variation and possibly 10 year period can be treated as long term variation period. Thus the time series values must be examined over few cycles of variation, which can decide long and short time variation.

In general, trend is a general, smooth, long term average tendency of the data variation and the increase and decrease should be in the same direction.

6.3 LINEAR AND NON-LINEAR TREND

When the data of time series is plotted on a graph, the cluster of points indicates the trend or variation. If points rally more or less around a straight line, it is called linear trend and when the change is slow or fast in the beginning and changes its rate later, it will form a non-linear trend. This is called curvilinear trend also. These are exhibited in Figs. 6.6 and 6.7 given below.

If the variations of data with reference to time pertain to a short period, say, few weeks or months etc., these are called short term variations. When time horizon is larger, say a few years, it can be termed as long term variation. These variations/trends can be linear or non-linear depending on the data obtained from actual business operations.

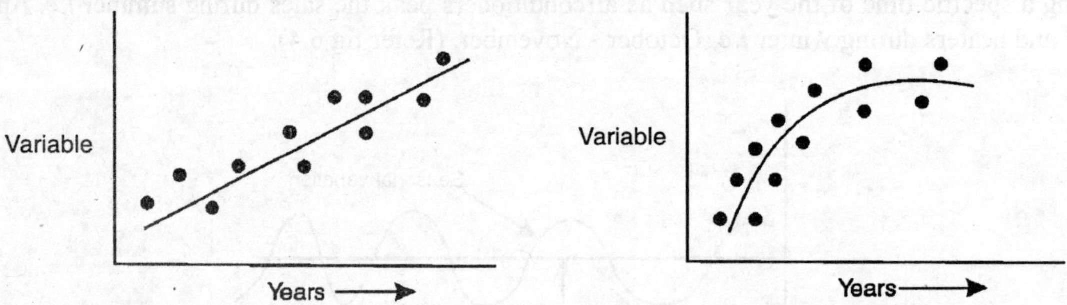

Fig. 6.6 Linear trend. *Fig. 6.7 Non-linear trend*

Uses of Trend

The study of variation or trend can be very useful for future study or future predictions. We can generally summarise the uses as follows.

1. The data variation analysis enables us to formulate general idea about pattern or the behaviour of the subject under study. We presume that under normal conditions, the increase or decrease of data should follow the same pattern if extended in time further. This is a great helping behaviour used in businesses for future predictions of sales, prices, salaries etc.
2. The trend also enables us to compare two or more time series over a period of time and draw useful conclusions.
3. Barring few isolated highs or lows, the time series values can give us either short term or long term projections.

6.4 TIME SERIES ANALYSIS

For analysing time series data, we can adopt following sequence of events

1. Identify various forces of influence responsible for causing variations in the series. This is called the study of environment around the phenomenon under study.
2. Study of the environmental factors individually to understand their individual impacts.
3. The direction of variation and various levels there of, can then be combined to understand the trend, so that its usage can be effectively made use of in future utilisation of the given

time series data.

Mathematical Models

There are two important models for studying the components of the time series.

(*a*) Additive model : In this case, various components can form the additive trend such as

$$y_t = T_t + S_t + C_t + I_t$$

Where y_t = value of the variable at a time t.

T_t = value of secular trend at time t.

S_t = value of the seasonal variation at time t.

C_t = value of the cyclic fluctuation at time t.

and I_t = value of the irregular fluctuation at time t.

The assumption for additive model is that all the four components operate independently and each would not have any effect on the other three. In most of the business situations, this assumption does not hold good as the effects are generally environmental and side effects would always be felt.

(*b*) Multiplicative model : Considering the ever changing environment, most of the business or economic time series would be characterised by the following model.

$$y_t = T_t \times S_t \times C_t \times I_t$$

For Time-Series analysis, we can use either the mathematical models or the curve fitting models. Additive or multiplicative models are established as per variable relationship pattern. Similarly, linear or non-linear trends can be utilised through "curve-fitting" method.

6.5 CURVE FITTING OF TRENDS

1. Linear trend in time series : When we observe a linear trend in the values of time series data points, we can fit a linear trend by the least square method.

The given linear equations can be written as follows

$$\hat{y} = a + bx$$

Where $\hat{y}$ = estimated value of the dependent variable

a = y intercept or starting point of the trend

b = slope of the trend line

x = independent variable

t = time series analysis

For fitting the linear trend by least square method, we can write various values as

slope $$b = \frac{\Sigma y.t - n\bar{y}\bar{t}}{\Sigma t^2 - n\bar{t}^2}$$

and

y-intercept $a = \bar{y} - b\bar{t}$

Where y = values of the dependent variable

t = value of independent variable *i.e.* time in time series

$\bar{y}$ = mean value of the values of the dependent variable

$\bar{t}$ = Average of the values of the independent variable 't'

n = number of observations in time series analysis

a = y intercept *i.e.* value of y, when $t = 0$

b = slope of the linear trend line

This is best fitting line by least square method from where the line can be established by using values of a and b.

2. Second Degree Trend in Time Series : In the last paragraph, we have described the method to deal with a time series, the data points of which fit a straight line and we have done so by fittting the straight line by least square method.

In this method, we are describing the time series analysis, best described by some curve and not a straight line. We can and often do use parabolic curve. This can be mathematically described as a second degree equation, the general form of this curve being

$$\hat{y} = a + bt + ct^2$$

Where $\hat{y}$ = estimate of the dependent variable

a, b, c = numerical constants

t = value of the time variable

Graphically, this curve can be drawn as in Fig. 6.8.

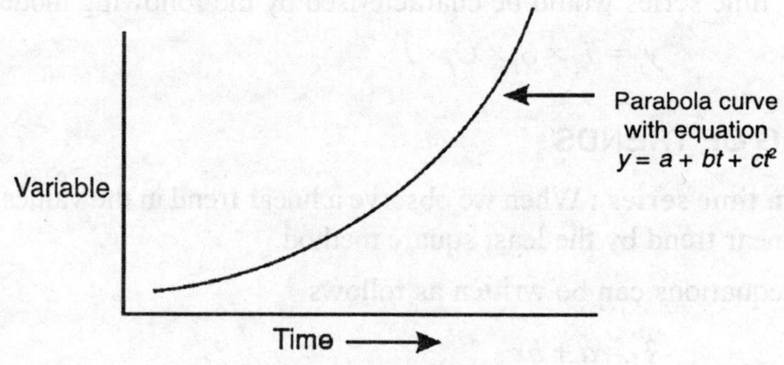

Fig. 6.8. Parabolic variation

For calculation of the values of the constants a, b and c, we can use the following three equations.

$$\Sigma y = na + b\Sigma t + c\Sigma t^2$$

$$\Sigma ty = a\Sigma t + b\Sigma t^2 + c\Sigma t^3$$

$$\Sigma t^2 y = a\Sigma t^2 + b\Sigma t^3 + c\Sigma t^4$$

and $b = \dfrac{\Sigma yt}{\Sigma t^2}$ etc.

3. Cyclic variation : It is the component of the time series that slows variation above and below the secular or long term trend line, when considered for a long period, say for more than a year.

In this case, the percentage of trend, can be obtained by the relationship

Percentage trend $= \dfrac{y}{\hat{y}} \times 100$

Where y = actual time series value

$\hat{y}$ = estimated trend value from the same point

Relative cyclic residual is another measure that can help analyse the seasonal trend. Thus

Relative cycle residual $= \dfrac{y - \hat{y}}{\hat{y}} \times 100$

The graphical representation of the cyclic variation can be done as in Fig 6.9.

The "Best Fitting" of curve can be and is being used extensively by the business managers to draw coherent conclusions. This can be used for cyclic, non-linear or even irregular variation pattern.

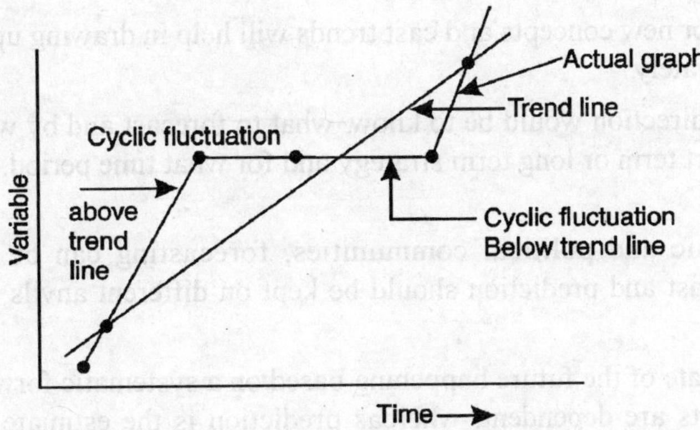

Fig. 6.9. Cyclic Variation

4. Seasonal variation : Seasonal variation, as described earlier, is a repetitive and predictable variation of the data points around the trend line, normally during the year or even less. By this study, we can establish not only the pattern of happenings as per past data, but also can. to a fairly good degree of accuracy, predict the behaviour of the phenomenon over the seasons during the year or year-after-year. The seasonal variations can be analysed by moving average method as described in para 6.8.

The relationships of variables with various movement patterns taken into consideration, is usefully employed to carry forward the data to the nearby future. The extension of trend data is then used for future forecasting in business operations.

5. Irregular variation : There is no definite pattern of this variation, nor there is any fixed time interval for its occurrence. Since this variation is highly unpredictable, there is no mathematical treatment given to this trend. Only we can isolate the cause of such a variation, thus, smoothing out the time series.

6.6 TIME SERIES ANALYSIS FOR FORECASTING

Forecasting is fundamental to Quantitative Approaches in Management and "We wish we had known it before" brings forecasting into business focus.

While introducing a new product, a product development plan in terms of its market demand, the quality of product and time estimation with respect to Market forces need to be worked out. It is essential to know in advance, by some reliable method, whether it will be a success or a failure, and how much efforts in terms of manpower and cost will be worthwhile. After identifying the market, product, manufacturing method, process planning and production capacity, we then have to establish, beyond reasonable doubt, how fast the product will be accepted in the market, how the growth pattern will develop and when it levels off. All these items of thought process will be answered if forecasts and predictions for the future are made rationally and methodically. Hence, the necessity of forecasting methods is established beyond doubt.

From the above statement, it is evident that the managers must be able to anticipate the future under various conditions. The quality of future predictions will speak for a good business in future growth. The future always had a great fascination for the humans and astrology, numerology and various other tools have been developed by the mankind for this "seeing or looking into the future." Some people use 'dream' knowledge for future prediction. But we cannot really depend on such methods fully, when it comes to decision making for the business propositions. No doubt, such things cannot really work fine in share market, or for weather predictions.

In business, where stakes (financial) are high, decisions have to be very deliberate and a large number of environmental factors along with their future behaviour need to be studied and used for decision making. The managers should be able to predict the demand for their products and services. For this, behavioural pattern to these parameters in the immediate past and probable development in terms of new technology or new concepts and cast trends will help in drawing up a future blue print more rationally and accurately.

The first step in this direction would be to know, what to forecast and by whom. We also need deciding whether it is short term or long term strategy and for what time period, the forecasts are to be made.

In business, economic and political communities, forecasting can be defined as per its applicability. Thus, forecast and prediction should be kept on'different anvils, while usage of the terms be specified.

A forecast is an estimate of the future happening based on a systematic forwarding of past data on which the future events are dependent, whereas prediction is the estimate of future obtained through subjective consideration other than just the past data. Thus basic necessity of forecast arises out of planning requirement and it is for the purpose of all levels of human organisations, be it individual or personal, industry and the government.

Forecasting, thus, is an integral part of planning process and hence no management can be successful without quality forecasts.

Any growth in business can be very uncertain but if we establish the trend of growth (say, through regression lines) based on past data, it can be safe to predict the future growth, if otherwise not disturbed by unforeseen circumstances or situations.

Forecasting helps in managerial decision-making process in the following ways :

1. Business decisions today are made based on the experiences of the past, either own or data collected by specified organisations, as relevant to the system under consideration.
2. Due to uncertainty of future events, forecasts, based on some reliable method, help in reducing the uncertainty of events in near future.
3. Forecasting can act as a good tool for those in control of the system, in evolving a firm base for their decisions. Specialists collecting information for forecasts thus use the information for systematic consideration and analysis. Thus, forecasting can play a very important role in relevant decision-making.

6.7 FORECASTING APPROACHES

1. Judgement Approach : It is a basic step in looking into the future with additional benefits of (*a*) articulating the participants thinking (*b*) broadening and firming up opinion (*c*) creating a consensus and (*d*) reaching a workable plan based on the forecast.

2. Statistical Approach : It attempts to extrapolate the past into the future and to exploit our fundamental belief that irregularities underlying the past will also prevail in the future or at least in the near future. Such analysis includes the examination of columns of data grouped in various ways and alternate graphical representations of data. Some of the examples of short/long term forecasts are given below :

Short-term forecasts are used for Manpower Planning, Equipment Policy, Budget allocation. Inventory Policy, Product development. Pricing policy, sales forecast and cash flows, whereas long term forecasts are useful for Innovations like growth of Science and Technology.

3. Mathematical Models in Forecasting : In formulation of a mathematical model for forecasting, we examine historical data and infer the nature and characteristic of the underlying process gathering the data. We then plot this data to obtain the following information.

(*a*) Trend (*b*) Seasonal Variation (*c*) Cyclic Variation

6.8 FORECASTING METHODS

Various forecasting methods can be classified as follows :

1. Subjective Forecasting : depends on the experience of the person in a particular trade. Experience and judgement are important. Two such methods are expert opinions and DELPHI method.

Expert Opinions : While taking general business decisions, the experience of the key managers is taken into account, because they are in a portion to indicate forecast of cost market information, prices or demand etc. Such a decision is called "Forecasting Through Expert Opinion." Such group or committee decisions can be biased due to personal preferences. Hence, it is better to avoid this bias as done in Delphi method.

Delphi Method : This method was developed by RAND Corporation as a technique for working out decision/forecasting without creating a bias amongst group members. In this method, a questionnaire list is circulated to certain panel of experts without disclosing the composition of the panel. Individual opinion (answers) are obtained, information sifted by the coordinator and opinion re-invited on revised questionnaire. Delphi coordinator edits, clarifies and summarises the data and forecast is thus obtained without creating any bias by the panel members. It allows multiple opinions and hence ensures improved information collection.

2. Structural and Economic Model : Use of mathematical approach in economic problems. Establish basic causes and build a function defining it.

Q (say launch product quantity) = f(price wage rate, GNP, Income of Customer)

$$= \alpha_0 + \alpha_1\, Pt + \alpha_2\, Wt + \alpha_3\, Yt$$

Where Pt = Price

Wt = wage rate

Yt = consumer income etc.

3. Deterministic time series Models : Let us define it as,

$Z_t = f(t)$, where Z_t = forecast variable at time t

Here data is a function of time t, such as

$\therefore$ $$Zt = a_0 + a_1 t + a_2 t^2 + \ldots\ldots\ldots$$

or $Zt = Ar^t$ (used for predicting population)

where r = rate of change or growth

4. Moving Averages/Exponential Smoothing Models : We use certain section of the past data for predicting the future. We assume by experience that change comes only after 1, 2, 3, 6 months etc.

5. *Regression Analysis* : A casual method by correlation of parameters of demand and factors causing any change.

Various forecasting models are useful for future forecast of events. Some of these are
- Judgemental method
- Statistical or Mathematical models
- Structural and Economic models.

Mathematical Models

Moving Averages (Time Series Model)

Underlying assumption in this method is

"Next months sale forecast = this months sales (actual)"

To establish the pattern, we develop the concept of moving averages.

Averages of last two Values *i.e.*, Forecast for March = 1/2 (actual sale of February and January)

$$F = \frac{1}{2}\,(S_1 + S_2).$$

Similarly weighted Average of last two values (if all the values do not have the same importance for future)

$$F = \frac{3S_1 + 2S_2}{3+2}$$ (With weightage for most recent observation as 3 and the previous as 2)

Here Sales of February are playing more decisive role in future sales.

Weighted average for last three values can be assumed as

$$F = \frac{7S_1 + 2S_2 + 1S_3}{7+2+1}$$ (Weightages given as 7, 2 and 1 for most recent previous and previous to that respectively)

where S_1 = most recent value, S_2 = next recent value and so on.

Hence, the general forecasting formula would be

$$F = \frac{w_1S_1 + w_2S_2 + w_3S_3 \ldots\ldots\ldots w_nS_n}{w_1 + w_2 + w_3 \ldots\ldots\ldots w_n}$$

Where w's are the weightages attached to the actual values sales of (*S*) for forecasts (*F*).

> In some specific situations, the semi-average and weighted-average model are useful. Exponential smoothing model is also a weighted average model.

Semi-Average method

This is slightly different approach to the forcasting procedure, wherein the time series data is divided into two equal parts with reference to the time period under consideration. In case, the time period is odd, then middle value can be eliminated. After this division of data, the average value of the time series data is calculated for both the parts. These averages are called semi-averages. These semi-averages are then plotted for the period as middle point of the time period (each half) and we obtain the trend line by joining these two points (plotted semi-averages). Corresponding values trend for each year, then, can be obtained either from the graph or from calculations.

Expontential Smoothing

It is refined version of moving Average. In moving average, we give equal weightage to most recent observations. Here we give reduced weightage for less recent observations/readings and we draw relationship of recent forecast and actual sales.

$$F_n = \alpha y_{n-1} + (1 - \alpha)F_{n-1}$$

Where F_n = present forecast

F_{n-1} = previous forecast

α = Smoothing constant

y_{n-1} = previous actual observations

Regression Analysis

In this case, we use the theory of curve fitting to the group of past data and use this curve for the projection of trend for the future.

Let $$\bar{x} = \frac{x_1 + x_2 + x_3 + \ldots\ldots x_n}{n}$$

Similarly $$\bar{x} = \frac{y_1 + y_2 + y_3 + y_4 \ldots\ldots y_n}{n}$$

Hence $\Sigma xy = x_1y_1 + x_2y_2 + \ldots\ldots x_ny_n.$

$\Sigma x^2 = x_1^2 + x_2^2 + x_3^2 + \ldots\ldots x_n^2.$

Now try and fit the straight line to this data.

If we treat the straight line as $y = a + bx$.

The value of a and b can be calculated from the following equations :

$$\Sigma y = na + b\Sigma x.$$

and $$\Sigma xy = a\Sigma x + b\Sigma x^2$$

Thus, we get the best fitting straight line as

$$y_e = a + bx.$$

Which can be used for projection of trend for future by using values of a and b from the above relationships of the data.

Least Square Method of Curve fitting

If actual value against forecast is different, then we calculate errors *i.e.* Forecast – actual = error

or $$e = d_f - d_a. = y_c - (a + bx)$$

Where d_f = forecast demand and d_a = actual demand

It can be used for Sd = $\sqrt{\dfrac{\Sigma e^2}{(n-1)}}$ where sd = standard deviation of estimation.

Considering two cases :

(*i*) straight line $y = a_0 + a_1x$.

(*ii*) Parabolic or quadratic curve $y = a_0 + a_1x + a_2x^2$. When there are n points (x_1, y_1) (x_2, y_2) etc., the constant a_0, a_1 can be calculated by solving

$$\Sigma y = a_0n + a_1 \Sigma x \text{ and } \Sigma xy = a_0 \Sigma x + a_1\Sigma x^2.$$

These are called normal equations for least square lines. In case of quadratic curve, we can determine the values of a_0, a_1 and a_2 by solving the following equations

$$\Sigma y = a_0n + a_1\Sigma x + a_2\Sigma x_2$$

$$\Sigma xy = a_0\Sigma x + a_1\Sigma x^2 + a_2\Sigma x^3$$

$$\Sigma x^2y = a_0\Sigma x^2 + a_1\Sigma x^3 + a_2\Sigma x^4$$

These are called normal equations for the least square parabola.

In mathematical models, the regression analysis and time series analysis are more commonly use methods for business forecasting. In some specific cases, the curve-fitting method is also usefully employed.

CHAPTER SUMMARY

Terms used

- **Cyclic fluctuation :** A type of variation in time series where fluctuation occurs above or below a secular trend line
- **Delphi method :** A judgemental method of forecasting, using a panel of experts, without announcing the panel members to other members of the panel.
- **Irregular variation :** It is the component of the time series, where the variation is totally unpredictable
- **Long term variation :** When variation occurs only during a long period say 2-3 or 10 years etc.
- **Moving average method :** When the prediction for future is based on most recent observations in time series, neglecting the old observations (of lesser importance)

- **Relative cyclic residue :** A measure of the cyclic variations, using percentage deviation from the trend point of the time series
- **Seasonal variation :** When the change occurs either during one year or even less.
- **Second degree equation :** A mathematical equation used to represent a parabolic curve. It is also called quadratic equation.
- **Secular trend :** When variation occurs over a long period of time.
- **Short term variation :** When variation occurs and is analysed only for few cycles of change.
- **Time series :** Collection of information of a phenomenon over a given regular interval, so as to identify the pattern of variation of the data.
- **Regression analysis :** A linear time series method of predicting future events based on least square curve fitting.

Relationships used

- Additive model

$$y = T_t + S_t + C_t + I_t$$

- Multiplicative model

$$y = T_t \times S_t \times C_t \times I_t$$

- Linear curve fitting

$$\hat{y} = a + bt$$

$$b = \frac{\Sigma yt - n\bar{y}\bar{t}}{\Sigma t^2 - n\bar{t}^2}$$

and $$a = \bar{y} - b\bar{t}$$

- Quadratic or parabolic curve fitting

$$\hat{y} = a + bt + ct^2$$

Equations

$$\Sigma y = na + c\Sigma t^2$$

$$\Sigma t^2 y = a\Sigma t^2 + c\Sigma t^4$$

and $$b = \frac{\Sigma ty}{\Sigma t^2}$$

- Percentage trend $= \frac{y}{\hat{y}} \times 100$
- Relative cyclic residue $= \frac{y - \hat{y}}{\hat{y}} \times 100$
- Moving average method of forecasting F $= \frac{1}{2}(S_1 + S_2)$ or $\frac{1}{n}(S_1 + S_2 + S_3 + ...)$ etc.
- Weighted average method $F = \frac{w_1 S_1 + w_2 S_2 + ...}{w_1 + w_2 + ...}$
- Exponential shooting method $F_n = \alpha y_{n-1} + (1 - \alpha)F_{n-1}$

- Forecast error $e = d_f - d_a$
- Standard deviation of estimation $Sd = \sqrt{\frac{\Sigma e^2}{(n-1)}}$

SOLVED PROBLEMS

Problem 6.1

From the actual sales given below, work out the forecasts for future months of the year using moving average/weighted moving average concept.

Months	Jan.	Feb.	March	April	May	June	July	Aug.	Sept.	Oct.	Nov.	Dec.
Sales (000's)	2.0	1.4	1.9	1.9	3.1	1.8	1.5	1.3	2.2	2.7	2.0	1.3

Solution :

Sl. No.	Months	Actual sales	Last month sales	Avg. of last 2 months	Weighted Avg. of last 2 months	Avg. of last 3 months	Weighted avg. for last 3 months
1.	Jan.	2.0	—	—	—	—	—
2.	Feb.	1.4	2.0	—	—	—	—
3.	March	1.9	1.4	$\left[\frac{1}{2}(1.4+2.0) = 1.70\right]$	$\left[\frac{1}{4}(3\times 1.4+2) = 1.64\right]$		—
4.	April	1.9	1.9	1.65	1.70	$\left[\frac{1}{3}(1.9+1.4+2.0) = 1.77\right]$	$\left[\frac{1}{10}(7\times 1.9+2\times 1.4+1\times 2.0) = 1.81\right]$
5.	May	3.1	1.9	1.90	1.90	1.73	1.85
6.	June	1.8	3.1	2.50	2.62	2.30	2.74
7.	July	1.5	1.8	2.45	2.32	2.27	2.07
8.	Aug.	1.3	1.5	1.65	1.62	2.13	1.72
9.	Sept.	2.2	1.3	1.40	1.38	1.53	1.39
10.	Oct.	2.7	2.2	1.75	1.84	1.67	1.31
11.	Nov.	2.0	2.7	2.45	2.50	2.07	2.40
12.	Dec.	1.3	2.0	2.35	2.28	2.30	2.16

Problem 6.2

For the data given in Problem 6.1, work out relevant future forecasts by exponential smoothing method using smoothing constant $\alpha = 0.7$.

Solution :

Exponential Smoothing Method

Months	*Actual Sales*	*Last Month Sales*	*Previous Forecast ($\alpha = 0.7$)*
1. Jan.	2.0	–	–
2. Feb.	1.4	2.0	3.0 (Judgement)
3. March	1.9	1.4	$(0.7 \times 2 + 0.3 \times 3) = 2.30$
4. April	1.9	1.9	$(0.7 \times 1.4 + 0.3 \times 2.30) = 1.67$
5. May	3.1	1.9	1.83
6. June	1.8	3.1	1.88
7. July	1.5	1.8	2.73
8. Aug.	1.3	1.5	2.08
9. Sept.	2.2	1.3	1.67
10. Oct.	2.7	2.2	1.41
11. Nov.	2.0	2.7	1.96
12. Dec.	1.3	2.0	2.48

α is selected based on judgement. Deviations can be calculated.

Mathematical methods by using concept of μ, and σ can be made use of.

Problem 6.3

From the given data, forecast the number of students expected to be admitted in 1992 and 1993.

Years :	1986	1987	1988	1989	1990	1991
Students :	15	17	18	20	21	22

Solution :

Years	*Data point (x)*	*Students (y)*	*(x)(y)*	x^2
1986	1	15	15	1
1987	2	17	34	4
1988	3	18	54	9
1989	4	20	80	16
1990	5	21	105	25
1991	6	22	132	36
	$\Sigma x = 21$	$\Sigma y = 113$	$\Sigma xy = 420$	$\Sigma x^2 = 91$

$$\therefore \quad \bar{x} = \frac{21}{6} = 3.5$$

$$\text{and} \quad \bar{y} = \frac{113}{6} = 18.82$$

$$b = \frac{\Sigma xy - n(\bar{x})(\bar{y})}{\Sigma x^2 - n(\Sigma \bar{x}^2)}$$

$$= \frac{420 - 6 \times 3.5 \times 18.82}{91 - 6 \times (3.5)^2} = 1.4$$

$$a = 18.82 - 1.4 \times 3.5 = 13.93$$

Best fitting straight line, therefore, would be.

$$y_e = 13.93 + 1.4x$$

Forecast for $x = 7$ is $y_7 = 23.73$ *i.e.*, for 1992

and for $x = 8$ $y_8 = 25.13$ *i.e.*, for 1993

Probem 6.4

The following data shows the exports of raw cotton and the value of imports of manufacturing goods into india for 7 years.

Crores of Rupees

Exports	42	44	58	55	89	98	60
Imports	56	49	53	58	67	76	58

Ascertain the regression equation of imports on exports and estimate the import when export in a particular year were to the value of Rs. 70 crores. [*C.A., May 1979*]

Solution :

Let us use the general straight line equation as Regression equation of y on x as $y = a + bx$.

Exports(x)	*Imports(y)*	x^2	*xy*
42	56	1,764	2,352
44	49	1,936	2,156
58	53	3,364	3,074
55	58	3,025	3,190
89	67	7,921	5,963
98	76	9,604	7,448
60	58	3,600	3,480
$\Sigma x = 446$	$\Sigma y = 417$	$\Sigma x^2 = 31{,}214$	$\Sigma xy = 27{,}663$

Here $b = \dfrac{\Sigma xy - n(\bar{x})(\bar{y})}{\Sigma x^2 - n(\bar{x})^2}$

$$= \frac{27{,}663 - 7\left(\frac{446}{7} \times \frac{417}{7}\right)}{31{,}214 - 7\left(\frac{446}{7}\right)^2} = 0.39$$

Calculating value of b and a,

$b = 0.39$ and $a = 34.72$

Hence, $y = 34.72 + 0.39\,x$

For $x = 70$, $y = 34.72 + 0.39 \times 70 = 62$

Hence, exports are Rs. 62 crores against the imports of Rs. 70 crores.

Problem 6.5

Use exponential smoothing technique to complete forecasts for the following series data under two situations, when smoothing constant is 0.3 and when smoothing constant is 0.7. Which forecast will you accept and why?

Period	1	2	3	4	5	6	7	8	9	10
Observation	27	30	32	31	28	27	30	33	33	31

[*C.A., May 1985*]

Solution :

For this problem, the basic exponential smoothing equation used is

$$F_t = \alpha x_1 + (1-\alpha) F_{t-1}$$

where F_t = forcast at time t (smoothed value)

α = smoothing constant $(0 < \alpha < 1)$

x_t = actual value of the observation at time t.

F_{t-1} = forecast (smoothed value) at time $t-1$.

With no value prior to period 1 given, the smoothed value of the observation for the first period will be presumed to be the actual value *i.e.*, 27. Now we can draw the tables for $\alpha = 0.3$ amd $\alpha = 0.7$ seperately.

Table For $\alpha_1 = 0.3$

Period	x_t	$e_t = (x_t - F_{t-1})$	$\alpha_1 e_t$	F_t	e_t^2
1	27	0	0.3×0 = 0	27	0
2	30	30 – 27 = 3.0	0.3 × 3 = 0.9	27.9	9.0
3	32	32 – 27.9 = 4.1	0.3 × 4.1 = 1.23	29.1	16.8
4	31	1.9	0.57	29.7	3.61
5	28	–1.7	–0.51	29.2	2.89
6	27	–2.2	–0.66	28.5	4.84
7	30	1.5	0.45	29.0	2.25
8	33	4.0	1.20	30.2	16.0
9	33	2.8	0.84	31.0	7.84
10	31	0	0	31.0	0
					$\Sigma e_t^2 = 63.23$

Table For $\alpha_2 = 0.7$

Period	x_t	$e_t = (x_t - F_{t-1})$	$\alpha_2 e_t$	F_t	e_t^2
1	27	0	0	27	0
2	30	3	2.1	29.1	9.0
3	32	2.9	2.03	31.13	8.41
4	31	–0.1	–0.07	31.0	0.01
5	28	–3.0	–2.1	28.9	9.0
6	27	–1.9	–1.33	27.6	3.61
7	30	2.4	1.68	29.3	5.76
8	33	3.7	2.59	31.9	13.69
9	33	1.1	0.77	32.7	1.21
10	31	–1.7	–1.19	31.5	2.89
					$\Sigma e_t^2 = 53.58$

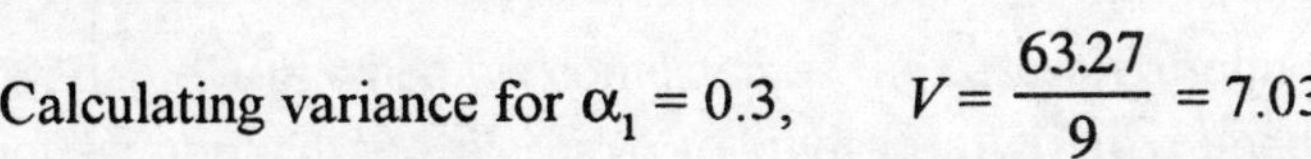

Calculating variance for $\alpha_1 = 0.3$, $V = \frac{63.27}{9} = 7.03$

Variance for $\alpha_2 = 0.7$, $V = \frac{53.58}{9} = 5.95$

Since variance for $\alpha = 0.7$ is less, we choose the forecast with the smoothing constant $(\alpha) = 0.7$.

Problem 6.6

Use method of least squares to determine sales for the year 1984. Following data is given :

Years	1978	1980	1981	1982	1983
Sales of regfrigerators	100	110	130	125	160

[*C.A., May* 1984]

Solution :

The straight line for the sales trend is assumed to be $y = a + bx$. We treat the base year as 1981.The calculations for various relations are as under :

Years (x)	*Value (y)*	x^2	*xy*
1978 (1)	100	1	100
1980 (2)	110	4	220
1981 (3)	130	9	390
1982 (4)	125	16	500
1983 (5)	160	25	800
$\Sigma x = 15$	$\Sigma y = 625$	$\Sigma x^2 = 55$	$\Sigma Xy = 2010$

Now, the relationships for calculating a and b are

$$\Sigma y = na + b\Sigma x$$

and $$\Sigma xy = a\Sigma x + b\Sigma x^2$$

Substituting the values from the table, we obtain

$$a = 96.5,\ b = 13.5$$

Hence, the sale trend is represented by the straight line

$$y = 96.5 + 13.5x$$

For 1984 forecast, we substitute value of $x = 6$ due to the base year selected as 1978.

$\therefore \quad y_{1984} = 96.5 + 13.5 \times 6 = 178$ refrigeration

Problem 6.7

Carry out a statistical analysis for the following data, using 95% confidence level for a normally distributed data around the mean.

Month	*Demand*	*Forecast*	*Month*	*Demand*	*Forecast*
1	100	—	7	110	98.9
2	95	100	8	115	102.2
3	85	98.5	9	105	106
4	95	94.5	10	100	105.7
5	100	94.7	11	95	104
6	105	96.3	12	85	101.3

Solution :

Error at any point of time

for month 2, $e = 95 - 100 = -5.$

for month 6, $e = 105 - 106 = -1.$

Working out e_t^2 for all the values,

$e_2 = -5$, $e_3 = +13.5$; $e_4 = -0.5$; $e_5 = -5.3$; $e_6 = 8.7$; $e_7 = 11.1$; $e_8 = 12.8$; $e_9 = -1$; $e_{10} = -5.7$; $e_{11} = 9$; $e_{12} = -16.3$ and hence $\Sigma e_t^2 = e_1^2 + e_2^2 + ... = 978.51$

Standard deviation for the forecasting system

$$\text{Sd} = \sqrt{\frac{\Sigma e_t^2}{n-1}} = \sqrt{\frac{978.51}{11-1}} = 9.89 \text{ as there are only 11 forecast values given}$$

For a stable process, when we are dealing with the normally distributed data with 95% confidence level, we operate the control chart at ±2 standard deviations around the mean of zero.

If we plot the errors on the control chart, we can observe that the values of forecast are within ±2σ limits and hence process is under control *i.e.*, demand pattern has not changed much.

Problem 6.8

Fit a trend line from the following data by using semi-average method

Year :	1973	1974	1975	1976	1977	1978
Profits (in '000 Rs.) :	100	120	140	150	130	20

[Andhra Pradesh University, B. Com. April 1982]

Solution :

For using semi-average method, we divide the data into two equal parts with reference to the time.

Year	*Profit (Rs.'000)*	*Semi Average*
1973	100	
1974	120	$\frac{360}{3} = 120$
1975	140	
1976	150	
1977	130	$\frac{480}{3} = 160$
1978	200	

Now plotting these semi-averages 120 and 160 against mid years of the corresponding period *i.e.* 120 for 1974 and 160 for 1977

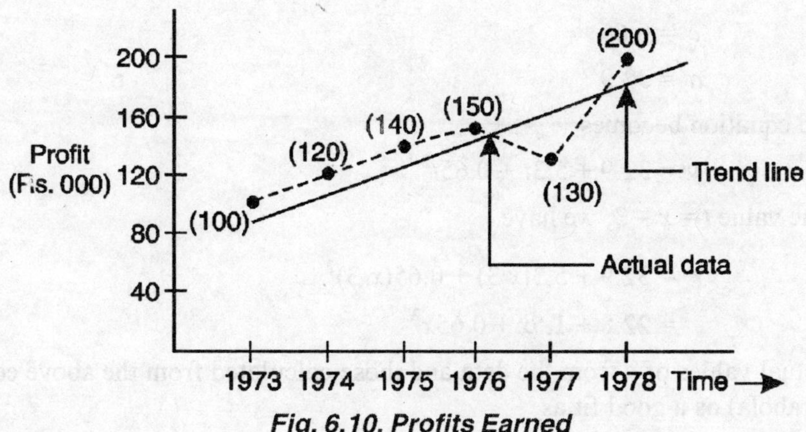

Fig. 6.10. Profits Earned

Problem 6.9

Fit an equation of the form $y = a + bx + cx^2$ to the data given below

x	:	1	2	3	4	5
y	:	25	28	33	39	46

[*Delhi Universtiy B.A. (Eco. Hons) 1982*]

Solution :

In this case, the value data sets are 5 and hence we use

$t = x - 3$

Then value can be plotted in the table such that $y = a + bt + ct^2$

where $t = x - 3$

x	y	$t = x - 3$	t^2	t^3	t^4	ty	t^2y
1	25	–2	4	–8	16	–50	100
2	28	–1	1	–1	1	–28	28
3	33	0	0	0	0	0	0
4	39	1	1	1	1	39	39
5	46	2	4	8	16	92	184
	$\Sigma y = 171$	$\Sigma t = 0$	$\Sigma t^2 = 10$	$\Sigma t^3 = 0$	$\Sigma t^4 = 34$	$\Sigma ty = 53$	$\Sigma t^2y = 351$

Using normal equations for solving for a, b and c

$$\Sigma y = na + b\Sigma t + c\Sigma t^2$$

$$\Sigma ty = a\Sigma t + b\Sigma t^2 + c\Sigma t^3$$

$$\Sigma t^2 y = a\Sigma t^2 + b\Sigma t^3 + c\Sigma t^4$$

substituting the values from the above table, we obtain

$$5a + 10c = 171 \quad \ldots(i)$$

$$10b = 53 \quad \ldots(ii)$$

and $$10a + 34c = 351 \quad \ldots(iii)$$

Solving (*i*) (*ii*) and (*iii*), we get

$$b = 5.3$$

$c = 0.65$

and $a = 32.9$

Thus the trend equation becomes

$$y = 32.9 + 5.3t + 0.65t^2$$

substituting the value $t = x - 3$, we have

$$\hat{y} = 32.9 + 5.3(x.3) + 0.65(x\text{-}3)^2$$

$$= 22.8 + 1.5x + 0.65x^2$$

By plotting actual values of y from the data and those calculated from the above equations, we find the curve (parabola) as a good fit as

$\hat{y}$ (for $x = 1$) $= 34.95 \simeq 25$

$\hat{y}$ (for $x = 2$) $= 28.4 \simeq 28$

$\hat{y}$ (for $x = 3$) $= 33.15 \simeq 33$

$\hat{y}$ (for $x = 4$) $= 39.2 \simeq 39$

and $\hat{y}$ (for $x = 5$) $= 45.55 \simeq 46$

Problem 6.10

On the basis of quarterly sales (in Rs. lakhs) of a certain commodity for the years 1961-65, the following calculations were made.

Trend $y = 25.0 + 0.6t$ **with origin at 1st quarter of 1961.**

where t **= time units (one quarter) and**

y **= quarterly sales (Rs. lakhs)**

Seasonal variations :

Quarter	1st	2nd	3rd	4th
Seasonal index	90	95	110	105

Estimate the quarterly sales for the year 1962 (use multiplicative model)

[*ICWA (Final), July 1972 (O.S.)*]

Solution :

Since first quarter of 1961 is origin

$t = 0$ for the first quarter

$t = 1$ for the 2nd quarter

$t = 2$ for the 3rd quarter

and $t = 3$ for the 4th quarter

Hence for 1962,

$t = 4$ for the first quarter

$t = 5$ for the 2nd quarter

$t = 6$ for the 3rd quarter

$t = 7$ for the 4th quarter

using multiplicative model

$$y = T_t \times S_t \times C_t \times I_t$$

Estimations for 1962 are

for 1st quarter $y = 25 + 0.6 \times 4 \quad = 27.4$

for 2nd quarter $y = 25 + 0.6 \times 5 \quad = 28.0$

for 3rd quarter $y = 25 + 0.6 \times 5 \quad = 28.6$

for 4th quarter $y = 25 + 0.6 \times 7 \quad = 29.2$

When seasonal indices are given, the actual estimated sales would be

for 1st quarter, sales $= 27.4 \times 0.9 = 24.66$

for 2nd quarter, sales $= 28.0 \times 0.95 = 26.60$

for 3rd quarter, sales $= 28.6 \times 1.10 = 31.46$

and for 4th quarter, sales $= 29.2 \times 1.05 = 30.66$

All these sales values are in Rs. lakhs.

PRACTICE PROBLEMS

6.11 Past data about the requirement of a material for manufacturing shop are given as under :

Months	*Requirement (Nos.)*
July 94	784
Aug. 94	863
Sept. 94	940
Oct. 94	960
Nov. 94	1030
Dec. 94	1150

(*a*) Using 3 months averages, forecast the demands for Jan., Feb., March and April 95.

(*b*) Compute the weighted 3 months average for Jan. 95 assuring weights as 0.4 for latest months, 0.35 and 0.25 for earlier months respectively.

6.12 From the data given in Problem 5.8., compute the exponential smoothing forecast for the month of Jan. 95, using smoothing factor as 0.7.

6.13 Indian Exports have experienced the following demand for its item A, during previous year. Assuming that straight line relationship fits in the data of demand, work out the demand for 2000.

Years	*No. of items*
1990	30
1991	32
1992	33
1993	35
1994	38
1995	41
1996	43
1997	46
1998	48
1999	52

6.14 Following table indicates number of rooms occupied in a 5-star Hotel during the last 4 years. Calculate the demand of rooms for the next coming year 2000.

Years	*Jan. to March*	*April to June*	*July to Sept.*	*Oct. to Dec.*
1996	2,050	2,462	2,127	1,938
1997	2,365	2,754	2,265	1,860
1998	2,560	2,963	2,150	2,055
1999	2,780	3,355	2,560	2,365

6.15 The past data for a production shop are given below :

Months	*Production hours*
April	680
May	540
June	560
July	610
August	650
September	740
October	850
November	900
December	970

(*i*) Compute the forecast of production load of the shop, using a 3-months average for forecasting the next months load.

(*ii*) Compute a three month weightage average for Jan., Feb., and March when the weightages are 3, 2 and 1 for the last and prior two consecutive months respectively.

6.16 From the data given in problem 5.12, compute an exponential smoothing forecast for the month of January, using Smoothing constant $\alpha = 0.4$ and compare this forecast with the figures obtained in the previous problem using moving average and weighted moving average criteria.

6.17 Workout the demands of production load on production shop with the data givne in problem 5.12. Considering the values of $\alpha = 0.3$ and $\alpha = 0.4$. How you find the forecasts actually comparing with the atual demand. Draw the exponential smoothing forecast curve with actual demand and comment.

6.18 In an office, the demand of work varies with the amount of business received in a business documentation centre. The number of typists required to meet the workload for the last 14 days is given in the table below.

Days	*Number of girl typists*	*Days*	*Number of girl typists*
1	10	8	10
2	11	9	12
3	12	10	11
4	12	11	14
5	13	12	15
6	13	13	16
7	+14	14	16

Using the simple exponential smoothing technique for forecasting future demands, comment on the forecasts against the actual deamand, if the smoothing constants used by the consultant are 0.3, 0.4 or 0.5.

6.19 The export level of a big export house is given below in terms of millions of rupees.

Years	*Export worth (Rs. millions)*
1986	13
1987	20
1988	19
1989	25
1990	28
1991	30
1992	32
1993	32
1994	33
1995	34
1996	35
1997	38
1998	43
1999	45

If the data indicate that straight line gives the best fit, compute the forecast for 2000 and 2001.

6.20 Using a 2-year cycle, work out the trend values for the following data :

Years :	1993	1994	1995	1996	1997	1998	1999
Sales (in Rs. 000) :	350	410	435	465	470	493	515

6.21 Explain the concept of linear regression and obtain lines of regression for the following data :

X :	1	2	3	4	5	6	7
Y :	9	3	10	11	11	13	14

Do these lines intersect at means X, Y ? [*C.A., Nov.,* 1983]

6.22 The experience of machine operators and their performance rating is given below :

Operator :	1	2	3	4	5
Experience (x) :	6	2	10	4	8
Performance rating (y) :	45	55	25	40	35

Calculate the regression line of performance rating (y) on experience (x). [*C.A., Nov.,* 1980]

6.23 This following table gives the ages and blood pressure of 10 women.

Age (*X*) :	56	42	36	47	42	49	60	72	63	55
BP (*Y*) :	147	125	118	128	145	140	155	160	149	150

(*i*) Find the correlation coefficient between X and Y.

given, r = correlation coefficient $= \dfrac{\Sigma xy}{\sqrt{\Sigma x^2 \Sigma y^2}}$

(*ii*) Determine the least square regression equation of y on x.

(*iii*) Evaluate the flood pressure of a women whose age is 45 years.

6.24 From the following data, calculate trend values by the method of least squares

Years :	1976	1977	1978	1979	1980	1981	1982	1983
No. of houses :	56	55	51	47	42	38	35	32

[*Rajasthan University, M.Com., 1981*]

6.25 Two lines of regression are given as follows :

$$6x + 10y - 119 = 0$$

$$-30x + 45y + 180 = 0$$

The variance of y is known to be 4 (*i.e.* $V_y = 4$). Find and $x = X - \bar{X}$ and $y = Y - \bar{Y}$

(*i*) The mean values of x and y.

(*ii*) The coefficient of correlation between x and y

(*iii*) The variance of $x(V_x)$ [*Rohtak University, M.B.A.*, 1982]

6.26 The table given below indicate the number of vehicles sold in a territory during last 5 years and the sale of tyres sold during the same period.

Years	***Vehicle sold***	***Types sold***
1995	500	1150
1996	550	1270
1997	700	1400
1998	700	1540
1999	730	1630

Find the regression equations to estimate the sale of tyres. Estimate the sale of tyres against the vehicle sale of 820.

6.27 The following data relate to the advertisement expenditure and sales :

	Ad. Expenditure (x) (*Rs. lakhs*)	*Sales (y)* (*Rs. crores*)
Arithmetic mean	20	90
Standard deviation	4	12
Correlation coefficient	+0.9	

(*i*) Calculate the two regression equations.

(*ii*) Evaluate the likely sales when advertisement expenditure is Rs. 30 lakhs.

(*iii*) What should be the likely Ad. expenditure for attaining sales of Rs. 120 crores?

[*Andhra University, M.Com.*, 1988]

6.28 While calculating the coefficient of correlation between two variables X and Y, the following results were obtained.

The number of observations $N = 25$, $\Sigma X = 125$, $\Sigma Y = 100$, $\Sigma X^2 = 650$ and $\Sigma Y^2 = 460$ and $\Sigma XY = 508$. It was however, later discovered at the time of checking that two pairs of observations (X, Y) were copied (6, 14) and (8, 6), while the values were (8, 12) and (6, 8) respectively. Determine the correct value of coefficient of correlation. Hence find the correct equations of the two lines of regression. [*ICWA, June* 1978]

6.29 A university had decided to use exponential smoothing technique ($\alpha = 0.35$) to forecast its intake level of students to organise various facilities accordingly. The actual data has been indicated in the table giveb below.

Years	*Actual Enrollment (in thousand)*	*Presumed Forecast*	*Forecast Error*	*Correlation (in 000)*	*New Forecast (in 000)*
1994	10.2	8.3	0.4	0.2	8.5
1995	11.4				
1996	12.3				
1997	13.0				
1998	13.4				
1999					

Use the above data to forecast the intake of students for 1998 and 1999. Also compute the forecast if the smoothing constant adopted is changed to 0.6.

6.30 How far does time series help in forecasting ?

If the average production level in a mill is given as follows :

Years	*Production in Million Tonnes*
1991	435
1992	415
1993	450
1994	463
1995	470
1996	482
1997	475
1998	490
1999	500

Fit a straight line trend and establish the forecast of production for the year 2000 and 2001.

6.31 The consumption of milk in a new colony is going up every quarter as noticed for the last four years. The consumption pattern in tabulated below :

Years Demand of milk in litres in four quarters

	I	*II*	*III*	*IV*
1996	1,250	1,260	1,270	1,280
1997	1,310	1,335	1,350	1,350
1998	1,370	1,395	1,415	1,500
1999	1,670	1,730	1,780	1,830

Can you forecast demand for the four quarters of the year 2000?

❖❖❖

CHAPTER 7

INTERPOLATION AND EXTRAPOLATION

7.1 INTRODUCTION

When the population is large, its study for all its aspects is difficult in terms of time consumption and the cost of carrying out such a study. Hence we normally resort to a large time gap for such continuous studies. Let us take the example of census for National Population. We normally carry out census every ten years say 1971, 1981, 1991 and 2001 etc. When we tabulate this data of population (say y) for the periods 1971, 1981, 1991, 2001 etc. (say , x), we can establish a relationship as $y = f(x)$ *i.e.* the population can be correlated to a year in which this is required to be known. But due to long time periods.'we don't exactly know the population level at any specified period say 1975, 1986 etc. But under certain assumptions it can be worked out based on the two extreme values of the period. The technique to work out such results for any period inside a given range is called interpolation.

Interpolation is a useful technique of estimation of the values of the dependent variable for any corresponding value of the independent variable. Extrapolation is similarly a technique of estimating dependent variable beyond the range of independent variable.

Hence interpolation can be defined as the technique of estimating the value of the dependent variable for any intermediatory value of the independent variable.

Similarly Extrapolation is defined as the technique of obtaining most likely value (predicted) for a certain value of the dependent variable from a given data of independent variable, outside the range of the available data.

Basically both the techniques *i.e.* inter polation as well as extra polation have the same principle of calculations under similar assumptions. Thus from a given set of data 1971-1981, for value in 1976, we use interpolation and for 1985, we use extrapolation.

The values of the independent variable x are termed as **arguments** whereas the corresponding values of the dependent variable y are known as **entries.**

7.2 ASSUMPTIONS

Before embarking on to the methods of calculation for polation inter or extrapolation; we have to set the rules of the game *i.e.* listing out various assumptions for such trends. Following are the assumptions made for such calculations

(a) There are no sudden peaks or falls in the values of the dependent variable for the period under study. The conditions for such variables should be normal and stable and no untoward or abnormal situation should arise during the study period. Random fluctuations should normally be avoided such as a period of national calamity, wars, political upheaval, abnormal labour strikes or sudden economical boom or recession. These conditions will not be taken into account during the study, because the effect of such abnormality will not be known for their levels of change.

This means that the relationship, between the independent and dependent variable should be generally a smooth curve, which is also continuous. To express this statement in mathematical terms, we can say that the given data can be represented by a polynomial of certain degree, which is determined by the following **Fundamental Theorem of Algebra.**

"One and only one polynomial curve of degree less than or equal to n passes through a given set of $n+1$ distinct points".

Therefore if we are having 4 set of entries (y), then y can be represented by a polynomial curve of third degree, such as $y = a + bx + cx^2 + dx^3$. In the similar manner, if the number of entries is only 3, the value of y can be expressed in the form of a curve of second degree polynomial as $y = a + b + cx^2$.

Thus we can summarise it as follows :

All the formulae of interpolation are based on the fundamental assumption that the given data can be expressed as a polynomial function of certain degree with fair degree of accuracy.

(b) The second assumption followed for this techniques is that **in the absence of the evidence to the contrary, there is regularity in the fluctuations so that the rate of change in the given data is uniform.** It brings home the fact that the rate of change or growth during the period under study has been uniform.

Thus for such studies to be of some value, there have to be sufficient data *i.e.* entries available for the trend of change to be studied with a high level of accuracy. The sufficiency of data in the form of arguments as well as entries will ensure (to a fair degree of accuracy) that the interpolated or extra polated values are reliable for their effective use.

7.3 ACCURACY OF ESTIMATES

Since the interpolation and extrapolation techniques are based on the assumptions enumerated in the preceding paragraph, to establish the accuracy of estimates obtained from such technique will depend on as to how much these assumptions are valid. If assumptions do not hold good, their usage will obviously result in wrong predictions. These techniques are used for finding out a missing value (interpolation) or forecasting a future value (extrapolation) in any area of life or in any discipline such as economics, social science, population study, Agricultural outputs etc. The accuracy of future prices, business growth for likely profits etc. can be dependent on how much the past data follows the rate of growth assumption.

In order to achieve worthwhile results from interpolation or extrapolation, some basic assumptions are to be adopted. These assumptions, basically, are the uniform pattern of increase or decrease of the values of the variables. Thus it is important that the relationship of variables is expressable as a polynomial function.

In case we use these techniques for sampling, then it becomes all the more important for the data to be accurate and reliable so that filled gaps may not vary widely from anticipated estimates. For the purpose of accuracy, we have to have a knowledge of possible fluctuations and nature of courses of events that are taking place around the phenomenon under study.

7.4. METHODS OF INTERPOLATION / EXTRAPOLATION (FINITE DIFFERENCES)

Following two methods can be adopted for the purpose of interpolation and extrapolation

(a) Graphical Method.

(b) Algebraic Method.

Graphical Method

This method is used by drawing the data as a graph since there are only two variables involved, we generally plot the independent variable along x-axis and the dependent variable along the y-axis. After obtaining various points based on data set, we draw a smooth free hand curve joining all these points. The curve now will represent the general trend of variation relationship of the two variables. From this curve various values desired (interpolation) for a specific value of a variable can be read. This aspect has since been discussed in chapter 6 under Time series Analysis.

Interpolation and extrapolation can be easily obtained either through the graphical method or else through the algebraic method. Graphical method produces approximate results, whereas the algebraic method is more specific or accurate, within the constraint limits.

Similarly, the values of x or y (corresponding) can be obtained by extending the curve for the future period *i.e.* beyond the period for which the data set have been obtained. This would become the case of extrapolation and future period estimates (forecasts) can thus be obtained after establishing the growth curve in the logical smooth extension manner.

Graphical method is useful when the series of data are correlated and there exists a historical periodical or cycle fluctuation. A sample example is given in figure 7.1 below

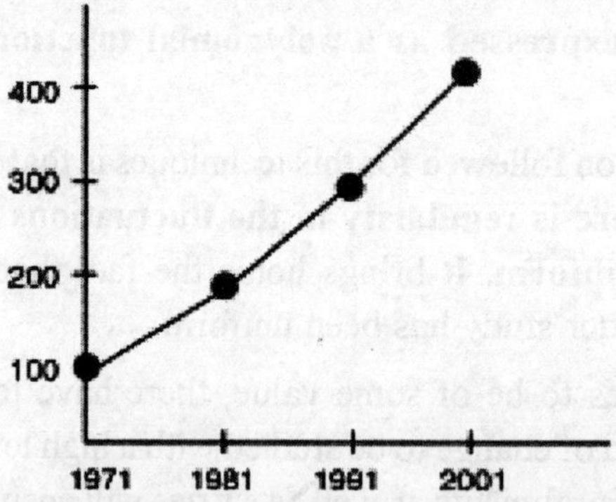

Fig 7.1 Data with connected Curve

Algebraic Method

We have already discussed some useful methods under forecasting and Time Series Analysis. These methods are followed under the given assumptions discussed in para 7.2 above. These methods are used extensively for interpolation or extrapolation of data for common usage in daily life. Now we shall be discussing some additional methods under specific trends.

1. Methods of Parabolic Curve fitting

Since the relationship of dependent and independent variable expressed as

$$y = f(x)$$

can be represented through fitting a polynomial curve to a given set of observations, provided the values of arguments (x) are at equal intervals. The basis of the method has already beam spelled out under the Fundamental Theorem of Algebra, (given below again)

"One and only one polynomial curve of degree less than or equal to n passes through a given set of $\eta + 1$ distinct points".

Thus any polynomial function of nth degree can be represented by

$$y = f(x) = ax^n + bx^{n-1} + cx^{n-3} + \dots\dots$$

where a, b, c etc. are $(n+1)$ constants, whose values can be obtained from $(n+1)$ equations by substituting the given values of x and y in the data form. By solving these $(n+1)$ equations, we obtain the values of constants a, b, c etc. to establish the trend of variation of the curve and then any value of y can be obtained by using required value of x in the above equation.

Solutions to these equations are tedious, if the degree of the relationship is large.

2. Methods of Finite Differences

The calculus of finite differences is quite convenient tool for interpolating figures when the arguments are of equal intervals. Let us define the operators Δ and E, before using these in the technique.

Let us have the equidistant values of the independent variable x as a, $a+h$, $a+2h$, ...$a+nh$, where a is known as the initial argument and h as the common interval of differences. Let us assume the corresponding values of y be.

$f(a), f(a+h), f(a+2h) \dots\dots\dots f(a+nh)$

These values are termed as entries.

Operator Δ: the differential operator, can be defined as

$$\Delta f(x) = f(x+h) - f(x)$$

where $\quad x = a, a+h, a+2h, \dots\dots$ etc

By using the values of x from above

$$\Delta f(a) = f(a+h) - f(a)$$

$$\Delta f(a+h) = f(a + h + h) - f(a+h)$$

and $\quad \Delta f(a+2h) = f(a+3h) - f(a+2h)$ and so on.

These differences given above are known as the first degree differences. By operating Δ on the first order differences, we get the second order differences, (denoted by Δ^2),

$$\Delta f(a) = \Delta[\Delta f(a)] = \Delta\,[f(a + h) - f(a)]$$

$$= \Delta^2 f(a + h) - \Delta\,f(a)$$

$$= [f(a + 2h) - f(a + h)] - [f(a + h) - f(a)]$$

$$= [f(a + 2h) - 2f(a + h)] - f(a)$$

and so on we can, similarly, obtain higher order differences also in the similar manner. These differences can be expressed in the table known as the table of Finite Forward Differences.

Methods of finite differences for interpolation is useful when the arguments are of equal interval. Through a systematic approach, the successive parameters can be progressed and appropriate desired values of dependent variable obtained.

TABLE 7.1. Table of Finite Forward Differences

Argument x	Entry $y = f(x)$	First differences $\Delta f(x)$	Second differences $\Delta^2 f(x)$
a	$f(a)$		
		$f(a+h) - f(a) = \Delta f(a)$	
$a + h$	$f(a + h)$		$\Delta f(a + h) - \Delta f(a) = \Delta^2 f(a)$
		$f(a+2h) - f(a + h) = \Delta f(a + h)$	
$a + 2h$	$f(a + 2h)$		$\Delta f(a + 2h) - \Delta f(a + h) = \Delta^2 f(a + h)$
		$f(a + 3h) - f(a + 2h) = \Delta f(a + 2h)$	
$a + 3h$	$f(a + 3h)$		$\Delta f(a+3h) - \Delta f(a + 2h) = \Delta^2 f(a + 2h)$
		$f(a + 4h) - f(a+3h) = \Delta f(a + 3h)$	
$a + 4h$	$f(a + 4h)$		

In the above table, $f(a)$ is known as the first entry in the table of finite differences and $\Delta f(a)$, $\Delta f(a + h)$, $\Delta f(a+2h)$........etc are known as the leading finite differences, Due to the diagonal form of the table, it is also called a table of Diagonal Differences.

The Method of finite differences can be operated through the concept of E and Δ operators. Both the operators can be used successfully for equal interval interpolation.

Operator ∇ : This operator ∇ is called by the name as Nebla of Greek alphabet and denotes the backward differences as follows.

$$\nabla f(x + h) = f(x + h) - f(x) = \Delta f(x)$$

Thus we can see that backward difference of $f(x + h)$ is the same as the forward difference of $f(x)$.

The backward differences table can be written as follows:

TABLE 7.2. Table of Backward Differences

Argument	Entry $y = f(x)$	First differences $\nabla f(x)$	Second differences $\nabla^2 f(x)$
a	$f(a)$		
		$f(a + h) - f(a) = \nabla f(a + h)$	
$a + h$	$f(a + h)$		$\nabla f(a + 2h) - \nabla f(a + h) = \nabla^2 f(a + 2h)$
		$f(a + 2h) - \nabla f(a+h) = \nabla f(a + 2h)$	
$a + 2h$	$f(a + 2h)$		$\nabla f(a + 3h) - \nabla f(a + 2h) = \nabla^2 f(a + 3h)$
		$f(a+ 3h) - f(a+ 2h) = \nabla f(a + 3h)$	
$a + 3h$	$f(a + 3h)$		$\nabla f(a + 4h) - \nabla f(a + 3h) = \nabla^2 f(a + 4h)$
		$f(a + 4h) - f(a + 3h) = \nabla f(a + 4h)$	
$a + 4h$	$f(a + 4h)$		

Operator E :

In case of the arguments at equal interval h, the operator E is defined as $E f(x) = f(x + h)$ *i.e.* the operator E is equivalent to increasing the argument by the interval of differencing.

Thus we can write other relationships of higher differences as

$$E^2 f(x) = E[Ef(x)] = E[f(x + h)] = [f(x + 2h)]$$

and
$$E^3 f(x) = E[E^2 f(x)] = f(x+3h)$$

and so on

In general, we can write,

$$E^n f(x) = f(x + nh)$$

where 'h' is the interval of differencing

In particular

$$Ef(0) = f(0+1) = f(1)$$
$$E^2 f(0) = f(2) \text{ and so on for interval of differencing} = 1$$

Relation between E and Δ.

Since
$$\Delta f(x) = f(x+h) - f(x)$$
$$= E\,f(x) - f(x)$$

$\therefore$
$$\Delta f(x) = (E-1)f(x)$$

or
$$\Delta = (E-1)$$

or
$$E = 1 + \Delta$$

3. Fundamental Theorem of Finite Differences

If $f(x)$ is a polynomial of nth degree in x, *i.e.*

if
$$f(x) = a_0 x^n + a_1 x^{n-1} + \ldots\ldots + a_n$$

then
$$\Delta^n f(x) = a_0(n!) = \text{constant}$$

and
$$\Delta^r f(x) = 0 \text{ if } r > n$$

Thus, the nth order differences of a polynomial of nth degree is constant and higher order differences are all zero.

4. Newton's Forward Differences Formula

Newton's formula of forward differences enables us to determine the polynomial form of the function $f(x)$ and hence estimate its value from any given value of x.

This formula (Newton's formula) is expressed as follows,

$$f(x) = f(a) + u\Delta f(a) + \frac{u(u-1)}{2!}\Delta^2 f(a) + \frac{u(u-1)(u-2)}{3!}\Delta^3 f(a) + \ldots\ldots$$

Where x is the period of interpolation, a its first argument in the differences table and

$$u = \frac{\text{Period of interpolation} - \text{Period of origin}}{\text{Interval of differencing}}$$

i.e.
$$u = \left(\frac{x-a}{h}\right)$$

Since the formula follows polynomial form, the last term of the formula depends on the number of entries. Thus for a $(n+1)$ number of entries, $f(x)$ can be expressed as a polynomial of nth degree and there will be terms only upto $\Delta^n f(x)$ as the remaining terms will be zeros as per fundamental theorem of finite differences.

Newton's formula given in this paragraph is commonly known as **Newton - Gregory Formula** for forward Interpolation.

5. Newton's Backward Differences Formula

This relationship is based on the backward differences ∇ and is useful, if the estimated value lies towards the end of the difference table. Thus

The Scientist Newton advocated a method of forward differences formula to obtain the polynomial expression for the mathematical function of the dependent variable in terms of independent variable. This formula is also known as Newton-Gregory Formula for forward differences. Formula for backward differences ius also very similar.

$$f(x) = f(a+nh) + u\Delta f(a+nh) + \frac{u(u-1)}{2!}\nabla^2 f(a+nh)$$

$$+\frac{u(u-1)(u-2)}{3!}\nabla^3 f(a+nh) + \ldots\ldots$$

where $(a + nh)$ is the last argument in the differences table and ∇, ∇^2, ... etc are the leading backward differences of the last entry and

$$u = \frac{x-(a+nh)}{h}$$

6. Binomial Expansion Method for Interpolating Missing Values.

Yet another effective method for interpolation is called Binomial expansion method, through which missing values in the intermediate range can be easily calculated algebraically.

In case, we have data of a nature that certain values of the dependent variables are missing from the data set, while the independent variable occurs at regular interval, then the missing values need be interpolated from the data based on the general trend of the variation. These missing values can be interpolated easily by using the concept of finite differences, in the following manner.

(i) Suppose we have $(n + 1)$ equidistant arguments, but the entry to any one of them is missing. In this case, we can say that we have n entries and data can be expressed as a polynomial of $(n + 1)$ degrees. *i.e.* $y = f(x)$ will be of $(n - 1)$ degrees and by fundamental theorem of finite differences, the nth and higher order differences will be zero. This can be expressed mathematically as

$$\Delta^{n-1} f(x) = \text{constant}$$

and $$\Delta^n f(x) = 0, \text{ for } x > n$$

If we take $$x = a, \text{ (the first argument)}$$

$$\Delta^n f(x) = 0$$

and $$(E-1)^n f(a) = 0$$

Expanding it binomially

$$[E^n - {}^nC_1 E^{-2} + {}^nC^2 E_{n-2} + \ldots\ldots + (-1)^n]\, f(a) = 0$$

or $$E_n f(a) - {}_nC_1 E^{n-1} f(a) + {}^nC_2 E^{n-2} f(a) + \ldots\ldots (-1)^n f(a) = 0$$

or $$f(a+nh) - {}^nC_1 f[a+(n-1)h] + \ldots\ldots (-1)^n f(a) = 0$$

We can interpolate the missing value from this equation.

(*ii*) If we are given $(n + 2)$ equidistant arguments and two entries are missing, as before, with n entries, we can obtain.

$$\Delta^n f(x) = 0 \text{ for } x > n$$

since we have two entries missing, we can get these by using following equations (taking $x = a$ and $x = a + h$)

$$\Delta^n f(a) = 0 \text{ and } \Delta^n f(a+h) = 0$$

or $$(E-1)^n f(a) = 0 \text{ and } (E-1)^n f(a+h) = 0$$

we can now expand these equations binomially and obtain the two missing values.

7.5 INTERPOLATION WITH ARGUMENTS AT UNEQUAL INTERVALS

So far, we have discussed the methods of interpolation when the values of the independent variable are at equal intervals. Hence the Newton's Difference Formula and Binomial Expansion Method can be used only for cases where entries corresponding to the equidistant values of arguments are available. But when we come across the cases of arguments at unequal intervals, these methods cannot be applied and we have to find an alternative method for solving such problems. These special techniques are as follows .

(*a*) Newton's Divided Difference Formula

(*b*) Lagrange's Formula

1. Newton's Divided Difference Formula

Before we discuss the above method, we first, have to understand the concept of Divided Difference. It is different from Formula for Differences, because in earlier cases, we used the differences between successive units, whereas now, we have to take into account the changes in the values of the arguments also, Thus the differences defined as taking into consideration the changes in the values of the arguments are known as Divided Differences.

Newton also suggested a method for estmiating the dependent variable through Divided difference concept. In this case, the changes in the values of arguements also have to be taken into account.

We can take the values of the arguments as a_0, a_1, a_2.....etc. which are not necessarily equidistant.

The corresponding values of the entries can, be taken as

$$f(a_0), f(a_1), f(a_2)...... \text{ etc}$$

Then the first order divided differences of $f(x)$ for the arguments a_0 and a_1 can be denoted and defined as follows

$$f(a_0, a_1) = \text{Divided differences of } y\text{'s with reference to two arguments } a_0 \text{ and } a_1$$

$$= \frac{f(a_1) - f(a_0)}{(a_1 - a_0)}$$

$$= \underset{a_1}{\triangle} f(a_0)$$

This is the ordinary difference divided by the corresponding difference between the arguments.

In the tabular form, we can represent the divided differences as follows.

Table 7.2 Table of Divided Differences

x	$f(x)$	$f(a_0, a_1)$	$f(a_0, a_1, a_2)$	$f(a_0, a_1, a_2, a_3)$
a_0	$f(a_0)$			
		$\frac{f(a_1)-f(a_0)}{(a_1-a_0)} = \triangle f(a_0)$		
a_1	$f(a_1)$		$\frac{\triangle f(a_1)-\triangle f(a_0)}{(a_2-a_0)} = \triangle^2 f(a_0)$	
		$\frac{f(a_2)-f(a_1)}{(a_2-a_1)} = \triangle f(a_1)$		$\frac{\triangle^2 f(a_1)-\triangle^2 f(a_0)}{(a_3-a_0)} = \triangle^3 f(a_0)$
a_2	$f(a_2)$		$\frac{\triangle f(a_2)-\triangle f(a_2)}{(a_3-a_1)} = \triangle^2 f(a_1)$	
		$\frac{f(a_3)-f(a_2)}{(a_3-a_2)} = \triangle f(a_2)$		
a_3	$f(a_3)$			

It can be drawn out that if $f(x)$ is a polynomial of the nth degree, then n^{th} order divided differences of $f(x)$ are constant and higher order differences as zeros.

Mathematically expressing,

$$\triangle^n f(x) = \text{constant}$$

$$\triangle^r f(x) = 0 \qquad \text{for } r > n$$

Now, we can write the Newtons Divided Difference Formula. If $f(a_0), f(a_1), f(a_2)......f(a_n)$ are $(n + 1)$ entries corresponding to the arguments $a_0, a_1, ... a_n$, when arguments are not necessarily equispaced, then Newton's Divided Difference Formula is given as

$$f(x) = f(a_0) + (x-a_0) \triangle f(a_0) + (x-a_0)(x-a_1) \triangle^2 f(a_0) + (x-a_0)(x-a_1)(x-a_2) \triangle^2 f(a_0) + ...$$
$$.... + (x-a_0)(x-a_1) .... (x-a_{n-1}) \triangle^n f(a_0)$$

Though it is most appropriate for the arguments of non-equal intervals, it can be used for equispaced arguments cases also.

2. Lagrange's Formula

It is another formula to be need in case of non-equispaced arguments. This was devised by Lagrange and hence is known after his name.

If $a_0, a_1, a_2, ... a_n$ are $(n+1)$ arguments not necessarily of equal intervals, and their corresponding entries are $f(a_0), f(a_1), f(a_2) .... f(a_n)$ etc. then the Lagrange's form of function $f(x)$ is given by

$$f(x) = \frac{(x-a)(x-a_2)......(x-a_n)}{(a_o-a_1)(a_0-a_2)......(a_0-a_n)} f(a_0) + \frac{(x-a_0)(x-a_2)......(x-a_n)}{(a_1-a_0)(a_1-a_2)......(a_1-a_n)} f(a_1)$$

$$+ ...... + \frac{(x-a_0)(x-a_1)......(x-a_{n-1})}{(a_n-a_0)(a_n-a_1)......(a_n-a_{n-1})}$$

Lagrange's Method of Divided differences is utilised when the arguments are non-equispaced. As a special case, Inverse Interpolation formula can be used for working out the corresponding value of the independent variable with reference to a given value of the dependent variable.

3. Inverse Interpolation

As a special case, if we have the values of a given set of x and $y = f(x)$ and we want to find the value of x for a certain value of y, we can use the concept of Inverse Interpolation. This is called inverse, because instead of finding out the value of y for a certain value of x, we now reverse the process of finding out the value of x for a given value of y. This formula is obtained from Lagrange's interpolation formula given above.

With usual notations, for 4 arguments a_0, a_1, a_2 and a_3;

These concepts are being used for specific problems.

$$f(x) = + \frac{[f(x)-f(a_1)][f(x)-f(a_2)][f(x)-f(a_3)]}{[f(a_0)-f(a_1)][f(a_0)-f(a_2)][f(a_0)-f(a_3)]} \times a_0$$

$$+ \frac{[f(x)-f(a_0)][f(x)-f(a_2)][f(x)-f(a_3)]}{[f(a_1)-f(a_0)][f(a_1)-f(a_2)][f(a_1)-f(a_3)]} \times a_1$$

$$+ \frac{[f(x)-f(a_0)][f(x)-f(a_1)][f(x)-f(a_3)]}{[f(a_2)-f(a_0)][f(a_2)-f(a_2)][f(a_1)-f(a_3)]} \times a_2$$

$$+ \frac{[f(x)-f(a_0)][f(x)-f(a_1)][f(x)-f(a_2)]}{[f(a_3)-f(a_0)][f(a_3)-f(a_1)][f(a_3)-f(a_2)]} \times a_3$$

CHAPTER SUMMARY

Important Terms used

- **Interpolation** : The technique of estimating the value of the dependent variable for any intermediate value of the independent variable, within the given range of independent variable.

- **Extrapolation:** The technique of estimating any future value of dependent variable for any value of the independent variable outside the given range. This is called forecasting or projections.
- **Interval of Differencing :** For equidistant set of values for the independent variables, the difference between various successive values (normally denoted by $\underline{h}$) .
- **Arguments :** The values of the independent variables.
- **Entries:** The values of the dependent variables corresponding to the given values of independent variables.
- **Difference Operator :** The difference between successive values of the entries in forward direction denoted by Δ.
- **Backward Difference Operator :** The difference between successive values of the entries in the backward direction, denoted by ∇.
- **Operator E :** It is equivalent to increasing the argument by the interval of differencing.
- **Divided Differences :** The differences defined on taking into consideration the changes in the values of the arguments, when the interval of differencing is not uniform.
- **Inverse Interpolation :** The interpolation in the reverse form by finding value of the independent variable for a given value of dependent variable.

Relationship Used

- $y = f(x) = a_0 x_n + a_1 x^{n-1} + \ldots a_{n-1} x + a_n.$
- $\Delta f(x) = f(x+h) - f(x)$ for $x = a, a+h, \ldots\ldots$ etc.
- $\Delta f(a) = f(a+h) - f(a)$
- $\Delta f(a+h) = f(a+2h) - f(a+h)$
- $\Delta f(a+2h) = f(a+3h) - f(a+2h)$
- $\Delta^2 f(a) = \Delta f(a+h) - \Delta f(a) = f(a+2h) - 2f(a+h) + f(a)$
- $\nabla f(x+h) = f(x+h) - f(x)$
- $\nabla f(x+h) = \Delta f(x)$
- $\nabla f(x) = \nabla f(a+h) = f(a+h) - f(a)$
- $\nabla f(a+2h) = f(a+2h) - f(a+h)$
- $\nabla^2 f(a+2h) = \nabla f(a+2h) - f(a+h)$
- $Ef(x) = f(x+h)$
- $E^2 f(x) = E[Ef(x)]$

  $= E[f(x+h)]$

  $= f[x+2h]$
- $\Delta f(x) = (E-1) f(x)$
- Newton's Forward Difference Formula

$$f(x) = f(a) + u\Delta f(a) + \frac{u(u-1)}{2!}\Delta^2 f(a) + \ldots\ldots$$

where $$u = \left(\frac{x-a}{h}\right)$$

- Newton's Backward Formula

$$f(x) = f(a+nh) + u\nabla f(a+nh) + \left(\frac{u(u-1)}{2!}\right)\nabla^2 f(a+nh) + \ldots\ldots$$

where $u = \dfrac{x-(a+nh)}{h}$

- Binomial Expansion equation for equidistant arguments

$$f(a+nh) - {}^nC_1 f(a+\overline{n-1}h) + nC_2 f(a+\overline{n-2}\,h)\ldots(-1)^n f(a) = 0$$

- Dividend Differences

$$\underset{a_1}{\Delta} f(a_0) = f(a_0, a_1) = \frac{f(a_1) - f(a_0)}{a_1 - a_0}$$

- Newton's Divided Difference Formula

$$f(x) = f(a_0) + (x-a_0)\,\Delta f(a_0) + (x-a_0)(x-a_1)\Delta_2 f(a_0) + \ldots\ldots$$

- Lagrange's Formula

$$f(x) = \frac{(x-a_1)(x-a_2)\ldots\ldots(x-a_n)}{(a_0-a_1)(a_0-a_2)\ldots\ldots(a_0-a_n)} \times f(a_0) + \frac{(x-a_0)(x-a_2)\ldots\ldots(x-a_n)}{(a_1-a_0)(a_1-a_2)\ldots\ldots(a_1-a_n)} f(a_1) + \ldots\ldots$$

SOLVED PROBLEMS

Problem 7.1

The following table gives the profit of a firm for the period 1971 to 1976. The figure for 1975 is missing. Interpolate the same by graphic method.

Year :	1971	1972	1973	1974	1975	1976
Profits : (Rs. in lakhs)	110	120	115	125	?	130

(Osmania University B.Com, April 1978)

Solution :

For solving the problem by graphic method, we plot the points of profit for various year as given in the problem.

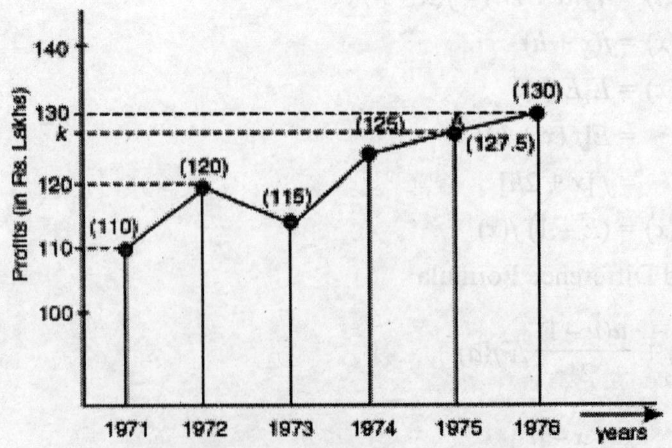

Fig 7.2 Profits for various years

We have plotted the time period (years) 1971 to 1976 on the x-axis and profit on y-axis. The points have been connected by straight lines, due to values climbing and falling. Now for interpolating the profit figure for 1975, we graw a perpendicular from x-axis to meet the profit line in point A. The conesponding point on the y-axis is obtained as k. The point k (value read from the graph) indicates Profit at Rs. 127.5 lakhs. Thus the estimated (interpolated) profit from 1975 is Rs. 127.lakhs. This may not be very accurate due to variation in the profits *i.e.* rising and falling. In actual practice, it may not, therefore, indicate the collect figure.

Problem 7.2

Interpolate the index number for 1970 from the following table.

Year	:	1968	1969	1971	1973
Index Numbers	:	100	107	157	212

(Punjab University B.Com II, Sept., 1982)

Solution :

Since no method has been specified, let us first solve it by the Graphical method. We are drawing years on x-axis and index numbers on the y-axis.

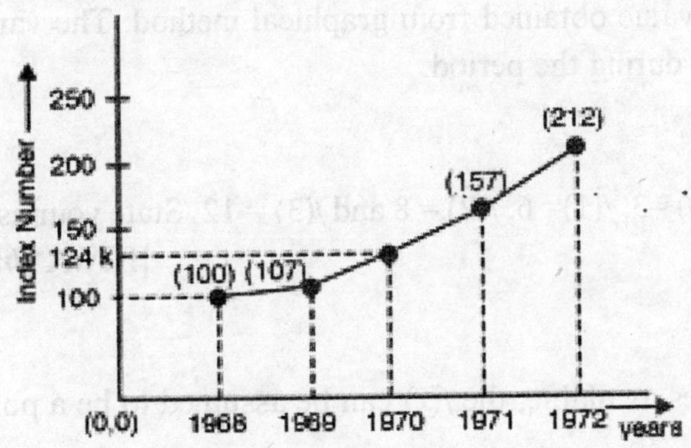

Fig 7.3 Index Numbers

The points obtained from plotting index numbers against various years have been connected by straight lines and So marked. We have to interpolate the index number for the year 1971. Taking a perpendicular from x-axis' to the drawn curve, it meets at point P (PL is'perpendicular from 1970 to the curve). Then we'project the point P to the y-axis as Pk, the point k establishing the corresponding index number for the year 1970. The value works out to 124, which is so marked.

Problem 7.3

Taking the data from Problem 7.2, solve the problem for interpolating index number for 1970 by using Algebraic method.

Solution :

Since the problem 7.2 has to be solved by using Algebraic method, we frame simultaneous equations in the following manner.

$$\Sigma y = na + b\Sigma x$$

and $$\Sigma xy = a\Sigma x + b\Sigma x^2$$

Taking the values and formulating the table for above equations

Year	(x)	(y)	x^2	xy
1968	1	100	1	100
1969	2	107	4	214
1971	4	157	16	628
1972	5	212	25	1060
	$\Sigma x = 12$	$\Sigma y = 576$	$\Sigma x^2 = 46$	$\Sigma xy = 2002$

Putting values in the equations

$$576 = 4a + 12b$$

and
$$2002 = 12a + 46b$$

Solving these equations, we obtain

$$b = 27.4$$

and
$$a = 62$$

substituting these values in the general equation $y = a + bx$, and putting value of x for 1970 3, we get

$$y = 62 + 274 \times 3 = 144$$

The value is near the value obtained from graphical method. The variation indicates the non-uniform trend of the index during the period.

Problem 7.4

Find $f(x)$: given that $f(0) = 3, f(1) = 6, f(2) = 8$ and $f(3) = 12$. State your assumptions, if any. Hence find $f(6)$. [ICWA (*Intermediate*), *June* 1976]

Solution :

Since there are 4 entries available, the $f(x)$ can be assumed to be a polynomial function of 3rd degree.

Let the function be defined as

$$y = ax^3 + bx^2 + cx + d$$

Putting the value of x, *i.e.* $x = 0, x = 1, x = 2$ and $x = 3$

$$f(0) = d = -3$$
$$f(1) = a + b + c + d = 6$$
$$f(2) = 8a + 4b + 2c + d = 8$$

and
$$f(3) = 27a + 9b + 3c + d = 12$$

Solving these equations for a, b, c and d, we obtain

$$d = -3$$
$$c = \frac{31}{2}$$
$$b = -8$$

and
$$a = \frac{3}{2}$$

From these values, the function $f(x)$ can be written as

$$f(x) = \frac{3}{2}x^3 - 8x^2 + \frac{31}{2}x - 3$$

To obtain $f(6)$, we substitute value of $x = 6$,

$$\therefore \quad f(6) = \frac{3}{2}(6)^3 - 8(6)^2 + \frac{31}{2}(6) - 3$$
$$= 126$$

Problem 7.5

Given the function $y = 3x^3 + x^2 - 2x + 1$, calculate the value of y corresponding to $x = 0$, $x = 1$, $x = 2$, $x = 3$, $x = 4$ and write the table of differences.

Solution :

Given function is

$$y = 3x^3 + x^2 - 2x + 1$$

Putting the values of $x = 0$, $x = 1$, 2, 3 and 4 respectively

$$y_0 = 1$$
$$y_1 = 3 \times 1 + 1 - 2 + 1 = 3$$
$$y_2 = 3 \times 2^3 + 2^2 - 2 \times 2 + 1 = 24 + 4 - 4 + 1$$
$$= 25$$
$$y_3 = 3 \times 3^3 + 3^2 - 2 \times 3 + 1 = 81 + 9 - 6 + 1$$
$$= 85$$
$$y_4 = 3 \times 4^3 + 4^2 - 2 \times 4 + 1 = 256 + 16 - 8 + 1$$
$$= 265$$

Now the table of differences can be written as follows

x	y_x	Δy_x	$\Delta^2 y_x$	$\Delta^3 y_x$	$\Delta^4 y_x$
0	1				
		2			
1	3		20		
		22		18	
2	25		38		64
		60		82	
3	85		120		
4	265	180			

Problem 7.6

Estimate the expectation of life at the age of 16 years by using the following data :

Age (in years) :	10	15	20	25	30	35
Expectation of life (year) :	35.4	32.3	29.2	26.0	23.2	20.4

[*Guru Nanak Dev University B. Com. II. 1983; ICWA(Intermediate), December; 1977*]

Solution :

The expected the requirement is to be worked out for an age of 16 years,which is in the begining of the data table. Hence we use Newton's Forward Differences Formula *i.e.*

$$y_x = y_u + u\Delta y_a + \frac{u(u-1)}{2!}\Delta^2 y_a + \frac{u(u-1)(u-2)}{3!}\Delta^3 y_a + \ldots\ldots$$

where $\quad u = \dfrac{x-a}{h}$

and x = year of interpolation
a = year of origin
h = common interval of differencing

In this case, we have

$$x = 16$$
$$a = 10$$
$$h = 5$$

$$\therefore \quad u = \frac{16-10}{5} = 1.2$$

Now we can write the table of forward differnces as follows :

x	y_x	Δy_x	$\Delta^2 y_x$	$\Delta^3 y_x$	$\Delta^4 y_x$	$\Delta^5 y_x$
10	35.4					
15	32.3	–3.1	0	–0.1		
20	29.2	–3.2	–0.1	0.5	0.6	–1.5
25	26.0	–2.8	0.4	–0.4	0.9	
30	23.2	–2.8	0	–0.4		
35	20.4					

Now substituting various values from the table, we obtain

$$y_{16} = 35.4 + 1.2(-3.1) + \frac{(1.2)(1.2-1)}{2} \times 0 + \frac{(1.2)(1.2-1)(1.2-2)}{6} \times (0.1)$$
$$\frac{(1.2)(1.2-1)(1.2-3)}{24} \times (0.6) + \frac{(1.2)(1.2-1)(1.2-2)(1.2-3)}{120} \times (-1.5)$$
$$= 31.7 \text{ years}$$

Problem 7.7

From the following table, find the number of workers falling in the earning group of Rs. 25 to Rs. 35.

Earnings in rupees	*No. of workers*
upto 10	50
upto 20	150
upto 30	300
upto 40	500
upto 50	700
upto 60	800

[*Rajasthan University, M.A.* (*Eco.*), *January 1976*]

Solution :

In order to find the number of workers falling in the earning group from Rs. 25 to Rs. 35, we have to calculate y_{35} and y_{25}. Also because the value 25 and 35 are in the beginning of the table, we use Newton's Forward Differences Formula.

since $u = \frac{x-a}{h}$

Here x = interpolation digit

a = origin digit

h = common interval of differencing

For y_{25}, $u = \frac{25-10}{10} = 1.5$ and for y_{35}, $u = \frac{35-10}{10} = 2.5$

Now we workout the table of forward differences

x	y_x	Δy_x	$\Delta^2 y_x$	$\Delta^3 y_x$	$\Delta^4 y_x$	$\Delta^5 y_x$
10	50					
		100				
20	150		50	0		
		150				
30	300		50	−50	−50	0
		200				
40	500		0	−100	−50	
		200				
50	700		−100			
		100				
60	800					

Using these values, we obtain,

$$y_{35} = 50 + (2.5) \times 100 + \frac{(2.5)(2.5-1)}{2} \times 50 + \frac{(2.5)(2.5-1)(2.5-2)}{6} \times 0$$

$$+ \frac{(2.5)(2.5-1)(2.5-2)(2.5-3)}{24} \times (-50) + \frac{(2.5)(2.5-1)(2.5-2)(2.5-3)(2.5-4)}{120} \times 0$$

$$= 396$$

Similarly, $y_{25} = 50 + (1.5) \times 100 + \frac{(1.5)(1.5-1)}{2} \times 50 + \frac{(1.5)(1.5-1)(1.5-2)}{6} \times 0$

$$+ \frac{(1.5)(1.5-1)(1.5-2)(1.5-3)}{24} \times (-50) + \frac{(1.5)(1.5-1)(1.5-2)(1.5-3)(1.5-4)}{120} \times 0$$

$$= 218$$

$\therefore \quad y_{35} - y_{25} = 396 - 218 = 178$

Problem 7.8

The following table shows the value of the function for different ages.

Age (in years)	:	20	30	40	50
Function value $f(x)$	:	5	7	11	15

Interpolate the function value for the age 27.

Solution :

Since the interpolation digit is towards the beginning of the data set, we can use Newton's Forward Differences method.

Here $u = \frac{x-a}{h}$

$$= \frac{27-20}{10} = 0.7$$

Table for Forward Difference

x	y_x	Δy_x	$\Delta^2 y_x$	$\Delta^3 y_x$
20	5			
		2		
30	7		2	
		4		−2
40	11		0	
		4		
50	15			

Hence by Newton's Formula

$$y_{27} = y_0 + u_0 y_a + \frac{u(u-1)}{2!}\Delta^2 y_a + \frac{u(u-1)(u-2)}{3!}\Delta^3 y_a + \ldots\ldots$$

$$= 5 + 0.7 \times 2 + \frac{(0.7)(0.7-1)}{2} \times 2 + \frac{(0.7)(0.7-1)(0.7-2)}{6} \times (-2)$$

$$= 5 + 1.4 - 0.21 - 0.09$$

$$= 6.1$$

Problem 7.9

The following results are given

$\sqrt[3]{27} = 3.0000$ $\sqrt[3]{28} = 3.0369$

$\sqrt[3]{29} = 3.0727$ $\sqrt[3]{30} = 3.1074$ using them, find $\sqrt[3]{26}$.

[ICWA (Intermediate), December 1981]

Solution :

As per the given values of the function, we can assume function $v_x = \sqrt[3]{x}$.

Then we have to obtain the value of y_{26} by using the values of y_{27}, y_{28}, y_{29} and y_{30}.

Since the value of interpolation y_{26} falls in the beginning of the data set, we use Newton's Foward Difference Formula.

Let us have $\quad u = \dfrac{x-a}{h}$

Here $\quad u = \dfrac{26-27}{1} = 1$

Working out the table of Forward Differences, we get

x	y_x	Δy_x	$\Delta^2 y_x$	$\Delta^3 y_x$
27	3.0000			
		0.0369		
28	3.0369		−0.0011	
		0.0358		0
29	3.0707		−0.0011	
		0.0347		
30	3.1074			

Putting these values in the Newton's Formula, we obtain

$$y_{26} = 3.0000 + (-1) \times 0.0369 + \frac{(-1)(-2)}{2} \times (0.0011) + \frac{(-1)(-2)(-3)}{6} \times 0$$

$$= 2.962$$

Thus the value of $\sqrt[3]{26}$ worksout to be 2.962

Problem 7.10

Using an appropriate formula for interpolation, estimate the number of students, who obtained less than 45 marks, from the following.

Marks	:	0-40	40-50	50-60	60-70	70-80
No. of students	:	31	42	51	35	31

[*Bangalore University B.Com; April 1978*]

Solution :

Since we have to obtain number of students obtaining less than 45 marks, we define out function y_x from less than cumulative frequeuncy level.

Working out the table of Forward Differences, by using this definition, we get

x	$f(x)$	y_x *less than cf*	Δy_x	$\Delta^2 y_x$	$\Delta^3 y_x$	$\Delta^4 y_x$
40	31	31	42			
				−9		
50	42	73	51		−25	
				−16		
60	51	124	35		+12	−37
				−4		
70	35	159	31			
80	31	190				

From the above values, we now can obtain y_{45},

Given here $x = 45$

$a = 40$

$h = 10$

$$\therefore \quad u = \left(\frac{x-a}{h}\right) = \left(\frac{45-40}{10}\right) = 0.5$$

$$\therefore \quad y_{(45)} = 31 + (0.5) \times 42 + \frac{(0.5)(-0.5)}{2} \times 9 + \frac{(0.5)(-0.5)(-1.5)}{6} \times (-25)$$

$$+ \frac{(0.5)(-0.5)(-1.5)(2.5)}{24} \times 37 = 48$$

Hence estimated number of students obtaining less than 45 marks are 48.

Problem 7.11

The following table indicates the sales of a certain commodity during the years 1971 to 2001. Estimates the sales for the year 1995 by using an appropriate interpolation method.

Years	:	1971	1981	1991	2001
Unit of Sales (in lakh)	:	46	68	80	95

Solution :

Since the year of interpolation is towards the later period of data set, we can use Newton's Backward Differences Formula

Preparing the table of Backward Differences

x	y_x	∇y_x	$\nabla^2 y_x$	$\nabla^3 y_x$
1971	46	22		
1981	68	12	−10	
1991	80	15	+3	13
2001	95			

For $u = \left(\frac{x-a}{h}\right)$

given $x = 1995$

$a = 2001$ Here a = last argument

$h = 10$

$$\therefore \quad u = \frac{1995-2001}{10}$$

$$= \frac{6}{10} = -\ 0.6$$

$$\therefore \quad y_{(1995)} = 95 + (0.6) \times (15) + \frac{(-0.6)(0.6+1)}{2!} \times 3 + \frac{(-0.6)(0.6+1)(0.6+2)}{6} \times 13$$

$$= 95 - 9 - 0.36 - 0.728$$

$$= 85$$

Hence the sales during the year 1995 will be approximately 85 lakh units.

Problem 7.12

The following table gives the quantity of airconditioners sold by a shopkeeper each year. Find the missing term by using a suitable method of interpolation.

Years	:	1995	1996	1997	1998	1999	2000
Number of air conditioners	:	44	95	155	?	240	350

Solution :

In this case, we have to use 1995 as the year of origin. Thus we have the data as follows :

x	:	0	1	2	3	4	5
$y(x)$	:	44	95	155	?	240	350

Since we have five entries, the function y_x can be taken as a polynomial of 4th degree hence by the fundamental theorem of finite differences.

For $\Delta^5 y_x = 0$ for all values of x

Hence $\Delta^5 y_0 = 0$

or $(E-1)^5 y = 0$

or $(E^5 - 5E^4 + 10E^3 - 10E^2 + 5E - 1)\, y_0 = 0$

or $y_5 - 5y_4 + 10y_3 - 10y_2 + 5y_1 - y_0 = 0$

using values of y_0, y_1, etc. from the table above, we obtain

$350 - 5 \times 240 + 10y_3 - 10 \times 155 + 5 \times 95 - 44 = 0$

or $10y_3 = 44 - 350 + 1200 + 1550 - 475$

$$y_3 = 192.5 = 193$$

Hence the shop keeper sells 193 units in the year 1998.

Problem 7.13

Solve the problem 7.12 by using another appropriate interpolation formula.

Solution :

Using Newton's Backward Differences method, we prepare the table accordingly.

Table of Backward Differences

x	y_x	∇y_x	$\nabla^2 y_x$	$\nabla^3 y_x$	$\nabla^4 y_x$	$\nabla^5 y_x$
0	44	51				
			9			
1	95	60		$a-224$		
			$a-215$		$834-4a$	
2	155	$a-215$		$610-3a$		$10a-1969$
			$395-2a$		$6a-1135$	
3	a					
4	240	$240-a$		$3a-525$		
			$a-130$			
5	350	110				

Since there are 5 entries, the function y_x can be taken as a polynomial of 4th degree and hence by fundamental theorem of finite differences.

or $\qquad \nabla^5 y_x = 0$

or $\qquad 10a-1969 = 0$

$\therefore \qquad a = \dfrac{1969}{10}$

$\qquad = 196.9 = 197$

Hence the missing data is 197

Problem 7.14

Estimate u_2 from the following table

x	:	1	2	3	4	5
$u_{(x)}$	:	2.0000	?	2.0646	2.0954	2.1253

State the necessary assumption made. [*ICWA (Intermediate), December 1980*]

Solution :

Since there are only 4 entries available, we can fit a polynomial curve of 3rd degree such that

$$\Delta^3 u(x) = \text{constant}$$

and $\qquad \Delta^4 u(x) = 0$ for all values of x

By the method of Binomial Expansion, we get

$$(E-1)^4\, u(x) = 0$$

or $\qquad (E^4 - 4E^3 + 6E^2 - 4E + 1)\, u(x) = 0$

or $u_5 - 4u_4 + 6u_3 - 4u_2 + u_1 = 0$

Substituting the given values here,

$$2.1253 - 4 \times 2.0954 + 6 \times 2.0646 + 4u_2 + 2.0000 = 0$$

or $4u_2 = 2.0000 + 2.1253 - 8.3816 + 12.3876$

or $u_2 = \frac{8.1313}{4}$

$= 2.0328$

Problem 7.15

Using appropriate method of interpolation, estimate the missing value of the data set, given below.

x	:	0	1	2	3	4
y	:	1	3	9	—	81

Solution :

Since there are four entries given, we can represent the data through a polynomial of the 3rd degree and hence, by the fundamental theorem of finite difference.

$\Delta^4 y_{(n)} = 0$ for all value more than 4.

i.e. $\Delta^4 y_0 = 0$

If we consider the missing value as p the table of differences can be drawn as follows.

x	y_x	Δy_x	$\Delta^2 y_x$	$\Delta^3 y_x$	$\Delta^4 y_x$
0	1				
		2			
1	3		4		
		6		$p-19$	
2	9		$p-15$		$124-4p$
		$p-9$		$105-3p$	
3	p		$90-2p$		
		$81-p$			
4	81				

Substituting these values in the above expression

$124 - 4p = 0$

$\therefore$ $p = 31$

Hence y_3, the missing value is 31.

Problem 7.16

Estimate u_2 from the following table

x	:	1	2	3	4	5
$u_{(x)}$	:	6	?	12	20	35

Solution

Since there are 4 entries given in the problem, we can fit a polynomial of 3rd degree to the data and by using the fundamental theorem of finite differences, we get

$$\Delta^4 u_{(x)} = 0$$

$$\Delta^4 u_{(1)} = 0$$

or $$(E-1)^4 u_1 = 0$$

or $$(E^4 - 4E^3 + 6E^2 - 4E + 1)u_1 = 0$$

or $$u_5 - 4u_4 + 6u_3 - 4u_2 + u_1 = 0$$

or $$35 - 4 \times 20 + 6 \times 12 - 4u_2 + 6 = 0$$

or $$4u_2 = 35 - 80 + 72 + 6 - 0$$

or $$u_2 = \frac{33}{2} = 8.25$$

Hence the missing value u_2 is 8.25.

Problem 7.17

From the following table, interpolate the missing values.

Year	:	0	1	2	3	4	5	6
Production (in '000 tonnes)	:	200	220	260	?	350	?	430

[*Kurukshetra University, B.Com. 1981*]

Solution :

Writing the data with usual notation

x	:	0	1	2	3	4	5	6
$y(x)$	:	200	220	260	y_3	350	y_5	430

Since there are five entries given, we can fit a polynomial of 4th degree to this data and using the fundamental theorem of finite differences, we can write

$$\Delta^5 y_x = 0$$

or $$(E-1)5\, y_0 = 0$$

or $$(E_5 - 5E_4 + 10E_3 - 10E_2 + 5E)y_0 = 0$$

or $$y_5 - 5y_4 + 10y_3 - 10y_2 + 5y_1 - y_0 = 0$$

Putting these value from the data set, we obtain

$$y_5 - 5 \times 350 + 10y_3 - 10 \times 260 + 5 \times 220 - 200 = 0$$

or $$y_5 + 10y_3 = 3450$$

Similarly $$\Delta^5(y_1) = 0$$

or $$(E^5 - 5E^4 + 10E^3 - 10E^2 + 5E - 1)y_1 = 0$$

or $$y_6 - 5y_5 + 10y_4 - 10y_3 + 5y_2 - y_1 = 0$$

substituting the various values from the above data set

$$430 - 5y_5 + 10 \times 350 - 10y_3 + 5 \times 260 - 220 = 0$$

or $$5y_5 - 10y_3 = 5010$$

Now solving (*i*) and (*ii*) for y_5 and y_3, we obtain

$$y_3 = 306$$

and $$y_5 = 390$$

Problem 7.18

Given the following table, find the function $f(x)$, assuming it to be a polynomial of the third degree in x.

x	:	0	1	2	3
$f_{(x)}$	:	1	2	11	34

[*ICWA*, (*Intermediate*) *June, 1975*]

Solution :

Since this is a case of four entries, of equal space of the variable x, we use Newton's Forward Differences Formula.

Working on the table of forward differences, we get

x	$y(x)$	$\Delta y(x)$	$\Delta^2 y(x)$	$\Delta^3 y(x)$
0	1			
		1		
1	2		8	
		9		6
2	11			
		23	14	
3	34			

For Newton's Forward difference formula

$$u = \frac{x-a}{h}$$

$$= \frac{x-0}{1} = x$$

$$\therefore \quad f(x) = 1 + (x \times 1) + \frac{(x)(x-1)(x-2)}{6} \times 6$$

$$= 1 + x + 4x\,(x-1) + x(x-1)(x-2)$$

$$= x^3 + x^2 - x + 1$$

Problem 7.19

Solve the problem 7.18 by Newton's Divided Differences formula.

Solution

For using Newton's Divided Differences Formula, we have to prepare the table of Divided Differences

Table of Divided Differences

x	y_x	Δy_x	$\Delta^2 y_x$	$\Delta^3 y_x$
0	1	$\frac{2-1}{1-0} = 1$	$\frac{9-1}{2-0} = 4$	$\frac{7-4}{3-0} = 1$
1	2	$\frac{11-2}{2-1} = 9$	$\frac{23-9}{3-1} = 7$	
2	11	$\frac{34-11}{3-2} = 23$		
3	34			

Using Newton's Divided Differences formula for the values so obtained.

$$f(x) = f(0) + (x-0)\ \Delta f(0) + (x-0)(x-1)\ \Delta_2 f(0) + (x-0)(x-1)(x-2)^2\Delta^2 f(0)$$

$$= 1 + (x \times 1) + x(x-1) \times 4 + x(x-1)(x-2) \times 1$$

$$= x^3 + x^2 - x + 1$$

It is the same function as obtained in Problem 6.18 above.

Problem 7.20

Using the data of problem 7.18, find the function $f(x)$ by using parabolic curve fitting method.

Solution :

Since there are four entries, we can fit a polynomial of 3rd degree. *i.e.*

$$f(x) = ax^3 + bx^2 + cx + d$$

Now putting values of x in this expression

$$f(0) = d = 1$$

$$f(1) = a + b + c + d = 2$$

$$f(2) = 8a + 4b + 2c + d = 11$$

$$f(3) = 27a + 9b + 3c + d = 34$$

Solving these equtions, for the values of a, b and c (d is already available as $d = 1$), we obtain

$$a = 1$$

$$b = 1$$

$$c = -1$$

$$d = 1$$

Hence the polynomial function will be written as

$$f(x) = x^3 + x^2 - x + 1$$

which is the same as obtained in problem 7.18 and 7.19

Problem 7.21

Given the following data, find the corresponding value of $f(x)$ for $x = 6$, by applying Newton's Divided Difference Method, (a case of non-equidistant arguments).

x	:	1	3	5	7	8	10
$f_{(x)}$	:	15	18	22	27	30	35

Solution :

Since we have to apply Newton's Divided Difference Method for solving it, we have to prepare the table of Divided Differences.

Table of Divided Differences

x	y_x	Δy_x	$\Delta^2 y_x$	$\Delta^3 y_x$	$\Delta^4 y_x$	$\Delta^5 y_x$
1	15					
		$\frac{18-15}{3-1} = 1.5$				
3	18		$\frac{2-1.5}{3-1} = 0.25$			
		$\frac{22-18}{5-3} = 2$		0		
5	22		$\frac{2.5-2}{5-3} = 0.25$		0	
		$\frac{27-22}{7-5} = 2.5$		0		−0.04
7	27		$\frac{3-2.5}{7-5} = 0.25$		−0.04	
		$\frac{30-27}{8-7} = 3$		−0.25		
8	30		$\frac{2.5-3}{8-7} = 0.5$			
		$\frac{35-30}{10-8} = 2.5$				
10	35					

Using Newton's Divided Difference Formula,

$$
\begin{aligned}
f_{(6)} &= 15 + (x-1)\,\Delta f(1) + (x-1)(x-3)\,\Delta^2 f(1) + (x-1)(x-3)(x-5)\Delta^3 f(1) \\
&\quad + (x-1)\,(x-3)(x-5)(x-7)\,\Delta f(1) + (x-1)(x-3)(x-5)(x-7)(x-8)\,\Delta^5 f(1) \\
&= 15 + (6-1) \times 1.5 + [(6-1)\,(6-3)] \times 0.25 + (6-1)\,(6-3)\,(6-5) \times 0 \\
&\quad + [(6-1)(6-3)(6-5)(6-7)] \times 0 + [(6-1)(6-3)(6-5)(6-7)(6-8)] \times 0.004 \\
&= 15 + 7.5 + 3.75 + 0 + 0 - 0.012 \\
&= 26.74
\end{aligned}
$$

Problem 7.22

Find the polynomial function $f(x)$, given that

$f(0) = 2$

$f(1) = 3$

$f(2) = 12$

$f(3) = 35$

Hence find $f(5)$. *[ICWA (Intermediate) June 1984]*

Solution :

Since it is a case of equidistant arguments *i.e.* 0, 1, 2, 3, we can either apply Newton's Forward or Backward Difference Formula. We can also apply Newton's Divided Difference Formula or the Lagrange's Formula. But when the arguments are not equally spaced, then only Newton's Divided Difference Formula or Lagrange's Formula can be used.

In this case, we try Lagrange's formula (through the arguments are equally spaced).

We can write the Lagrange's Formula as follows

$$f_{(x)} = \frac{(x-1)(x-2)(x-3)}{(0-1)(0-2)(0-3)} \times f(0) + \frac{(x-0)(x-2)(x-3)}{(1-0)(1-2)(1-3)} \times f(1) + \frac{(x-0)(x-1)(x-3)}{(2-0)(2-1)(2-3)} \times f(2)$$

$$+ \frac{(x-0)(x-1)(x-2)}{(3-0)(3-1)(3-3)} \times f(3)$$

$$= \frac{x(x-1)(x-3)}{(-1)(-2)(-3)} \times 2 + \frac{x(x-2)(x-3)}{(1)(-1)(-2)} \times 3 + \frac{x(x-1)(x-3)}{(2)(1)(-1)} \times 12 + \frac{x(x-1)(x-2)}{3(2)(1)} \times 35$$

$$= -\frac{1}{3}(x^3 - 6x^2 + 11x - 6) + \frac{3}{2}(x^3 - 5x^2 + 6x) - 6(x^3 - 4x^2 + 3x) + \frac{35}{6}(x^3 - 3x^2 + 2x)$$

$$= x^3\left(-\frac{1}{3}+\frac{3}{2}-6+\frac{35}{6}\right) + x^2\left(2-\frac{15}{2}+24-\frac{35}{2}\right) + x\left(-\frac{11}{2}+9-18+\frac{35}{3}\right) + 2$$

$$= x^3 + x^2 - x + 2$$

To find $f(5)$, we substitute the value of $x = 5$, in the expression

$$\therefore f(5) = (5)^3 + (5)^2 - (5) + 2$$

$$= 125 + 25 - 5 + 2$$

$$= 147$$

Problem 7.23

The mode of a certain frequency curve $y = f(x)$ is attained at $x = 9.1$ and the value of the frequency function $f(x)$ for $x = 8.9, 9.0$ and 9.3 are respectively equal to 0.3, 0.35 and 0.25. Calculate the approximate value of $f(x)$ at the mode. *[ICWA (Intermediate) December 1978]*

Solution :

Organizing the data in the usual form

x	$a_0 = 8.9$	$a_1 = 9.0$	$a_2 = 9.3$
$f(x)$	$f(a_0) = 0.30$	$f(a_1) = 0.35$	$f(a_2) = 0.25$

Since mode of the frequency distribution can be obtained at $x = 9.1$ we can get the value of $f(9.1)$ at mode, by using Lagrange's Formula

$$\therefore f(x) = \frac{(x-9)(x-9.3)}{(8.9-9)(8.9-9.3)} \times (0.30) + \frac{(x-8.9)(x-9.3)}{(9-8.9)(9-9.3)} \times (0.35) + \frac{(x-8.9)(x-9)}{(9.3-8.9)(9.3-9)} \times (0.25)$$

$$\therefore f(x) = \frac{(9.1-9)(9.1-9.3)}{(8.9-9)(8.9-9.3)} \times (0.30) + \frac{(9.1-8.9)(9.1-9.3)}{(9-8.9)(9-9.3)} \times (0.35) + \frac{(9.1-8.9)(9.1-9)}{(9.3-8.9)(9.3-9)} \times (0.25)$$

$$= 0.36$$

Thus the value of the function at mode $(x = 9.1) = 0.36$

Problem 7.24

Given

$$\log_{10}(654) = 2.8156$$
$$\log_{10}(658) = 2.8182$$
$$\log_{10}(659) = 2.8189$$
$$\log_{10}(661) = 2.8202$$

Find, by using Lagrange's interpolation Formula, $\text{Log}_{10}(656)$,

[Retain Four decimal places in your answer] *[ICWA(Intermediate), June 1978]*

Solution :

As per the given data, $f(x) = \log_{10}(x)$,

Putting the data in the normal form,

x	$a_0 = 654$	$a_1 = 658$	$a_2 = 659$	$a_3 = 661$
$f(x)$	2.8156	2.8182	2.8189	2.8202

We have to obtain $f(x)$, when $x = 656$ or $f(x) = \log_{10}(656)$

Using $f(x) = f(656) = \log_{10}(656)$

$$= \frac{(656-658)(656-659)(656-661)}{(654-658)(654-659)(654-661)} \times 2.8156$$

$$+ \frac{(656-654)(656-659)(656-661)}{(658-654)(658-659)(658-661)} \times 2.8182$$

$$+ \frac{(656-654)(656-658)(656-661)}{(659-654)(659-658)(659-661)} \times 2.8189$$

$$+ \frac{(656-654)(656-658)(656-659)}{(661-654)(661-658)(661-659)} \times 2.8702$$

$$= \frac{3}{14}(2.8156) + \frac{3}{2}(2.8182) - 2 \times 2.8189 + \frac{2}{7} \times 2.8202 = 2.8168$$

Problem 7.25

The values of x and $y = f(x)$ are given below

x	3	5	6	7	9
y	10	12	15	17	20

Find the value of x, when $y = 18$

Solution :

This is a case of reverse interpolation, because we have to find the value of x for a given value of $y = f(x)$.

Using formula for inverse interpolation, we utilize the values as follows.

for $a_0 = 3$, $f(a_0) = 10$
$a_1 = 5$, $f(a_1) = 12$
$a_2 = 6$, $f(a_2) = 15$
$a_3 = 7$, $f(a_3) = 17$
and $a_4 = 9$, $f(a_4) = 20$

We have to find the value of x when $f(x) = 18$

$$\therefore \quad x = \frac{[(18-12)(18-15)(18-17)(18-20)]}{[(10-12)(15-12)(15-17)(15-20)]} \times 3 + \frac{[(18-10)(18-15)(18-17)(18-20)]}{[(12-10)(12-15)(12-17)(12-20)]} \times 5$$

$$+ \frac{[(18-10)(18-12)(18-17)(18-20)]}{[(15-10)(10-12)(10-17)(10-20)]} \times 6 + \frac{[(18-10)(18-12)(18-15)(18-20)]}{[(17-10)(17-12)(17-15)(17-20)]} \times 7$$

$$+\frac{[(18-10)(18-12)(18-15)(18-17)]}{[(20-10)(20-12)(20-15)(20-17)]}$$

$$= 1.54 + 1.00 + 3.84 + 1.08 = 7.46$$

Hence the value of x for $f(y) = 18$ is 7.46

PRACTICE PROBLEMS

7.26. (*a*) What do you understand by 'Interpolation'? Show clearly necessity of interpolation by taking a few concrete examples.

(*b*) Give the assumptions and importance of the method of interpolation.

[*Punjabi University, M.A.(Eco.,) 1983*]

7.27. (*a*) Explain the terms 'argument' and 'entry' as applicable in the interpolation.

(*b*) Define the difference operators Δ and E showing there relationship as $\Delta = E - 1$

7.28. Explain situations clearly where the following methods of interpolation can be used

(*a*) Newton's Forward Differences Formula

(*b*) Newton's Backward Differences Formula

(*c*) Newton's Divided Differences Formula

7.29. What do you understand by the terms 'interpolation' and 'extrapolation'? Discuss briefly their necessity and usefulness in statistical studies.

[*Himanchal Pradesh University, M.A.(Eco.) February 1982*]

7.30. What is the utility of interpolation and extrapolation to businessmen? Mention the chief methods of interpolation, giving the conditions under which they are suitable.

[*Kurukshetra University, B.Com. II september 1982*]

7.31. Explain Graphical Methd and Algerbraic Method of interpolation. State, under what situations, these can be used. Also discuss their relative merits.

7.32. Explain the Binomial Expansion Method for interpolation of missing obersvations. Also state assumptions used.

7.33. How would you use the difference operators Δ and E for estimation of (*a*) one missing (*b*) two missing observations in a data set? Clearly specify the assumptions applied.

7.34. Enumerate and explain various methods used for interpolating the values of the dependent variables, when the values of the independent variables are

(*a*) at equal intervals (*b*) not at equal intervals

7.35. What do you understand by the following terms

(*a*) Forward Differences (*b*) Backword Difference

(c) Divided Differences

Also write the expression for Divided Differences in the form of a table where there are four arguments and four corresponding entries available.

7.36. The following table gives the values of a certain function $y = f(x)$ for some equidistant values of x.

x	:	14	20	26	32	38	44
y	:	110	192	308	464	666	920

Find graphically (*i*) The value of y when $x = 40$ and
(*ii*) The value of x when $y = 400$ [*ICWA (Final), July 1972(O.S.)*]

7.37. Explain the meaning of interpolation. The following table gives the expectation of life at different ages. Find the expectation of life at the age of 49 years.

Age (years)	35	45	55	65	75
Expectation of life (years)	34	26	18	12	10

[*Himanchal Pradesh University, M.A.(Eco.) July 1984*]

7.38. What do you understand by interpolation? Estimate the number of students for 1953 from the data given below.

Years	1948	1950	1952	1954
Number of students	50	79	102	113

[*Guru Nanak Dev University, B.Com. II. September 1983*]

7.39. By Newton's or by any other algebraic method, find the number of persons, who probably will be travelling if the rate is 4.2 in the following table.

Rate	5.0	4.5	4.6	3.5	3.6
Passengers	30,000	40,000	60,000	1,00,000	1,50,000

[*Punjabi University M.A. (Eco.) 1978, Pubjab University M.A. (Eco.) 1979*]

7.40. From the following figures, find the premium payable at the age of 40:

Age (in years)	20	25	30	35
Annual Premium (in Rs.)	28	31.25	35	41

[*Kurukshatra University, B.Com. 1980*]

7.41. Given the following table, construct a difference table and from it, estimate y, when $x = 0.35$, by using Newton's Backward interpolation formula

x	0	0.1	0.2	0.3	0.4
y	1	1.095	1.179	1.251	1.310

(Answer to be given correct to 3 decimal places) [*ICWA (Inter), June 1978*]

7.42. Estimate by Newton's method of interpolation, the expectation of life at age 32 from the following data:

Age	10	15	20	25	30	35
Expectation of life	35.3	32.4	29.2	26.1	23.2	20.5

7.43. The population of a district for different years is given below. Find out the population for 1982

Year	1977	1978	1979	1980	1981
Population (in million)	17	20	36	44	60

7.44. The following are the marks obtained by 492 candidates in a certain examination.

Not more than	*Students*
40 marks	212
45 marks	296
50 marks	368
55 marks	429
60 marks	460
65 marks	481

70 marks	490
75 marks	492

Find the number of candidates who scored more than 42 but nor more than 45.

[*Punjab University, M.A.* (*Eco.*) 1980, *Punjabi University M.A.* (*Eco.*) 1979]

7.45. From the following data, estimate number of persons earning wages between Rs. 25 and Rs. 35.

Wages in Rs.	*No. of Persons*
upto 10	50
upto 20	150
upto 30	300
upto 40	500
upto 50	700

[*Guru Nanak Dev University, B.Com., 1980*]

7.46. The following table gives the quantity of cement in thousand of tonnes manufactured each year. Find the missing term by a suitable Algebraic method of interpolation.

Year	1962	1964	1966	1968	1970	1972
Current Quantity	44	90	?	180	270	390

[*Madras University, B.Com., April 1976*]

7.47. Given, $u_{50} = 99, u_{52} = 907, u_{53} = 841, u_{55} = 773$ estimate u_{51} and u_{54} under suitable assumptions.

[*ICWA (Inter), December 1984*]

7.48. The number of member of International Statistical Society are :

Year	1970	1971	1972	1973	1974	1975	1976	1977	1978	1979
Number of members	845	867	?	846	821	772	?	757	761	796

Make the best estimate you can of the members in 1972 and 1976.

[*Punjab University B.Com. 1980*]

7.49. Interpolate the missing figures from the following data

X	5	10	15	20	25	30	35
Y	8	?	25	?	40	50	60

[*Punjabi University M.A.* (*Eco.,*) *December 1983*]

7.50. Estimate the production for the year 1955 and 1965 with the help of following table.

Year	1940	1945	1950	1955	1960	1965	1970
Production in tonnes	20	22	26	?	35	?	43

[*Kurushatra University, B.Com. II, April 1982*]

7.51. Obtain an estimate of the missing figure in the following table.

x	4	5	6	7	8
$f(x)$	3.11	2.96	?	2.77	2.70

[*ICWA (Intermediate) December 1983*]

7.52. Interpolate the two missing figures with the help of a suitable formula :

Year	1950	1951	1952	1953	1954	1955	1956
Production (in millions)	76.6	78.7	?	77.7	78.7	?	80.6

[*Mysore University, B.Com. April 1982*]

7.53. Interpolate the index number for 1970 from the following table,

Year	1968	1969	1971	1972
Index Number	100	107	157	212

[*Punjab University, B.Com. II, September 1982*]

7.54. Find the missing values in the following (use Binomial Method)

x	2	3	4	5	6	7
y	5.99	7.92	9.49	?	12.59	14.07

[*Kurukshetra University, B.Com. 1978*]

7.55. Find the missing value from the following figures by the Binomial Method of interpolation.

Year	1970	1971	1972	1973	1974	1975
Value	141	131	145	?	149	173

[*Kurukshetra University, B.Com. 1979*]

7.56. By using Langranges Method, estimate the number of persons whose income is Rs. 19 and more but doesn't exceed Rs. 25 from the following table :

Income in Rs.	*No. of persons*
1 and not exceeding 9	50
10 and not exceeding 19	70
19 and not exceeding 28	203
28 and not exceeding 37	406
37 and not exceeding 46	304

[*Rajasthan University, M.Com. 1976*]

7.57. Determine the percentage of criminals under 35 years of age

Age	*Percentage of criminals*
under 25 years	52.0
under 30 years	67.3
under 40 years	84.1
under 50 years	94.4

[*Punjab University, B.Com. 1973, Nagpur University, B.Com. 1974*]

7.58. Use Lagranges interpolation Formula to find $f(x)$, when $x = 0$ given the following table.

x	−1	−2	2	4
$y(x)$	12	13	14	16

7.59. The values of x and y are given below

x	5	6	9	11
$y(x)$	12	13	14	16

Find the value of y when $x = 10$ by using Lagranges method.

[*Punjab University M.A.* (*Eco.*) 1978]

7.60. The following table gives the normal weight of a baby during the first six months of life :

Age in months	0	2	3	5	6
Weight in lbs	5	7	8	10	12

Estimate the weight of the baby at the age of 4 months.

[*ICWA* (*Final*), *January, 1970* (*O.S.*)]

7.61. Calculate the population in 1976 (estimate) from the population of a country during the four censuses :

Year	1941	1951	1961	1971
Population (in crores)	29	31	32	35

[*Punjab University, M.A.* (*Eco.*) 1976]

7.62. Using the Lagranges Formula of interpolation, find from the data given below the number of workers earning between Rs. 30 and Rs. 40.

Earnings in Rs.	15–20	20–30	30–45	45–55	55–70
No. of workers	73	97	110	180	140

[*Guru Nanak Dev University, B.Com. 1981*]

7.63. State Lagranges interpolation Formula and its differences in use from the Newton's interpolation formula

Given the table of values

x	1.40	1.60	1.70	1.80
$f(x)$	0.9855	0.9995	0.9917	0.9737

Find $f(1.75)$

[*ICWA (Intermediate) December, 1984*]

7.64. State Lagranges Formula of interpolation, Given the table of values

x	35.5	35.5	39.5	40.5
$f(x)$	1175	1280	2180	2020

[*ICWA(Intermediate), December, 1983*]

7.65. By using the most suitable method, estimate the business done in 1980 from the following data

Years	1977	1978	1979	1981	1982
Business done (in lakhs Rs.)	1570	2350	3650	5250	7800

[*Punjab University, B.Com. II, April 1983*]

❁❁❁

CHAPTER 8

INDEX NUMBERS

8.1 INTRODUCTION

In daily life, things keep changing. The prices of various commodities in the market vary at some rate over a period of time. In order to be updated on such changes, we need some way to guess it, so that we can be prepared to meet this change. If we have bought a grocery item today, we may be interested to know what the price we would have to pay if we are buying either the same item or any suitable item in the category after 6 month or so. In business area, a manager may be interested to know how the raw material prices have increased over last one year, so that he can cater for such changes in his budget for the year. May be some changes indicate the trend of increase on the regular basis, so that future planning could be more accurate. For such variations, we may analyse the degree of change in the form of index numbers.

The concept of Index Number is extensively used in quite a few business applications such as calculation of capital gains for Income-tax purposes. Index Number is thus, a measure of change in a given variable under study. It is the proportionate value of the variable with reference to an assumed base value.

8.2 DEFINITION OF INDEX NUMBER

It is the measure of change in the variable under study over a period of time. When we calculate a proportional or ratio value over a given base value, it is called index number. For ease of calculation of ratio, we treat the base value of 100 *i.e.* if last year's price of a commodity was Rs. 600 and present price is Rs. 700, then the ratio of price is $\frac{700}{600} = 1.16$.

If we take Rs. 600 as the base price, taking it as value 100, then the index for the commodity for this year would be

$$1.16 \times 100 = 116$$

Such like indices are used in calculation of price changes, population changes, inflation or volume changes in business activity.

For making it amply clear, let us take a case of profits earned by a business house and calculate the index established by them for their internal consumption. Refer Table 8.1. for the purpose.

TABLE 8.1. Measurement of Profit Index

Year	*Profit earned (Rs. crores)*	*Ratio*	*Index (base 1995)*
1995	55	55/55 = 1.0	1.0×100 = 100
1996	63	63/55 = 1.15	1.15×100 = 115
1997	70	70/55 = 1.27	1.27×100 = 127
1999	81	81/55 = 1.47	1.47×100 = 147
2000	85	85/55 = 1.54	1.54×100 = 154
2001	91	91/55 = 1.65	1.65×100 = 165
2002	94	94/55 = 1.71	1.71×100 = 171
2003	98	98/55 = 1.78	1.78×100 = 178

Similarly, various indices can be worked out for establishing cost of living, payment of income tax on short term or long term capital gains etc.

8.3. TYPES OF INDEX NUMBERS

Generally speaking, we can used three types of index numbers

1. Price index
2. Value index
3. Quantity index

Price Index : It is the most commonly used index. It compares the prices of various commodities from one period to another. We may have steel price index, sugar price index, vegetables or estables price index etc. For the purpose, a well known price index is called consumer price index (CPI). it is tabulated at regional or National level so as to establish the price levels of various consumer goods and services. This is an effective measure and useful index of cost of living.

Value Index : The price index does not measure only the cost of living, it takes into account the total monetary worth, like change in the exchange rate of rupee against other world currencies such as dollar or pound. While calculating the value, the price and quantity, both are considered and therefore it is more useful an index. Here it is change in a variable in its useful or utitlity value.

Quantity index : In this case, the change in the variable is measured in quantity or the mere number. For example, we measure the numerical ratio increase in numbers for the population increase or the number of employee change in organized or unorganized sector.

To have a useful interpretation of various important variables, we can use the index numbers in the following areas.
- Price (called Price index)
- Value (called Value index)
- Quantity (called Quanity index)

Hence the index is like time series where the increase in the variable is studied over a specified period of time taking a particular period as base point. In addition, it can also be used to indicate the change in the given variable in different situations or in different locations. India being a vast country, we may be collecting CPI (consumer price index) for various locations separately like CPI for North, South, East and West India. This would amount to comporative CPI for various location, also comparative CPI for various good or services to establish that cost of living in Delhi is higher than that in Hyderabad.

Composite Index Numbers

While individual single indices may indicate changes in a given variable over a period of time, we may use a composite index for working out index of general goods and services together. Let us take the calculation of general price index for consumer items in the market, as given in the table 8.2.

TABLE 8.2. Composite Price Index

Year	*Value of goods (Rs. crores)*	*Ratio*	*Index (base 1995)*
1995	42.5	42.5/42.5 = 1.0	1.0×100 = 100
1996	45.3	45.3/42.5 = 1.07	1.07×100 = 107
1997	47.5	47.5/42.5 = 1.12	1.12×100 = 112
1998	49.2	49.2/42.5 = 1.16	1.16×100 = 116
1999	51.5	51.5/42.5 = 1.21	1.21×100 = 121
2000	53.0	53.0/42.5 = 1.25	1.25×100 = 125
2001	53.9	53.9/42.5 = 1.27	1.27×100 = 127
2002	54.8	54.8/42.5 = 1.29	1.29×100 = 129

The use of index numbers can be tricky if the data collected for a specific purpose is not complete, authentic or reliable. In addition, all the values of the data may not be equally important for the purpose of desired study. Such problems must be addressed before making use of the index numbers for business situation.

8.4 DIFFICULTIES IN USE OF INDEX NUMBERS

While using index numbers, some major causes of worry must be guarded such as follows :

Data collection : In order to establish the use of index number, the basic data used for the purpose must be reliable, authentic and suitable for the purpose. Sufficient data also is required to arrive at a worthwhile information deduction.

Compatibility of indices : When we try and compare the indices arrived at, the basic data must be compatible for type of comparison. For example, it is not enough to collected data on increase in sales of cars unless we can correlate the side changes *i.e.*Index of an salary increases or cost of fule etc.

Weightage of factors for comparison : In case of inappropriate importance given to various factors responsible for calculation of index, the calculated value will be found distorted and may not be the true representative of the decision variable. If we weigh some changes more important than relevant ones, the distortion is bound to occur. Proper balancing would help like the increase in sales of cars as a result of decrease in their prices or decrease in fuel prices.

Base value : If we select inappropriate base, then distortion can be large, Taking a year of large increase in prices due to abnormal assignable causes may not be appropriate base. Also may be a large consumption of a commodity at the time of natural calamity may not reflect correct index level at this base year.

8.5 METHODS OF CALCULATION OF INDEX NUMBERS

We generally use the following methods for calculation of index numbers :

1. Unweighted aggregate index
2. Weighted aggregate index.
3. Average of Relatives method
4. Quantity and value index.

Unweighted Aggregate Index

This is the simplest method of calculating aggregate index. All the values or data collected are used with equal importance for each. Hence the simple method of calculating index is the major advantage.

In can be expressed mathematically as

$$I_{(u)} = \frac{\Sigma Q_i}{\Sigma Q_0} \times 100$$

Where $I(u)$ = unweighted aggregate index.

Q_i = quantity of each element in the data points for the year of calculations.

Q_0 = quantity of each element of the data points in the base year.

The major disadvantage of the method is that all the factors or elements of the study may not be contributing in the same proportion (importance) towards the index.

Weighted aggregate index

There are some factors or the important elements leading to major changes in the variable than the other factors. It is done in most of the cases in actual life situations. Allotting proper weightage or importance to relevant factor will result in more reliable index.

Mathematically, we may represent the index by the following relationship

$$I_{(w)} = \frac{\Sigma P_i Q}{\Sigma P_0 Q} \times 100$$

Where $I_{(w)}$ = weighted aggregate price index under.

P_i = price of each commodity in the current year.

P_0 = price of related commodity in the base year.

Q = weight or importance for the factor.

The more important question that arises from this so called reliable index calculation is as to what quantitites are used for calculations. We may be using these quantities in the following manner.

(*i*) Quantities consumed during the base year

(*ii*) Quantities consumed during the index year

(*iii*) Quantities consumed during a specified (chosen) year

Based on these three ways, we have three different methods for calculating indices.

Laspeyres Method

This method is used for the index calculation for weighted aggregate system, when the quanitites used are that consumed during the base year. Thus the relationship of index calculation is modified as under

$$I_{(WL)} = \frac{\Sigma P_i Q_0}{\Sigma P_0 Q_0} \times 100$$

Where Q_0 = quantities consumed during the base year.

and $I_{(WL)}$ = weighted index by Laspeyres method.

This method is named after its inventor or the statistician, who developed it.

By using this method, since the quantity base is the same, direct comparison is possible, where as the major disadvantage is that the consumption variation over a period under study is not considered.

The calculation of index number can be done through various methods, depending on the specific situation. These methods are

- Unweighted aggregate index method
- Weighted aggregate index method
- Laspeyres method
- Paasche method
- Fixed-weight aggregate method

Paasche method

When we utilise the quantities consumed during the current year, the weighted aggregate index uses this method. The method was developed by the person under whose name this method is known.

The relationship for index calculation undergoes the change as follows :

$$I_{(WP)} = \frac{\Sigma P_i Q_i}{\Sigma P_0 Q_i} \times 100$$

Where $\quad Q_i$ = quantity consumed during the current or index year

and $\quad I_{(WP)}$ = weighted aggregate index calculated by Paasche method.

The major advantage of this method is collection of data for quantities of each index year. Also due to continuously changing prices, the comparison may be effective.

As an alternative to the above-mentioned methods of calculating index numbers, we can use Average of Relative method by comparing the current prices to the base-time prices and then using the average concept for index calculation.

Fixed-weight aggregate method

This is the third technique used for calculating index under assigned weights in a composite comparison system. It is similar to both the methods described above *i.e.* Laspeyres methods as well as Paasche method, the difference being in the use of quantities consumed during a specified period (neither in that year nor in the current year). The weights assigned for a fixed or representative period are called fixed weights.

Thus, the Index calculation relationship undergoes the change as follows :

$$I_{(wf)} = \frac{\Sigma P_i Q_2}{\Sigma P_0 Q_2} \times 100$$

Where $\quad I_{(wf)}$ = Weighted aggreagate index with fixed weightages

P_i = Current period prices

P_0 = Base period prices

Q_2 = Fixed assigned weights from a representative period

It is more advantageous due to the fact that it caters for the price flexibility in selecting the base year and also allotting a fixed importance level from the representative period selected for the purpose.

Average of Relatives Method

Unweighted average of relatives method

In the last paragraph, we have discussed the methods of calculating indices by three different methods. As an alternate measure, we can work out the average of relatives method to construct an index.

In order to calculate the weighted average of relatives method, we can compare the ratio of current prices to the base prices and then the index is calculated by multiplying the rate by 100. We, then, take the average of all the ratios summed up together. The general relationship now undergoes the change as follows.

Unweighted average of relative price index

$$= \frac{\sum \frac{P_i}{P_0}}{n} \times 100$$

Where P_1 = current period price

P_0 = base period price

n = number of elements in the composite

This would be different from unweighted index as it is mean or the average value of the index.

Weighted average of relatives method

In case of weighted average, we multiply the ratios of current and base prices by 100 and then by the weight or the importance of each ratio. Thus the relationship used for this purpose can be written as follows

Weighted average of the relatives price index

$$= \frac{\sum\left(\frac{P_i}{P_0}\times 100\right)(P_nQ_n)}{\sum P_nQ_n}$$

Where P_nQ_n = Price and quantities that will establish value for the weight or importance assigned to the given ratio.

P_0 = base period price

P_n = current period price

Thus weighted average for all the three methods of calculating can be found out by using appropriate values. The values could be

P_0Q_0 for base period

P_iQ_i for current period

P_2Q_2 for fixed period

Where P_2 = fixed period price

The relationships can accordingly be changed as follows

Weighted average of relative price index

$$(i) \text{ with base period weightage} = \frac{\sum\left[\left(\frac{P_i}{P_0}\times 100\right)(P_0Q_0)\right]}{\sum P_0Q_0}$$

$$(ii) \text{ with fixed period weightage} = \frac{\sum\left[\left(\frac{P_i}{P_0}\times 100\right)(P_2Q_2)\right]}{\sum P_2Q_2}$$

In a situation, where unweighted average may not be useful or accurate, the weighted average of relative method can be used for price index calculation.

Quantity and value indices

So far we have been discussing basically the Price Index, most commonly used. For the quantity and value indices also, the general concept and resultant mathematical relationships can be developed.

In the difficult times of inflation, a quantity index may become more appropriate as it will establish a better and more reliable measure of the variations in the output of materials and the finished goods. Similarly, prices may fluctuate, but quantity of agricultural produce may give better idea of production levels.

Quantity Index :

As for the price index, the weighted average of relatives quantity index can be worked out by using the following mathematical relationship.

Weighted Average of Relatives quantity index

$$= \frac{\sum\left[\left(\frac{Q_i}{Q_0}\right)\times 100\right](P_nQ_n)}{\sum P_nQ_n}$$

Where Q_i = quantity for the current period

Q_i = quantity for the base period

P_nQ_n = prices and quantities for deciding weightages for various ratios.

$n = 0$ for base period

$n = i$ for current period

$n = 2$ for fixed period

There are similar methods suggested for calculating the indices for quantity as well as value (a combination of price and quantity). The actual use depends on the specific situation.

Value Index :

This index measures the changes in the total value of the variable. Since value is a combination of price and quantity, it can be called a composite index. The only negative issue is that composite value index does not distinguish the variations in individual values of price or quantity separately.

CHAPTER SUMMARY

Important Terms used

- **Consumer Price Index :** Indicates the variations in the prices of a given set of consumer items prepared either at regional level or at National level.
- **Fixed-weight aggregates method :** When weightage or importance to the variable is allotted based on a given specified fixed period.
- **Index number :** A ratio of the variable value at the current level to the base level, *i.e.* the ratio of variable change over a period.
- **Laspeyres method :** In calculation of aggregate index, the method uses the weights as the quantities consumed during the base period.
- **Paasche method :** Allocation of weights based on quantities consumed during the current period, is done in this method.
- **Percentage relative :** Ratio of the current value to a base value with the result multipled by 100. It is also called index.
- **Price index :** Compares levels of prices from one period (the current) to another (the base) period.
- **Quantitiy index :** An index comparing the quantity of the variable during a given period by time.
- **Unweighted aggregates index :** Using all the values or data collected for study and allocating same importance to all the values.

- **Unweighted average of relatives method :** Working out the index number by dividing the present or current level of the variable to its base value, multiplied by 100 and then dividing the summation of percentage values by the number of products to result in average value.
- **Unweighted aggregates index :** Using all the values considered, but assigning importance or weights to individual ratios.
- **Weighted average of relatives method :** Constructing the index number by allotting weightages to values of each element in the composite.

Relationship used

- Unweighted aggregates quantity index $= \dfrac{\sum Q_i}{\sum Q_0} \times 100$

Where
i = the current period
0 = the based period
Q = quantity

- Weighted aggregates price index $= \left(\dfrac{\sum P_i Q}{\sum P_0 Q} \times 100\right)$

Where
P_i = price at current period
P_0 = price at the base period
Q = weight or importance of value

- Laspeyres index $= \dfrac{\sum P_i Q_0}{\sum P_0 Q_0} \times 100$
- Paasche index $= \dfrac{\sum P_i Q_i}{\sum P_0 Q_i} \times 100$
- Fixed weight aggregate price index $= \dfrac{\sum P_i Q_2}{\sum P_0 Q_2} \times 100$
- Unweighted average of relatives price index $= \dfrac{\sum\left(\dfrac{P_i}{P_0}\right) \times 100}{n}$
- Weighted average of relatives price index $= \dfrac{\sum\left[\left(\dfrac{P_i}{P_0} \times 100\right)(P_n Q_n)\right]}{\sum P_n Q_n}$

- Weighted average of relatives price index = $\dfrac{\sum\left[\left(\dfrac{P_i}{P_0}\times 100\right)(P_0Q_0)\right]}{\sum P_0Q_0}$

- Weighted average of relatives quantity index = $\dfrac{\sum\left[\left(\dfrac{Q_i}{Q_0}\times 100\right)(Q_nP_n)\right]}{\sum Q_nP_n}$

SOLVED PROBLEMS

Problem 8.1

Following prices are indicated for 1995 (base year) and for 2000 (the current year). Calculate the unweighted aggregates price index for the data

Variables	*Prices*	
	1995	*2000*
Tomatoes (per kg)	Rs. 15.00	Rs. 19.00
Egg (per dozen)	Rs. 20.00	Rs. 24.00
Petrol (per litre)	Rs. 22.50	Rs. 30.70
Juices (per litre)	Rs. 61.00	Rs. 69.00

Solution :

For computing price index (unweighted) we have

$$\Sigma P_i = \text{Rs. } 19 + 24 + 30.60 + 69 = \text{Rs. } 142.70$$

$$\Sigma P_0 = \text{Rs. } 15 + 20 + 22.50 + 61 = \text{Rs. } 118.50$$

∴ Unweighted aggregates price index

$$= \frac{142.70}{118.50}\times 100 = 120$$

Problem 8.2

Given the same price levels as in problem 8.1, calculate the weighted aggregates price index, if the quantities consumed as follows

Tomatoes	3000 kg
Egg	2000 dozens
Petrol	6200 litres
Juices	520 litres

Solution :

Preparing the table for calculation of price, index we get

Variables	*Quantities*	*Prices*		*Weighted levels*	
		(P_0) 1995	*(P_i) 2000*	*P_0Q*	*P_iQ*
Tomatoes	3000 kg	Rs. 15.00	Rs. 19.00	45,000	57,000
Egg	2000 dozens	Rs. 20.00	Rs. 24.00	40,000	48,000
Petrol	6200 litres	Rs. 22.50	Rs. 30.70	1,39,500	1,90,300
Juices	520 litres	Rs. 61.00	Rs. 69.00	31,720	35,880

Here $\Sigma P_0Q = 2{,}66{,}220$

and $\Sigma P_iQ = 3{,}31{,}220$

∴ Weighted Aggregates Price Index

$$= \left(\frac{\Sigma P_iQ}{\Sigma P_0Q}\right) \times 100$$

$$= \frac{3{,}31{,}220}{2{,}66{,}220} \times 100$$

$$= 124.4$$

Problem 8.3

By using laspeyres method, calculate the weighted price index for the year 2003 when the given data indicates the prices and consumption levels of various commodities.

Commodities	*Base Price (1997)*	*Current Price (2003)*	*Average quantity consumed (1997)*
Potatos (per kg)	Rs. 5.10	Rs. 4.50	4000 kgs
Milk (per litre)	Rs. 14.00	Rs. 17.00	800 litres
Eggs (per doz)	Rs. 21.00	Rs. 24.00	2000 dozens
Bread (per loaf)	Rs. 17.50	Rs. 19.00	350 loaves

Solution :

For working out Laspeyres price index, we prepare the table as follows :

Commodities	*Price in 1997 (P_0)*	*Price in 2003 (P_i)*	*Quantity in 1997 (Q_0)*	*P_0Q_0*	*P_iQ_0*
Potatos (per kg)	Rs. 5.10	Rs. 4.50	4000 kgs	20,400	18,000
Milk (per litre)	Rs. 14.00	Rs. 17.00	800 litres	11,200	18,200
Eggs (per doz)	Rs. 21.00	Rs. 24.00	2000 dozens	42,000	48,000
Bread (per loaf)	Rs. 17.50	Rs. 19.00	350 loaves	6,125	6,650

From the above calculations

$$\Sigma P_0Q_0 = \text{Rs. } 79{,}725$$

$$\Sigma P_iQ_0 = \text{Rs. } 87{,}850$$

$$\text{Laspeyres price index} = \frac{\Sigma P_i Q}{\Sigma P_0 Q_0} \times 100$$

$$= \frac{87.850}{79.725} \times 100$$

$$= 110$$

Problem 8.4

Using the price level as given problem 8.3, calculate Paasche price index, if the quantities consumed during the year 2003 are as follows

Potatos (per kg)	4000 kgs
Milk (per litre)	650 litres
Eggs (per doz)	2500 dozens
Bread (per loaf)	350 loaves

Solution :

For working out Laspeyres price index, we prepare the table as follows :

Commodities	*Price in 1997* (P_0)	*Price in 2003* (P_1)	*Quantity in 2003* (Q_0)	P_0Q_i	P_iQ_i
Potatos (per kg)	Rs. 5.10	Rs. 4.50	3,650 kgs	18,615	16,425
Milk (per litre)	Rs. 14.00	Rs. 19.00	650 litres	9,100	12,350
Eggs (per doz)	Rs. 21.00	Rs. 24.00	2500 dozens	52,500	60,000
Bread (per loaf)	Rs. 17.50	Rs. 19.00	350 loaves	6,125	6,650

From the above calculations

$$\Sigma P_i Q_i = \text{Rs. } 95{,}425$$

$$\Sigma P_0 Q_i = \text{Rs. } 86{,}340$$

$$\therefore \text{Paasche Index} = \frac{\Sigma P_i Q_i}{\Sigma P_0 Q_i} \times 100$$

$$= \frac{95.425}{86.340} \times 100$$

$$= 110$$

Problem 8.5

A unit of manufacturing has been purchasing following items from the market for the last 10 years. Over a period of 10 years, the prices have gone up. The Unit calculated the average consumption levels as given below. Calculate the fixed-weight aggregates price Index, so as to give confidence to the materials manager about his budget for the year 2004.

Commodities	*Price in 1995*	*Price in 2004*	*Consumption in 1999*
Steel (per ton)	Rs. 5.10	Rs. 4.50	4000 kgs
Water pumps (per litre)	Rs. 14.00	Rs. 17.00	800 litres
Eggs (per doz)	Rs. 21.00	Rs. 24.00	2000 dozens
Bread (per loaf)	Rs. 17.50	Rs. 19.00	350 loaves

Solution :

For working out Laspeyres price index, we prepare the table as follows :

Commodities	*Price in 1997*	*Price in 2004*	*Quantity in 1997*		
	(P_0)	(P_1)	(Q_0)	P_0Q_2	P_iQ_2
Steel (per ton)	Rs. 50,000	Rs. 80,000	150 tons	75 lakhs	120 lacs
Water pumps (unit)	Rs. 50,000	Rs. 80,000	3500 Nos.	1750 lakhs	2800 lacs
Motors (unit)	Rs. 2,60,000	Rs. 3,50,000	570 Nos.	1482 lakhs	1995 lacs
Engines (unit)	Rs. 12,00,000	Rs. 17,00,000	30 Nos.	360 lakhs	510 lacs

We get ΣP_0Q_2 = Rs. 3667 lacs

and ΣP_iQ_2 = Rs. 5425 lacs

∴ Fixed weight aggregates index

$$= \frac{\Sigma P_iQ_2}{\Sigma P_0Q_2} \times 100$$

$$= \frac{5425}{3667} \times 100$$

$$= 148$$

Since the manager knows the present index of pricing of his products as 148, he can (on the average) reliably base his budget on this information.

Problem 8.6

Based on the data given in problem 8.3 calculate the weighted average of relatives index.

Solution :

Working out the table for the index

Commodities	(P_0)	(P_i)	(Q_0)	$\left(\frac{P_i}{P_0}\right) \times 100$	P_0Q_0	$\left(\frac{P_i}{P_0}\right) \times 100\ (P_0Q_0)$
Potatos	Rs. 5.10	Rs. 4.50	4000	88.23	20,400	17,99,892
Milk	Rs. 14.00	Rs. 19.00	800	135.71	11,200	15,19,952
Eggs	Rs. 21.00	Rs. 24.00	2000	114.28	42,000	47,99,760
Bread	Rs. 17.50	Rs. 19.00	350	108.57	6,125	6,64,991

From the above calculations, we obtain the values

$$\Sigma P_0 Q_0 = \text{Rs. } 79{,}725$$

and $$\Sigma\left[\left(\frac{P_i}{P_0}\right)\times 100(P_0 Q_0)\right] = 87{,}84{,}595$$

∴ Weighted Average of the relatives index

$$= \frac{\Sigma\left[\left(\frac{P_i}{P_0}\right)\times 100(P_0 Q_0)\right]}{\Sigma P_0 Q_0}$$

$$= \frac{87{,}87{,}595}{79{,}725}$$

$$= 110$$

It can be seen that index number is the same as calculated from weighted price index (Laspeyres Method)

PRACTICE PROBLEMS

8.7 Company A has been providing four models of motor cycles since 2000. For 4 years the sales volumes have been going up and so have been the prices. These have been tabulated below :

Model	***Average Price***				***Units sold in thousands***			
	2000	***2001***	***2002***	***2003***	***2000***	***2001***	***2002***	***2003***
I	Rs. 32,000	34,000	35,000	41,000	5.1	4.3	4.6	5.7
II	Rs. 27,000	29,000	30,000	32,000	3.5	3.7	4.5	6.1
III	Rs. 25,000	27,000	30,000	32,000	4.7	5.1	5.7	6.8
IV	Rs. 35,000	38,000	41,000	45,000	3.8	4.3	4.3	5.8

Calculate the weighted average of relative price index for the year 2003 as the base and weightage.

8.8 Sports gears have been selling at the price levels indicated in the table below. Calculate the weighted average of relatives quantities indices using price and quantities from 1997 to compute the value weights with 1997 as the base year

Items	***Quantity sold***			***Price 1997 (Rs.)***
	1997	***1998***	***1999***	
Bats	510	605	695	710
Gloves	1100	1200	1400	355
Balls	2500	2700	2100	410
Clothes (pairs)	50	60.	75	910

8.9 An appliances shopkeeper has been keeping watch on the sales volume and prices of items sold by him during the last four years. Using 1999 as the base year, advise him of the price Index for 2003 based on the following information.

Products	Prices (in Rs.)			
	1999	*2000*	*2001*	*2002*
Washing machine	15,000	16,000	17,000	18,000
Refrigerator	10,000	12,000	13,000	15,000
Microwave oven	35,000	41,000	43,000	45,000
Dishwasher	16,000	18,000	20,000	21,000

8.10 Compute the weighted aggregates quantity indices for each year using year 2000 as base year and weights for the prices.

Products	*Volumes exported (in thousand of tons)*				*Price per ton in 2000 (Rs.)*
	1998	*1999*	*2000*	*2001*	
Wheat	4.6	6.7	4.3	5.4	30,000
Rice	4.9	7.3	6.5	6.5	1,20,000
Soyabean	4.7	5.8	3.8	2.1	70,000

8.11 An electronics product shop has been selling three types of calculators namely the business, scientific and the basic education models. The sales information is given below.

Model	*Sales (in thousand) Nos*				*Price in 2000 (Rs.)*
	1999	*2000*	*2001*	*2002*	
Business	5.3	5.5	6.5	8.3	14,000
Scientific	3.5	3.7	4.6	4.9	20,000
Basic educational	7.9	8.5	9.6	10.5	5,000

Calculated the weighted average of relatives quantity index using price and quantity of year 2001 to compute the weights and the base year.

8.12 The sales manager of ABC company was trying to work out the travel budget for his sales people. He had the following information collected from previous years.

Sales persons	*Expenditure on taxis (Rs.)*				*Average rate per km.*
	1999	*2000*	*2001*	*2002*	
A	10,500	11,700	13,000	15,000	3.50
B	9,300	10,000	13,000	15,000	3.60
C	10,000	9,500	8,000	9,000	3.55
D	11,300	12,500	15,000	18,000	3.70
E	10,300	12,000	13,500	14,500	3.60
F	9,000	10,500	12,000	15,000	3.50

For the manager to arrive at logical variation in his budget, calculate the unweighted average of relatives index for each year taking 1999 as the base year.

8.13 National Dairy and Development Board (NDDB) conducted a survey and the following information was obtained. Construct a Laspeyres index with year 2000 as the base year.

Product	*Average price per unit (Rs.)*			*Total quantity in 2000 (in thousands)*
	2000	*2001*	*2002*	
Cheese (kg)	30	33	35	2,000
Milk (litre)	16	17	19	5,000
Butter (kg)	25	28	30	5,500

8.14 A regional engineering college (REC) in Andhra Pradesh has spent the following amounts for recruiting new students for various departments.

Department	***Expenses for year (Rs.)***			
	2000	***2001***	***2002***	***2003***
Mechanical	1,62,000	1,75,000	1,90,000	2,05,000
Civil	1,73,000	1,82,000	2,01,000	2,10,000
Textiles	1,50,000	1,65,000	1,93,000	2,03,000
Electrical	1,75,000	1,89,000	1,98,000	2,11,000

Calculate an unweighted average of relatives index for each year using 2000 as base year.

8.15 A fast food restaurant has been creating data bank by collating information about previous sales and they want to understand the trend of variation in demand. Data for analysis is given below.

Item	***Unit price (Rs.)***			***Quantity sold (in thousands)***		
	2001	***2002***	***2003***	***2001***	***2002***	***2003***
Sandwich	35	38	40	200	215	219
French fries	15	18	22	410	450	510
Burgers	11	12	13	850	950	1080
Pizzas	75	80	88	870	900	950

Calculate fixed weight aggregate for each year using 2001 as base year and quantities in 2002 for weight.

CHAPTER 9

DECISION ANALYSIS

9.1 INTRODUCTION

Basic functions of any manager in day-to-day performance of his job are planning, organising, monitoring and controlling. In all these functions, he has to take a number of decisions, small or big. Thus, decision-making becomes an integral part of any management proccss. The decisions are based on the criteria decided by the organisational objectives of business. Utility, minimisation of cost or time, maximisation of profits are some of the criteria for good business decisions. Normally, there are combination of factors, which decide, a particular outcome of the decision and at times, these may be in conflict. Adhering to high quality level may effect the time and cost criterion, but credibility of the firm to secure future orders or to establish its market share with a certain level of competitors may be very necessary and hence a trade off decision amongst time-cast-performance parameters becomes a matter of utmost importance. There are large number of external factors responsible to modify the decision and decision-maker has to recognise factors like attitude or interest of stock holders or employees and unions. Government policies or change in Regulatory framework may be a major factor playing its cards in major decision making processes. Normally it is the change of decisions, when problems are faced in business. Rationality of Decision making and their improvement bring out the best in a Decision-Maker. Hence, deep analysis of previous decisions and that of complexities of the given environment help the process of coherent, and effective decision-making. Quality of decision-making depends on the input qualitatively and quantitatively.

The basic function of any business manager is decision-making for various purposes. The quality of decision-making depends on the quantity and quality of information available to him or utilised by him. Decision theory is a systematic approach for such a function.

Often inputs or consequences are not fully known and uncertainty prevailing amongst the input parameter creates complications for quality decision-making. Decision theory provides a method for a rational decision-making under given circumstances.

In the previous chapters, we have described models with different parameters inter-reacting under different environmental conditions. The models are formulated based on input information, where parameters are known or are assumed to be known with certainty, while in others, uncertainty can prevail to varying degree. On certain situations are dealt with by assuming parameters following various probability distribution functions. In this chapter, we are trying to work out a formal analytical framework for the decision maker, under uncertainty conditions. Decision maker, in this case, has to make a choice among several courses of action available to him. Due to uncertainty in decision variables relationship and environmental conditions being under constant change as business and time proceeds, the best the decision maker can adopt is the best under the circumstances. Uncertainty has to be tackled with certain amount of risk that the future is likely to materialise. Calculated risk, therefore, becomes a handy tool to reach a worthwhile optimum decision. This analysis is termed as Decision Analysis.

9.2 DECISION TABLES

The quantity of information may be available in large proportions for a number of decision parameters. This information should be structured in the form of a matrix or table, denoting the inter-relationship of various parameters useful for decision-making.

The necessary quantitative data collected or known for a given problem can be arranged in the standard tabular form known as Decision Table or Pay-off Table. The main objective of the Pay-off table is to organise the given known data in very structured format, so that its analysis becomes systematic. The decision table generally contains the following elements:

1. Various alternatives or courses of action (finite)
2. The states of nature
3. The probabilities of the occurrences
4. The resultant pay-offs (conditional) or the outcome.

The tabulated form of this information is also given the name of Pay-off Matrix. A sample pay-off table or decision table or pay-off matrix is given below:

States of Nature	*Alternatives*		
	Bonds	*Stocks*	*Fixed Deposits*
Growth	5	7	10
Stagnation	15	10	–5
Inflation	2	3	7

9.3 DECISION-MAKING PROCESS

As described under 9.1 and 9.2. the decision-making process follows under-given steps.

1. Identify all possible states of nature *i.e.*, events available or affecting the decision.
2. List out various courses of action open to the decision maker. These finite number of courses of action will facilitate the decision maker to decide under controlled parameters.
3. Identify the pay-offs for various strategic solutions under all known events or states of nature. Variation of acts and events will be helpful to identify the outcomes or pay-off for various combinations.
4. Decision to choose from amongst these alternatives under given conditions with identified payoffs. This step may involve the judgement or any additional information helping the decision-making process.

9.4 DECISION-MAKING CATEGORIES

Decision can be broadly divided into four major categories:

1. Strategic Decisions. These are those decisions which have the impact on the broad policy of the organisation and hence have long-term effects, such as decisions on type of market the business is aimed at or the product mix to cater for the varieties of the product line.

2. Tactical Decisions. These are day-to-day decisions having impact on immediate business environment and the resultant outcome.

3. Administrative Decisions. These are the decisions affecting the organisational structure of the firm for optimisation of its utility and performance. Selection of plant location, type of distribution system or level of man-machine ratio are termed as Administrative decisions.

4. Operating Decisions. These are the decisions taken to operate the organisation at a particular performance level and to keep the objectives well under control. Product pricing, Resources Scheduling or Inventory decision such as re-order level or payment schedules are some of the operating decisions.

9.5 DECISION-MAKING ENVIRONMENTS

Decision models are based on the type of input information available to the decision makers. Under the input information umbrella, there are four types of decision environments, namely—

1. Decision-making under certainty
2. Decision-making under uncertainty
3. Decision-making under risk
4. Decision-making under conflict.

Decision-making is not always easy due to the level of operation. While the strategic decisions affect the operations on a long-term basis, tactical administrative or operating decisions may not permit a long time schedule to the business manager.

Decision-Making Under Certainty

Decision-making under certainty are easiest to operate as information available is known with definite results. Linear programming, Break even analysis, goal, programming. Transportation and Assignment Models are some examples of decisions under certainty.

Decision-Making Under Uncertainty

In the absence of past data, it is not possible to estimate the probabilities of occurrence of different states of nature. The decision maker has no method of computing the expected payoff for any strategy. Launching a new product with no information a bout action or strategy of the competitors falls under this category. The choice ‘of the strategy will have to be based on Company policy, experience and the judgement of the decision maker.

Following methods can be used for such situations:

(*a*) Maximin criterion
(*b*) Minimix criterion.
(*c*) Maximax criterion
(*d*) Laplace criterion
(*e*) Hurwicz Alpha criterion
(*f*) Regret criterion

The application of these methods has been illustrated in problem 9.1.

Decision-Making Under Risk

Under this condition, the decision-making is probabilistic and the person making decision cannot predict the outcome of an event. By selecting a particular course of action, he can expect a variety of outcomes or a combination of outcomes. Hence, the risk involved in taking a particular decision is large and this risk is reflected in deciding possible occurrence of a state of outcome. In order to reach the best possible decision, probability distribution of the occurrences will have to be decided based on past data and then the best course can be decided based on largest expected profit value. Hence, the concept of Expected Monetary Value (EMV) is to be understood and used as a criterion for decision-making.

$$\text{EMV } (C_i) = \sum_{i=1}^{n} p_i O_i$$

Where C_i = Course of action i

p_i = Probability of occurrence of outcome O_i

n = number of possible outcomes

O_i = the pay-off expected or outcome of action i

This can be understood from problems 9.2 and 9.3

The decision-making process is always affected by the expected future happenings. Thus decisions under uncertainty or risk have an element of approximation and hence a culmination of all possible environmental factors.

Decision-Making Under Conflict

Conflict in decision-making arises when there are more than one option open for optimality, due to the action of others in the field. Thus decision-making has to take into account the strategy of the competitor also, because the outcome greatly depends not only on our own decisions but largely upon the action taken by the competitor in the similar field.

9.6 SOME IMPORTANT CONCEPTS

Expected Value of Perfect Information (EVPI)

When the situation is probabilistic, there is no control on the occurrences of a given state of nature. If the decision maker had exact information, the situation would be entirely different *i.e.*, with more authentic and exact information available, the decision quality would improve. Thus, the expected value with perfect information will be the expected or the average outcome of the states of nature of the level of information. Therefore, we can calculate the expected value of perfect information (EVPI) with the help of the best alternatives for each state of nature and multiply the pay-off with its probability of occurrence.

Thus, Expected Value with Perfect Information (EVPI).

= (Best outcome of first state of nature) × (Probability of first state of nature) + (Best outcome of second state of nature) × (Probability of second state of nature) +.......+ (Best outcome of the last state of nature) × (Probability of last state of nature).

This expected value with Perfect Information will, thus be the additional or improved value achieved due to perfect information

Thus EVPI = EPPI - EMV

Where EPPI = Expected Profit with Perfect Information

And EMV = Expected Monetary Value

In the relationship described above, the Expected Profit with Perfect Information (EPPI) would mean the maximum obtainable expected monetary value based on perfect information. Let us take the case of increase in the price of a given product. If we anticipate the possibility of price increase and if we know what the competitor would do, then decision made will be easier with more confidence. The manufacturer will be able to adopt the optimal course of action with certainty, if he knows that the competitor would not raise the price, if he acted to raise the price of his manufactured product. This is possible due to completely reliable or perfect information.

Expected Opportunity Loss (EOL)

There is yet another method of maximising the monetary value. This is the way of minimising the expected opportunity loss or expected value of regret. This is obtained by using the difference between the pay-off value of the most favourable course of action and some other course of action. This is considered loss of opportunity by not choosing the most useful or favourable course of action. From a given state of data (information) we can calculate the opportunity loss by subtracting all outcomes from the maximum obtainable payoff or outcome for all states of nature. The opportunity loss for each course of action, then is termed as conditional opportunity joss and expected opportunity loss for any course of action would be the conditional opportunity loss multiplied by its probability of occurrence. These concepts have been used in problem 9.4.

9.7 DECISION TREE ANALYSIS

Often in analysing decisions, the decision maker, apart from considering 'all the choices open to him as well as the uncertainties associated, will have to identify the time sequence in which various actions and consequent events would occur. Decision-making involves several stages, and at each stage, each of the choice open will result in a different outcome and pay-off. These can be represented by the tree formation listing out all events and resultant outcomes.

Since decision quality depends on the quantity and quality of information used, more the information, better the decision will be made. Hence, the concept of expected monitory value and expected value of perfect information are useful in Decision theory.

As can now be understood from the description given above, a decision tree would consist .of nodes, branches, probabilities and the resultant pay-offs. It can also be seen that the square indicates a decision point. There are a number of branches leading from this square (decision point) indicating various courses of action open to the decision maker. At the end of each branch, there is a node denoted by a circle and it is called a chance node. Various outcomes emerge out of the chance node with their associated probability estimates. The net result of each outcome is indicated against each node branch. (Refer Fig. 9.1).

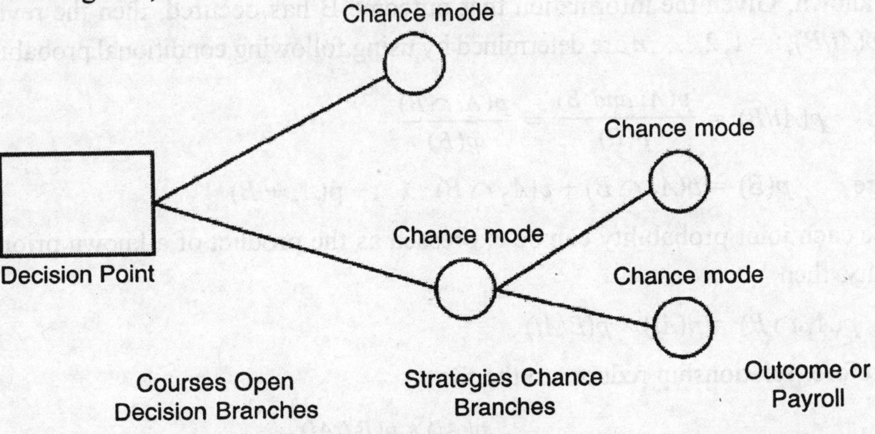

Fig. 9.1. Decision Tree

It is also evident from the above figure that there are branches from the decision node as well as from the chance nodes. These are named as decision branches and chance branches respectively. The probabilities associated with each branch is indicative of the likelihood that a particular.-action would be assumed within the given situation. The pay-off written against each chance branch can be positive or negative depending on the nature of event. Revenue of sale or, Profits can be represented as positive pay-off, whereas expenditure or losses can be represented as negative pay-off.

The stages of the decision tree would depend on the level of decision-making. If there are series of decisions to be made, say, likely profits for 5 years span, it will be a multistage decision tree case for spans of 1, 2, 3, 4 and 5 years decisions.

9.8. POSTERIOR PROBABILITES AND ANALYSIS

The quality of decision-making depends on the quality of inputs information and a major source of improved new information is the search and evaluation of old decisions. Due to the improved information, new alternatives can be considered, due to which the effects and resultant consequences can be duly modified or restated. The uncertainty of uncontrolled parameters result in reconsidered state of nature and therefore the likelihood of their occurrence can be revised. This normally has the impact on the expected pay-off. The existing information can thus be compared with the impact of newly acquired information in the form of expected value and the cost of the new information and it is then determined whether the new information is worth acquiring.

The method of improving the quality of decision by a business manager is constant upgradation of the information received. Even a minor change in the information level can make a major contribution to the quality of decision. An Algebraic method has been suggested through Baye's Theorem, establishing the improvement of quality (probability) through added information.

The initial probability statement used to evaluate expected, pay-off this termed as a "prior probability Distribution" whereas the statement which has been revised in the light of new information acquired is called a "Posterior Probability Distribution". It is new evident that what is posterior to one sequence of state of nature becames the prior to other yet to happen. The effects and relationship of prior probability to the posterior probability can be computed with the help of "Baye's Theorem. The analysis of problems using these probabilities with reference to the revised pay-offs with new, information, is thus called prior-posterior analysis.

Baye's Theorem or Bayesian Decision Rule

The general farm of the Baye's Theorem can be stated as follows:

Let $A_1, A_2, \ldots\ldots A_n$ be mutually exclusive and collectively exhaustive outcomes. The related prior probabilities can be expressed as $p(A_1), p(A_2) \ldots p(A_n)$. As a result or further experiment, there be an outcome B whose conditional probabilities, can be expressed as $p(B/A_1); p(B/A_2); \ldots\ldots p(B/A_n)$ and are known, Given the information that outcome B has occured, then the revised probabilties known, $p(Ai/B), i = 1, 2 \ldots\ldots n$ are determined by using following conditional probability relationship.

$$p(Ai/B) = \frac{p(Ai \text{ and } B)}{p(B)} = \frac{p(Ai \cap B)}{p(B)}$$

where $\quad p(B) = p(A_1 \cap B) + p(A_2 \cap B) \ldots\ldots + p(A_n + B)$

Since each joint probability can be expressed as the product of a known prior and conditional probability, then

$$p(A_1 \cap B) = p(Ai) \times p(B/Ai)$$

Therefore, relationship reduces to the form

$$p(Ai/B) = \frac{p(Ai) \times p(B/Ai)}{p(A_1)p(B/A_1) + p(A_2)p(B/A_2) + \ldots\ldots p(A_n)p(B/A_n)}$$

The Baye's theorem relationship is extensively used to determine the effect of new information and decision makers can utilise the concept to decide whether the information is worth acquiring and what is the concept to decide whether the information is worth acquiring and what is the resultant advantage *i.e.*, pay-off and at what cost.

9.9. DECISION-MAKING WITH UTILITIES

Under normal circumstances, the decision maker the decision based on EMV criterion described in this chapter under 'Decision Theory'. This should be a good measure for decision-making under risks conditions. But there are times when either the measure of EMV is not good enough a reason for decision making or else the monetary value cannot really be assigned to the decision, if the usefulness of the decision has some alternate course to consider.

There can be three situations, when EMV criterion is not going to or likely to produce desired result.

1. When decision maker cannot assign some of the outcomes of his or her decision in terms of EMV or monetary denefit.
2. Risks need be judged in terms of short terms or long term gains. The perception of the decision maker is valied in this case. Some persons do not mind risk of short term losses, if there are long terms gains anticipated.Other can be the orther way round. A person may be happy, if he gets Rs. 10,000 today as a sure money, rather than waiting for one year for enhancement of this amount to Rs. 2,50,000 when he bets it in horse racing or in shares. This is because of risk-taking capability.
3. EMV assumes a linear relationship of the outcome with its utility or value. This is explained by the concept that the value of the money decreases with lapse of time due to market conditions of inflation etc. and hence 'One bird in hand' is considered better than two in, the bush for which you are not sure they will remain two, by the time you get them. Today's gain can be multiplied better due to the fact that it is available today and is certain.

Due to these reasons, the concept of utility is useful phenomenon to explain the decision theory under utility consideration'.

This can be explained by a simple example. Let us consider the decision maker to be needing money for his son's education. If he can get this money of say Rs. 2,00,000 from a friend today, he can put it to use. And hence a promise of Rs. 5,00,000 by another friend after a lapse of 2 years is no use to him and if it comes to him only if he gets it after friends house is sold. In this case, the monetary value of Rs. 5 lakhs is lower for him than Rs. 2 lakhs today, for which he has the immediate need.

Sometimes the business decisions are dependent on the utility value of the decision. Hence the Expected Monitory Value (EMV) may not be a true refection of things to come. In such cases, the concept and theory of utility should be made use of.

9.10 THE UTILITY CONCEPT

This concept of utility of a commodity or an outcome for a decision maker is difficult to apply, but Von Neumann and Morgenstern proposed that the utility can be expressed as a measure of the value of an outcome. It indicates that each individual has different preference from amongst various choices or alternatives available or offered to him. This preference is called utility. If we can evaluate, a person's preference or utility by proper reasoning, the risk taking characteristics of the person can be found out. The measure of utility is done in an arbitrary unit called "utiles".

As per the concept suggested by Von Neumann and Morgenstern, in any decision making, where there is risk involved, the person will go in for the alterative or option with maximum utility. The measure of the utility function or expected utility is done in a similar way as done for any expected value *i.e.* by mutliplying the probabilities by the corresponding outcome or pay-off and then adding all these values. The utility is measured on the cordinal scale. This means that if a 10% discount on an item is twice as important as getting 15% discount on another item, we say that cordinally (say 1, 2,......... etc.) 10% discount on item A is *twice* as important on 15% discount on another item B for the same benefit. This is called establishing relationship between money value and the utility value. In case of risky decisions, these are based on the utility value of the proposal.

For the purpose of utility application, some basic assumptions are necessary to set the basis of decision-making. These are
- Transitivity
- Continuity
- Certainty Equivalent.
- Risk Premium

The Assumptions

For explaining the decision-making on utility concept, we follow certain assumptions described below:

1. *Transitivity*—When an individual is found to have indifferent attitude towards two alternatives, it is means that he has the same utility Jor both the proposals.
2. *Continuity*—When the individual is having preference to proposal A over B ,and B over C, Then the utility is better in case of A than C.
3. *Certainty Equivalent*—For a risky situation, when an individual prefers to pay Rs. 100 for an item while the other individual is prepared to pay only Rs. 75, we say that utility of Rs. 100 for A is equivalent to the utility of Rs. 75 for B. This is called Certainty Equivalent (CE), under risky situations.
4. *Risk Premium (RP)*—Having understood the concept of EMV and CE, we can deduce that the difference of the two measures is called Risk Premium (RP) *i.e.*,

$$\text{Risk Premium} = \text{Expected Monetary Value} - \text{Certainty Equivalence}$$

or

$$RP = EMV - CE$$

For a risk-taker, the value of RP will he negative as he is prepare to risk more than hope for the return. This concept is useful in day-to-day business, where risks are taken based on the perception of the decision maker to achieve better results.

Utility Function and Measures

Von-Neumann and Morgenstern proposed an index for the measurement of utility. It is designed for predictive purposes and allows to predict which of several bets a person would prefer and thus enables him to take decisions.

As per utility theory, expected utility of a risky alternatives is defined as the aggregate of the products of the utility values of all its possible outcomes and their respective probabilites.

Utility Function or Utility Curves

We have seen that expected monetary value (EMV) and Expected Utility (EU) are calculated in the similar way. But it is difficult to relate money to the utility. This is generally done in the form of a graph called utility curves. Since these curves describe the relationship of money and utility, *i.e.*, connecting monetary value in terms of utility, these are called utility functions also.

Since the expected utility (EU) of a risky situation is conceptualised as the aggregate total of the products of the individual utility values of all possible outcomes *i.e.*,

$$EU = \sum_{i=1}^{n} pi\ ui$$

where ui = individual utility for $i = 1, 2 \ldots\ldots n$

and pi = corresponding probabilities of these utility outcomes $i = 1, 2, \ldots\ldots n$

The concept of utility functions can be explained by constructing the curve by measuring the attitude of the decision maker towards his risk taking attitude and capacity. The curves are described as follows :

Psychological Reactions to Risks

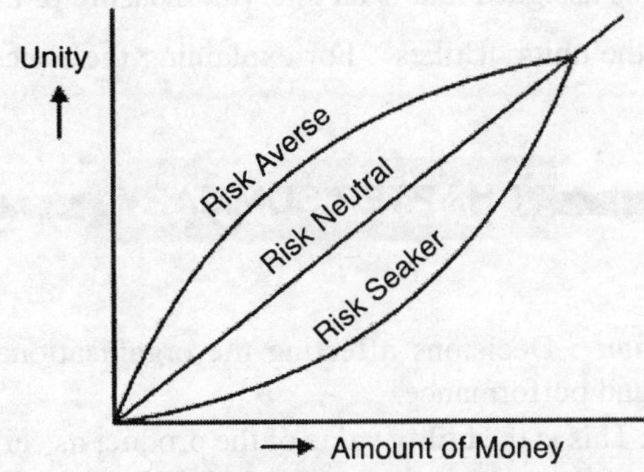

Fig. 9.2. Utility Concept

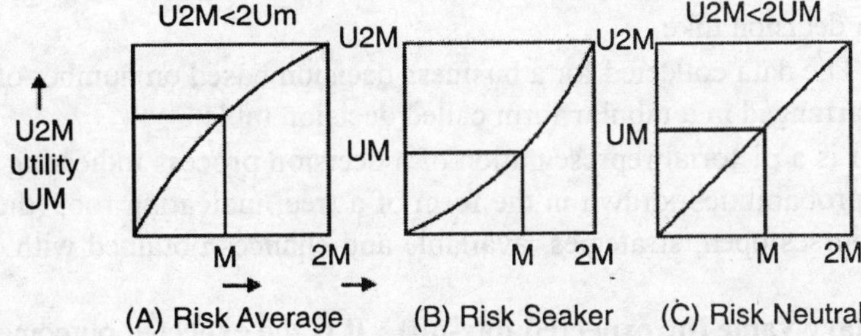

Fig. 9.3. Risk Reactions

The utility functions of risk-averse, risk seekers and risk-neutral decision makers are given above. It may be observed from part (*a*) of the figure that, if *N* be a certain sum of money, then the utility of an amount double than that represented by *N*, equal to 2*N*, is less than twice the utility of the amount M. Thus U2M < 2UM. Similarly, from the part (*b*) and (*c*) respectively, it is clear that for a risk-seeker U2M > 2UM while U2M = 2UM for a risk neutral individual.

The increasing slope of the utility function of a risk-seeker indicates that he has increasing marginal utility of money. Thus, when his cash position improves, he places more value on each additional rupee that he would get. For a Risk-averse, on the other hand, the marginal utility of money is decreasing. The linear utility function for a risk-neutral implies a constant marginal utility of money for him. His utility varies in direct proportion to the monetary value.

> The concept of utility can best be illustrated with the help of utility curves under different risk perceptions. Risk is an inherent part of the business, but calculated risk with environmental analysis, brings better results.

9.11 UTILITY MEASUREMENT

Von-Neumann Morgenstern Method

When the decision maker makes a subjective assessment of the value of the quantity of money, in case of situations involving risk, it is called the utility of money as explained in the opening paragraph of this chapter. For measuring such a. utility, we can adopt three different systems.

1. Nominal of classifications
2. Ordinal or ranking
3. Cardinal or interval

The Von-Neumann and Morgenstern method of measuring the utility is the Cardinal system wherein a unit or a number is assigned that is an interval. measure of a characteristic,

Utility is measured in the units "Utilies". For explaining the concept, problem 9.16 has been illustrated.

CHAPTER SUMMARY

Terms used

- **Administrative Decision :** Decisions affecting the organisational structure of the firm for optimisation of utility and performance.
- **Certainty equivalent :** This is the utility value of the product as certain amount equivalent. *e.g.* under condition of risk, if Person A is paying Rs. 100 for an item but B is ready to pay Rs. 75. Then Rs. 75 is certainty equivalent for A under risky condition.
- **Conditional pay-off :** It is the level of outcomes for a combination of strategies for a business. *i.e.* elements of a decision take.
- **Decision table :** The data collected for a business decision based on number of alternatives for two variables is arranged in a tabular form called decision table.
- **Decision tree :** It is a pictorial representation of a decision process indicating alternatives and their associated probabilities; drawn in the form of a tree, indicating root (the decision point) and branches (courses open, strategies, available and chances obtained with conditional pay-off).
- **Expected monetary value (or expected pay-off) :** It is the expected outcome of the situation from all available alternatives. It is the product of the conditional pay-off with the corresponding value of the probability
- **Expected opportunity loss (EOL) :** It is the minimum value expected from the represent situation, when we estimated the expected loss for not doing the best. It is the product of conditional opportunity loss (difference between the most favourable opportunity and the opportunity availed) with the relative probability of occurrence.
- **Expected value of perfect information (EVPI) :** In probabilistic situations, the improvement in the expected value of the Outcome due to better available information.
- **Hurwicz alpha criterion :** It is a decision-making method under conditions at uncertainty, considering the best and the worst outcomes and using Alpha as the level-of importance.
- **Laplace criterion :** Under uncertain conditions, when we use equal probability for all opportunities it is, called laplace criterian of decision-making.
- **Maximax criterion :** For uncertain conditions, a decision made base on best of the best alternatives.
- **Maximin criterion :** A decision under uncertainty using the best opportunity for the most pessimistic outcomes.
- **Minimax criterion :** A decision based on the minimum level of the best possible outcomes, under uncertainty conditions.
- **Operating decisions :** Decisions taken to operate the organisation at a particular, performance level and to keep the objectives under control.
- **Risk premium :** It is the difference of the expected pay-off and the certainty equivalent for a decision maker.
- **Tactical decisions :** Day-to-day short term decisions having impact on immediate business environment.
- **Transitivity :** When an individual is formed to have indifferent attitude towards two alternatives, thus having same utility for both the proposals.

- **Utility :** The value of the proposal for an individual for its immediate use.
- **Utility function :** It is the measures of expected utility of a risky situations and is the product of conditional utility of the proposal with the probability of its acceptances.

Relationships used

- $EMV = \sum_{1}^{n} p_i o_i$
- EVPI =EPPI – EMV where EPPI = expected profit with perfect information
- Baye's theorem $P(A_i/B) = \frac{p(A_i) \times p(B / A_i)}{\Sigma[p(A_i) \times p(B / A_i)]}$
- RP = EMV – CE
- $EU = \sum_{1}^{n} p_i u_i$

SOLVED PROBLEMS

Problem 9.1

A company has to choose one of the three types of Biscuits, Cream, Coconut and Glucose. Sales expected during next year are highly uncertain. Marketing Department estimates the profits considering manufacturing cost, promotional efforts and distribution set up etc., as given in the table below.

Types of Biscuits	*Profits on estimated level of sales (in lakhs) for quantities*		
	5,000	*10,000*	*20,000*
Cream (C)	15	25	45
Coconut (Co)	20	55	65
Glucose (G)	25	40	70

Maximin Criterion: In using the maximin criterion, the decision maker adopts a pessimistic approach and tries to maximise his security in the face of a highly uncertain situation. For worst situation, the pay-offs are 15, 20 and 25 for C, Co and G respectively. Even at the pessimistic level, the manager tries to make the best of the situation reaching the decision as Glucose, pay-off being the best amongst the worst. This maximises the minimum pay-off. Hence, company will launch Glucose biscuits (G).

Minimax Criterion: In this case, maximum pay-offs are 45, 65 and 70 in three cases. In order, to gain at least the minimum of these maximas, minimum pay-off is 45 for cream (C). Hence, the strategy will be to launch Cream biscuits (G).

Maximax Criterion: In this case, the decision -maker become totally optimistic and chooses the strategy that makes the best of the best. The largest pay-off for each type are 45, 65 and 70. The maximum pay-off being 70, we choose to launch Glucose biscuits (G).

Laplace Criterion: When decision maker has no definite information about the probability of occurrence of various states of nature, he makes simple assumption that each is equally likely. Therefore, the probability of each to occur is $^1/_3$.

Expected pay-offs are :

$$E(C) = {}^1/_3 \times 15 + {}^1/_3 \times 25 + {}^1/_3 \times 45 = 28.33$$

$$E(Co) = {}^1/_3 \times 20 + {}^1/_3 \times 55 + {}^1/_3 \times 65 = 46.67$$

$$E(G) = {}^1/_3 \times 25 + {}^1/_3 \times 40 + {}^1/_3 \times 70 = 45$$

The strategy for 'Coconut' expects the maximum pay-off. Hence, the decision would be to launch Coconut Biscuits (Co).

Hurwicz Alpha Criterion : Maximin and Maximax are two extremes on the scale of optimism. It would be progmatic to assume that a business manager's attitude would fall somewhere in between rather than at either extremes. Leonid Hurwicz, therefore, propounds a combination of the two criteria in what is known as Hurwicz Alpha Criterion.

In this case, the decision maker's degree of optimism is represented by α, the coefficient of optimism, varying between 0 and 1; α = 0 denoting total pessimism and α = I, total optimism.

A decision index *Di* is defined by

$Di = \alpha Mi + (1 - \alpha)\, mi$ where

Mi = Max. pay-offs from any of the outcomes resulting from the *i*th strategy.

and mi = min. pay-off from any of the outcomes resulting from the *i*th strategy.

For each strategy, the value of decision index is found and strategy with the highest values of outcome is chosen.

Let us assume α = 0.6 in this particular example.

$$Di(C) = (0.6 \times 45) + (1–0.6) \times 15 = 33$$

$$Di(Co) = (0.6 \times 65) + (1–0.6) \times 20 = 47$$

$$Di(G) = (0.6 \times 70) + (1–0.6) \times 25 = 52$$

The strategy chosen, therefore, would be to launch Glucose (G) producing the best outcome *i.e.*, 52.

Regret Criterion : Loss of opportunity is a common phenomenon in the business world. The Regret Criterion the dissatisfaction associated with not having got the best that would have been possible if the state of nature of occur were known in advance.

A measure of regret of an outcome is the opportunity cost computed as the difference in pay-off of the outcome and the largest pay-off which could have been obtained under the corresponding state of nature. The table so obtained is also called Opportunity Loss Table (OL table).

Revised pay-off (substracting pay-off from highest of that event) *i.e.*, Regret pay-off.

	5,000	*10,000*	*20,000*	*Max. Regret*
Cream (C)	(25-15)	(55-25)	(70-45)	30
Coconut (Co)	(25-20)	(55-55)	(70-65)	5
Glucose (G)	(25-25)	(55-40)	(70-70)	15

Minimum of max regret is 5 corresponding to coconut biscuits. Hence we choose to launch Coconut (Co) biscuits.

Comparison

Criterion	*Strategy*

Maximim	Glucose
Minimax	Cream
Maximax	Glucose
Laplace	Coconut
Hurwicz Alpha	Glucose
Regret	Coconut

The choice of the decision maker is the reason for inconsistency in the above results. It is method of converting a state of decision under 'uncertainty' to state of risk' or 'certainty'. The personality of the decision maker plays an important role in these decisions.

Problem 9.2

A trading company of Delhi is considering expansion of its activities and planning to open a marketing office at Kanpur to boost the sales in North-East U.P. It is to be decided whether to operate from the existing office at Delhi and cover the area by frequent travelling or else establishing the office the Kanpur.

The connected pay-offs and probabilities of two alternatives are as under :

Alternatives	*States of nature*	*Probability*	*Pay-off (Rs. in lakhs)*
A. Operate from Delhi	(*i*) increase in demand by 30%	0.60	50
	(*ii*) no appreciable change	0.40	5
B. Open office at Kanpur	(*i*) increase in demand by 30%	0.70	40
	(*ii*) no appreciable change	0.30	–10

Expected pay-off for alternative A = (0.60 × 50) + (0.40 × 5) = Rs. 32 lakhs

Expected pay-off for alternative B = (0.70 × 40) + [(0.30) × (–10)] = Rs. 25 lakhs

The expected pay-off for alternative A being higher, it is advisable to operate from Delhi.

As seen from the pay-offs new office at Kanpur would entail certain capital expenditures which may not be justified if the sales do not pick-up. Hence calculated risk may be taken to operate from Delhi only.

Problem 9.3

Under an employment promotion programme, it is proposed to allow sales of newspapers on the buses during off-peak hours. The vendor can purchase the newspaper at a speical discounted rate of 25 paise per copy against the selling price of 40 price. Any unsold copies are, however a dead loss. A vendor has estimated the following probability distribution for the number of copies demanded.

Number of copies demanded	:	15	16	17	18	19	20
Probability	:	0.04	0.19	0.33	0.26	0.11	0.07

How many copies should he order so that his expected profit will be maximum ?

[*Punjab University, M.B.A., 1983*]

Solution :

From the data given in the problem, it is evident that the number of copies to be purchased by the vendor would vary between 15 and 20 depending on the demand pattern. We therefore, establish the profit level pattern for 15 to 20 copies. The results are tabulated below:

Demand	Probability	Conditional pay-off for purchase level (Rs.)						Expected pay-off for the purchase level (Rs.)					
		15	16	17	18	19	20	15	16	17	18	19	20
15	0.04	2.25	2.00	1.75	1.50	1.25	1.00	0.09	0.08	0.07	0.06	0.05	0.04
16	0.19	2.25	2.40	2.15	1.90	1.65	1.40	0.427	0.456	0.408	0.361	0.313	0.266
17	0.33	2.25	2.40	2.55	2.30	2.05	1.80	0.742	0.792	0.841	0.759	0.676	0.594
18	0.26	2.25	2.40	2.55	2.70	2.45	2.20	0.585	0.624	0.663	0.702	0.637	0.572
19	0.11	2.25	2.40	2.55	2.70	2.85	2.60	0.247	0.264	0.280	0.297	0.313	0.286
20	0.07	2.25	2.40	2.55	2.70	2.85	3.00	0.157	0.168	0.178	0.189	0.199	0.210
		Total expected profit						2.248	2.384	2.440	2.368	2.188	1.968

Working out has been done for a unit profit of Re. 0.15 for sold newspapers and loss of Re. 0.25 for unsold papers. Papers purchased in the excess of demand are total loss. For example, for a combination of Demand as 15 against a purchase of 15, the net pay-off = 15 × 0.5 = Rs. 2.25 as total profit (no copies left unsold).

For any demand more than purchase, profit remain as per sold copies (purchase level). But when demand is lower than the pruchase level, say purchased copies being 18 but demand is only 16, there will be only 16 sold and 2 wasted. Thus, profit

= 16 × 0.15 – 2 × 0.25 = Rs. 2.40 – 0.50 = Rs. 1.90 (Reflected in the table as 1.90 and marked.)

Thus, we can infer that the maximum profit strategy of the vendor would be to purchase 17 copies of the newspaper everyday. (marked as 2.440)

Problem 9.4

A manufacture finds the opportunity to increase his business beyond his present on existing production capacity. In order to decide whether to increase the production capacity, he would need a reliable information about increase in demand of the product, based on which only, he can commit his resources. He has two choices open to him, firstly, the expansion of the existing capacity with a cost of Rs. 8 lakhs or the modernisation of the plant at a cost of Rs. 5 lakhs. The time required for implementation of both the options is expected to be the same. While considering the demand pattern, he estimates the high demand situation at a probability of 0.35 as compared to the moderate rise in demand at 0.65 probability. He also estimates that he would be spending an additional amount of Rs. 12 lakhs for expansion against Rs. 6 lakhs for modernisation, if the demand rise is high, whereas in case of moderate demand increase, the expenditurre involved would be Rs.7 lakhs for expansion or Rs. 5 lakhs for modernisation process.

(*a*) Calculate the conditional profits under various combinations.

(*b*) Establish expansion or modernisation so as to maximise its expected monetary value.

(*c*) Work out EPPI, EVPI and EOL.

Solution :

We have the following states of nature and courses of action.

Let S_1 = state of high demand

S_2 = state of moderate demand

A_1 = courses of action as expansion

A_2 = course of action as modernisation

The probabilities as

P_1 = probability of high demand = 0.35

P_2 = probability of moderate demand = 0.65

Calculations for conditional profits values are as under

States of Nature	Conditional profits (Rs.) with courses of action A_1	A_2
S_1 (high demand)	12 – 8 = 4 lakhs	6 – 5 = 1 lakh
S_2 (moderate demand)	7 – 8 = 1 lakh	5 – 5 = 0 lakh

∴ Expected Monetary values can be calculated as under :

$$\text{EMV}(A_1) = 4 \times 0.35 + (-1) \times 0.65$$
$$= \text{Rs. } 0.75 \text{ lakhs}$$
$$\text{EMV}(A_2) = 1 \times 0.35 + (0) \times 0.65$$
$$= \text{Rs. } 0.35 \text{ lakhs}$$

In order to maximise the EMV, therefore, the manufacturer would choose the course of action as Expansion (A_1), due to its higher resultant EMV.

Now to calculate EVPI and EPPI, we choose the optimal course of action for state of nature and then multiply b the corresponding probability. These are shown as under :

State of nature	Probability	Optional Course of Action	Optimal Courses of Action (Rs.) Conditional Profit	Expected Profit
S_1	0.35	A_1	4 lakhs	Rs. 4 × 0.35 = 1.40 lakhs
S_2	0.65	A_2	0	Rs. 0 × 0.65 = 0
				Hence EPPI = 1.40 + 0 = Rs. 1.40 lakhs

The optimal EMV related to course of action A_1 is Rs. 0.75 lakhs

Hence EVPI = EPPI – EMV
= 1.40 – 0.75
= Rs. 0.65 lakhs

This is the cost of getting perfect information on demand pattern.

The opportunity loss vlaues are calculated as under :

States of Nature	Probability	Conditional Profit (Rs.) A_1	A_2	Conditional Opportunity Loss (Rs.) A_1	A_2
S_1	0.35	4 lakhs	1 lakhs	4 – 4 = 0	4 – 1 = 3
S_2	0.65	–1 lakhs	0	0 – (–1) = 1	0 – 0 = 0

Hence, EOL (A_1) = 0 × 0.35 + 1 × 0.65 = Rs. 0.65 lakhs

and EOL (A_2) = 3 × 0.35 + 0 × 0.65 = Rs. 1.05 lakhs

As Evident, the manufacture would try and minimise his opportunity loss and hence would choose course of action A, i.e. Expansion.

Problem 9.5

A manufacturer is faced with a problem of fast change of technology and hence, fast change in the product line. At this point of time, the research and development wing of the organisation has suggested an improved new product with easy acceptance. It will cost the manufacturer Rs. 60,000 for the pilot testing and development testing before establishing the product in the market. The organisation has 100 customers and each customer, might purchase, at the most, one unit of the product, due to its cost and newness. The selling price suggested is Rs. 6,000 for each unit and selling estimate is Rs. 2,000 for each unit.

The probability distribution for proportion of customers buying the product is estimated as follows:

Proportion of Customers	*Probability*
0.04	0.1
0.08	0.1
0.12	0.2
0.16	0.4
0.20	0.2

Work out the expected opportunity, losses and suggest whether the manufacturer should develop the product or not.

Solution :

Let '*p*' be proportion of customers, who purchase the new product. The conditional profit would be governed by the relationship as

$$(6,000 - 2,000) \times 100p - (60,000) = \text{Rs. } (40,000p - 60,000)$$

The conditional profit and opportunity loss are given as under :

Nature of State (proportion of customers)	*Prob.*	*Conditional Profit (Rs.)* A_1 *(develop the product)*	A_2 *(Do not develop)*	*Opportunity Loss (Rs.)* A_1	A_2
0.04	0.1	–44,000	0	44,000	0
0.08	0.1	–28,000	0	28,000	0
0.12	0.2	–12,000	0	12,000	0
0.16	0.4	4,000	0	0	4,000
0.20	0.2	20,000	0	0	20,000

Hence, $\text{EOL}(A_1) = 44,000 \times 0.1 + 28,000 \times 0.1 + 12,000 \times 0.2 + 0 \times 0.4 + 0 \times 0.2 = \text{Rs. } 9,600$

$\text{EOL}(A_2) = 0 \times 0.1 + 0 \times 0.1 + 0 \times 0.2 + 4,000 \times 0.4 + 20,000 \times 2 = \text{Rs. } 5,600$

To seek minimisation of opportunity loss, the manufacturer should not develop the product.

Problem 9.6

A food products company is contemplating the introduction of a revolutionary new product with new packaging to replace the existing product at same price (S_1) or a moderate change in the composition of the existing product with a new packaging at a small increase in price (S_2) or a small change in the composition of the existing except the word 'New' with a negligible increases in price (S_3). The three possible states of nature of events are (*i*) high increases in sales (N_1). (*ii*) no change in sales (N_2) and (*iii*) decreases in sales (N_3). The marketing department of the company worked out the pay-offs in terms of yearly net profits for each course of action for these events (expected sales). This is represented in the following table.

States of Nature	*Courses of Action* S_1	S_2	S_3
N_1	7,00,000	5,00,000	3,00,000
N_2	3,00,000	4,50,000	3,00,000
N_3	1,50,000	0	3,00,000

Which strategy should the choose on the basis of (*a*) Maximin criterion, (*b*) Maximax criterion, (*c*) Minimax Regret criterion, (*d*) Laplace criterion. [*M. D. University, M.B.A. 1983*]

Solution :

For applying various criteria, we will modify the table for the specific parameters under consideration.

(*a*) *Maximin Criterion* : Here we have to select maximum of the minimum pay-offs against each course of action. Hence the table will be used as follows :

	Courses of Action		
States of Nature	S_1	S_2	S_3
N_1	7,00,000	5,00,000	3,00,000
N_2	3,00,000	4,50,000	3,00,000
N_3	1,50,000	0	3,00,000
Minimum pay-off	1,50,000	0	3,00,000

Hence applying the maximin criterion, we have the course of action S_3 as the optimal decision, this being the maximum pay-off of all the minimas (*i.e.* 1,50,000; 0; and 3,00,000).

(*b*) *Maximax Criterion*: Here the outcome recommeded should be the maximum pay-off of all the maximas of the three courses of action. The maximum pay-off against these courses of action are

$S_1 \longrightarrow 7,00,000$ $S_2 \longrightarrow 5,00,000$ $S_3 \longrightarrow 3,00,000$

The maximum of three is relating to S_1 (*i.e.* 7,00,000). This will be the optimal decision under this criterion.

(*c*) *Minimax Regret*: Here we, first have to calculate the Regret or the opportunity loss for each state of nature. Thus, the Regret table will be as under :

States of Nature	S_1	S_2	S_3
N_1	7,00,000–7,00,000	7,00,000–5,00,000	7,00,000–3,00,000
N_2	4,50,000–3,00,000	4,50,000–4,50,000	4,50,000–3,00,000
N_3	3,00,000–1,50,000	3,00,000–0	3,00,000–3,00,000

or

States of Nature	S_1	S_2	S_3
N_1	0	2,00,000	4,00,000
N_2	1,50,000	0	1,50,000
N_3	1,50,000	3,00,000	0
The maximum regrets	1,50,000	3,00,000	4,00,000

The minimax Regret Criterion applications will indicate the course of action with the minimum of maximum regrets *i.e.*, 1,500,000 which relates to S_1.

(*d*) *Laplace Criterion* : In this criterion, we assume that each course of action has a probability of occurence as equal. Since there are three courses of action available, the probability of occurences associated with would be $^1/_3$. The expected pay-off table, thus, gets converted as under :

Courses of Action *Expected pay-off*

S_1 $\frac{1}{3}[7,00,000 + 3,00,000 + 1,50,000] = 38.3 \times 10^4$

S_2 $\frac{1}{3}[5,00,000 + 4,50,000 + 0] = 31.6\% \times 10^4$

S^3 $\frac{1}{3}[3,00,000 + 3,00,000 + 3,00,000] = 30.0 \times 10^4$

The best pay-off is related to course of action S_1 as evident from the above values. Thus, the course of action to be adopted should be S_1 *i.e.* a product with increased price and new packaging.

Problem 9.7.

A typical decision tree has been drawn as below.

Workout the best option suggested.

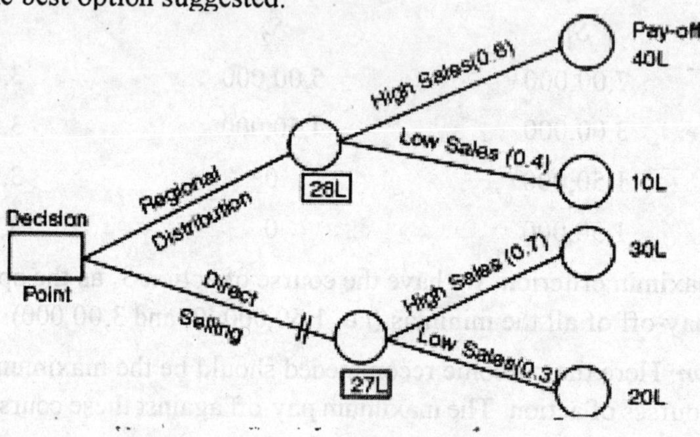

Fig. 9.4.

Solution :

Expected pay-off can be calculated to decide profitable or optimal strategy.

Expected pay-off for regional distribution $= 0.6 \times 40 + 0.4 \times 10 = 28L$

Expected pay-off for direct selling $= 0.7 \times 30 + 0.3 \times 20 = 27L$

Since in this case, pay-off for regional distribution is more than that for direct selling, setting up distribution network regionally is more profitable. These are represented on the tree as given above and then discarded option (direct selling in this case) is scissored out as done.

Problem 9.8

Expected value. of an alternate course of action is the sum of the values of all the predicted outcomes for the alternative multiplied by their respective probabilities. The table gives different alternatives for sales under given situations.

		Outcomes	
		High sales	*Low sales*
Probability→		(0.40)	(0.60)
Company	A	+ 45,000	–10,000
	B	+ 80,000	–25,000
	C	+ 30,000	+ 5,000

Solution :

Decision tree for the problem can be drawn as follows :

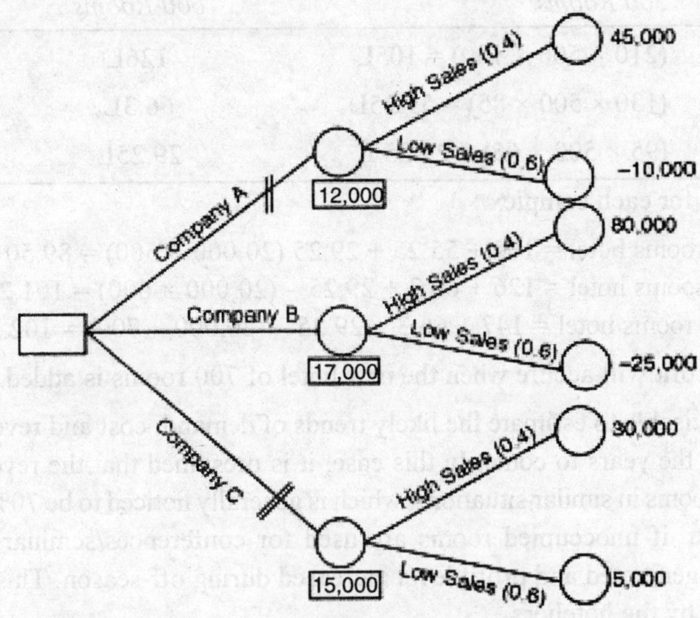

Fig. 9.5. Decision Tree

EMV(A) = (0.4) (45,000) + (0.60) (–10,000) = 12,000
EMV(B) = (0.4) (80,000) + (0.60) (–25,000) = 17,000
EMV(C) = (0.4) (30,000) + (0.60) (+5,000) = 15,000

The maximum benefit accrues when you invest in company B as it given you the greatest expected return in sales.

Problem 9.9

A hotel management is planning to add another 700 room hotel to their chain. Existing occupancy has been found to be an average of 70% on annual basis. It has been estimated that the cost per room per annum is Rs. 20,000. Following data based on demand at simlar hoterls of the chain has been tabulated.

Season	*Number of days*	*Daily demand*	*Average cost per occupied room per day*
Peak Season	210	700	100
Normal Season	130	600	85
Slack Season	90	500	65

(*a*) Prepare a pay-off table for a complex with 500, 600 and 700 rooms.

(*b*) Advise management as to the number of rooms it should construct under new proposal.

(*c*) How to utilise spare capacity due to poor occupancy rate ?

Solution :

(*a*) Pay-off table :

Season	*500 Rooms*	*600 Rooms*	*700 Rooms*
Peak	(210 × 500 × 100) = 105L	126L	147L
Normal	(130 × 500 × 85) = 55.25L	66.3L	66.3L
Slack	(95 × 500 × 65) = 29.25 L	29.25L	29.25L

(*b*) Annual profits for each complex :

Profit for 500 rooms hotel = 105 + 55.25 + 29.25 (20,000 × 500) = 89.50 lakhs
Profit for 600 rooms hotel = 126 + 66.3 + 29.25 – (20,000 × 600) = 101.25 lakhs
Profits for 700 rooms hotel = 147 + 66.3 + 29.25 – (20,000 × 700) = 102.55 lakhs

Thus, maximum profit will accure when the new hotel of 700 rooms is added.

(*c*) It would be advisable to estimate the likely trends of demand, cost and revenue to ascertain profitability in the years to come. In this case, it is presumed that the revenue is based on occupancy of rooms in similar situations, which is generally noticed to be 70% of the available accommodation. if unoccupied rooms are used for conferences/seminars etc. additional income can be generated and profit level increased during off-season. This is generally the trend followed by the hoteliers.

Problem 9.10

A businessman has two independent investments A and B available to him, but he lacks the capital to undertake both. of them simultaneously. He can choose to take A first and then stop, or if A is successful, then take B or *vice-versa.* The probability of success on A is 0.7, while for B, it is 0.4. Both investments require an initial capital outlay of Rs. 2,000 and both return nothing, if the venture is unsuccessful. Successful completion of A will return Rs. 3,000 (over cost), whereas successful completion of B will return Rs. 5,000 (over cost). Draw the decision tree and determine the best strategy. [*C.A., May 1985*]

Solution :

The tree with reference to the available information can be drawn as follows :

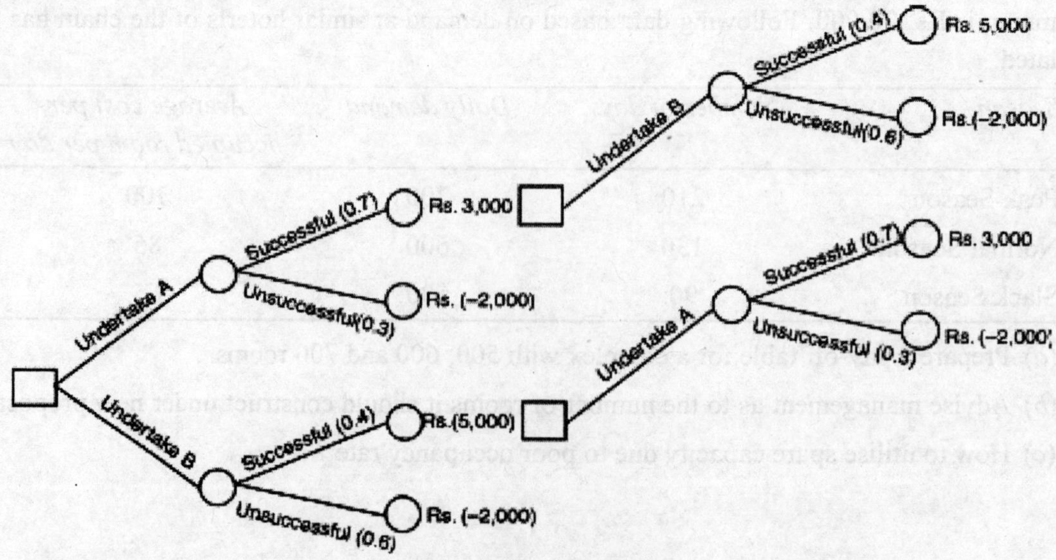

Fig 9.6. Decision Tree

From Fig. 9.6., we can deduce that there are three decision points with 4 strategies

(*i*) Undertake A and stop

(*ii*) Undertake B and stop

(*iii*) If A successful, undertake B

(*iv*) If B successful, undertake A

Now, we work out various pay-off levles for all the three decision points.

Strategy (i) Undertake A and stop.

Investment has a return of Rs. 3,000 with probability 0.7

Hence, expected pay-off = 3,000 × 0.7 = Rs. 2,100

If unsuccessful, the loss is capital investment of Rs. 2,000 with probability 0.3. Hence, expected pay-off or loss due to failure = (–) 2,000 × 0.3
= (–600)

Expected Profit = Rs. 2,100 – 600 = Rs. 1,500

For Stop, Profit = 0

∴ Net Expected Profit = Rs. 1,500

Strategy (ii) undertake B and stop

Success of venture B, Pay-off = Rs. 5,000

Probability = 0.4

∴ Expected Profit = 5,000 × 0.4 = Rs. 2,000

Failure of Venture B, Pay-off = Rs. (–2,000)

Probability = 0.6

Expected Profit = –2,000 × 0.6 = Rs.(–1,200)

For Stop, Profit = Zero

Hence, Net profit = Rs. 2,000 – 1,200 = Rs. 800

Strategy (iii) undertake A and if successful, undertake B

Success of A, Pay-off = Rs. 3,000 + 800

Probability = 0.7

Expected Profit = Rs. 3,800 × 0.7
= Rs. 2,660

Success of B, Pay-off = Rs. 5,000 + 1,500

Probability = 0.3

Expected Profit = Rs. 6,500 × 0.3
= Rs. 1,950

Failure of A, Profit = Rs. (–) 600

Failure of B, Profit = Rs. (–) 1,200

∴ Expected Profit from A = Rs. 2,660 – 600
= Rs. 2,060

Expected Profit from B = Rs. 1,950 – 1,200
= Rs. 750

Strategy (iv) undertake B, if sucessful undertake A

The profits expected have been calculated in strategy (*iii*)

The results are tabulated as follows :

Events	Probability	Courses of Action or Strategies			
		(i)	*(ii)*	*(iii)*	*(iv)*
A & B successful	0.7 × 0.4 = 0.28	3,000	5,000	8,000	8,000
A successful, Not B	0.7 × 0.6 = 0.42	3,000	(2,000)	1,000	(2,000)
B successful, Not A	0.3 × 0.4 = 0.12	(2,000)	5,000	(2,000)	3,000
A & B both unsuccessful	0.3 × 0.6 = 0.18	(2,000)	(2,000)	(2,000)	(2,000)
Expected Pay-offs		1,500	800	2,060	750

Since expected value or profit from strategy (*iii*) is the maximum, we adopt strategy of undertaking A and if successful, undertake B.

Problem 9.11

A person has two independent investements A and B available to him, but he can undertake only one at a time due to certain constraints. He can choose A first and then stop, or if A is successful, then take B or *vice versa*. The probability of success of A is 0.6, while for B it is 0.4. Both the investments require an initial capital outlay of Rs. 10,000 and both return nothing, if the venture is unsuccessful. successful completion of A will return Rs. 20,000 (over cost) and successful completion of B will return Rs. 24,000 (over cost). Draw decision tree and determine the best strategy.

[*C.A., May 1988*]

Solution

The problem is similar to problem 9.10 given above. The decision tree can be drawn as follows :

(*i*) Accept A and stop, expected profit = (20,000 × 0.6) – (10,000 × 0.4) = Rs. 8,000

(*ii*) Accept B and stop, expected profit = (24,000 × 4) – (10,000 × 0.6) = Rs. 3,600

(*iii*) Accept A Expected Profit = (20,000 + 36,000) × 0.6 – (10,000 × 0.4)
= Rs. 10,160

(*iv*) Accept B Expected Profit = (24,000 + 8,000) × 0.4 + (– 10,000 × 0.6)
= Rs. 6,800

It can be deduced that the best strategy is to accept A and then undertake B after A's success.

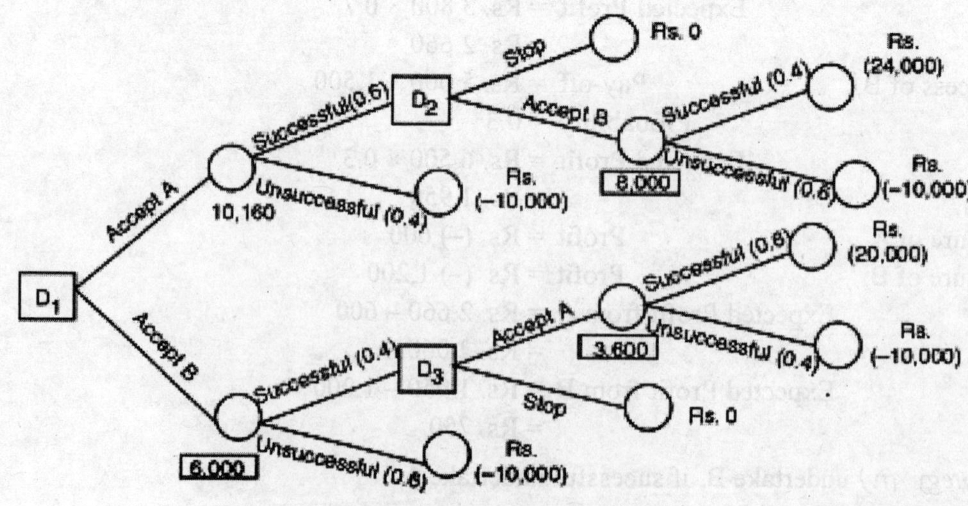

Fig. 9.7. Decision Tree

The expected profit from various alternatives as strategies can be calculated in the similar manner as done in problem 9.10.

Problem 9.12

Matrix company is planning to launch a new product, which can be introduced initially in Western India or int the entire country. If the product is introduced only in Western India, the investment outlay will be Rs. 12 million. After 2 years, Matrix can evaluate the project to determine, whether it should cover the entire country. For such expansion, it will have to incur an additional investment of Rs. 10 million. To introduce the profit in the entire country right in the beginning whould involve an outlay of Rs. 20 million. The product, in any case, will have a life of 5 years, after which the plant will have zero net value.

If the product is introduced only in Western India, demand would be high or low with the probabilities of 0.8 and 0.2 respectively and annual cash inflow of Rs. 4 million and Rs. 2.5 million respectively.

If the product is introduced in the entire country right in the beginning, the demand would be high or low with probabilities of 0.6 and 0.4 respectively and annual cash inflows of Rs. 5 million respectively.

Based on the observed demand in Western India, if the product is introduced in the entire country, the following probabilities would exist for high and low demand on all India basis.

Western India	*Whole Country*	
	High demand	*Low demand*
High demand	0.90	0.10
Low demand	0.40	0.60

The hurdle rate applicable to this project is 12 per cent.

(*a*) Set up a decision tree for the investment situation.

(*b*) Advise Matrix company on the investment policy it should follow. Support your advice with appropriate reasoning. [*ICWA, June 1990*]

Solution

Based on the supplied information, the decision tree is as follows :

Calculations for D_2, $8 \times 0.9 + 5 \times 0.1 = 7.7 \times 3$ years – less cost 10 = Rs. 13.1 million

For D_3, $8 \times 0.4 \times 5 \times 0.6 = 6.2 \times 3$ years – less cost 10 = Rs. 8.6 million

For D_1, $8 \times 0.6 \times 5 \times 0.4 = 6.8 \times 5$ years – cost 20

= Rs. 14 million for whole country.

and $(4 \times 2 + 13.1) \times 0.8 + [(2.5 \times 2)] \times 0.2 = 19.6$ – cost 9.0

= Rs. 7.60 million for Western India

Hence, we advise Matrix company to launch the product over the entire country to gain maximum advantage.

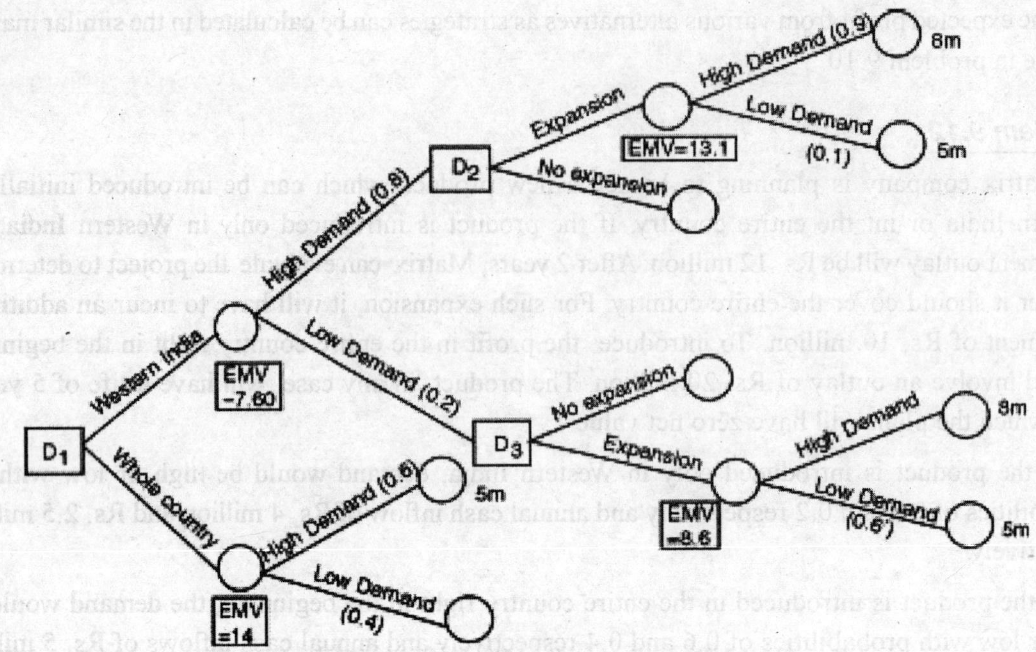

Fig. 9.8. Decision Tree

Problem 9.13

A businessman wants to plain expansion with the knowledge that prices will not increase. His market analysis indicates 65% price stability. But he wants to be at least 80% sure before his commitment. A consultant suggests 75% probability of non-increase of prices. Suggest if expansion should be planned by the businessman.

Solution

Here $P\left(\frac{Ai}{B}\right)=\frac{0.65\times 0.75}{(0.65\times 0.75)+(0.35\times 0.25)}$

Since it is more than 80% required, it means prices will not increase and expansion can be planned.

Problem 9.14

A company is trying to weigh its options whether to go for spending money on market research or not. Market situation is highly probabilistic and it is given in the table below :

Sales	*Expected Returns (Rs. in lakhs)*		
	Poor Market(P)	*Fair Market(F)*	*Good Market(G)*
High	0.5	1.0	1.5
Medium	0	1.5	2.5
Low	0.5	2.0	3.5

The probabilities of markets being poor, fair or good is 0.3, 0.5 and 0.2. As per further investigation, the market research establishes actual chances of market impact as follows :

Actual	$Poor(p_1)$	$Fair(p_2)$	$Good(p_3)$
P	0.7	0.2	0.1
F	0.2	0.7	0.1
G	0	0.2	3.5

Calculate : (*a*) the conditional expected loss

(*b*) expected value of perfect information(EVPI)

(*c*) the expected loss based on market research.

(*d*) the cost of market research.

Solution :

(*a*) *The conditional profit*

Market Sales	*Prior Probability*	*Course of Action*		
		High	*Medium*	*Low*
P	0.3	0.5	0	0.5
F	0.5	1.0	1.5	2.0
G	0.2	1.5	2.5	3.5

The expected conditional opprotunity losses will be calculated by subtracting each pay-off from the maximum pay-off of each event.

Hence, the conditional opoortunity losses are given as follows :

State of Nature	*Prior Prob.*	*Conditional losses*			*Expected opportunity losses (Rs. lakhs)*		
		High	*Medium*	*Low*	*High*	*Medium*	*Low*
P	0.3	0	0.5	0	0	0.15	0
F	0.5	1.0	0.5	0	0.5	0.25	0
G	0.2	2.0	1.0	0	0.4	0.2	0
				EOL =	0.9	0.6	0

(*b*) Expected opportunity loss for medium sale being minimum *i.e.*, 0.6, whereas the opportunity loss under perfect information would be zero. Hence, the expected value of perfect information would be Rs. 0.6 lakhs or Rs. 60,000.

(*c*) The marginal and joint probabilities are given below :

State of Nature		*Conditional Probability*					
		$p(p_1/P_s)$	$p(p_2/F_s)$	$p(p_3/G_s)$	$p(P_S \cap P_1)$	$p(F_S \cap p_2)$	$P(G_S \cap p_3)$
P	0.3	0.7	0.2	0.1	0.21	0.06	0.03
F	0.5	0.2	0.7	0.1	0.1	0.35	0.05
G	0.2	0	0.2	0.8	0	0.04	0.16
Hence,				$p(p_1) = 0.31$;	$p(p_2) = 0.45$;	$p(p_3) = 0.24$	

We now have to revise prior probabilites as per Baye's Theorem relationship as follows :

State	*Probability*	*State of Nature*	*Posterior Probability = p*	$(P_s/p_1) = \frac{p(p_1 \cap p_3)}{p(p_1)}$
p_1	0.31	P	0.21/0.31	= 0.677
		F	0.1/0.31	= 0.323
		G	0/0.31	= 0
p_2	0.45	P	0.06/0.45	= 0.133
		F	0.35/0.45	= 0.778
		G	0.04/0.45	= 0.089
p_3	0.24	P	0.03/0.24	= 0.125
		F	0.05/0.24	= 0.208
		G	0.16/0.24	= 0.667

We, therefore, recalculate the EMVs based on the revised probability as per new information.

State of Nature	*Forecasted or Revised Outcome*								
		I			*II*			*III*	
	Prob.	*COL*	*EOL*	*Prob.*	*COL*	*EOL*	*Prob.*	*COL*	*EOL*
P	0.68	0	0	0.13	0.5	0.065	0.12	0	0
G	0.32	1.0	0.32	0.78	0.5	0.39	0.21	0	0
G	0	2.0	0	0.09	1.0	0.09	0.67	0	0
Posterior EOL			= 0.32			0.545			0

(*d*) Now, to calculate the expected value of the market research

State of Nature	*Revised Probability*	*EOL*	*EVSI*
p_1	0.31	0.32	0.099
p_2	0.45	0.545	0.245
p_3	0.24	0	0
		Revised EOL	Rs. 0.344 lakhs

Thus, the EOL has been reduced from Rs. 60,000 to Rs. 34,400, due to improved information out of market research. The net gain achieved is Rs. 60,000 – 34,400 = Rs. 25,600, which will be the maximum amount the company can spend on market research.

Problem 9.15

A landlord wants to decide on the type of crop to be planted on his farm. The yield largely depends on the amount and time of rainfall. He estimates the profit due this state of nature as follows :

Rainfall	*Estimated Profit (Rs. per acre)*		
	Crop P	*Crop Q*	*Crop R*
Substantial	7,000	2,500	4,000
Moderate	3,500	3,500	4,000
Low	1,000	4,000	3,000

Based on the previous experience, he allocates the probabilites of the type of rainfall as 0.2, 0.3, and 0.5 for substantial, moderate and low rainfall. In order to be more confident, he approaches the Met department and obtains the following forecasts for the current season.

Rainfall	*Estimated Probabilites*		
	Crop P	*Crop Q*	*Crop R*
Substantial	0.7	0.25	0.05
Moderate	0.3	0.6	0.1
Low	0.1	0.2	0.7

Determine which crop the landlord should opt for and also find out, whether it will be worthwhile to obtain the forecast, if the services are to be paid for.

Solution :

(*a*) Let the states of nature of rainfall be R_1, R_2 and R_3 corresponding to substantial, moderate and low rainfall. The table for the expected profit can be computed as follows :

States of Nature	*Prior Probabilities*	*Conditional Profit (Rs.)*			*Expected Profit (Rs.)*		
		P	*Q*	*R*	*P*	*Q*	*R*
R_1	0.2	7,000	2,500	4,000	1,400	500	800
R_2	0.3	3,500	3,500	4,000	1,050	1,050	1,200
R_3	0.5	1,000	4,000	3,000	500	2000	1,500

The maximum EMV is Rs. 3,550 and it is for crop Q and hence the landlord should opt for crop Q.

(*b*) The revised information based on Met Forecast can be denoted as F_i (i = 1, 2, 3) for substantial, moderate and 7.15low rainfall respectively. The likely probabilites (revised) can be computed as per the following table:

States of Nature	*Forecast Livelihood*		
	$p(F_{11}/Ri)$	$p(F_{21}/Ri)$	$p(F_{31}/Ri)$
R_1	0.7	0.25	0.05
R_2	0.3	0.6	0.1
R_3	0.1	0.2	0.7

The EPPI can be calculated based on the maximum profit basis for various crops under different rainfall conditions.

Thus, EPPI = 0.2 × 7,000 + 0.3 × 4,000 + 0.5 × 4,000

= Rs. 4,600

Hence, EVPI = EPPI – Max. EMV

= Rs. 4,600 – 3,550

= Rs. 1,050

For the forecast results, the prior and posterior probabilites are calculated as under :

State of Nature	Prior Prob.	Outcome	Conditonal Prob. $p(F_i/Ri)$	Joint Probability $p(Fi/Ri) = p(Ri) \times p(Fi/Ri)$		
				1	2	3
R_1	0.2	F_1	0.7	0.14	—	—
		F_2	0.25	—	0.05	—
		F_3	0.05	—	—	0.01
R_2	0.3	F_1	0.3	0.09	—	—
		F_2	0.6	—	0.18	—
		F_3	0.1	—	—	0.03
R_3	0.5	F_1	0.1	0.05	—	—
		F_2	0.2	—	0.10	—
		F_3	0.7	—	—	0.35
Marginal Probabilities =				0.28	0.33	0.39

The posterior probabilities are computed as follows :

Outcome	Probabilites $p(F_i)$	States of Nature	Posterior Prob.
F_1	0.28	R_1	0.14/0.28 = 0.5
		R_2	0.09/0.28 = 0.32
		R_3	0.05/0.28 = 0.18
F_2	0.33	R_1	0.05/0.33 = 0.15
		R_2	0.18/0.33 = 0.55
		R_3	0.10/0.33 = 0.03
F_3	0.39	R_1	0.01/0.039 = 0.025
		R_2	0.03/0.39 = 0.076
		R_3	0.35/0.39 = 0.897

Now we calculate revised EMV for the adjusted or revised probability due to the new information.

State of Nature	F_1 Prob.	COL	EOL	F_2 Prob.	COL	EOL	F_3 Prob.	COL	EOL
R_1	0.5	0	0	0.15	500	75	0.025	3,000	60
R_2	0.32	4,500	1440	0.55	500	275	0.076	0	0
R_3	0.18	3,000	540	0.03	0	0	0.897	1,000	900
Posterior EOL =			1,980			350			960

The expected value of the new information will be as follows :

Outcome	Probability	EOL	EVSI
F_1	0.28	1980	554.4
F_2	0.33	350	115.5
F_3	0.39	960	374.4
			Total = 1044.3

Thus, the landlord has to pay Rs. 1044.3 for hiring the net information, which is fairly high with reference to the gain/profit in deciding crop Q is Rs. 3,550. Hence it is not worth calling for additional information from Met department.

Problem 9.16

A person has two choices to choose from

Choice 1 : Winning Rs. 25,000 or nothing with 50/50 chance on a bet.

Choice 2 : A sure gift of Rs. 10,000

Suggest the most likely choice chossen by him.

Solution :

If he decides on choice 2, he is a person of the nature to win with 100% certainity of winning Rs. 10,000 He does not take a 50/50 chance of gaining Rs. 25,000. If the gift amount with certainty is reduced to Rs. 8,000, he may still opt for choice 2. If we keep redcuing this amount, he will hesitate to take the same decision as the sum now may not attract him easily. He first becomes indifferent, at a level called Certainty. Monetary Equivalent (CME) of the bet. Let us presume that his CME level is Rs. 2,000. To plot the effective utility curve, we assign a utility value (a number) say 10 to the choice 1 *i.e.* utility of Rs. 25,000 and utility value 0 to getting nothing (*i.e.* zero).

Now the individual is indifferent to

(*i*) Winning Rs. 25,000 or nothing with 50% chance.

(*ii*) A definite gain of Rs. 2,000.

Symbolically, the utility of Rs. 25,000 with a probability of 0.5 is equivalent to the utility of Rs. 2,000 with probability of 1.0.

Thus, $\frac{1}{2}U_{25,000} + \frac{1}{2}U_0 = \frac{1}{2}U_{2,000}$

Hence, $U_0 = 0$

and $U_{25,000} = 10.0$

$\therefore$ $U_{2,000} = \frac{1}{2} \times 10 + \frac{1}{2}(0) = 5$ units

Points on the utility curves therefore, can be obtained as

Rs.	*Units*
25,000	10
2,000	5
0	0

By the same logic, we can obtain some more points on the utility curve for odds against the sure gift, and indifference points can be obtained for the decision maker.

When we obtain the monetary outcomes duly converted into utility values, we multiply these by their probabilties to get the total expected utility for each strategy. The strategy optimising utility function of the decision maker is the optimal strategy.

Problem 9.17

The manager of a firm has two alternatives to choose from for the next quarter.

(*a*) To take a contract to, supply an item to a company which would result in a sure profit of Rs. 20,000.

(*b*) To make and introduce a new product in the market. The likely profit/loss possibilities along with the expected probabilties also given. Also shown are the utility values associated with the various profit levels.

Profit/loss	–20,000	0	20,000	40,000	80,000
Probability	0.1	0.2	0.3	0.3	0.1
Utility	–0.50	0	0.45	0.7	1.20

Determine which course of action would be preferred by the manager when he wanted to maximise (*i*) the EMV and (*ii*) the expected utility.

Solution :

Profit/Loss	*Probability*	*Utility*	*Exp. Profit*	*Exp. Utility (Prob. × Utility)*
–20,000	0.1	–0.50	–2,000	–0.050
0	0.2	0	0	0
20,0000.3	0.45	6,000	0.135	
40,0000.3	0.7	12,000	0.210	
80,0000.1	1.2	8,000	0.120	
		Total	24,000	0.415

Interpretation of the Result

(*i*) Expected profit of alternative (*a*) is 20,000 whereas for alternative (*b*) it is 24,000. So the manager decides alternative (*b*) for max profit.

(*ii*) Exp. Utility for (*a*) is 0.45 (sure profit of 20,000) but expected utility for alternative (*b*) is 0.415. So Manager decides alternative (*a*) for max utility.

Problem 9.18

Current assets of a businessman are worth Rs. 80,000. The utility pattern at various levels are given below :

Assets	60,000	70,000	80,000	90,000	1,00,000	1,10,000
Utility	0.24	0.38	0.50	0.60	0.67	0.72

(*a*) He is offered a bet in which he has 60% chance of gaining 20,000 and a 40% chance of losing 20,000. Should he accept the offer?

(*b*) Alternatively, he is offered participation in two bets each involving a gain of Rs. 10,000 with prob. 0.6 and loss of 10,000 with 40% chance. Should he decide differently than in (*a*).

Solution :

(*a*)

Outcome	*Assets*	*Utility*	*Probability*	*Expected Utility*
Gain	1,00,000	0.67	0.6	0.402
Loss	60,000	0.24	0.4	0.096
			Total	0.498

With 80,000 assets he has the utility 0.5 whereas in alt (*a*) it gets reduced to 0.498. So, he does not accept the offer.

(*b*)

Choices	*Assets*	*Utility*	*Probability*	*Expected Utility*
Losses both bets	60,000	0.24	0.4 × 0.4 = 0.16	0.0384
Losses one	80,000	0.5	0.6 × 0.4 = 0.24	0.12
Wins both	1,00,000	0.67	0.6 × 0.6 = 0.36	0.2412
			Total	0.3996

Hence, he still decides not to accept the offer.

Problem 9.19

A company is considering an investment which would utilise all its funds available for investment. It is expected that either of the two instantaneous events can occur, with the following results :

Event	*Conditional Net Monetary Value (Rs.)*	*Probability of Event*
A	5,00,000	0.6
B	–25,000	0.4

Assuming the company has the utility functions which may be approximated as follows :

$u = -0.002\, y^2 \qquad \text{if } y < 2{,}000$

$u = y \qquad \text{if } y \geq 2{,}000$

(*i*) Is it desirable to undertake the venture on the basis of the assumed function?

(*ii*) What would be the decision if the expected pay-off criterion is used?

(*iii*) Offer your comments on the answers for (*i*) and (*ii*) obtained. [*C.A. Nov., 1988*]

Solution :

Based on the utility functions, the utilities of investment are calculated as follows :

for $y = 5{,}00{,}000 \qquad u = y = 5{,}00{,}000$

for $y = -\,25{,}000 \qquad u\,(-25{,}000) = -0.002(-25{,}000)^2$

$= -12{,}50{,}000$

Thus, calculating the expected utility, we have

Event	*Conditional Net Monetary Value(Rs.)*	*Conditional Utility*	*Probability*	*Expected Utility*
A	5,00,000	5,00,000	0.6	3,00,000
B	–25,000	–12,50,000	0.4	–5,00,000
			Net expected utility =	–2,00,000

(*i*) Hence, it is not desirable to undertake the venture on the basis of this assumed utility function.

(*ii*) The expected pay-off can be calculated as follows :

Event	*Conditional Net Monetary Value(Rs.)*	*Probability*	*Expected Pay-off (Rs.)*
A	5,00,000	0.6	3,00,000
B	–25,000	0.4	–10,000
		Total	2,90,000

Hence, venture should be undertaken based on the expected pay-off criterion.

(*iii*) The decision based on the two criteria are contradictory. This is due to inadequate data for expected pay-off criterion.

PRACTICE PROBLEMS

9.20 Calculate the loss table from the following pay-off table.

Action	*Events* E_1	E_2	E_3	E_4
A_1	50	300	–150	50
A_2	400	0	100	0
A_3	–50	200	0	100
A_4	0	300	300	0

Suppose that the probabilites of the events in this table are

$$P(E_1) = 0.15, P(E_2) = 0.45, P(E_3) = 0.25 \text{ and } P(E_4) = 0.15$$

Calculate the expected pay-off and expected loss to each action.

[*M.D. University, M.B.A., 1983*]

9.21 A mineral processing company wants to decide about the number of spare gear trains it has to order out at the time of placing order for a high horsepower gear box connected to a grinding unit. Although the life of a gear can be as high 30 years and more, sudden failures cannot be ruled out. In case of failure, it would be expensive and time consuming to get a spare gear-train. The cost would be Rs. 2,00,000 including the loss of production due to down time of the equipment. If ordered-out with gear-box, a gear-train would cost only Rs. 10,000 per unit. The following data is based on an analysis of past experience of 100 gear boxes.

Number of spare gear trains required :	0	1	2	3	4
Number of gear boxes requiring the spares :	3	4	2	1	0

Your are expected to advise the optimal order size. [*Poona University, M.B.A. 1982*]

9.22 A company, which operates a chain of lunch rooms, plans to install a unit in either of two locations. The company feel that the probability of a unit being successful in location X is $^3/_4$ and that, if it is successful it will make an annual profit of Rs. 4,00,000. If it is not successful, the company will lose Rs. 1,00,000 per year. The probability of a unit making success in location Y is only ½, but if it does succeed, the annual profit will be Rs. 6,00,000. If it does not succeed in location Y, the annual loss will be Rs. 1,20,000. Where should the company locate the new unit so as to maximise its expected gain?

[*Banaras University, MMS, 1984*]

9.23 A milkman buys milk at Rs. 2 per litre and sells it for Rs. 2.50 per litre. Unsold milk has to be thrown away. The daily demand in litres has the following probabilistic distribution.

Litres	46	48	50	52	54	56	58	60	62	64
Probability	0.01	0.03	0.06	0.1	0.2	0.25	0.15	0.1	0.05	0.05

If each day's demand is independent of previous day's demand, how many litres should be ordered everyday?

[*Rajasthan University, M.B.A., 1982*]

9.24 A company is contemplating whether to produce a new product. If it decides to produce the product, it must either install a new division which needs a cash outlay of 4 lakhs rupees, or work overtime with overtime expenses of Rs. 1.5 lakhs. If the company decides to install a new division, it needs the approval of the government and the company feels that there is a 70% chance of getting the approval.

A market survey has revealed the following facts regarding the magnitude of sales for the new product :

Magnitude of sales	*Probability*	*Resulting Profit(in Rs. lakhs)*
High	0.45	15
Medium	0.30	7
Low	0.20	3
NIL	0.05	–5 (Loss)

However, by resorting to overtime; the company will not be in a position to meet the high magnitude of sales. It will be able to satisfy upto the level of medium magnitude only, even if high magnitude of sales results.

Solve the problem to suggest which option should be selected? [*C.A., Nov., 1989*]

9.25 A person has two independent investments A and B available to him; but he can undertake only one at a time due to certain constraints. He can choose A first and then stop, or if A is successful then take B or *vice versa*. The probability of success of A is 0.6, while for B, it is 0.4. Both investments require an initial capital outlay of Rs. 10,000 and both return nothing if the venture is unsuccessful. Successful completion of A will return Rs, 20,000 (over cost) and successful completion of B will return Rs. 24,000 (over cost). Draw decision tree and determine the best strategy.

[*C.A., May 1988*]

9.26 A sensual cosmetic co. has developed a new perfume which management feels, has a tremendous potential. It not only interacts with the wearer's body chemistry to create a unique fragrance, but is especially long lasting. A total of Rs. 10 lakhs has already been spent on its development. Two marketing plans have been devised.

(i) The first plan follows the company's usual policy of giving small samples of the new product when other items in the company's product lines are purchased and placing advertisements in women's magazines. This plan would cost Rs. 5 lakhs and it is believed that it might result in a high, moderate or low market response with probability of 0.2, 0.5 and 0.3 respectively. The net profit excluding development and promotion cost, in these cases would be Rs. 20 lakhs, Rs. 10 lakrs and Rs. 1 lakh respectively. If it later appeared that the market response is going to be low, it would still be possible to launch a TV ad campaign. This would cost another Rs. 7.5 lakhs. It would change response to high or moderate as previously described but with probability of 0.5 each.

(ii) The second marketing plan is much more aggressive than the first. The emphasis would be heavily upon TV advertising. The total cost of this plan would be Rs. 15 lakhs, but the market response would be either excellent or good, with probabilities of 0.4 and 0.6 respectively. The profit excluding the development and promotion costs, would be Rs. 30 lakhs and Rs. 25 lakhs for the two outcomes.

Advise on the sequence of strategy to be followed by the company. *[ICWA, Dec., 1987]*

9.27 Mr. Basu is interested in developing and marketing new drug. The cost of extensive research to develop the drug would be Rs.1,00,000. The manager of research programme said that there is a 60% chance that the drug will be developed successfully. The market potential is assessed as follows with present value of profits.

Market conditions	*Probability*	*Present Value of Profits*
Large market potential	0.1	500
Moderate maket potential	0.6	220
Low market potential	0.3	80

The present value figures do not include the cost of research. While Mr. Basu was considering. This proposal, another similar proposal came up, which also required the investment of Rs. 1,00,000. The present value of profit for the second proposal was Rs. 1,20,000. The return on the investment in the second proposal is almost certain.

1. Draw a decision tree for Mr. Basu, indicating all choices and events.
2. What decision Mr. Basu, should take regarding investment of Rs. 1,00,000.
3. If Mr. Basu is a risk averter should he change the decision given by you?

[Bombay University, MMS]

9.28 A manager has a choice between (i) a risky contract promising Rs. 7 lakhs with probability 0.6 and Rs. 4 lakhs with prob. 0.4. and (ii) a diversified portfolio consisting of two contacts with indepenqent outcomes and each promising Rs. 3.5 lakhs with prob. 0.6 and Rs. 2 lakhs with prob. 0.4. Construct a decision tree for using EMV criteria. Can you arrive at the decision using EMV criteria. *[Poona University, M.B.A. 1982]*

9.29 The demand pattern of the cakes made in a bakery is as follows:

No. of cakes demanded :	0	1	2	3	4	5
Probability :	0.05	0.1	0.25	0.30	0.20	0.10

If the preparation cost is Rs. 2 per unit and selling price is Rs. 4 per unit, how many should the baker make to maximise his profits? *[Poona University, M.B.A., 1983]*

9.30. A distributor of a certain product incures holding cost of Rs. 100 per unit per week and shortage cost of Rs. 300 per unit. The data on the sales of the product are given below:

Weekly Sales (units)	:	0	1	2	3	4	6	7	8
Frequency (No. of weeks)	:	0	0	5	10	15	5	0	0

How many limits should the distributor buy every week? Also find EVPI.[*C.A., Nov., 1986*]

9.31 You have a new furnace installed. The dealer offers to sell you spare fuel pumps at Rs. 200 each, if you buy them during installation. The pumps sell for Rs. 500 in retail. These pumps cannot be repaired if they fail. Manufacturer's records indicate the following probability of fuel pumps failures during the furnaces life time.

Failures	:	0	1	2	3	4
Probability	:	0.1	0.3	0.4	0.1	0.1

Ignoring installation and holding costs, how many spare fuel pumps should be purchased during installation? [*Delhi University, M.B.A., Dec., 1987*]

9.32 The estimated sales of proposed types of perfumes are as under:

Types of Perfumes	*Estimated Sales (Units)* *Rs. 20,000*	*Rs. 10,000*	*Rs. 2,000*
A	25	15	10
B	40	20	5
C	60	25	3

Make decisions under minimax and Laplace method.[*Sardar Patel University, B.B.A., 1987*]

9.33 A company receives shipments of certain items. It should decide whether to accept or reject the shipment, on the basis of inspection of a sample selected from the shipment. From the past experience, it is known that the percentage of defectives in a batch of shipment is either 0, 2 or 5, the probabilities for which are 0.5, 0.3 and 0.2 respectively. The company can accept only those batches which have no defectives. The cost of rejecting a good batch *i.e.* the batch with no defectives is Rs. 200. The cost of accepting a batch with 2 per cent defectives is Rs. 400 and the cost of accepting a batch with 5% defectives is Rs. 600.

A sample of 10 items has been selected from the shipment and two items are found to be defective. The conditional probability of getting 2 defectives in a sample of 10 items a batch of 0, 2 and 5 per cent defectives are calculated as 0.083, 0.185 and 0.265 respectively. Determine whether the shipment should be accepted. [*CA., Nov., 1989*]

9.34 A company has two options: either invest in a large plant (Investment Rs. 50 lakhs) or in a small plant (outlay Rs. 25 lakhs). In the latter option, after 1 year, depending on the market response, it can expand by investing Rs. 30 lakhs further. Market survey puts the market response into two categories, good and bad. The chances of good response initially are 0.6 and bad response 0.4. However, if the initial response is good, subsequent response will be good with probability of 0.9. Similarly if initial response is bad, subsequent response is likely to be bad with probability 0.9. The estimated pay-offs are:

Period	*Small plant*		*Large plant*	
	good	*bad*	*good*	*bad*
Initial year	15	5	20	5
Subsequent years (cumulative)	60	20	80	20

Advise the company what option to adopt. [*ICWA, Dec., 1988*]

9.35 The Oil India Corporation is considering whether to go for an offshore oil drilling contract to be awarded in Bombay High. If they bid, value would be Rs. 600 million with a 65% chance of gaining the contract. They may set up a new drilling operation or move already existing operation, which has proved successful, to the new site. The probability of success and expected returns are as follows:

Outcome	*New Drilling Operations*		*Existing Operations*	
	Prob.	*Exp. Revenue (Rs. Million)*	*Prob.*	*Exp. Revenue (Rs. Million)*
Success	0.75	800	0.85	700
Failure	0.25	200	0.15	350

If the corporation does not bid, or lose the contract, they can use Rs. 600 million to modernise their operation. This would result in a return of either 5% or 8% on the sum invested with probabilities 0.45 and 0.55. (Assume all costs and revenues have been discounted to present value).

(*i*) Construct a decision tree for the problem showing clearly the course of action.

(*ii*) By applying an appropriate decision, criterion, recommend whether or not the Oil India Corporation should bid the contract. [*ICWA, June 1989*]

9.36 An oil drilling company is considering the purchases of mineral rights on a property for Rs. 100 lakhs. The price includes tests to indicate whether the property has type A geological formation or type B geological formation. The company will be unable to tell the type of geological formation until the purchase is made. It is known, however, that 40% of the land in this area has type A formation and 60% type B formation. If the company decides to drill on the land, it will cost Rs. 200 lakhs. If the company does drill, it may hit on oil well, gas well or a dry hole. Drilling experience indicates that the probability of striking an oil well is 0.4 on type A and 0.1 on type B formation. Probability of hitting gas is 0.2 on type A and 0.3 on type B formation, The estimated discounted value from an oil well is Rs. 1,000 lakhs and from a gas well Rs. 500 lakh. This includes every thing except cost of mineral rights and cost of drilling. Use decision tree approach and recommend whether the company should purchase the mineral rights? [*ICWA, June 1987*]

9.37 A firm is planning to develop and market a new drug. The cost of extensive research to develop the drug has been estimated at Rs. 1 lakh. The manager of the research programme has found that there is 60% chance that the drug will be developed successfully. The market potential has been estimated as follows :

Market Conditions	*Probability*	*Present Value of Profits (Rs.)*
Large market potential	0.1	50,000
Moderate market potential	0.6	25,000
Low market potential	0.3	10,000

The present value figures do not include the cost of research. While the firm is considering this proposal, a second proposal almost similar comes up for consideration. The second one also requires an investment of Rs. 1 lakh, but the present value of all profits is Rs. 12,000. Of course, the returns on investment in the second proposal is certain.

(*i*) Draw a decision tree indicating all events and choices of the firm

(*ii*) What decision the firm should take regarding the investment of Rs. 1 lakh.

[*ICWA, Dec., 1986*]

9.38 The owner of a boat has estimated the following distribution of demand for a particular kind of boat.

No. of demand :	0	1	2	3	4	5	6
Probability :	0.14	0.27	0.27	0.18	0.09	0.04	0.01

Each boat costs him Rs. 7,000 and he sells them for Rs. 10,000 each. Boats that are left unsold at the end of the season must be disposed off for Rs. 6,000 each. How many should be stocked so as to maximise his expected profit? *[Delhi University, M.Com., 1988]*

9.39 A wholesaler of sporting goods has an opportunity to buy 5,000 pairs of ski's that have been, declared surplus by the government. The wholesaler will pay Rs. 50 per pair and can obtain Rs. 100 a pair by selling skis to retailers. The price is well established, but the wholesaler is in doubt as to how many pairs he will be able to sell. Any skis left over, he can sell, to discount outlet at Rs. 20. After a careful consideration of the historical data, the wholesaler assigns probabilistic demand as follows:

Retailers demand	1,000 pairs	3,000 pairs	5,000 pairs
Probability	0.6	0.3	0.1

(*i*) Compute the conditional monetary and expected monetary values.
(*ii*) Compute the expected profit with a perfect predicting device.
(*iii*) Compute the EVPI.

9.40 The probability distribution of monthly sales of an item is as follows.

Monthly sales (units) :	0	1	2	3	4	5	6
Probabilities :	0.01	0.06	0.25	0.30	0.22	0.10	0.06

The cost of carrying inventory (unsold during the month) is Rs. 30 per unit per month and the cost of unit shortage is Rs. 70. Determine optimum stock to minimise expected cost. *[CA., May 1987]*

9.41 The owner of a stall has introduced a new item of food. The cost of manufacture is Re. 1 per piece and he can sell it at Rs. 3 per piece. Since the item is perishable any left over items are worthless. He expects the demand to vary between 10 and 15. How many pieces should be manufactured for net maximum profit? Use minimax and laplace criteria.

9.42 A small industry finds from the past data, that the cost of making an item is Rs.25 and the selling price of the item is Rs. 30, if it is disposed off within the week, and it could be disposed off at Rs. 20 per item in the end of the week.

Weekly Sales :	< 3	4	5	6	7	≥ 8
No. of Weeks :	0	10	20	40	30	0

Find the optimum number of items per week the industry should produce. *[C.A., May 1986]*

9.43 A physician purchases a particular vaccine on Monday each week. The vaccine must be used within the following week, otherwise it becomes worthless. The vaccine costs Rs. 2 per dose and the physician charges Rs. 4 per dose. In the past 50 weeks; the physician has administrated the vaccine in the following quantities.

Doess per week :	20	25	50	60
Number of weeks :	5	15	25	5

Determine how many doses the physician should buy every week. *[Delhi University, M. Com., 1983]*

9.44 A firm makes pastries which it sells at Rs. 8 per dozen in special boxes containing one dozen each. The direct cost of the pastries for the firm is Rs. 4.50 per dozen. At the end of the week, the state pastries are sold off for a lower price of Rs. 2.50 per dozen. The overhead expenses attributable to pastry production are Rs. 1.25 per dozen. Fresh pastries are sold in special boxes which cost 50 paise each and the state pastries are sold wrapped in ordinary paper. The probability distribution of demand per week is as under:

Demand (in dozens)	:	0	1	2	3	4	5
Probability	:	0.01	0.14	0.2	0.5	0.1	0.05

Find the optimal production level of pastries per week. *[Delhi University, M.Com., 1986]*

9.45 A modern home appliances dealer finds that the cost of holding a mini cooking range in stock for a month is Rs. 200 (insurance, minor deterioration, interest on borrowed capital etc.). Customers who cannot obtain a cooking range immediately tend to go to other dealers and he estimates that for every customer, who cannot get immediate delivery, he loses an average of Rs. 500. The probabilities of demand of 0, 1, 2, 3, 4, 5 mini cooking ranges in a month are 0.05, 0.1, 0.2, 0.3, 0.2 and 0.15 respectively. Determine the optimal stock level of cooking ranges. Also find EVPL. *[Delhi University, M.B.A., 1990]*

9.46 The investment staff of TNC Bank is considering four investment proposals for a client: shares, bonds, real estate and savings certificates. These investments will be held for one year. The past data regarding four proposals are given below:

Shares: There is a 25 per cent chance that the shares will decline by 10 per cent, a :30 per cent chance that they will remain stable and a 45 per cent chance that they will increase in value by 15 per cent. Also the shares under consideration do not pay any dividends.

Bonds: These bonds stand a 40 per cent chance of increase in value by 5 per cent and 60 per cent chance of remaining stable and yield 12 per cent.

Real Estate: This proposed has a 20 per cent chance of increasing 30 per cent in value, a 25 per cent chance of increasing 20 per cent in value, a 40 per cent chance of increasing 10 per cent in value, a 10 per cent chance of remaining stable and a 5 per cent chance of losing 5 per cent of its value.

Saving Certificates: These certificates yield 8.5 per cent with certainty.

Use a decision tree to structure the alternatives to the investment staff and using the expected value criterion, choose the alternative with the highest expected value. *[C.A., Nov., 1990]*

9.47 Matrix Company is planning to launch a new product, which can be introduced initially in Western India or in the entire country. If the product is used only in Western India, the investment outlay will be Rs. 12 million. After two years, Matrix can evaluate the project to determine whether it should cover the entire country. For such expansion, it will have to incur an additional investment of Rs. 10 million. To introduce the product in the entire country right in the beginning would involve an outlay of Rs. 20 million. The product in any case, will have a life of 5 years, after which the plant will have zero net value. If the product is introduced only in Western India, demand would be high or low with the probabilities of 0.8 and 0.2 respectively and annual cash flow of Rs. 4 million and Rs. 2 million respectively. If the product is introduced in the entire country, right in the beginning, the demand would be high or low with probabilities of 0.6 and 0.4 respectively and annual cash inflows of Rs. 8 million and Rs. 5 million respectively.

Based on the observed demand in Western India, if the product is introduced in the entire country.

The following probabilities would exist for high and low demand on all India basis.

Western India	*Whole country*	
	High demand	*Low demand*
High demand	0.90	0.10
Low demand	0.40	0.60

The hurdle rate applicable to this project is 12 per cent.

(*a*) Set up a decision tree for the investment situation.

(*b*) Advise Matrix Company on the investment policy it should follow. [*ICWA, June 1990*]

9.48 Construct the decision tree diagram from the given data.

Decision Di	*Probability of decision Di, given research R*	*Outcome number*	*Probability of outcome xi given D P(xi | Di)*	*Pay-off value of outcome xi (Rs. '000)*
Develop	0.5	1	0.6	600
		2	0.3	–100
		3	0.1	0
Do not develop	0.5	1	0.0	600
		2	0.0	–100
		3	1.0	0

9.49 For the given data, work out the most preferred decision and relevant expected values after drawing the applicable decision tree.

Demand	*Probability*	*Courses of Action*		
		New plant	*Overtime*	*Subscontracting*
Low	0.2	–150	–50	50
Medium	0.3	30	70	100
High	0.5	200	100	40

9.50 Investor wants to invest in a project and his information is probabilistic with respect to the returns on investments. The information has been tabulated as under

Investment Amount (Rs.)	*Probability*
10,00,000	0.65
–50,000	0.35

The utility function is approximated thus

$U = -0.002\,x^2$ if $x < 5{,}000$

and $U = 1.003\,x$ if $x \geq 5{,}000$

Should the investment be planned by the investor, taking EMV as well Expected utility criterion into account.

9.51 The project planned to be undertaken by company A is based on the Government policy. In case of favourable policy, with the probability of 0.7, the net profit expected of the project is Rs. 30 lakhs, whereas if the policy announced is unfavourable towards this project with the probability of 0.3, the company is likely to get into a loss of Rs. 5 lakhs. Should the project be planned to be undertaken by the company A. The company can approximate the utility function as follows

$u = -0.004\,y.$ if $y < -2{,}00{,}000$

$= y + 0.01,\ \sqrt{|\ |}$ if $y \geq -2{,}00{,}000$

Would you recommend the project worth considering for implementation ?

9.52 The utility function for a manager is given below

Amount (Rs.)	*Utility index*
−1,20,000	0.00
−1,00,000	0.20
−60,000	0.30
−10,000	0.35
40,000	0.50
60,000	0.60
1,00,000	0.85
2,00,000	1.00

The manager has been offered a contract promising a net profit of Rs. 1,00,000 with a probability of 0.6 and a loss of 40,000 with the probability of 0.4. Should he accept the contract ? Consider both the criteria *i.e.*, EMV criterion as well as expected utility criterion.

9.53 A certain output is manufactured at Rs. 2 and sold at Rs. 4 per unit. The product is such that if it is produced but not sold during a week's time, it becomes worthless. The weekly sales recorded in the past are as follows :

Demand per week	20	25	40	60
Number in weeks	5	15	25	5

Suggest the optimal action which should be taken by the manufacturer of the output.

[*C.A. Final, Nov., 1984*]

9.54 A grocer is faced with a problem of how many items to be stocked to meet tomorrow's demand.

Purchasing price Rs. 8 per item

Selling price Rs. 10 per item

Total demand of items per day	*Number of days each demand level was recoreded*
25	20
26	60
27	100
28	20

(*a*) What should be the optimal decisioin of the grocer concerning the items to be stocked? Assuming that the grocer has a perfect knowledge, what should be his expected profit?

(*b*) Briefly explain the different decision rules usually adopted in context of decision-making under conditions of uncertainty. [*Poona University, M.B.A., 1982*]

9.55 Explain some methods, which are useful for decision-making under condition of uncertainity. Illustrate each by an example. [*Punjab University, M.B.A. 1979*]

9.56 Indicate the difference between decision-making under risk and uncertainty in statistical decision theory. [*Osmania University, M.B.A. 1982*]

❖❖❖

CHAPTER 10

THEORY OF PROBABILITY

10.1 INTRODUCTION

In the previous chapters, we have discussed the data collection, presentation and development of certain statistical techniques for effective utilisation of such data either in the form of concentration, dispersion or lack of symmetry (*i.e.* the measure of central tendency, dispersion through standard deviation, range skewness or Kurtosis; correlation and regression etc.). In these discussions, we have applied these concepts directly in various business situations in order to arrive at some useful inference for managerial decision-making.

However, in actual life situations, the decisions are required to be taken under highly complex and uncertain circumstances.

We know that there are only very few things that happen when we know it should happen. When a unique thing happens, and we know the outcome, it is called a deterministic or predictable phenomenon. Some established laws of science can be put in this category, such as a definite chemical reaction or a physical law like Boyle's law. But most of things that happen in our day-to-day life do not follow a set rule and results cannot be predicted,, nor we ever know that it will happen. These are called unpredictable phenomena.

Since actual happenings in any business scenario are uncertain, business managers find it difficult to take decisions. But there is no way out of it. Hence environmental analysis helps in such uncertain situations. Probability theory is a great help in worth-while analysis.

In a business scene, most of the managerial decisions are uncertain and since we cannot foresee the future with certainty, we have to depend on "The best possible" or "would be tomorrow" concepts. Thus, under such uncertain situations, managers have to base their decisions on certain assumptions and take a chance of an occurrence. The outcome of an interview for a job, reaching the place of work at a certain specified time, getting elected.to the body of experts or in an election, are all matters of chance. Some of us can call it as 'luck', some others as 'gamble'. Under such uncertain conditions, therefore, we are forced to take a chance under certain 'risk' level. This risk or uncertainty is called probability. Some of the examples can be quoted as expression of probable occurrences.

1. The sales of either this season or next season.
2. The life of a battery or a bulb.
3. The outcome of tossing of a coin; head or tail
4. Getting through an examination or promotion board.

In our day-to-day life, we often use such language as "we are not sure whether we will win or not", "we might win this match of football against Dempos". This all shows the concept of probability in real life situation.

Such situations can be handled through collection of relevant and useful information and then analysing it. Information can, generally, be collected through a sample as it is neither practical nor feasible and economical to collect data for the entire population (unless and until, it is either mendatory or so critical). In case of sample information, there is tremendous risk of taking an erronous decision because of the limited data of the sample. But we are at least sure of decision rather than hunch (based on very limited or practically no information) Through some well established techniques, such risks can he minimised. Whatever degree of care that we take for sample information, there is an element of certain degree of error. This estimation of error is, hence, important in all such situations. The estimation of error helps the decision maker to ascertain how close the information is to that of actual population happening. The greater the error, the greater is the risk involved in decision-making. Evaluation of risk, in these situations, can be done in terms of probability.

The concept of probability and its use for decision-making is very old. Quite a substancial research has been and is being done. In business complexity, such as current, the theory of probability is utilised for forecasting in various situations. These area could be demand pattern, investments, inventory or even new product launching.

10.2 DEVELOPMENT OF PROBABILITY

Probable origin of the word "Probability" is from the games of gambling, such as throwing of a dice or a coin or a game of cards. As per history, the first book on the subject was noticed having been written by Jerome Cardan (1501 - 1576), an Italian mathematician. The book was titled "Book on Games of Chances", though published only in 1663. Then a systematic and scientific theory of probability was produced by a French Mathematician Blaise Pascal (1623 - 62) and Pierre de Fermat (1601 - 65), while solving a problem for sharing the stake in an incomplete gambling match by a French gambler and nobleman Chevalier-de-Mere. The solution to this problem resulted in the methodical and scientific development of the Theory of Probability. Some further work was done by James Bernoulli (1654 - 1705), A. De-Moivre(1667 - 1754). Then Thomas Bayes (1702 -61) introduced the concept of Inverse Probability. French Mathematician Pierre - Simon de Laplace published his book in 1812 by the name, *i.e.,* "Theorie Analytique des Probabilities" (Theory of Analytical Probability). In addition, some Russian mathematicians like Chebychev (1821 - 94), A. Markov (1856 - 1922) Liapouoff, and Kolmogorov etc. made great contribution to the subject. Now much developed concepts are used extensively in the form of 'Decision Analysis'.

10.3 AREAS OF UTILISATION OF PROBABILITY THEORY IN BUSINESS

Some of the areas, where the "Theory of Probability" or "Decision Theory" is now used extensively are listed under :

1. Forecasting of demands
2. Investment problems
3. Stocking Patterns
4. New product launching etc.

10.4 PERMUTATIONS AND COMBINATIONS

Since meaning of Permutation is 'arrangement' and that of combination is 'group', the concept of permutation and combination indicates the system of arranging a group of data in various forms or series, such as three digits 1, 2, 3 can be arranged as 123, 132, 231, 213, 312, 321 *i.e.* in 6 ways or if we take two at a time. then it is 12, 23, 31, 13, 21, 32, also in 6 ways. Here the order of the elements in these cases is immaterial.

In general, the words Permutations and Combinations can be defined in the following way.

Permutation : Permutation of n different objects taken r at a time, denoted by $^{n}p_{r}$ is an ordered arrangement of only r objects out of n objects.

Various mathematical expressions relating to the concept are as follows :

1. The number of different permutations of n different taken r at a time without repetition is

$$^np_r = n\,(n-1)\,(n-2)\,\ldots\ldots(n-r+1)$$

$\therefore$ $\quad {}^3p_2 = 3 \times 2 = 6$

and $\quad {}^4p_3 = 4 \times 3 \times 2 = 24$

and $\quad {}^np_n = n\,(n-1)\,(n-2)\ldots\ldots,1.$

This expression $^np_n = n\,(n-1)\,(n-2)\ldots\ldots,1.$ is also expressed as $n!$ or $\lfloor n$, and is called factorial n.

Hence $\quad 5! = 5 \times 4 \times 3 \times 2 \times 1 = 120$

By convention, $\quad \lfloor 0 = 0! = 1$

$$\therefore \quad {}^np_r = \frac{n!}{(n-r)!}$$

2. The number of different permutations of n different objects, taken r at a time with repetition is

$$^np_r = n^r$$

Hence $\quad {}^np_n = n^n$

3. The number of permutations of n different objects all at a time is $(n-1)!$
4. When all the objects are not alike, but may be like for a certain number, say n_1, n_2 etc, Then the number of permutations for such objects can be written as

$$\frac{n!}{n!n_2!\ldots\ldots n_k!}$$

5. If one operation can be performed in p different ways and another operation in q different ways, then the two operations, when associated together can be performed in $p \times q$ ways.

Combination : A combination of n different objects taken r at a time, denoted by ^nC_r or (n_r), is a selection of only r objects out of n objects, without any regard to the order of the arrangement.

Some of the mathematical expressions for combinations under different conditions are as under :

1. The number of different combinations of n different objects taken r at a time, without repetition is given by

$$^nC_r = (n_r) = \frac{n!}{r!(n-r)!}\text{; when } r \le n$$

$$= \frac{^nP_r}{r!}$$

$^nC_0, {}^nC_1, {}^nC_2 \ldots\ldots {}^nC_n$ are called Binomial Coefficients and $^nC_0 = 1 = {}^nC_n$

2. $^nC_r = {}^nC_{n-r}$
3. $^nC_r + {}^nC_{r-1} = {}^{n+1}C_r$
4. $^nC_0 + {}^nC_1 + {}^nC_2 + \ldots\ {}^nC_n = 2^n$

• Permutation is an ordered arrangement of objects in a systematic manner, whereas combination indicates the way these objects are arranged. These concepts are extensively used in Probability Theory.

10.5 TERMINOLOGY

Equally likely : When all the happenings of an event have equal chance of outcome.

This is also called "**uniform probability Model**" is $P(A) = \frac{m}{n}$.

Exhaustive Cases : Total number of possible outcomes is called 'Exhaustive Cases' For tossing of two balanced coins will result in (H, H) (H, T) (T, T) (T, H). While there are only two outcomes of a single coin tossing H or T, there are 4 such outcomes for tossing 2 coins. Thus total number of exhaustive cases are 2^2. It can be proved by continuing tossings of 3, 4, 5 or 6 faced dices or coins that if there are '*r*' cards, drawn out of *n* cards the exhaustive cases will be $^nC_r = \binom{n}{r}$

Experiment : It is any operation of data collection or observations where outcomes are subject to variation.

Favourable Cases : The number of outcomes of a random experiment which results in the happening of an event is called the favourable case to that event.

While using probability theory for business decisions, there are some useful assumptions to be specified. Hence some important terms have been defined so as to use these while developing probability for various events.

Thus in tossing two coins there can be only 2 cases favourable to head outcome *i.e.* HT or TH (exactly one head) or HH only one favourable to H as two heads.

Independent Event : When the events are such that the happening of one does not affect the happening of the other, the events are called 'Independent'. As an example, getting 'Head (H) at one throw does not affect getting 'H' again on the next throw. Thus we can keep getting H continuously as it is not affected by getting 'H' in the previous throw. Thus getting a 'Head' will be an independent event.

While doing the same experimentation with a pack of cards, after picking a card from the pack, the next card picking will be affected by earlier picking if the card is not replaced back into the pack. Thus. after the replacement of the picked card, the original pack will give "Independent Event" of getting the same card again.

Mutually Exclusive Event : Two or more events are called Mutually exclusive if the happening of any one of them excludes the happening of all others in the same experiment. Thus, in a game of tossing the coin, at one time, we can either get only head or only tail. Thus 'Head' or 'Tail' are mutually exclusive events in this experiment. Similarly, while throwing a dice with 6 faces, event of getting any one face (*i.e.* 1, 2, 3. 4, 5 or 6) will be mutually exclusive as at one time only one face can result out of the throw.

Random Experiment : An experiment is called Random only when conducted repeatedly under essentially homogeneous condition, result not necessarily being unique.

Sets Theory : The concept can be seen from chapter 5 of this, book. The laws of Sets Theory can be used extensively for probability theory in terms of all its Algebra.

Sample points and sample space : When a trial is performed, it gives rise to an outcome these outcomes are called events or sample points. A collection of all possible outcomes is called a sample space.

Statistical Independence : It means that statiscally, the happening of one event has no effect on the happening of the other.

Trial and Event : Performance of random experiment is called a 'Trial' and the outcome is called an 'Event'. It can be understood as follows :

Of all the possible outcomes in a Sample space of a random experiment, some outcomes satisfy a specified description. We call it as an 'Event'.

Tossing of three coins can be written as

$$S = \{HHH, HTH, THH, TTH, HHT, HTT, THT, TTT\}$$

Here (HHH) is called an Event of getting all Heads and (TTT) as event of getting all Tails. These two events are disjoint.

Thus an event may be defined as an non-empty subset of the sample space.

If two events A and B are disjoint, They cannot happen simultaneously, their intersection set is a null set. Thus $A \cap B = \phi$ or $P(A \cap B) = P(\phi) = 0$.

This will indicate that A and B are mutually exclusive. The concept can be enlarged to the probability concept of events such as $P(A) = \frac{n(A)}{n(S)} = \frac{n(A)}{N}$, where $n(A)$ is the number of happenings favourable to event A and $n(S) = N$ is the number of all possible points of sample space.

10.6 DEFINITION OF PROBABILITY

In simple language, it refers to the chances of happening of an event. When we say that chances of good crop due to moderate rains is eighty per cent, it means that there is a probability of 0.8 of having moderate rains and the resultant good crop. We can thus define "Probability" as follows :

"The probability of an event is the proportion of the times the event is expected to occur when the experiment is repeated under identical conditions".

Sample Space : The sample space is the collection of all possible distinct outcomes of an experiment and hence for the concept of probability, sample space would be defined. It can be either discrete or continuous based on the outcome, when sample space has a finite number of elements, it is called "Discrete sample space". The elements in this case can be counted with integers, such as occurance of head or tail on tossing of a coin or tossing of two coints or an successive tossings. First toss resulting in Head can get H or T (Head or Tail) on second toss and similarly first toss Tail can again result in H or T, In the case of continuous-sample space, the outcomes may be infinite or sample space-having infinite elements such as distance travelled by a car with sample capacity of full may be varying. Thus the distance travelled is a continuous'sample space, *i.e.* space = $\{d : d \geq 0\}$ *i.e.* a set of all read numbers larger or equal to zero. It can be summarised as follows:

The set of all possible outcomes of a random experiment is known as Sample Space and is denoted by S. It is the exhaustive cases of a random experiment. The outcomes of the experiment are called sample points. These are written as $n(s)$ *i.e.,* the sample points in s.

Thus, if we toss a coin at random, the sample space $S = \{H, T\}$ and $n(S) = 2$.

If we toss two ceins at random, then

$$S = \{(H\,T), \times (H\,T)\}$$

$$= \{HH, HT, TH, TT\}$$

and $n(S) = 4$

10.7 METHOD OF DETERMINING PROBABILITY OF AN EVENT

For the purpose of detemining probability of an events, approaches can be adopted

1. The Classical approach
2. The Bayesian approach

The Classical Approach : Under this concept, we can assume that outcome of any event or experiment is equally likely. Then we can assign same probability to each outcome. Thus when we toss a balanced coin, the chances of getting head or tail are the same. Hence it is called equally likely concept and probability assigned to the outcome of head or tail in this case will be the same or 0.5 each.

For utilisation of uncertainty (probability) in business situations, the concept needs to be understood, so that, when applied, it produces effective outcome of the events under consideration and decisions can be fairly accurate.

Similarly, an unbiased dice having 6 faces have the chances of getting any face as equally likely. Thus chances of getting any one face is 1/6 of tossing. The probability of 1/6 is, hence, assigned to each outcome. Similarly we can say that probability of 'odd number' event will be 3/6 *i.e.* chances of (1, 3, 5) out of (1, 2, 3, 4, 5, 6) outcomes and hence probability is 0.5. If we take the case of cards, getting a card of Ace of spade is 1/52, since there is only one probability (only one Ace of spade in the pack) due to one outcome out of 52 cards. If we wanted to know the chance of an Ace, then it will be 4/52 (since there are 4 Aces in 52 cards).

Similarly if there are 5 items defective out of 300 items manufactured, we say that probability of getting a defective item is 5/300. The other way of expressing probability in a classical approach is based on the assumption that each time when an experiment is repeated several (large number) times and each trial has no influence on subsequent repetitions, this getting m outcomes of an event out of n experimentations, we say that the probability of occurrence of such an event is P(A) =

$$\lim_{n\to\infty}\frac{m}{n}=p$$

There are two basic approaches for probability calculations. One is to determine the likely outcome of a specified random experiment and other for enhancing the quality of decision based on added information. Bayesian approach is very useful in decision improvement.

Here $\left(\frac{m}{n}\right)$ ratio is referred to as "relative frequency" of the event in n trials. For example, if we 520 heads out of 1000 tosses, the probability of head will be $\frac{520}{1000}=0.52$. If we repeat the tossing another 1000 times and get 495 heads, the probability becomes $\frac{520+495}{2000}=0.5075$. If we further repeat the experiment independent of earlier tossings and get another 491 heads out of 1000 tossings, the probability becomes $\frac{520+495+491}{3000}=0.502$.

We can see that the larger the experiment tossings, more the value of probability tends towards 0.5.

Since m cannot be negative, the extreme values of the outcomes can vary between 0 and 1 only. Thus we can say that $0 \le p \le 1$ and any probability of an event lies between 0 and 1.

The Bayesian Approach : When the level of outcome is not known, *i.e.* the event may not have occured earlier or may not occur again under the same circumstances or in the same form, the managers have to depend upon their "feeling about a situation". Thus, this type of probability is called "Subjective Probability" and based on the managers' "degree of rational belief". The assignment of probability will be based on the type and level of knowledge and experience of the manager coupled with his beliefs and convictions. Hence the .manager's decision will depend upon his own subjective assessment and situation judgement. This probability will also vary between 0 and 1, the 'zero' reflecting the belief that event is not going to occur and 'one' that the event is definitely going to occur.

10.8 SETS THEORY

Definition

In modern mathematics, the concept of sets is a very useful fundamental development. It has very wide ranging applications in general life, business and management. The terminology is used as a set of products, a set of workers or a set of decisions etc. In order to make useful utilisation of sets in the analysis of various business decisions, the set theory needs to be understood, so that many complex problems can be resolved by logical interpretation of set theory.

For the sake of definition, "A set is a well defined collection of objects." Individual objects forming the set are called set members or elements of the set. For example, a set of integers from 1 to 50, will contain its elements 1, 2, 3, …… 50, each one of them being called an element of the set of all such outcomes.

The representation of a set is done with the help of its elements written inside brackets, such as

Set A = {1, 3, 5, 7, 9} is a set of all odd integers from 1 to 10.

Set B = {Civil, Mechanical, Electrical, Computer Science, Textiles} is a set of department in an Engineering college.

Set C = {Male adult, Female adult, Male Child, Female child,} is a set of the members of a family.

It may be noted that the sequence of the elements in a set of representation is not important. Thus {2, 4, 6, 8} and {8, 6, 4, 2} represents the same set.

> The concept of set i.e. the group of data (elements) for a given situation is utilised for probability working out given a number of parameters affecting the outcome. Various business decisions can be reached by systematic application of the Sets Theory.

Description of Set

In describing a set, we can either write all its elements in brackets as given above or it can also be written as the characteristic that the elements are required to possess.

The example of characteristic description is given as {*x*/ *x* possessing the underlined chacteristics} such as {*x* / *x* being even integers upto and including 40}

This helps, when writing all the elements of the set is lengthy and cumbersome.

The sets are normally denoted by Capital letters as given above. The symbol ∈ stands for the description "belong to". Thus

If $A = \{1, 3, 5, 7, 9\}$

and $B = \{3, 5, 7\}$

Then $B \in A$ means that set *B* belongs to *A*. Thus all elements of *B* belong to set *A*. Similarly $3 \in A$ means that element *x* (=3) belongs to set *A*.

Similarly a symbol ∉ indicates the status "does not belong to". Thus $4 \notin A$ means that element 4 does not belong to set *A*.

In the description given with regard to the characterstic, the vertical line/means "such that". Hence $A = \{x / x$ being an odd number from 1 and 10$\}$ means that the values of the elements of set A have been defined as only odd number between 1 to 10. Thus it means $A = \{1, 3, 5, 7, 9\}$.

Power of a set : The number of elements in a set is called the power of a set and is denoted by $|A|$ for set *A*. There may be a finite number of a elements in a given set *A*, such as $A = \{1, 2, 3, 4, 5, 6\}$ has a definite number of elements and its power is 6.

When we describe a set $B = \{x / x$ is an integer$\}$, the set *B* has indefinite number of elements.

When there are no elements in a set, it is called a "null or empty" set and is denoted as ϕ. For clarification {0} is not a null set as it has one element 'zero' and its power is one.

Elementary concepts of set

Universal set : A set describing all the objects that are possible points of interest in a problem is called Universal set. It is the largest set of elements.

Thus A = {*x*/*x* indicates world population} is a universal set with all human beings of the world as its members or elements, whereas B = {*x*/*x* is the male population of the world} is not a universal set as it does not contain the total population or the female population. It is represented by S.

Subset of a set : Set A is called the subset of B, if all the elements of A are also the elements of B. This is denote by the symbol ⊂. If

$$A = \{2, 4, 6, 8, 10\}$$

and $$B = \{4, 6, 8\}$$

and $$C = \{3, 6\}$$

Then all the elements of B are also the elements of A. Hence symbolically $B \subset A$

Where as all the elements of C are not the elements of A or B, then we write

$$C \not\subset A, C \not\subset B.$$

It can be established that if a set A has *n* elements, the total number of subsets is given by 2^n.

Equality of two sets : When all the elements of one set are also the elements of the second set and they are equal in value, both the sets are called Equal. *i.e.*, sets A and B are equal sets if $A \subset B$ and $B \subset A$.

Let $$A = \{21, 22, 23, 24, 25\}$$

and $$B = \{25, 24, 23, 22, 21\}$$

$$C = \{25, 23, 22, 24, 21\}$$

Then $$A \subset B, B \subset A, B \subset C$$

Then $$A \subset B = C.$$

Complement of a set : The complement of a set A is the set of all the elements of a universal set, which donot belong to A. The complement is denoted A' or $\overline{A}$.

Thus, let the universal set S = {2, 4, 6, 8, 10, 12, 14}

and A = {4, 8, 12}

The complement set A = A' = A = {2, 6, 10, 14} we can thus say (in board sense) that

(*a*) Complement of a universal set is a null set

(*b*) Complement of a null set is a universal set.

Difference of two sets : A set of elements belonging to A, but not to B, is a difference set.

Thus $$A - B = \{x / x \in A; x \notin B\}$$

Definitions and illustrations of various types of sets bring out, how the given data can be grouped and analysed. Accordingly the sets can be operated for different business situations.

Operations of sets

Union of two sets : The union of two sets A and B is the set of elements which belong to A or to B or to both. It is denoted by $A \cup B$.

Hence if A = {2, 4, 6, 8, 10}

and B = {8, 10, 12}

then $A \cup B$ = {2, 4, 6, 8, 10, 12}

Intersection of two sets : The intersection of two sets A and B is a set of elements that belong to both A and B. It is denoted by $A \cap B$. Thus

If $$A = \{2, 4, 6, 8, 10\}$$

and $$B = \{4, 6, 10, 12\}$$

Then $$A \cap B = \{4, 6, 10\}$$

It can be written symbolically as $A \cap B = \{x / x \in A \text{ and } x \in B\}$

Difference of two sets : The difference of two sets A and B is the set of elements, which belong to A, but do not belong to B. It is denoted as A – B.

Hence $\quad A - B = \{x / x \in A \text{ and } x \not\subset B\}$

For Example if $\quad A = \{2, 4, 6, 8, 10\}$

and $\quad B = \{4, 6, 8, 12\}$

Then $\quad A - B = \{2, 10\}$

We can also establish that

$$A - B = \{x / x \in A; x \notin B\}$$
$$= \{x / x \in A; x \in \overline{B}\}$$
$$= A \cap \overline{B}$$

Venn diagram

Venn diagram is a pictorial representation of a set. Each set is denoted by a circle. The universal set is represented as a rectangle. However the size of the rectangle or the circle is immaterial as it does not indicate any measure of the number of elements in a set.

Venn diagram is the pictorial representation of various concepts/types of sets used for business situations. Union, intersection or combination concepts are easy to understand through Venn diagrams.

Universal set : A rectangle denotes the universal set S and is drawn as.

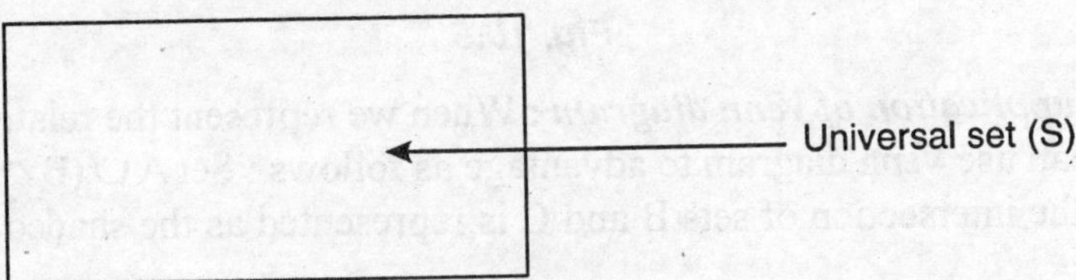

Fig. 10.1

Union of two sets : If A and B are represented by two circles and if we have to find the union of two sets *i.e.*, common elements to both the sets, we denoted it as shaded area in Fig. 10.2.

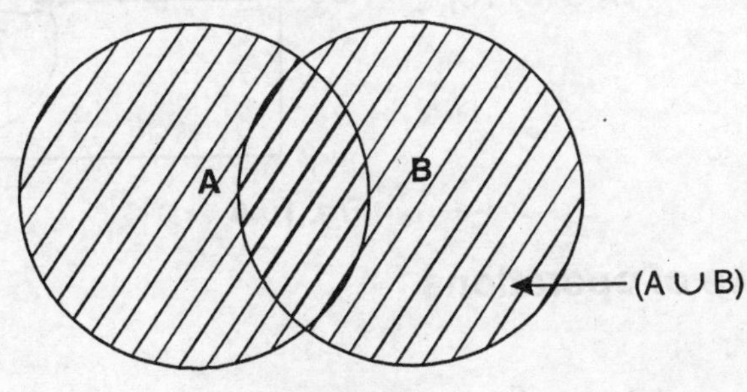

Fig. 10.2

Intersection of two sets : Since intersection of two sets is the set belonging to A or B or both, the Venn diagram representation can be drawn as shown in Fig. 10.3., the shaded indicating intersection of A and B *i.e.*, $A \cap B$.

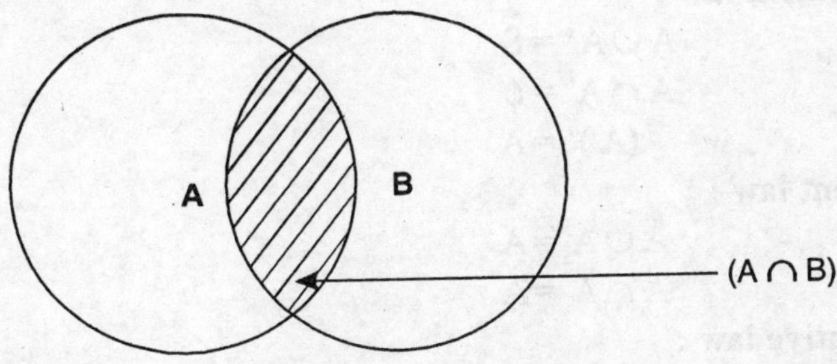

Fig. 10.3

Difference of two sets : The set of elements belonging to set A but not to set B, is the set of difference. It can be represented as given in Fig. 10.4. below.

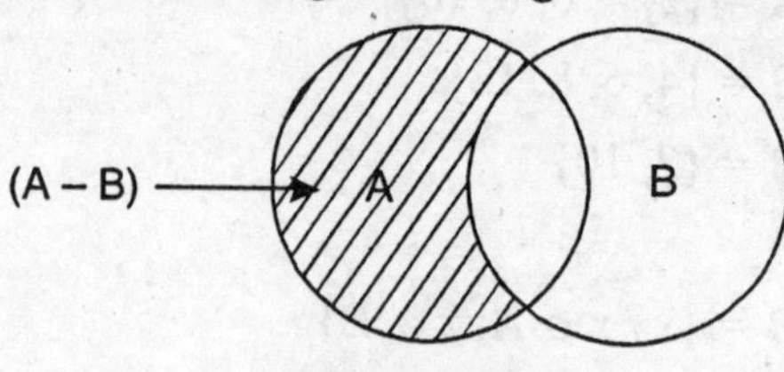

Fig. 10.4

Complementary set : A set A, whose elements donot belong ot a universal set is complementary set and is denoted as given Fig. 10.5. below (shaded area).

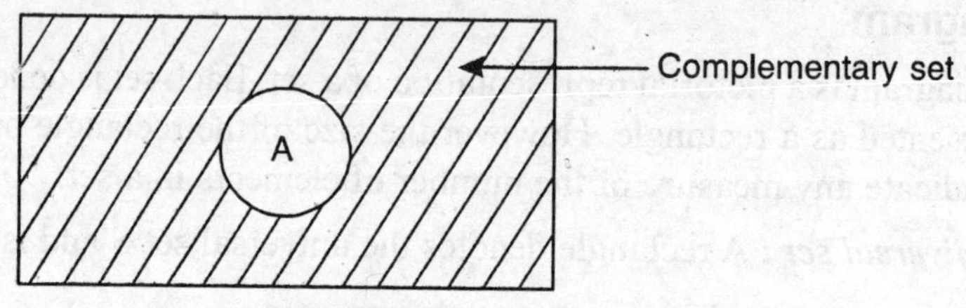

Fig. 10.5

Based on the basic concepts of sets and associated Venn diagrams, the laws of operation of sets have been simplified, which makes it easy to apply under different situations.

Enhanced application of Venn diagram : When we represent the relationship of more than 2 sets, we can use Venn diagram to advantage as follows : Set $A \cup (B \cap C)$ means, union of set A with the intersection of sets B and C is represented as the shaded area in Fig. 10.6.

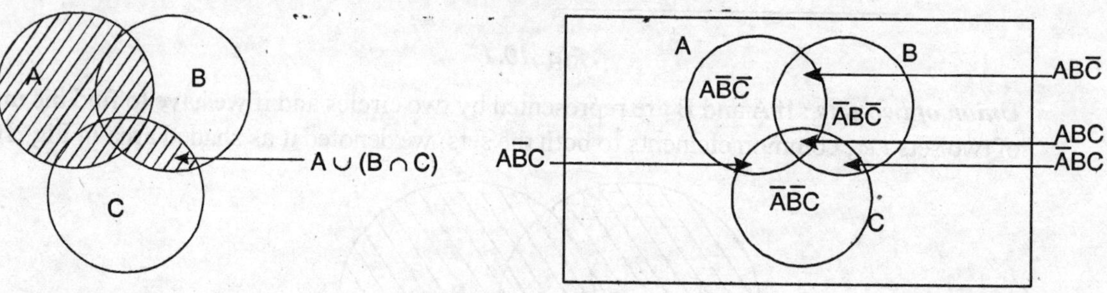

Fig. 10.6

Fundamental laws of operations

1. Indentity law :

$$A \cup \phi = S$$
$$A \cup S = S$$
$$A \cap \phi = \phi$$
$$A \cap S = A$$

2. Complement law :

$$A \cup A' = S$$
$$A \cap A' = \phi$$
$$(A')' = A$$

3. Idepotent law :

$$A \cup A = A$$
$$A \cap A = A$$

4. Cumulative law :

$$A \cup B = B \cup A$$

and $$A \cap B = B \cap A$$

5. Law of difference :

$$A - \phi = A$$
$$A - A = \phi$$

6. Associative law :

$$(A \cup B) \cup C = A \cup (B \cup C)$$
$$(A \cap B) \cap C = A \cap (B \cap C)$$

7. Distributive law :

$$A \cup (B \cap C) = (A \cup B) \cap (A \cup C)$$
$$A \cap (B \cup C) = (A \cap B) \cup (A \cap C)$$

8. De Morgan's laws :

$$(A \cup B)' = A' \cap B'$$

and $$(A \cap B)' = A' \cup B'$$

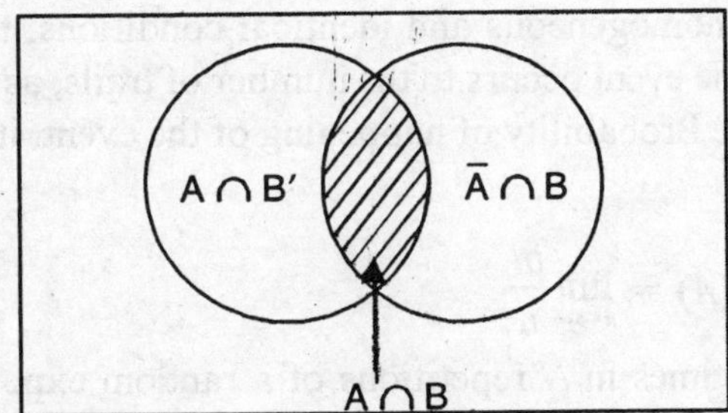

Fig. 10.7

Mathematical, statistical and axiomatic probabilities have their utility, under various types of activities or events considered for decision-making. The description given here clarifies the difference of use under different situations.

10.9 TYPES OF PROBABILITIES

We can define probabilities under certain given circumstances and the types of probabilities described below are as follows :

1. Mathematical or Priori probability
2. Statistical probability or probability as long run relative frequency
3. Axiomatic probability
   (*a*) Marginal probability
   (*b*) Joint probability
   (*c*) Conditional probability or postenior probability

Mathematical probability (Priori Probability)

If we carry out a random experiement of *N* exhaustive mutually exclusive and equally likely outcomes, out of which *m* are favourable to *A*, an event, then the probability of occurrence of even *A*, is denoted by

$$P(A) = \frac{\text{Favourable number of outcomes for } A}{\text{Exhaustive number of cases}}$$

$$= \frac{m}{N}$$

This is called Bernoullis definition of Probability

Similarly $P(\bar{A}) = \dfrac{\text{Favourable number of cases for } A}{\text{Exhaustive number of cases}}$

$$= \frac{N-m}{N} = \left(1 - \frac{m}{N}\right)$$

$P(\bar{A}) = 1 - P(A)$ (Thus $P(A)$) = Probability of A not – happening)

$\therefore$ $P(A) + P(\bar{A}) = 1$

Since m and N are non-negative integers, $P(A) \geq 0$ and since $m \leq N$, $P(A) \leq 1$.

Hence $0 \leq P(A) \leq 1$.

Notionally, if $P(A) = 0$, then A is called a null event and if $P(A) = 1$, then A is termed as a certain event.

Statistical probability

Axiomatic probability for statistically independent activities can be understood for two or more activities happening together. The differentiation of marginal and joint probability and also conditional probability has been brought out clearly.

Von Mises describes the definition of statistical probability as "If an experiment is performed repeatedly under essentially homogeneous and identical conditions, then the limiting value of the ratio of the number of times the event occurs to the number of trails, as the number of trails becomes indefinitely large, is called the Probability of happening of the event, it being assumed that the limit is finite and unique."

Thus $$P(A) = \lim_{n \to \infty} \frac{m}{n}$$

When event A occurs m times in N repetitions of a random experiement and N is sufficiently large.

Axiomatic probability

(*a*) *Marginal probabilities under statistical independence* : As explain above, the events can either be dependent or independent, we describe here only statistically independence events. Statistical independence means that the happening of one event has no effect on the happening of the other. The simple probability of occurrence of an event such as probability of getting "Head" in an unbiased with is 0.5 (Total occurrences head or tail and if head occurs, tail cannot occur). Similarly P(T) = 0.5

This means that tossing outcome of an unbiased coil will be the event (either head or tail) independent of the other. This is called marginal probability under statistical independence.

(*b*) *Joint prorbabilties under statistical independence* : When two or more independent events occur together, their probability of occurrence is called joint probability. Thus joint probability of two independent events can be written as

$$P(AB) = P(A) \times P(B)$$

where $P(AB)$ = Probability of A and B occuring togther.

$P(A)$ = marginal probability of A

$P(B)$ = marginal probability of B

Thus for a fair coin, probability of Tails on two successive tosses will be

$$P(T_1 T_2) = P(T_1) \times P(T_2) = 0.5 \times 0.5 = 0.25$$

If we extend the concept for further tossing of unbaised coin, we can get

$$P(T_1\, T_2\, T_3) = P(T_1) \times P(T_2) \times P(T_3)$$
$$= 0.5 \times 0.5 \times 0.5 = 0.125$$

This concept can be illustrated in the form of a probability tree

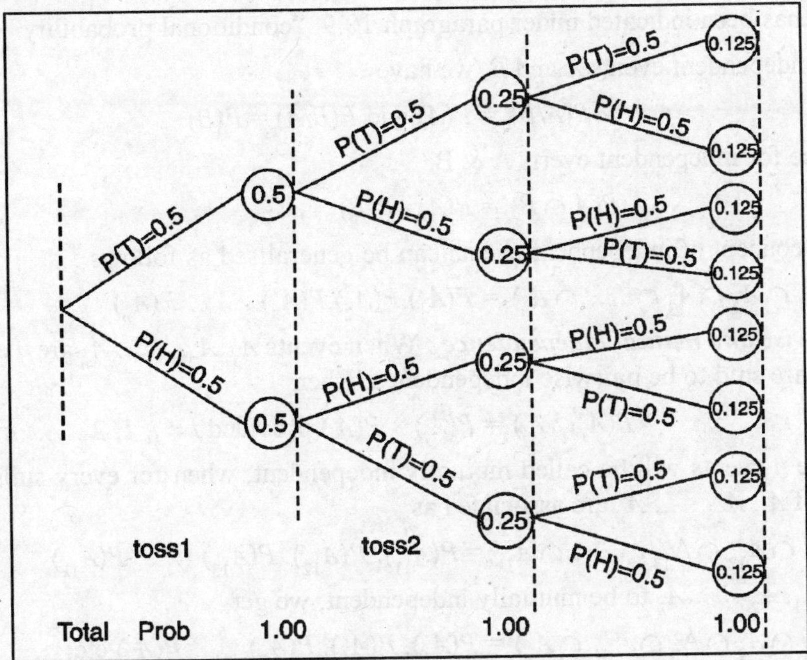

Fig. 10.8. Probability tree for 3 tosses

(c) *Conditional probability* : When we wish to describe the probability of simultaneous happening of two events A and B, we write

$$P(A \cap B) = P(A) \, . \, P(B/A) \text{ provided } P(A) \neq 0$$

similarly $\quad P(B \cap A) = P(B) \times P(B/A)$ provided $P(B) \neq 0$

Where $P(B/A)$ is called the conditional probability of happening of B under the premise that A has occured. Similarly $P(A/B)$ will be conditional probability of happening of event A provided B has happened.

Various laws of probability have been designed for their easy application. The probability tree is an illustration to indicate the concept vividly.

10.10. THEOREM OR LAWS OF PROBABILITY

Additive law of probability : Probability of occurance of at least one of the two events A and B is indicated as :

$$P(A \cup B) = P(A) + P(B) - P(A \cap B)$$

This has already been explained under paragraph 10.9 above and it is called "Addition theorem of probability" or "additive law of probability". Veen Diagram given below classifies is further

For mutually exclusive events, $A \cup B = \phi$ and hence

$$P(A \cap B) = 0$$

Therefore for mutually exclusive events,

$$P(A \cup B) = P(A) + P(B)$$

The theorem now can be generalised for mutually exclusive or disjoint events as under

$$P(A_1 \cup A_2 \cup A_3 \cup ... \cup A_n) = P(A_1) + P(A_2) + P(A_3) + \; ...... P(A_n)$$

Multiplicative law of probability (Theorem of compound probability) : This theorem states that the probability of simultaneous happening of two events A and B can be written as

$$P(A \cap B) = P(A), P(B/A), \text{ when } P(A) \neq 0$$

or $\quad P(B \cap A) = P(B), P(A/B)$, when $P(B) \neq 0$

This has been indicated under paragraph 10.9. "conditional probability"

For independent events A and B, we have

$$P(A/B) = P(A) \text{ and } P(B/A) = P(B)$$

Hence for independent everts A & B,

$$P(A \cap B) = P(A) \,.\, P(B)$$

This concept of independent events can be generalised as follows :

$$P(A_1 \cap A_2 \cap A_3 \cap \ldots\ldots \cap A_n) = P(A_1).P(A_2).P(A_3). \ldots\ldots P(A_n)$$

Pairwise and mutual independence : When events $A_1, A_2, \ldots\ldots A_n$ are n events of space S, then are said to be pairwise independence, when

$$P(A_i \cap A_j) = P(A_i) \times P(A_j) \text{ provided } i \neq j, 1, 2 \ldots\ldots n$$

These n events will be called mutually independent, when for every subset $A_{11}, A_{12} \ldots\ldots$ etc. of $A_1, A_2 \ldots\ldots A_n$ are associated as

$$P(A_{11} \cap A_{12} \cap A_{13} \cap \ldots\ldots \cap A_{1k}) = P(A_{11}).\, P(A_{12}).\, P(A_{13}) \ldots\ldots P(A_{1k})$$

For $A_1, A_2 \ldots\ldots A_n$ to be mutually independent, we get

$$P(A_1 \cap A_2 \cap A_3 \cap \ldots\ldots \cap A_n) = P(A_1).\, P(A_2).\, P(A_3) \ldots\ldots P(A_n) \text{ etc.}$$

and total number of conditions for mutual independence will be

$$n_{c_2} + n_{c_3} + \ldots\ldots n_{c_n} = (n_{c_2} + n_{c_1} + \ldots\ldots n_{c_n}) - n_{c_0} - n_{c_1}$$

Thus mutual independence implies pairwise independence, but the converse is not necessarily true.

The law of total probability : The general multiplication rule leads to an alternative rule called the "Rule of Total Probability". An event A can occur either when an event B occurs or when it does not occur. Thus A can be written as the disjoint union of $A \cap B$ and $A \cap \overline{B}$.

or $\quad P(A) = P(A \cap B) + P(A \cap \overline{B})$

or $\quad P(A) = P(B)P\left(\dfrac{A}{B}\right) + P(\overline{B})P\left(\dfrac{A}{\overline{B}}\right)$

This is called the rank of total probability.

The effective use of conditional probability for an improvement in the probability of decision-making has been suggested under 'Posterior probability' concept given under Baye's Theorem.

Baye's theorem has been written basedon poisterior probability of such events (explained under conditional probability)

10.11 INVERSE PROBABILITY AND BAYE'S THEOREM

A very important and useful application of conditional probability is the computation of unknown probabilities, based on past data or information. When an event occurs through one of the various mutually disjoint events, then the conditional probability that this event has occurred due to a particular reason or event is termed as "Inverse Probability". This is also called Posterior Probability as against the 'Priori Probability' of the first occurrence. The rule or the theorem enunciatims and explaining the procedure for its calculation was suggested by a British Mathematician Thomas Bayes (1763). Since it is a concept of revision of probability based on some additional information, it shows the improvement towards certainty level of the event. Thus it has wide ranging application in Business and its management.

Bayes Theorem : If an event A can only occur in conjuction with n mutually exclusive and exhaustive events $B_1, B_2, \ldots.. B_n$, and if A actually happens, then the probability that it was proceeded by an event B (for A conditional probabilities of A given B_1 ,A given B_2.... A given B_n are known) and if marginal probabilities $P(B_i)$ are also known, then the Posterior Probability of event B. given that event A has occurred is given by

$$P\left(\frac{B_i}{A}\right) = \frac{P\left(\frac{A_a}{B_i}\right).P(B_i)}{\Sigma P\left(\frac{A}{B_i}\right).P(B_i)} = \frac{P(B_i).P\left(\frac{A}{B_i}\right)}{P\left(\frac{A}{B_i}\right).P(B_i) + P\left(\frac{A}{B_2}\right).P(B_2)+...}$$

Since $B_1, B_2, ...B_n$ are mutually exclusive and collectively exhaustive, then the event A is bound to occur with either $B_1, B_2 ......B_n$. In other words,

$$A = AB_1 \cup AB_2 \cup AB_3 \cup ... \cup AB_n$$

$$\therefore \quad P(A) = P(AB_1) + P(AB_2) + ...P(AB_n)$$

$$= P\left(\frac{A}{B_1}\right).P(B_1) + P\left(\frac{A}{B_2}\right).P(B_2) + ...$$

Hence $$P\left(\frac{B_1}{A}\right) = \frac{P\left(\frac{A}{B_1}\right).P(B_1)}{\Sigma P\left(\frac{A}{B_i}\right).P(B_i)}$$

10.12 RANDOM VARIABLE

The decision-making gets complicated when there are number of alternatives' available and the outcomes of each alternative is not very easy to determine. But any Business Manager faces this dilemma at all points of time and hence makes a decision based on the best information available to him at that point of time. He also has to evaluate, in his own mind, whether the information is complete, unbiased and authentic. The quantity and quality of data available for decision-making becomes important to understand the quality of decision made. Due to uncertainty of information due to dynamic situation of the Business, a decision-maker has to depend on uncertain outcome, which is termed as a Random Variable.

Random Variable is a numerically valued function on any data space. The concept is useful in case of probability calculation, because events occur randomly and are generally unpredictable in real life situation. Use of Random Variable is very helpful in such experiments.

A Random variable, therefore, is a numerically valued function defined on a sample space. A sample space for a random experiment (the experiment, whose outcomes depend on chance) is a set of all possible outcomes of the experiment. Thus Random variable is a function, which takes real values which are determined by the outcomes of the random experiment. It must be understood here that the random variable denotes possible values of the outcomes before the event has taken place. After the experiment has been performed and say we get 2 heads as a result of throw of two coins, then 2 is not a random variable. We can in simple language say that any unknown real quantity, for which probability assignment can be made for all intervals in the real space is called a Random Variable. When we assign probabilities as given below, we can say that the random variable takes the values between the interval of Rs. 100 and 300 crores with a probability of 0.25.

Profits (Rs. in Crores)	*Probability*
100–300	0.25
300–500	0.40
500–800	0.20
800–1000	0.15

A Random variable may be discrete or continuous. It is discrete if the set of all possible values is finite or can be organised in the form of a sequence, whereas a continuous variable is the one capable of taking all values in the interval.

10.13 MOMENTS

If X is a discrete Random Variable with probability function $p(x)$, then

$$\mu'_r = r\text{th moment about any point (arbitrary) A,}$$
$$= \Sigma(x - A)^r\, p(x)$$
$$\mu_r = r\text{th moment about mean } (\bar{x})$$
$$= \Sigma(x - \bar{x})^r\, p(x)$$

$\therefore$ Mean $(\bar{x}) = \Sigma x\, p(x)$

and variable $(x) = \mu_2 = \Sigma(x - \bar{x})^2, p(x)$

In case of a continious Random Variable, these values take the shape of integral instead of summation.

Moments and mathematical expectation are both used for understanding the use of random variables and their frequency distributions.

10.14 MATHEMATICAL EXPECTATION

If x is a random variable which can assume any one of the values $x_1, x_2, x_3, \ldots x_n$ with respective probabilities $p_1, p_2, p_3, \ldots p_n$, then the Mathematical Expectation of X is defined as

$$E(x) = p_1x_1 + p_2x_2 + \ldots\, p_nx_n = \Sigma p \times x$$

Where $\Sigma p_i = p_1 + p_2 + \ldots\ldots p_n = 1.$

If X is a random variable with probability distribution $\{x, p(x)\}$ then $E(X) = \Sigma x, p(x)$.

The Mathematical Expectation is also called the Expected value of X.

In case the freqeucny distribution of the random variable X is given as

x	:	x_1	x_2	$\ldots x_n$
f	:	f_1	f_2	$\ldots f_n$

Then $$\bar{x} = \frac{f_1x_1 + f_2x_2 + \ldots\ldots f_nx_n}{N}$$

$$= \frac{f_1}{N}x_1 + \frac{f_2}{N}x_2 + \ldots \frac{f_2}{N}x_n$$

But we know that expression $\frac{f_1}{N}$ means that the favourable number of cases to x_i out of N cases (exhaustive) are f_i, then $= p_i$ $\frac{f_i}{N} = pi$

Hence $$\bar{x} = p_1x_1 + p_2x_2 + \ldots p_nx_n$$

Therefore we can safely say that the mathematical expectation of a random variable is its Arithmetic Mean.

Note : If an experiment is conducted repeatedly over large number of times under similar homogenous conditions, then the average of the actual outcomes is the expected value, but it is not in any sence, a value which one can expect to occur in a particular experiement. In a game of chance, suppose a player gains 'a' while winning and loses 'b' while not winning. If p and q are the probabilities of a win and a failure in a single trial, we regard loss as negative gain and hence his expected gain will be

$$a \times p + (-b)q = ap - bq.$$

If the mathematical expected gain of a player is zero, then the game is fair, otherwise it is biased towards one or the other player depending on positive or negative value of the expected gain.

Theorems on Expectation

1. $E(C) = C$; where C is a constant
2. $E(CX) = CE(X)$; where C is a constant
3. $E(aX + b) = a\,\Sigma(X) + b$; where a and b are constant
4. $E(X + Y) = E(X) + E(Y)$; where X, Y are Random Variables
5. $E(XY) = E(X).E(Y)$
6. $\sigma_x^2 = \text{Var}(X)$

$$= \frac{1}{N}\Sigma f_1(x_1 - \bar{x})^2$$

$$= E[X - \bar{x}]^2$$

$$= E[X - E(X)]^2$$

$$= E(X^2) - [E(X)]^2$$

$$= \Sigma x^2 p(x) - [\Sigma(x.px)]^2$$

7. $\text{Vari}(X \pm C) = E(X \pm C) - E(X \pm C)^2$

$$= E[(X \pm C) - E(X \pm C)]^2$$

$$= E[X \pm E(X)]^2$$

$$= \text{Var}(X)$$

8. $\text{Var}(aX) = a^2\,\text{Var}(X)$
9. $\text{Var}(c) = 0.$

CHAPTER SUMMARY

Terms used

- **Axiomatic probability :** Probability based on certain properties or postulates as defined by Kolmogorov.
- **Bayes theorem :** Defines conditional probability under statistical dependence.
- **Classical probability :** The number of outcomes favourable to the occurrence of one event divided by the total number of outcomes (when events are equally likely).
- **Collectively exhaustive events :** All the possible outcomes of an experiment.
- **Conditional probability :** The probability of happening of one event, provided the other eveni has occurred.
- **Event :** One or more of the possible outcomes of something happening.
- **Experiment :** The process of observing a phenomenon that has variation in its outcomes.
- **Joint probability :** The probability of two events, occurring together.

- **Mathematical expectation :** It is the expected value of a given variable.
- **Marginal probability :** The probability of a single event
- **Mutually exclusive event :** The events that cannot happen together.
- **Posterior probability :** The probability that has been obtained as a result of additional information,called perfect information.
- **Prior probability:** Probability obtained prior to receiving new information.
- **Probability:** The proportion of an event the times is expected to occur under identical conditions of experiment.
- **Probability tree:** A graphical representation of possible outcomes of a series of experiments and their resultant probabilities.
- **Random variable:** A numerically valued function defined on a sample space.
- **Sample space:** Total number of happening of an event. This may be either discrete or continuous.
- **Statistical dependence :** The condition when the probability of some event is dependent on, or affected by the occurrence of another or some other event.
- **Statistical Independence :** The condition when the occurrence of one event has no effect on the probability of occurrence of another event.
- **Venn Diagram :** A pictorial representation of probability concept in which a sample space is represented as a rectangle or a circle and the events in the sample space are represented as portion of this space.

Important relationship used

- Probability of an event = $P(A)$
- $P(A) = m/n$
- $P(A \text{ or } B) = P(A) + P(B)$ for mutually exclusive events
- $P(A \text{ or } B) = P(A) + P(B) - P(AB)$ for non-mutually exclusive events
- Joint probability $P(AB) = P(A) + P(B)$ for independent events
- Conditional probability $P(B/A)$ = probability of an event B, given that A has occured.
- Conditional probability $P(B/A) = P(B)$ when events are statistically independent.
- $P(B/A) = \dfrac{P(B/A)}{P(A)}$ for dependent events
- $P(A/B) = P(A/B) / P(B)$ for dependent events
- $P(AB) = P(A/B) \times P(B)$ for dependent events
- $P(BA) = P(B/A) \times P(A)$ for dependent events
- ${}^nC_r = \dfrac{n!}{r!(n-r)!}$
- ${}^nP_r = n!(n-r)!$
- $P(A) + P(A) = 1$
- Baye's Theorem

$$P\left(B_i/A\right) = \frac{P\left(A/B_i\right) \times P(B_i)}{\Sigma P\left(A/B_i\right) \times P(B_i)}$$ for mutually exhaustive events

SOLVED PROBLEMS

Problem 10.1

Four cards are drawn at random from a pack of 52 cards. Find the probability that

(*i*) We get a King, a Queen and an Ace

(*ii*) All are diamonds

(*iii*) There is one card of each suit

(*iv*) There are two black and two red cards.

Solution :

When we draw 4 cards out of a pack of 52 cards, there can be $^{52}C_4$ ways. This is the exhaustive number of happenings.

(*i*) When we draw a King (out of 4 kings), there can be $^4C_1$ ways. Similarly a Queen and an Ace can be drawn in $^4C_1$ ways.

Thus probability of drawing a King, a Queen and an Ace out of 52 cards.

$$= \frac{^4C_1 \times {}^4C_1 \times {}^4C_1}{^{52}C_4} = \frac{4 \times 4 \times 4}{^{52}C_4}$$

(*ii*) All diamonds are 13 in numbers and to draw any 4 out of these we can do it in $^{13}C_4$ ways.

Hence probability of drawing all the 4 cards as diamonds $= \frac{^{13}C_4}{^{13}C_4}$.

(*iii*) One card of each suit can be drawn in (one out of 13 cards of each suit) $^{13}C_1$ ways. Hence probability of one card of each suit

$$= \frac{^{13}C_1 \times {}^{13}C_1 \times {}^{13}C_1 \times {}^{13}C_1}{^{52}C_4}$$

(*iv*) Drawing of 2 black and 2 red cards, can be done out of 26 black and 26 red cards. Hence their happening will be done in $^{26}C_2$ ways each.

Hence the probability of drawing 2 black and 2 red cards

$$= \frac{^{26}C_2 \times {}^{26}C_2}{^{52}C_4}$$

Problem 10.2

A bag contains 4 white, 5 red and 6 green balls. Three balls are drawn at random. What is the chance that a white a red and a green ball is drawn ?

[*Punjab University, B. Com.*, 1974, *Meerut University, M. Com.*, 1975]

Solution :

There are total of 4 + 5 + 6 = 15 balls. To draw 3 balls, out of the bag, we allow $^{15}C_3$ ways.

One white ball can be drawn in $^4C_1$ ways.

One red ball can be drawn in $^5C_1$ ways.

and one green ball can be drawn in $^6C_1$ ways.

Thus probability of drawing one white, one red and one green ball

$$= \frac{^4C_1 \times ^5C_1 \times ^6C_1}{^{15}C_3}$$

Thus probability of drawing one white one and one green ball

$$= \frac{4_{C_1} \times 5_{C_1} \times 6_{C_1}}{15_{C_3}}$$

$$= \frac{4 \times 5 \times 6}{(15 \times 14 \times 13)/(3 \times 2)}$$

$$= \frac{24}{91}$$

Problem 10.3

A bag contains 20 tickets marked with numbers 1 to 20. One ticket is drawn at random. Find the probability that it will be a multiple of (*i*) 2 or 5, (*ii*) 3 or 5.

[Bombay University, B.Com., May 1978]

Solution :

One ticket out of 20 can be drawn in $^{20}C_1 = 20$ ways.

(*i*) Cases favourable to get number of the ticket as

(*a*) a multiple of 2 are 2, 4, 6, 8, 10, 12, 14, 16, 18, 20 (10 ways)

(*b*) a multiple of 5 are 5, 10, 15, 20 (4 ways)

10 and 20 being common, a ticket having a number as multiple of or 5 will be drawn in 10 + 4 – 2 = 12 ways.

Hence probability of number being multiple of 2 or 5 = $\frac{12}{20}$ = 0.6.

(*ii*) Cases for number as multiple of 3 are 3, 6, 9, 12, 15, 18 (6 ways). Cases for number as multiple 5 are 4 (given below)

There is one number 15 occuring in both the cases

∴ Cases favourable to a number as multiple of 3 or 5 will be 6 + 4 – 1 = 9

∴ Probability of a number being a multiple of 3 or 5 = $\frac{9}{20}$ = 0.45

Problem 10.4

The following data show the length of life of wholesole grocers in a particular city.

Length of life (years)	*Percentage of wholsalers*
0—5	65
5—10	16
10—15	9
15—25	5
25 and over	5
	100

(*i*) During the period studied, what is the probability that a entrant to this profession will fail within 5 years?

(*ii*) That he will survive at least 25 years?

(*iii*) How many years would he have to survive to be among the 10 per cent longest survivors?

[*Kurukshetra University, M. Com.*, (*Eco.*), 1974]

Solution:

Given total number of cases = 100

(*i*) The entrant to the profession will fail within 5 years and the favourable cases for such an eventuality is 65.

Hence probability of the new entrant failing within 5 years.

$$= \frac{65}{100} = 0.65$$

(*ii*) A wholesaler will survive at least 25 years if his life in the profession is 25 years and above.

Hence probability of surviving at least 25 years.

$$= \frac{5}{100} = 0.05$$

(*iii*) To be in the list of 10% longest survivors, he has to be in the range of life of 15 years or above. Hence he has to survive at least 15 years in the profession to be among the 10% longest survivors.

Problem 10.5

n persons are seated on n chairs at a round table. Find the probability that two specified persons are sitting next to each other. [*Delhi University, B.A.*(*Eco. Hons.*) 1992]

Solution.:

Exhaustive number of outcomes for n persons to be sitting on n chairs = $(n-1)!$

Total number of favourable cases for two persons sitting together (out of n) = $(n-2)!$ and these two persons can sit of mutually exchange seats in 2! ways.

Hence proabability that two specified persons are sitting next to each other

$$= \frac{(n-2)!2!}{(n-1)!} = \frac{2}{(n-1)}$$

Problem 10.6

There are 4 hotels in a certain town. If 3 men check into hotels in day, what is the probability that each checks into a different hotel?

Solution.:

Each person can check into any hotel in $^4C_1$ ways.

Hence three persons can check into any hotel in $^4C_1 \times {}^4C_1 \times {}^4C_1 = 64$ ways.

If one persons checks into one hotel, he can do it in $^4C_1$ ways = 4 ways.

Other person can check into a hotel (3 remaining) in $^3C_1$ ways = 3 ways.

Third person can check into a hotel (2 remaining) in $^2C_1$ ways = 2 ways.

Hence each men checking into a different hotel will have $^4C_1 \times {}^3C_1 \times {}^2C_1$

$$= 4 \times 3 \times 2 = 24 \text{ ways}$$

$$\therefore \text{ Required probability } = \frac{24}{64} = 0.375$$

Problem 10.7

A committee of four has to be formed from among 3 economists, 4 engineers, 2 statisticians and a doctor.

(*i*) What is the probability that each of the four professions is represented on the committee?

(*ii*) What is the probability that the committee consists of the doctor and at least one economist?

[*Delhi University, B.A.* (*Eco. Hon.*) 1983]

Solution :

We have to form a committee of 4 out of 3 + 4 + 2 + 1 = 10 members. Exhaustive number of cases

$$= {}^{10}C_4 = \frac{10 \times 9 \times 8 \times 7}{4 \times 3 \times 2} = 26.$$

(*i*) Favourable number of cases for the committee to have one of each profession

$$= {}^3C_1 \times {}^4C_1 \times {}^2C_1 \times {}^1C_1 = 3 \times 4 \times 2 \times 1 = 24$$

$\therefore$ Required probability for all professions to be represented on the committee

$$= \frac{24}{210} = 0.114$$

(*ii*) Probability of having a doctor and at least one economist

$$p = p\text{ (doctor + economist + 2 others)}$$
$$+ p\text{ (doctor + two economists + 1 other)}$$
$$+ p\text{ (doctor + three economists)}$$
$$= \frac{{}^1C_1 \times {}^3C_1 \times {}^6C_2}{{}^{10}C_4} + \frac{{}^1C_1 \times {}^3C_2 \times {}^6C_1}{{}^{10}C_4} + \frac{{}^1C_1 \times {}^3C_2}{{}^{10}C_4}$$

$$= \frac{45 + 18 + 1}{(210)} = 0.3048$$

Problem 10.8

In a certain college, the students engage in various sports in the following proportions.

Foot ball (F)	:	60% of all students.
Basket ball (B)	:	50% of all students.
Both Foot ball and Basket ball	:	30% of all students.

If a student is selected at random, what is the probability that he will

(*i*) Play foot ball or basket ball

(*ii*) Play neither sports?

[*Delhi University, B.A.* (*Eco. Hons.*) 1983]

Solution :

Given $P(F) = 0.6$

$P(B) = 0.5$

and $P(F \cap B) = 0.3$

(*i*) For probability that a student selected will play either foot ball or basket ball, the relationship is

$$P(F \cup B) = P(F) + P(B) - P(F \cap B)$$
$$= 0.6 + 0.5 - 0.3 = 0.8$$

(*ii*) When student play neither sports, then we have to use

$$P(F \cap \overline{B}) = 1 - P \text{ (he plays at least one of the two games)}$$
$$\text{Alternately} = 1 - 0.8 = 0.2$$

or $P(\overline{F} \cap \overline{B}) = P(\overline{F}).P(\overline{B})$

$$= [1 - P(\overline{F})].[1 - P(B)]$$
$$= [1 - 0.6]\ [1 - 0.5]$$
$$= 0.4 \times 0.5 = 0.2$$

Problem 10.9

The probability that a contractor will get a plumbing contract is $\frac{2}{3}$ and that the probability that he will not get an electric contract is $\frac{5}{9}$. If the probability of getting at least one contract is $\frac{4}{5}$, what is the porbability that he will get both the contracts? [*C.A. (Inter), May 1979*]

Solution :

Given $P(A) = \frac{2}{3}$ and $P(\overline{B}) = \frac{5}{9}$

$$\therefore \quad P(B) = 1 - P(\overline{B}) = 1 - \frac{5}{9} = \frac{4}{9}$$

$$P(A \cup B) = \text{Prob. that he gets at least one cotract} = \frac{4}{5}$$

or $P(A) + P(B) - P(A \cap B) = \frac{4}{5}$

$$\therefore \quad P(A \cap B) = \frac{2}{3} + \frac{5}{9} - \frac{4}{5} = \frac{14}{45}.$$

Problem 10.10

A problem in statistics is given to three students *A*, *B* and *C*. whose chances of solving it are $\frac{1}{3}$, $\frac{1}{4}$ and $\frac{1}{5}$ respectively. Find the probability that the problem will be solved.

[*Shivaji University, B. Com.*, 1978]

Solution :

Given here $P(A) = \frac{1}{3}, P(B) = \frac{1}{4}, P(C) = \frac{1}{5}$

$$P(\overline{A}) = 1 - \frac{1}{3} = \frac{2}{3}$$

$$P(\overline{B}) = 1 - \frac{1}{4} = \frac{3}{4}$$

$$P(\overline{C}) = 1 - \frac{1}{5} = \frac{4}{5}$$

If the problem is solved, at least one of the students should be able to solve it. Thus

$$P(A \cup B \cup C) = 1 - P(\overline{A \cap B \cap C}) = 1 - P(\overline{A}).P(\overline{B}).P(\overline{C})$$

$$= 1 - \left[\frac{2}{3} \times \frac{3}{4} \times \frac{4}{5}\right]$$

$$= \frac{3}{5}$$

Problem 10.11

The odds that A speaks the truth are 3:2 and the odds that B speaks the truth are 5:3. In what percentage of cases are they likely to contradict each other on an identical point?

[*AIMA., Dip. in Mgmt.*, 1977]

Solution :

Let $P(A)$ = Prob. that A speaks the truth = $\frac{3}{5}$

and $P(B)$ = Prob. that B speaks the truth = $\frac{5}{8}$ {given above}

For contradiction on a point

(*i*) Either A speaks the truth and B tells a lie *i.e.* $(A \cap \overline{B})$

(*ii*) Or A tells a lie and B speaks the truth $(A \cap B)$

Then for probability for contradiction = $P(i)$ + P(ii)

$$= P(A \cap \overline{B}) + P(\overline{A} \cap B)$$

$$= P(A)P(\overline{B}) + P(\overline{A}).P(B) = \frac{3}{5} \times \frac{3}{8} + \frac{2}{5} \times \frac{5}{8} = 0.475$$

Problem 10.12

There are 5 while and 7 red balls in a bag. A ball is drawn and then replaced. What is the probability that a white and a red ball are drawn in that order ? What would be the probability if the balls drawn are not put back into the bag? [*Meerut University, M.Com. 1972*]

Solution :

(*i*) If balls are replaced, then

Let $P(W)$ = Prob. of drawing a white ball

and $P(R)$ = Prob. of drawing a red ball

For drawing a white and then a red ball, the prob. will be

$$P(W \cap R) = P(W) \,.\, P(R)$$

$$= \frac{5}{12} \times \frac{7}{12} = \frac{35}{144}$$

(*ii*) When balls are not replaced, then two events are indepedent

Then $$P(W \cap R) = P(W) \times P\left(\frac{R}{W}\right)$$

When the ball is not replaced, for the red ball, there will be only 11 balls left

Hence prob. of drawing a red ball = $\frac{7}{11}$

$$\therefore \quad P(W \cap R) = \frac{5}{12} \times \frac{7}{11} = \frac{35}{132}$$

Problem 10.13

A box contains 3 red and 7 white balls. One ball is drawn at random and in its place, a ball of the other colour is put in the box. Now one ball is drawn at random from the box. Find the probability that it is red. [*Bombay University, B.Com., 1975*]

Solution :

Let A bet the event of while ball on first draw.

and B the vent of red ball on the first draw.

C the event of red ball in the second draw.

Given here $P(A) = \frac{3}{10}$, $P(B) = \frac{7}{10}$

Getting a red ball in the second draw can be possible

(*i*) When white is drawn in first draw and red in the second

(*ii*) When a red ball is drawn in the first draw and red again in the second draw.

Probability that red ball is drawn in the second draw,

$$= P(i) + P(ii)$$

$$= P(A \cap C) + P(B \cap C)$$

$$= P(A) \times P\left(\frac{C}{A}\right) + P(B) \times P\left(\frac{C}{B}\right)$$

$$= \frac{7}{10} \times P\left(\frac{C}{A}\right) \times \frac{3}{10} \times P\left(\frac{C}{B}\right)$$

For calculating $P\left(\frac{C}{A}\right)$ and $P\left(\frac{C}{B}\right)$, we consider the cases separately.

When we draw a white ball first it is replaced by a red ball. Hence there will be 4 red and 6 white balls.

$$\therefore \quad P\left(\frac{C}{A}\right) = \frac{4}{10}$$

Similarly, $$P\left(\frac{C}{B}\right) = \frac{2}{10}$$

∴ Total prob. of a red ball on the second draw

$$= \frac{7}{10} \times \frac{4}{10} + \frac{3}{10} \times \frac{2}{10}$$

$$= \frac{28}{100} + \frac{6}{100} = \frac{34}{100} = 0.34.$$

Problem 10.14

The products of three factories producing the same product are known to be 3 per cent, 4 per cent and 5 per cent defective. One unit is selected at random from the products of each factory. Find the probability that at least two of them will not be defective.

[AIMA Dip. in Mgmt., July 1981]

Solution :

Let $P(A) = 0.03, P(B) = 0.04, P(C) = 0.05$

Thus $P(\bar{A})$ = not defective $= 0.97$, $P(\bar{B}) = 0.96$, $P(\bar{C}) = 0.95$ when a unit is randomly selected from the product of each factory, then

$$p = P(\bar{A} \cap \bar{B} \cap C) + P(\bar{A} \cap B \cap \bar{C}) + P(A \cap \bar{B} \cap \bar{C}) + P(\bar{A} \cap \bar{B} \cap \bar{C})$$
$$= P(\bar{A})P(\bar{B})P(C) + P(\bar{A}).P(B).P(\bar{C}) + P(A).P(\bar{B}).P(\bar{C}) + P(\bar{A}).P(\bar{B}).P(\bar{C})$$
$$= (0.97 \times 0.96 \times 0.05) + (0.97 \times 0.04 \times 0.95) + (0.03 \times 0.96 \times 0.75) + (0.97 \times 0.96 \times 0.95)$$
$$= 0.9954$$

Problem 10.15

There are three bags containing gold, silver and both combined. Bag A contains 2 gold coins, Bag B contains 2 silver coins and bag C contains 1 gold and 1 silver coins. What is the probability of selecting bag A out of the three bags ?

Solution :

Since bags are identical of selecting bag *A* is $\frac{1}{3}$. When we draw a coin from one the bags, and it turns out t be gold we persume that it was not bag *B*, and hence the probability of selection of bag A is 0.5. But when we calculate this posterior probability with the help of Baye's theorem, the actual proabability will be given by

$$P\left(\frac{A}{G}\right) = \frac{P(AG)}{P(G)} = \frac{P\left(\frac{G}{A}\right).P(A)}{P\left(\frac{G}{A}\right)P(A) + P\left(\frac{G}{B}\right)P(B) + P\left(\frac{G}{C}\right)P(C)}$$

$$= \frac{1 \times \frac{1}{3}}{\left(1 \times \frac{1}{3}\right) + 0 + \left(\frac{1}{2} \times \frac{1}{3}\right)} = \frac{2}{3}$$

Problem 10.16

Two sets of candidates are competing for the positions one the Board of Directors of a company. The probabilities that the first and the second sets will win are 0.6 and 0.4 respectively. If the first set wins, the probability of introducing a new product is 0.8 and the corresponding probability if the second set wins is 0.3 what is the probability that the product will be introduced?

[*Delhi University, M.Com., 1976, C.A. (Inter), Nov. 1978*]

Solution :

We are given the following information $P(S_1) = 0.6$, $P(S_2) = 0.4$, $P\left(\frac{I}{S_1}\right) = 0.8$, $P\left(\frac{I}{S_2}\right) = 0.3$

Where I is the event of introduction of the product and S_1, S_2 the two sets of the candidates. We can achieve even I in the following manner

(*i*) First set (S_1) wins and product is introduced *i.e.* $S_1 \cap I$ occurs.

(*ii*) Second set (S_2) wins and product is Introduced *i.e.* $S_2 \cap I$ occurs

Thus $I = (S_1 \cap I) \cup (S_2 \cap I)$

$$P(I) = P(S_1 \cap I) + P(S_2 \cap I)$$

$$= P(S_1) \times P\left(\frac{I}{S_1}\right) + P(S_2) \times P\left(\frac{I}{S_2}\right)$$

$$= 0.6 \times 0.8 + 0.4 \times 0.3$$

$$= 0.6$$

Problem 10.17

A company has two plants to manufacture scooters. Plant I manufactures 80 per cent of the scooters and plant II manufactures 20 per cent. At plant 1,85 out of 100 scooters are rated standard quality or better. At plant II only 65 out of 100 scooters are rated standard quality or better.

(*i*) What is the probability that scooter selected at random came from plant I if it is known that the scooter is of standard quality ?

(*ii*) What is the probability that the scooter came from plant II if it is known that the scooter is of standard quality?

[*Delhi University, MBA. 1976, M. com., 1978*]

Solution :

Let S be the event of Standard Scooter Quality

S_1 the event that Scooter is manufactured at plant I

S_2 the event that Scooter is manufactured at plant II

Thus, we are given $P(S_1) = 0.80, P(S_2) = 0.2, P\left(\frac{S}{S_1}\right) = 0.85, P\left(\frac{S}{S_2}\right) = 0.65$

(i) $$P\left(\frac{S_1}{S}\right) = \frac{P(S_1)P\left(\frac{S}{S_1}\right)}{P(S_1).P\left(\frac{S}{S_1}\right) + P(S_2)P\left(\frac{S}{S_2}\right)}$$

$$= \frac{0.8 \times 0.85}{(0.8 \times 0.85) + (0.2 \times 0.65)}$$

$$= 0.84$$

$$P\left(\frac{S_2}{S}\right) = \frac{P(S_2)P\left(\frac{S}{S_2}\right)}{P(S_1).P\left(\frac{S}{S_2}\right) + P(S_2)P\left(\frac{S}{S_2}\right)}$$

$$= \frac{0.2 \times 0.65}{(0.8 \times 0.85) + (0.2 \times 0.65)} = 0.16$$

Problem 10.18

In a bolt factory machines A, B, C manufacture respectively 25%, 35% and 40% of the total of their output 5, 4, 2 per cent are defective bolts. If A bolt is drawn at random from the product and is found to be defective, what are the probabilities that it was manufactured by machine A, B and C?

[Delhi University, MBA, 1978]

Solution:

Given event D as bolt defective

and E_1, E_2, E_3 as bolt manufactured by A, B, C.

We have to find out $P\left(\frac{E_1}{D}\right), P\left(\frac{E_2}{D}\right)$ and $P\left(\frac{E_3}{D}\right)$

Given data $P(E_1) = 0.25$

$P(E_2) = 0.35$

$P(E_3) = 0.40$

and $P\left(\frac{D}{E_1}\right) = 0.05, P\left(\frac{D}{E_2}\right) = 0.04\ P\left(\frac{D}{E_3}\right) = 0.02$

Then $$P\left(\frac{E_1}{D}\right) = \frac{P(E_1).P\left(\frac{D}{E_1}\right)}{\Sigma P(E_1).P\left(\frac{D}{E_1}\right)}$$

$$= \frac{0.25 \times 0.05}{(0.25 \times 0.05) + (0.35 \times 0.04) + (0.04 \times 0.02)} = 0.36$$

Similarly $$P\left(\frac{E_2}{D}\right) = \frac{P(E_2).P\left(\frac{D}{E_2}\right)}{\Sigma P(E_2).P\left(\frac{D}{E_2}\right)}$$

$$= \frac{0.35 \times 0.04}{0.0345} = 0.41$$

and $$P\left(\frac{E_3}{D}\right) = \frac{P(E_3).P\left(\frac{D}{E_3}\right)}{\Sigma P(E_1)P\left(\frac{D}{E_1}\right)}$$

$$= \frac{0.4 \times 0.02}{0.0345} = 0.23$$

Problem 10.19

If we draw two cards from a pack

(*i*) Successively with replacement

(*ii*) Successively without replacement.

Find the probability distribution of a number of aces.

Solution :

Here the Random Variable X is the number of aces obtained in a draw from a pack of 52 cards, while we draw 2 cards *i.e.* X taking the values 0, 1, 2.

(*i*)Probability of drawing an ace $= \frac{4}{52} = \frac{1}{13}$

Probability of two aces $= P(X = 2)$

$$= P(\text{Ace}) \times P(\text{Ace})$$

$$= \frac{1}{13} \times \frac{1}{13} = \frac{1}{169}$$

Probability of one Ace and one non-ace

$$= P(x = 1)$$

$$= P(\text{Ace and Non-Ace}) + P(\text{Non-Ace, Ace})$$

$$= \frac{1}{13} \times \frac{12}{13} + \frac{12}{13} \times \frac{1}{13} = \frac{24}{169}$$

Probability of no ace $= P(X = 0)$

$$= \frac{12}{13} \times \frac{12}{13} = \frac{144}{169}$$

The distribution function will be

x	:	0	1	2
$p(x)$	:	$\frac{144}{169}$	$\frac{24}{169}$	$\frac{1}{169}$

(*ii*) When cards are drawn without replacement, the exhaustive number of cases, will be $^{52}C_2$ for two cards out of 52

$$\therefore \quad P(X=0) = P(\text{Non-Ace}) = P(\text{both Non-Aces})$$

$$= \frac{^{48}C_2}{^{52}C_2} = \frac{188}{221}$$

$$P(X=1) = P(\text{one Ace, other Non-Ace})$$

$$= \frac{^{4}C_1 \times {^{48}C_1}}{^{52}C_2} = \frac{32}{221}$$

$$P(X=2) = P(\text{both Aces})$$

$$= \frac{^{4}C_2}{^{52}C_2} = \frac{1}{221}$$

Hence the probability distribution function of X will be

x	:	0	1	2
$p(x)$	:	$\frac{188}{221}$	$\frac{32}{221}$	$\frac{1}{221}$

Problem 10.20

A company estimates the net profit on a new product it is launching to be Rs. 30,00,000 during the first year, if it is successful, Rs. 10,00,000 if it is moderately successful and a loss of Rs. 10,00,000 if it is unsuccessful. The firm assigns the following probabilities to first years's prospects for the product successful 0.15, moderately successful 0.25. What are the expected values and standard deviation of the first year net profit for this prodcut. [*C.A. (Final), May 1979*]

Solution :

The given value are

x(profits)	:	30,00,000	10,00,000	–10,00,000
$p(x)$(Probability)	:	0.15	0.25	0.60
$x\,p(x)$	:	4,50,000	2,50,000	–6,00,000
$x^2p(x)$	:	1,35,000	25,00,000	6,00,000

$$\text{Expected profit} = E(X) = \Sigma xp(x)$$

$$= 4{,}50{,}000 + 2{,}50{,}000 - 6{,}00{,}000$$

$$= 1{,}00{,}000$$

$$\text{Var }(X) = \Sigma x^2 p(x) - [\Sigma x\, p(x)]^2$$

$$= (1{,}35{,}00{,}000 + 25{,}00{,}000 + 6{,}00{,}000) - (1{,}00{,}000)^2$$

$$= 21{,}90{,}000$$

$$\sigma_x = \sqrt{2.19} \text{ million} = \text{Rs. } 1.48 \text{ million}$$

Problem 10.21

A Random Variable X is defined as the sum of faces when a pair of dice is thrown. Find the expected value of X.

[Calcutta University, B.A. (Eco. Hons.), 1979. Punjab University, M.A. (Eco.), 1982,]

Solution :

If X denotes the sum of points obtained on a pair of dice, then the probability distribution can be written as

x	2	3	4	5	6	7	8	9	10	11	12
$p(x)$	$\frac{1}{36}$	$\frac{2}{36}$	$\frac{3}{36}$	$\frac{4}{36}$	$\frac{5}{36}$	$\frac{6}{36}$	$\frac{5}{36}$	$\frac{4}{36}$	$\frac{3}{36}$	$\frac{2}{36}$	$\frac{1}{36}$

$$E(X) = \Sigma x\, p(x)$$

$$= 2 \times \frac{1}{36} + 3 \times \frac{2}{36} + 4 \times \frac{3}{36} + \ldots 12 \times \frac{1}{36}$$

$$= \frac{252}{36} = 7.$$

Problem 10.22

A restaurant serves two special dishes A and B to its customers consistings of 60% men and 40% women. 80% of men order dish A and the rest B. 70% of women order dish B and the rest A. In what ratio of A and B should the restaurant prepare the two dishes?

[Bombay University B. Com. April 1982]

Solution :

Let us write the probabilities of happenings

Let $P(m)$ = Probability of men customers

$P(w)$ = Probability of women customers

Hence $P(A/m) = 0.8$

$P(B/m) = 0.2$

similarly $P(B/w) = 0.7$

$= 0.3$

and $P(m) = 0.6$

$P(w) = 0.4$

since dishes A and B are ordered either by men or women, we can write

$$P(A) = P[A \cup m) \cup (A \cap m)]$$

$$= PA \cup m) + P(A \cap m)$$

$$= P(m) \times P(A/m) + P(w) + P(A/w)$$

$$= (0.6 \times 0.8) + (0.4 \times 0.7)$$

similarly

$$P(B) = P(m) \times P(B/m) + P(w) \times P(B/w)$$

$$= (0.6 \times 0.2) + (0.4 \times 0.7)$$

$$= 0.4$$

Hence the restaurant should prepare the two dishes A and B in the proportion of 0.6 and 0.4 *i.e.* 3:2.

Problem 10.23

There are two containers A and B. Container A has 4 red balls and 6 black balls, whereas container B holds 3 red balls and 2 black balls. If we draw a black ball, find the probability of this ball oming from container A.

Solution :

In order to solve this problem, let us go systematically through successive experiments

Stage I — We first find the probability of selection of container A or B.

(*a*) While selecting containers, it could be either A or B, both having same chance of selection. If we denote probabilites as $P(A)$ and $P(B)$ respectively for container A and B. Then

$$P(A) = P(B) = \frac{1}{2}$$

Thus probability of a black ball coming either from container A or container B is $\frac{1}{2}$ each.

Stage II — Now we perform the experiment of drawing a black ball from one of the two containers selected at stage I.

(a) Drawing a ball from either of the containers have two possibilities – either it is a red ball or a black ball. Let the outcome of the black ball be denoted by y_1 and that of red ball of y_2. It may be noted that only one of these outcomes would occur.

(*b*) If the ball is drawn from container A, the probabilites associated with the outcome of the colour of the ball will be conditional as $P(y_1|A)$ or $P(y_2|A)$ *i.e.*

Probability of drawing a black ball from A = $P(y_1|A)$

and probability of drawing red ball from A = $P(y_2|A)$

Similarly, if the ball is drawn from container B, then

conditional probability drawing black ball from $B = P(y_1|B)$

and conditional probability of drawing red ball from $B = P(y_2|B)$

(*c*) Now, we have four conditional probabilites, two for drawing a red ball and two for black ball.

Hence, $P(y_1|A) = 6/10$ and $P(y_2|A) = 2/5$

Similarly $P(y_1|B) = 4/10$ and $P(y_2/B) = 3/5$

These probabilities are identified are represent the probabilities that stage II outcome will occur when it is known that stage I outcomes have occured.

We now require the probability of selecting a balck ball belonging to container A. Thus we have to calculate the conditional probability $P(y_1|A)$.

From conditional probability relationship.

$$P(A|y_1) = \frac{P(A \cap y_1)}{P(y_1)}$$

and $$P(y_1|A) = \frac{P(y_1 \cap A)}{P(A)}$$

$$\therefore \quad P(A \cap y_1) = P(A|y_1).P(y_1)$$

$$P(y_1 \cap A) = P(A).P(y_1|A)$$

Since $P(y_1)$ is the probability of drawing a black ball, it can be obtained in two ways; either we draw the black ball from container A or from container B. This would mean that either y_1 and A occur simultaneouslyor y_1 and B occur simultaneously.

Therefore $\quad P(y_1) = P(y_1 \cap A) + P(y_1 \cap B)$

$$= P(A).P\left(\frac{Y_1}{A}\right) + P(B).P\left(\frac{Y_1}{B}\right)$$

$$\therefore \quad P(A|y_1) = \frac{P(A).P\left(\frac{y_1}{A}\right)}{P(A).P\left(\frac{y_1}{A}\right) + P(B).P\left(\frac{Y_1}{B}\right)}$$

This is Bayesian's probability rule. Substituting the values.

$$P(A|y_1) = \frac{\frac{1}{2}\times\frac{6}{10}}{\left(\frac{1}{2}\times\frac{6}{10}\right)+\left(\frac{1}{2}\times\frac{2}{5}\right)} = \frac{3}{5}$$

This is probability of drawing a black ball out of container A.

If we have to calculate the probability of drawing a black ball out of container B,

$$\text{Then} \quad P(B|y_1) = \frac{P(B)P\left(\frac{y_1}{B}\right)}{P(B).P\left(\frac{y_1}{B}\right) + P(A).P\left(\frac{y_1}{A}\right)}$$

$$= \frac{\left(\frac{1}{2}\times\frac{4}{10}\right)}{\left(\frac{1}{2}\times\frac{4}{10}\right)+\left[\frac{1}{2}\times\frac{6}{10}\right]}$$

$$= \frac{2}{5}$$

PRACTICE PROBLEMS

10.24 Define independent and mutually exclusive events. Can two events be mutually exclusive and independent simultaneously? Support your answer with an example. *[Delhi University. M.B.A.. 1973]*

10.25 (*a*) Discuss briefly various schools of thought on probability. Discuss their limitations, if any.

(*b*) Discuss the different school of thought on the interpretation of probability? How does each school define probability? *[Delhi University, M.B.A., 1976]*

10.26 State and prove the addition law of probability for any two events A and B. Rewrite the law when A and B are mutually exclusive. *[Bombay University, B.Com., April 1983]*

10.27 State and prove the Multiplication of probability. How is the result modified if events are not independent. *[Delhi University, B.A. (Eco. Hons.), 1985]*

10.28 State the axioms of probability. *[Delhi University, B.A. (Eco. Hons.). 1984]*

10.29 Explain with examples the rules of Addition and Multiplication in Theory of probability. *[Calicut University, M.Com., 1975, C.A. (Inter). Nov., 1977]*

10.30 Explain the meaning of conditional probability of an event. State the addition and multiplication rules of probability. *[Delhi University, B.A. (Eco. Hons.).1982]*

10.31 What do you understand by conditional probability? If Prob. (A + B) = Prob. (A) + Prob (B), are the two events A and B mutually exclusive? *[Delhi University, M.A. (Eco. Hons.).1977]*

10.32 Define Random variable and Mathematical Expectation. How do you use the concept in a Business situation?

10.33 The Federal Match Company has forty female employees and sixty male employees. If two employees are selected at random, what is the probability that (*i*) both will be males, (*ii*) both will be females. (*iii*) there will be one of each sex?

Since the three events are collectively exhaustive and mutually exclusive, what is the sum of the three probabilities? *[Punjab University, B.Com., April 1978]*

10.34 If a single draw is made from a pack of 52 cards, what is the probability of securing cither an acr of spade or a jack of clubs? *[Allahabad University, M.Com.. 1970]*

10.35 There are 17 balls, numbered from 1 to 17 in a bag. If a person selects one ball at random, what is the probability that the number printed on the ball will be an even number greater than 9? *[C.A. (Inter). Nov.. 1985]*

10.36 Four cards are drawn from a full pack of cards. Find the probability that two are spades and two are hearts. *[Bombay University. B.Com., 1974]*

10.37 A bag contains 7 white and 9 black balls. Two balls are drawn in succession at random. What is the probability that one of them is white and the other is black? *[Madras University. M.B.A.. 1976]*

10.38 Let E denote the experiment of tossing a corn three times in succession. Construct the sample space S. Write down the elements of two events E_1 and E_2 where E is the event that the number of heads exceeds the number of tails and E_2 is the event of getting head in the first trial. Find the probabilities $P(E_1)$ and $P(E_2)$; assuming that all the elements of S are equally likely to occur. *[ICWA (Final), June 1984]*

10.39 Probability that a man will be alive 25 years hence is 0.3 and the probability that his wife will be alive 25 years hence is 0.4. Find the probability that 25 years hence (*i*) both will be alive, (*ii*) only the man will be alive, (*iii*) only the woman will be alive, (*iv*) at least one of them will be alive. *[Bombay University, B.Com., Nov. 1980]*

10.40 A committee of 4 persons is to be appointed .from 3 officers of the Production department, 4 officers of the Purchase department, 2 officers of the Sales department and one Charted Accountant. Find the probability of forming the committee in the following manner. [(*i*) There must be one from each category, (*ii*) It should have at least one from the purchase department, (*iii*) The Chartered Accountant must be in the committee. *[C.A. (Inter). May 1983]*

10.41 A Chartered Accountant applies for a job in two firms *X* and *Y*. He estimates that the probability of his being selected in firm *X* is 0.7 and being rejected at *Y* is 0.5, and the probability of at least one of his application being rejected is 0.6. What is the probability that he will be selected in one of the firms? *[Punjab University, B.Com., Sept. 1980]*

10.42 A piece of equipment will function only when all the three components *A, B* and *C* are working. The probability of A failing during one year is 0.15, that of *B* failing is 0.05 and that of C failing is 0.6. What is the probability that the equipment will fail before the end of one year?[*Delhi University, M.B.A., 1982, AIMA (Dip. in Mgmt.), July 1980*]

10.43 A man is dealt 4 spade cards from an ordinary pack of 52 cards. If he is given 3 more cards, find the probability p that at least one of the additional cards is also a spade.
[*Delhi University, B.A. (Eco. Hons.), 1985*]

10.44 Find the probability of throwing 6 at least once in six throws with a single dice.
[*Calcutta University, B.A. (Eco. Hons.), 1976, Kurukshetra University, B.Com., Sept. 1975*]

10.45 The probability that a person stopping at a petrol pump will get his tyres checked is 0.12. The probability that he will get his oil checked is 0.29 and the probability that he will get both checked is 0.07.

(*i*) What is the probability that a person stopping at this pump will have neither his tyres nor oil checked?

(*ii*) Find the probability that a person who has his oil checked will also have his tyres checked.
[*Delhi University. B.A. (Eco. Hons.), 1980*]

10.46 Six persons toss a coin turn by turn. The game is won by players who first throws head. Find the probability of success of the fourth player. [*Delhi University, B.A. (Eco. Hons.) 1982*]

10.47 A person is known to hit the target in 3 out of 4 shots, where as another person is known to hit the target in 2 out of 3 shots. Find the probability of the targets being hit at all when they both try.[*Punjab University, B.Com., 1981*]

10.48 Suppose it is 11 to 5 against a person who is now 38 years of age living till he is 73 and 5 against 3 against B now 43 living till he is 78. Find the chance that at least one of these persons will be alive 35 years hence. [*Bombay University, B.Com., 1974*]

10.49 A card is drawn at random from a well shuffled pack of cards. What is the probability that is a heart or a queen? [*C.A. (Inter), May 1982*]

10.50 A candidate is selected for interview for three posts. For the first post, there are 3 candidates, for the second are 4 and for the third, there are 2. What are his chances of getting at least one post? [*C.A. (Inter), May 1981*]

10.51 A salesman has a 60 per cent chance of making a sale to each customer. The behaviour of successive customer is independent. If two customers A and B enter, what is the probability that the salesman will make a sale to A or B? [*AIMA (Dip. in Mgmt.), 1977*]

10.52 A statistical experiment consists of asking 3 housewives at random if they wash their dishes with brand X detergent. List the elements of the sample space S using the letter Y for yes and N for no. List the elements of the event. "The second woman interviewed uses brand X". Find the probability of this event if it is assumed that all the elements of S are equally likely to occur. [*ICWA (Final), June 1983*]

10.53 If $P(A) = 0.3$, $P(B) = 0.2$ and $P(C) = 0.1$, and A, B, C are independent events, find the probability of occurrence of at least one of the three events A, B and C.
[*Bombay University, B.Com, Oct.,1973*]

10.54 A sub-committee of six members is selected at random from the fifteen members of a committee, ten of whom are men and five women. Find the probability that the sub-committee
(*i*) Includes exactly 5 men
(*ii*) Includes at least 2 women.
[*Delhi University, B.A. (Eco. Hons.) 1982*)

10.55 If a dice is rolled 3 times, what is the probability of 5 coming up at least once?
[*C.A. (Inter), Nov.. 1985*]

10.56 Two six-sided dice are tossed at a time. Find the probability of getting one dot side of the first dice and five dot side of the second dice. *[Rajasthan University, M.Com., 1976]*

10.57 From a computer tally based on employee records, the personnel manager of a large manufacturing firm finds that 15 per cent of the firms' employees are supervisors and 25 per cent of the firms employees are college graduates. He also discovers that 5 per cent of the firm's employees are both supervisors and college graduates. Suppose that an employee is selected at random from the firm's personnel records, find the

(*i*) Probability of selecting a person who is both a college graduate and a supervisor and

(*ii*) Probability of selecting a person who is neither a supervisor nor a college graduate. *[Delhi University. M.B.A., 1977]*

10.58 The odds against student X solving a business statistics problem are 8 : 6 and odds in favour of student Y solving the same problem are 14 : 16.

(*i*) What is the chance that the problem will be solved if they both try independently of each other?

(*ii*) What is the probability that neither solves the problem? *[C.A. (Inter), Nov., 1979]*

10.59 An electronic device is made up of three components A, B and C. The probability of failure of the component A is 0.01, that of B is 0.1 and that of C is 0.02, in some fixed period of time. Find the probability that the device will work satisfactorily during that period of time assuming that the three components work independently of one another. *[Bombay University, B.Com., April' 72]*

10.60 Suppose two six-faced dice are thrown 10 times. What is the probability of getting double six in at least one of the throws? *[Delhi University, M.Com., 1970]*

10.61 If three coins are tossed simultaneously, what is the probability that they will all fall alike? *[Punjab University, M.A. (Eco.), 1977]*

10.62 A husband a wife appear in an interview for two vacancies in the same post. The probability of husband's selection is 1/7 and that of the wife's selection is 1/5. What is the probability that

(*a*) Both of them will be selected
(*b*) Only one of them will be selected
(*c*) None of them will be selected? *[Punjab University, B.Com., 1980]*

10.63 Three tokens marked 1, 2 and 3 are placed in a bag and one is drawn and replaced. The operation being repeated three times, what is the probability of obtaining a total of 6? *[Delhi University, B.A. (Eco. Hons.), 1979]*

10.64 A and B toss an ordinary dice alternately in succession. The winner is one who throws an ace first. If A is the first to throw, calculate their probabilities of winning the game. *[Meerut University. M.Com., 1975]*

10.65 A, B and C in that order, toss a coin. The first one to throw a head coin wins. What are their respective chances of winning? Assume that the game may continue indefinitely. *[Meerut University, M.Com., 1975]*

10.66 A and B alternately cut a pack of cards and the pack is suffled after each cut. If A starts and the game is continued until one cuts a diamond, what are the respective chances of A and B first cutting a diamond? *[Delhi University, B.Com., 1976]*

10.67 A bag contains 8 white and 7 black balls. 4 balls are'drawn one by one without replacement. What is the probability that white and black balls appear alternately? *[Bombay University, B.Com., April 1983]*

10.68 A manager has two assistants and he bases his decision on information supplied independently by each of them. The probability that he makes a mistake in his thinking is 0.005. The probability that an assistant gives wrong information is 0.3. Assuming that the mistakes made by the manager are independent of the information given by the assistants, find the probability that he reaches a wronp decision.

[*Delhi University. M.B.A.. Dec., 80. Bombay, B.Com., April '76*]

10.69 Three group of workers contain 3 men and 1 woman, 2 men and 2 women and 1 man and 3 women respectively. One worker is selected at random from each group. What is the probability that the group selected consists of 1 man and 2 women?

[*Meerut University, M.Com., 1975, Nagpur University, M.Com., 1976*]

10.70 An urn contains 10 white and 6 black balls. Find the probability that a blindfolded person in one draw shell obtain a white ball, and in the second drawn (without replacing the first one) a black ball. [*Punjab University, B.Com., Sept., 1981*]

10.71 The personnel department of a company has records, which show the following analysis of its 200 engineers.

Age	*Bachelor's degree only*	*Master's degree*	*Total*
Under 30	90	10	100
30 to 40	20	30	50
Over 40	40	10	50
Total	150	50	200

If one engineer is selected at random from the company, find

(*a*) The probability he has only a bachelor's degree

(*b*) The probability he has a Master's degree given that he is over 40.

(*c*) The probability he is under 30, given he has only a bachelor's degree

[*Delhi University, M.B.A.. 1977; Punjab University, B.Com., 1979*]

10.72 Two digits are selected at random from the digits 1 through 9. If the sum is even, find the probability P that both are odd. [*Delhi University, B.A. (Eco. Hons.), 1984*]

10.73 The following table gives the details of the consumer preference for a new product to be introduced in the market.

No. of Consumers	*Like*	*Dislike*	*Neutral*
Male	500	250	125
Female	200	350	75

What is the probability that a consumer selected at random from the group will be

(*i*) A male who disliked the product.

(*ii*) One who like the product, given that the person is a female.

(*iii*) Either male one who dislike the product. [*Bombay University, B.Com., May 1982*]

10.74 In a survey study of a randomly selected sample of 1,000 individuals were asked whether they were planning to buy a new car in the next 12 months. A year later, the same persons were interviewed again to find out whether they actually bought a new car. The response to both interviews is cross tabled in the following table:

Second interview	*First Interview*		
	Planners	*Non-planners*	*Total*
Buyers	50	150	200
Non-Buyers	200	600	800
Total	250	750	1000

If a person selected at random was found to be a buyer, what is the probability that

(*i*) He was a planner

(*ii*) He was a non-planner? [*Udaipur University, M.Com., 1975*]

10.75 A restaurant serves two special dishes, *A* and *B* to its customers consisting of 60% men and 40% women. 80% of men order dish *A* and the rest *B*. 70% of women order dish *B* and the rest *A*. In what ratio of *A* to *B* should the restaurant prepare the two dishes? [*Bombay University, B.Com., April 1982*]

10.76 Suppose that a product is produced in three factories *A*, *B* and *C*. It is known that factory A produces twice as many items as factory B, and that factory *B* and *C* produce the same number of products. Assume that it is known that 2 percent of the items produced by each of the factories *A* and *B* are defective while 4 percent of those manufactured by factory *C* are defective. All the items produced in three factories are stocked, and an item of product is selected at random, what is the probability that this item is defective? [*Madras University, M.A. (Eco.) Dec., 1976*]

10.77 In a certain university, the percentage of Hindus, Muslims and Christians among students are 50, 25 and 25 respectively. If 50% of Hindus, 90% of Muslims and 80% of Christians are smokers, find the probability that a randomly selected smoker student is a Muslim. [*Punjab University, M.A. (Eco.), 1981*]

10.78 There are 4 boys and 2 girls in Room No.1 and 5 boys and 3 girls in Room No.2. A girl from one of the two rooms laughed loudly. What is the probability that the girl who laughed loudly was from Room No.2? [*Rajasthan University, M.Com., 1978*]

10.79 A manufacturing firm produces steel pipes in three plants with daily production volumes of 500, 1000 and 2000 units respectively. According to past experience it is known that the fraction of defective outputs produced by the three plants are respectively 0.005, 0.008 and 0.06. If a pipe is selected from a day's total production and found to be defective, find out (*i*) From which plant the pipe comes (*ii*) What is the probability that it came from the first plant? [*Delhi University, M.Com., 1973*]

10.80 A factory produces a certain type of outputs by three types of machines. The respective daily production figures are

Machine I	:	3,000 units
Machine II	:	2,500 units
Machine III	:	4,500 units

Past experience shows that one per cent of the output produced by machine I is defective. The corresponding fraction of defectives for the other two machines are 1.2 per cent and 2 per cent respectively. An item is drawn at random from the day's production run and is found to be defective. What is the probability that it comes from the output of (*a*) Machine I, (*b*) Machine II, (*c*) Machine III?

[*Delhi University, M.Com., 1975 ; AIMA (Dip. in Mgmt.). Jan., 1979*]

10.81 It is known that 40% of the students in a certain college are girls and 50% of the students are above the median height. If 2/3 of the boys are above the median height, what is the probablity that a randomly selected student, who is below the median height is a girl? (Answer the problem preparing a joint probability table). [*C.A. (Inter), Nov.. 1985*]

10.82 A survey conducted over last 25 years indicated that in 10 years winter was mild, in 8 years it was cold and in the remaining 7 years it was very cold. A company sells 1000 woollen coats in a mild a mild year, 1300 in a cold year and 2000 in very cold year. You are required to find the yearly expected profits of the company, if a woollen coat costs Rs. 173 and it is sold to stores for Rs. 248. [*C.A. (Inter), Nov., 1983*]

10.83 Food products Ltd. have introduced a new item of food delicacy. The company has calculated that the cost of manufacture is Rs. 1 per piece and that what would be unsold at the end of a day is a dead loss. The demand is a variable and the following probability distribution of demand is expected :

Number of pieces demanded	:	10	11	12	13	14	15
Probability	:	0.07	0.10	0.23	0.38	0.12	0.10

[AIMA (Dip. in Mgmt.), Jan., 1980]

10.84 A random variable X has the following probability distribution:

X	:	1	0	1	2
Probability	:	1/3	1/6	1/6	1/3

Compute the expectation of X. *[Calcutta University, B.A. (Eco. Hons.), 1977]*

10.85 If the probability that the value of a certain stock will remain the same is 0.46, the probability that its value will increase by Rs. 0.50 or Rs. 1.00 per share are respectively 0.17 and 0.23, and the probability that its value will decrease by Rs. 0.25 per share is 0.14, what is the expected gain per share? *[Delhi University, B.A. (Eco. Hons.), 1984]*

10.86 Suppose an insurance company offers a 45 year old man Rs. 1000 one year term insurance policy for an annual premium of Rs. 12. Assume that the number of deaths per thousand is 5 for persons in this age group. What is the expected gain for the insurance company on a policy of this type? *[Delhi University, M.B.A., 1972]*

10.87 The monthly demand for transistors is known to have the following probability distribution.

Demand (n)	:	1	2	3	4	5	6
Probability	:	0.10	0.15	0.20	0.25	0.18	0.12

Determine the expected demand for transistors? Also obtain the variance. Suppose the cost (C) of producing 'n' tansistors is given by the rule $C = 10{,}000 + 500\ n$. Determine the expected cost. *[Madras University, M.B.A., (Eco.), Dec., 1976]*

❖❖❖

CHAPTER 11

PROBABILITY DISTRIBUTIONS

11.1 INTRODUCTION

While tabulating various data in order to obtain a worthwhile decision result out of it, we have used the concept of frequency distribution in chapter 2. In those discussions, we listed out all possible outcomes of an experiment and then worked out the distribution of those observations taking into account the observed frequencies for various values.

Due to uncertain nature of happening of events/activities in real-life situation, the concept of frequency distribution of data is more useful as Probability Distribution. Random experiments producing results of such random happening is then utilised for decision formulation.

In addition, in the chapter 10 on Theory of Probability, we then expanded the concept to the chances of happening of all such events, which the data indicate. This was indicative of the phenomenon that the outcomes may vary and due to uncertainty of events, the concept of probability can be associated with the frequency distribution in the form of probability distribution. In fact, we can now call the probability distribution as theoretical frequency distribution. Some aspect of this variation of outcomes / decisions under conditions of uncertainty has also been discussed.

11.2 CONCEPT OF PROBABILITY DISTRIBUTION

While discussing the theory of probability, we used the fair coin concept. The outcomes of throwing or tossing such a coin can be written in the following manner :

First toss	*Second toss*	*Probability of four possible outcomes*
H	T	$0.5 \times 0.5 = 0.25$
T	T	$0.5 \times 0.5 = 0.25$
H	H	$0.5 \times 0.5 = 0.25$
T	H	$0.5 \times 0.5 = 0.25$
		Total Prob $= 1.00$

If we consider, say, a case of getting heads from the outcome of three coins tossed simultaneously, we get the result as

Outcome :	HHH	HTH	THH	TTH	HHT	HTT	THT	TTT
No. of heads :	3	2	2	1	2	1	1	0

This can be described as the outcome of a random experiment, in which we assign a real number X, (In this case, the number of heads obtained as part of the above experiment) then

$$X_1 = 3, X_2 = 2, X_3 = 2, X_4 = 1, X_5 = 2, X_6 = 1\ ;\ X_7 = 1 \text{ and } X_8 = 0$$

We can also represent the above result in the following manner

Numarical value of X as the event :	X = 0	X = 1	X = 2	X = 3
Outcome of the event :	(TTT)	(HTT,THT,TTH)	(HHT, HTH, THH)	(HHH)

Thus random variable can be defined as a real value function on the sample space taking values on the real line $P(-\infty, \infty)$

We can define the above concept as $pi = P(x = X_L)$; $i = 1, 2, \ldots n$

This is called proabability of x.

or $\quad p(x) = P(X = x)$

and $\quad \Sigma pi = p_1 + p_2 + \ldots p_n = 1.$

If we define distribution function $F(X)$. Where X is discrete random variable.

then $\quad F(x) = P(X \leq x)$

or $\quad F(x) = p(1) + p(2) + \ldots p(x)$

$\therefore \quad p(x) = F(x) - F(x-1)$

$$\therefore \quad F(X) = \int_{-\infty}^{x} p(x)dx$$

The function $F(x) = P(x = x_i)$ or $p(x)$ is called the probability function and a set of all possible pairs *i.e.* $[x, p(x)]$ is called "the probability distribution of the random variable x" as defined above. The probability distribution is an expression describing the variation in a population.

Experimentation of events results in deciding the sample space, so that all elementary outcomes can be listed out along with the probability of happening attached to each outcome.

11.3 TYPES OF PROBABILITY DISTRIBUTIONS

The probability model of an experiment has two major ingredients :

1. The sample space containing all the elementary outcomes.
2. The attachment of a probability (Chance) to each such elementary outcome.

Since a random variable associates a numerical value with each elementary outcome, as described in the previous paragraph, this random variable represents some characteristic, which can be measured on a defined scale. If the defined scale is continuous over a period of interval of numbers, it is called a continuous random variable. Since the value of the random variable is directly related to the elementary outcome, these values can be associated with probabilities. Such a list of values of the random variable and their associated probabilities is called the probability distribution of the random variable.

There are two catergories of probability distributions

(*i*) Continuous probability distribution

(*ii*) Discrete probability distribution

When probability can take only some definite values such as 12 for the number of months in a year or 24 as the hours during the day, or 60 as the number of students in a particular class, it is called a discrete probability distribution.

As against this, when the variable being considered for analysis is allowed to take any value from within a given range, we call it as continuous probability distribution, because we cannot list out all the possible outcomes or values.

Continuous Probability Distribution :

We can use two types of probability distributions in business problems analysis. It can be either a mass distribution or the cumulative distribution.

Mass Distribution Function : When we consider a discrete random variable X, which can take the possible values (*i.e.*, listing of the set of all possible distinct values of the random variable), $x_1, x_2, x_3, \ldots, x_n$, we can write

$$P_i = P(X = x_i) \text{ where } i = 1, 2, 3, \ldots n.$$

This is known as the probability of X_i and satisfies the following conditions.

$$P_i = P(X = x_i) \geq 0$$

and $$\Sigma p_i = p_1 + p_2 + p_n = 1$$

Then the function $p_i = P(X = x_i)$ or $p(x)$ is called the probability function or probability mass function of the Random Variable x. The set of all possible value $\{x, p(x)\}$ is called the Probability Distribution of the random variable X.

Continuous Distribution Function : As against this concept in case of a continuous random variable, we donot assign the probability at a specific point, but over an interval of the random variable, in that case the probability $p(x)dx$ is defined as the probability that the random variable assumes in a small interval (dx) *i.e.*, $(x, x + dx)$, then $p(x)$ is called the probability density function of the random variable X. Refer Fig. 11.1.

Mass Distribution Function, Continuous Distribution Function and Cummulative probability function are normally used in relation to the business situations depending on the assigning the values of probability to a random variable.

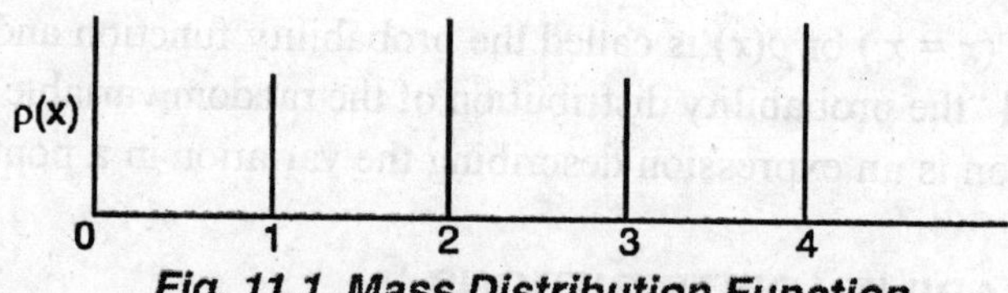

Fig. 11.1. Mass Distribution Function

Cumulative Probability Function : If Random Variable X is discrete with probability function $p(x)$, then the distribution function is defined as $F(x) = P(X \leq x)$

If X takes ntegral values say 1, 2, 3..... n etc. then

$$F(x) = P(X = 1) + P(X = 2) + P(X = 3) + P(X = x)$$
$$= p(1) + p(2) + p(3) + \ldots p(x)$$
$$\therefore \quad P(x) = F(x) - p(x - 1)$$

Hence if X takes only positive integer values, then probability function can be obtained from Distribution function based on the equation $p(x) = F(x) - p(x - 1)$.

If X is a continuous random variable with probability density function $p(x)$, then the distribution functions is given as

$$F(x) = P(X \leq x) = \int_{\infty}^{x} p(x)dx$$

This is illustrated in Fig. 11.2.

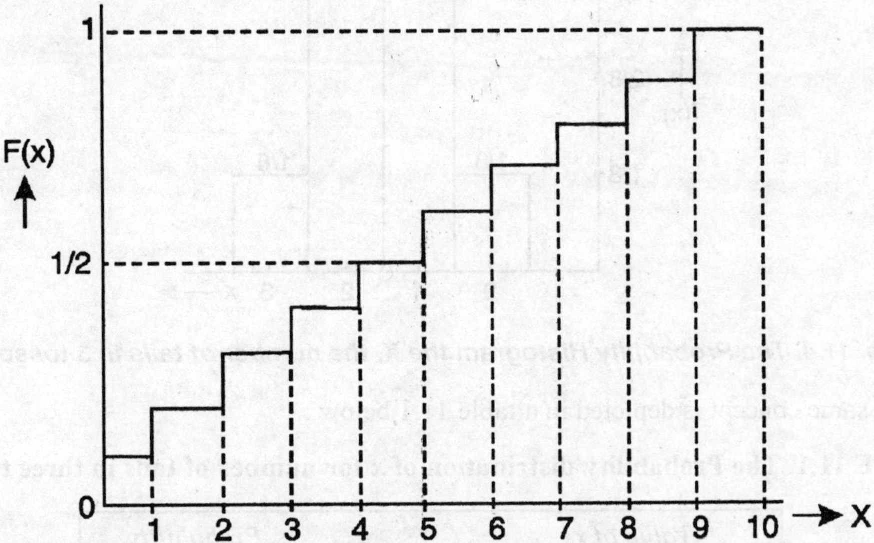

Fig. 11.2. Cumulative Distribution Function of a Random Variable.

The discrete probability distribution is a concept used when the discrete random variable is associated with distinct numerical values of the variable.

Discrete Probability Distribution :

The probability distribution of a discrete random variable X is a list of the distinct numerical values of the variable alongwith their associated probabilities.

Let us take the case of tossing of coin in a three-trial experiment. (discussed above under the concept).

When $x = 0$, the probability of getting no tail = 1/8 (all HHH only 1out of 8).

When $x = 1$, the probability of getting one tail (variable x denotes the obtaining of tail on a toss = 3/8). [i.e. HTH, THH and HHT i.e 3 out of 8 outcomes]

Similarly when $x = 2$, probability of getting 2 tails = 3/8

and when $x = 3$, probability of getting 3 tails = 1/8

This can be drawn on the diagram as indicated below (Fig. 11.3.)

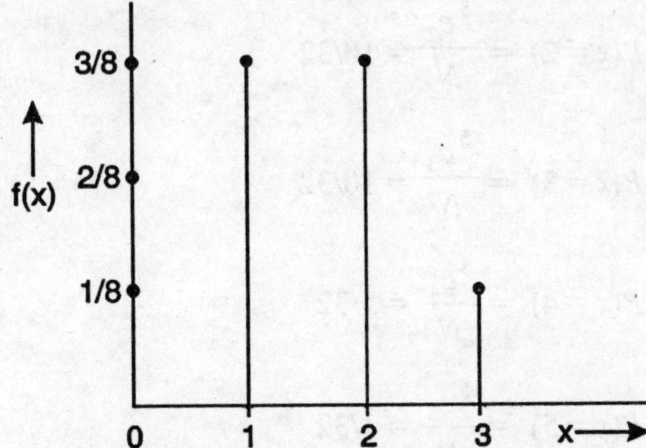

Fig. 11.3. Discrete Probability distribution

The same can be presented in the form of probability histogram as follows :

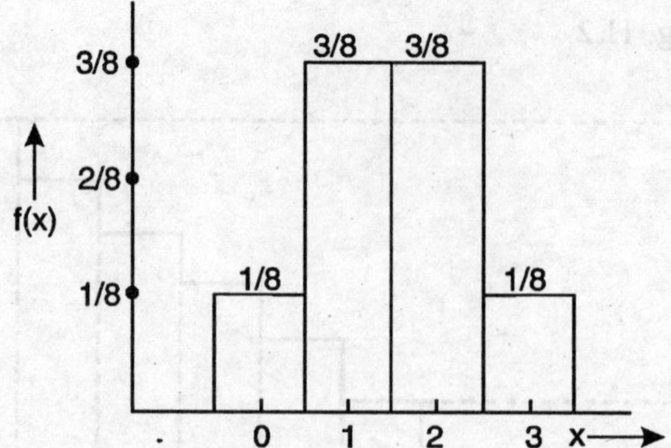

Fig. 11.4. The Probability Histogram the X, the number of tails in 3 tosses of a coin

The same concept is depicted in a table 11.1 below :

The concept of 'combination' and its associated frequency distribution (i.e., Binomial distribution) is usefully employed for calculation of the randomly happening events for various values of the random variable.

TABLE 11.1. The Probability distribution of *x* for number of tails in three tosses of a coin

Value of x	*Probability*
0	1/8
1	3/8
2	3/8
3	1/8
Total	1

When we conduct experiment of 5 trials, the probability can be worked out as follows :

$$P(x=0) = \frac{{}^{n}C_0}{N} = \frac{{}^{5}C_0}{32} = 1/32$$

$$P(x=1) = \frac{{}^{5}C_1}{N} = 5/32$$

$$P(x=2) = \frac{{}^{5}C_2}{N} = 10/32$$

$$P(x=3) = \frac{{}^{5}C_3}{N} = 10/32$$

$$P(x=4) = \frac{{}^{5}C_4}{N} = 5/32$$

$$P(x=5) = \frac{{}^{5}C_5}{N} = 1/32$$

The distribution chart as well as probability histogram can be drawn as follows *i.e.* Fig. 11.5. and 11.6. respectively

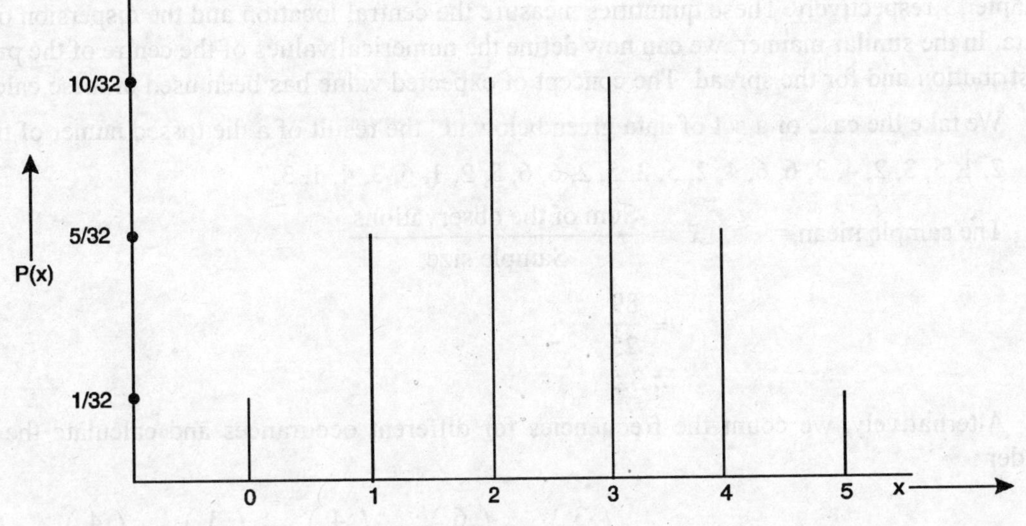

Fig. 11.5. Bar Chart

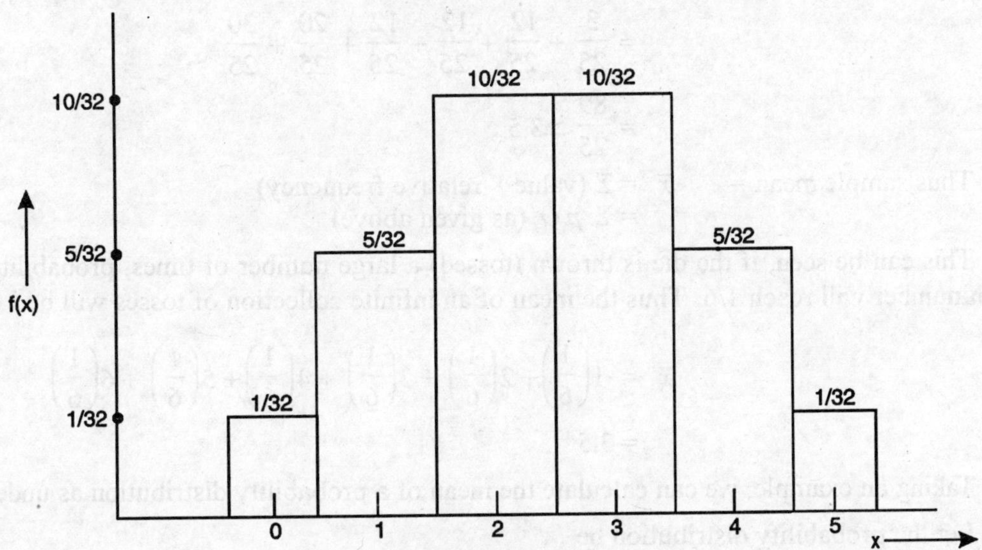

Fig. 11.6. Probability Histogram

The expected value of the random variable results from the concept of probability of an outcome as a result of experimentation. The value is the summation of the product of corresponding probability with its outcome.

11.4 EXPECTED VALUE OF A RANDOM VARIABLE

Expected value concept can be obtained from the decision theory. The expected value is the product of each value of the random variable and its probability of occurance. Thus,

$$EMV = \sum_{i=1}^{n} P_i O_i$$

where EMV = expected monitory value of the variable

P_i = Probability of ith outcome

O_i = conditional value of ith outcome

Expected losses may be calculated in similar manner.

11.5 MEAN AND STANDARD DEVIATION OF A PROBABILITY DISTRIBUTION

We have discussed the concept of sample mean $\bar{x}$ and standard deviation(s) in chapter 2 and chapter 3 respectively. These quantities measure the central location and the dispersion of a set of data. In the similar manner, we can now define the numerical values of the centre of the probability distribution and for the spread. The concept of expected value has been used in these calculations.

We take the case of a set of data given below i.e. the result of a die tossed numer of times.

2, 1, 5, 3, 2, 4, 3, 6, 6, 4, 2, 5, 2, 5, 2, 6, 6, 5, 2, 1, 6, 3, 4, 1, 3.

$$\text{The sample mean} = \quad \bar{x} = \frac{\text{Sum of the observations}}{\text{Sample size}}$$

$$= \frac{89}{25}$$

$$\simeq 3.5$$

Alternatively, we count the frequencies for different occurances and calculate the mean as under :

In the manner similar to calculation of mean and standard deviation of the variable, we use the concept of EMV for working out the mean value of the random variable.

$$\bar{x} = 1\left(\frac{3}{25}\right) + 2\left(\frac{6}{25}\right) + 3\left(\frac{4}{25}\right) + 4\left(\frac{3}{25}\right) + 5\left(\frac{4}{25}\right) + 6\left(\frac{5}{25}\right)$$

$$= \frac{3}{25} + \frac{12}{25} + \frac{12}{25} + \frac{12}{25} + \frac{20}{25} + \frac{30}{25}$$

$$= \frac{89}{25} \simeq 3.5$$

Thus sample mean = $\bar{x} = \Sigma$ (value × relative frequency)

$= \Sigma\ p_i O_i$ (as given above)

This can be seen, if the die is thrown (tossed) a large number of times, probability of getting each number will reach 1/6. Thus the mean of an infinite collection of tosses will be

$$\bar{x} = 1\left(\frac{1}{6}\right) + 2\left(\frac{1}{6}\right) + 3\left(\frac{1}{6}\right) + 4\left(\frac{1}{6}\right) + 5\left(\frac{1}{6}\right) + 6\left(\frac{1}{6}\right)$$

$$= 3.5$$

Taking an example, we can calculate the mean of a probability distribution as under :

Let the probability distribution be

x	:	0	1	2	3	4	5
$p(x)$	:	0.11	0.22	0.13	0.16	0.21	0.17

Then the mean of the random variable x is

$$\bar{x} = \Sigma x_i\, p(x_i) = 0 \times 0.11 + 1 \times 0.22 + 2 \times 0.13 + 3 \times 0.16 + 4 \times 0.21 + 5 \times 0.17$$

$$= 2.65$$

The Mean of an Expected Value

In the similar manner, as worked out in the earlier example, the expected outcome of an event can be decided as under :

Money payment	:	Rs. 10,000	Rs. 20,000	Rs. 30,000
Proability of payment	:	0.81	0.15	0.04

The expected value $E(x) = \bar{x} = \Sigma\ p_i O_i$

$$= 10{,}000 \times 0.81 + 20{,}000 + 0.15 + 30{,}000 \times 0.04$$

$$= \text{Rs } 11{,}220$$

Such cases can be related to chance payments for, say, an insurance policy payment under different conditional clauses or receipt of prize money under "condition apply" provisions etc.

The spread of a Probability Distribution

The concept of the expected value of a random variable can be extended to workout the numerical value of the spread of a probability distribution.

When we take the mean value of the random variable as μ and the deviation denoted as $(x - \mu)$. then the variance of the random variable is defined as the expected value of the squared deviation $(x - \mu)^2$. Thus, if the observed values of the random variable are taken as $(x_1 - \mu)^2, (x_2 - \mu)^2, (x_3 - \mu)^2$, ... $(x_k - \mu)^2$ etc. and if the probabilities associated with such deviation are p_1, p_2, p_3 .... p_k etc, then the expected value of $(x - n)^2$ can be obtained as follows :

$$\text{Variable of } X = \sum_{1}^{K} (\text{deviation})^2 \times (\text{probability})$$

$$= (x_1 - \mu)^2 p_1 + (x_2 - \mu)^2 p_2 + \ldots\ldots\ldots\ldots (x_k - \mu)^2 p_x$$

$$\therefore \quad \sigma^2 = \Sigma(x_i - \mu)^2 p_i \qquad i = 1, 2, 3, \ldots\ldots\ldots\ldots k$$

and

$$= sd(x) = +\sqrt{\text{var}(x)}$$

$$= +\sqrt{(x_i - \mu)^2 p_i} \qquad i = 1, 2, 3, \ldots\ldots\ldots\ldots k$$

The expression in a further simplified form can be written as

$$\sigma^2 = \sum_{1}^{k} x_i^2 p_i - \mu^2$$

This expression can be used for an example as under

Let x	:	0	1	2	3	4
$p(x)$	:	0.1	0.2	0.3	0.4	0.1

Then calculating values of $\Sigma x_i^2 p_i = 5.2$

and $\quad \mu = \Sigma x_i p_i = 2.0$

$$\sigma^2 = 5.2 - (2)^2 = 1.2$$

and $\quad \sigma^2 = \sqrt{1.2}$

$$= 1.095$$

The concept of the expected value of the random variable can be extended to work out the value of the spread of the probability distribution.

11.6 THEORETICAL PROBABILITY DISTRIBUTIONS

Under certain given conditions, these observed or empirical frequency distributions can be approximated by some standard known theoretical distributions. These theoretical distributions are very helpful to the decision makers in various business decisions. In the population, the values of the variable may follow distribution according to some law of probability and hence these distributions are termed as "Theoretical Probability Distributions". These laws may either be based on 'priori' considerations or on 'posteriori' inferences. Thus these theoretical probability distributions indicate the behaviour of the variable under certain known or given conditions. These distributions may be discrete or continuous, depending upon whether the random variable behaves with discrete or continuous values. In this chapter, we will define some of the well known probability distributions may be discrete or continuous, depending upon whether the random variable behaves with discrete or continuous values.

We will be discussing some important discrete distributions such as Binomial, Poisson and hyper geometric distributions, whereas some main continuous distributions such as Normal, exponential and uniform distributions will also be discussed.

Binomial distribution

This distribution is also called "Bernoulli's Distribution" after the name of the discoverer James Bernoulli (1654 - 1705). It was published in 1713.

For explaining the distribution, let us discuss the experiment conducted, whose outcomes are classified into two mutually exclusive and collectively exhaustive categories. Let us say these are 'success' and 'failure'. Few important examples can be item being defective or not defective when manufactured products are inspected; an oil well may or may not yield oil on digging experiment, or a student either passing an exam or failing in it. Similar experiment can be performed on a coin, by tossing of which, we either get head or tail. When we conduct this experiment, all the outcomes are independent and one outcome in not affected by the other. We can, hence, say that probability of success (head) is 1/2 and so is the probability of failure (tail) as 1/2 and it is constant for each toss.

Binomial Distribution is established with the help of actual experiments, where random trials are conducted and it is said that outcome of each trial can either be success or failure. When independent trials are repeated a finite number of times, the result is tabulated as a Binomial Distribution.

Successsive trials are called Bernoullis trials, if the following conditions are fulfilled :

1. There are two and only two possible outcomes of each trials either success or failure (S or F).
2. The random experiment is performed repeatedly (successive trails) a finite and fixed number of times.
3. All the trails are independent if outcome of one trial is not affected by the outcome of the other.
4. The probability of the occurance of success (S) is the same at each trail. If we call this probability P(S) = p, then the probability of failure (F) is equal to P(F) = $1-p=q$ and it also remains the same from one trial to another.

To explain the concept further, let us consider X as the number of successes in n Bernoulli's trials with the probability of a success p in each trial, we can now say that X is a random variable capable of taking values 0, 1, 2----n and the probability distribution of the random variable X is called 'Binomial Probability Distribution' with parameters n and p.

Let us consider a case of n = 3, where we may be finding the probability of zero success, one success, two and three success. The possible values of X are 0, 1, 2 or 3. The corresponding outcomes are tabulated below.

For	$X = 0$,	outcomes	*FFF*
For	$X = 1$,	outcomes	*SFF*
			FSF
			FFS
For	$X = 2$,	outcomes	*SSF*
			SFS
			FSS
and	For $X = 3$	outcomes	*SSS*

Thus we can derive a possible relationship that the total number of outcomes are 8, which is 2^3. In general, we can say that the probability of any outcomes of S or F with n = 3, will be

$$p^{(\text{no. of Ss in the sequence})} \times q^{(\text{no. of Fs in the sequence})}$$

and the coefficients of these are just the number of possible outcomes with the given Ss and Fs.

Thus,

$$p(X = 0) = q^3$$
$$p(X = 1) = 3pq^2$$
$$p(X = 2) = 3\,p^2q$$
$$p(X = 3) = p^3$$

Hence in general, the probability of exactly x successes and $(n - x)$ failures in n Bernoulli's trails, each with success probability p is given by,

$$P(X) = (n_x)p^x\, q^{n-x};\ x = 0, 1, 2, \ldots n$$

$$= \frac{n!}{x!(n-x)!}p^x q^{n-x}$$

where $\qquad n! = n(n-1)(n-2) \ldots 3, 2, 1$

This expression for $P(X)$ is known as the probability function of the Binomial Distribution with the parameters n and p. These parameters n and p completely define the distribution, since $q = 1 - p$ is also well defined. Random variable X takes only integer values and hence this distribution is Discrete Probability Distribution.

For n trials, the binomial Prabability distribution consists of $(x + 1)$terms, the successive coefficients being

$${}^nC_0, {}^nC_1, {}^nC_2 \ldots\ldots {}^nC_{n-1}, {}^nC_n.$$

Since $\qquad {}^nC_0 = {}^nC_n$, first and last coefficients are 1.

Also Since $\qquad {}^nC_r = {}^nC_{n-r}$, hence Binomial coefficients will be symmetric

For all values of x,

$$(1 + x)^n = {}^nC_0 + {}^nC_1x^1 + {}^nC_2\,x^2 + \ldots\ldots + {}^nC_n\,x_n$$

Putting $x = 1$, we have,

$$(1 + 1)^n = {}^nC_0 + {}^nC_1 + {}^nC_2 + \ldots\ldots {}^nC_n$$

Thus, the sum of all binomial coefficients will be 2^n.

This can be obtained and understood by Pascal's triangle also.

Through finite number of independent trials, it can be established that there is a set pattern of the co-efficients of the Binomial values. This pattern is depicted as Pascal's triangle.

Pascal's Triangle

Value of n	Binomial coefficients	(Sum 2^n)
1	1 1	2
2	1 2 1	4
3	1 3 3 1	8
4	1 4 6 4 1	16
5	1 5 10 10 5 1	32
6	1 6 15 20 15 6 1	64
7	1 7 21 35 35 21 7 1	128

and so on. It can be seen that always first and the last coefficients are unity (1) and each term in the above table can be obtained by adding the two terms of either side of it, in the preceeding line. This shows that binomial coefficients are symmertric and the sum of the coefficients is 2^n.

Characterstics of Binomial Distribution

We can prove that Mean of Binomial constant $= np$

and variance $\mu_2 = \sigma^2 = npq$

we can also prove that $\mu_3 = npq(q-p)$

and $\mu_4 = npq[1 + 3\,pq\,(n-2)]$

Moment coefficients of skewness is,

$$\beta_1 = \frac{(q-p)^2}{npq}$$

$$\gamma_1 = \frac{q-p}{\sqrt{npq}}$$

$$\beta_2 = 3 + \frac{(1-6pq)}{npq}$$

and $$\gamma_2 = \frac{(1-6pq)}{npq}$$

From the values of N number of experiments, a distribution pattern emerges and can be accordingly drawn to show that the Binomial distribution is symmetrical with its mean *np* and variance *npq*.

For easy use, elaborate statistical tables have been prepared to give all the binomial probabilities for various values of its parameters *n* and *p*. These tables are appended at the end of this book. In these tables of binomial distribution, entries for $f_b(x/n, p)$ are given for values of *p* in the range $0 < p \leq 0.5$., whereas for $p > 0.5$, the values can be obtained by the symmetry relation.

$$f_b(x/n,p) = f_b[(n-x)/n, (1-p)]$$

Fitting of Binomial Distribution

As given in the earlier sections, when a random experiment is carried out consisting of n trials and all binomial conditions are satisfied, the frequency of *x* successes is given by.

$$N \times p(x) = N \times n_{C_x} p^x q^{n-x}$$

where N = Number of experiments repeated

and $x = 0, 1, 2, \ldots\ldots n$

Thus we can work out the theoretical frequencies of *x* success as $N q^n$, $NC_1 pq^{n-1}$ .... $NC_x p^x q^{n-x}$...Np^n, etc., for values of $x = 0, 1, 2\ldots x,\ldots n$ etc. If *p* is known (probability of success), then the frequencies expected can be known from the above expression. However, if *p* is not known and we wish to be use Binomial distribution, we can first find the mean of the given frequency distribution as,

$$\bar{x} = \frac{\Sigma fx}{\Sigma f}$$

If $\bar{x} = np$

Then *p* can be estimated as $\frac{\bar{x}}{n}$ and then expected frequencies can be easily obtained.

Application of Binomial Distribution

As per the given Binomial conditions the Binomial Distribution is applicable only when samples are chosen from an infinite population with replacement so that the success probability remains the same during all the trails. But it can be used in many situations with excellent approximation. The acceptance or rejection of the lot for defective products based on the sample meeting or not meeting the quality standards is one such example. For small sample size, it is very good approximation, although the sample is taken from finite population with replacement.

Poisson Distribution

Poisson Distribution was derived by a French Mathematician D. Poisson (1781 - 1840) and it was considered to be a limiting case of Binomial Distribution, under the following conditions.

(*i*) The number of trials is infinitely large *i.e.*, $n \to \infty$

(*ii*) The constant probability of success (p) for each trial is infinitely small *i.e.* $p \to 0$.

(*iii*) $np = m$ is finite.

Under the above given conditions, the Binomial Distribution tends towards the probability function of Poisson Distribution,

Then $$p(x) = P(X = x) = \frac{e^{-m}m^x}{x!}, \text{ when } x = 0, 1, 2, \ldots$$

where X is the number of successes and $m = xp$ and $e = 2.71828$ [The base of Natural logarithms].

For making it worthwhile to understand, let us write down the Binomial probability function and apply the above three conditions to approximate it to the Poisson probability function.

Poisson Distribution was suggested by Poisson as a limiting case of Binomial Distribution, in which case, the number of trials is very large and the constant probability of success of each trial is infinitely small.

Conditions are $$n \to \infty$$
$$p \to 0$$
$$np = m$$

and $$q = 1 - p = 1 - \frac{m}{n}$$

Since, $${}^nC_x\, p^x q^{n-x} = \frac{n!}{x!(n-x)!} p^x q^{n-x}$$

$$= n(n-1)(n-2)\ldots[n-(x-1)]\left(\frac{m}{n}\right)^x \left(1 - \frac{m}{n}\right)^{n-x}$$

$$= \frac{m^x}{x!}\left[\frac{n}{n}.\frac{n-1}{n}.\frac{n-2}{n}\ldots\frac{n-(x-1)}{n}\right]\left(1-\frac{m}{n}\right)^{n-x}$$

$$= \frac{m^x}{x!}\left(1-\frac{1}{n}\right)\left(1-\frac{2}{n}\right)\ldots\left(1-\frac{x-1}{n}\right)\left(1-\frac{m}{n}\right)^n\left(1-\frac{m}{n}\right)^{-x}$$

If $n \to \infty$,

Then $$\frac{m^x}{x!}\lim_{n\to\infty}\left(1-\frac{1}{n}\right) \times \lim_{n\to\infty}\left(1-\frac{2}{n}\right) \times \ldots \times \lim_{n\to\infty}\left(1-\frac{m}{n}\right)^n \times \lim_{n\to\infty}\left(1-\frac{m}{n}\right)^{-x}$$

$$= \frac{m^x}{x!} \times (1-0) \times (1-0) \ldots (1-0) \lim_{n\to\infty}\left(1-\frac{m}{n}\right)^n \times \lim_{n\to\infty}\left(1-\frac{m}{n}\right)^{-x}$$

$$= \frac{m^x}{x!}\, 1 \times e^{-m} \times 1 = \frac{e^{-m}m^x}{x!}$$

Thus Poisson probability function

$$p(x) = P(X = x) = \frac{e^{-m}m^x}{x!}$$

Thus Poisson Probability Distribution is another discrete probability distribution, which can be applied when an event occurs at random points in space. The example of the Poisson Distribution can be the queuing system at any queue situation, be it in Post office or in a service station or even in a telephone booth.

For the queuing systems, we normally write the Poisson Probability Distribution function as,

$$P(X = x) = \frac{e^{-\lambda}\lambda^{x}}{x!}$$

where λ represents the probability of x in unit time interval. Thus, λ is the average rate of occurrence.

Properties of Poisson Distribution

If the random variable X indicates the number of events occurring in a given interval and it follows the Poisson Distribution with paramete λ, then

$$E(X) = \lambda \text{ and } V(X) = \lambda$$

and Hence Standard Deviation $S(X) = \sqrt{\lambda}$

In case of Poisson Distribution, the parameter used is $np = m$ where the mean value m is finite. The probability function is related to the base of natural logarithm, i.e., accordingly the mean, variance and mode values can be worked out.

The Poisson Distribution is skewed to the right and as λ increases, the Poisson distribution will be close to the bell-shaped continuous curve. There are two important properties of Poisson Distribution.

1. If X and Y are two independent random variable, having Poisson Distribution with parameters λ_1 and λ_2, respectively, then the random variable $(X + Y)$ will have Poisson Distribution with mean $(\lambda_1 + \lambda_2)$
2. If X and Y are two independent random variable having Poisson Distribution, with means λ_1 and λ_2. then the conditional distribution of X, given $X + Y = a$ will be a Binomial with $p = \frac{\lambda_1}{\lambda_1 + \lambda_2}$ and $n = a$.

Mode of Poisson Distribution

The Poisson Distribution has the mode at

$$X = x \text{ if } p(x) > p(x-1)$$

$$\text{and } p(x) > p(x+1)$$

When m or λ is an integer, the Poisson Distribution is bi-nodal at points $X = x$ and $X = x - 1$.

When m or λ is not an integer, then the Poisson Distribution is uni-nodal, the nodal value at integral part of m or λ.

For fitting a Poisson Distribution to a given frequency distribution, we compute the mean $\bar{x}$ of the given distibution and then put $m = \bar{x}$. When m is known, the probability of the Poisson Distribution can be obtained as follows :

Variable value (x):	0	1	2
Probability $p(x)$:	e^{-m}	me^{-m}	$\frac{m^2 e^{-m}}{2!}$
Theoretical frequency $f(x) = Np(x)$:	Ne^{-m}	$mNp(0)$	$\frac{m}{2}Np(1)$...etc.

Hyper geometric Distribution

When we consider the case of random sampling without replacement, the basic conditions of independence of trials in Bernoulli's distribution does not hold. Hence in such cases, we cannot use the Binomial Distribution. We then consider the utilisation of Hypergeometric Distribution, which is more appropriate for such situations. When the trials are carried out without replacement, the probability of success changes in each trial. Let us take the case of a pack of cards, where there are 52 cards, 13 cards of one suit and hence, when we want to pick up an ace of hearts, the probability will be $1/13$. For second trial, there will be only 12 cards left (first drawn card not replaced in the pack) and hence probability of picking up ace of heart from these cards will be $1/12$. Similarly, if we have drawn an ace of heart in the first trial itself, the probability of picking up ace of heart in the second trial will be zero, since card drawn (ace of heart) has not been replaced and there is no ace of heart left in the remaining 12 cards.

In general, when we are using samples out of a finite population of size N, the population can be divided into two groups, defectives and non-defectives. If there are D defectives, these will be $(N-D)$ non-defectives in the groups. Now when we pick up defectives, out of a sample of n items, the number $(n-x)$ should come from the population of $(N-D)$ elements of the population. Thus the probability distribution of X, in such cases, known as Hypergeometric Distribution is given by,

$$P(X=x) = \frac{(D_x)\binom{N-D}{n-x}}{(N_n)} \quad \text{for } x = 0, 1, 2, \ldots n$$

The mean of such distribution will be $= np$ where $p = \dfrac{D}{N}$

and Standard Deviation $= \sqrt{npq\left(\dfrac{N-n}{N-1}\right)}$, where $q = 1-p$.

Here the term $\left(\dfrac{N-n}{N-1}\right)$ is called the finite population correction factor when n is very small and N very large, this factor will be close to 1 and the Hyper Geometric Distribution will be an approximation to the Binoamial Distribution.

- Hyper-geometric Distribution is a specific case of Binomial Distribution, whose random sampling is achieved without replacement of the variable in the successive trials.

Normal Distribution

One such distribution is commonly known as Normal probability distribution or Normal distribution. It is most widely used probability distribution for continuous random variables. It is also most important continuous theoretical distribution because most of the data relating to business, social or physical situations conform to or can be approximated to the Binomial and the Poisson distributions.

Normal Distribution was discovered by an English Mathematician De-Moivre (1667–1754) in the year 1733 while solving the problem of game of chance. This distribution is also called as Gaussian Distribution due to its use for theory of accidental errors by Karl Friedrick Gauss (1777–1855). Normal distribution curve is bell shaped and symmetrical with two parameters, the mean μ and the standard deviations σ. For normal distribution, the probability function of a random continuous variable is given by

$$f(x) = \frac{1}{\sqrt{2\pi\sigma}} \exp^{(x-\mu)^2/2\sigma^2}$$

$$= \frac{1}{\sqrt{2\pi}\sigma} e^{-\frac{(x-\mu)^2}{2\sigma^2}} ; -\infty < n < \infty$$

Where π and e are the constant as $\pi = \frac{22}{7}$ and

$$e = 2.71828 \text{ (base of Natural Logarithms)}$$

$$\therefore \quad \sqrt{2\pi} = 2.5066$$

If we use a normally distributed random variable Z, with a mean 0 and standard deviation 1, then the probability density function of Z is given by,

$$f(Z) = \frac{1}{\sqrt{2\pi}} e^{-z^2/2} ; -\infty < Z < \infty$$

This random variable Z is called a standardised normal variate as $Z = \frac{x - E(x)}{\sigma_x} = \frac{x - \mu}{\sigma}$

Normal Distribution is the most useful and most commonly used distribution. It is a symmetrical distribution in a specific case with its mean as zero and variance and standard variation as unity.

These expression can be seen to be following the relationship as given below :

$$E(Z) = E\left(\frac{x-\mu}{\sigma}\right) = \frac{1}{\sigma} E(x - \mu)$$

$$= \frac{1}{\sigma} [E(x) - E(\mu)]$$

$$= \frac{1}{\sigma} (\mu - \mu) = 0$$

$$\text{Var}(Z) = \text{Var}\left[\frac{x-\mu}{\sigma}\right] = \frac{1}{\sigma^2} \text{Var}(x - \mu)$$

$$= \frac{1}{\sigma^2} = \text{Var}(x)$$

$$= \frac{1}{\sigma^2} .\sigma^2 = 1$$

Thus the standard Normal variate Z has mean 0 and SD 1. Hence the probability density function of Z is transformed into (as given above)

$$f(Z) = \frac{1}{\sqrt{2\pi}} e^{-z^2/2}, -\infty < z < \infty.$$

The normal distribution of X is written symbolically as $N(\mu, 0)$. The probability density curve is symmetric about the mean μ and the standard deviation σ indicates the spread of the normal curve in terms of the probabilities of various intervals around μ. There are standard tables available for the normal density curve indicating probability as

$\mu \pm \sigma$ containing 68.3% probabilities

$\mu \pm 2\sigma$ containing 95.5% probabilities

and $\mu + 3\sigma$ containing 99.7% probabilities

Also Mean = Mode = Median = μ.

The probabilities are indicated as the area under the normal curve, which is given is Fig. 11.7.

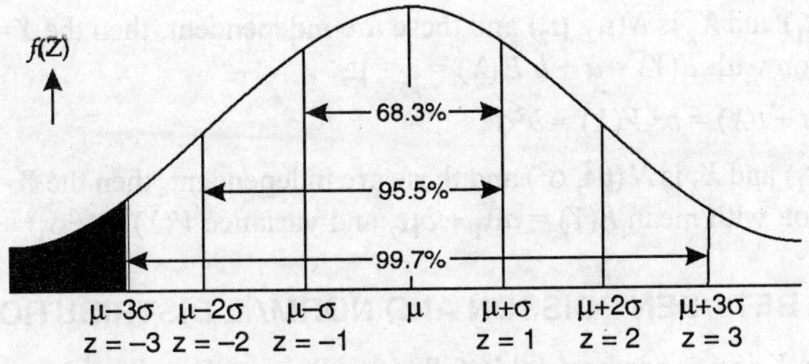

Fig. 11.7. Normal Distribution

The tables for Normal probabilities are given at the end of this book.

Relation Between Binomial and Normal Distribution

Normal Distribution is a specific limiting case of the Binomial Distribution under the following given conditions.

(*i*) The number of trials n is very large; $n \to \infty$.

(*ii*) p and q are not very small.

Then for binomial variate x, with parameters n and p.

$$E(x) = np$$

$$\text{Var}(x) = npq,$$

Hence

$$Z = \frac{X - E(X)}{\sigma_n}$$

$$= \frac{X - np}{\sqrt{npq}} \text{ tends to } Z\text{-variate,}$$

As earlier brought out, Normal Distribution is a specific case of Binomial distribution, whose mean value changes from *np* to zero and the variance from *npq* to unity. Due to its symmetry of curve about the mean value, it is very useful for probability calculations.

11.7. USE OF NORMAL TABLES

Since the tables indicate the area under the normal curve to the left of the point Z, we can denote it as

$$\text{Area }(Z) = P(Z \leq z)$$

Since the curve is symmetrical about the mean μ,

Then, $\text{Area }(-a) = \text{Area }(a)$

Hence $(Z = -a) = (Z = a)$

and, $P(a \leq z \leq b) = \text{Area }(b) - \text{Area }(a)$

$$P(-a \leq z \leq a) = \text{Area }(a) - \text{Area }(-a) = 2\text{ Area }(a)$$

This is clearly indicated in figure 11.8. given below.

In the table for negative values of z, the area has been marked to the left of z as indicated.

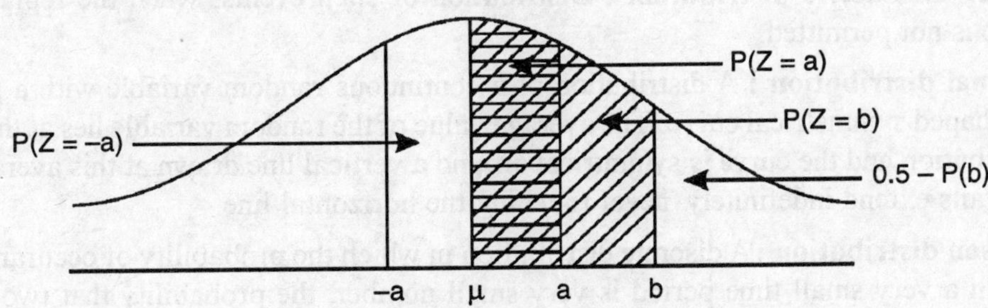

Fig 11.8. Probability from tables

If X_1 is $N(\mu_1, \sigma_1)$ and X_2 is $N(\mu_2, \mu_2)$ and these are independent, then the $Y = aX_1 + bX_2$ will have a normal distribution with $E(Y) = a + b\ E(X) = a + \mu$,

and $V(Y) = V(a + bX) = b^2\ V(X) = b^2\sigma^2$.

If X_1 is $N(\mu_1, \sigma_1)$ and X_2 is $N(\mu^2, \sigma^2)$ and these are independent, then the $Y = aX_1 + bX_2$ will have a normal distribution with mean $E(Y) = a\mu_1 + b\mu_2$ and variance $V(Y) = a^2\sigma_1{}^2 + b^2\sigma^2{}_2$.

11.8. RELATION BETWEEN POISSON AND NORMAL DISTRIBUTION

Let us consider X as a random variable following Poisson Distribution with parameter λ, then

$$E(X) = \lambda$$

$$\text{and } \operatorname{var}(X) = \sigma^2 = \lambda$$

Thus standard Poisson variate will become $\dfrac{X - E(X)}{\sigma_x}$

or $\dfrac{x-\lambda}{\sqrt{\lambda}}$ when $\lambda \to \infty$.

It can thus be seen that this variate tends to be a standard Normal variate if $\lambda \to \infty$. Therefore Normal Distribution can be regarded as a limitting case of Poisson Distribution with parameter λ, tending to lead to unifimity $(\lambda \to \infty)$.

CHAPTER SUMMARY

Terms used

- **Bernoulli's Process :** A process in which each trial has only two possible outcomes, the probability of the outcome of any trial remains the same over a period of time and that the trials are statistically independent.
- **Binomial Distribution :** A discrete Distribution specifying the results of an experiment known as Bernoull's process.
- **Continuous Probability Distribution :** A probability Distribution in which a variable is allowed to take any value within a specified range.
- **Continuous Random variable :** A random variable allowed to take any value within a specified range.
- **Expected value :** A weighted average of the outcomes of an experiment.
- **Expected value of a Random variable :** The sum of the products of each value of the random variable with that value's probability of happening.
- **Hyper Geometric distribution :** Distribution of such events, when the replacement of the value is not permitted.
- **Normal distribution :** A distribution of a continuous random variable with a single peaked, bellshaped symmetrical curve. The average value of the random variable lies at the centre of the distribution and the curve is symmtrical around a vertical line drawn at this average value. The two tails extend indefinitely, never touching the horizontal line.
- **Poisson distribution :** A discrete distribution in which the probability of occurance of an event within a very small time period is very small number, the probability that two or more such events will occur within the same time interval is effectively zero and the probability of occurance of the event within one time period is independent of where that time period is.

- **Probability distribution :** A list of outcomes of an experiment with the probabilities expected to be associated with these outcomes.
- **Random variable :** A variable that takes different values as a result of the outcome of a random experiment.
- **Standard normal probability distribution :** A normal probability distribution, with mean $\mu = 0$ and standard deviation $\sigma = 1$.

Relationships used

- Probability of r successes = $p(r) = {}^n c_r\, p^r\, q^{x-r}$ in Bernoullis trials

where p = probability of success

and q = probability of failure

$(q = 1 - p)$

- Mean of binomial distribution $\mu = np$
- Standard deviation of a binomial distribution $\sigma = \sqrt{npq}$
- Probability of discrete random variable occurring in a Poisson Distribution

$$p(x) = \frac{\lambda^x e^{-\lambda}}{x!} \text{ or } \frac{e^{-m} . m^x}{x!}$$

- Poisson Distribution as approximated to normal distribution. Then

$$p(x) = \frac{(np)^x e^{-xp}}{x!}$$

- Normal variate

$$z = \frac{x - \mu}{\sigma}$$

Where x = value of the random variable.

μ = mean of the distribution

σ = standard deviation of the distribution

z = number of standard deviations from x to the mean of this distribution.

- Probability function of a random continuous variable $f(z) = \frac{1}{\sqrt{2\pi\sigma}} . e^{\frac{(x-\mu)^2}{2\sigma^2}}$

SOLVED PROBLEMS

Problem 11.1

For a given $n = 5$, and $p = 0.4$, obtain the binomial distribution probability for all values of X.

Solution.

For $n = 5$, and $p = 0.4$

$$P(X = x) = {}^nC_x\, p^x\, q^{n-x}$$

$$= {}^5C_x\, p^x\, q^{5-x}$$

We can now tabulate the values of probabilities for all values of x, where $x = 0, 1, 2, 3, 4$ and 5.

TABLE 11.1.
Probability Distribution in 5 Bernoulli's Trials for N = 5 and P = 0.4

x	${}^5C_x$	$p^x q^{5-x}$	${}^5C_x p^x q^{5-x}$
0	1	$(0.6)^5 = 0.07776$	0.07776
1	5	$(0.4)(0.6)^4 = 0.05184$	0.25920
2	10	$(0.4)^2(0.6)^3 = 0.03456$	0.34560
3	10	$(0.4)^3(0.6)^2 = 0.02304$	0.23040
4	5	$(0.4)^4(0.6) = 0.01536$	0.07680
5	1	$(0.4)^5 = 0.01024$	0.010240

This distribution of probability can be drawn on a histogram as follows (see Fig. 11.9 below).

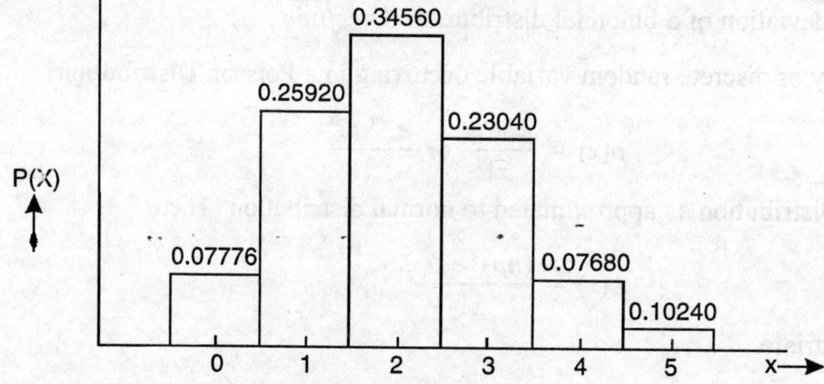

Fig.11.9. Histogram Binomial Distribution (n = 5, p = 0.4)

Problem 11.2

Define Binomial Distribution. What is the probability of guessing correctly at least six of the ten answers in a True, False objective test? [*ICWA (Final), Dec.*, 1979]

Solution :

Given here $p = 1/2$ and hence $q = 1/2$

(Since it is either True or False, $p = 1/2$ for each)

By Binomial probability distribution, the probability of x correct answers, at least 6 out of 10 questions, will be.

$$p(x) = p(6) + p(7) + p(8) + p(9) + p(10)$$

$$= \left(\frac{1}{2}\right)^{10} [{}^{10}C_6 + {}^{10}C_7 + {}^{10}C_8 + {}^{10}C_9 + {}^{10}C_{10}]$$

$$= \frac{1}{1024} [{}^{10}C_4 + {}^{10}C_3 + {}^{10}C_2 + {}^{10}C_1 + 1]$$

$$= \frac{1}{1024} \left[\frac{10 \times 9 \times 8 \times 7}{4 \times 3 \times 2} + \frac{10 \times 9 \times 8}{3 \times 2} + \frac{10 \times 9}{2} + 10 + 1\right]$$

$$= \frac{386}{1024}$$

Problem 11.3

If the chance that the vessel arrives safely at a port is 9/10, find the chance that out of 5 vessels expected, at least 4 will arrive safely. [*Delhi University*, *B.Com.* (*Hons.*) *1980*]

Solution :

Given here p = probability of vessel arriving safely

$$= \frac{9}{10}$$

$$\therefore \quad q = 1 - \frac{9}{10} = \frac{1}{10}$$

By binomial probability law, the probability of x vessels arriving safely is given by,

$$p(x) = {}^nC_x\ p^x\ q^{n-x} = {}^5C_x\, p^x\ q^{5-x}$$

Probability for at least 4 vessels arriving safely will be,

$$p(4) + p(5) = \left(\frac{1}{10}\right)^2 [{}^5C_4\ .\ 9^4 + {}^5C_5\ .\ 9^5] = \frac{91854}{100000}$$

$$= 0.91854$$

Problem 11.4

With the usual notations, find p for a binomial random variable X, if $n = 6$, and $9P(X = 4) = p(X = 2)$ [*Delhi University M.Com. 1975*]

Solution :

For a random variable X with p as probability of success *i.e.* parameters (6, p) the probability function can be written as.

$$p(x) = p(X = x) = {}^nC_x p^x\ q^{n-x} \text{ for } x = 0, 1, 2, 3, 4, 5, 6$$

Here we have been given

$$9P(X = 4) = P(X = 2)$$

or $$9 \times {}^6C_4 p^4\, q^2 = 6_{C_2}\, p^2\, q^4$$

or $$9p^2 = q^2$$

Substituting the value $q = (1 - p)$,

$$9(p^2) = (1 - p)^2$$

$$= 1 + p^2 - 2\text{p}$$

or $$8p^2 + 4p - 2p - 1 = 0$$

or $$(4p - 1) = 0 \text{ or } 2p = -1$$

$$\therefore \quad p = \frac{1}{4} \text{ or } p = -\frac{1}{2}$$

Since p cannot be negative, $p = -\frac{1}{2}$ is rejected

Hence $$p = \frac{1}{4}$$

Problem 11.5

Comment on the following : For a binomial distribution, mean = 7 and variance = 11.

[*ICWA (Final), Dec.*, 1977]

Solution :

For a binomial distribution,

$$\text{Mean } = np = 7$$

and $$\text{variance } = npq = 11$$

For these relations, we get $q = 1.6$ (impossible). Since probability cannot be greater than 1, the statement is wrong.

Problem 11.6

8 coins are tossed at a time, 256 times. Find the expected frequencies of success (getting a head) and tabulate the results obtained. [*C.A.(Inter), May 1975*]

Solution :

Given here $N = 256$ and $n = 8$ and $p = q = \frac{1}{2}$ (getting head or tail)

∴ Frequency of x successes will be $= N\,p(x)$

$$= 256 \times {}^8C_x \left(\frac{1}{2}\right)^8 = {}^8C_x$$

The expected Binomial frequencies can now be tabulated as under

Number of heads (x) :	0	1	2	3	4	5	6	7	8
Expected Frequency :	1	8	28	56	70	56	28	8	1

Problem 11.7

Fit a Poisson Distribution to the following data and calculate the theoretical frequencies.

x :	0	1	2	3	4
f:	123	59	14	3	1

[*Gujarat University, B.Com., 1975*]

Solution :

Given data :

x :	0	1	2	3	4
f:	123	59	14	3	1
fx :	0	59	28	9	4

From the above table, $\Sigma f = 200$, $\Sigma fx = 100$

Now to calculate mean,

$$\bar{x} = \frac{\Sigma fx}{\Sigma f}$$

$$= \frac{100}{200} = 0.5$$

If the data follow the Poisson Distribution

$$x = \lambda$$

∴ Theoretical frequencies will be given by

$$f(x) = Np(x)$$

$$= N\frac{e^{-\lambda}\lambda^x}{x!}$$

The table can now be worked out for theoretical frequencies.

If $x = 0,$ $\quad f(x) = N\frac{e^{-\lambda}\lambda}{0!} = 200 \times e^{-0.5} = 121$

$x = 1,$ $\quad f(x) = \frac{200e^{-0.5}\lambda^1}{1!} = 61$

$x = 2,$ $\quad f(x) = \frac{200e^{-0.5}\lambda^2}{2!} = 15.3$

$x = 3,$ $\quad f(x) = \frac{200e^{-0.5}\lambda^3}{3!} = 2.5$

for $x = 4,$ $\quad f(x) = \frac{200e^{-0.5}\lambda^4}{4!} = 0.3$

∴ $\quad \Sigma f \simeq 200$

Problem 11.8

From a population of candles of 25 pieces, we find that 5 have been found to be broken. If we examine the candles, with a sample size of 5, what is the probability of having (*a*) less than 2 broken, (*b*) no broken candle.

Solution :

Given : as per normal notation,

$$N = 25, D = 5, n = 5$$

(*a*)Probability of less than 2 broken will be

$$P(x < 2) = P(x = 0) + P(x = 1)$$

$$P(x = 0) = \frac{\binom{5}{0}\binom{25-5}{5-0}}{\binom{25}{5}} = \frac{\binom{20}{5}}{\binom{25}{5}} = 0.292$$

$$P(x = 1) = \frac{\binom{5}{1}\binom{25-5}{5-1}}{\binom{25}{5}} = \frac{5\binom{20}{4}}{\binom{25}{5}} = 0.456$$

$$P(x < 2) = 0.292 + 0.456$$
$$= 0.748$$

(*b*) for no broken candles case,

$$P(x = 0) = \frac{\binom{5}{0}\binom{25}{5}}{\binom{25}{5}} = \frac{\binom{20}{5}}{\binom{25}{5}}$$

=0.292 (as worked out under (a)).

Problem 11.9

While conducting population survey of a city, the enumerator noticed that 40% of the male population were illiterate. If the trend continues, workout the probability that out of a random sample of 2,00,000 males population, the number of illiterates will be (*i*) less than 75,000; (*ii*) more than 82,000.

Solution :

(*i*) In this problem, if we denote x as the random variable indicating number of males in the city of sample size 2,00,000, we have

$$n = 2{,}00{,}000$$
$$p = 40\% \text{ or } 0.4$$

Hence $q = 1 - 0.4 = 0.6$ (non-illiterate)

$$np = 2{,}00{,}000 \times 0.4 = 80{,}000$$
$$npq = 80{,}000 \times 0.6 = 48{,}000$$
$$\sqrt{npq} = \sqrt{48{,}000} = 219$$

Hence the distribution of the population of the population is (80,000, 219).

(*ii*) When $x \le 75{,}000$, then,

$$Z_1 = \frac{75{,}000 - 80{,}000}{\sqrt{48{,}000}} = -\frac{5000}{219}$$
$$= -22.8$$

When $x > 82{,}000,\ Z_2 = \frac{82{,}000 - 80{,}000}{219}$

$$= \frac{2{,}000}{219}$$
$$= 9.13$$

Both the values of Z are very high. Hence the probability of illiterates in the range of 75,000 and 82,000 are infinitely small.

Problem 11.10

If a manufacturer produces the eatables in a box of average weight of 1kg with a variance of 0.01 kg. While packing these boxes, he uses the packaging for 100 boxes in one lot for easy transportation. If we consider the weights of each box to be statistically independent, find the probability that the packaging box has a weight of less than 102 kg or more than 101 kg.

Solution :

Since each box has its weight statistically independent, the packaging unit will follow a normal distribution as each of these would represent the sum of weights as 100 kg.

$$\text{Mean weight of packaged box} = \mu n = 100 \times 1 = 100 \text{ kgs}$$

and $$\text{variance} = \sigma_n^2 = 0.01 \times 100 = 1 \text{ kg}$$

$\therefore$ $$\text{standard deviation} = \sigma\sqrt{n} = \sigma\sqrt{n} = 1 \text{ kg}$$

(i) For probability that a package will have a weight less than 102 kg *i.e.* $P(x < 102 \text{ kg})$

$$\therefore\ z = \left[\frac{x-\mu_n}{\sigma\sqrt{n}}\right] = \frac{102-100}{1} = 2$$

$$\begin{aligned}\therefore\ P(\bar{x} < 102) &= P(z < 2)\\ &= 0.5 + P(0 < z < 2)\\ &= 0.5 + 0.4772\\ &= 0.9772\end{aligned}$$

This probability is same as the probability of one box having less than 1.02 kg weight.

(*ii*) For probability of a packaged unit will have weight more than 101 kg, we calculated the value of z, viz.

$$z = \frac{101-100}{1} = 1$$

$$\begin{aligned}\therefore\ P(\bar{x} > 101) &= P(z > 1)\\ &= 0.5 + P(0 < z < 1)\\ &= 0.5 + 0.3413\\ &= 0.1587\end{aligned}$$

Thus the probability of the packaged unit having weight more than 101 kg will be 0.1587.

Problem 11.11

The mean weight of life of certain cutting tool is 41.5 hours, with a standard deviation of 2.5 hours. What is the probability that a simple random sample of size 50 drawn from this population will have a mean between 40.5 hours and 42 hours.

[*M.B.A., Delhi University, 1982; M.B.A., BIT, Ranchi University, 1985*]

Solution :

According to the usual normal notations, we are given

$$\mu = 41.5 \text{ hours}$$

and $$\sigma = 2.5 \text{ hours}$$

$$\sigma_{\bar{x}} = \frac{\sigma}{\sqrt{n}} = \frac{2.5}{\sqrt{50}}$$

$= 0.3536$

The required probability is given by

$P(40.5 \leq x \leq 42)$

$$z_1 = \frac{40.5 - 41.5}{0.3536}$$

$$= -2.828$$

$$\text{and } z_2 = \frac{42 - 41.5}{0.3536}$$

Hence the required probability $= P(40.5 \leq x \leq 42)$

$= P(-2.828 \leq z_1 \leq 0) + P(0 \leq z_2 \leq 1.414)$

$= 0.4977 + 0.4207 = 0.9184$

This can be illustrated by the normal distribution diagram as follows

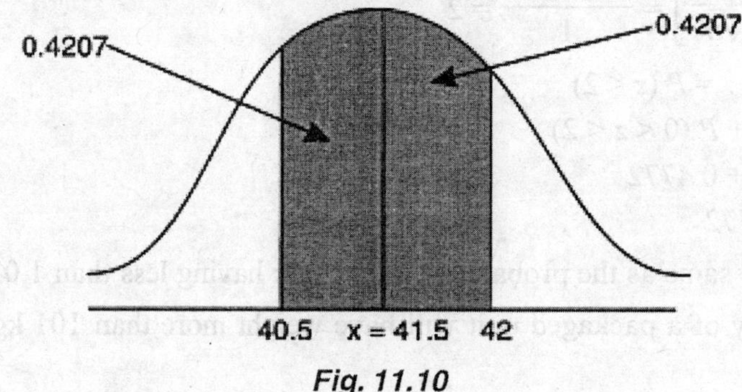

Fig. 11.10

Problem 11.12

A Sales Tax Officer has reported that the average sales of the 500 businesses that he has to deal with during a year amount to Rs. 36,000 with a standard deviation of Rs. 10.000. Assuming that the sales in these businesses are normally distributed, find

(*i*) The number of businesses the sales of which are over Rs. 40,000

(ii) The percentage of businesses, the sales of which are likely to range between Rs. 30,000 and Rs. 40,000.

(*iii*) The probability that the sales of a business selected at random will be over Rs. 30,000.

Proportions of Area under the Normal curve—

Z:	0.25	0.40	0.50	0.60
Area:	0.0987	0.1554	0.1915	0.2257

[*Himachal University, M.Com., July 1982*]

Solution :

If we denote X as the random variable following the normal distribution with $X \sim N(\mu, \sigma)$, given are

$\mu = 36,000$

and $\sigma = 10,000$

(*i*) The probability of the sales being over 40,000 will be given by

$P\ (x > 40{,}000)$

When $X = 40{,}000$, $\mu = 36{,}000$, $= \sigma = 10{,}000$

$$Z = \frac{x-\mu}{\sigma} = \frac{40{,}000 - 36{,}000}{10{,}000} = 0.4$$

$\therefore\ P\ (x > 40{,}000) = 0.5 - P\ (0 \le Z \le 0.4)$

$= 0.5 - 0.1554 = 0.3446$

Total number of business houses = 500

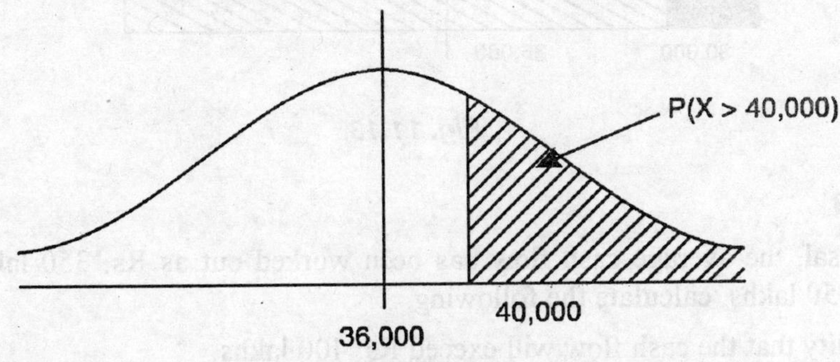

Fig. 11.11

$\therefore$ Number of business over 40,000 sales = 500 × 0.3446

= 172

(*ii*) When sales vary between 30,000 and 40,000, we have to calculate its probability $P\ (30{,}000 < x < 40{,}000)$.

When $X = 30{,}000$, $Z = \dfrac{30{,}000 - 36{,}000}{10{,}000} = -0.6$

and when $X = 40{,}000$, $Z = 0.4$ [calculated above in (ii)]

Hence $P\ (30{,}000 < x < 40{,}000) = P\ (-0.6 < z < 0.4)$

$= P\ (0.6 < z < 0) + P\ (0 < z < 0.4)$

$= P\ (0 < z < 0.6) + P\ (0 << 0.4)$

$= 0.2257 + 0.1554$

$= 0.3811$

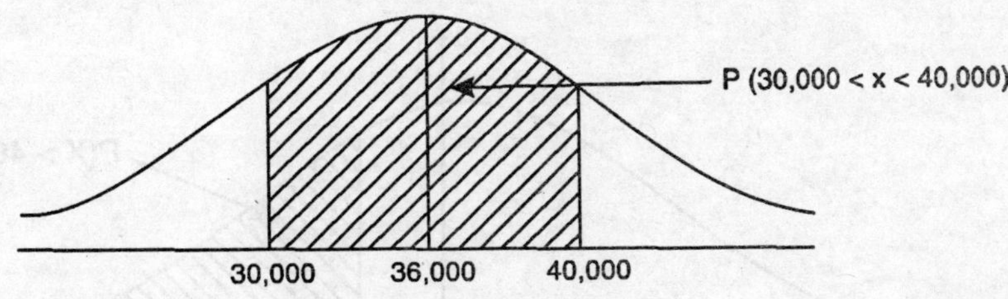

Fig. 11.12

Hence percentage of businesses with sales in the range 30,000 to 40,000 will be 38% (approx.).

(*iii*) For probability of sales being over Rs. 30,000, we take

$$P(x > 30{,}000) = P(Z > -0.6) = P(-0.6 < z < 0) + 0.5$$
$$= P(0 < Z < 0.6) + 0.5$$
$$= 0.2257 + 0.5 = 0.7257.$$

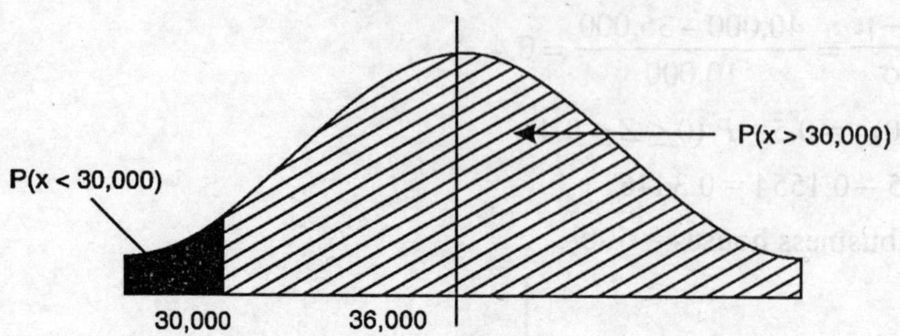

Fig. 11.13.

Problem 11.13

For a proposal, the average cash flow has been worked out as Rs. 350 lakhs with standard deviation of Rs. 50 lakhs, calculate the following.

(*i*) Probability that the cash flow will exceed Rs. 400 lakhs.

(*ii*) Probability that cash flow will be between 300 and 400 lakhs.

Solution :

Given data indicates the values $\mu = 350$ lakhs

and $\sigma = 50$ lakhs.

If cash flow is assumed to be following normal distribution, then we can with the relationship as :

$$Z = \frac{x - \mu}{\sigma}$$
$$= \frac{x - 350}{50}$$

(*i*) Now, to consider the value of Z for cash flow x exceeding 400, we get

$$Z = \frac{400 - 350}{50} = 1$$

For this value Z = 1, probability from the table = 0.3413

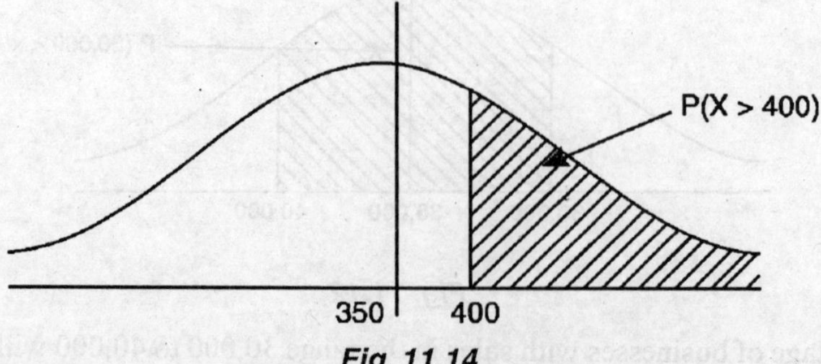

Fig. 11.14

The figure of the normal curve indicates that the area for (x > 400) will be as given by $P(x > 400)$ *i.e.*, to the right of $Z = 1$, (refer Fig. 12.12 above).

This area will be $= 0.5 - P\,(Z = 1)$

$= 0.5 - 0.3413$

$= 0.1587$

Hence probability of cash flow exceeding Rs. 400 lakhs will be 0.1587.

(*ii*) For cash flow between 300 lakhs and 40 lakhs, we have to calculate both the probabilities and then find the intermediate area (probability) as clear from the Fig. 12.13.

In this case
$$Z_1 = \frac{X_1 - \mu}{\sigma} = \frac{300 - 350}{50} = -1$$

$$Z_2 = \frac{X_2 - \mu}{\sigma} = \frac{400 - 350}{50} = 1$$

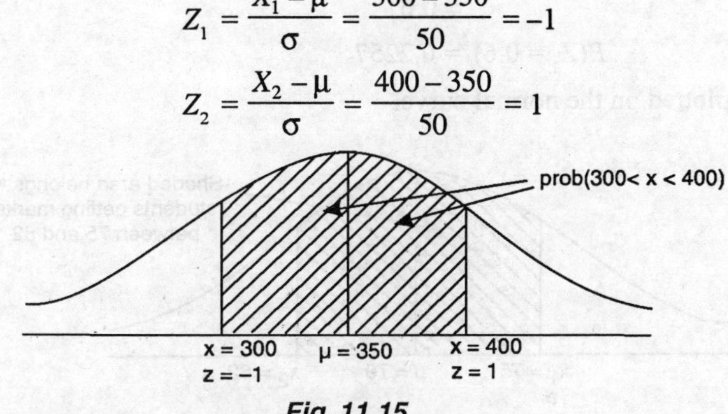

Fig. 11.15

Hence the probabilities will be worked out separately for $Z = -1$, and $Z = 1$.

Prob $(X = 300) = P\,(Z = -1) = 0.3413$

Prob $(X = 400) = P\,(Z = 1) = 0.3413$

Prob $(300 < X < 400) =$ Prob $(X \geq 300)$ + Prob $(X \leq 400)$

$= 0.3413 + 0.3413$

$= 0.6826$

Problem 11.14

The average test marks in a particular class is 79. The standard deviations is 5. If the marks are distributed normally, how many students, in a class of 200 did not receive marks between 75 and 82 ? Given,

$P_r\,(0 \leq Z \leq 0.7) = 0.2580$

$P_r\,(0 \leq Z \leq 0.8) = 0.288$

$P_r\,(0 \leq Z \leq 0.6) = 0.2257$

When Z is a Standard Normal Variate. [*Punjab University, M.A. (Eco.), 1982*]

Solution :

Given in the problems,

Z = Standard Normal Variable

$\mu = 79$

$\sigma = 5$

Hence to obtain the probability (percentage) of students not receiving marks between 75 and 82, we calculate the values of Z_1 for 75 and Z_2 for 82 and then with the help of the Normal distribution table and the Normal curve, we calculate the percentage of students desired,

$$Z_1 = \frac{X_1 - \mu}{\sigma} = \frac{75 - 79}{5}$$

$$= -0.8$$

Hence $P(Z_1 = -0.8) = 0.288$

$$Z_2 = \frac{X_2 - \mu}{\sigma} = \frac{82 - 79}{5}$$

$$= 0.6$$

Hence $P(Z_2 = 0.6) = 0.2257$

This can be plotted on the normal curve.

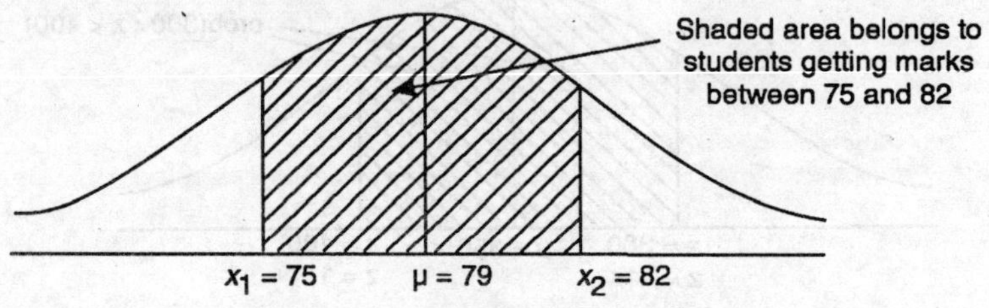

Fig. 11.16

Since shaded area indicates probability of students getting marks between 75 and 82, the area not shaded will indicate probability of students not getting marks between 75 and 82.

Hence Students not getting marks between 75 and 82

$$= 1 - P(75 < x < 82)$$

$$= 1 - P(-0.8 < Z < 0.6)$$

$$= 1 - [P(0 < Z < 0.8) + P(0 < Z < 0.6)]$$

$$= 1 - [0.288 + 0.2257]$$

$$= 0.4863$$

This number of students not getting marks between 75 and 82 = Np

$$= 200 \times 0.4863 \simeq 97.$$

PRACTICE PROBLEMS

11.15 What do you understand by 'Binomial Distribution'? What are its main features? *[Himachal University, M.Com., 1982]*

11.16 Obtain the variance of a binomial distribution and show that the variance cannot exceed. $n/4$. *[ICWA (Final), June 1983]*

11.17 "A Binomial distribution need not necessarily be a symmetrical distribution". Do you agree with the statement? Give reasons. *[Delhi University, B.A. (Eco Hons.), 1985]*

11.18 Obtain an expression for the mean of the binomial distribution in terms of the number of trials and the probability of success. *[Delhi University, B.A. (Eco. Hons.), 1983]*

11.19 State the distinctive features of the Poisson Distribution. When does this tend to a normal distribution? *[Delhi University, B.Com. (Hons.) 1983]*

11.20 What do you understand by Binomial distribution? What are its features? Three perfect coins are tossed together, what is the probability of getting at least one head?
[Delhi University, B.Com., (Hons.), 1982]

11.21 Briefly answer the following:
(*i*) Salient features of Poisson Distribution
(*ii*) Importance of sample size. *[Osmania University, M.B.A., April 1999]*
(*iii*) Binomial Distribution *[Osmania University, M.B.A., July 2000]*

11.22 The following statement cannot be true, why? "The mean of a binomial distribution is 4 and its standard deviation is 3".
[ICWA (Final), Dec. 1979]

11.23 If the mean of the binomial distribution is 3 and variance is 3/2, find the probability of at least 4 successes. *[Bombay University, B.Com., Nov., 1980]*

11.24 The mean of binomial distribution is 4 and its standard deviation is $\sqrt{3}$. What are the values of *n*, *p* and *q* with usual notation? *[Delhi University, B.A. (Eco. Hons.), 1982]*

11.25 A discrete random variable *X* has mean equal to 6 and variance equal to 2. If it is assumed that the underlying distribution of *X* is binomial, what is the probability that $5 \leq X \leq 7$?
[Delhi University, B.A. (Eco. Hons.). 1987]

11.26 Five coins are tossed 3200 times. Find the frequencies of the distribution of heads and tails and tabulate the results. Calculate the mean number of successes and standard deviation.
[C.A. (Inter), May 1977]

11.27 Five fair coins were tossed 100 times. From the following outcomes calculate the expected frequencies.

No. of heads up :	0	1	2	3	4	5
Observed frequencies :	2	10	24	38	18	8

[Delhi University, B.Com. (Hons.), 1984]

11.28 Comment on the following:
For a Poisson Distribution. Mean = 8 and variance = 7. *[ICWA (Final), Dec., 1977]*

11.29 If 5% of the electric bulbs manufactured by a company are defective, use Poisson Distribution to find the probability that in a sample of 100 bulbs ; (i) None is defective ; (ii) 5 bulbs will be defective. (Given : $e^{-5} = 0.007$)
[ICWA (Final), Dec., 1979]

11.30 Between the hours 2 PM and 4 PM, the average number of phone calls per minute coming through the switch board of a company is 2.35. Find the probability that during one particular minute, there will be at least 2 phone calls (Given : $e^{-2.35} = 0.095374$)
[ICWA (Final), June 1984}

11.31 A manufacturer of blades knows that 5% of his products are defective. If he sells blades in boxes of 100 and guarantees that not more than 10 blades will be defective, what is the probability (approximately) that a box will fail to meet the guaranteed quality?
[ICWA (Final), June 1978]

11.32 If a random variable *X* follows the Poisson Distribution such that $P(X = 1) = P(X = 2)$, find
(a) The mean of the Distribution
(b) P(*X*=0) *[Delhi University, M.Com., 1974 ; ICWA (Final), Dec., 1974]*

11.33 It is known from past experience that in a certain plant, there are on the average 4 industrial accidents per month. Find the probability that in a given year, there will less than 4 accidents. Assume Poisson Distribution ($e^{-4} = 0.0183$) *[Bombay University, B.Com., Oct., 1981]*

11.34 Assuming that one in 100 births is a case of twins, calculate the probability of 3 or more sets of twins on a day when 40 births occur. Compare the results obtained by using

(i) The Binomial distribution, and (ii) Poisson approximation.

11.35 Write down the probability function of a Poisson Distribution whose mean is 2. What is its variance? Give 4 examples of Poisson Variable *[Bombay University, B.Com., April 1981}*

11.36 The standard deviation of a Poisson Distribution is 2. Find the probability that $X = 3$.

(Given $e^{-4} = 0.0183$) *[ICWA (Final), Dec., 1980]*

11.37 Define a Poisson Distribution.

If X be a Poisson Variate with parameter 1. find $P(3 < X < 5)$. *[ICWA (Final). June 1983]*

11.38 If 2% of electric bulbs manufactured by a certain company are defective, find the probability that in a sample of 200 bulbs, (i) less than 2 bulbs ; (ii) more than 3 bulbs are defective. (Given : $e^{-4} = 0.0183$) *[ICWA (Final). June 1980]*

11.39 A manufacturer of pins knows that on an average 5% of his products are defective. He sells pins in the boxes of 100 and guarantees that not more than 4 pins will be defective. What is the probability that a box will meet the guaranteed quality? (Given : $e^{-5} = 0.0067$)

[Meerut University, M.Com., 1975 : ICWA (Final), Dec., 1982]

11.40 Find the probability of at least 5 defective bolts found in a box of 200 bolts if it is known that 2 per cent of such bolts are expected to be defective (assume Poisson Distribution and $e^{-4} = 0.0183$) *[ICWA (Final). Dec.. 1985]*

11.41 Using Poisson approximation to the Binomial Distribution, solve the following problem :

If the probability that an individual suffers a bad reaction from a particular injection is 0.001, determine the probability that out of 2000 individuals (*i*) exactly three : (*ii*) more than two individuals will suffer a bad reaction (Given : $e^2 = 7.4$)

11.42 In a certain factory, turning out razor blades, there is a small chance $\frac{1}{500}$ for any blade to be defective. The blades are supplied in packets of 10. Use Poisson distribution to calculate the-approximate number of packets containing no defective, one defective and two detective blades respectively in a consignment of 10,000 packets.

[Allahabad University. M.A. (Eco.). 1977]

11.43 The distribution of typing mistakes committed by a typist is given below. Assuming a Poisson Model, find the expected frequencies.

Mistakes per page :	0	1	2	3	4	5
No. of Pages :	142	156	69	27	5	1

[Delhi University, M.B.A.. April 1952 : M.Com.. I976]

11.44 Five hundred television sets are inspected as they come off the production line and the number of detects per set is recorded below.

Estimate the average number of defects per set and the expected frequencies of 0, 1. 2. 3 and 4 defects, assuming Poisson Distribution.

No. of defects (X) :	0	1	2	3	4
No. of Sets :	368	72	52	7	1

[Delhi University. M.B.A., Nov.. 1980]

11.45 Suppose that waist measurement W of 800 girls are normally distributed with mean 66 cm. and standard deviation 5 cm. Find the number N of girls with waists

(i) Between 65 and 70 cm.

(ii) Greater than or equal to 72 cm. [*Delhi University. B.A. (Eco Hons.), 1985*]

11.46 Assume the mean height of soldiers to be 68.22 inches with a variance of 10.8 inches. How many soldiers in a regiment of 1,000 would you expect to be (i) over six feet tall and (ii) below 5.5 feet. Assume heights to be normally distributed.

[*Punjab University. M.A. (Eco.), 1980*]

11.47 Compare the salient features of Binomial and Normal Distributions. Give appropriate examples from real life situations in business and management for suitability of their applications. [*Osmania University. M.B.A., March/April 1999*]

11.48 Balances in Saving's Accounts in a bank have an average of Rs. 1,200 and SD of Rs. 400. Assuming that the accounts are normally distributed, estimate the number of accounts having balances between Rs. 1,000 and Rs. 1,500 (Given the areas under normal curve between o and $Z = \dfrac{x - \overline{x}}{\sigma}$ are 0.1915 and 0.2734 for Z = 0.5 and Z = 0.75 respectively).

[*Osmama University, M.B.A., March/April, 1999*]

11.49 A workshop produces 5,000 units per day. The average weight of the units is 140 kgs. with standard deviation of 8 kgs. The variable weight follows a normal distribution. Find the number of units weighing less than 145 kgs. [*Osmania University, M.B.A.. April 1998*]

11.50 What are the characteristics of Binomial and Poisson Probability Distributions?

[*Osmania University, M.B.A., Sept., 1998*]

11.51 Assuming that the distribution is normal and if a student is selected at random, what is the probability that his *1Q* will be (i) above 165, (ii) between 140 and 155 and (iii) less than 145.

[*Osmania University, M.B.A., Sept., 1998*]

11.52 Describe the characteristics of Normal Distribution. Explain how t-distribution is different from Normal Distribution. [*Osmania University, M.B.A., Sept., 1998*]

11.53 Fit a binomial distribution

X	0	1	2	3	4	5	6	7
Y	7	6	19	35	30	23	7	1

[*Osmania University, M.B.A., July 2000*]

11.54 The arithmetic mean of purchases per day by a customer in a large store is Rs. 25 with a standard deviation of Rs. 10. If on a particular day, 100 customers purchased for Rs. 37.80 or more, estimate the total number of customers who purchased from the store that day. Given that the normal area between $t = 0$ to $t = 1.28$ is 0.4000, where t is a standard normal variate.

[*Bombay University, B.Com., April 1983*]

11.55 (i) A normal distribution has 77.0 as mean. Find its Standard Deviation if 20 per cent of the area under the curve lies to the right of 90.0.

(ii) A random variable has a normal distribution with 10 as standard deviation. Find its mean if the probability that the random variable takes on a value less than 80.5 is 0.3264.

[*Delhi University, B.A. (Eco. Hons.) 1980*]

11.56 A set of examination marks is approximately normally distributed with a mean of 75 and standard deviation of 5. If the top 5% of students get A grade and the bottom 25% get grade F, what mark is the lowest A and what mark is the highest F?

[*Bombay University, B.Com., Oct., 1976*]

11.57 The weekly wages of 1,000 workmen are normally distributed around a mean of Rs. 70 and with a standard deviation of Rs. 5. Estimate the number of workers whose weekly wages will be, (i) Between Rs. 70 and 72 (ii) Between Rs. 69 and 72 (iii) More than Rs. 75 (iv) Less than Rs. 63 (v) More than Rs. 80. Also estimate the lowest weekly wages of the 100 highest paid workers. *[Delhi University, B.A. (Eco. Hons.), 1977]*

11.58 In a normal distribution, 31% of the items are under 45 and 8% are over 64. Find the mean and standard deviation of the distribution.

[Delhi University. B.A. (Eco. Hons.), 1978; Punjab University. M.A. (Eco.), Oct.. 1950]

❖❖❖

CHAPTER 12

SAMPLING THEORY AND SAMPLING DISTRIBUTIONS

12.1 INTRODUCTION

To obtain information or its analysis about a given population is not very easy nor it may be feasible when the population is large. We then find a method which can speak about the characteristics of a total population based on the analysis of certain representative members of that population. This gives rise to 'Theory of Sampling'. The sample is a small part or a representative section selected from a population. The process of such a selection is called 'Sampling'. Therefore, we can say that Sampling Theory is the study of relationship existing between the population and the samples obtained from the population.

Population being aggregate of very large number of members, or a very vast information, may be not even easy to collect, is not feasible to be studied for complete enumeration. It may be very cumbersome, time and effort consuming or may be very costly process, not serving the purpose due to delay in collection of information, even after incurring heavy cost. Information not collected in time may be worthless, if decision-making gets affected due to its non-availability. Even after collection of large information, it may take very long time for its structuring and analysis. Hence 'Sampling Theory' is a very handy tool for day-to-day decision-making environment.

A large population may not be easy to study for various inferences. It may be very costly and time-consuming to study total population. Hence sampling method is adopted to draw timely conclusions from limited study.

It, therefore, becomes essential to draw inferences for the total population based on the analysis carried out on some of its members, information about whom can be collected easily and their selection itself can be structured in a definite way, so that this sample analysis can be relied upon and deployed for the total population. Thus, samples help us in determining the reliability of the estimates. This can be achieved by taking different samples from the same parent population and then by comparing analysis results obtained from different samples.

12.2. SAMPLING THEORY

When we decide to undertake the survey of the entire population, such as population of the country, the data is collected from each and every member of the family from across the country. We can also collect information about the salary structure of an organisation by obtaining data of all the employees of that organisation. This is Population Data Collection Process. We can then use this data to analyse and obtain various characteristics of the population, such as number of males and females in the country, the range of their ages, the number of persons in an organisation paid in a certain range of salary or their correlation of salary with their educational background or salary relationship with reference to their age groups etc. The average, mean or range parameters can be worked out from such vast data collected.

In this process, a very coherent and correct information is made available about the total population. Thus, we can enumerate the advantage of the population survey as follows.

1. The relevant respective data for every unit or sub-group of the population can he compiled.
2. The analysis based on this data is very accurate and reliable.
3. The population data so obtained can be used for future study for comparing certain changed future characteristics from this accurate data.

It is important to make the sample, a true representative of the population. Hence authentic, reliable and sufficient data should be obtained as sample to use it for decision purposes.

Though there are distinct advantages of the population or Census Method, the time. effort, and cost required to carry out such a survey is very large and may not be worthwhile every now and then. This method should be used sparingly for a large population or else can be utilised for smaller population groups.

Sampling, therefore, should be resorted to. because it can be done faster and the analysis results can be used as fairly reliable. Sampling involves the study of a small group of the target population sector or unit. Sampling Method is most desired under the following situations :

1. The population is very large (almost infinite) and survey is either practically impossible to conduct or is undesirable from the cost effectiveness angle of such a survey.
2. When information or analysis is required at short notice for a quick decision-making process, it is better to obtain quick results by Sample Survey.
3. When we are trying to carry out 'destructive testing of a group of units' it is preferred to rely on sample testing rather than study of all units.
4. When cost of conducting total population survey is prohibitive, we better rely on sample survey.
5. The reliability of the Census or Population survey also cannot be guaranteed, due to vastness of the data and its defective structuring. In such cases, sample reliability can be used with same degree of usefulness.

Since the data volume in a sample survey is limited, it is possible to pay attention to all relevant elements and more authentic results can be expected and that too at limited cost and effort level. To augment reliability further, a number of sample studies can be compared, spending again limited time and money.

The sampling theory is widely used as a very useful tool in day to day working such as tasting tea and coffee, home food for salt or sugar, testing of bulbs in the shop before buying, tasting grapes from the seller's baskets or testing students (on 3 hrs. test basis) for their quality of performance.

12.3. PARAMETERS AND CHARACTERISTICS

When we conduct surveys, we aim at obtaining some useful information about the attributes of certain entities. The attributes selected for the study or survey are called characteristics and the units possessing these characteristics are termed as elementary units. We are normally concerned with certain measurable characteristics of these units or with the number of proportions of such units marked by the presence or absence of some qualitative characteristic. The study of the qualification of workers or employees in an organisation will be treated as qualitative characteristic, whereas the salary structure study of a group of people is known as quantitative characteristic. Thus, the sampling unit is an elementary unit such as the organisation for which salary structure is being studied. The sample is then defined as an aggregate of the sampling units actually chosen in obtaining a representative subset from which inferences about the population can be drawn.

The statistical constants of the population like mean (μ), the variance (σ^2), the skewness (β_1), kurtosis (β_2), moments (μ_r), correlations coefficients (r) etc., are knwon as parameters and we can compute similar statistical constant for the sample drawn from the given population.

Considering a finite population of N units with $y_1, y_2, \ldots y_N$ observations of the populations units, we can set select a sample of size n units from this population. If $x_1, x_2, x_3 \ldots\ldots x_n$ are the observations of the sample units, then

$$\mu = \frac{1}{N}(y_1 + y_2 + \ldots y_N) = \frac{1}{N}\sum_{i=1}^{N} y_i$$

$$\sigma^2 = \frac{1}{N}[(y_1 - \mu)^2 + (y_2 - \mu)^2 + \ldots] = \frac{1}{N}\sum_{i=1}^{N}(y_i - \mu)^2$$

From sample observations,

$$\bar{x} = \frac{1}{n}\sum_{x=1}^{n} x_i$$

and $$s^2 = \frac{1}{n}\Sigma(x_i - \bar{x})^2$$

We can say that sample statistics are functions of sample observations and we write $t = t(x_1, x_2, \ldots x_n)$

If a statistic $t = t(x_1, x_2, x_3, \ldots x_n)$ is said to be an unbiased estimate of the population parameter θ, if $E(t) = \theta$. Then

$$E\text{ (Statistics)} = \text{Parameter.}$$

12.4. BASIC SAMPLING CONCEPTS

In order to establish the relationship of sample parameters to population parameters, important relationship must be derived. For this purpose, some sampling concepts must be understood.

Sampling Population Relationship : If we draw a sample of size n from a given finite population of size N, then the total number of possible samples is

$$^nC_n = \frac{N!}{n!(N-n)!} = k$$

Now we can compue $\bar{x}$, s^2 etc. for $t = t(x_1, x_2 \ldots x_n)$

$$\text{and Var}(t) = \frac{1}{k}\sum_{i=1}^{k}(t_i - \bar{t})^2$$

Standard Error : The standard deviation of the sampling distribution of a statistic is known as its Standard Error. Thus

$$\text{SE}(t) = \sqrt{\text{Var}(t)}$$

$$= \sqrt{\left[\frac{1}{k}\sum_{i=1}^{k}(t_i - t)^2\right]}$$

This concept is extremely useful in testing the statistical hypothesis by $Z = \frac{t - E(t)}{SE(t)} \sim N(0,1)$.

If n is large. If (Z) < 1.96 then $|t-E(t)|<1.96\ SE(t)$. Then the difference $t-E(t)$ is not significant at 5% level of significance. The difference is just the fluctuation of the sampling and data do not provide any evidence against null hypothesis, which may, therefore, be accepted. However if $|Z| > 1.96$ or $|t - E(t)| > 1.96\ SE(t)$, then the difference is regarded as significant and null hypothesis is rejected at 5% level of significance.

The reciprocal of *SE* of a statistic gives a measure of the precision or the reliability of the estimate of the parameter.

Speed, economy, adaptability and scientific approach used in collection and analysis of samples must be adopted for an effective study.

Law of Statistical Regularity : In the words of L.R. Conner, "The law of statistical regularity lays down that a group of objects chosen at random from a higher group tends to possess the characteristic of that larger group". Thus if the sample size increases, the sample is more likely to reveal the true characteristics of the population. It also establishes that the sample should be selected at random from the population.

Principle of Inertia of Large Numbers : From the above rule *i.e.* "Law of Statistical Regularity" emerges the Principle of Inertia of large Numbers, which can be stated as "other things being equal, as the sample size increases, the results tend to be more reliable and accurate".

Principle of Persistence of Small Numbers : If some of the items in a population possess distinct characteristics from the remaining items, then the tendency would be revealed in the sample values also. It means that the tendency of the charcteristic will be persisted in sample observations also in large samples.

Principle of Validity : A sample design is said to be valid if it obtains valid results and estimates about the population parameters.

Principle of Optimisation : It stressess the necessity of obtaining optimum results in terms of efficiency and the cost of the sampling design with the sources available.

12.5. SAMPLING UTILITY

As described earlier in the chapter, there are distinct advantages of sampling method over the population enumeration method. These can he summarised as speed, economy, adaptability and scientific approach. It also ensures a great administrative convenience by avoiding requirement of large resources. Though there are chances of large sampling errors, a carefully designed and scientifically executed sample survey can provide very reliable results. It also offers a scope of better results due to execution of large number of samples and comparison of their results to establish reliability. However, the sample method can be made more useful by

1. Drawing the sample in a scientific manner.
2. Using appropriate sampling design.
3. Ensuring an adequate (fairly large) sample size.

In the words of **Frederick F. Stephen** – "Samples are like medicines. They can be harmful when they are taken carelessly or without the knowledge of their effects. Every good sample should have a proper label with instructions about its use".

12.6. STEPS IN SAMPLE SURVEY (SAMPLING PROCEDURE)

For the reasons stated above, the planning and execution of the sample survey should be immaculate with following structured steps:

1. *Objectives and Scope of the Survey* : We should have specific, clear and concrete objective and scope of the survey to be conducted, so that collection of irrelevant data can be avoided and wastages of resources minimised.

2. *Defining the Population to be Sampled* : With aim being clear, the target population for the relevant statistic should be well defined, so that unnecessary population units can be left out from the survey.

3. *The Frame and Sampling Units* : We should select the population capable to division into small sample units, so that enumeration is made easy and simultaneous. A sampling unit should be specific, unambiguous, stable and appropriate for the requirement. The list and other acceptable material to serve as a guide for information collection is called a Frame. An updated good frame will help in collection of quality data and hence is a great help in achieving good results out of sample survey.

4. *Data Collection :* Since aim is known, frame is updated, the data to be collected gets specified. This will help in getting all the relevant information within the cost and time estimate of the survey.

5. *Schedule :* Data can be collected by deciding a structured schedule or a set of questionnaire, which can be obtained in writing from the respondents. Care should be taken to frame questionnaire very clearly to the point, without ambiguity, in view of the knowledge, understanding and the general level of respondents.

6. *Collection of Information :* The relevant information either in the form of structured data set or questionnaire can be collected by direct personal interviews or by mail questionnaire method. Choice between the two depends on time, cost, urgency or ambiguity of the survey. Non-respondents can disturb the balance of information and to be guarded against.

7. *Selection of Sampling Design :* The sampling plan should be decided before execution of the sample survey. Simple Random Sampling, Stratified Random Sampling, Systematic Sampling etc., be decided in advance based on the situation due to the object of the survey, nature of population, cost involved or the time availability for the sample survey.

Survey for collection of sample observations must be unbiased, timely and random. A systematic approach has been suggested for carrying out a sample survey.

8. *Field Work :* For reliable results, the data collected should be reliable and hence sampling errors should be eliminated. For this purpose, the ground work should be properly designed, organised and monitored by proper selection and training of the field workers. It is very desirable to provide adequate and frequent supervisory monitoring on the field work.

9. *Pilot Survey :* Initially, we should resort to conduct of pre-test or a guide survey for establishing usefulness of the survey. Hence a pilot survey on miniature scale should be conducted first to establish authenticity of the method, level of questionnaire and training and knowledge of the survey field staff. It will improve the quality of the outcome of the result.

10. *Summary and Analysis :* Once the planning and execution of survey has been completed, we have to organise analysis of the collected data. The analysis involves the following:

(*a*) Scrutiny and editing of the data
(*b*) Proper tabulation of data as per parameters
(*c*) Statistical analysis
(*d*) Reports, summary, conclusions and recommendations.

For this purpose, we need designing and utilising appropriate statistical techniques, so as to minimise errors at every stage. The report should be concise, logical and clear cut so that its usefulness can be established.

12.7. ERRORS IN SAMPLE SURVEY

Depending on the type of population and sampling technique, the level of competence of the surveyor, the data availability and its structuring, there may be inaccuracies arising in any statistical investigation and these may arise during any phase such as collection of information, processing, analysis or interpretation of the data. These inaccuracies are called 'Errors' and may be of two types *(a)* Sampling errors, and *(b)* Non-sampling errors.

Sampling Errors : While studying the characteristics of a population, we take only a small portion of data in the form of the sample and the quality of this data in the sample survey may not truely represent the basic structure of the population, the results thereby differing from the population results. This is called Sampling Error. Even if the sample is highly random and representative of the population, some error is natural. This error is attributed to the fluctuations of the sample data. Thus sampling error will be present in any sampling survey results and not in the census method.

These errors may be creeping in either due to faulty selection of the sample or an intentional random data substitution in the sample. Even analysis method selection may lead to different results with built-in sampling errors. The errors reduce when we increase the sample size as now the data tend towards the population. It is demonstrated in Fig. 12.1.

The errors in sampling do creep in, if due care is not exercised for proper method. Natural or unnatural errors must be reduced to the minimum, so that collected data becomes useful.

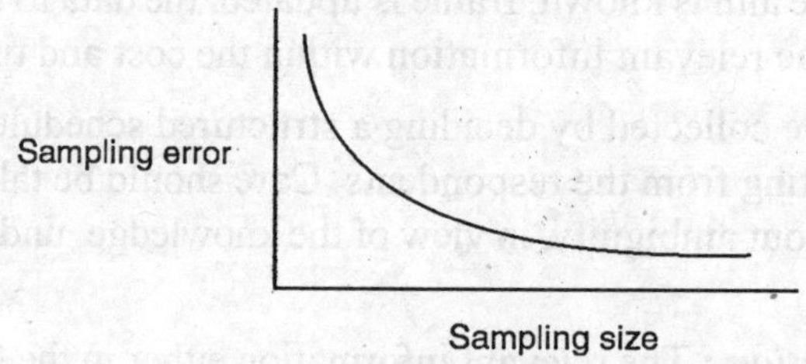

Fig. 12.1. Sampling Error

Non-Sampling Error : These errors arise as a consequence of certain factors, which can be controlled by human intervention, such as proper selection, planning and careful execution of the sample survey. These types of errors are due to certain assignable causes, which can be traced and controlled. They, obviously, will be present in sample survey as well as in census survey, infact more in census survey due to large data. The possible causes can be faulty planning (aim of survey not very clear), imperfect questionnaire, selection of interviewers being unplanned, or non-coherent answers by the sample subjects or respondents, either due to self interest or inadequate knowledge or even due to ego or prestige problems. Then there may be a similar bias introduced by the investigator himself either due to his self-interest or poor training, non-response or improper coverage (to suit his convenience). Then we may find publication errors arising out of poor printing or proof reading problems etc.

These may be biased or unbiased errors in the sample survey (or even in census survey) as described in the reasons above. Bias may be introduced either due to intention of the investigator or by his faulty instrumentation. The bias can be due to poor or faulty response of the respondents or in the processing techniques. The unbiased errors can creep in during investigation based on small samples, but will he minimised when sample size is increased. The unbiased errors do not grow with the increase in the number of observations, but have a tendency to reduce during final analysis. These unbiased errors are thus inversely proportional to the number of observations

12.8. TYPES OF SAMPLING (RANDOM AND NON-RANDOM METHODS)

For achieving desired correct results from a sample survey, the execution of sample design is of utmost importance and hence proper selection of the sampling method becomes imperative. The Sampling Techniques can be broadly classified into following categories: viz. probability and non-probability sampling.

Probability Sampling

The probability sampling is the scientific technique which draws sample from the population based on the application of probability methods, wherein each unit of the population has some predefined probability of inclusion of an event into the drawn sample. The samples will therefore be selected in the following manner:

1. Each unit is drawn on the basis of randomness
2. Each unit has the same chance of being selected
3. Probability of selection of a unit is proportional to the sample size.

Thus the samples are drawn based on random procedure and not on any judgemental method. It attaches a objective measure of precision to the results achieved by such samples.

The probability sampling techniques are described below:

(*a*) ***Simple Random Sampling*** : Sampling design in this case is based on some probability laws. In a random sampling, the elements of the sample are drawn at random and the choice of each element follows some probability law. In this case, each element will, then, be chosen based on the same law. Thus every possible element has the same chance of drawing as the others.

If we have a population of N elements, we can select n sets of elements out of such a population (where n is fairly large), and the possible sets of n elements will be ${}^{N}C_{n}$, following the same probability of selection for every such set of elements. The basic aim is to achieve randomness in drawing the elements of a sample to ensure all possible samples to have the same chance of being selected. We can use either lottery system or the Random Number table system, both either with replacement of the drawn number or without replacement.

In lottery system, all the elements .of the population are allotted identical identification, say same type and size of paper with element numbers written on each. After proper folding the papers in the same manner and thorough mixing of these papers, we can choose any paper at random without any bias either through the container system or taking out each paper blindly. Thus. if we have 200 students and we have to nominate only 10 to the students welfare council, we can use 200 paper written numbers or names and by selecting any first 10 out the container having all the 200 papers, we can constitute the council in a very fair manner. When N is very large, this method becomes cumbersome and difficult to manage.

Random sampling must be adopted, so as to make individual observations to be as close to the population as possible. Various types of random samplings can be used depending on the quality of population.

In that case, we use the method of Random Number Tables (tables attached at the end of the book). From the Random Number Tables, the numbers can be selected from the list, where numbers have already been arranged in Random order. We can select Numbers either through the rows or through columns. Various Random Number Tables in use are :

(*i*) Tippetts (1927) — 10,400 sets of four-digit Random Numbers

(*ii*) Fisher and Yates (1938) — Table of Random Numbers with 1,500 sets of ten-digit Random Numbers.

(*iii*) Kendall and Babinton Smiths (1939) — Consisting of 1,00,000 digits grouped into 25,000 sets of 4 digit Random numbers.

(*iv*) Rand Corporation (1955) — Table of Random Number of 2,00,000 sets of five-digit Random Numbers.

(*v*) Table of Random Numbers — (ISI Series, Calcutta) by C.R. Rao, Mitra and Mathai.

(*b*) ***Stratified Sampling :*** In Simple Random Sampling, we draw very homogeneous samples and the individual elements are drawn from the whole universe or population. In some situations, we can classify the population into some specified distinct class of element sets such as Men and Women classes (out of total population). When we draw a random sample out of each of these classified groups, we call such samples as Stratified Samples. Thus, if we divide the seats on the welfare council, say 5 for men and 5 for women, then we have to draw Random samples from two different groups (Men and women). Hence there is no possibility of drawing more than 5 elements from Men's group, so also from the women's group. Thus we ensure there is no probability of more than 5 men or 5 women on the council. There is distinct advantage of such a sample based on specific situation. Thus, stratification is an effective sampling tool to create homogeneous class samples rather than the total. We ensure homogeneity among the class elements only. It is a more representative sample for the study in this case.

(c) ***Cluster Sampling :*** Cluster sampling consists of forming suitable groups or clusters and then collecting relevant information of all the elements in a sample of clusters as per the appropriate sampling design. The advantage of the cluster sampling is the cost involved; because the data collected from the nearby elements is easier, cheaper, faster and more convenient than by observing units scattered over a wide region.

Cluster sampling, Area sampling, multi-stage and multi-phase sampling can be effective methods under certain specific circumstances and must be judiciously adopted.

For explaining the concept, we can divide a town into various blocks and then using Random Sampling Technique for each block for collection of information about their income groups. For a similarly placed people in a block, this type of sampling will be more useful.

(d) ***Multi-stage Sampling :*** As described above, we can see that use of cluster sampling technique under certain circumstances is cheaper, but it is less efficient than the individual sampling. Thus as a combination, we can use Multistage Sampling, in which we can select cluster samples and then studying only a sample of units in each cluster. This is called Two-stage Sampling. Similar concept can be extended to bring in Multistage sampling, where sampling units at each stage are the cluster of units of the next stage and the observations are selected in stages, sampling at each stage being done from each of the sampling units. This method is more efficient than the direct sampling and less efficient than the cluster sampling. The diagrammatic representation is given in Fig. 12.2 below:

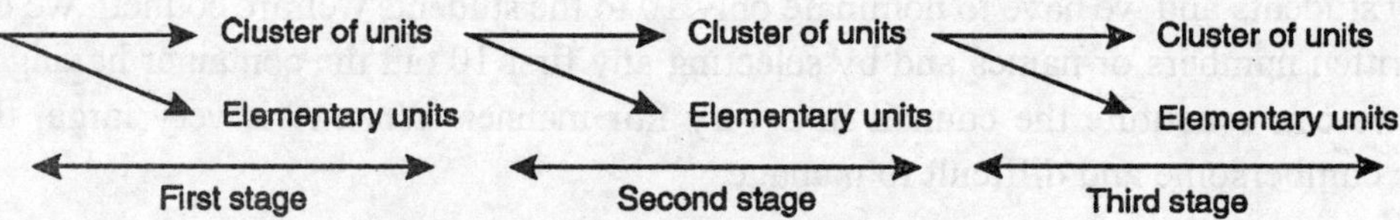

Fig. 12.2. *Multistage sampling units*

It may be noted that the sampling process at each stage may be either random or stratified. Multistage sampling is more flexible as compared to other methods of sampling.

(e) ***Area Sampling :*** When we use cluster sampling concept for the elementary units of population is a particular geographical area, it is called 'Area Sampling'. In this case, we can study the community behaviour index of a particular community living in a particular locality or part of the country, such as Tamil population in Tamil Nadu, Jats in Haryana, Brahmins in U.P. or Gujjars in Rajasthan or J & K etc. But selection of sample in each area should be random for enumerated elements. Thus the enumeration of elements is necessary only in the limited number of selected areas.

(f) ***Multi-phase Sampling :*** This type of sampling is adopted when sampling units of the same type are the objects of different phases of observation. In this case, all the units of a phase in a sample are studied with respect to the same characteristics. If we want to collect information about capital employed by all members of 300 companies, we can add information about source of financing about another 100 companies, this type of sampling will be treated as Two-phase sampling. The concept can be extended to Multiphase Sampling. In this case information collected during one phase is then used in the second or subsequent phases.

(g) ***Systematic Sampling :*** A very simple form of sampling for its design and execution is used when the members of a population are arranged in an order. The order corresponding to consecutive members. In this type of sampling, the first sample unit is selected at random and the remaining units are automatically selected on a definite sequence at equal spacing from one another. For example, if we want to select 50 candidates out of 1,000 names arranged systematically, we can select any 20 at random (*i.e.*, $K = \frac{N}{n} = \frac{1,000}{50}$) and the corresponding candidates for a call centre job will be selected based on a selected number basis (say 4), we then have candidates with serial numbers, 4. 24, 44, 64 etc. and can have 50 such candidates for the first set of interviews.

Non-Probability Sampling

As against the Probability Sampling, the Non-Probability Sampling is a procedure of selection of a sample without the use of randomization. It is based on convenience or judgement and hence is likely to be biased. The sampling variation in such a case is very uncertain and cannot be estimated.

In this category, we have following types of sampling :

(*a*) ***Convenience sampling*** : In this case, we can adopt sampling on the convenience basis such as filling up means from the telephone directory. ·

(*b*) ***Quota sampling*** : In this case, we can adopt sampling based on a quota of information out a specific population such as condidates under one category of job fixed for the interview.

We can first sample out the total population based on categories as per quota list and then selection of these lists without any fixed procedure. For admission to an institute, there may be quota fixed such as general category 50%, SC/ST category 40% ad NR1 quota 10%. It then depends on the interviewer, what name he selects for each quota list, if there is no rules formed.

(c) ***Judgemental sampling*** : We can also follow a judgemental method of non-probability sampling, when the sample elements are either picked up on previous experience basis or with no set rule procedure, but based on hunch. It is also called as opinion sampling. This is used only when there is better evidence or selection procedure in vogue.

In some case, some short-cut methods of sampling such as convenience sampling, quota sampling or judgemental sampling are adopted based on the manager's convenience.

12.9. LAW OF LARGE NUMBERS AND THE CENTRAL LIMIT THEOREM

Law of Large Numbers :

The law of large numbers has been defined and stated in different forms. The latest formulation stated by Prof Khintchine has been known under his name as Khintchine Theory of large Numbers.

It is defined in terms of the random variable S or $\overline{X}$ where $\overline{X} = \left(\frac{S}{n}\right)$.

It states that if we have $x_1, x_2, \ldots\ldots x_n$ as n independent and identically distributed random variables with mean and variance of the distribution of $\overline{X}$ or $\left(\frac{S}{n}\right)$ being

$$E(\overline{X}) = \mu$$

and $$V(\overline{X}) = \frac{\sigma^2}{n}$$

then, as the sample size n becomes very large, the probability that a particular value $\overline{x}$ of the random variable $\overline{X}$ will be very close to the population mean μ, is very close to 1. In other words, it means that the larger the size of the sample drawn from a population, the smaller the variations in the values of $\overline{X}$ and consequently, the closer a particular sample mean $\overline{x}$ to the population mean μ.

The Central Limit Theorem

From the above, it can be seen that the distribution of the sum S of n independent and identically distributed random variables has mean $E(S) = \mu n$ and variance $\sigma^2{}_s = \sigma^2{}_n$.

It can thus be seen that as the number of random variables in S increases, the centre of the distribution of S will shift farther away to the right along the horizontal axis, with variance becoming larger and larger. This, thus, becomes the basis of the central limit theorem. The main unique characteristic of this theorem is that its application requires no precondition on the distribution of the random variable ($x_1, x_2, x_3, \ldots x_n$).

The Central limit Theorem describes the distribution pattern of random variables selected from any population, tending to be described by the Normal Probability Distribution.

The central limit theorem was first introduced by DeMoivre during the early eighteen century. The theorem states that the distribution of sum S of n independent, identically distributed random variables ($x_1, x_2, x_3, \ldots x_n$) selected from any population, will tend to be described by the normal probability distribution with mean μn and variance $\sigma^2 n$ as n increases larger and larger. In other words, the sampling distribution of sample means approaches to a normal distribution, irrespective of the distribution of the population from which the sample is taken. Approximation to the normal distribution becomes closer with increase in the sample size.

Thus we can write

$$S = X_1 + X_2 + X_3 + \ldots\ldots X_n$$

When $X_1, X_2, \ldots$ Xn are n independent random variables. (Whatever be the distribution) and it is a normal variate.

Similarly mean μ and variance σ^2 for X are

$$\mu = \mu_1 + \mu_2 + \ldots\ldots + \mu_n = n\mu_i$$

where μ_i and $\sigma^2{}_i$ are the mean and variance of X_i consequently, the standardized variate

$$Z = \frac{S - \mu_n}{\sigma / \sqrt{n}}$$

is normally distributed with mean 0 and variance 1. This theorem furnishes a practical method of computing approximate probability values associated with sums of arbitrarily distributed independent random variable of S. For defining the required probabilites, the cumulative probability distribution function of S can be written as

$$P(S<s) = P\left[\left(\frac{S-\mu_n}{\sigma/\sqrt{n}}\right) < \left(\frac{s-\mu_n}{\sigma/\sqrt{n}}\right)\right]$$

where s is a particular value of S, based on a sample size n. thus

$$Z = \frac{S - \mu_n}{\sigma / \sqrt{n}}$$

and $$z = \frac{s - \mu_n}{\sigma / \sqrt{n}}$$

we can write $P(S < s) = P(Z < s)$

The cumulative probability distribution function of $\bar{X}\left(=\frac{S}{n}\right)$ can be defined as

$$P(\bar{X} < \bar{x}) = \left[\left(\frac{\bar{X}-\mu}{\sigma\sqrt{n}}\right) < \left(\frac{\bar{x}-\mu}{\sigma/\sqrt{n}}\right)\right]$$

or $$P(X < x) = P(Z > z)$$

where $$Z = \frac{\bar{X}-\mu}{\sigma/\sqrt{n}}$$

and $$z = \frac{x-\mu}{\sigma/\sqrt{n}}$$

In this case, z is a particular value of Z variate, corresponding to the sample mean value $\bar{x}$ based on the sample of size n. From these two relationships, the probabilities obtained will be the same and the accuracy of the probabilities so obtained will depend on the actual distribution of the random variables x_i, and sample size n. If the population being sampled is normal, the two cumulative probability functions will give exact probabilities irrespective of how small n may be, but if the population is not normal, then for accurate or fairly accurate probabilties, n needs to be large enough to generate a distribution of S or $\bar{X}$, which is quite near normal. Hence the large size of the sample *i.e.* larger value of n will decide how accurate the described probabilties are obtained. The larger is the value of n, the more accurate will be the probabilities. When the general distribution of the population is not known, we normally adopt a general rule of $\bar{x} \geq 30$ to obtain fairly accurate results.

As it is important to adopt randomness during observation collection, it is also important that sufficient number of observations are collected to draw useful inference. Hence determination of sample size becomes important.

12.10. SAMPLE SIZE DETERMINATION

Selection of sample is very important if the information so collected is of any use to the decision making. The sample has to be a true representative of the target population. Similarly the sample size is equally important so as to speak the useful information for its proper analysis. Thus depending on the method of sampling adopted, following precautions are to be observed while selecting sample size.

Simple random sampling : In this case, the sample should be so drawn that each and every unit in the target population has an equal and independent chance of being include in the sample.

Stratified random sampling : In this case, a properly arranged proportional allocation of sample elements or sample fraction should be organised for optimum allocation from each stratified area.

Systematic sampling : In this case, we select the first sample unit at random and the remaining with as per automatic equal spacing. The size of the sample could emerge out of steps or spacings adopted *i.e.*

$$n = \frac{N}{K}$$

where n = sample size

N = population size

K = sample interval or spacing

12.11. SAMPLING DISTRIBUTIONS

We have discussed the laws of large numbers and also the central limit theorem. Now we use these concepts to develop sampling distribution. Sampling distribution means that we take a sample from the given population and study the way various parameters of this sample are distributed. The mean and the standard deviation of the sampling distribution are written as $\bar{x}$ and s respectively.

Sampling distributions constitute the basis of statistical inference and play an important role in decision-making process. If we take number of samples of equal size from the population, the probability distribution of all the possible values of given statistics from all the possible samples of equal size is termed as sampling distribution.

If we take $x_1, x_2, \ldots\ldots x_n$ random independent variables of sample size n from a population having the same mean μ, then

$$\bar{x} = \frac{x_1 + x_2 + x_3 + \ldots\ldots + x_n}{n}$$

Through the use of Central limit Theorem, we can draw the sampling distribution of the random variables. With sufficient volume of observations form a probability distribution for an infinite population.

and

$$\bar{X} = E(x) = E\left[\frac{x_1 + x_2 + x_3 + \ldots + x_n}{n}\right]$$

$$= \frac{1}{n}[E(x_1) + E(x_2) + \ldots E(x_n)]$$

$$= \frac{1}{n}[\mu + \mu + \ldots \mu]$$

$$= \frac{1}{n}.n\mu = \mu$$

Thus it can be seen that mean of a sampling distribution of sample means is the same as the mean of the population. From the diagram given below, we can observe that sampling distributions closely approximate a normal distribution.

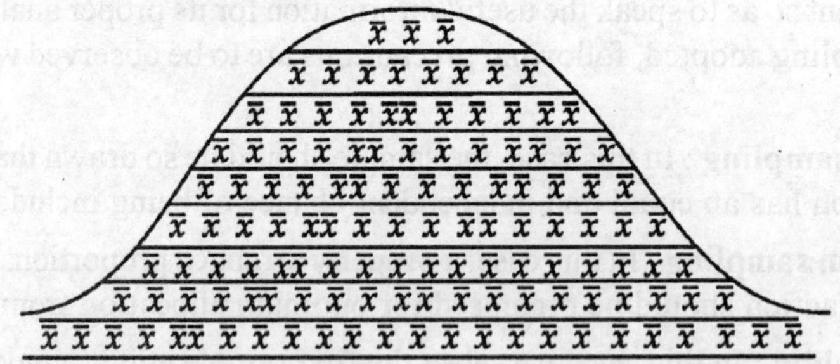

Fig. 12.3. ***Sampling Distribution of Sample means***

The mean of the sampling distribution is given the same symbol as that for the mean of the population *i.e.* μ, but the standard deviation of the sampling distribution is called standard error of mean and is denoted as $\sigma_{\bar{x}}$ indicating that it is for sampling distribution of means. The relation of standard error of sampling that to the standard deviation of the population is given below.

$$\sigma_{\bar{x}} = \frac{\sigma}{\sqrt{n}}$$

This relationship is valid only when the population is infinite or the samples are chosen from a finite population without replacement. Thus,

$$\sigma_{\bar{x}}^2 = \text{Var}(\bar{x}) = \text{Var}\left[\frac{x_1 + x_2 + \ldots\ldots + x_n}{n}\right]$$

$$= \frac{1}{n^2}\,[\text{Var}(x_1) + \text{Var}(x_2) + \ldots\ldots\ \text{Var}(x_n)]$$

$$= \frac{1}{n^2}\,n\sigma^2$$

$$\therefore \qquad \sigma_{\bar{x}} = \frac{\sigma}{\sqrt{n}}$$

Before embarking on the sampling distribution, it is necessary to make assumptions about the population parameter. We can use any value for a parameter, depending on the quality of population but there is no theoretical limit to the number of sampling distribution for the same sample size that can be drawn from the given population. The distribution of one static may differ from that of another statistic. Thus the shape of the distribution of $\bar{x}$ will differ from that of s, even though both the parameters are computed from the same sample.

Through the use of sampling distribution concept, we can develop various values of important parameters such as mean and variances.

It is interesting to notice that the mean of the sampling distribution is the same as the mean of the population. Also the observed standard deviation of a sample is close to the standard deviation of the population values. However the standard deviation of the sample is calculated as follows.

$$\boxed{s = \sqrt{\frac{\Sigma(x-\bar{x})^2}{n-1}}}$$

and not $\quad s = \sqrt{\dfrac{\Sigma(x-\bar{x})^2}{n}}$

Due to smaller denominator, it gives slightly larger value of standard deviation. Thus the estimated standard deviation of the population is slightly larger than the observed standard deviation of the sample.

Sampling Distribution of the Mean

If the population distribution is normal, the sampling distribution of the mean ($\bar{x}$) is also normal for all sample sizes.

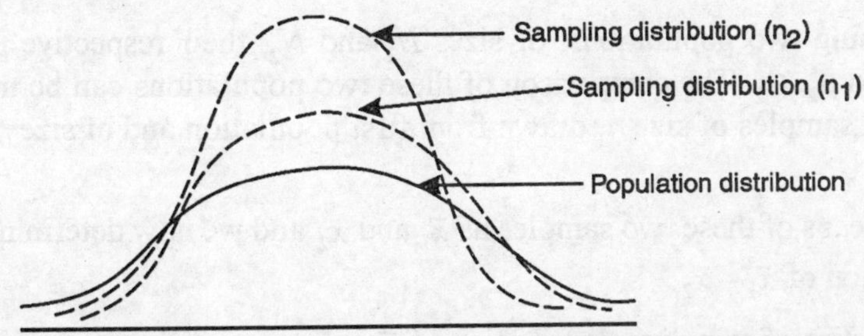

Fig. 12.4. Relationship of population and sampling distribution of mean

Important properties of the sampling distribution of mean are

(*a*) Its mean is equal to the population mean, $\mu_{\bar{x}} = \mu$

(*b*) Standard deviation $\sigma_{\bar{x}} = \dfrac{\sigma}{\sqrt{n}}$

(*c*) It is normally distributed

In practice, population mean may not be easily available and hence standard deviation of the sample is used in its place.

$$\therefore \qquad \sigma_{\bar{x}} = \frac{s}{\sqrt{n}}$$

where s = standard deviation of the sample

Normally, for all survey and research, the samples are chosen without replacement, which is contrary to the assumption of central limit theorem. Hence a correction factor has to he applied to cater tor the proportion of observations not included in the sample.

If N is the population finite size, then we apply a correction factor as $1-\frac{n}{N}=\frac{N-n}{N}$, When N is large, this would be approximated to $\frac{N-n}{N-1}$. Therefore, in case of sampling from a finite population, sample being chosen without replacement, the sampling distribution of a sample mean will have mean $\mu_{\bar{x}} = \mu$ and standard error

$$\sigma_{\bar{x}} = \frac{\sigma}{\sqrt{n}}\sqrt{\frac{(N-n)}{(N-1)}}$$

Hence
$$Z = \frac{\bar{x}-\mu}{\frac{\sigma}{\sqrt{n}}\sqrt{\frac{(N-n)}{(N-1)}}}$$

There are relationships available for highlighting the distribution of sample means, sample medians as well as of the differences of means from two populations.

Distribution of Sample Medians

If the population is large and can be approximated to the normal distribution with the mean μ and the standard deviation σ, the medians of random samples of size n are distributed with a mean μ and standard deviation $1.2533\frac{\sigma}{\sqrt{n}}$. If the value of n is large, this distribution is nearly normal.

Thus
$$\sigma_{\text{Med}} = 1.2533\left(\frac{\sigma}{\sqrt{n}}\right)$$

Sampling Distribution of the Differences between Two Means

If we are analysing two populations, of sizes N_1 and N_2, their respective parameters can be denoted as μ_1, σ_1 and μ_2, σ_2. The comparison of these two populations can be made based on two Independent random samples of size n_1 drawn from first population and of size n_2 from the second population.

We denote the means of these two samples as $\bar{x}_1$ and $\bar{x}_2$ and we now determine the properties of a sampling distribution of $\bar{x}_1 - \bar{x}_2$.

Important properties of sampling distribution of $\bar{x}_1 - \bar{x}_2$ are

(*a*) $\mu(\bar{x}_1 - \bar{x}_2) = \mu_{\bar{x}_1} - \mu_{\bar{x}_2} = \mu_1 - \mu_2$

(*b*) $\sigma_{(\bar{x}_1-\bar{x}_2)} = \sqrt{\sigma^2_{\bar{x}_1} + \sigma^2_{\bar{x}_2}}$

$$= \sqrt{\frac{\sigma_1^2}{n_1} + \frac{\sigma_{x_2}^2}{n_2}}$$

(*c*) If $\bar{x}_1$ and $\bar{x}_2$ are means of the independent samples drawn from two large populations, the sampling distribution of $\bar{x}_1 - \bar{x}_2$ will be normal if the samples are fairly large sized.

Sampling Distribution of the Number of successes

If a random sample of size *n* is chosen from a population, where elements belong to two mutually exclusive categories, then the sampling distribution of the number of successes will be binomial distribution if the sampling is done with replacement. If sampling is done without replacement, the distribution will he hypergeometric.

Then $\mu = np$

and $\sigma = \sqrt{npq}$ as per binomial probability model.

Sampling Distribution of Proportions

A population proportion is defined as

$$\pi = \frac{X}{N}$$

where X = number of elements in a sample for a trial

N = total number of items in the population

Similarly a sample proportion can be written as

$$p = \frac{x}{n}$$

If a random sample of size *n* is obtained with replacement, the sampling distribution (p) obeys the binomial probability law

Then $\mu_p = \pi$

and $\sigma_p = \sqrt{\dfrac{\pi(1-\pi)}{n}}$

For value of *n* being large ($n \geq 30$), this will be closely normally distributed. When the sampling is made without replacement, then we apply the correction factor.

$$\sigma_p = \sqrt{\frac{N-n}{N-1}}\sqrt{\frac{\pi(1-\pi)}{n}}$$

Like sampling distribution for means, we can use the distribution for proportions as well as differences of two proportions from different populations.

Sampling Distribution of the Differences of Two proportions

As discussed in the case of difference of means of samples from two populations, we can obtain similar results for the difference of proportion from two binomially distributed populations with parameters π_1, π_2 respectively, when random samples of sizes n_1 and n_2 are drawn from their respective populations

Then $\mu_{(P_1-P_2)} = \mu_{P_1} - \mu_{P_2} = \pi_1 - \pi_2$

and $\sigma_{(P1-P2)} = \sqrt{\sigma^2_{P_1} + \sigma^2_{P_2}}$

If n_1 and n_2 are large *i.e.* $n_1, n_2 \geq 30$, then the sampling distribution of differences of proportions can be considered close to normal distribution.

12.12 SMALL SAMPLING THEORY

While discussing the central limit theory in the proceeding paragraphs, we had the case of samples being of large size. It was discussed that the sampling distribution of the sample statistic is normal or can he approximated to normal. For this purpose either the population from which the sample has been chosen is normal or that the sample size is large enough to represent the population in true way. Only in such cases, we have been able to use central limit theory. As per this theory, we have discussed the distribution of the sample mean to be normally distributed regardless of the sample size. Generally as sample of size $n \geq 30$ is considered to be a large mean or sample proportion respectively and if we apply central limit theory, we can use the distribution sample variance S^2 (when σ^2 is not known) to be normal when the population is normal and the sample size is large.

In the last chapter, we have established the relationship.

$Z = \dfrac{\overline{X} - \mu}{\sigma / \sqrt{n}}$ in order to define the standard normal variate. But in case ot a situation, when either the population variance σ^2 is not known or the sample size is small, then we cannot use S^2 as the unbiased estimator of σ^2, In case of sample size being small, it is seen that the sample distribution will be *t*-distribution. In this case, sample size n being less than 30, the central limit theorem will not be applicable and sample variance S^2 can no longer be used as an unbiased estimator of σ^2 *i.e.* the population variance.

When sample size is small, say observations less than thirty, some standard relationships for sample mean and related analysis are developed. For this purpose, some important probability distributions are used.

The student's *t* - distribution was obtained and published by WS Gosset. but under a changed name as "student". In addition, we also have *F* - distribution. *Z* - distributions and χ^2 -distribution in addition to Binomial and Poisson distributions for small sample applications. Binomial and Poisson Distributions have been discussed in earlier chapters. Now we will be discussing the others.

Degrees of Freedom

Before discussing the distributions, let us first understand the concept of "Degrees of Freedom". Degree of Freedom is normally denoted by a Greek symbol υ (pronounced as nu). It is the number of useful items of information generated by the sample of a given size with respect to the estimation of a given population parameter.

If we have a sample of size *n* as having the values of $x_1, x_2, x_3, ... x_n$, then the sum of these values

$$s = x_1 + x_2 + x_3 + ... x_n = \sum_{i=1}^{n} x$$

is a value that is obtained by us. If we arbitrarily assign any values of all other terms, say (n – I) terms, we can get the nth value automatically. Let us take a case of

$$\Sigma x = x_1 + 2 + 3 + 4 = 19$$

This expression has 5 terms and we assign values of 4 terms as 19, 2, 3 and 4. Then the value of the 5th terms is automatically determined as $x_1 = 10$. In this case, there are 5 – 1 = 4 degrees of freedom as other values can be assigned to $n - 1$ observations (here $n = 5$). Freedom to assign any values 10, the *n*th term, is restricted because this value is known to us to be the sum or otherwise.

Thus if *n* is the number of observations (sample size *n*), and *k* is the number of independent constants that can be estimated from the given data, $n - k$ is the degrees of freedom.

Students *t*-distribution :

While discussing the sampling distribution of mean, two assumptions were made :

(*a*) the mean of the population (μ) is known, and

(*b*) the standard deviation of the population (σ) is also known.

This means that the sample size n is large enough to justify the above assumption and that σ can be replaced by the sample mean (s). If we are not in a position to know μ and σ. *i.e.* if the sample size is not large, we can define a new variable (Students *t*-variable), given by the relationship.

$$t = \frac{\bar{x} - \mu}{s / \sqrt{n}}$$

where $s = \sqrt{\frac{(x_1 - \bar{x})^2}{n-1}}$ (SD of the sample)

When we compare *t*-distribution with standard normal variate $Z = \frac{x - \mu}{\sigma / \sqrt{n}}$ we can observe that *t* differs from *Z*, such that *t* contains sample deviation whereas *Z* contains the population deviation. By this explanation, we can draw a benefit that *t*-distribution can be used for analysis even with the knowledge of sample mean (s) only. In practice *t*-distribution is very close to *Z*-distribution, except when sample size *n* is very small. Similar to *Z*-tables, we have *t*-distribution tables also available, indicating various values of *t* for different degrees of freedom. The number of degrees of freedom for a sample size *n* is $(n - 1)$.

t-distribution and F-distribution are two important sampling distributions utilised for small sample cases.

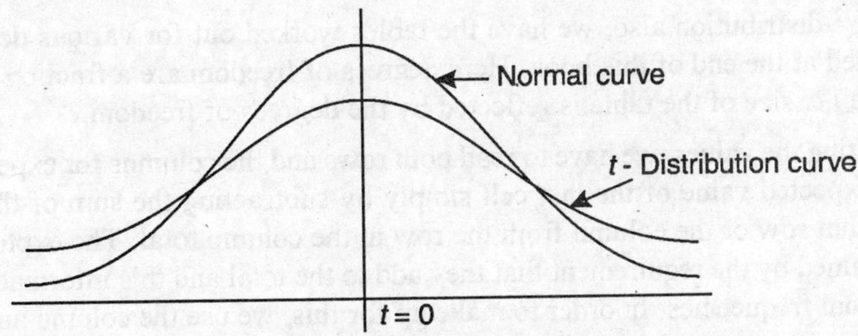

Fig. 12.5. Normal and t-distribution curve

The probability density curve of the *t*-distribution is uninodal and symmetric about $t = 0$. The variability of *t* is higher than that of Z and it decreases as the degrees of freedom increase. In that case, with increasing degrees of freedom, *t*-distribution tends to coincide with the normal distribution curve, as given in Fig. 12.5

This distribution has also been discussed in chapter 13, where it has been used for testing of hypothesis.

F-Distribution :

The *F*-Distribution is defined as the distribution of ratio of the sample variance of two normal populations. Thus if we represent s_1^2 as the sample variance of the first and s_2^2 the sample variance calculated on the basis of sample drawn from the second population, then

$$F = \frac{s_1^2}{s_1^2}$$

This relationship follows a *F*–Distribution with $(n_1 - 1)$ and $(n_2 - 1)$ degrees of freedom. This ratio is kept more than unity by selecting s_1 higher than s_2, so that the larger variance figures in the numerator. These ratios have seen tabulated and are appended at the end of this book for reference for various values of degrees of freedom.

Chi-Square Distribution : The Chi-square distribution is also represented as χ^2-distribution.

While conducting an experiment, we find the observed frequency of a random variable based on the observations obtained. If the random variable behaves in an organised fashion following a probability distribution, we can work out the expected frequency of the variable. The Chi-square (χ^2) is the measure of the extent to which the observed frequency and the expected frequency agree, χ^2-is defined by the relationship

$$\chi^2 = \sum_{i=1}^{n} \frac{\left[f_{i(0)} - f_{i(e)}\right]}{f_{i(e)}}$$

Where $f_{i(0)}$ is the observed frequency and $f_{i(e)}$, the estimated frequency of the random variable, In general, χ^2-distribution depends on the degrees of freedom as depicted in Fig. 12.6 below:

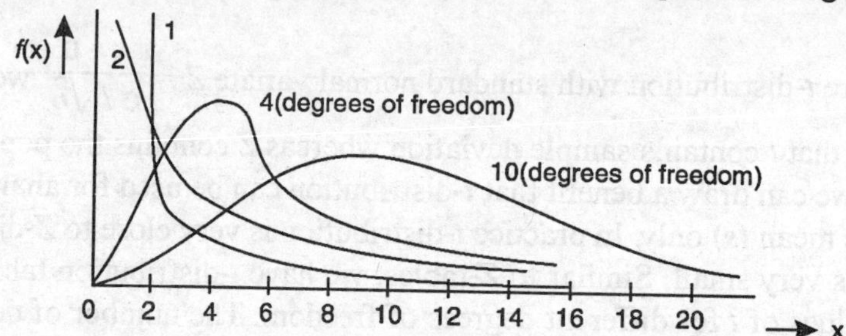

Fig. 12.6 Shape of χ^2-distribution for various degrees of freedom

Chi-square distribution is the most effectively used sampling probability distribution for analysing the small sample data. This distribution draws the accuracy from the observed and the expected observations.

In case of χ^2-distribution also, we have the tables worked out for various degrees of freedom and are appended at the end of this book. Here degrees of freedom are a fraction of the number of calls $r \times k$ table *i.e.* size of the table is reflected by the degrees of freedom.

For calculating the values, we have to read both rows and the columns for expected frequencies, obtaining the expected value of the last cell simply by subtracting the sum of the other expected frequencies in that row or the column from the row in the column total. The exptected frequencies are thus constrained by the requirement that they add to the total and this information is utilised for obtaining the final frequencies. In order to make up for this, we use the column and row degrees of freedom column minus one and row minus one respectively. Hence we obtain the degrees of freedom for the table as,

(Number of row – 1) × (Number of column – 1)

Thus if we are reading 3 rows and 4 columns, the degree of freedom will be (3 – 1) × (4 – 1) = 6

These have been defined in next chapter for use in hypothesis testing

12.13 SAMPLING FROM NON-NORMAL POPULATIONS

In the entire discussion in preceeding paragraphs, we have assumed that the populations are normally distributed. In such a case, the sampling distribution of the mean also has been assumed to be normal. When such as assumption does not hold *i.e.*, when we encounter populations which are not normally distributed, the behavior of the sampling distribution of the mean would be possibly different from being normal. We now analyse such a situation.

Let us consider a case to calculate the probability of sample mean between two values, which are not equally spread from the mean value (μ)

Considering a case of battery distributor, we select 6 users of the car batteries and collect the data, as to how long these batteries have survived.

Cars	Car No. 1	Car No. 2	Car No. 3	Car No. 4	Car No. 5	Car No. 6
Battery life (years)	3	2	3	4	2	4

We can calculate the mean life of the battery $= \dfrac{3+2+3+4+2+4}{6} = \dfrac{18}{6} = 3$ years

It is too small a sample to approximate it or assume it to be normal. Now taking sample means based on 3 cars at a time.

Sample 1 Mean $= \dfrac{3+2+3}{3} = \dfrac{8}{3} = 2.67$ years

Sample 2 Mean $= \dfrac{2+3+4}{3} = \dfrac{9}{3} = 3.00$ years

Sample 3 Mean $= \dfrac{3+4+2}{3} = \dfrac{9}{3} = 3.00$ years

Sample 4 Mean $= \dfrac{4+2+4}{3} = \dfrac{10}{3} = 3.33$ years

Sample 5 Mean $= \dfrac{2+4+3}{3} = \dfrac{9}{3} = 3.00$ years

Sample 6 Mean $= \dfrac{4+3+2}{3} = \dfrac{9}{3} = 3.00$ years

Sum of the means = 18.00 years

$\therefore$ Average mean $= \mu_{\bar{x}} = \dfrac{18}{6} = 3$ years

Thus we can see that the sample mean and the population mean, both are same.

If we increase the population size and take samples of different sizes, we can plot the sampling distribution of the mean for different size samples. We can easily establish that the sampling distribution very quickly approach the normal distribution whatever be the shape of the population distribution.

Following things would energe from the above discussion.

(i) The mean of the sampling distribution of the mean will equal the population mean, regardless of the sample size.

(ii) As the sample size increases, the sampling distribution of the mean will approach normality. regardless of the shape of the population distribution.

CHAPTER SUMMARY

Terms used

- **Census :** The examination or collection of information for every element of the population.
- **Clusters :** Within a population, groups that are essentially similar to each other or variable values almost at the same level, although various groups may have wide variations.
- **Cluster sampling :** A method of random sampling in which the population is divided into groups or clusters and then selecting random samples out of these clusters.
- **Finite population :** A population having a definite or limited size.
- **Infinite population :** A population in which there is no theoretical limit for the observations and hence all elements of the population cannot be studied.
- **Judgement sampling :** A method of selecting a sample from a population based on personal knowledge or expertise of a person. Only the identified elements will be sampled out.

- **Parameters :** Values that indicate the characteristics of a population.
- **Random or probability sampling :** A method of selecting a sample from a population in which all the items in the population have an equal chance of being included in the sample.
- **Sample :** A part of the elements or observations in a population, selected for examinations or study of the population.
- **Sampling distribution of the mean :** A probability distribution of all the possible means of sample.
- **Sampling distribution of a statistic :** A probability distribution of all the possible values of a statistic may have for a given sample size.
- **Sampling error :** Variation among sample statistics due to chance.
- **Sampling with replacements :** A sampling procedure in which sampled items are replaced back in the population, so that it may find its place in the sample again.
- **Sampling without replacement:** A sampling procedure in which an element picked up once for a sample, is not replaced back and hence further sampling is done out of remaining elements. Item included in the sample cannot, therefore, appear in the sample again.
- **Simple random sampling :** Method of selecting samples that allow each possible elements an equal opportunity of being chosen and each element in the population has one equal chance of being included in the sample.
- **Standard error :** The standard deviation of the sample distribution of a statistic.
- **Standard error of the mean :** The standard deviation of the sampling distribution of the mean.
- **Statistical inference :** The process of making inference about populations from the information contained in the samples.
- **Statistics :** Measures describing the characteristic of a sample.
- **Stratefied sampling :** A method of random sampling, in which the population is divided into homogeneous groups and elements within each groups are selected randomly according to one of the two rules (a) a specified number of the elements is drawn from each group or (b) equal number of elements are drawn from each group and the results are weighted according to the groups proportion of the total population.
- **Systematic sampling :** A method of sampling in which elements are sampled out from the population in time, order or space.

Relationship used

- $$\sigma_{\bar{x}} = \frac{\sigma}{\sqrt{n}}$$
- $$z = \frac{\bar{x} - \mu}{\sigma_{\bar{x}}}$$
- $$\sigma_{\bar{x}} = \frac{\sigma}{\sqrt{n}}\sqrt{\frac{N-n}{N-1}}$$

  Where N = size of the population and n = sample size
- $$s^2 = \frac{1}{n}\Sigma(x_i - \bar{x})^2 \text{ (large sample)}$$

- standard error $SE_{(t)} = \sqrt{\left[\frac{1}{k}\sum_{1}^{k}(t_i - \bar{t})^2\right]}$

- $s = \sqrt{\frac{(x_i - \bar{x})^2}{n-1}}$ (sample size small)

- $F = \frac{s_1^2}{s_2^2}$

- $\chi^2 = \sum_{i}^{n} \frac{\left[f_{i(o)} - f_{i(e)}\right]}{f_{i(e)}}$

SOLVED PROBLEMS

Problem 12.1

Considering a population of 3, 5, 7, 9, 10, 4, 7, 8, 11, 13, 12, 8, 6, 7, 10; find the probability that the sample mean is more than 6 and less than 7, in all possible sample of size 15, provided the samples are drawn with replacement.

Solution :

The values of population are

3, 5, 7, 9, 10, 4, 7, 8, 11, 13, 12, 8, 6, 7 and 10

The mean of the population $= \frac{\Sigma x}{N}$

or $\mu_{\bar{x}} = \mu = \frac{120}{15} = 8$

Standard deviation of population : σ

$$= \sqrt{\frac{(8-3)^2 + (8-5)^2 + (8-7)^2 + (8-9)^2 + (8-10)^2 + (8-4)^2 + (8-7)^2 + (8-8)^2 + (8-11)^2 + (8-13)^2 + (8-12)^2 (8+6)^2 + (8-8)^2 + (8-7)^2 + (8-10)^2}{15}}$$

$$= \sqrt{\frac{25+9+1+1+4+16+1+9+25+16+4+1+4}{15}}$$

$= 2.78$

The sample standard deviation

$$\sigma_{\bar{x}} = \frac{\sigma}{\sqrt{n}}$$

$$= \frac{2.78}{\sqrt{15}}$$

$= 0.72$

The situation can be drawn on the normal curve as follows

We how calculate the value of z with respect of $\bar{x}_1$ and $\bar{x}_2$ given as $\bar{x}_1 = 6$ and $\bar{x}_2 = 7$.

$$z_1 = \frac{\bar{x}_1 - \mu}{\sigma_{\bar{x}_1}}$$

$$= \frac{6-8}{0.72} = 2.78$$

$$\text{and } z_2 = \frac{7-8}{0.72} = -1.39$$

$$\therefore \quad P(6 \le \bar{x} \le 7) = P(-2.78 \le z \le -1.39)$$

$$= P(-2.78 < z < 0) - P(-1.39 < z < 0)$$

$$= 0.4973 - 0.4177$$

$$= 0.0796$$

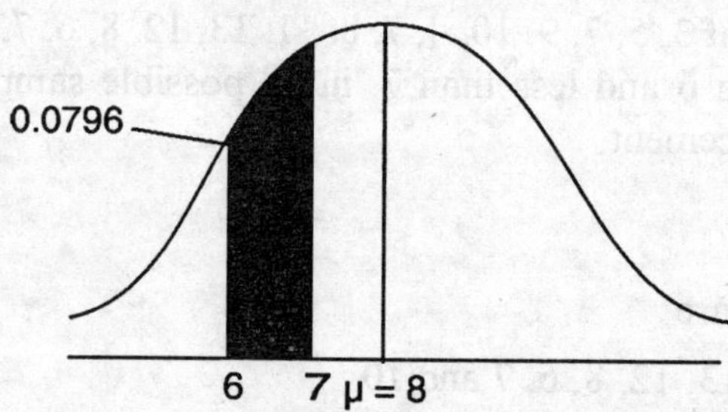

Fig. 12.7

Problem 12.2

If we have the following data from a sample-number of products manufactured during the day each hour as 55, 57, 65, 62, 58, 64, 63, 70. If the mean production is 60, calculate the value of t.

Solution :

Given $x_1 = 55$, $x_2 = 57$, $x_3 = 65$ and so on.

$$\therefore \quad \bar{x} = \left(\frac{x_1 + x_2 + ...x_8}{8}\right)$$

$$= \frac{55+57+65+62+58+64+63+70}{8} = 61.75$$

$$s = \sqrt{\frac{(x_i - \bar{x})^2}{n-1}}$$

$$= \sqrt{\frac{(-6.75)^2 + (-4.75)^2 + (3.25)^2 + (0.25)^2 + (-2.75)^2 + (1.25)^2 + (8.25)^2}{8-1}}$$

$$= \sqrt{\frac{45.56 + 22.56 + 10.56 + 0.0625 + 7.56 + 5.06 + 1.56 + 68.06}{7}} = 4.9$$

$$t = \frac{x - \mu}{s / \sqrt{n}}$$

$$= \frac{61.75 - 60}{4.8 / \sqrt{8}}$$

$$= \frac{1.75 \times 2.82}{4.8}$$

$$= 1.02$$

The degrees of freedom = $n - 1 = 8 - 1 = 7$

Problem 12.3

When we select a sample of 400 products and we found that 55 products are on the preferred list of users, find the mean proportion and the number of products in use. Also work out the standard deviation.

Solution :

$$\text{The mean proportion } (p) = \frac{55}{400} = 0.1375$$

$\therefore$ Average number of products in use $= np$

$$= 400 \times 0.1375$$

$$= 55$$

$$\text{Standard Deviation} = \sqrt{npq} = \sqrt{400 \times 0.1375 \times 0.8625}$$

$$= 6.89$$

Problem 12.4

Let us consider two sets of observations as

A : 55, 56, 70, 69, 68, 58, 60, 63, 68, 58

B : 20, 25, 24, 27, 19, 28, 30, 31, 28, 27

Calculate the value of F.

Solution :

Here for sample A

$$\bar{x}_1 = \frac{55 + 56 + 70 + 69 + 68 + 58 + 60 + 63 + 68 + 58}{10} = 62.5$$

$$s_1^2 = \frac{(\Sigma x_i - \bar{x})^2}{(n-1)}$$

$$= \frac{56.25 + 42.25 + 56.25 + 42.25 + 30.25 + 20.25 + 6.25 + 0.25 + 30.25 + 20.25}{(10-1)}$$

$$= 33.83$$

Similarly for sample B,

$$\bar{x}_2 = \frac{20+25+24+27+19+30+31+28+27}{10}$$

$$= 25.9$$

$$\therefore \quad s_2^{\,2} = \frac{34.81+0.81+3.61+1.21+47.61+4.41+16.81+26.01+4.41+1.21}{9}$$

$$= 15.65$$

$$\therefore \quad F = \frac{s_1^2}{s_2^2} = \frac{33.83}{15.65}$$

$$= 2.16$$

The value of F is 2.16 for degrees of freedom (9,9).

Problem 12.5

Calculate the χ^2-value from the following data

	A	B	C
Observed frequency :	25	29	27
Expected frequency :	23	28	29

Solution :

The data given above obtain to $f_{i(o)}$ and $f_{i(e)}$

Then
$$\chi^2 = \sum_{i=1}^{3} \frac{\left[f_{i(0)} - f_{i(e)}\right]^2}{f_{i(e)}}$$

$$= \frac{(25-23)^2}{23} + \frac{(29-28)^2}{28} + \frac{(27-29)^2}{29}$$

$$= 0.173 + 0.036 + 0.138$$

$$= 0.347$$

The degrees of freedom = (3 – 1) = 2

Problem 12.6

A random sample of 700 units from a large consignment showed that 200 were damaged. Find (*i*) 95%, (*ii*) 99% confidence limits for the proportion of the damaged units in the consginment.

Solution :

Given here $n = 700$

and
$$p = \frac{200}{700} = \frac{2}{7}$$

$$q = 1 - p = \frac{5}{7}$$

$$\therefore \quad SE(p) = \sqrt{\frac{pq}{n}} = \sqrt{\frac{2}{7} \times \frac{5}{7} \times \frac{1}{700}}$$

$= 0.017$

(*i*) For 95% confidence limits for *P*, we have

$$p \pm 1.96\sqrt{\frac{pq}{n}} = 0.286 \pm 1.96 \times 0.017$$

$$= (0.319, 0.253)$$

(*ii*) For 99% confidence limits for *P*, we get

$$p + 2.58\sqrt{\frac{pq}{n}} = 0.286 \pm 2.58 \times 0.017$$

$$= (0.330, 0.242)$$

Problem 12.7

A research worker wishes to estimate the mean of a population by using sufficiently large sample. The probability is 95% that the sample mean is not at variance with the true mean by more than 25% of the standard deviation. How large a sample he should obtain ?

Solution :

Given $P|(\bar{x}-\mu)| \leq 25\% \text{ of } SD = 0.95$

Hence $P|(\bar{x}-\mu)| \leq \frac{\sigma}{\sqrt{n}} = 0.95$

or $P|(\bar{x}-\mu)| \leq 1.96\,\frac{\sigma}{4} = 0.95$

Hence $\frac{\sigma}{4} = 1.96\,\frac{\sigma}{\sqrt{n}}$

$\therefore$ $n = (4 \times 1.96)^2 \simeq 62$

Problem 12.8

A random sample of 100 items taken from a large batch of articles contains 5 defective items, (*a*) Set up 96 per cent confidence limits for the proportion of the defective items in the batch, (*b*) If the batch contains 2,696 items, set up 95% confidence interval for the proportion of defective items. [*ICWA (Final), June 1974*]

Solution :

(*a*) We have been given $n = 100$ and defectives = 5

Hence $p = \frac{5}{100} = 0.05$ Hence $q = 0.05 = 0.95$

$$SE(p) = \frac{\sqrt{pq}}{n} = \frac{\sqrt{0.05 \times 0.95}}{100}$$

For 96% confidence limits, we have (from the table normal curve)

$P(-2.05 \leq Z \leq 2.05) = 0.96$

Hence confidence limits are $p + 2.05 \frac{\sqrt{pq}}{n} = 0.05 + 2.05 \times 0.022 = (0.095, 0.005)$

(*b*) Here we have N = 2,669. Then the 95% confidence limits for P will be given by

$$p + 1.96\ SE(p) = p \pm 1.96 \sqrt{\frac{pq}{n}\left(\frac{N-n}{n-1}\right)}$$

$$= 0.05 \pm 1.96 \sqrt{\frac{0.05 \times 0.95}{2,669} \times \frac{(2,669 - 100)}{(100 - 1)}}$$

$$= 0.05 \pm 1.96 \times 0.0215$$

$$= (0.092, 0.008)$$

PRACTICE PROBLEMS

12.9 What is the difference between Statistic and Parameter as used in Sampling Theory? What is Sampling Distribution of a statistic? Explain it by taking a particular statistic. *[ICWA (Final), June 1979]*

12.10 Describe briefly the law of Statistical Regularity and state its applications in the economic and social spheres. *[Nagarjuna University, B.Com., April 1980]*

12.11 What are the main objectives of sampling? Compare and contrast the merits and drawbacks of sample and census studies? *[Punjab University, M.Com., (Eco.) 1978]*

12.12 What is a statistical error? Explain the difference between a statistical error and a 'mistake'? Describe the various measures of statistical errors. *[Allahabad University, B.Com., 1979]*

12.13 What are statistical errors? What are the sources of errors? Explain the methods of measuring them. *[Mysore University, B.Com., Nov., 1981]*

12.14 Distinguish between census and sample methods. Compare their relative merits and demerits. *[Mysore University, B.Com., Nov., 1981]*

12.15 Describe the advantages of sample surveys over complete enumeration giving examples in support of your arguments.

What is simple random sampling? How would you estimate the total labour force in the State by random sampling? *[Punjab University, M.Com. (Eco.), 1978]*

12.16 Explain briefly the reasons for the increasing popularity of sampling methods. Explain briefly any two methods of sampling which help us to obtain a representative sample. *[C.A. (Inter), May 79]*

12.17 Enumerate the various methods of sampling and describe two of them mentioning the situations where each one is to be used. *[Punjab University, M.B.A., 1977]*

12.18 Bring out the important features of (*i*) Systematic Sampling (*ii*) Stratified Sampling. *[Delhi University, B.Com., 1982]*

12.19 Distinguish between random sampling and stratified sampling suppose if it is desired to survey petrol buying habits of car owners in a particular city, how would you proceed about it? Draw a brief questionnaire for the purpose. *[Punjab University, B.Com., 1979]*

12.20 Discuss the various techniques which may be used for carrying out a sample survey. Explain how you will minimise sampling errors and biases while using these techniques.
[Himachal University, M.Com., 1982]

12.21 Three sampling plans to determine the quality of, manufactured product are given below;
(*i*) Inspect every 10th item. (*ii*) Inspect one item every 10 minutes. (*iii*) Inspect a random sample of 6 during each hour's production
State the sampling design in each case. Which one is the most appropriate? Give reasons.
[Bombay University, B.Com., Nov.. 1980]

12.22 Write a note on sampling and its uses. [C.A. *(Inter.), May 1981, May 1982]*

12.23 Describe briefly any three methods of sampling. *[C.A. (Inter), Nov., 1981]*

12.24 While collecting data, under what circumstances would you prefer
(*a*) Random sampling to deliberate sampling
(*b*) Stratified sampling to simple random sampling
Is quota sampling same as stratified sampling? *[Madras University. B.Com.,1974]*

12.25 Distinguish between simple random sampling and stratified random sampling. Describe a procedure of drawing a random sample of size 3 from a population of size 11 by "without replacement" method. *[ICWA (Final), Dec.,* 1979]

12.26 Distribution of children in three schools is as follows :

School :	**A**	**B**	**C**
Number of children :	400	550	250

Using the following random numbers draw a random sample of size 24 given that the children have 1 to 400. 1 to 550 and 1 to 250 as their roll numbers in the three schools respectively. Explain the method.

24, 12, 26, 65, 51, 27, 69, 90, 64, 94, 14, 84, 54, 66, 72, 61, 19, 63, 02, 31, 92, 96, 26, 17, 73, 41, 83, 55, 53, 82, 30, 53, 22, 17, 04, 10, 27, 41, 22, 82, 35, 68, 52, 33, 69, 03, 78, 89, 75, 99,75, 56, 72, 07, 17, 74. 41, 65, 31, 46, 43, 22, 86, 33, 79, 85, 78, 34, 76. 19, 53, 15, 26, 74. 33. *[Bombay University, B.Com., May 1978*]

12.27 Determine the mean of distribution of the sample means, the population means being 19.5. 55, 195.6, 23.6, 179.5.

12.28 The diameter of the shaft is on the average 20 cm. We select random samples of 15 shafts choosing a shaft at every hour of working. If the measurements obtained are 20.56. 20.89. 20.5. 19.69, 19.90, 20.35, 19.58, 20.05. 19.96 and 20.85, calculate the *t*-values.

12.29 Two operations on a machine produce certain defective parts according to the following data.

Operation :	**A**	**B**
Defectives :	6	10
Non-defectives :	154	200

Calculate the value of χ^2.

12.30 From the sample of 250 workers in an organisation, the indication was received that if the actual proportion of workers having their loyalty to the union is *(a)* 15%, *(b)* 20%, *(c)* 30%, *(d)* 50%. find the probability of getting a sample proportion that differs by more than 5% from the actual proportions.

12.31 Find the mean of the distribution of sample proportion when the proportion in the population being sampled is 45%.

12.32 A random sample of 500 sarees was taken from a ship consignment ready for export shipping. On inspection, the defective sarees were taken aside and their numbers came out to be 95. Calculate the standard error and the range in which these defective sarees will lie.

12.33 Using the two types of promotional campaigns P and Q, the products sold in cities were as under, P : 916, 360, 815, 725, 856, 245, 460, 595

Q : 810, 400, 500, 650, 550, 530, 750, 890

Calculate the value of F-distribution.

12.34 Out of a sample of 120 childrens in a village, 76 were administered a drug for prevention of a particular disease. Out of these 76 childrens, 24 were attacked by the disease where as 12 children were not attacked by the disease, who were not administered the drug. Prepare table showing actual and expected frequencies and use χ^2-test to determine whether or not the new drug was affective (The value of χ^2-distribution from the table at 5 df (degree of freedom) at 0.05 level is 3.84). *[Osmania University, M.B.A., Sept., 1998]*

12.35 In a post office, three clerks are assigned to process the incoming mail. The first clerk A_1 processes 30%, the second clerk A_2 processes 40% and the third clerk A_3 processes 30%. The error rate of A_1, A_2 and A_3 are 0.05, 0.06 and 0.04 respectively. A mail selected at random from the days output found to have an error. What is the probability that the mail was processed by the second clerk A_2 ? *[Osmania University, M.B.A., April 1998]*

❖❖❖

CHAPTER 13

THEORY OF ESTIMATION AND TESTING OF HYPOTHESIS

13.1 INTRODUCTION

So far we have studied the inference of the population characteristics based on some samples drawn from it in a scientific manner, because census method is time consuming, costly, and at times impractical. These concepts have already been discussed in chapter on 'Sampling Theory'. The samples are expected to give close results regarding the population provided samples are drawn to make them representative of the population. These results can now be generalised if we know, how much these generalisation conditions are valid. We, then, can estimate the population parameter with the degree of confidence. The techniques used for the purpose are dealt with in statistics by "Statistical Inference", which is classified into two main categories :

1. Theory of Estimation ;
2. Testing of Hypothesis.

Due to high level of uncertainty in business operations, the decisions are not always definite and hence are valid under certain assumptions made on the basis of environmental factors. Hence we call it as "Estimation of Business Parameters".

13.2 THEORY OF ESTIMATION

When we want to estimate certain population parameters such as mean, variance, proportions and correlation with the help of samples statistics, the problem becomes important from the point of view of decisions for business. This is because the business decisions need verification of statements or assumptions as per the information available. When a manager wants to verify or compare his company's performance in any field, be it administrative, technical, quality related or financial during certain period, he will need referring to the Theory of estimation. Estimation of future demand of the product, average future life of the product, quality of production (defect percentage) or the quality of equipment are some of the important parameters, which help in planning the future scientifically. In estimation of these parameters. the sampling distribution of a statistic and its standard error will play a very important role as sampling system can save a lot of time, effort and money and results may be very useful.

13.3 TYPES OF ESTIMATES

The theory of estimation for such results was founded by Prof. R.A Fisher around 1930. This theory can be divided into two parts (*i*) **Point Estimation,** (*ii*) **Interval Estimation.** As can be understood from names, point estimation provides a single numerical value for the estimate of the population parameter, whereas in Interval Estimation, a probable range is specified, within which the true value of the parameter may be expected to lie.

Estimator

An estimator is a sample statistic used to estimate the population parameter, useful for decision-making. For example, sample mean $\bar{x}$ can be treated as a good estimator of the population mean μ. and the sample proportion can be made use of for the purpose of population proportions.

Estimate

When we use a specific numerical value of the estimator, this is called an estimate. Thus An estimate is a specific observed value of the population parameter.

Since estimates are the best help available to the decision-maker, he obtains the estimate either at a definite value basis or values valid in a given interval of parameter range. Thus point and interval estimates are obtained as the requirement of the decision.

Point estimate : is a single number *i.e.* numerical value as estimation of the parameter of the population and hence not always enough to show the validity or correctness of the estimate. It may not be possible to locate either the extent or the cause of the 'not correct estimate'. In order to ensure the reliability of the estimate, we might have to add the measure of error to deduce worthwhile information.

Interval estimate : which is a range of values of the parameter and may be a better measure of population parameter. This estimate will indicate the error in two ways (*a*) by the extent of the range of the values and (*b*) by the probability of the true population parameter lying within that range.

13.4 CRITERION OF A GOOD ESTIMATOR

Four different criteria can be used to specify whether an estimator is good or not. A good estimate or estimator should satisfy the following conditions :

1. Unbiased
2. Consistent
3. Efficient
4. Sufficient

Unbiased Estimator : The statistic $X = f(x_1, x_2, \ldots x)$ as a function of observations is said to be unbiased estimate,

If $E(X) = \theta$. This indicates that the mean value of the sampling distribution should be equal to the parameter. When sample mean is $\bar{x}$ and population mean is μ, Then $E(\bar{x}) = \mu$. from the above relation. Similarly, if p is the sample proportion, it is unbiased estimate of the population proportion P *i.e.*

$$E(p) = P$$

Now, sample variance $s^2 = \frac{1}{n}\sum_{i=1}^{n}(x_i - \bar{x})^2 = \frac{1}{n}\sum(x_i - \bar{x})^2$ is not an unbiased estimate of the population variance σ^2, but

$S^2 = \frac{1}{n-1}\sum(x_i - \bar{x})^2$ provides an unbiased estimate of the population variance.

$\therefore \qquad E(s^2) = \sigma^2$, but $E(S^2) = \sigma^2$

Thus $\qquad ns^2 = (n-1)\,S^2$

$$\therefore \qquad S^2 = \frac{n}{(n-1)}(s^2) \simeq s^2 \text{ (when sample size } n \text{ is large)}$$

Hence for large samples $\sigma^2 = s^2$

If $(Ex) \neq \theta$, then the statistic X is said to be biased estimate and $E(X) = b + \theta$

Where b is called the "amount of bias" in the estimate. If $b > 0$, the X is positively biased and if $b < 0$, it will be negatively biased.

$$\text{Now} \qquad E(s^2) = \frac{(n-1)}{n}E(S^2) = \left(1 - \frac{1}{n}\right)\sigma^2$$

This is less than σ^2. Hence σ^2 is the estimated value of s^2, which is negatively biased by an amount $\left(-\frac{\sigma^2}{n}\right)$.

Consistent Estimator : A statistic $(X) = f(x_1, x_2, \ldots x_n)$ based on a sample size n is called consistent estimator of the parameter θ, if it converges' in probability to θ. *i.e.*

$$\lim_{n\to\infty} p(x_n \to \theta) = 1$$

For any distribution, sample mean $\bar{x}$ is a consistent estimator of the population mean, sample proportion p a consistent estimator of population proportion P and sample variance s^2 a consistent estimator of the population variance σ^2. However, a consistent estimator may not be unbiased. Consistency is a property belonging to large sample size *i.e.* $n \to \infty$. Then Var $(X) \to 0$ for $n \to \infty$.

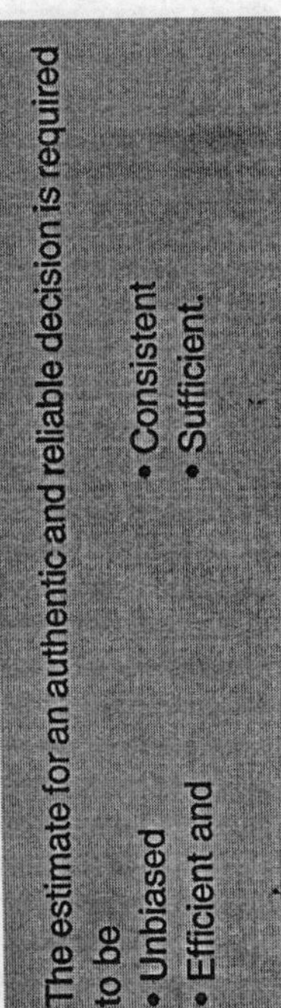

Efficient Estimator : If we consider the sample from a normal population $N(\mu, \sigma^2)$, then both sample mean $\bar{x}$ and sample median (Md) are unbiased and consistent estimator of the population mean μ. Whereas the variances are

$$\text{Var}(\bar{x}) = \frac{\sigma^2}{n}$$

$$\text{and Var}(Md) = \frac{\pi\sigma^2}{2n} = 1.57\frac{\sigma^2}{n} \text{ for large samples.}$$

Hence Var $(\bar{x}) <$ Var (Md) for large samples.

When we describe the above relationship, we can say that in the sampling from a normal population, the variance of the sampling distribution of mean $\bar{x}$ is less than that of the Median (Md) for very large value of n. Then we say that $\bar{x}$ is more efficient than Md.

"If x is the most efficient estimator of a parameter θ, with variance v and x_1. any estimator parameter with variance v_1, then

$$E = \frac{v}{v_1}$$

and hence $E \leq 1$

Sufficient Estimator : A statistic is called a sufficient estimator of population parameter θ, if it contains all the population parameter information in the sample.

The sample mean $\bar{x}$ is sufficient estimator of the population mean μ and sample proportion p is sufficient estimator of the population proportion P. We are to remember, (*i*) If a sufficient estimator exists for a parameter, it is also the most efficient estimator

(*ii*) It may or may not be unbiased, but is always consistent.

(*iii*) A minimum variance unbiased estimator exists only if there exists a sufficient estimator for it.

13.5 METHODS OF POINT ESTIMATION

The most commonly used methods for obtaining the Point Estimation are as under:

1. Method of Maximum Likelihood
2. Method of Least Squares
3. Method of Moments
4. Method of Minimum Variance
5. Method of Minimum Chi-square
6. Method of Inverse Probability Theory

For the purpose of obtaining a point value estimate, the decision-maker can make use of various methods, whatever be suitable and easily applicable for the problem in question.

The Method of Point estimation based on least square has already been dealt with in chapter 15. Similarly, the Method of Inverse Probability Theory has been discussed in Chapter 17 (Baye's Theory of Posterior Probability). We are now discussing two important Methods *i.e.* Method of maximum likelihood and Method of Moments.

Method of Maximum Likelihood : It is one method, which is most commonly and widely used in business situations for the purpose of estimating the population parameter.

Let us consider a random sample of size n as $x_1, x_2, x_3, \ldots x_n$ from a population denoted by $p(x,\theta)$. Here θ is the unknown parameter to be estimated.

$$\text{Let L} = p[x_1, x_2, x_3 \ldots\ldots x_n]$$

By the principle of maxima and minima, the Maximum Likelihood Estimator (MLE as it is commonly known) is the solution under the following conditions:

$$\frac{\partial L}{\partial \theta} = 0 \text{ and } \frac{\partial^2 L}{\partial \theta^2} < 0$$

L and log L attain their extreme values (max. or min.) at the same value of θ, since log L is the non-decreasing function of L.

$$\frac{1}{L}\frac{\partial L}{\partial \theta} = 0 \text{ or } \frac{\partial}{\partial \theta}(\log L) = 0.$$

When $x_1, x_2, x_3 \ldots\ldots x_n$ is a random sample of size n for a Normal Population $N(\mu, \sigma^2)$, where σ^2 is known, but μ is unknown parameter.

$$L = L(\mu) = \sum_{i=1}^{n}\left[\frac{1}{\sigma\sqrt{2_\pi}} e^{\frac{-1/2(x_i-\mu)^2}{\sigma^2}}\right]$$

$$= \left(\frac{1}{\sigma\sqrt{2\pi}}\right)^n \frac{-1}{{}_e 2\sigma^2}\sum_{i=1}^{n}(x_i-\mu)^2$$

$$\text{or } \log L = -n\log\left(\sigma\sqrt{2\pi}\right) - \frac{1}{2\sigma^2}\sum_{i=1}^{n}(x_i-\mu)^2$$

$$= c - \frac{1}{2\sigma^2}\sum_{i=1}^{n}(x_i - \mu)^2$$

$$\frac{\partial}{\partial u}(\log L) \quad = 0 - \frac{1}{2\sigma^2}\sum_{i=1}^{n}2(x_i - \mu)\times(-1)$$

If $\frac{\partial}{\partial u}(\log L) \quad = 0$

Then $\frac{1}{\sigma^2}\Sigma(x_i - \mu) \quad = 0$

or $\Sigma(x_i - \mu) \quad = 0$

or $\mu \quad = \frac{\Sigma x_i}{n} = x$

Similarly $\frac{\partial^2}{\partial \mu^2}(\log L) \quad = \frac{1}{\sigma^2}\sum_{i=1}^{n}(-1)$

$= \frac{1}{\sigma^2}\times(-n) = -\frac{n}{\sigma^2}$ It is < 0.

Hence MLE for μ is the sample mean $\bar{x}$ and $\sigma^2 = s^2$, *i.e.* MLE for the variance σ^2 is provided by the sample variance s^2.

It may be remembered that MLEs are consistent and most efficient estimators and are asymptotically normally distributed about the true value of the parameter.

Method of Moments : In this method, we equate the moments of the population to the moments of the samples and then solve these equations to obtain the value of the estimate of the population parameters.

Let us consider a binomial distribution of sample of size n, and if P is the parameter to be estimated, we can write

$$nP \quad = \bar{x} \text{ or } P = \frac{\bar{x}}{n}$$

Variance $nPQ \quad = nP(1 - P) = s^2$ where $Q = (1 - P)$

When we know the values of the sample parameters, the population parameter can be estimated. It is very useful method for estimating the theoretical frequencies of a given distribution by fitting an appropriate probability distribution. The other concepts, are beyond the preview of this book.

For an interval estimate within a certain specified range of parameters, various methods based on the confidence limits of mean or standard deviation can be used to advantage.

13.6 METHODS OF INTERVAL ESTIMATION

While we obtain a single value of the statistic for the estimation of the population parameter, there are situations of the fluctuations in these values and hence the single value may not be the satisfactory estimate. Under these situations, we try and obtain a range of the statistic in which the parameter may be satisfying the population characteristic. We use technique of Interval Estimation in such situation. This method was adopted by Neyman and consists of determination of two constants c_1, and c_2 such that

$$P[c_1 < c_2 \text{ for a given value of } x] = I - \alpha.$$

In this case, α is known as the level of significance and the interval (c_1, c_2) as the range in which the parameter θ (unknown for the population) is expected to lie. This is called level of confidence or confidence Interval or Fiducial Interval. The values of c_1 and c_2 are called confidence limits and the factor $(1 - \alpha)$ as the confidence coefficient.

Thus if $\alpha = 0.05$, then the confidence limit is 95%

Confidence Limits for Mean

In case of large samples, $(n \to \infty)$ from an infinite population, with mean μ and variance σ^2, the sample mean $\bar{x}$ will be given by

$$Z = \frac{\bar{x} - \mu}{\sigma / \sqrt{n}} \text{ for } N(0, 1)$$

For area under the normal curve (normal probability)

$$P(-1.96 \leq Z \leq 1.96) = 0.95$$

or

$$P\left[\bar{x} - \frac{1.96\sigma}{\sqrt{n}} \leq \mu \leq \bar{x} + \frac{1.96\sigma}{\sqrt{n}}\right]$$

Thus 95% confidence limits for population mean are $x \pm 1.96\ \sigma/\sqrt{n}$ where s is known and it indicates 95% confidence interval for estimating μ.

Similarly $x \pm 2.58\ \sigma/\sqrt{n}$ indicate confidence interval at 99% for estimation of population mean μ

The confidence limits for mean or standard deviation are good values for Interval estimate. These limits can be drawn for various level of confidence desired by the Decision maker, the normal being either 95% or 99%.

Confidence Limits for Standard Deviation

For large samples, we can define sample variance as Var (s) for a sample of size n $(n \to \infty)$ from an infinite population of variance σ^2.

$$\text{Var}(s) = \frac{\sigma^2}{2n}$$

Hence $(1 - \alpha)$ % confidence limits for the standard deviation of population (σ) are given by

$$s \pm Z_a\ SE(s) = s \pm Z_a \sqrt{\frac{\sigma^2}{2n}}$$

Where value of Z_α for different levels of significance is given at the end of this book.

Confidence Limits for Difference of Means

If $\bar{x}_1$ and $\bar{x}_2$ are the sample means of two large and independent samples selected randomly with sizes n_1 and n_2 from two infinite populations with means μ_1 and μ_2 and standard deviations σ_1 and σ_2, then the relationship of confidence limits of differences of means $(\mu_1 - \mu_2)$ at $(1 - \alpha.)$ confidence coefficient can be written as

$$\bar{x}_1 - \bar{x}_2 \pm Z_a SE(\bar{x}_1 - \bar{x}_2)$$

or

$$\bar{x}_1 - \bar{x}_2 \pm Z_a \sqrt{\frac{\sigma_1^2}{n_1} + \frac{\sigma_2^2}{n_2}}$$

Confidence Limits for Difference of Proportions

When we consider p_1 and p_2 as the sample proportions of large and independent random samples of size n_1 and n_2 from infinite populations with proportions P_1 and P_2, then

$$E(p_1 - p_2) = P_1 - P_2$$

$$\text{and Var } (p_1 - p_2) = \frac{P_1Q_1}{n_1} + \frac{P_2Q_2}{n_2}$$

$$\therefore \text{ Z} = \frac{(p_1 - p_2) - (P_1 - P_2)}{\sqrt{\frac{P_1Q_1}{n_1} + \frac{P_2Q_2}{n_2}}} \sim N(0, 1)$$

Hence the confidence limits for the difference of proportions $P_1 - P_2$ at the level of significance α are given by

$$p_1 - p_2 \pm Z_\alpha \sqrt{\left(\frac{p_1q_1}{n_1} + \frac{p_2q_2}{n_2}\right)}$$

If P is not known then, we can write $E[SE(P)] = \sqrt{\left[\frac{pq}{N} + \frac{(N-n)}{n-1}\right]}$.

13.7 TESTING OF HYPOTHESIS

In order to estimate decision variables with confidence, certain assumptions used are to be validated. The validation of the assumptions is done through "Testing of Hypothesis".

We have already discussed that the inductive inference can be used for deciding the characteristics of the population based on the sample study. The inherent risks in such decision-making processes may give rise to some serious business repercussions. During the process of such decisions, we normally streamline the analysis by making some assumptions under which the uncertainly of decisions can be controlled. To reduce risks, we check whether all these assumptions hold good during the pendency of the decision. For this purpose, theory of probability plays a very prominent role and the statistical theory used is called "Testing of Hypothesis". The theory of testing of hypothesis was used by J. Nagman and E.S. Pearson to arrive at decisions under uncertain circumstances but based on samples of fixed sizes. When the sample size is not fixed, another technique known as "Sequential Testing" was advocated by Abraham Bald. We are discussing only Testing of Hypothesis in this chapter.

We can define a statistical hypothesis as a statement about the population or the probability distribution defining a population. In testing of hypothesis, we, therefore, plan techniquess which can tell us whether the assumptions made during the study of population based only some representation random sample are valid or not or how long they remain valid. Thus the decision problem is either to accept the hypothesis (H_0) true or reject H_0 (equivalent version is accept H_1 as true). Out of these two hypotheses, H_0 and H_1 one is called the "Null hypothesis" and the other as "alternative hypothesis". Normally, notionally H_0 is defined as null hypothesis and H_1 as alternative hypothesis.

Let us use an information that a business manager thinks that his product will he preferred by the consumers by more than 40% of the potential consumers, otherwise the product may not he launched. Hence we write the null hypothesis that the true proportion p of the consumers preferring the product as H_0: $P < 0.4$ and hence the alternative hypothesis $H_1 : p \geq 0.4$. Now the manager holds this view that the preference proportion of the product will be less than 0.4 till such time it is otherwise established to the contrary by actual sample results. Thus the decision manager starts with negative thinking and revises his thinking on getting overwhelming evidence from the sample that it is not true.

When the hypothesis completely specifies the population, it is called a simple hypothesis, otherwise it will be called a composite hypothesis.

The simple hypothesis for sampling from a normal population $N(\mu, \sigma^2)$ can be specified as H: $\mu = \mu_0$ and $\sigma^2 = \sigma_0^2$.

For accepting or rejecting a hypothesis, we must ensure a definite evidence from the sample. Thus "The acceptance of a statistical hypothesis is due to insufficient evidence provided by the sample to reject it and does not necessarily imply that it is true".

Steps Involved in Hypothesis Testing

The process of testing the hypothesis involve following steps.

1. State the hypothesis parameters clearly as to what is to be confirmed or tested.
2. Formulate the null and alternative hypothesis with the help of the problem.
3. Specify the test statistic that best reflects the relative merits of H_0 and H_1.
4. Separate out the set of values of the test statistic into two distinct areas, the rejection area and acceptance area, so that H_0 reject means H_1 accept.
5. Observe the sample data, compute the value of the test statistic and apply the decision rule in 4 above.

For hypothesis testing, a systematic approach is necessary so as to reach a plausible optimal solution. The types of errors that can creep in during such a testing are to be understood and taken care of, while reaching a worthwhile decision.

Types of Errors in Testing of Hypothesis

Since there is a risk involved in decision-making based on the sample theory, there may be errors in the decision making or accepting or rejecting a null hypothesis (H_0) after knowing the results of a sample from the population. From the point of decision, four alternatives can be thought of

Reject H_0 when actually it is not true. (*i*)
Accept H_0 when it is true. (*ii*)
Reject H_0 when it is true. (iii)
Accept H_0 when it is false. (*iv*)

We can see that (*i*) and (*ii*) are correct decisions, whereas (*iii*) and (*iv*) are wrong decisions. These can be shown diagrammatically as given in Fig. 13.1 below.

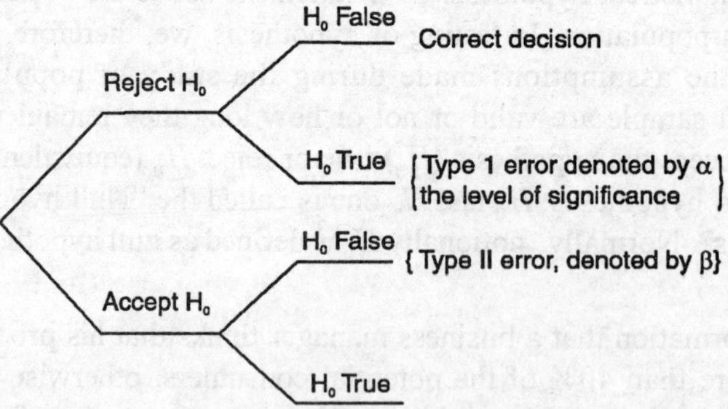

Fig. 13.1. Type I and Type II errors

As indicated above in Fig. 13.1. these errors in taking wrong decisions are termed as Type I errors or Type II errors. Type I errors are more serious, because we are taking a decision, when we have correct hypothesis and have rejected it. as in this case, the losses will be of far more greater consequences, compared to a case when we accept the proposal when it is actually false. As Type I error is more serious. it is customary to control α at a predetermined low level and to choose a test procedure to minimise β. Type I or Type II errors are not normally explicitely quantifiable and hence it is difficult for the decision maker to make a logical assessment of the level of tolerance of such errors. Type I errors are generally kept very low, to the level of 0.01 to 0.05. These values are called level of significance, which is the maximum level of probability of risk acceptance. By this we mean that if a level of significance is chosen as 0.05 or 5%, then we have 5% chance that we reject the hypothesis when it should have been accepted, *i.e.* in 95% chance, we have made the correct decision.

In summary α = Prob. of rejecting a good lot

β = Prob. of accepting a bad lot

The size of Type I errors (α) is called Producer's risk whereas the size of Type II errors (β) is called consumer's risk.

Power of the Test

We have β = Prob. (Type II errors)

= Prob (Accept H_0 when H_0 is false or H_0 is true)

$\therefore$ Prob. (Accept H_0 when H is true)

= 1 – Prob. (Accept H_0 when H_0 is false)

= 1 – β.

Hence to minimise type II error *i.e.* β, we should maximise $1 - \beta$. The term $(1 - \beta)$ is called the Power of the test. Thus in testing of hypothesis, we aim at fixing α and then minimise β *i.e.*, maximise $(1 - \beta)$, the Power of the test.

The concept of 'Power of the Test' has been brought in to take care of errors during testing. The Power of the test devotes the minimisation of type II error, i.e., maximise the power of the test for batterment of decision.

13.8 LARGE SAMPLE TESTS

Hypothesis Testing of Means

Let us assume and discuss a normal population with standard deviation known or in the second case, when standard deviation is not known.

When standard deviation is known :

Consider at normal population $N/(\mu, \sigma^2)$ where σ is known, but μ is not known. We choose a random sample $x_1, x_2, .x_3, \ldots x_n$ and we wish to lest the hypothesis regarding the value of μ. We can formulate the null and alternative hypotheses as

$$H_0 ; \mu = \mu_0 ; \quad H_1 : \mu \neq \mu_0 \qquad (i)$$

or $$H_0 ; \mu = \mu_0 ; \quad H_1 : \mu > \mu_0 \qquad (ii)$$

or $$H_0 ; \mu = \mu_0 ; \quad H_1 : \mu < \mu_0 \qquad (iii)$$

Where μ_0 is a specified value.

In situation (*i*), the alternative hypothesis is two sided, whereas in situation (*ii*) and (*iii*) it is one sided. We now proceed to locate the critical region or rejection region for the hypothesis.

The mean of the sample.

$\bar{x} = \dfrac{\Sigma x_i}{n}$ and the critical region is given by R : $|\bar{x} - \mu_0| \geq C$. where C is such that

$$P\, P[\bar{x} - \mu_0 | \geq C | H_0| = \alpha$$

In order to find the value of C, we use the sampling distribution of $\bar{x}$. The sampling distribution of $\bar{x}$ is normal with mean μ and standard deviation $\sigma/\sqrt{n}$. and hence $Z = \dfrac{\bar{x} - \mu_0}{\sigma / \sqrt{n}}$ has a normal distribution with mean 0 and standard deviation 1. We have the tables available for $N(0,1)$ (given at the end of the book) and we can find the value of $K_{\alpha/2}$, such that $P[|Z| \geq K_{\alpha/2}] = \alpha$

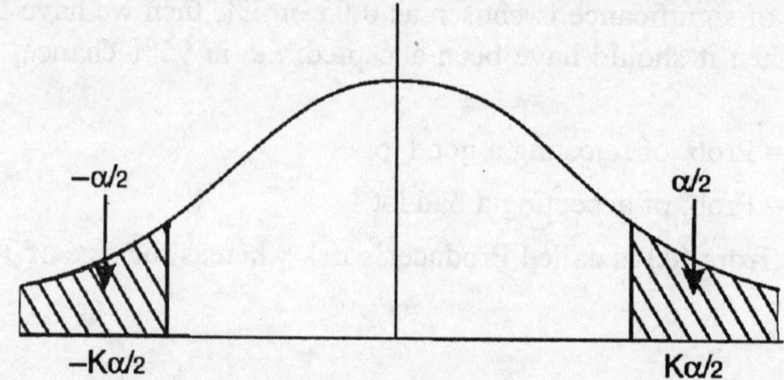

Fig. 13.2. Prob. of type I error for normal distribution (Two tail test)

The shaded area in Fig. 13.2 gives the Probability α for normal variate $K_{\alpha/2,}$ on both sides of the mean.

Since Normal Distribution Curve is symmetrical about the mean value of the parameter, i.e., mean, its shape can be made use of the various tests such as one-tail test or two-tail test.

Thus $\quad |Z| \geq K_{\alpha/2}$

or $\quad \dfrac{\bar{x} - \mu_0}{\sigma/\sqrt{n}} \geq K_{\alpha/2}$

or $\quad |x - \mu_0| \geq K_{\alpha/2}\dfrac{\sigma}{\sqrt{n}}$

Hence our critical region is $R : |\bar{x} - \mu_0| \geq e$.

or $\quad C = K_{\alpha/2} \cdot \dfrac{\sigma}{\sqrt{n}}$ is the critical region for a as level of significance.

Thus the critical region $R : |\bar{x} - \mu_0| \geq C$

or $\quad R : |Z| \geq K_{\alpha/2}$

We specify the value of α, the level of significance and numerical value of $K_{\alpha/2}$ can be obtained from the normal table.

Now that we have defined the critical region (or the rejection region), we obtain the sampte information of Z.

If $|Z| > K_{\alpha/2}$ H_0 is rejected as against H_1 at α level of significance. As can be seen from the normal, tables af the end of the book, the most common used values of α and the corresponding values of $K_{\alpha/2}$, are given below :

α	:	0.1	0.05	0.025	0.01
$K_{\alpha/2}$	:	1.645	1.96	2.240	2.275

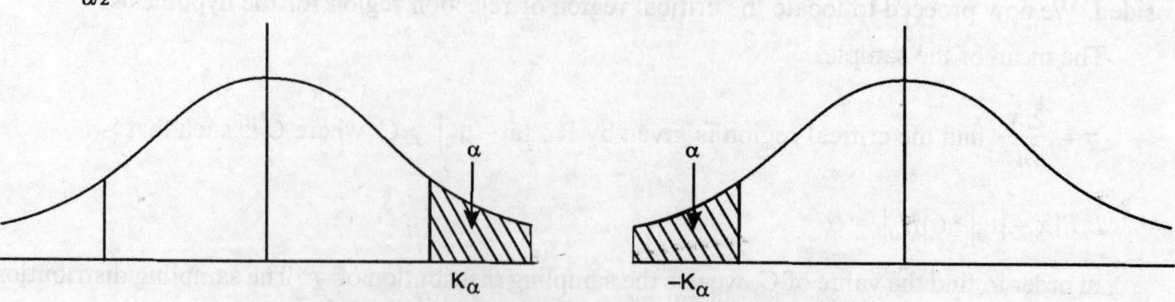

Fig. 13.3. One tail test - Normal Distribution

The rejection regions are

$$R = Z \quad \geq K_{\alpha/2} \text{ for situation } (ii)$$

and $$R : Z \leq - \; K_{\alpha/2} \text{ for situation } (iii)$$

The commonly used values of α and corresponding values of K_α are given below.

α	:	0.1	0.05	0.025	0.01
$K_{\alpha/2}$	:	1.280	1.645	1.96	2.326

Hypothesis Testing of Proportions

If the data available is classified as per the frequencies of the parameters, then binomial distribution tends towards the normal distribution and if p is the proportion of success with sample size *(n)* (very large sample), we can use the binomial distribution. The mean of the number of successes will be np and standard deviation as $\sqrt{\dfrac{pq}{n}}$, where $q = 1 - p$. Then the test statistic will be

$$Z = \frac{\overline{P} - p}{\sqrt{\dfrac{pq}{n}}}$$

For testing the hypothesis, we can formulate the null and alternative hypotheses and locate the rejection region using normal distribution as approximation to the Binomial distribution.

Tests for Equality of Population Mean

In this case, the null hypothesis will be formulated

$$H_0 : \mu_1 = \mu_2$$

Where μ_1 is the population mean of population 1 and μ_2 that of population 2.

Then various relationship for the test statistic will be

$$Z = \frac{\bar{x}_1 - \bar{x}_2}{\sqrt{\dfrac{\sigma_1^2}{n_1} + \dfrac{\sigma_2^2}{n_2}}} \text{ with usual notations} \qquad (i)$$

If $\sigma_1 = \sigma_2 = \sigma$, then the value can be written as

$$Z = \frac{\bar{x}_1 - \bar{x}_2}{\sigma\sqrt{\dfrac{1}{n_1} + \dfrac{1}{n_2}}} \qquad (ii)$$

However, if σ is not known, then it has to be estimated from the sample standard deviation (s) as follows

$$s = \sqrt{\frac{(n_1 - 1)s_1^2 + (n_2 - 1)s_2^2}{(n_1 + n_2 - 2)}}$$

and then test of statistic is calculated as

$$t = \frac{\bar{x}_1 - \bar{x}_2}{s\sqrt{\left(\dfrac{1}{n_1} + \dfrac{1}{n_2}\right)}}$$

This has t-distribution with $(n_1 + n_2 - 2)$ degrees of freedom.

Various parameters are chosen to bring out the testing for hypothesis. These can be either mean, proportions, equality of means or else the difference between proportions of two populations.

Testing of Difference Between Proportions

If two samples are drawn from two different populations, and p_1, p_2 represent the proportions of successes, we can establish whether their difference are significant or not.

Null hypothesis will be $H_0 : p_1 = p_2$

and test statistic is given by

$$Z = \frac{p_1 - p_2}{\sqrt{\frac{p_1 q_1}{n_1} + \frac{p_2 q_2}{n_2}}} \text{ with usual notations.}$$

Testing Equality of Variances of Two Normal Populations

Let σ_1^2 and σ_2^2 be the variances of two normal populations we wish to test the null hypothesis.

$H_0 : \sigma_1^2 = \sigma_2^2$

For such a test, it will be convenient to use the ratio of sample variances s_1^2/s_2^2 because s_1^2/s_2^2 follows the F-distribution. In order to establish the rejection region, the alternative hypothesis can be

Testing of hypothesis can also be done through the equality of variances of two normal populations, i.e., comparing whether two normal populations have same variance or not.

$H_1 : \sigma_1^2 > \sigma_2^2$ (*i*)

$H_1 : \sigma_1^2 < \sigma_2^2$ and (*ii*)

$H_1 : \sigma_1^2 \neq \sigma_2^2$ (*iii*)

After working out the values of s_1^2/s_2^2 the value of F can be compared from the F-table (given at the end of this book) and if the calculated value falls within the rejection region, the null hypothesis H_0 is rejected in favour of H_1, as per the relationships given below.

$$R : \frac{s_1^2}{s_2^2} \geq F_\alpha[(n_1 - 1), (n_2 - 1)]$$

The rejection region is the left tail of $F_\alpha[(n_1 - 1). (n_2 - 1]$. When $s_2^2 > s_1^2$, then the rejection region is the right tail of $F_\alpha[(n_2 - 1), (n_1 - 1]$ and the cut-off point can be read from the table.

Using $\frac{s_1^2}{s_2^2}$ as a test statistic, the level of significance α (region of acceptance) is the interval

$$\frac{1}{F_{\alpha/2}(n_2 - 1, n_1 - 1)} < \frac{s_1^2}{s_2^2} < F_{\alpha/2}[(n_2 - 1), (n_1 - 1)]$$

and the rejection region now falls outside this interval.

13.9 SMALL SAMPLE TESTS (CHI-SQUARE TEST)

We have already discussed the tests of significance when samples sizes are large. But when sample size is small, we use the sample distribution of the statistic t as $Z = \frac{t - E(t)}{SE(t)}$

This distribution is not normal and hence normal test cannot be applied in such cases. For such cases, we apply sample tests depending on the sample size n. the square of a standard normal variable is called a "Chi-Sqaure variate" with 1 degree of freedom. Thus if X *is* a random variable following a normal distribution, with mean μ and standard deviation σ, then the square of the normal variate

$\left(\frac{x - \mu}{\sigma}\right)^2$ is a Chi-square (Written as χ^2, a Greek alphabet) variate with 1 degree of freedom.

$$\therefore \qquad \chi^2 = \sum_{i=1}^{\nu}\left(\frac{x_i - \mu_i}{\sigma_i}\right)^2$$ follows the Chi-Square distribution with ν degree of freedom.

The Probability Density function of the Chi-Square distribution is given by

$$p(\chi^2) = \frac{1}{2^{\nu/2}\,\tau_{(\nu/2)}}\, e^{-\chi^2/2}(\chi^2)^{\nu/2-1} \ ; \ 0 < \chi^2 < \infty$$

where τ_ν is the Gamma function and is given as

$$\tau_\nu = (\nu - 1)! \text{ if } \nu \text{ is a positive integer}$$

and $$\tau_\nu = (\nu - 1)\,\tau_{(\nu-1)} \quad \nu > 1$$

The probability curve of the χ^2 - distribution can be drawn as follows (Refer Fig. 13.4 below) with χ^2 axis being asymptotic to the probaiblity curve (χ^2).

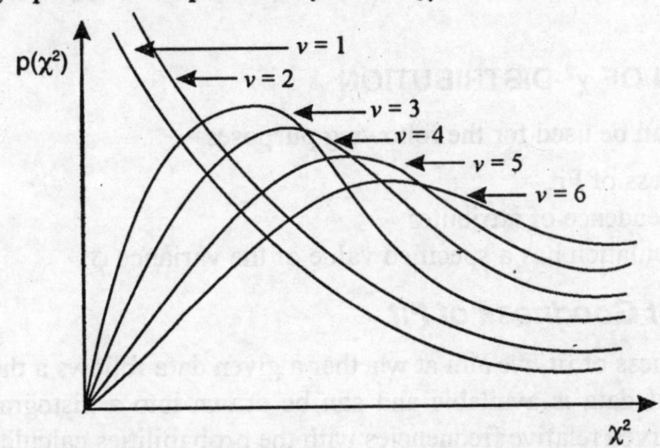

Fig. 13.4. Probability Curve of χ^2-distribution

Constants of χ^2-Distribution

With ν - degree of freedom, various contants of χ^2-distribution are as follows.

(*a*) Mean = ν

(*b*) Mode = $\nu - 2$

(*c*) Variance = 2ν

(*d*) Moments $\mu_1 = 0$

$$\mu_2 = 2\nu$$

$$\mu_3 = \delta\nu$$

$$\mu_4 = 4\delta\nu + 12\nu^2$$

$$\beta_1 = \frac{\mu_3^{\,2}}{\mu_2^{\,3}} = \frac{8}{\nu}$$

$$r_1 = \sqrt{\frac{8}{\nu}}$$

$$\beta_1 = \frac{\mu_4}{\mu_2^{\,2}} = \frac{4\delta\nu + 12\nu^2}{4\nu^2} = 3 + \frac{12}{\nu}$$

$$r_2 = \beta_1 - 3 = \frac{12}{\nu}$$

> The situation of hypothesis testing changes a bit while dealing with small samples (generally the samples with $n < 30$, i.e., sample size smaller than thirty observations). The valid distributions in such cases can be either chi-square distribution or else t, F or Z distributions.

(*e*) Pearson's Coefficient of skewness

$$Sk = \frac{\text{Mean} - \text{Mode}}{\text{Standard Deviaiton}} = \frac{\nu - (\nu - 2)}{\sqrt{2\nu}}$$

$$= \sqrt{\frac{2}{\nu}}$$

(*f*) for large ν,

$$Z = \frac{\chi^2 - E(\chi^2)}{S.D(\chi^2)} = \frac{\chi^2 - \nu}{\sqrt{2\nu}}$$

This is normally good enough for ν, over 30.

(*g*) Addition $\sum_{i=1}^{k} \chi_i^2 = \chi_1^2 + \chi_2^2 + \ldots\ldots\ \chi_k^2$ with $n_1 + n_2 + \ldots\ldots\ n$ degrees of freedom

13.10 APPLICATION OF χ^2-DISTRIBUTION

Chi-square distribution is quite prominantly and consistantly used for testing of small samples. The tests adopted under this distribution are :
- goodness of fit test
- independence of attributes
- specified value of the variance.

This distribution can be used for the following purposes

1. χ^2-test of goodness of Fit.
2. χ^2-test for independence of attributes
3. To test if the population has a specified value of the variance σ^2.

Chi-Square Test of Goodness of Fit

In testing the goodness of fit, we aim at whether a given data follows a theoretical distribution. This can be analysed if data is available and can be drawn into a histogram and observing the comparison of the observed relative frequencies with the probabilities calculated from the tables of a particular distribution. The test used for testing the goodness of fit is known as the χ^2-test, wherein Chi-Square (χ^2) is the measure of the relative discrepancy between the observed and the expected frequencies. Thus

$$(\chi^2) = \sum_{i=1}^{k} \left(\frac{f_{i(o)} - f_{i(e)}}{f_{i(e)}} \right)^2$$

Where $f_{i(o)}$ is the observed frequency of ith class

$f_{i(e)}$ is the expected frequecy of ith class

and k is the number of the classes. The above relationship can also be written as

$$\chi^2 = \sum_{i=1}^{k} \frac{f_{i(o)}^{\ 2}}{f_{i(e)}} - n$$

Because $\Sigma f_{i(o)} = \Sigma f_{i(e)} = n$

The degrees of freedom are calculated as $\nu = k - r - 1$, where r = no. of independent parameters estimated from sample observation.

The values of $f_{i(o)} - f_{i(e)}$ can be calculated as the deviation of the observed frequency and estimated frequency of each class and squaring it up, we can calculate the value of χ^2. Then

(*i*) Under the null hypothesis that the theory fits the data well, it will follow the χ^2-distribution with $\nu - 1$ degrees of freedom.

(*ii*) If the values *of* χ^2 *so* obtained from the calculation is less than the corresponding tabulated value, then it is said to be non-significant at the required level of significance, which means that deviation can be attributed to chance. Thus the data donot provide us any evidence against the null hypothesis and hence null hypothesis may, therefore, be accepted at the required level of significance and it can be inferred that there is a good fit between the theory (assumption) and the experiment.

On the other hand, if the calculated value of χ^2 is greater than the tabulated value it is said to be significant. We can thus say that the discrepancy between the observed,and the expected frequencies cannot be attributed to chance and hence we reject the null hypothesis.

The rejection region can be seen from the Fig. 13.5 given below.

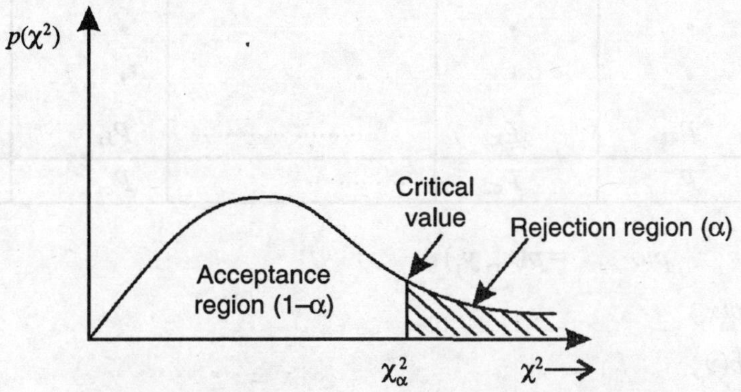

Fig. 13.5 Rejection Region of χ^2 Statistic.

The value χ^2_n (α) is known as the upper (right-tailed) α-per cent critical value of the χ^2 for n degrees of freedom and is thus tabulated for different values of n and α from the table given at the end of this book.

The conditions for the validity of χ^2-test are as under:

(*i*) The total frequency N should be reasonably large.
(*ii*) The sample observations should be independent
(*iii*) The constraints on the cell frequencies should be linear.
(*iv*) No theoretical frequency should be small.
(*v*) The data should be given in the original units.

> For Chi-square test certain important assumptions are made such as frequency, to be fairly large and sample observations random. For the purpose of test, the constraints on the cell-frequencies are that these should be linear and small.

χ^2- Test as a Test of Independence of Attribute

Sometimes, we have to establish whether two characteristics or attributes manifest themselves independently or in some related way. For establishing it, we first formulate the contingency table of two attributes x and y with k mutually exclusive and collectively exhaustive categories of x and categories of y, as given below.

Contingency Table

x \ y	y_1	y_2	y_3	y_i	*Total*
x_1	n_{11},	n_{12}	....	n_{11}	n_{10}
x_2	n_{21},	n_{22}	....	n_{21}	n_{20}
•	•	•	•	•	•
•	•	•	•	•	•
•	•	•	•	•	•
x_k	n_{k1},	n_{k2}	....	n_{ki}	n_{ko}
Total	n_{o1}	n_{o2}	....	n_{oi}	n

Now, we can prepare a table of probabilities in place of frequencies and the reused table probabilities is given below.

Table of Probabilities

x \ y	y_1	y_2		y_i	*Total*
x_1	p_{11},	p_{12}	....	p_{1i}	p_{10}
x_2	p_{21},	p_{22}	....	p_{2i}	p_{20}
•	•	•		•	•
•	•	•	•	•	•
•	•	•	•	•	•
x_k	p_{k1},	p_{k2}	....	p_{ki}	p_{k0}
Total	p_{o1}	p_{o2}		p_{oi}	1

In this table, $pio \quad = p(x_1, y_1)$

and $pio \quad = p(x_i)$

and $poj \quad = p(y_j)$

If $x.$ and y_1 are independent for all values of i and j, then for independence of x and y

$$p(x_i, y_j) = p(x_i)\, p(y_j) \qquad \text{for all } i = 1, 2, \ldots k$$

and $j = 1, 2, \ldots\ldots l$

Hence null hypothesis will be

$$H_o : pij = pio \times poj$$

The cell frequencies are given by *n. pio.poj* and can be tested for independence by χ^2 - test with $(k - l)\,(1 - l)$ degrees of freedom.

For the purpose of comparing attributes, the tabular form suggested is very handy to bring out the probability of attributes clearly. An easy approach is also available for testing of population variances through chi-square distribution.

χ^2 – *Test for the Population Variance*

When we want to test if the given normal population has a specified variance, *i.e.* $\sigma^2 = \sigma_0^{\,2}$, then we formulate a null hypothesis as

$H_0 : \sigma^2 = \sigma_0^{\,2}$, if

$x_1, x_2, x_3 \ldots x_n$ is a random sample of size n from the given population, then under null hypothesis.

$$\chi^2 \quad = \sum_{i=1}^{n} \frac{(x_i - \bar{x})^2}{\sigma_n^{\,2}} = \frac{n / s^2}{\sigma_0^{\,2}}$$

It follows χ^2-distribution with (n - I) degrees of freedom, when $s^2 = \frac{1}{n}\sum (x_1 - \bar{x})^2$ denotes the sample variance. It can be applied only if the population has normal distribution and when sample size is large ($n > 30$), then

$$\sqrt{2\chi^2} \quad = N\left(\sqrt{2x - 1,1}\right)$$

and then we apply normal test

$$Z \quad = \sqrt{2\chi^2} - \sqrt{2n - 1} \sim \nu\,(0, 1)$$

13.11 NON-PARAMETRIC TESTS

During the discussion in the previous paragraphs, we have made restrictive assumptions about the population from which the samples are drawn. Most of the cases discussed required either the large samples or the population was considered to have normal distribution. To a large extent, these assumptions were valid in day-to-day life situations, where most of the business decision could be taken based on these approximations or assumptions. These assumptions, however, may not always be true *i.e.* the populations arc not necessarily normally distributed. And because of the reason, in certain situations, the use of the normal curve may not be appropriate. Thus for such situations, we have to adopt different techniques to solve such problems.

These techniques are called "Non-Parametric Tests". We are going to discuss the following important tests

1. Sign Test
2. Mann - Whitney *U*-Test
3. Run Test
4. Kolmogorov - Smirnov (One Sample) Test
5. WILCOXON signed - Rank Test
6. Kruskal - Wallis *H*-Test

In addition to chi-square test, some non-parametric tests are also available to deal with different situations. These tests are also meant for situations where the samples are not normally distributed.

Sign Test

This test is based on the sign of a pair of observations and does not depend on the magnitude of the observations. The null hypothesis in this case is that there is no real difference between the two sets of observations. For a null hypothesis $H_0 : x = y$, we assign positive value for $H_1 : x > y$ and negative value for $H_1 : x < y$. While grading various parameters, we allocate plus (+) sign to $(x - y)$ *i.e.* if the score for x is higher than that for y, it is allotted + sign. If the scores for x and y are the same, we assign + value and for lower x score, we assign negative sign for $x - y$.

After this allocation, we count the number of positive signs and work out its proportion (p) of the signs. Thus the hypothesis formulated will be

$$H_0 : p = 0.5$$

and $$H_1 : p \neq 0.5$$

Having worked out the proportion (p) for the positive signs, we use the binomial distribution for the purpose of locating the rejection region. Again for large values of n, Binomial distribution can be approximated to Normal distribution and the following relationship can be used.

$$SD = \sqrt{\frac{pq}{n}} = \sqrt{\frac{0.5 \times 0.5}{n}}$$

and the normal variate $$Z = \frac{P - p}{\sqrt{\frac{pq}{n}}}$$

Mann Whitney U-Test

This test is useful to establish whether the two independent samples have been drawn from the same population. It would also help in establishing whether the samples drawn are from two different populations having the same distribution. The method used here is ranking the information for the acceptance of the null hypothesis.

For carrying this test, we first pool the information of the two samples under test, it is then arranged in the ascending order and ranked. If there are n_1 items or observations in sample 1 and n_2

in sample 2, R_1 the sum of the ranks of observations in sample 1 and R_2 the sum of the ranks of observation in sample 2, the test statistic U is defined as :

$$U = n_1 n_2 + \frac{n_1(n_1+1)}{2} - R_1$$

Thus U- represents the measurement of the difference between the ranked observations of the two samples.

If the null hypothesis that $n_1 + n_2$ observations come from the identical (or the same) populations. then U has the sampling distribution mean $= \frac{n_1 n_2}{2}$ and the Standard Deviation $= \frac{n_1 n_2 (n_1 + n_2 + 1)}{12}$.

The sampling distribution of U can be approximated to the normal distribution for n_1 and n_2 if n_1 and $n_2 \geq 10$. In that situation, we can work out the rejection region from a given level of significance. If the calculated value of U falls in this region, the null hypothesis is rejected. Thus it establishes that there is difference between the two populations.

We can also compute the value of U statistic as follows

$$U = n_1 n_2 + \frac{n_2(n_2+1)}{2} - R_2$$

Whether we calculate the value of U based on earlier relationship or this one, the inference drawn will he the same.

A point to be noted here is that in case of tie in ranking.(Variable having the repeat or same value), the both will be granted average rank $\left(\frac{r_1 + r_2}{2}\right)$ where r_1 should have been the rank of 1 and r_2 for the other same valued observations. In case of three observations having the repeat values, the average method is followed again for their ranking, each being awarded $\frac{r_1 + r_2 + r_3}{3}$ value.

While sign test is used for comparing two variable values based on their plus and minus sign (not actual values), the Mann-Whitney test is based on U-statistic through ranking the observations of two variables, either in descending or ascending order and then using U-statistic assuming that U-distribution approximates the Normal distribution.

Run Test

The third test *i.e.*, The Run Test being discussed here is used to test the samples for randomness of their order. The method followed is to first combine the observation of the two samples and then to arrange them in the ascending order. A run is defined as the sequence of the elements of the same type. If x_1, x_2, x_3 are first three observations from first sample, it is called one run. If the runs are well mixed, then we accept the null hypothesis that samples are random. If we have long run *of x or y* at the extremes, then H_0 is rejected. Also if there are few funs, we also reject H_0..

For n_1, and n_2, each being larger than 10, we can write the distribution of the number of runs *(r)* is asymptotically normal, with

$$E(r) = \frac{2n_1 n_2}{n_1 + n_2} + 1$$

$$\text{and SD}(r) = \sqrt{\frac{2n_1 n_2(2n_1 n_2 - n_1 - n_2)}{(n_1 + n_2)^2(n_1 + n_2 - 1)}}$$

and then we calculate

$$Z = \frac{r - E(r)}{\sqrt{\text{Var}(r)}}$$

If Z falls in the rejection zone, we reject H_0, otherwise accept H_0.

Kolmogorov- Smirnov Test (One Sample Test)

This particular test is very similar to the Chi-Square test goodness of fit, but difference is that it compares the distribution on an ordinal scale. It involves specifying the cumulative frequency distribution under the null hypothesis and then comparing it with the observed cumulative frequency distribution. Let us have $F_o(x)$ as the theoretical cumulative distribution under the null hypothesis H_o and $S_n(x)$ as the cumulative distribution of the observed values, then the test-statistic is expressed as

$$D = \text{Maximum} \mid F_o(x) - S_n(x) \mid$$

And at 5% level of significance, the critical value of D for large samples is given by $\frac{1.96}{\sqrt{n}}$ where n is the sample size. For testing the results, we reject null hypothesis H_o, if the calculated value of D exceeds the critical value obtained from the above expression.

The Run test is used to test the samples for randomness of their order through combination of the values of both the samples together and then arranging them in ascending or descending order and then testing for the randomness.

Wilcoxon Signed - Rank Test

During the discussion on the sign test, we have used the method of testing based on plus-minus sign of the differences of the parametric values. We use this difference of $(x - y)$ as a single sample observation and the population mean and then test the null 'hypothesis based on) $\mu - \mu_0$, where μ_0 is the population mean. Since the sign test has been based on the plus and minus sign only for the differences, the magnitude of the differences have been ignored. Now we discuss a test that would take the plus and minus sign as well as the magnitude of the differences. This test was suggested by Frank Wilcoxon (1945) and it is commonly known after his name as Wilcoxon signed rank test. We will he using this test tor the following hypothesis.

$H_0 : \mu = \mu_0$ *i.e.* $H_0 : \mu = \mu_0$

or $H_0 : \mu_1 = \mu_2$ $H_0 : \mu_1 = \mu_2$

and $H_1 : \mu_1 - \mu_2 = d_0$ *i.e.* $\mu_1 > \mu_2$ and $H_1 : \mu_1 - \mu_2 = d_0$

The differences of the observations are denoted by $d_i = D_i - d_0$

where $D_i = x_i - y_i$

These differences are obtained from the sample observations and are designated along with their signs. We neglect those differences which are zeros and other differences are assigned ranks as 1. 2, 3 .... etc. starting from the smallest difference in magnitude (not considering the respective signs).When the differences are equal in magnitude, these are allotted ranks equal to the average of the ranks that could have been assigned if the differences were not equal. This is the same procedure of allocating ranks as in case of Spearman's Rank method of correlation. After all the ranking has been done, we, then, add all the rank values against positive (plus) differences and these are written as s_+. Similarly we add all the negative rank values and are written as s_-. Lowest of these values is denoted as s. We have these sums whose values will be different in repeated sampling experiments.

Now if the null hypothesis states that $\mu = \mu_0$ or $\mu_1, = \mu_2$, then logically the values of s_+, s_- will be approximately the same. If it is not so, *i.e.* if alternate hypothesis states either $\mu_1 > \mu_2$ or $\mu > \mu_0$ for a sample size n and value of s_+ is sufficiently large and s_- sufficiently small. the H_0 will be rejected in favour of H_1.

Similarly the null - hypothesis will be rejected in favour of alternative hypothesis defined as $\mu < \mu_0$, $\mu_1 < \mu_2$ or $\mu_1 - \mu_2 < d_0$, if the value of s_+ is sufficiently small and value of s - sufficiently large for a sample size n.

Similarly the two sided alternative hypothesis defined as $\mu_1 \neq \mu_0$; $\mu_1 \neq \mu_2$; $\mu_1 - \mu_2 \neq d_0$ will be accepted when the value of s (*i.e.* lower of the two s_+ and s_-) is sufficiently small in relation to s_+ (when $s_- < s_+$) or in relation to s_- (when $s_- > s_+$)

Kruskal – Wallis Test

This test can be applied for null hypothesis, when different populations have identical distributions and we select k independent random samples from these populations. In order to proceed with this test. we first combine all observations from each of k samples and all the observations $n = n_1 + n_2 +$ .... n_k are arranged in the ascending order. If we find that two observations are equal, then ranking is again done on the basis of average of the otherwise possible ranks as in case of the test above or in case of Spearnean's Rank correlation analysis. These rank values are then identified whether these pertain to samples of size n_1 or n_2. The ranks pertaining to different samples are then added and sum of these ranks for each sample is denoted as $t_1, t_2, t_3, \ldots\ldots\ t_k$ etc. We then apply the test in the following manner.

$$H = \frac{12}{n(n+1)}\left[\frac{t_1^2}{n_1} + \frac{t_2^2}{n_2} + \ldots\ldots \frac{t_k^2}{n_k}\right] - 3(n+1)$$

This expression is resembling of χ^2- distribution with degrees of freedom as $\upsilon = k - 1$, provided each sample consists of 5 or more observations. After computing the value of H, we reject H_0 at α-level of significance if the computed value of $H > \chi^2_\alpha$ with $\upsilon = k - 1$ degrees of freedom. If not, the null hypothesis is accepted.

We can find the value of H, if one or more sets have two or more equal observations.

$$\text{Modified} \quad H' = \frac{H}{C}$$

where C is the correction factor, and its value is

$$C = 1 - \sum_{J=1}^{s} \frac{(0_j^3 - 0_j}{(n^3 - n)}$$

where s is the number of sets with two or more equal observations and t_j is the number of equal observations in the jth set. In this case also, H_o is rejected at a level of significance if computed value of $H, > \chi^2_\alpha$. Otherwise it is accepted.

13.12. TESTS OF SIGNIFICANCE BASED ON t, F AND Z DISTRIBUTION

The tests discussed so far pertain to business decisions where large samples can be obtained and their characteristics can be utilised to draw inferences about the population characteristics, from which such samples are drawn. But when the sample size is small, say $n \leq 30$, then the sample may not represent the population in its true characteristics and the normal tests may not be useful for such decisions. We, therefore, now discuss certain specific tests known as Exact Sample Tests, which have been developed to deal with such situations.

The initial and important research and developmental work on Exact Sample Theory was done by William S. Gosset. an Irish brewery employee. He had been publishing his work under the name "Student" and hence the statistic developed was named as "student" t-distribution (1908). The concept was later refined by Prof. R. A. Fisher. Now we shall discuss these distributions by the name of t. F and Z-distributions and tests on the basis of these distributions.

The Wilcoxon-signed Rank test is a step forward over sign test. In this case, we work out the hypothesis testing based on the differences of the sample values and then ranking the differences for camparing the means of the samples. Kruskal-Wallis test is similar to Spearman's Rank test for diferent populations with identical distributions.

Exact Sample Tests

For discussions on the Exact Sample Tests, we make and follow the fundamental assumptions given below,

1. The parent population from which the sample is drawn is Normally Distributed.
2. The sample drawn is random and independent.

Students' *t*-Distribution

For the large sample tests for mean, we had discussed the statistic as

$Z = \dfrac{\bar{x}-\mu}{\sigma/\sqrt{n}} \sim N(0, 1)$ with usual notations and the curve of distribution was asymptotic. When the population variance σ^2 was not known, we replaced σ^2 by S^2 (the sample variance for small samples) and hence obtained $S^2 = \dfrac{1}{n-1}\Sigma(x-x)^2$ or $ns^2 = (n-1)\,S^2$. We had then replaced σ^2 by S^2 and applied Normal tests. But student *t*-distribution devised by Gosset established that the sampling distribution of the statistic.

$\dfrac{\bar{x}-\mu}{S/\sqrt{n}}$ was applicable to small samples, but it was not near Normal Distribution. He gave a statistic as

$$t = \frac{x-\mu}{S/\sqrt{n}}$$

where $x = \dfrac{\Sigma x}{n}$

and $S^2 = \dfrac{1}{n-1}\sum(x-\bar{x})^2$ is unbiased estimate of the population variance σ^2 Gosset indicated that t-statistic follows student's *t*-distribution with $\nu = (n-1)$ degrees of freedom with probability density function.

$$p(t) = \text{Const.}\ \frac{1}{\left(1+\dfrac{r^2}{\nu}\right)^{(\nu+1)/2}} : -\infty < t < \infty.$$

The constant in this equation is calculated by the area under the probability curve $p(t)$, (total area = 1), given by $\int_{-\infty}^{\infty} p(t)\,dt = 1$

$$\text{Hence Constant} = \frac{1}{\sqrt{\nu}\,\beta\left(\dfrac{1}{2},\dfrac{\nu}{2}\right)}$$

Where $\beta\,(m, n)$ is the Beta function defined by $\beta\,(m, n) = \dfrac{\tau_m \tau_n}{\tau_{(m+n)}}$: $m > 0, n > 0$

Where Gamma $m(\tau_m)$ is given by

$\tau_m = (m-1)\,\tau_{(m-1)}$

and $t_m = (m-1)!$ if m is a positive integer.

A specific test under *t*-distribution has been suggested by making assumptions that the population for the sample drawn should be normally distributed and that the samples drawn are random with observations independent.

Properties of t-Distribution

1. Moments $\mu^1_{(2r+1)}$ (about origin) = 0

μ^1 (about origin) = 0, Mean = 0

$\mu_{(2r+1)}$ (about origin) = $m^1_{(2r+1)}$ (about mean)

$$\mu_{2r} = \frac{(2r-1)(2r-3)\ldots5.3.1}{(v-2)(v-4)\ldots.(v-2r)}$$

$$= \frac{v(2r-1)}{(v-2r)}\mu_{(2r-2)}$$

$$\beta_1 = \frac{\mu_3^1}{\mu_2^1} = 0,\ \beta_2 = \frac{\mu_4}{\mu_2^2} = 3\left(\frac{v-2}{v-4}\right).$$

2. The curve is uninodal with Mean = Median = Mode = 0.

3. *t*-distribution depends only on 'Sample size $v = n - 1$, nor on population parameters for v large. ($v > 30$), *t*-distribution approximates to Normal distribution as can be seen from Fig. 13.6.

> *t*-distribution has few specific properties such as the distribution curve being uninodal and the distribution depends on the sample size (large sample). Also that the distribution varies from $-\infty$ to ∞, it is bell-shaped but more platikurtic than normal distribution, with wider dispersion.

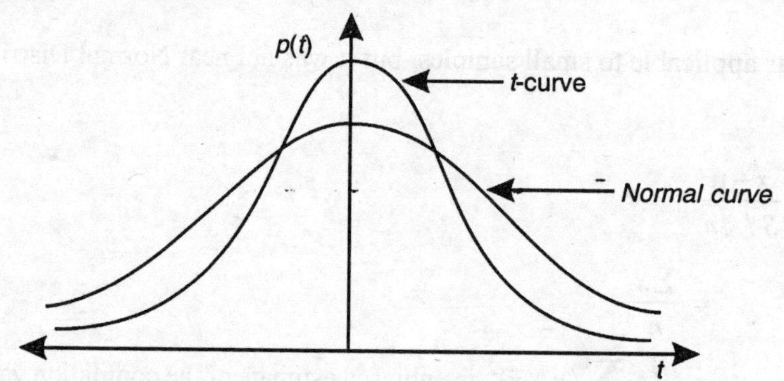

Fig. 13.6 Comparison between Normal and t-curve

4. *t*-distribution varies from $-\infty$ to ∞ as in case of normal distribution

5. *t*-distribution is also bell-shaped and symmetrical about mean zero as in the case of normal distribution.

6 . It is more platikurtic them the normal distribution

7. It has more dispersion than the standard normal distribution

Critical Values of t-Distribution

The critical values of *t*-distribution at level of significance α and required degree of freedom v. for two tail test are given by

$P[|t|] > t_v(\alpha) \quad = \alpha$

or $P[|t|] > t_v(\alpha)\,| \quad = 1 - \alpha$

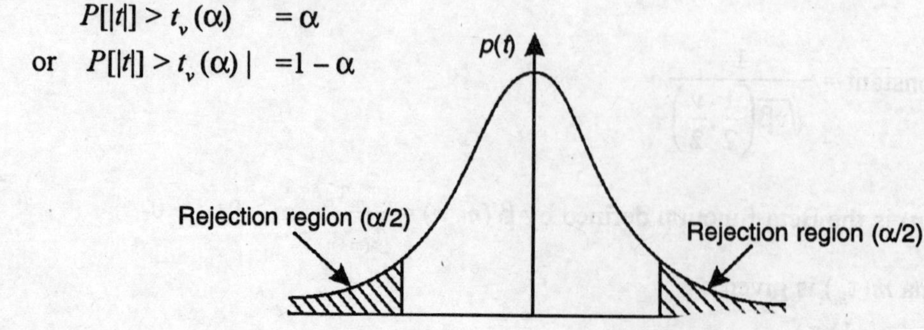

The values of t-distribution have been tabulated by Fisher and Yates for degrees of freedom v and different levels of significance α. These values figure at the end of this book.

Applications of t-Distribution

This distribution can be used in business decisions for the following purposes:

1. t-test for significance of single mean when population variance is not known.

2. t-test for significance of the difference between two sample means, when population variance are equal but not known.

3. t-test for significance of an observed sample correlation coefficient.

t- Tests for Single Mean

We formulate the null hypothesis $H_0 : \mu = \mu_0$ (Poulation mean = μ_0) *i.e.*, when there is significant difference between sample mean and the population mean and the fluctuation is sample fluctuation.

Under H_0, we test the t-statistic

$$t = \frac{\bar{x} - \mu_0}{S / \sqrt{n}}$$

where $$x = \frac{\Sigma x}{n} \text{ and } S^2 = \frac{1}{n-1} - \Sigma (x - x)^2.$$

It follows t-distribution with $(n - 1)$ degrees of freedom. The calculated value of t can then be compared with the tabulated values of t for $(n - 1)$ degrees of freedom at certain level of significance If the calculated value of $| t |$ is greater than the tabulated value of t, the difference is significant and H_0 is rejected and *vice-versa.*

Prof. R.A. Fisher, later defined hiw own t-distribution as

$$t = \frac{X}{\sqrt{Y/n}} \text{ where } X \sim N(0,1)$$

and Y is an independent χ^2-variate with n degrees of freedom.

It follows the student's t-distribution with n degrees of freedom and

$$p(t) = \frac{1}{\sqrt{n}\beta\left(\frac{1}{2}, \frac{n}{2}\right)\left(1 + \frac{t^2}{n}\right)^{(n+1)/2}} ; -\infty < t < \infty.$$

Confidence limits for μ are given by

$$\mu = \bar{x} \pm t_\alpha (v) \times \frac{S}{\sqrt{n}}$$

These can be used for testing of hypotheses. We can use the t-statistic in numerical problem as

$$t = \frac{\bar{x} - \mu_0}{\sqrt{S^2 / n}} = \frac{x - \mu_0}{\sqrt{S^2 / (n-1)}} \sim t_{(n-1)}$$

t-distribution can be used for testing the significance of single mean, when population variance is not known and also for testing the significance of difference of means between two sample means. It can also be utilised to test significance of sample correlation coefficient.

t-Test for Difference of Mean

When we use two independent random samples as $x_1, x_2, \ldots x_n$ and $y_1, y_2, \ldots y_n$ from the given Normal populations having same mean, we set the null hypothesis as $H_0 : \mu_x = \mu_y$.

Under the assumptions $\sigma_x^2 = \sigma_y^2 = \sigma^2$, the test-statistic under these situation is

$$t = \frac{\bar{x} - \bar{y}}{S\sqrt{\frac{1}{n_1} + \frac{1}{n_2}}}$$

and $S^2 = \frac{1}{(n_1 + n_2 - 2)}\left[\Sigma(x-\bar{x})^2 + \Sigma(y-y)^2\right]$ is an unbiased estimate of common population variance σ^2 of the two samples.

We can now compare the calculated value of $|t|$ for $(n_1 + n_2 - 2)$ degrees of freedom at a given level of significance. Null hypothesis H_0 can be accepted if calculated vale of $|t|$ is within the acceptance zone or else rejected.

Professor R.A. Fisher, who suggested the *t*-distribution concept suggested its use under specific situations and accordingly hypothesis testing could be done.

Paired t-Test for Difference of Means

A very special situation can be considered when the sample size of two samples drawn from a Normal population with equal means are same *i.e.*, $n_1 = n_2 = n$ and the two samples are not completely independent.

In such cases, we take $d_i = x_i - y_i$. Under the null hypothesis that the increments are just by chance and not attributable to a particular cause.

Then $H_0 : \mu_x = \mu_y$

The best statistic $t = \frac{d}{S/\sqrt{n}} = \frac{d}{\sqrt{S^2/\sqrt{n}}}$

Where $d_i = x_i - y_i$ and $d = \frac{1}{n}\sum_{i=1}^{n} d_i$

and $S^2 = \frac{1}{(n-1)}\sum(d-\bar{d})^2 = \frac{1}{(n-1)}\left[\sum d^2 - \frac{(\Sigma d)^2}{n}\right]$

t-Test for significance of observed sample correlation coefficient

When we have a random sample (x_i, y_i) of size n drawn from a bivariate Normal Distribution and let r be the correlation coefficient, then our problem is to find if this correlation coefficient r is significant of any correlation between the variable in the population.

Prof. R.A. Fisher proved that under the Null hypothesis $H_0 : \rho = 0$, *i.e.*, the variable are un-correlated in the population. We use statistic.

$$t = \frac{r}{\sqrt{1-r^2}}\left(\sqrt{n-2}\right) \sim t_{n-2}$$

t-follows the student's *t*-distribution with $(n-2)$ degrees of freedom when n is the sample size. 95% confidence limit for ρ.

$$r \pm t_{0.05}(n-2) \times SE(r) = r \pm r_{0.05}(n-2) \times \left(\frac{1-r^2}{\sqrt{n}}\right)$$

F-Distribution

This is another specific distribution for testing of hypothesis based on the sample distribution and it does not involve any population parameter. It depends only on the degrees of freedom n_1 and n_2.

It we take X as a Chi-square variate with n_1 degrees of freedom and Y as the independent Chi-Square variate with n_2 degrees of freedom, then we can define the F-Statistic as

$$F = \frac{X / n_1}{Y / n_2}$$

This distribution follows F-distribution of G.W. Snedecor with probability density function given by

$$p(F) = y_0 \cdot \frac{F^{\left(\frac{n_1}{2}-1\right)}}{\left(1+\frac{n_1}{n_2}F\right)^{\frac{n_1+n_2}{2}}} : 0 \leq F < \infty$$

Where y_0 is a constant, which is determined by the area under the curve of F-distribution, the total area being 1.

$$\text{or} \quad \int_0^{\infty} p(F)\,dF = 1$$

$$\text{and hence} \quad y_0 = \frac{\left(\frac{n_1}{n_2}\right)^{n_1/2}}{\beta\left(\frac{n_1}{2}, \frac{n_2}{2}\right)}$$

Where $\beta\ (m, n)$ is defined in an earlier paragraph.

The Snedecor's F-distribution can be converted into Fisher's Z-distribution. which shall be described later in this chapter.

The F-distribution, suggested by Snedecor is useful for testing of hypothesis based on the sample distribution, without involving any population parameter. Thus it is dependent only on the degress of freedom.

Critical Values of F-Distribution

The area under the curve for F-distribution is defined in the tables given at the end of this book. This tables give the values of the critical region of the F-distribution by the right-tail areas *i.e.* $P[F > F_\alpha(n_1, n_2)] = \alpha$ as shown in Fig. 13.8.

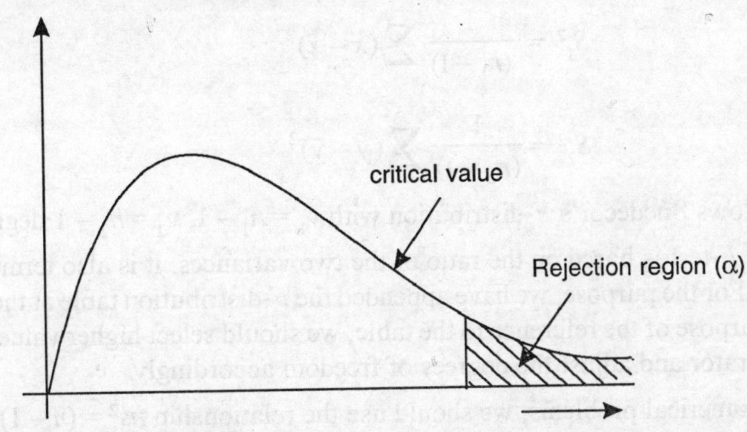

Fig. 13.8 Critical Value of F-Distribution

Main Features of F-Distribution

(*a*) Mean $= \dfrac{n_2}{n_2 - 2}$; $n_2 > 2$

(*b*) $\text{Var}_{(F)} = \simeq 2\left(\dfrac{1}{n_1} + \dfrac{1}{n_2}\right)$

(*c*) Mode $(F) = \dfrac{n_2(n_1 - 2)}{n_1(n_2 + 2)}$ If $F > 0$, Mode exists only if $n_1 > 2$

(*d*) Karl Pearson's Coefficient of Skewness is

$$S_k = \frac{\text{Mean - Mode}}{\sigma} > 0$$

Hence *F*-distribution is highly positively skewed

(*e*) The probability $P(F)$ increases steadily till its peak value (Corresponding to the modal value, which is less than 1) and then decreases slowly to become asymptotic till $F \to \infty$ (*i.e.*, right tail). This is clear from Fig. 13.8.

(*f*) $\dfrac{1}{F} = \dfrac{Y/n_2}{X/n_1} \sim F(n_2, n_1)$ with *F*-distribution of degrees of freedom reversed *i.e.* (n_2, n_1)

F-distribution is gainfully utilised for comparing the variance ratio of two populations. It is used even in case of multiple-correlation, sample correlation ratio, linear regression as well as for testing the equality of several population means.

Applications of F-Distribution

1. ***F*-test** for Equality of Population variances : When we wish to find out if two normal populations have the same variance, we use *F*-test. Let $x_1, x_2, \ldots\ldots x_{n1}$ be a random sample of size n_1 from first population with variance σ_1^2 and $y_1, y_2 \ldots y_{n2}$ from random sample of size n_2 from the second Normal population of variance σ_2^2 (both samples being independent).

   We can formulate the Null hypothesis as $H_0 : \sigma_1^2 = \sigma_2^2 = \sigma^2$.

$$F = \frac{S_1^2}{S_2^2} \sim F(n_1 - 1, n_2 - 1)$$

   Where S_1^2 and S_2^2 are unbiased estimates of the common population variance σ^2 and are given by

$$S_1^2 = \frac{1}{(n_1 - 1)} \sum (x - x)^2$$

   and
$$S_2^2 = \frac{1}{(n_2 - 1)} \sum (y - \bar{y})^2$$

   It follows Snedecor's *F*-distribution with $v_1 = n_1 - 1$, $v_2 = n_2 - 1$ degrees of freedom.

   Since *F*-test is based on the ratio of the two variances. it is also termed as **Variance Ratio Test**. For the purpose, we have appended the *F*-distribution table at the end of this book. For the purpose of the reference to the table, we should select higher value of the variance as the numerator and adjust the degrees of freedom accordingly.

   For numerical problems, we should use the relationship $ns^2 = (n - 1) S^2$

2. ***F*-test** for testing the sample Multiple Correlation

3. **F-test** for testing the significance of observed sample correlation ratio.
4. **F-Test** for testing the linearity of Regression
5. **F-test** for testing the Equality of Several Population Means.

Relation between t, F and χ²-Distribution

t and F-distribution : If a statistic t follows students t-distribution with n degrees of freedom, then its square (t^2) follows Snedecor's F-distribution with (l, n) degrees of freedom.

Thus if $t \sim t_n$, $t_2 \sim F(l, n)$

Thus $F = t^2 = \left[\dfrac{\bar{x} - \mu}{S/\sqrt{n}}\right] \sim F\,(l, n)$ and apply F-test for the best of hypothesis

F and χ²-distribution : $n_1 F = \chi^2$ *i.e.*, $F = \dfrac{\chi^2}{n_1}$

and let $n_2 \to \infty$, then we get χ^2-distribution with n_1 degrees of freedom.

Fisher's Z-Distribution

We have already utilised the t-test for null bypothesis $H_0 : \rho = 0$, to establish that the variables are uncorrelated in the population. In sampling from a bivariate normal population, in which variables are correlated, the distribution of statistic t is not normal even for large samples, Hence R.A. Fisher suggested a transformation from r to a new variable Z (Hence we call it as Z-Transformation also), Such that

$$Z = \frac{1}{2}\log_e\left(\frac{1+r}{1-r}\right)$$

Prof. Fisher proved that even for small samples, the distribution of Z will approximately be normal with mean.

$$\xi = \frac{1}{2}\log\left(\frac{1+\rho}{1-\rho}\right)$$

and variance $1/(n-3)$ *i.e.*,

$$Z = \frac{1}{2}\log\left(\frac{1+\rho}{1-\rho}\right) \sim N\left(\xi, \frac{1}{n-3}\right)$$

This transformation can be used for testing

1.If the correlation coefficient in the population has a specified value

2.If r differes significantly from $\rho = 0$, then t-test may be preferred *i.e.*, $U = \dfrac{Z - \xi}{\sqrt{1/(n-3)}}$ $\sim N(0,1)$

3.If two independent sample correlation coefficients r_1 and r_2 differ significantly

$$Z = \frac{Z_1 - Z_2}{\sqrt{\left(\frac{1}{n_1 - 3}\right) + \left(\frac{1}{n_2 - 3}\right)}} \sim N(0,1)$$

By comparing the value of Z with 1.96 or with 2.58, we may accept or reject the null hypothesis H_0 at 5% or 1% level of significance respectively.

Professor R.A. Fisher also suggested a transformation from Snedecor's t-distribution to Z-distribution. He proved that even for small samples, the distribution of Z will approximately by normal with modified mean. This distribution is used for correlation coefficients.

13.13 ANALYSIS OF VARIANCE (ANOVA)

While discussing Testing of Hypothesis, we have narrated various tests performed to find suitable correlation among various populations either in terms of their means or proportions. We have discussed χ^2– (chi-square) test to examine the difference among more than two sample proportions to find whether these samples have been drawn from populations, each having the same proportion. Now we are trying to obtain the method to test the significance of the differences among more than two sample means. Thus by using a technique called Analysis of Variance (ANOVA), we want to establish and draw inferences whether the samples in use for analysis have come from populations having the same mean.

Let us take the case of decision on the price of a new product to be launched in the market. Why such a decision is required is to ascertain as to what price would be appropriate to achieve best sales. Various price levels are seen to influence the quantities of sales and for the purpose, we select four samples from five different sales markets in randomly situated locations. We record the observations of actual sales for the products with different price tags. For discussion sake, let us record these observations.

Analysis of Variance (ANOVA) is an import method of comparing the variances of the two populations having the same mean. It tests the significance of variation between same mean.

TABLE 13.1. Sales Due to Different Price Levels

	Observations					*Total*	*Mean*
	1	*2*	*3*	*4*	*5*		$\bar{x}$
Price level I	5	7	10	8	5	35	7
Price level II	8	5	8	9	10	40	8
Price level III	5	9	8	7	6	35	7
Price level IV	10	8	9	8	10	45	9

Grand Mean = $\bar{\bar{x}}$ =7.75

This experiment shows that when the price levels vary, the sales volumes vary and the mean sales also vary. Thus we can ascertain that price difference does affect the change in the sales volumes.

Response, Factors and Treatments

In this case, the dependent variable is sales volume and the independent variables are price levels. The dependent variable is also called the **Response** variable and the independent variables (four price levels) are called **Factors**. Different levels of a factor are called Treatments. In the case explained above, we term the sales volume as Response variable whereas the price of the product is a factor. The various price levels (four in this case) are treatments. Now we have to study whether the effects of various treatments is different on the response variable and if so, how to estimate this difference. This is done with the help of a technique called "Analysis of Variance (ANOVA), as described in subsequent paragraphs.

Some other business situations, where this technique is useful are KPL (Kilometre per litre) consumption for different types of petrol grades or testing of training methods for better learning curve or the initial grades of pay offered to students from different Business schools etc.

One-Factor Analysis of Variance

When we wish to study the effect of various treatments of a single factor (say price) on the response variable (say sales), we call it as One-Factor Analysis of Variance. It is also called one-way Analysis of Variance.

In the initial stage, we establish whether there is a significant difference statistically between the treatment means. When we represent

μ = mean of the population of all possible values of and

μ_1, μ_2, μ_3 .. = mean values of the treatments.

From this data, we try and formulate hypothesis for testing. We wish to find whether these four levels of price are forming part of the product range from the same population. The Null hypothesis can be written as

$H_0 \quad : \mu_1 \quad = \mu_2 = \mu_3 .... = \mu$

Against this, the Alternative hypothesis can be written as

$H_1 \quad : \mu_1 \quad \neq \mu_2 \neq \mu_3$ etc.

or else H_1 : at least 2 of μ_1, μ_2, μ_3 etc. are different

i.e. at least two treatments have different effects as the response variable.

The interpretation of results can be used to conclude whether price variation does have an effect on sales or not. Does the price variation significantly affect the sales volumes or not? Thus, if we find that differences among the treatments means are too large to attribute it to chance sampling error, we can infer that the method used to study market response on the product for various price levels does influence the level of sales and hence a suitable price can be adopted for effective launching of the product.

13.14 BASIC CONCEPTS IN ANOVA

For using this technique, we must assume that each of the samples is drawn from a normal population and that each of these populations have the same variance. When sample size is large, even this assumptions may not be necessary as the sample size itself will take care of the results.

In the example taken by us in the previous paragraph, (refer table 13.1) our null hypothesis states that the four populations have the same mean. If it was true, we need not obtain means of individual treatments. We could use the mean for the entire set of observations (20 in numbers) to establish the mean of the population. This overall population also have a variance σ^2.

The important terms used in ANOVA methodology are Response, Factors and Treatments. The relationships of these terms help in drawing the testing to a close decision.

The methodology adopted in the Analysis of variances is based on the comparison of two different estimates of the variance σ^2 for our overall population. One estimate would be examining the variance among the four sample means, which are 7, 8, 7 and 9, whereas the other estimate of the population variance is determined by the variation within the samples themselves *i.e.*

Treatment I : 5, 7, 10, 8 and 5

Treatment II : 8, 5, 8, 9 and 10

Treatment III : 5, 9, 8, 7 and 6

Treatment IV : 10, 8, 9, 8 and 10

Now we can compare these two estimates of the population variance. Both the estimates of σ^2 should approximately, be the same or equal, if null hypothesis is to be true. If the values differ significantly, null hypothesis is not true.

13.15 STEPS IN ANALYSIS OF VARIANCE

For analysis of variance, we adopt the following steps :

1. Determine one estimate of the population variance from the variance among the sample means. This variance is called between - treatment variance.

2 Determine the other estimate of the population variance from the variance within the samples. This is called within - treatment variance *i.e.* variance in response variable for a given treatment.

3. Now compare these two estimates. If these estimates are approximately equal in value, then we accept the Null-hypothesis. If the 'between - treatment variance' is significantly different or larger than the 'within-treatment variance', we can reject the Null hypothesis.

Calculating the Between - Treatment Variance

As per step 1 in the Analysis of Variance, we have to obtain the estimate of variance of the population from the variance between various treatments.

$$\text{Sample variance} = s^2 = \frac{\Sigma(x-\overline{x})}{(n-1)}$$

In this case of between-treatment variance, we have to establish the variation of each treatment mean from the overall grand mean of the observations. Hence the formula undergoes a change as follows :

$$S_{\overline{x}}^2 = \frac{\Sigma(\overline{x}-\overline{\overline{x}})^2}{k-1}$$

where $\overline{x}$ = sample mean for each treatment

$\overline{\overline{x}}$ = grand mean for all observations/population

k = number of treatments (samples)

For 'ANOVA' testing, we follow a systematic approach consisting of various steps and each step is adopted in that sequence. First step is calculating the between-treatment variance.

since standard error of the mean is defined as the standard deviation of all possible samples of a given size, we can write the formula as

$$\sigma_{\overline{x}} = \frac{\sigma}{\sqrt{n}}$$

where $\sigma_{\overline{x}}$ = standard deviation of mean of all sample means

σ = standard deviation of the population

n = sample size

Therefore we can write

$$\sigma^2 = n\,\sigma_{\overline{x}}^2$$

$$= s_{\overline{x}}^2 \times n$$

$$= \sqrt{\frac{(2\times30\times20)\,(2\times30\times20-30-20)}{(30+20)^2(30+20-1)}}$$

This can be calculated, because values of $\overline{x}$ and $\overline{\overline{x}}$ are obtained for k samples, each of size n.

The difficulty experienced in these calculations will arise, where all the samples or treatments are not of the same size. In that case, we can use weighted average system by multiplying each sample value by its own size n_j

$$\text{Thus} \quad \hat{\sigma}_b^2 = \frac{\Sigma n_j\left(\overline{x}_j-\overline{\overline{x}}\right)^2}{(k-1)} = n_1\left(\overline{x}_j-\overline{\overline{x}}\right)^2 + n_2 + \left(\overline{x}_j-\overline{\overline{x}}\right)^2 \ldots\ldots$$

where $\hat{\sigma}_b^2$ = Estimate of the population variance based on the variance among the samples (Between-treatment variance)

n_j = size of the jth sample

$\bar{x}_j$ = sample mean of the j th sample

$\bar{\bar{x}}$ = grand mean

k = number of samples

From the example given in Table 13.1, we can calculate this estimate of variance as follows,

$$\hat{\sigma}_b^2 = 5\Sigma\left(\bar{x}_j - \bar{\bar{x}}\right)^2 \Big/ (k-1)$$

$$= \frac{5\left[(7-7.75)^2 + (8-7.75)^2 + (7-7.5)^2 + (9-7.75)^2\right]}{4-1}$$

$$= 4.58$$

Calculating the Within-Treatment Variance :

While calculating the other estimate of variance *i.e.* Within-Treatment Variance as per step 2, we use the formula for sample means as

$$s^2 = \frac{\Sigma(x-\bar{x})^2}{n-1}$$

Introducing standard error concept

$$\hat{\sigma}_w^2 = \Sigma\left(\frac{n-1}{n-k}\right) s^2$$

when sample sizes are not the same, we an modify the relationship as

$$\hat{\sigma}_w^2 = \Sigma\left(\frac{n_j - 1}{n_T - k}\right) s_j^2$$

where $\hat{\sigma}_w^2$ = second estimate or Within-Treatment Variance

n_j = size of the jth treatment /sample

n_T = Total sample size = Σn_j

k = number of treatments

From the example of Table 13.1, we can now calculate the within treatment variance $\hat{\sigma}_w^2$ as follows

$$\hat{\sigma}_w^2 = \frac{(5-1)\left[\Sigma \dfrac{(x_j-\bar{x})^2}{(n-1)}\right]}{(20-4)}$$

$$= \frac{4}{16} \times \frac{1}{4} [(5-7)^2 + (7-7)^2 + (10-7)^2 + (8-7)^2 + (5-7)^2 + (8-8)^2$$
$$+ (5-8)^2 + (8-8)^2 + (9-8)^2 + (10-8)^2 + (5-7)^2 + (9-7)^2$$
$$+ (8-7)^2 + (7-7)^2 + (6-7)^2 + (10-9)^2 + (8-9)^2 + (9-9)^2$$
$$+ (8-9)^2 + (10-9)^2]$$

$$= \frac{1}{16}[4+1+9+4+9+1+4+4+4+1+1+1+1+1]$$

$$= \frac{46}{16} = 2.9$$

In the second step for ANOVA we calculate the within-treatment variance so that the variances of Step 1 and Step 2 can then be compared.

Finding F-Ratio and Testing of Hypothesis

As per step 3 of the Analysis of variance, we now compare these two estimates so obtained as follows (as per F-ratio)

$$F\text{-Ratio} = \frac{\textit{First or Between Treatment Variance}}{\textit{Second or Within Treatent Variance}}$$

$$= \frac{\hat{\sigma}_b^2}{\hat{\sigma}_w^2}$$

$$= \frac{4.58}{2.9}$$

$$= 1.58$$

Interpreting the F-Ratio

Having obtained the F-ratio as the comparison of'two estimates, we interpret the results. If this ratio is unity, then we accept the null-hypothesis and if not the null-hypothesis is rejected. In this case, the F - ratio is not unity. Hence we reject the Null hypothesis

In Step 3, the two variances, namely between and within treatment, are then compared. The ratio is called F-ratio. For testing or interpreting, the calculated ratio value is then correlated to the Standard F-ratio value from the standard F-tables.

13.16 SUM OF SQUARES METHOD

There is yet another slightly different method for analysis of variance. Instead of calculating the variances of the two steps given above, we can base the analysis on sum of squares only *i.e.* within-treatments and between-treatments.

To test the null hypothesis, we first concentrate on the variations within the treatments *i.e.* $\bar{x}_1, \bar{x}_2$, $\bar{x}_3$ and $\bar{x}_4$ etc and then we consider the variation of these means with the grand mean *i.e.* within treatments values. As discussed earlier, these two variations should not differ significantly, if null hypothesis is to be accepted as true. If the estimates based on these two variations are largely or statistically significantly different, null hypothesis is liable for rejection.

We first calculate sum of the squares between the sample means as follows :

$SS_{(b)}$ = sum of the squares between the treatment means

$$= \Sigma n_p \sum_{r=1}^{r} \left(\bar{x}_p - \bar{\bar{x}}\right) = n_1\left(\bar{x}_1 - \bar{\bar{x}}\right)^2 + n_2\left(\bar{x}_2 - \bar{\bar{x}}\right)^2 + \ldots\ldots..$$

where $SS_{(b)}$ = Sum of the squares between rows or treatments. It is also called Treatment it sum of squares or between-treatment sum of squares

$\bar{x}_p$ = average or mean value at level p (say $x_1 = 7$)

$\bar{\bar{x}}$ = overall mean of the observations

n = number of observations at each treatment level

p = treatment level or treatment levels (*i.e.* 1. 2, 3 or 4)

r = number of treatments

As an example, let us apply the formula to the problem solved by variance method. Here, we have

$$n_p = 5 = n$$

$$\bar{x}_1 = 7 : \bar{x} = 8,\ \bar{x}_3 = 7,\ \bar{x}_4 = 9$$

$$\bar{\bar{x}} = 7.75$$

$$r = 4$$

and, $\quad p = 1, 2, 3 \text{ and } 4$

$$\therefore \quad SS_{(b)} = 5\left[(7-7.75)^2 + (8-7.75)^2 + (7-7.75)^2 + (9-7.75)^2\right]$$

$$= 5[4.33] = 21.65$$

and Mean sum of square (between) $= \dfrac{SS_{(b)}}{df} = \dfrac{21.65}{4-1} = 7.22$ (df = degrees of freedom)

or, $\quad MSS_{(b)} = 7.22$

In the similar manner, the sum of the squares within the treatments can be calculated by the relationship

$$SS_{(w)} = \sum_{i=1}^{np}\sum_{r=1}^{r}\frac{\left(x_{i_p} - \bar{x}_p\right)^2}{(5-1)}$$

where $\quad SS_{(w)}$ = sum of the squares of variations within the treatments. This is calculated within treatment value of sum of the squares

x_{ip} = number of observation at each treatment level

$\bar{x}_{ip}$ = mean of the values of each treatment level

p = number of treatments i.e. 1, 2, 3 or 4 etc

r = number of treatments say 4 etc

By the calculation based on the example quoted above,

$$SS_{(w)} = [(5-7)^2 + (7-7)^2 + (10-7)^2 + (8-8)^2 + (5-8)^2 + (8-8)^2 + (10-9)^2]/(5-1)$$

$$= 46$$

We can now convert sum of the squares (within) also to the Mean sum of the squares by dividing it by degrees of freedom.

$$\therefore \quad MSS_{(w)} = \frac{SS_{(w)}}{df} = \frac{SS_{(w)}}{N-r}$$

$$= \frac{46.0}{20-4}$$

$$= 2.875$$

Now to work out F - ratio, we get

$$F\text{-ratio} = \frac{MSS_{(b)}}{MSS_{(w)}}$$

$$= \frac{7.22}{2.875}$$

$$= 2.53$$

From F-ratio tables, for a degree of freedom of (4,16), we get the value as 3.24 at 95% confidence level.

There is yet another method for ANOVA. It is called 'Sum of Square Method'. But it is based on comparison of Mean sum of squares between and within the treatments to obtain the F-ratio. For testing, standard F-ratio values are used.

The value of F-static indicates that we are well within the range of acceptance of null hypothesis at 95%, confidence level.

We can now convert these calculations to the ANOVA table as follows

TABLE 13.2 AVOVA Table

Source of variation	*Variation sum of the squares*	*Degrees of freedom*	*Variance estimate Mean sum of squares*	*F-ratio*
Between variation (between - treatments)	$SS(b) = \sum n_p\left(\bar{x}_p\bar{x}\right)^2$	$n-1 = 4-1$	$MSS_{(b)} = \frac{SS_{(b)}}{df}$	$\frac{MSS_{(b)}}{MSS_{(w)}}$
	$= 21.65$	$=3$	$= \frac{21.65}{3} = 7.22$	$= \frac{7.22}{2.88} = 2.53$
Within variation	$SS_{(w)} = \sum n_p \frac{(x_p - \bar{x})^2}{n-1}$	$N-k = 20-4$	$MSS(w) = \frac{SS_{(w)}}{df}$	
	$= 46$	$= 16$	$= \frac{46}{16} = 2.875$	
Total variation	$SS_{(T)} = 21.65 + 46$ $= 67.65$	$N-1 = 20-1$ $= 19$		

From the table of F-dislribution, we get the value of F-statistic for degrees of freedom (4. 16), 95% level of confidence as 3.24, which is higher than the value obtained. Thus the value of F - statistic is within the acceptance zone and hence null hypothesis is true or accepted. It is the same result as in case of earlier method.

In case of F-ratio, the concept of Degrees of Freedom is important. The method of calculating and using degrees of freedom for the numerator and denominator of the F-ratio has been described.

13.17 USE OF F-DISTRIBUTION : DEGREES OF FREEDOM

As explained in earlier chapter on testing of hypothesis, each F-distribution would have a pair of degrees of freedom, one for the numerator and the other for the denominator. We should calculate both these degrees of freedom before applying the value of F - statistic from the table as it can be read only with reference to both the degrees of freedom.

For numerator,

Number of degrees of freedom in the numerator of the F - ratio = (number of samples - I)= (k - 1)

Here we have it as (5 - 1) = 4

For denominator,

Number of degrees of freedoft. in the denominator of the F-ratio = $S(n_j - k) = (n_T - k)$

Here we have it as (20 – 4) = 16

Therefore we have read the value of F-statistic at 95% CL, for values of degrees of freedom as (4, 16)

13.18 PRECAUTIONS ABOUT USE OF *F*-RATIO

The discussion about the hypothesis can be useful, only if the samples are representative of the given population under study. In the case that has been discussed, we had only 5 samples each at price variation level and there are only 4 price levels obtained. The results may not have been effective, because the samples are of very small magnitude and if we had large number of samples with large number of observations, the calculations would have been tedious.

In this case, we have also discussed only one factor *i.e.* price level. Hence we call it only One-factor ANOVA or one-way ANOVA. When we introduce number of factors for variation effects, the calculations would be tedious again. But the method just described is fair enough under the situation. Due precautions should be taken while using *F*-ratio for such complex situations (which is the case in large number of business problems).

In case of advanced problems, use of computers is advised, by using appropriate software developed for the purpose. One such software is SAS. We can also use Minitab ANOVA procedure for the purpose.

CHAPTER SUMMARY

Important Terms Used

- **Alpha (α)** : The Probability of a type 1 error.
- **Alternative hypothesis** :The conclusion drawn when the given data does not support the provision of null-hypothesis.
- **Analysis of variance (ANOVA)** : A statistical technique used to test the equality of three or more sample means and to ascertain whether the samples have been obtained from the same population.
- **Beta (β)** : The probability of a type II error.
- **Chi-square distribution** : A family of probability distributions, differentiated by their degrees of freedom, used to test a number of difference hypothesis about variances, proportions and distributional goodness of fit.
- **Confidence Interval**: A range of values that have some specified probability of including the true population parameter value.
- **Confidence level** : The probability that is associated with the interval estimate of a population statistic, including how reliable these are for inclusion in the population parameter.
- **Confidence limits** : The upper and lower boundaries of a confidence interval.
- **Consistent estimator** : An estimator that yields values more closely approaching the population parameter as the sample size increases.
- **Critical value** : The value of the standard statistic, beyond which the null hypothesis is rejected.
- **Contingency table** : A table having designated number of rows and columns, each row corresponding to a level of one variable, the entries in the table being relative frequencies of the combination.
- **Degree of Freedom** : The number of values in a sample we can specify freely once something is known about the sample.
- **Efficient estimator** : An estimator with a smaller standard error than that for some other estimator of the population parameter.
- **Estimate** : A specific value of the estimator.
- **Estimator** : A sample statistic used to estimate a, population parameter.

- ***F*- Distribution :** A family of distributions for two parameters used primarily to test hypothesis regarding their variances.
- **Goodness of fit test:** A statistical test to ascertain whether a significant difference exists between observed frequency distribution and theoretical probability distribution.
- **Hypothesis :** An assumption adopted regarding the population parameter.
- **Interval estimate :** A range of values to estimate a population parameter.
- **Lower-Tailed test :** One-tailed hypothesis-in which a sample value much lower than hypothesis population value will lead the analysis to rejection of the null hypothesis.
- **Null Hypothesis :** The assumptions about the population parameter to be tested for it to be true.
- **One-tailed test:** A hypothesis test, in which there is only one rejection zone *i.e.* when we concern ourselves only for one directional values of the parameter under test.
- **Point estimate :** A single value of the estimate of the population parameter.
- **Power of the test :** A measure to minimise the type II error.
- **Significance level :** A value denoting the percentage of sample values outside certain limits, assuming that the null-hypothesis is correct.
- **Students *t* - distribution** : It is a probability distribution used when sample size is small ($x < 30$) and the population standard deviation is not known.
- **Sufficient estimator**: An estimator that uses all the information available for estimating a particular parameter.
- **Two-tailed test :** A hypothesis test in which the null-hypothesis is rejected, if the sample value is significantly higher or lower than the hypothesized value of the parameter
- **Type I error :** Rejecting a nult hypothesis when it is true.
- **Type II error :** Accepting a nult hypothesis when it is false.
- **Two - sample test :** Hypothesis test based on samples taken from two populations in order to compare their means or proportions.
- **Unbiased estimator :** An estimator of a population parameter that, on average, assumes values above the population parameter and to some extent even below the population parameter.
- **Analysis of Variance (ANOVA) :** A statistical technique used for testing the variation in more than two sample means in order lo establish whether the samples have heen laken from lhe having the same mean.
- **Between-Treatment Variance :** An estimation of the population variance derived from among the sample means.
- **Factors :** Independent parameters affecting a certain business decision
- ***F*- distribution :** A family of distribution differentiated by two parameters (degrees of freedom numerator and degrees of freedom for the denominator) used to lest the hypothesis about variances.
- **F-ratio :** A ratio used in the analysis of variance.
- **Response variable :** The dependent variable in case of ANOVA is culled Response variable
- **Treatment :** The levels of the factors affecting the dependent variable.

Relationship used

- $$\hat{\sigma} = s = \sqrt{\frac{(x-\bar{x})}{(n-1)}}$$

- $\hat{\sigma}_{\bar{x}} = \frac{\hat{\sigma}}{\sqrt{n}} \times \sqrt{\frac{N-n}{N-1}}$
- $\hat{\sigma}_{\bar{p}} = \sqrt{\frac{pq}{n}}$
- $\mu_{\bar{p}} = p$
- $\hat{\sigma}_{\bar{x}} = \frac{\hat{\sigma}}{\sqrt{n}}$ **(for infinite population)**
- $z = \frac{x-\mu}{\sigma_{\bar{x}}}$
- $\hat{\sigma}_{\bar{x}_1-\bar{x}_2} = \sqrt{\frac{\hat{\sigma}_1^2}{n_1} + \frac{\sigma_2^2}{n_2}}$
- $\hat{\sigma}_{\bar{x}_1-\bar{x}_2} = \sqrt{\frac{\hat{\sigma}_1^2}{n_1} + \frac{\sigma_2^2}{n_2}}$
- $s_\rho^2 = \frac{(n_1-1)s_1^2 + (n_2-1)s_2^2}{n_1+n_2-2}$
- $\hat{\sigma}_{\bar{x}_1-\bar{x}_2} = s_p\sqrt{\left(\frac{1}{n_1} + \frac{1}{n_2}\right)}$
- $\hat{\sigma}_{\bar{p}_1-\bar{p}_2} = \sqrt{\left(\frac{p_1q_1}{n_1} + \frac{p_2q_2}{n_2}\right)}$
- $p = \left[\frac{n_1p_1 + n_2p_2}{n_1+n_2}\right]$
- $\chi^2 = \frac{(n-1)_s{}^2}{\sigma^2}$
- **Power of the test = (1 – β) (maximize)** **Where β is type II error**
- $F = \frac{s_1^2}{s_2^2}$
- $F(n, d, \alpha) = \frac{1}{F[d, n, (1-\alpha)]}$ **for upper tail test**
- $f_c = \frac{RT \times CT}{n}$ RT = Row total, CT = column total
- $s_{\bar{\bar{x}}}^2 = \frac{\Sigma(\bar{x} - \bar{\bar{x}})}{k-1}$
- $\sigma^2 = \sigma_{\bar{x}}^2 \times n$

- $$\hat{\sigma}^2_{\bar{x}} = \frac{\Sigma n_j(\bar{x}_j - \bar{\bar{x}})}{(k-1)}$$
- $$\hat{\sigma}^2_{\bar{x}} = \frac{(n_j - 1)}{(n_T - k)} s_j^2$$
- $$F - \text{ratio} = \frac{\hat{\sigma}^2_b}{\hat{\sigma}^2_w}$$
- Degrees of freedom for numerataor = (number of samples – 1) = $(k-1)$
- Degrees of freedom for denominator = $\Sigma(n_j - 1) = n_T - k$

SOLVED PROBLEMS

Problem 13.1

While checking the quality of a product, one particular dimension was varying slightly due to changes in the machine setting, though μ and σ were not much at variation. The target value of mean μ was $\mu_0 = 50$ and $\sigma = 2.5$ Dimensions checked by the inspector based on sample procedure were 43, 1, 50, 41, 53, 52, 47, 54, 51, 45, 48 and 47. Formulate the null hypothesis and test the same.

Solution :

The target value of mean is 50. Hence null hypothesis will be $H_0 : \mu_0 = 50$

If the production is to be guarded against decreasing value of μ, the alternative hypothesis will be $H_1 : \mu_0 < 50$.

For testing the hypothesis, we work out the Standard Normal variate Z.

$$Z = \frac{\bar{x} - \mu_0}{\sigma / \sqrt{n}}$$

Here $$\bar{x} = \frac{\Sigma x}{n} = \frac{43+51+50+41+........47}{12}$$

$= 48.5$

Now $\bar{x} = 48.5, n = 12$ and $\sigma = 2.5$

Hence $$Z = \frac{48.5 - 50}{2.5/\sqrt{12}} = -2.078$$

For a 5% level of significance, the critical region will be

$R : Z \leq -1.645$

But $Z = -2.078 < -1.645$

This means that μ is significantly less than expected. Hence at 5% level of significance H_0 is rejected.

Problem 13.2

In a factory, the following null hypothesis is formulated for its defect levels.

$H_0 \quad : \mu \leq 60$

$H_1 \quad : \mu > 60$

From an inspection report, the samples showed the following values, $n = 16$, $\sigma = 12$ and $\bar{x} = 62$ Test the hypothesis.

Solution :

For the given values, Normal Variate

$$Z = \frac{\bar{x} - \mu}{\sigma / \sqrt{n}}$$

$$= \frac{62 - 60}{12 / \sqrt{16}} = \frac{2 \times 4}{12}$$

$$= \frac{8}{12} = 0.667$$

At 5% level of significance Rejection region will be R : 1.64. The value of Z being less than the Rejection region, the value falls in the acceptance region. Hence H_0 is accepted.

Problem 13.3

In a restaurant, the average sales of Pizzas is 200 per day. Due to a new office building in the vicinity, the sales increased during first 27 days, and these were found to be 205, 215, 216, 220, 225, 236, 240, 241, 245, 250, 216, 240, 238, 204, 217, 219, 225, 235, 196, 193, 215, 168, 190, 216, 218, 222, 219. Discuss that the sales of Pizzas have increased.

Solution :

The average sales figures are 200 per day.

The hypothesis are

$$H_0 : \mu = 200$$

$$H_1 : \mu > 200$$

For the sample sales for 27 days

$$\bar{x} = \frac{\sum x}{n} = \frac{5924}{27} = 219$$

The standard deviation of sample

$$s = \sqrt{\frac{(x_i - \bar{x})^2}{n-1}}$$

$$= \sqrt{\frac{196+16+9+1+36+289+441+484+676+961+9+441+361 +225+4+0+36+256+529+676+16+2601+841+9+1+9+0}{27-1}}$$

$$= 18.73$$

The calculated value of the test statistic will be

$$t = \frac{\bar{x} - \mu}{s / \sqrt{n}} = \frac{219 - 200}{18.73 / \sqrt{27}}$$

$$= \frac{19 \times 5.2}{18.73} = 5.27$$

At 5% level of significance, the rejection region is $|t| \geq 1.711$ (table for t- distribution)

Since value of t falls beyond the rejection region, the hypothesis is rejected in favour of null hypothesis.

Problem 13.4

From a certain process, it was concluded that on the average there are 15 per cent defectives. The new material purchased was used in the process and it was noticed that out of total output of 400 units, 48 were found to be defective. Would you accept the new material?

Solution :

From given data

$$p = \frac{48}{400} = 0.16$$

The test statistic $Z = \frac{\bar{p} - p}{\sqrt{pq/n}}$

$$= \frac{(0.15 - 0.16) \times 20}{\sqrt{0.16 \times 0.84}} = \frac{-0.2}{0.367} = -0.545$$

For 5% level of significance, the rejection region is $R : Z < -1.65$. The tested statistic value is not within this range of rejection.

Hence the hypothesis is accepted.

Problem 13.5

Before an increase in excise duty on tea, 400 people out of a sample of 500 persons were found to be tea drinkers. After an increase in duty, 400 people were tea drinkers in a sample of 600 people. Using standard error of proportion, state whether there is a significant decrease in the consumption of tea. *[Delhi University, M. Com., 1978, C.A. (Inter), May1977]*

Solution :

With Standard Notations, given are

$$n_1 = 500 \text{ and } n_2 = 600$$

$$p_1 = \frac{400}{500} = 0.8 \text{ and } p_2 = \frac{400}{600} = 0.67$$

The null hypothesis is $H_0 : p_1 = p_2$

Alternative hypothesis $H_1 : p_1 > p_2$ or $H_1 : p_1 < p_2$

Under the null hypothesis,

$$Z = \frac{p_1 - p_2}{SE(p_1 - p_2)} = \frac{p_1 - p_2}{\sqrt{PQ\left(\frac{1}{n_1} + \frac{1}{n_2}\right)}}$$

$$\text{Where} \quad P = \frac{n_1p_1 - n_2p_2}{n + n_2} = \frac{400+400}{500+600} = 0.73$$

$$Q = 1 - P = 0.27$$

$$Z = \frac{0.8 - 0.67}{\sqrt{0.73 \times 0.27 \times \left[\frac{1}{500} \times \frac{1}{600}\right]}} = 4.81$$

For 5% level of significance Z > 1.645 and for 1% level of significance Z > 2.33

Calculate value of Z is even greater than 3 (one tail test). Hence it is highly significant change in tea drinking. The null hypothesis is rejected.

Problem 13.6

The average number of defective articles in a certain factory is claimed to be less than the average for all the factories. The average for all the factories is 30.5. A random sample of 100 defective articles showed the following distribution.

Class Limits	*Number*
16 – 20	12
21 – 24	22
26 – 30	20
31 – 35	30
36 – 40	16

Calculate the mean and the standard deviation of the sample and use it to test the claim that the average is less than the figure for all the factories at 5% level of significance. Given $Z(-1.645) = 0.95$. [*C.A. (Inter), May 1979*]

Solution :

Null hypothesis $H_0 : \mu = 30.5$.

Alternative $H_1 : \mu < 30.5$

Table for computing Mean and SD of the Sample

Class Limits	*Number* (*f*)	*Mid pt* (*x*)	$d = \frac{x-28}{5}$	*fd*	*fd*²
16 – 20	12	18	–2	–24	48
21 – 25	22	23	–1	–22	22
26 – 30	20	28	0	0	0
31 – 35	30	33	1	30	30
36 – 40	16	38	2	32	64
	$\Sigma f = N = 100$			$\Sigma fd = 16$	$\Sigma fd^2 = 164$

Hence $\bar{x} = 28 + \frac{5 \times 16}{100} = 28.8$

$$s = i \times \sqrt{\frac{\Sigma fd^2}{N} - \left(\frac{\Sigma fd}{N}\right)^2}$$

$$= 5 \times \sqrt{\frac{164}{100} - \left(\frac{16}{100}\right)^2}$$

$$= 5 \times 1.27 = 6.35$$

Since sample is very large $\sigma^2 = s^2$

$\therefore \quad \sigma = 6.35$

For large sample, we can use normal variate relationship

$$\therefore \quad Z = \frac{\bar{x} - \mu}{\sigma / \sqrt{n}} = \frac{28.8 - 30.5}{6.35 / \sqrt{100}} = -2.67$$

Since $Z < -1.96$, the difference is significant at 5% level of significance for a single tail test. Hence we reject the null hypothesis which means that the claim of the factory about its low defectives level is valid.

Problem 13.7

The mean height of 50 male students who showed above average participation in college athletics was 68.2 inches with a standard deviation of 2.5 inches while 50 male students who showed no interest in such participaation had a mean height of 67.5 inches with a standard deviation of 2.8 inches. Test the hypothesis that male students who participated in college athletics are taller than other male students. *[Delhi University, M.A. (Eco.), 1981]*

Solution :

Given here,

$n_1 = 50,\ \bar{x} = 68.2,\ S_x = 2.5$

$n_2 = 50,\ \bar{y} = 67.5,\ S_y = 2.8$

Null hypothesis $H_0 : \mu_x = \mu_y$

Alternative hypothesis $H_1 : \mu_x > \mu_y$ (right tail test)

Calculating the value of Z,

$$Z = \frac{\bar{x} - \bar{y}}{\sqrt{\frac{S_x}{n_1} + \frac{S_y}{n_2}}} \text{ at } N(0.1)$$

$$= \frac{68.2 - 67.5}{\sqrt{\left(\frac{6.25}{50} + \frac{7.84}{50}\right)}} = 1.3188$$

Since $Z < 1.96$, the difference in the hights of student of two categories is not significant at 5% level of significance. Hence the Null hypothesis is accepted as the data is consistent with Null hypothesis.

Problem 13.8

The figures below are *(a)* the frequencies of a distribution and *(b)* the frequencies of the normal distribution having the same mean standard deviation and total frequency as in *(a)*.

(a) 1, 12, 66, 220, 495, 792, 924, 992, 495, 220, 66, 12, 1

(b) 2, 15, 66, 210, 484, 799, 944, 799, 484, 210, 66, 15, 2

Solution :

We wish to test the null hypothesis that normal distribution is a good fit to the given frequency distribution, which in technical terms, means athat there is no significant difference between the observed frequencies and the theoretical frequencies.

Table for Computation of χ^2

Observed frequency $f_{(o)}$	*Estimated frequency* $f_{(e)}$	$f_{(o)} - f_{(e)}$	$(f_{(o)} - f_e)^2$	$\frac{(f_0 - f_e)^2}{f_e}$
$\left.\begin{matrix}1\\12\end{matrix}\right\}13$	$\left.\begin{matrix}2\\15\end{matrix}\right\}17$	– 4	16	0.94
66	66	0	0	0.00
220	210	10	100	0.48
495	484	11	121	0.25
792	799	– 7	49	0.06
924	944	– 20	400	0.42
792	799	– 7	49	0.06
495	484	11	121	0.25
220	210	10	100	0.48
66	66	0	0	0.00
$\left.\begin{matrix}12\\1\end{matrix}\right\}13$	$\left.\begin{matrix}15\\2\end{matrix}\right\}17$	– 4	16	0.94
N = Σf = 4,096		$\Sigma (f_o - f_e) = 0$		$\left[\frac{\Sigma(f_o - f_e)^2}{f_e}\right] = 3.88$

Thus, $\chi^2 = \Sigma\left[\frac{(f_0 - f_e)^2}{f_e}\right]$

$= 3.88$

And degrees of freedom (*n* being 13)

$= 13 - 1 - 2 - 2 = 8$

It is because we loose 1 degree of freedom for linear constraint, 2 due to estimation of λ and σ^2 and 2 due to pooling of first and last frequencies (<5)

Tabulated value of χ^2 for 8 degrees of freedom at 5% level of significance is 15.507. Calculated value of χ^2 being less, null hypothesis is accepted.

Problem 13.9

We have been given a frequency distribution in the table below. Using the χ^2-test of goodness of fit, verify whether the given distribution follows poisson distribution.

x	:	0	1	2	3	4	5	6	7
$f_{(o)}$	:	10	30	40	50	35	20	10	5

Solution :

In the given situation, we wish to establish that for $f_{i(o)}$ given for the parameter x follows closely the Poisson distribution. Hence null hypothesis will be whether x follows Poisson Distribution for establishing this. We use χ^2 test for goodness of fit,

We work out $\bar{x} = \left(\frac{\Sigma f_i x_i}{\Sigma f}\right)$

$$= \frac{595}{200} \simeq 3$$

For Poisson Probability Distribution using $\lambda = 3$, we calculate the expected frequencies from the expected Poisson Probabilities.

x :	0	1	2	3	4	5	6	7
Poisson Probabilities P_i :	0.050	0.149	0.224	0.244	0.168	0.101	0.050	0.034
Expected frequencies np_i :	10.0	29.8	44.8	44.8	33.6	20.2	10.0	6.8

Now χ^2– is given by

$$\chi^2 = \Sigma \frac{f_{i(o)}^2}{f_{i(o)}} - n$$

$$= \frac{10^2}{10} + \frac{30^2}{29.8} + \frac{40^2}{44.8} + \frac{50^2}{44.8} + \frac{35^2}{33.6} + \frac{20^2}{20.2} + \frac{10^2}{10} + \frac{5^2}{6.8} - 200$$

$= 1.63$

The degrees of freedom $v = k - r - 1$

$= 8 - 1 - 1 = 6$

For level of significance at 5% and degrees of freedom as 6, the tabulated value of $\chi^2 = 12.59$ (see table from the book).

Hence the rejection region is $R : \chi^2 \geq 12.59$

Here the calculated value of χ^2 falls we below the rejection region or in the acceptance region.

Hence the null hypothesis is accepted at 5% level of significance. Hence Poisson Distribution fits well to the given data.

Problem 13.10

A certain drug was administered to 456 males out of a total 720 in a certain locality to test its efficacy against typhoid. The incidence of typhoid is shown below. Find out the effectiveness of the drug against the disease. (The table value of χ^2 for 1 degree of freedom at 5% level of significance is 3.84)

		Infection	*No infection*	*Total*
Administering the drug	:	144	312	456
Without administering the drug	:	192	72	264
Total	:	336	384	720

[*Delhi University, M.B.A.,1977*]

Solution :

We set up the null hypothesis that the two attributes *i.e.* administration of drug and incidence of typhoid are independent *i.e.* the drug is effective against typhoid.

Hence under the hypothesis of independence.

$$f_{i(e)}\ (144) = \frac{336 \times 456}{720} = 212.8$$

$$f_{i(e)}\ (192) = \frac{336 \times 264}{720} = 123.2$$

$$f_{i(e)}\ (312) = \frac{456 \times 384}{720} = 243.2$$

$$f_{i(e)}\ (72) = \frac{384 \times 264}{720} = 140.8$$

Table for Computing the value of χ^2

$f_{i(0)}$	$f_{i(e)}$	$f_{i(0)} - f_{i\,(e)}$	$[f_{i(0)} - f_{i(e)}]^2$
144	212.8	– 68.8	$(68.8)^2$
192	123.2	68.8	$(68.8)^2$
312	243.2	68.8	$(68.8)^2$
72	140.8	–68.8	$(68.8)^2$

Hence $\quad \chi^2 = \Sigma \dfrac{\left[f_{i(o)} - f_{i(e)}\right]^2}{f_{i(e)}}$

$$= (68.8)^2 \left[\frac{1}{212.8} + \frac{1}{113.2} + \frac{1}{243.2} + \frac{1}{140.8}\right]$$

$= 4733.44 \times 0.0240 = 110.60$

Degrees of freedom $= (k-1)\,(l-1) = (2-1)\,(2-1) = 1$

Table value of χ^2 $= 3.84$ for 1 degree of freedom (given)

Since calculated value of χ^2 is >> tabulated value of χ^2, the difference is highly significant. This the null hypothesis is rejected at 5% level of significance. We thus conclude that the drug is highly effective against typhoid.

Problem 13.11

A sample of 20 observations gave a standard deviation 3.72. Is this compatible with the hypothesis that the sample is drawn from a normal population with variance 4.35?

Solution :

Given here $n = 20$, $s = 3.72$, $\sigma^2 = 4.35$. Under the null hypothesis H_0 that the sample is drawn from normal population with $\sigma^2 = 4.35$, we work out χ^2 statistic

$$\chi^2 = \frac{ns^2}{\sigma^2} = \frac{20 \times (3.72)^2}{4.35} = 63.60$$

Table value of $\chi^2_{0.05}$ for $(n-1)$ or. 19 degree of freedom = 30.144

Since χ^2 calculated > χ^2 tabulated, the value difference is highly significant and hence null hypothesis is rejected at 5% level of significance. It shows that the sample has not been drawn from a normal population with $\sigma^2 = 4.35$ (variance).

Problem 13.12

During a contest, the following results were obtained showing the preference of judges in terms of marks allocated to various contestants.

Contestants	*Judge No. 1*	*Judge No. 2*
1	9	7
2	6	5
3	2	4
4	6	7
5	5	3
6	9	5
7	6	7
8	8	7
9	2	5
10	6	8
11	8	8
12	9	9
13	5	6
14	4	6
15	3	5
16	5	6
17	9	7
18	8	8
19	6	5
20	7	6

From the above data, work out the effectiveness of the grading procedure.

Solution :

From the data, we work out the proportion (p) of the positive signs, by assigning positive signs to the contestants awarded higher grades / marks by judge 1 than judge 2. Thus we get the following data :

Contestant No.	*Positive or Negative*
1	9 – 7 = + 2 (+) sign
2	6 – 5 = + 1 (+) sign
3	2 – 4 = – 2 (–) sign
4	6 – 7 = – 1 (–) sign
5	5 – 3 = +2 (+) sign
6	9 – 5 = + 4 (+) sign
7	6 – 7 = – 1 (–) sign
8	8 – 7 = + 1 (+) sign
9	2 – 5 = –3 (–) sign

(Contd...)

10	$6 - 8 = -2$ (–) sign
11	$8 - 8 = 0$ (0) sign (unusable)
12	$9 - 9 = 0$ (0) sign (unusable)
13	$5 - 6 = -1$ (–) sign
14	$4 - 6 = -2$ (–) sign
15	$3 - 5 = -2$ (–) sign
16	$5 - 6 = -1$ (–) sign
17	$9 - 7 = +2$ (+) sign
18	$8 - 8 = 0$ (0) sign (unusable)
19	$6 - 5 = +1$ (+) sign
20	$7 - 6 = +1$ (+) sign

Counting the plus signs (out of 17 usable observations), $p = \frac{8}{17} = 0.47$

Hence $q = 1 - p = 1 - 0.47 = 0.53$ and $n = 20$

Now we test the null hypothesis $H_0 : p = 0.5$

and $H_1 : p \neq 0.5$

Here sample proportion is $P = \frac{8}{20} = 0.4$

$$\therefore \quad Z = \frac{P - p}{\sqrt{\frac{pq}{n}}} = \frac{0.4 - 0.47}{\sqrt{\frac{0.47 \times 0.53}{20}}}$$

$$= -\frac{0.07}{0.12}$$

$$= -0.583$$

At 5% level of significance $-1.645 \leq Z \leq 1.645$

The value of Z (calculated) falls within the range of acceptance. Hence the null hypothesis is accepted. Thus both the judges have no perceivable difference in their grading system.

Problem 13.13

Given two samples having the following observation values, establish the sample belonging to the ne population or from identical population using Mann-Whitney U-test.

X : 450, 750, 925, 820, 770, 650, 575, 975, 1050, 1450

Y : 775, 475, 580, 900, 625, 525, 1050, 450, 820, 1160

Solution :

For using Mann Whitney U-test, for null hypothesis that both the samples x and y come from the same or identical population, we first arrange the pooled observations of x and y in the ascending order;

Thus the pooled information in ascending order is as follows.

Observation	*Rank*	*Series*	*Observation*	*Rank*	*Series*
450	1.5	X	775	11	Y
450	1.5	Y	820	12.5	X
475	3	Y	820	12.5	Y
525	4	Y	900	14	Y
575	5	X	925	15	X
580	6	Y	975	16	X
625	7	Y	1050	17.5	X
650	8	X	1050	17.5	Y
750	9	X	1160	19	Y
770	10	X	1450	20	X

Now we can list out the ranks for each series.

Ranks for X : 1.5, 5, 8, 9, 10, 12.5, 15, 16, 17.5, 20

Ranks for Y : 1.5, 3, 4, 6, 7, 11, 12.5, 14, 17.5, 19

The sum of ranks for $X = 114.5$

The sum of ranks for $Y = 95.5$

For the two samples, we have $n_1 = 10, n_2 = 10$; $R_1 = 114.5, R_2 = 95.5$

$\therefore$ U-statistic is given by

$$U = n_1 n_2 + \frac{n_1(n_1+1)}{2} - R_1$$

$$= \left[10 \times 10 + \frac{10 \times 11}{2}\right] - 114.5$$

$$= 110.5 - 114.5 = -4.0$$

The mean of the U-statistic $= \dfrac{n_1 n_2}{2} = \dfrac{10 \times 10}{2} = 50$

and SD of U-statistic $= \sqrt{\dfrac{n_1 n_2 (n_1 + n_2 + 1)}{12}}$

$$= \sqrt{\frac{10 \times 10(10+10+1)}{12}} = 10.22$$

From the values of mean and standard deviation, we now calculate the value of Z (as $n_1 = n_2 =$ 10) for U = – 4

$$\therefore\ Z = \frac{-4-50}{13.22} = -4.1$$

The value of Z falls well outside the limite of acceptance zone for 5% level of significance ($-1.645 \leq Z$).

Hence, the null hypothesis is rejected.

Problem 13.14

In a class, there are 30 boys and 20 girls. These students are selected for getting into the bus for the picnic according to their pattern of arrival as given below.

G, B, G, G, G, B, B, B, G, B, G, B, B, G, G, G, B, G, G, B, B, G, B, B, B, G, B, B, G, G, B, B, G, G. B, B, B, G, G, B, B, B, B, G, B, B, B,'B, B, B.

From this sequence of arrival, can we conclude, if the arrival pattern is random?

Solution :

In this case, we have to establish the null hypothesis that the students arrive in a random manner.

Here n_1 = 30 Boy

n_2 = 20 Girls.

r = number of runs = 24

Since n_1 and n_2 are greater than 10, the normal approximation can be used for sample distibution.

$$E(r) = \frac{2n_1 + n_2}{n_1 + n_2} + 1$$

$$= \frac{2 \times 30 \times 20}{30 + 20} + 1 = 25$$

$$SD(r) = \sqrt{\text{Var}(r)}$$

$$= \sqrt{\frac{2n_1n_2(2n_1n_2 - n_1 - n_2)}{(n_1 + n_2)^2(n_1 + n_2 - 1)}}$$

$$= \sqrt{\frac{(2 \times 30 \times 20)\,(2 \times 30 \times 20 - 30 - 20)}{(30 + 20)^2(30 + 20 - 1)}}$$

$$= \sqrt{\frac{1200 \times 1150}{2500 \times 49}}$$

$$= 3.35$$

$$Z \text{ statistic} = \frac{r - E(r)}{\sqrt{\text{Var}(r)}} = \frac{24 - 25}{3.35}$$

$$= -0.299$$

For 5% level of significance, acceptance region is - 1.645 ≤ Z. Hence, the calculated value of Z falls in acceptance region. Hence, H_o is accepted.

Problem 13.15

We wish to conduct a survey for preference of certain colours (shades) of cars in order to devise a customer satisfaction policy. The survey indicates the following results.

Shade	***Preference by customers (Nos.)***
White	150
Baize	70
Light Blue	140
Dark Brown	90

Do these results indicate a strong preference towards a shade?

Solution :

We formulate the null hypothesis H_o : no preference for a shade. In order to establish hypothesis, let us work out the results using Kolmogorov-Smirnou One Sample Test with the n = 450 (given). We first calculate the test Stastistic.D) for the data given above.

Shade Preferred	*No. of Customers Liking the Shade (f)*	*Perference Probability*	*Cumulative Theoretical Probability $F_o(x)$*	*Observed Cumulative Probability $S_n(x)$*
White	150	0.333	0.25	0.333
Baize	70	0.156	0.50	0.489
Light Blue	140	0.311	0.75	0.800
Dark Brown	90	0.200	1.00	1.000

Calculating values of $D = [F_o(x) - S_n(x)]$, we get,

for White colour $D_w = 0.083$

for Baize $D_b = 0.01$

for light blue $D_{lb} = 0.05$

for dark brown $D_{db} = 0.00$

The Calculated Cumulative Value of $D = D_w + D_b + D_{lb} + D_{db}$

$= 0.083 + 0.011 + 0.05$

$= 0.144$

$$\text{The Critical Value of D} = \frac{1.36}{\sqrt{n}}$$

$$= \frac{1.36}{450} = 0.064$$

Since the calculated value ot D exceeds the critical value of D, the null hypothesis H is rejected. Thus the prospective car buyers show significant preference for various shades.

Problem 13.16

Ten Cartons are taken at random from an automatic filling machine. The mean net weight of cartons is 11.8 oz and the standard deviation is 0.15 oz. Does the sample mean differ significantly from the intended weight of 12 oz ? you are given for $\nu = 9$, $t_{0.05} = 2.26$.

[Delhi University, M.B.A. 1977]

Solution :

Given in the problem, we have $n = 10$, $\bar{x} = 11.8$ oz, $s = 0.15$ oz and $\mu = 12$ oz. We formulate the null hypothesis as

$$H_0 : \mu = 12 \text{ oz.}$$

Alternative hypothesis $H_1 : \mu \neq 12$ oz.

For testing, we work out t-statistic (small sample size)

$$t = \frac{\bar{x} - \mu}{\sqrt{S^2 / n}}$$

$$= \frac{\bar{x} - \mu}{\sqrt{s^2 / (n-1)}}$$

$$= \frac{11.8 - 12}{\sqrt{0.15 / (10-1)}} = -4.0$$

The tabulated value of t for $(n - 1)$ *i.e.*, $v = 9$ degrees of freedom is given to us as 2.26 at 5% level of significance.

Since calculated $|t|$ is greater than the tabulated value, this is outside the acceptance zone. Hence the null hypothesis is rejected at 5% level of significance, which means that the sample mean differs significantly from the population mean, $\mu = 12$ oz.

Problem 13.17

The means of two random samples of size 9 and 7 are 196.42 and 198.82 respectively. The sum of the squares of the deviations from the mean are 26.94 and 18.73 respectively. "Can the samples be considered to have been drawn from the same normal population?

[AIMA (Dip. in Mgmt.), August 1979]

Solution :

The given information can be written as

$n_1 = 9$; $\bar{x} = 196.42$ and $\Sigma (x - \bar{x})^2 = 26.94$

$n_2 = 7$; $\bar{y} = 198.82$ and $\Sigma (y - \bar{y})^2 = 18.73$

Now Null hypothesis is formulated as

Null hypothesis $H_0 : \mu_x = \mu_y$

Alternative hypothesis $H_1 : \mu_x \neq \mu_y$

Under the null hypothesis, the t-statistic is given by

$$t = \frac{\bar{x} - \bar{y}}{S \Big/ \sqrt{\frac{1}{n_1} + \frac{1}{n_2}}}$$

and
$$S^2 = \frac{1}{(n_1 + n_2 - 2)} \left[\Sigma(x - \bar{x})^2 + \Sigma(y - \bar{y})^2 \right].$$

$$= \frac{1}{(9 + 7 - 2)} [26.94 + 18.73]$$

$$= 3.26$$

Hence
$$t = \frac{196.42 - 198.82}{\sqrt{3.26 \Big/ \left[\frac{1}{9} + \frac{1}{7} \right]}}$$

$$= -2.64$$

Tabulated value of t for $(n_1 + n_2 - 2) = 14$ degrees of freedom at 5% level of significance is 2.15

Since calculated $|t|$ is greater than tabulated value of t, the null hypothesis is rejected.

Problem 13.18

An IQ test was administered to 5 persons before and after they were trained. The results are given below

Candidates	:	I	II	III	IV	V
IQ before training	:	110	120	123	132	125
IQ after training	:	120	118	125	136	121

Test whether there is any change in IQ after the training programmes, given $t_{0.01}(n) = 4.6$

[C.A. (Inter), May 1980]

Solution :

We have two dependent small samples of sizes $n_1 = n_2 = 5$ and these are paired together due to cause of training. We wish to test the null hypothesis $H_0 : \mu_1 = \mu_2$.

The test statistic $t = \dfrac{\bar{d}}{S/\sqrt{n}}$

Given here $d_1 = 110 - 120 = -10$

Similarly $d_2 = 2, d_3 = -2, d_4 = -4, d_5 = 4$

$$\therefore \bar{d} = \frac{\Sigma d}{n} = \frac{-10+2+2-4+4}{5}$$

$$= -2$$

$$\text{and } S^2 = \frac{1}{(n-1)}\left[\Sigma d^2 - \frac{(\Sigma d)^2}{n}\right]$$

$$= \frac{1}{4}\left[140 - \frac{100}{5}\right] = 30$$

$$\therefore t = \frac{\bar{d}}{S/\sqrt{n}} = \frac{-2}{30/(\sqrt{5})} = 0.149$$

The calcualted value of t is 0.149, which is much smaller than the tabulated value given for 1% level of significance at 4 degrees of freedom. Hence the Null hypothesis is accepted *i.e.*, there is no significant change in the IQ before and after the training.

Problem 13.19

A random sample of 27 pairs of obsrevations from a normal population gives a correlation coefficient of 0.42. Is it likely that the variables in the population are uncorrelated ?

[Bombay University, B.Com., 1976]

Solution :

Given in the problem $n = 27$ and $r = 0.42$

We get null hypothesis as $H_0 : \rho = 0$ and $H_1 : \rho \neq 0$.

We calculate test statistic $t = \dfrac{r \times \sqrt{n-2}}{\sqrt{1-r^2}} = \dfrac{0.42\sqrt{25}}{\sqrt{1-(0.42)^2}} = 2.31$

From the tables, the $t_{0.05}$ for 5% level of significance at 25 degrees of freedom is 2.06, which is less than the calculated t-value. Hence the null hypothesis is rejected at 5% level of significance.

Problem 13.20

The time taken by workers in performing a job by Method I and Method II is given below:

Method I : 20 16 26 27 23 22

Method II : 27 33 42 35 32 34 38

Do the data show that the variance of the time distribution from population from which these samples are drawn donot differ significally? *[AIMA (Dip. in Mgmt.), July /978]*

Solution :

We can formulate the null hypothesis as

$H_0 : \sigma^2{}_1 = \sigma^2{}_2$

Now to compute sample variances, we tabulate the observations

Method I

x	$d_1 = x - 22$	d_1^2
20	– 2	4
16	– 6	36
26	4	16
27	5	25
23	1	1
22	0	0
	$\Sigma d_1 = 2$	$\Sigma d_1{}^2 = 82$

Method II

y	$d_2 = y - 35$	d_2^2
27	– 8	64
33	– 2	4
42	7	49
35	0	0
32	– 3	9
34	– 1	1
38	3	9
	$\Sigma d_2 = -4$	$\Sigma d_2{}^2 = -136$

Calculating Sample Variances

$$S_1^2 = \frac{1}{(n_1 - 1)} \Sigma(x - \bar{x})^2 = \frac{1}{(n_1 - 1)}\left[\Sigma d_1^2 - \frac{(\Sigma d_1)^2}{n_1}\right]$$

$$= \frac{1}{5}\left[82 - \frac{4}{6}\right] = 16.266$$

$$S_2^2 = \frac{1}{(n_2-1)}\Sigma(y-\bar{y})^2 = \frac{1}{(n_2-1)}\left[\Sigma d_2^2 - \frac{(\Sigma d_2)^2}{n_2}\right]$$

$$= \frac{1}{6}\left[136 - \frac{16}{7}\right] = 22.286$$

Since $S_2^2 > S_1^2$, we use S_2^2 in the numerator, with reversed df.

$$\therefore \; F = S_2^2/S_1^2 = \frac{22.286}{16.266} = 1.37 \text{ at degrees of freedom } (6.5).$$

From the F tables, the tabulated value of $F_{0.05}$ (6,5) = 4.95

Since the calculated value of F is less than the tabulated value at 5% level of significance the null hypothesis $H_0 : \sigma_1^2 = \sigma_2^2$ is accepted, to conclude that the variability of the time distributions in the two populations is the same.

Problem 13.21

If we use a random sample of 20 observations (pairs) with $r = 0.5$, can we suggest that this sample has been drawn from a population (bivariate) having a correlation coefficient as 0.6? Work out 95% confidence limits for the population correlation coefficients.

Solution :

Given data indicate $n = 20$ and $r = 0.5$

We formulate the Null-hypothesis as $H_0 : \rho = 0.6$

Alternative hypothesis $H_1 : \rho \neq 0.6$

Calculating the Z-statistic from the above data

$$Z = \frac{1}{2}\log_e\left(\frac{1+r}{1-r}\right)$$

$$= 1.1513 \log_{10}\left(\frac{1+r}{1-r}\right)$$

$$= 1.1513 \log_{10}\left(\frac{1.5}{0.5}\right) = 0.5493$$

$$\xi = 1.1513 \log_{10}\left(\frac{1+\rho}{1-\rho}\right)$$

$$= 1.1513 \log_{10}\left(\frac{1.6}{0.4}\right) = 0.6932$$

Under H_0, the test statistic

$$U = \left(\frac{Z-\xi}{\sqrt{1/(n-3)}}\right) \sim N(0,1)$$

$$= (0.5493 - 0.6932) \times \sqrt{17}$$

$$= -0.5933$$

Since $|U| < 1.96$, it is not significant at 5% level of significance or 95% confidence level, 95% confidence limits for ρ are

$$|U| \leq 1.96$$

$$\text{or } |Z-\xi| \leq 1.96 \times \frac{1}{\sqrt{n-3}} = 0.4754$$

Thus ξ limits are

$$0.5493 - 0.4754 \leq \xi \leq 0.5493 + 0.4754$$

$$\text{or } 0.0739 \leq \xi \leq 1.0247$$

$$\text{when } \quad \xi = 0.0739 = \frac{1}{2} \log\left(\frac{1+\rho}{1-\rho}\right)$$

$$= 1.1513 \log_{10}\left(\frac{1+\rho}{1-\rho}\right)$$

$$\therefore \quad = \rho = 0.07$$

$$\text{When } \quad \xi = 1.0247 = 1.1513 \log_{10}\left(\frac{1+\rho}{1-\rho}\right)$$

$$\text{Then } \quad \rho = 0.77$$

Thus 95% confidence limits for ρ are 0.07 to 0.77

Problem 13.22

A doctor has a large number of patients waiting for consultation. A patient noted that each time he come to meet the doctor, he had to wait 5, 7, 15, 10, 8, 20, 15, 18, 12 and 14 minutes before getting his turn to go inside the doctor's chamber. Doctor has generally indicated that patient does not have to wait for him for more than 15 minutes. Using the sign test, establish the waiting criteria of the doctor at 5% level of significance.

Solution :

For formulation of testing hypothesis

$H_0 : \mu = 15$

$H_1 : \mu < 15$

and given $\alpha = 0.05$

Replacing the differences with +or –sign, we get

$d_1 = x_1 - 15 = 5 - 15 = -10$ minus

$d_2 = x_2 - 15 = 7 - 15 = -8$ minus

$d_3 = x_3 - 15 = 5 - 15 = -0$ minus

$d_4 = x_4 - 15 = 10 - 15 = -5$ minus

$d_5 = x_5 - 15 = 8 - 15 = -7$ minus

$d_6 = x_6 - 15 = 20 - 15 = +5$ minus

$d_7 = x_7 - 15 = 16 - 15 = +1$ minus

$d_8 = x_8 - 15 = 18 - 15 = +3$ minus

$d_9 = x_9 - 15 = 12 - 15 = -3$ minus

$d_{10} = x_{10} - 15 = 14 - 15 = -1$ minus

Here value greater than 15 are 3

Now H_0 is to be rejected in favour of H_1, only if

$H_0 : p = 0.5$
$H_1 : p < 0.5$

Here $p = \frac{3}{9} = 0.33$ (Since one valued d_3 is ignored)

$$\therefore \quad z = \frac{x - np}{\sqrt{npq}}$$

$$= \frac{x - n/2}{\sqrt{\frac{n}{4}}} \quad \left(\text{Since } p = q = \frac{1}{2}\right)$$

$$= \frac{3 - 4.5}{1.5}$$

$$= -1$$

Since the tabulated value of z at 0.05 level of significance is – 1.64, the contention of the doctor is established *i.e.*, H_0 accepted.

Problem 13.23

Using the data in problem 13.22, test the hypothesis using Wilcoxon Signed rank test.

Solution :

The given data can be organised in the following manner.

x_i	:	5	7	15	10	8	20	16	18	12	14
D_i	:	−10	−8	0	−5	−7	5	1	3	−3	−1
Ranks	:	9	8		5.5	7	5.5	1.5	3.5	3.5	1.5

Now $s_+ = 5.5 + 1.5 + 3.5 = 10.5$

$s_- = 9 + 8 + 5.5 + 7 + 3.5 + 1.5 = 34.5$

Here s = smaller value of s_+ *i.e.* $s = 10.5$

Since $s_+ < s_-$, U_{s+} + or $U_s = \frac{n(n+1)}{4}$

$$= \frac{9(9+1)}{4} = 22.5$$

$$\therefore \quad z = \frac{s - U_{s\_}}{T_{s\_}} = 22.5$$

Since $T_s^2 = \frac{n(n+1)(2n+1)}{24} = \frac{9(9+1)(18+1)}{24}$

$\therefore \quad T_s = 7.8$

$$\therefore \quad z = \frac{3.35 - 22.5}{7.8}$$

$$= 1.53$$

Since value of z at 0.05 level of significance is 1.64 the statistic completed is written the acceptance zone and hence H_0 is accepted

Problem 13.24

For the given tabulated values, test the hypothesis that the samples have been taken from the population with same distribution and that at 5% level of significance, there is no appreciable or significant difference in the parameter value

Sample No.	*Values of parameters*		
	1	2	3
1	11	12	14
2	14	12	17
3	16	15	12
4	12	14	16
5	10	12	13

Solution :

Hypothesis $H_0 : \mu_1 = \mu_2 = \mu_3$

$H_1 : \mu_1 \neq \mu_2 \neq \mu_3$

given $\alpha = 0.05$

For calculation of test statistic

$H' = H/C$

where $H = \dfrac{12}{n(n+1)}\left[\Sigma\dfrac{t_i^2}{n_i}\right] - 3(n+1)$

and $C = 1 - \dfrac{\Sigma(0_j^3 - 0_j)}{n^3 - n}$

Parameter	1			Parameter	1	2	3
Value	10			Value	12	12	12
Rank	1			Rank	5	5	5
Parameter	1			Parameter	3		
Value	11			Value	13		
Rank	2			Rank	8		
Parameter	1,	2,	3	Parameter	2		
Value	14,	14,	14	Value	15		
Rank	10	10	10	Rank	12		
Parameter	1	3		Parameter	3		
Value	16	16		Value	17		
Rank	13.5	13.5		Rank	5		

$\therefore\ t_1 = 1 + 5 + 2 + 10 + 13.5 = 31.5$

$t_2 = 5 + 10 + 12 = 27$

$t_3 = 5 + 8 + 10 + 13.5 + 15 = 51.5$

Total $= 31.5 + 27 + 51.5 = 110$

$$\therefore\ H = \frac{12}{15(15+1)}\left[\frac{(31.5)^2}{5}+\frac{(27)^2}{5}+\frac{(51.5)^2}{5}\right]-3(15+1)$$

$$= 4.25$$

$$\text{and } C = 1-\left[\frac{(3^3-3)+(3^3-3)+(3^3-3)+(2^3-2)+(2^3-2)}{15^3-15}\right] = 0.975$$

$$\therefore\ H' = \frac{4.25}{0.975} = 4.35$$

For $\upsilon = 3-1 = 2$, and $\alpha = 0.05$, the tabulated value of $\chi^2_{0.05} = 5.99$. Hence H_0 is accepted.

Problem 13.25

The data given below pertain to a research work carried out to establish the effectiveness of a learning course conducted by a consultant for a business organization (given are the marks obtained by three groups so formed, after the course terminated)

Persons	*Marks Obtained*			
	Test I	*Test II*	*Test III*	*Test IV*
1	45	50	51	47
2	35	51	48	39
3	40	48	45	45
4	38	45	38	38
5	40	35	39	38
6	37	38	42	42
7	41	40	43	40

Establish whether results achieved show the training method to be effective

Solution :

The problem can be solved by the technique of ANOVA so as to establish that the variation in the level of learning produced in the form of marks obtained is significant or not, such that the effectiveness of the training course can be commented upon.

We first obtain the mean of each test *i.e.* $\bar{x}_1$, $\bar{x}_2$, $\bar{x}_3$ and $\bar{x}_4$

$$\bar{x}_1 = \frac{45+35+40+38+40+37+41}{7} = 39$$

$$\bar{x}_2 = \frac{50+51+48+45+35+38+40}{7} = 43.8$$

$$\bar{x}_3 = \frac{51+48+45+38+39+42+43}{7} = 43.7$$

$$\bar{x}_4 = \frac{47+39+45+38+38+42+40}{7} = 41.3$$

The grand mean= $\bar{\bar{x}} = \dfrac{\Sigma \bar{x}}{k}$

$$= \frac{39 + 43.8 + 43.7 + 41.3}{4}$$

$$= 42$$

Now we obtain the values of between - treatments and within - treatments variances

$$\hat{\sigma}_b^2 = n\Sigma \frac{\left(\bar{x}_p - \bar{\bar{x}}\right)^2}{(k-1)}$$

$$= \frac{7}{4-1}\left[(39-42)^2 + (43.8-42)^2 + (43.7-42)^2 + (41.3-42)^2\right]$$

$$= 39.25$$

$$\hat{\sigma}_w^2 = \frac{4-1}{[(7\times4)-4]}\left[(45-39)^2 + (35-39)^2 + (40-39)^2 + (38-39)^2\right.$$
$$+ (40 - 39)^2 + (41 - 39)^2 + (50 - 43.8)^2 + (51 - 43.8)^2 + (48 - 43.8)^2$$
$$+ (45 - 43.8)^2 + (35 - 43.8)^2 + (38 - 43.8)^2 + (40 - 43.8)^2 + (51 - 43.7)^2$$
$$+ (48 - 43.7)^2 + (45 - 43.7)^2 + (38 - 43.7)^2 + (39 - 43.7)^2 + (42 - 43.7)^2$$
$$+ (43 - 43.7)^2 + (47 - 41.3)^2 + (39 - 41.3)^2 + (45 - 41.3)^2 + (38 - 41.3)^2$$
$$\left.+ (38 - 41.3)^2 + (42 - 41.3)^2 + (40 - 41.3)^2\right]$$

$$= \frac{3}{24}\ [36 + 16 + 1+1+1+4+38.5+51.8+23+1.4+77.5+33.6$$
$$+14.4+53.3+18.5+1.7+32.5+22+2.9+0.5$$
$$+32.5+5.3+13.7+5.3+5.3+0.5+1.7]$$

$$= \frac{1}{8} \times 495.4 = 61.92$$

$\therefore \qquad F - \text{ratio} = \dfrac{\hat{\sigma}_b^2}{\hat{\sigma}_w^2}$

$$= \frac{39.25}{61.92} = 0.63$$

Since the ratio is far away from unity, the null hypothesis that the results for all the seven persons are consistent, is rejected.

Problem 13.26

In the given data, daily production levels of 16 persons are available as follows.

Training Method	*Daily outputs in number of units*					
A	15	18	11	19	22	
B	17	22	21	18	27	
C	15	16	24	22	19	18

Check, if the training method has been effective

Solution :

We çan establish the efficacy of the training method by comparing variances of production obtained by these persons

We calculate means of production by each method.

For Method A, $\bar{x}_A = \dfrac{15+16+11+19+22}{5} = 17$

For Method B, $\bar{x}_B = \dfrac{17+22+21+18+27}{5} = 21$

For Method C, $\bar{x}c = \dfrac{15+16+24+22+19+18}{6} = 19$

Also, $\bar{\bar{x}}$ = grand mean = 19

we state the hypithesis on follows :

$H_0 : \mu_1 = \mu_2 = \mu_3$ (null hypothesis)

$H_1 = \mu_1 \neq \mu_2 \neq \mu_2$ (alternative hypothesis)

For establishing the above hypotheses results, we adopt ANOVA technique, where

$$\hat{\sigma}_b^2 = \frac{\sum n_j(\bar{x}-\bar{\bar{x}})^2}{(k-1)}$$

and $$\hat{\sigma}_w^2 = \Sigma(\bar{x}-\bar{\bar{x}})^2\left[\frac{n'_j-1}{n_T-k}\right]$$

Now, we calculate these values from the table below.

n	$\bar{\bar{x}}$	$\bar{x}$	$(\bar{x}-\bar{\bar{x}})$	$[\bar{x}-\bar{\bar{x}}]^2$	$n[\bar{x}-\bar{\bar{x}}]^2$
5	19	17	17–19 = –2	4	5 × 4 = 20
5	19	21	21 – 19 = 2	4	5 × 4 = 20
6	19	19	19 – 19 = 0	0	6 × 0 = 0

$$\therefore \sum n[\bar{x}-\bar{\bar{x}}] = 20 + 20 + 0 = 40.$$

$$\hat{\sigma}_b^2 = \frac{\sum n[\bar{x}-\bar{\bar{x}}]^2}{k-1}$$

$$= \frac{40}{3-1} = 20$$

$$s_1^2 = \frac{\Sigma(x-\bar{x})^2}{n-1}$$

$$= \frac{70}{5-1} = 17.5$$

$$s_2^2 = \frac{62}{5-1} = 15.5$$

$$s_3^2 = \frac{60}{6-1} = 12.0$$

$$\therefore \quad \hat{\sigma}_w^2 = \left(\frac{4}{13}\right) 17.5 + \frac{4}{13}(15.5) + \frac{5}{13} \cdot (12)$$

$$= 14.77$$

Now F-ratio $= \dfrac{\hat{\sigma}_b^2}{\hat{\sigma}_w^2}$

$$= \frac{20}{14.77} = 1.35$$

For all the means to be same for all samples indicating that the samples have been taken from population of the same means, this ratio should be unity.

In this case, since the F-ratio is not unity, we reject the null hypothesis. This means that the methods followed for training new workers for production produces different effects on persons.

Problem 13.27

The marketing manager of a company is contemplating the price of a new product and has three prices worked out, Rs. 105, 110 and 115. In order to decide what price he should fix, he carries out an experiment of sales in an upcoming market. He selects 3 samples in 4 geographical location markets and the sales of the new product are recorded at the end of the week. These are given in the table below.

Sales in location	*Price Levels*		
	Rs. 105	*Rs. 110*	*Rs. 115*
A	8	7	4
B	12	10	8
C	10	6	7
D	9	8	9
E	11	9	7

Please advice the marketing manager, whether the price levels have significant influence over the sales levels or not.

Solution :

Though determination of optimal price for the new product is the prime concern of the marketing manager, it would need an extensive experiment based on host of factors. Let us first carry out the analysis only to establish the basic question, if the variation in price would affect the sales of the product significantly.

To carry out this analysis, we use the technique of ANOVA, wherein we will establish if the average sales in all the geographical markets would be any different from the overall sales average *i.e.* if the individual means of each price level has the same influence on the population means of the total sales.

For use of ANOVA, let us go step by step

First work out the null hypothesis

$H_0 : \mu_1 = \mu_2 = \mu_3 = \mu$ (the population mean)

Alternative hypothesis can be written as

$H_1 : \mu_1 \neq \mu_2 \neq \mu_3$

To test this hypothesis, we go to ANOVA methodology

Let us now obtain, $\bar{x}_1$, $\bar{x}_2$, $\bar{x}_3$ and $\bar{\bar{x}}$ from the given data

Here $\mu_1 = \bar{x}_1 = \dfrac{8+12+10+9+11}{5} = 10$

$$\mu_2 = \bar{x}_2 = \frac{7+10+6+8+9}{5} = 7$$

and taking all the observations into account.

$$\bar{\bar{x}} = \frac{8+12+10+9+11+7+10+6+8+9+4+8+7+9+7}{15}$$

$= 8.33$

Step 1 : Calculate sum of the squares and the variance of between - treatment values. (Here there are 3 treatments of a single factor price and hence it is a case of one-factor or one way analyis variance). The response variable here is the sales volume

$$\therefore \; SS_{(b)} = \sum_{p=1}^{r} n_p\left(\bar{x}_p - \bar{\bar{x}}\right)^2$$

$$= 5\left\{(10-8.33)^2 + (8-8.33)^2 + (7-8.33)^2\right\}$$

$= 23.3$

$\therefore$ **Mean sum of square i.e., between variance estimate**

$$MSS_{(b)} = \frac{SS_{(b)}}{r-1}$$

$$= \frac{23.3}{3-1} = 11.65$$

Step 2 : Calculating the within - variance estimate, we have

$$SS_{(w)} = \sum_{i=1}^{n_p}\sum_{p=1}^{n}\left(x_{i_p} - \bar{x}_p\right)^2$$

$$= (8-10)^2 + (12-10)^2 + (10-10)^2 + (9-10)^2$$
$$+ (11-10)^2 + (7-8)^2 + (10-8)^2 + (6-8)^2$$
$$+ (8-8)^2 + (9-8)^2 + (4-7)^2 + (8-7)^2 + (7-7)^2 + (9-7)^2 + (7-7)^2$$

$= 34$

Mean sum of square *i.e.* within – variance estimate

$$MSS_{(w)} = \frac{SS_{(w)}}{N-r}$$

$$= \frac{34}{(15-3)} = 2.8$$

Step 3 : Now we obtain F-ratio for these variances

$$F\text{–ratio} = \frac{MSS_{(b)}}{MSS_{(w)}}$$

$$= \frac{11.65}{2.8} = 4.16$$

This can be written the form of ANOVA table as follows :

ANOVA Table

Source of variation	*Variation area*	*Degree of freedom*	*Variance*	*F-ratio Estimate*
Between - treatments	$SS_{(b)} = 23.3$	$r-1=3-1=2$	$MSS_{(b)} = \frac{23.3}{2} = 11.65$	$\frac{MSS_{(b)}}{MSS_{(w)}} = \frac{11.65}{2.8} = 4.16$
within-treatments	$SS_{(w)} = 34$	$N-r=15-3=12$	$MSS_{(w)} \frac{34}{12} = 2.8$	

In order to test the null hypothesis, we have to go to the table of F - distribution to obtain F - statistic value for the degrees of freedom as follows

for Numerator, df = 2

for Denominator. df = 12

From the F - distribution table, we obtain the F - statistic for 95% confidence level as 3.89. The calculated value of the F - statistic is well above the value at 95% CL. Hence it falls in the rejection zone.

The null hypothesis, therefore, is not true as F - statistic is significant at the 0.05 level of significance.

PRACTICE PROBLEMS

13.28 Comment breifly on the two terms - parameter and statistic as used in Sampling Theory. What is meant by the sampling distribution of a statistic? Define standard error of a statistic.

[ICWA (Final), June 1978 : C.A. (Inter), Nov., 1978]

13.29 What is standard error of a statistic? What does it measure? Name two fields where it is used.

[ICWA (Final). June 1977]

13.30 Explain the following with reference to testing of hypothesis

(*i*) Type 1 error and Type II errors

(*ii*) Critical region

(*iii*) Power of a test
(*iv*) Most powerful test [*Bombay University, B.Com., 1976*]

13.31 Explain the following terms (Mention only the essential points)
(*i*) Statistic and Parameter
(*ii*) Critical region
(*iii*) Standard error [*ICWA (Final), June 1983*]

13.32 Explain the assumptions in large sample theory. Distinguish clearly between large sample and small sample tests of significance. Are small sample tests valid for large samples? [*Bombay University. B.Com., 1974*]

13.33 Outline the procedure for large sample tests and discuss their theoretical basis. Comment on the assumptions made. [*Bombay University. B.Com., 1975*]

13.34 Discuss the large sample test for testing the equality of two population means.

13.35 Discuss the Chi-Square test of goodness of fit of a theoretical distribution to an observed frequency distribution. State the conditions for the validity of χ^2 test. [*Delhi University, M.Com.,* 1975]

13.36 Discuss the χ^2-test of goodness of fit of a theoretical distribution to an observed frequency distribution. How are the degrees of freedom ascertained when some parameters of the theoretical distribution have to be estimated from the data? State the conditions for the validity of χ^2-test. [*Gujarat University. M.Com., 1980*]

13.37 What is χ^2 -test of goodness of fit? What precautions are necessary while applying this test. [*Delhi University, M.B.A, 1977*]

13.38 Define Student's *t*-Statistic and write its probability density function.

13.39 (*a*) Explain the *t*-test for testing the significance of the difference between two sample means. State the assumptions while formulating it.

(*b*) Explain the *t*-test for testing the significance of an observed sample correlation.

13.40 Define Fisher's Z-transformation. How do you test the significance of the difference between sample correlation and the hypothetical value of population correlation (ρ)? Also how do you test the significance of difference between two independent sample correlation coefficients?

13.41 Define Snedecor's *F*-statistic and write its probability density function. Also list out the main features of the *F*-probability distribution.

13.42 While discussing the *F*-test for testing the equality of the two sample variances, list out the assumption made.

13.43 Define estimation theory and write its importance in decision-making in the situation of uncertainty. Also explain Point Estimation and Interval Estimation.

13.44 Define the following terms (*a*) Unbiased statistic (*b*) Consistent Statistic (*c*) Efficient statistic and (*d*) Sufficient statistic.

13.45 Explain why a random sample of size 25 is to be preferred to a random sample of size 20 to estimate the population mean [*Delhi University, B.A. (Eco. Hons.), 1987*]

13.46 Work out Point Estimate and Interval Estimate for the population mean μ and population proportion P from random sample of size n from a large population at a level of significance 0.05 and 0.01. Would it be different if the population to select random sample from is finite?

13.47 Describe the method of selecting a sample and determine its size for a desired degree of accuracy and level of significance α, while considering the sample distribution of mean and proportion.

13.48 A population consists of five numbers (2, 3, 6, 8, 11). Consider all possible samples of size two which can be drawn with replacement from this population. Calculate the standard error of the sample mean. *[ICWA (Final), June 1978]*

13.49 A random sample of 500 pineapples was taken from a large consignment and 65 of them were found to be bad. Show that the standard error of proportion of bad ones in a sample of this size is 0.015 and deduce that the percentage of bad pineapples in the consignment almost certainly lies between 8.5 and 17.5.

[Bombay University. B.Com., 1974, ICWA (Final), June 1984]

13.50 A random sample of 700 units from a large consignment showed that 200 were damaged. Find *(i)* 95% and *(ii)* 99% confidence limits for the proportion of damaged units in the consignment. *[Bombay University, B.Com., April 1978]*

13.51 A random sample of 100 items taken from a large batch of articles contains 5 defective items, (*a*) set up 96 per cent confidence limits for the proportion of defective items in the batch, (*b*) If batch contains 2,696 items. Set up 95% confidence interval for the proportion of defective items. *[ICWA (Final), June 1974]*

13.52 Out of 20,000 customers ledger accounts, a sample of 600 accounts was taken to test the accuracy of posting and balancing wherein 45 mistakes were found. Assign limits within which the number of defective cases can be expected at 95% level. *[C.A. (Inter), May 1976]*

13.53 In a marketing survey for the introduction of a new product in a town, a sample of 400 persons was taken. When they were approached for sale, 80 of them purchased the product. Find 95% confidence limits for the percentage of persons who would buy the product in the town. *[Bombay University, M.Com., April 1982]*

13.54 In a random sample of 400 items from a large consignment, 20 items were found to be defective. Find 99% confidence limits for the percentage of defectives in the consignment.

[Bombay University, B.Com., April 1983]

13.55 In measuring reaction time, a psychologist estimates that the standard deviation is 0.95 sec. How large a sample of measurements must be taken in order to be 95% confident that the error of his estimate of mean will not exceed 0.01 sec.? *[ICWA (Final), Dec., 1976]*

13.56 In a sample of 1,000 TV viewers, 340 watched a particular programme. Find 99% confidence limits for the percentage of all viewers who watch this programme.

[Bombay University, B.Com., 1973; Himachal University, M.Com., July 1979]

13.57 In a sample of 400 oranges from a large consignment, 40 were considered bad. Estimate the percentage of defective oranges in the whole consignment and assign limits within which the percentage will probably lie. *[C.A. (Inter), Nov., 1975]*

13.58 A life insurance company has 1,500 policies averaging Rs. 2,000 on lives at age 40. From the experience table; it is found that of 1,00,000 alive at the age of 30, as many as 90,000 were alive at age of 31. Find the lower and upper values of the amount the company will have to pay out in insurance during the year. *[C.A. (Inter), May 1982]*

13.59 A factory is producing 50,000 pairs of shoes daily. From a sample of 500 pairs, 2% were found to be of sub-standard quality. Estimate the number of pairs that can be reasonably expected to be spotted in the daily production and assign limits at 95% of level of confidence.

[C.A. (Inter), May 1979]

13.60 In a sample survey of 1,000 housewives in a city, 23% preferred a particular brand of pressure cooker. Find 99 per cent confidence limits for the percentage of all housewives in the city preferring that brand of cooker. *[Bombay University. B.Com., Oct., 1974]*

13.61 In a sample of 900 stockholders of companies, 400 stated that their major aim in holding stocks is capital appreciation. What is the 90% confidence range within which lies the population proportion of stockholders who hold stocks for capital appreciation. (Area between $t = 0$ and $t = 1.64$ is 45% where t is Standard Normal Variate).

[Bombay University, B.Com., April 1981]

13.62 A manufacturer claimed that at least 95% of the equipment which he supplied to a factory conformed to specifications. An examination of a sample of 200 pieces of equipment revealed that 18 were faulty. Test his claim at a significance level of (*i*) 0.05 ; (*ii*) 0.01.

[ICWA (Final) Dec.. 1977, C.A. (Inter). Nov., 1979]

13.63 In a random sample of 400 persons from a large population, 120 were females, can it be said that males and females are in the ratio 5:3 in the population? Use 1% level of significance.

[Bombay University. B.Com.. Nov., 1982]

13.64 In a sample of 400 parts manufactured by a factory, the number of defective parts was found to be 30. The company, however, claimed that only 5% of their product is defective. Is the claim reasonable. *[ICWA (Final), June 1975]*

13.65 A die was thrown 9.000 times and of these, 3,220 yielded a 3 or 4. Is this consistent with the hypothesis that the die was unbiased. *[ICWA (Final), June 1983]*

13.66 If a coin is tossed at random 400 times and tail turns up 160 times, can the coin be regarded as unbiased?

13.67 A dice is thrown 49,152 times and of these 25,145 yielded either 4 or 5 or 6. Is this consistent with the hypothesis that the die must be unbiased? *[ICWA (Final), June 1980]*

13.68 A candidate at an election claims 90% of support of all voters in a locality. Verify his claim if in a random sample of 400 voters from the locality. 320 supported his candidature. Use 5% level of significance. *[Bombay University. B.Com., May 1982]*

13.69 In a sample of 600 students of a certain college, 400 are found to use dot pens. In another college. from a sample of 900 students, 450 were found to use dot pens. Test whether the two colleges are significantly different with respect to the habit of using dot pens. (Null and alternative hypothesis should he stated clearly). *[ICWA (Final), Dec., 1982]*

13.70 A machine produced 20 defective articles in a batch of 400. After overhauling, it produced 10 defectives in a batch of 300. Has the machine improved? *[C.A. (Inter), Nov., 1981]*

13.71 An airline must allocate available seating space between first class passengers and economy class passengers. The null hypothesis is that 20 per cent of the passengers fly first class, but management recognises the possibility that the percentage could be more or less. A random sample of 400 passengers includes 70 passengers holding first class tickets. Can the null hypothesis be rejected at the 10 per cent level of significance?

[AIMA (Dip. in Mgmt.), July 1981]

13.72 A company has the head office at Calcutta and branch at Bombay. The Personnel Director wanted to know, if the workers at two places would like the introduction of a new plan of work and a survey was conducted for this purpose. Out of a sample of 500 workers at Calcutta, 62% favoured the plan. At Bombay, out of a sample of 400 workers 41% were against the new plan. Is there any significant difference between the two groups in their attitude towards the new plan at 5% level ? *[C.A. (Inter), May 1983]*

13.73 While throwing 5 dice 30 times, a person obtained success 23 times, securing a 6 which was considered a success. Can we consider the difference between the observed and the expected results as being significantly different? *[C.A. (Inter), Nov., 1975]*

13.74 In a sample of 500 people in Kerala, 280 are tea drinkers and the rest are coffee drinkers. Can we assume that both coffee and tea are equally popular in this state at 1% level of significance?

[C.A. (Inter), May 1978]

13.75 In a certain district A, 450 persons were considered regular consumers of tea out of a sample of 1,000 persons. In another district B, 400 were regular consumers of tea out of a sample of 800 persons. Do these facts reveal a significant difference between the two districts as far as tea drinking habit is concerned? Use 5% level. [*C.A. (Inter), Nov., 1975*]

13.76 A firm found with the help of a sample survey of a city (size of the sample 900), that $\frac{3}{4}$th of the population consumes things produced by them. A firm then advertised the goods in paper and on radio. After one year, a sample of size 1,000 reveals that proportion of consumers of the goods produced by the firm is $\frac{3}{4}$th. Is this rise significant to indicate that the advertisement was effective? [*AIMA, (Dip. in Mgmt.), 1977*]

13.77 Two groups A and B consist of 100 people each who have a disease. A serum is given to group A but not to group B. It is found that in groups A and B, 75 and 65 people, respectively recover from the disease. Test the hypothesis that the serum helps to cure the disease. [*ICWA (Final), June 1984*]

13.78 An advertising company claims that 40% of the people, who saw an advertisement put out on the television by the company remembered the name of the product 24 hours after they had seen the show. In a sample survey conducted 24 hours after the show, 152 out of 400 persons remembered the name of the product advertised. Test if the claim of the company can be accepted at a level of significance of one per cent. [*Punjab University, M.A. (Eco.), 1976*]

13.79 A candidate for an election from a large constituency thinks that he will win the election if at least 45% of the electorate vote for him. He therefore, conducts the sample survey to enable him to decide whether he should stand for the election or not. The survey covers 10,000 voters and it is found that 4,420 voted for him. Advise him as to whether he should stand for the election, stating clearly the level of significance and other assumptions on which you base your conclusion. [*Bombay University, B.Com., Oct., 1975*]

13.80 (*a*) A sample of size 100 students, is taken from a large population. The mean height of these students is 64 inches and the SD is 4 inches. Can it be reasonably regarded that in the population, mean height is 66 inches at 5% level of significance?

(*b*) Electric bulbs manufactured by companies X and Y gave the following results:

	X	Y
Number of bulbs :	100	100
Mean life in hrs. :	1,300	1,248
SD in hrs. :	82	93

State whether there is any significant difference in the mean life of two makes. [*AIMA (Dip. in Mgmt.), Dec.,1997*]

13.81 The sizes of components produced by a machine are normally distributed. It is required that the size should be between 15.63 cm and 15.84 cm and it is known that 2.872% of the production is rejected for being oversize and 1.072% of the production is rejected for being undersized.

(*a*) Calculate the mean of the component sizes.
(*b*) Obtain the SD of the component sizes.
(*c*) Calculate the range that would contain the middle 50% of the production.

[*AIMA (Dip., in Mgmt.) Dec. 1997*]

13.82 A weighing machine without any display was used by an average of 320 persons with a standard deviation of 50 persons. When an attractive display was used on the machine, the average for 100 days increased by 15 persons. Can we say that the display did not help much ? Use a level of significance of 0.05. *[Bombay University, B.Com., Oct., 1981]*

13.83 A random sample of 400 items is found to have a mean of 82 and standard deviation of 18. Find 95% confidence limits for the mean of the population from which the sample is drawn. *[Bombay University, B.Com., 1977]*

13.84 A random sample of 100 articles selected from a batch of 2,000 articles shows that the average diameter of the articles is 0.354 with a standard deviation 0.048. Find 95% confidence interval for the average of this batch of 2,000 articles. *[ICWA (Final), Dec., 1979; Calcutta University, M.Com., 1972]*

13.85 The average number of defective articles in a certain factory is claimed to be less than the average for all the factories. The average of all the factories is 30.5. A random sample of 100 defective articles showed the following distribution.

Class limits	*Number*
16-20	12
21-25	22
26-30	20
31-35	30
36-40	16

Calculate the mean and standard deviation of the sample and use it to test the claim that the average is less than the figure for all the factories at 5% level of significance. Given $Z = -1.645$. *[C.A. (Inter), May 1979]*

13.86 Given that the standard deviation of household expenditure from a pilot survey is Rs 7.2. What minimised sample should be taken to ascertain the mean level of expenditure so that we can be 95% confident that the population mean expenditure lies within Rs. 2.00 either way of mean expenditure. *[Delhi University, B.A. (Eco. Hon.) 1983]*

13.87 A sample of 400 male students is found to have a mean height of 171.38 cm. Can it be reasonably regarded as a sample from a large population with mean height of 171.17 cm. and standard deviation of 3.30 cm ? *[ICWA (Final), June 1980]*

13.88 A Pharmaceutical firm maintains that the mean time for a drug to take effect is 24 minutes. In a sample of 400 trials, the mean time is 26 minutes with a standard deviation of 4 minutes. Test the hypothesis that the mean time is 24 minutes against the alternative that it is not equal to 24 minutes. Use a level of significance of 0.05. *[Bombay University, B.Com., April 1981]*

13.89 A random sample of 1,000 members is found to have a mean of 3.67 cm, Can it be reasonably regarded as a random sample from a population with mean 3.25 cm. and standard deviation 2.35 cm ? *[Punjab University. M.A. [Eco.), Oct. 1981]*

13.90 A sample of size 400 was drawn and the sample mean was found to be 99. Test whether, it could have come from a normal population with mean 100 and variance 64 at 5% level of significance. *[Delhi University, M.A. (Bus. Eco,), 1977]*

13.91 A sample of 100 iron bars is said to be drawn from a large number of bars whose lengths are normally distributed with mean 4 ft. and standard deviation 0.6 ft. If the sample mean is 4.2 ft., can the sample be regarded as a truly random sample? (Null hypothesis and assumptions should be stated clearly) *[ICWA (Final), June 1982]*

13.92 The mean breaking strength of the cables supplied by a manufacturer is 1,800 with a standard deviation 100. By the new technique in the manufacturing process, it is claimed that the breaking strength of the cables has increased. In order to test the claim, a sample of 50 cables is tested. It is found that the mean breaking strength is 1850. Can we support the claim at 1% level of significance? *[ICWA (Final), Dec., 1980]*

13.93 Daily sales figures of 40 shopkeepers showed that their average sales and standard deviation were Rs. 528 and Rs. 60 respectively. Is the assertion that daily sales on the average is Rs. 400 contradicted at 5% level of significance by the sample?

[Delhi University, B.A. (Eco. Hons.), 1982]

13.94 An educator claims that the average IQ of American College Students is at most 110, and that in the study made to test this claim, 150 American college students selected at random had an average IQ of 111.2 with standard deviation of 7.2. Use a level of significance of 0.01 to test the claim of the educator. *[Delhi University, B.A. (Eco. Hons.), 1985]*

13.95 A random sample of 400 flower stems has an average length of 10 cm. Can this be regarded as a sample from a large population with mean 10.2 cm and standard deviation 2.25 cm?

[Delhi University, B.A. (Eco. Hons.), 1982]

13.96 The arithmetic mean of a sample of 100 items drawn from a large population is 52. If the standard deviation of the population is 7, test the hypothesis that the mean of the population is 55 against the alternative that the mean is not 55. Use 5% level of significance.

[Bombay University, B.Com, April 1982]

13.97 An auto company decided to introduce a new six-cylinder car, whose mean gas consumption is claimed to be lower than that of the existing auto-engine. A sample of 50 new cars was taken and tested for gas consumption test runs. It was found that the mean gas consumption of the 50 cars was 30 miles per gallon with standard deviation of 3.5 miles per gallon. Test for the company at 5% level of significance whether the claim that the new ear gas consumption is 28 miles per gallon on the average is acceptable. *[AIMA (Dip. in Mgmt.), 1977]*

13.98 A random sample of size 100 from a large population gave the following distribution

Value :	10-20	20-30	30-40	40-50	50-60
Frequency :	13	20	45	13	9

Test the hypothesis that this sample comes from a population with mean 40, you are given that the population standard deviation is 10. *[Bombay University, B.Com., 1976]*

13.99 From the following data, obtained from a sample of 1,000 persons, calculate the standard error of the mean.

Earning (in Rs.) :	0-10	10-20	20-30	30-40	40-50	50-60	60-70	70-80
No. of persons :	50	100	150	200	200	100	100	100

If the average of the population were Rs. 42, what conclusion do you arrive at about the reliability of the sample. *[C.A. (Inter), Nov., 1976]*

13.100 A sample of 100 workers in a large plant gave a mean assembly time of 294 seconds, with a standard deviation of 12 seconds in a time and motion study. Provide a 95% confidence interval for the mean assembly time for all the workers in the plant.

[Bombay University, B.Com., Nov., 1982]

13.101 A random sample of 200 consumer accounts at a large brokerage firm is selected for the purpose of estimating the mean number of transactions per year for each consumer. The sample mean is 43 and standard deviation is 12. Determine 99% confidence interval for the mean number of all consumer accounts of the firm. *[Bombay University, B.Com., May 1982]*

13.102 A random sample of 225 items from a normal population (mean not known) gives mean as 10.5 and standard deviation as 2.1. What are the intervals of dimensions for (*a*) 95% (*b*) 99% confidence limits?

13.103 In order to make a survey of the buying habits, two markets A and B are chosen at two different parts of a city. 400 women shoppers are chosen at random in market A. Their average weekly expenditure on food is found to be Rs. 250 with a standard deviation of Rs. 40. The figures were Rs. 220 and Rs. 55 respectively, in the market B, where also 400 women shoppers are chosen at random. Test at 1% level of significance whether the average weekly food expenditure of the two populations of shoppers are equal.
[AIMA (Dip. in Mgmt.), Jan., 1980; ICWA (Final). June]

13.104 The mean yield of wheat from district A was 210 Ibs. with SD = 10 lbs. per acre from a sample of 100 plots. In another district B, the mean yield was 220 lbs. with SD = 12 lbs. from a sample of 150 plots. Assuming that the standard deviation of the yield in the entire stale was 11 lbs., test whether there is any significant difference between the mean yield of crops in the two districts. *[Rajasthan University, M.Com., 1975; C.A. (Inter), May 1976]*

13.105 A manufacturer of spark plugs claims that 3% of the items supplied by him are defective. A random sample of 500 plugs is found to have 20 defective items. Test the claim of the manufacturer at 95% confidence limits *i.e.*, P ± 1.96SE(P).
[Osmania University, M.B.A., March/April 1999]

13.106 Out of a sample of 120 children in a village, 76 were administered a drug for prevention of a particular disease. Out of these 76 children, 24 were attacked by the disease, whereas 12 children not attacked by the disease were not administered the drug. Prepare a chart showing actual and expected frequencies and use χ^2-test to determine whether the new drug was effective. (The value of χ^2-distribution from the table at 11 degrees of freedom (d.f.) at 0.05 level is 3.84) *[Osmania University M. B. A., March/April 1997]*

13.107 A machine is designed to produce insulated washers with an average thickness of 0.025 cms. A random sample of 10 washers was found to have an average thickness of 0.024 cms. and standard deviation of 0.002 cms. Test the significance of the deviation. (Take the tabulated value of t for 9 d.f. at 0.05 level as 2.262). *[Osmania University. M.B.A., March/April 1997]*

13.108 For a random sample of 10 persons fed on diet A, the increases in weight in pounds in certain period were 10, 6, 16, 17, 13, 12, 8, 14, 15, 9

For another sample of 12 persons on diet B, the increases in weight in the same period were 1, 13,22, 15, 12, 14, 18, 8, 21.23, 10, 17

Test at 5% level of significance whether diets A and B differ significantly as regards their effect on increase in weight. *[Osmania University, M.B.A., March/April 1998]*

13.109 The management of a company claims that the average weekly income of their employees is Rs. 1,900. The trade union disputes this claim stressing that it is rather less. An independent survey of 150 randomly selected employees showed an average of Rs. 1,850 with a standard deviation of Rs. 300. Would you accept the view of the management or the trade union?
[Osmania University, M.B.A., April 1998]

13.110 The volume of retail sale of clothes is classified as low. moderate and high according to the volume of sales. Sales during the four quarters of calendar year are given next :

Volume of Sale	*Quarter I*	*Quarter II*	*Quarter III*	*Quarter IV*
Low	18	10	07	5
Moderate	17	16	17	20
High	5	14	26	35

Is there a significant evidence in the above data, to show that the volume of retail sale of clothes depends on the period of sale? What is the rationale behind the choice of the test you would apply? *[Osmania University, M.B.A., April 1998]*

13.111 Three methods are used in a production process. Test at 5% level of significance whether the three methods can be considered to be equivalent as far as outputs are concerned.

Method I :	70	72	75	80	83		
Method II :	100	110	108	112	113	120	107
Method III :	60	65	57	84	87	73	

[*Osmania University, M.B.A., April 1998*]

13.112 (*a*) Compare and contrast small and large sample tests.

(*b*) Ten female respondents are exposed to an advertising campaign about a fairness cream. The results are given below :

Respondent Number :	1	2	3	4	5	6	7	8	9	10
Score Before	35	37	38	36	40	35	30	38	36	38
Score After	40	38	39	36	44	45	35	37	40	45

Test whether the advertising campaign is successful at $\alpha = 0.05$.

[*Osmania University, M.B.A., July 2000*]

13.113 A random sample of 120 college teachers was asked their opinion whether more or less emphasis should be placed on teacher's research as a basis of promotion. The survey produced the following results.

		Arts	*Science*	*Engineering*
	More	20	20	10
Emphasis on	To some extent	15	10	15
Research	Less	15	5	20
	Total	50	35	45

Find out, whether there is an association between emphasis on research and the faculty group (use $\alpha = 0.05$)

13.114. The following data show the number of claims processed per day for a group of four insurance company employees observed for 6 days. Test the hypothesis that the employee's mean claims per day are all the same. ($\alpha = 0.05$)

Employee 1	*Employee 2*	*Employee 3*	*Employee 4*
10	7	9	7
12	5	8	12
9	9	8	10
7	7	7	9
8	9	6	8
10	7	6	10

13.115 (*a*) What is a hypothesis? Explain the process of testing a hypothesis in detail using business examples.

(*b*) A detergent soap manufacturer claims that his soap brand A outsells his soap brand B on the average by Rs. 500 per month. A study is undertaken to test this claim with a sample of 200 retail shops. They had an average sale of brand A and brand B worth Rs. 5,500 and Rs. 4,925 per month with SD's respectively as Rs. 400 and Rs. 350. Use appropriate statistics to test the claim of the manufacturer and comment at $\alpha = 0.05$.

[*Osmania University M.B.A., Sept., 1998*]

13.116 The following data are the outputs per day from three machines when operated by four mechanics.

Mechanics	*Machines*		
	A	B	C
1	44	48	38
2	37	40	36
3	45	38	32
4	40	44	44

Test whether (*i*) Mean productivity is same for mechanics
(*ii*) Mean productivity is same between mechanics.

[*Osmania University, M.B.A., July 2000*]

13.117 The means of two samples of 1,000 and 2,000 individuals are 67.5 inches and 68.0 inches respectively. Can the samples be regarded as drawn from the same population of standard deviation 2.5 inches? [*Punjab University, M.A. (Eco.). 1981*]

13.118 Given the following data of the two distributions,

Distt.	*Mean*	*Sd*	*Sample size*
A	100	12	80
B	95	10	70

test whether the difference between the sample mean is significant.

[*Himachal University, M.A. (Eco.), July 1984*]

13.119 A company claims that its light bulbs are superior to those of a competitor on the basis of a study, which showed that the sample of 40 of its bulbs had an average lifetime of 628 hours of continuous use with a standard deviation of 27 hours, while the sample of 30 bulbs made by the competitor had an average lifetime of 619 hours,of continuous use with a standard deviation of 25 hours. Check at 5% level of significance whether this claim is justified.

[*Delhi University, B.A. (Eco. Hons.). 1980*]

13.120 Intelligence tests on two groups; One group consisting of 121 girls and the other consisting of 81 boys gave the following results.

Group of girls Mean = 84, Standard Deviation = 10

Group of boys Mean = 81, Standard Deviation = 12

Exaimine if the difference between the sample means is significant

[*ICWA (Final), Dec. 1981*]

13.121 A college conducts both day and night classes intended to be identical. A sample of 100-days students yields examination result as under -

$\bar{x} = 72.4$, $\sigma_x = 14.8$

A sample of 200 - night students yields examination result as under

$\bar{x} = 73.9$, $\sigma_x = 17.9$

Are the two means statistically equal at 10% level [*C.A. (Inter), Nov,1985*]

13.122 The following figures show the distribution of digits in numbers chosen at random from a telephone directory.

Digit :	0	1	2	3	4	5	6	7	8	9	Total
Frequency :	1,026	1,107	997	996	1,075	933	1,107	972	964	853	10,000

Test whether the digits may be taken to occur equally frequently in the directory. (The table value of χ^2 for 9 d.f. at 5% level of significance is 16.92).

[Delhi University, M.B.A., 1973; Delhi University. M.A. (Eco.), 1972]

13.123 The theory predicts the proportion of beans, in the four groups A, B, C and D should be 9:3:3:1. In an experiment among 1600 beans, the numbers in the four groups were 882, 313, 287 and 118. Does the experimental result support the theory? (The table value of χ^2 for 3 d.f. at 5% level of significance is 7.81). *[Delhi University, M.B.A., 1975]*

13.124 The number of automobile accidents per week in a certain community were as follows ; 12, 8, 20, 2, 14, 10, 15, 6, 9, 4. Are these frequencies in agreement with the belief that accident conditions were the same during this 10 week period?

[Kurukshetra University, M.A. (Eco.),74]

13.125 Records taken of the number of male and female births in 800 families having four children are given below.

No. of births		*Frequency*
Male	*Female*	
0	4	32
1	3	178
2	2	290
3	1	236
4	0	64

Test whether the data are consistent with ithe hypothesis that the bmomial law holds and the chance of a male birth is equal to that of a female birth.

[Kurukshetra University, M.A. (Eco.), 1973]

13.126 In an experiment on the immunization of goats from Anthrax, the following results were obtained. Derive your inference on the efficacy of the vaccine.

	Died of Anthrax	*Survived*	*Total*
Innoculated with Vaccine	2	10	12
Not innoculated	6	6	12
Total	8	16	24

13.127 Two researchers adopted different sampling techniques while investigating the same group of students to find the number of students falling in different intelligence levels. The results are as follows:

Researcher	*No. of Students in each Level*				*Total*
	Below average	*Average*	*Above average*	*Gennius*	
X	86	60	44	10	200
Y	40	33	25	2	100
Total	126	93	69	12	300

Would you say that the sampling techniques adopted by the two researchers *are significantly* different? Given 5% value of χ^2 for 3 d.f and 4 d.f are 7.82 and 9.49 respectively)

[Delhi University, M.B.A., April 1981; Delhi University, M.Com., 1977]

13.128 A sample of 200 observations gave a standard deviation 3.72. Is this compatible with the hypothesis that the sample is from a normal population with variance 4.33?

[Kurukshetra University, M.Com., 1975]

13.129 Test the hypothesis that $\sigma = 8$; given that $s = 10$ for a random sample of size 51.

[Kurukshetra University, M.A.(Eco)., 1974]

13.130 200 digits are selected at random from a set of tables. The frequencies of the digits were.

Digits :	0	1	2	3	4	5	6	7	8	9
frequencies :	18	19	23	21	16	25	22	20	21	15

Use the χ^2- test to assess the correctness of the hypothesis that the digits were distributed in equal numbers in the tables from which these were chosen.

[Bombay University, B.Com., 1975]

13.131 A survey of 200 families having three children selected at random gave the following results.

Male births :	0	1	2	3
No. of families :	40	58	62	40

Test the hypothesis that the male and female births are equally likely at 5 per cent level of significance.

[Delhi University, M.Com., 1980]

13.132 A sample analysis of examination results of 500 students was made. It was found that 220 had failed, 170 had secured a third class, 90 were placed in second class and 20 got first class. Are these figures commensurate with the general examination results which is in ratio of 4 : 3 : 2 : 1 for the various categories respectively? (The table value of χ^2 for 3 d.f. at 5% level of significance is 7.81).

[Delhi University, M.B.A.. 1972]

13.133 A die is thrown 120 times and the frequencies of various faces are as follows :

Face No. :	1	2	3	4	5	6
Frequency :	10	15	25	25	18	27

Test whether the die was fair.

[Punjab University, M.A. (Eco.), 1981]

13.134 In the accounting department of a bank, 100 accounts are selected at random and examined for errors. The following result has been obtained

No. of errors :	0	1	2	3	4	5	6
No. of occounts :	35	40	19	2	0	2	2

Does the information verify that errors are distributed according to poisson's probability Law?

[Delhi University, M.Com.. 1979]

13.135 Two groups of 100 people each were taken for testing the use of a vaccine. 15 persons contracted the disease out of the innoculated persons, while 25 contracted the disease in the other group. Test the efficacy of the vaccine using χ^2-value. At 5% level of significance for one degree of freedom, the value of $\chi^2 = 3.84$.

[C.A. (Inter). Nov., 1890]

13.136 A random sample of 600 men in one town contained 500 smokers. After an increase in the price of tobacco, a sample of 500 men in the same town contained 400 smokers.

Show (*a*) by use of χ^2 *(b)* by finding the standard error of the difference of proportions, that there is significant decrease in smoking.

[Punjab University, M.A. (Eco.), 1977]

13.137 A certain drug is claimed to be effective in curing colds. In an experiment on 164 people with colds, half of them were given the drug and the half of them sugar pills. The patient's reactions to the treatment are recorded in the following table.

	Helped	*Harmed*	*No effect*
Drug	52	10	20
Sugar pills	44	12	26

Test the hypothesis that the drug is no better than sugar pill for curing colds.

[AIMA (Dip. in Mgmt.), Jan., 1980; Delhi University. M.B.A.. 1974]

13.138 Two groups of certain types of patients, A and B, each consisting of 200 people are used to test the effectiveness of a new serum. Both groups are treated identically except that the group A is given the serum while group B is not. It is found that 140 and 120 of groups A and B respectively, recover from the disease. Is this observed result sufficient evidence for the conclusion that the new serum helps to cure the disease if we are willing to assume a risk of 0.01? *[Delhi University, M.Com., 1979]*

13.139 (a) Discuss the importance of χ-test. How is it used to test the association between attributes?

(*b*) In a survey of 200 boys, of which 75 were intelligent, 40 had skilled fathers, while 85 of unintelligent boys had unskilled fathers. Do these figures support the hypothesis that skilled fathers have intelligent boys? Use χ^2-test. Value of χ^2 for 1 degree of freedom at 5% level is 3.84. *[C.A. (Inter). Nov., 1982]*

13.140 From the adult male population of four large cities, random samples of sizes given below were taken and the number of married and single men recorded. Do the data indicate any significant variation among the cities in the tendency of men to marry?

City	*A*	*B*	*C*	*D*	*Total*
Married	137	164	152	147	600
Single	32	57	56	35	180
Total	169	221	208	182	780

[Meerut University, M. Com., 1975]

10.141 A researcher wants to determine whether or not there exists a relationship between the incomes of salesmen and their educational background. For this purpose, he has obtained information as given in the following table on 400 randomly selected salesmen.

Income group	*No. degrees*	*Bachelor's degree*	*Post graduate degree*	*Total*
Annual income under Rs. 6,000	55	77	28	160
Annual income between Rs. 6000 and Rs. 10,000	42	72	66	180
Annual income over Rs. 10,000	23	31	6	60

Test by means of χ^2 analysis (at 5% alpha risk), if there is an association between incomes of salesmen and their educational background. *[Delhi University, M.B.A., 1980]*

13.142 A machine is designed to produce insulating washers for electrical devices of average thickness 0.02 cm. A random sample of 10 washers was found to have an average thickness of 0.024 cm. with a standard deviation of 0.002 cm. Test the significance of the deviation. Value of *t* for 9 degrees of freedom at 5% level is 2.262. *[C.A. (Inter), Nov., 1980]*

13.143 The mean weekly sales of the chocolate bar in candy store was 146.3 bars per store. After an advertising campaign the mean weekly sales in 22 stores for a typical week increased to 153.7 and showed a standard deviation of 17.2. Was the advertising campaign successful? *[AIMA (Dip. in Mgmt.), Jan., 1979]*

13.144 A machinist is making engine parts with axle diameter of 0.700 cm. A random sample of 10 parts shows a mean diameter of 0.742 cm. with a standard deviation of 0.040 cm. Compute the statistic you would use to test whether work is meeting the specification. Also state how you would proceed further. *[Punjab University, M.A. (Eco.). Oct., 1981]*

13.145 The yield of alfalfa from six test plots is 2.75, 5.25, 4.50, 2.50, 4.25 and 3.25 tonnes per hectare. Test at 5 per cent level of significance whether this supports the contention that the true average yield for this kind of alfa is 3.50 tonnes per hectare.

[Delhi University, B.A. (Eco. Hons.), 1981]

13.146 A random sample of size 20 from a normal population gives a sample mean of 42 and sample standard deviation of 6. Test the hypothesis that the population mean is 44, State clearly the alternative hypothesis you allow for and the level of significance adopted.

[C.A. (Inter). Nov., 1974]

13.147 Price of shares of a company on the different days in a month were found to be 66, 65. 69, 70, 69. 71, 70. 63, 64 and 68. Discuss whether the mean price of the shares in the month is 65.

[Delhi University, M.Com., 1977]

13.148 A Fertilizer mixing machine is set to give 12 kg. of nitrate for every quintal bag of fertilizer. Ten 100 kg. bags are examined. The percentage of nitrate are as follows : 11, 14, 13, 12, 13, 12, 13,14, 11, 12. Is there reason to believe that the machine is defective? Value of t for 9 d.f. is 2.262.

[C.A. (Inter), Nov.. 1982]

13.149 From a population of college students10 students were randomly selected. Their weekly pocket money was observed as

Student No. :	1	2	3	4	5	6	7	8	9	10
Pocket Money (in Rs.) :	20	22	21	15	25	19	18	20	21	22

Test whether the sample supports that on an average, the students get Rs. 25 as pocket money.

[Punjab University, M.A. (Eco.), 1982]

13.150 A salesman is expected to affect an average sale of Rs. 3,500. A sample test revealed that a particular salesman had made the following sales; Rs. 3,500, Rs. 2,500. Rs. 3,400, Rs. 5,200, Rs. 3,000 and Rs. 2,000. Using 0.05 level of significance, conclude whether his work is below standard or not.

[C.A. (Inter), May 1983]

13.151 What do you understand by point estimate and interval estimate? A sample of 10 television tubes produced by a company showed a mean lifetime of 1,200 hrs. and a standard deviation of 10 hrs. Estimate (*i*) the mean and (*ii*) the standard deviation of the population of all television tubes produced by this company. Are the estimates obtained by you unbiased?

[Punjab University, M.A. (Eco.), 1981]

13.152 The foreman of ABC mining company has estimated the average quantity of iron ore extracted to be 36.8 tonnes per shift and the sample standard deviation to be 2.8 tonnes per shift, based upon a random selection of 4 shifts. Construct a 90% confidence interval around these estimates (At 10% level of significance, the table value of t for 3 d.f. is 2.353]

[C.A. (Inter). Nov., 1983]

13.153 The nicotine content in milligrams of two samples of tobacco were found to be as follows:

Sample A :	24	27	26	21	25	
Sample B :	27	30	28	31	22	36

Can it be said that two samples came from normal population having the same mean?

[AIMA (Dip. in Mgmt.), July 1978]

13.154 Two types of batteries are tested for their length of life and the following data are obtained

	No. of samples	*Mean life in Hours*	*Variance*
Type A :	9	600	121
Type B :	8	640	144

Is there a significant difference in the two means? Value of t for 15 degrees of freedom at 5% level is 2.131. *[C.A. (Inter). (NS). Nov., 1982]*

13.155 A group of 5 patients treated with medicine A, weigh 42, 39, 48, 60 and 41 kgs. Second group of 7 patients from the same hospital treated with medicine B weigh 38, 42, 56, 64, 68, 69 and 62 kgs. Do you agree with the claim that medicine B increases the weight significantly? (The value of t at 5% level of significance for 10 d.f. is 2.2281). *[ICWA (Final). June 1979]*

13.156 The average number of articles produced by two machines per day are 200 and 250 with standard deviation of 20 and 25 respectively on the basis of records of 25 day's production. Can you regard both the machines as equally efficient at 1% level of significance? *[C.A. (Inter), May 1980]*

13.157 A certain stimulus administered to each of 12 patients resulted in the following changes in blood pressure : 5, 3, 8, –1, 3, 0, –2, 1, 5, 0. 4, 6. Can it be concluded that the stimulus in general will be accompanied by an increase in blood pressure? (Given for 11 degrees of freedom, t 0.05 = 2.201) *[ICWA (Final), Dec., 1980]*

13.158 You are given the following data about the life of the two brands of bulbs.

		Mean Life	*Standard Deviation*	*Size of Sample*
Brand A	:	2000 hrs.	250 hrs.	12
Brand B	:	2230 hrs.	300 hrs.	15

Do you think there is significant difference in the two bulbs? *[Delhi University, M.B.A., April 1982]*

13.159 *A.* random sample of 20 daily workers of state A were found to have average weekly earning of Rs. 44 with sample variance 900. Another sample of 20 daily workers from state B were found to earn on an average Rs. 30 per week with sample variance 400. Test whether the workers in state A are earning more than those in state B. *[Punjab University, M.A. (Eco.), 1981]*

13.160 Two working designs were under consideration for adoption in a plant. A time and motion study shows that 12 workers using design A have a mean assembly time of 300 seconds with a standard deviation of 12 seconds and that 15 workers using design B have mean assembly time of 335 seconds with a standard deviation of 15 seconds. Is the difference in the mean assembly time between the two working designs significant at 1 per cent level of significance?

The following table gives some t-values, which may be used.

Level of Significance	*Degrees of Freedom*		
	25	26	27
$\alpha = 0.05$	2.06	2.06	2.06
$\alpha = 0.01$	2.79	2.78	2.77

[Delhi University, M.Com., 1975]

13.161 Two salesmen A and B are working in a certain district. From a sample survey conducted by the head office, the following results were obtained. State whether there is any significant difference in the average sales between the two salesmen.

	A	*B*
Number of Sales	20	18
Average Sales (Rs.)	170	205
Standard Deviation (Rs.)	20	25

[C.A. (Inter), Nov., 1977]

13.162 The sales data of an item in six shops before and after a special promotional campaign under:

Shops	*A*	*B*	*C*	*D*	*E*	*F*
Before Campaign	53	28	31	48	50	42
After Campaign	58	29	30	55	56	45

Can the campaign be judged to be a success? Test at 5% level of significance.

[*C.A. (Inter). Nov., 1983*]

13.163 A company is interested in knowing if there is a difference in the average salary received by foremen in two divisions. Accordingly samples of 12 foremen in the first division and 10 foremen in the second division were selected at random. Based upon experience, foremen's salaries are known to be approximately normally distributed and the standard deviations are about the same.

	First Division	*Second Division*
Sample size	12	10
Average montly salary of foremen (in Rs.)	1,050	980
Standard Deviation of salaries (Rs.)	68	74

The table value of t for 20 d.f. at 5% level of significance is 2,086.

[*Delhi University, M.B.A. 1976*]

13.164 Measurements performed on random samples of two kinds of cigarettes yielded the following results on their nicotine content (in milligrams)

Brand A :	21.4	23.6	24.8	22.4	26.3
Brand B :	22.4	27.7	23.5	29.1	25.8

Use the 1 per cent level of significance to check on the claim that Brand B has a higher nicotine content than Brand A. [*Delhi University, B.A., (Eco. Hons.) 1981*]

13.165 Memory capacity of 10 students was tested before and after training. State whether training was effective or not from the following scores :

Roll No. :	1	2	3	4	5	6	7	8	9	10
Before training :	12	14	11	8	7	10	3	0	5	6
After training :	15	16	10	7	5	12	10	2	3	8

(For $v = 9$, $t_{0.05} = 2.26$) [*Himachal University, M.Com., July 1981*]

13.166 A research study shows that the incomes of a random sample of 6 junior engineers in industry A are Rs. 630, 650, 680, 690, 710 and 720 per month. The same study shows that the income of random sample of 10 junior engineers in industry B are Rs. 610, 620, 650, 660, 690,700,710, 720 and 730 per month. Do you find any significant difference in the incomes of the junior engineers in industries A and B? Use t-test to answer the questions.

Degrees of freedom :	12	13	14	15	16
t at 5% :	2.179	2,160	2,145	2.131	2,120

13.167 Measurement of the fat content of two kinds of ice cream, Brand A and Brand B, yielded the following sample data:

Brand A :	10.5	14.0	10.6	12.9	10.0	per cent
Brand B :	12.9	10.0	12.4	10.5	12.7	per cent

Discuss how you will test the null hypothesis: $\mu_a = \mu_b$ (where μ_a and μ_b are the respective true average fat content of the two kinds of ice-cream), against the alternative hypothesis

$\mu_a \neq \mu_b$, at the level of significances $\alpha = 0.05$ [Outline the procedure without doing numerical calculations] *[Punjab University. M.A., (Eco.), 1982]*

13.168 Eleven students of a class were given a test in statistics. They were given two months special coaching and thereafter, were given a second test. Marks obtained in two tests are given below :

Student :	1	2	3	4	5	6	7	8	9	10	11
I-test :	23	20	19	21	18	20	18	17	23	16	19
II-test :	24	19	22	18	20	22	20	20	23	20	18

Do the marks indicate the special coaching has benefited the students. [For 10 d.f. at 5% level of significance, the table value of $t = 2.23$) *[Rajasthan University. M.Com., 1976]*

13.169 Choose the right answer:
Two samples of size 10 and 12 are taken from a population and the means tested for significance of difference. The number of degree of freedom is (*a*) 22, (*b*) 21, (*c*) 20, or (*d*) none of these. *[CA (Inter), May, 1982]*

13.170 Two laboratories carry out independent estimates of particular chemical in a medicine produced by a certain firm. A sample is taken from each batch, halved and the seperate halves sent to the two laboratories. The following data is obtained.

No. of samples	10
Mean value of the difference of estimates	0.6
Sum of the squares of the differences (from their mean)	20

Is the difference significant? (Value of t at 5% level for 9 d.f. is 4.262) *[C.A. (Inter), May 1982]*

13.171 A certain diet newly introduced to each of the 12 pigs resulted in the following increase in body weight: 6. 3, 8, –2, 3, 0, –1, 1, 6, 0, 5 and 4. Can you conclude that the diet is effective in increasing the weight of pigs? (Given $t_{0.05}(11) = 2.20$). *[ICWA (Inter), Dec., 1985]*

13.172 A random sample of 27 pairs of observations from .a normal population gives a correlation coefficient of 0.42. Is it likely that the variables in the population are uncorrelated? *[Bombay University, B.Com., 1976]*

13.173 A correlation coefficient of 0.2 is discovered in a sample of 28 pairs. Use *Z* test to find out, if this is significantly different from zero. *[C.A. (Inter). (NS). Nov.. 1982]*

13.174 In a sample of 8 observations, the sum of the squared deviations of items from their mean was 94.5. In another sample of 10 observations, the value was found to be 101.7. Test whether the difference is significant at 5% level. You are given that at 5% level, critical value of *F* for $v_1 = 7$ and $v_2 = 9$ degrees of freedom is 3.29 and for $v_1 = 8$ and $v_2 = 10$ degrees of freedom, its value is 3.07. *[C.A. (Inter). May 1979]*

13.175 In one sample of 10 observations, the sum of the squares of the deviations of the sample values, from the sample mean was 120 and in the other sample of 12 observations, it was 314. Test whether the difference is significant at 5 per cent level. (Apply *F*-test). *[AIMA (Dip. in Mgmt.). August 1979]*

13.176 The random samples were drawn from two normal populations and the following results were obtained.

Sample I :	16	17	18	19	20	21	22	24	26	27		
Sample II :	19	22	23	25	26	28	29	30	31	32	35	36

Obtain estimates of the variances of the populations and test whether the two populations have the same variances. *[C.A. (Inter)., Nov., 1981]*

13.177 Two sample were drawn from two normal populations. From the following data, test whether the two samples have the same variance at 5% level.

Sample I :	60	65	71	74	76	82	85	87		
Sample II :	61	66	67	85	78	63	85	86	88	91

[*C.A. (Inter), May 1983*]

13.178 A study was carried out on the advertising methods of a brand of product. The unit sales achieved by five stores were recorded as under

Method I	78	85	82	88	79
Method II	93	87	85	85	85
Method III	81	92	77	83	81
Method IV	79	83	71	78	78

(a) Work out the mean unit sales at each production level and calculate the overall mean.

(b) Estimate the between - treatment variance of the population

(c) Estimate the within - treatment variance from the variances within the samples

(d) Calculate the F - ratio. Also establish whether the four methods of advertisement produce different effects on the sales volumes.

13.179 Given the values of measurements in five samples, can we conclude whether these samples come from the populations having the same means. Use 0.05 level of significance.

Sample 1	15	17	19	21	22		
Sample 2	18	21	17	23	29		
Sample 3	22	25	18	19	27	22	21
Sample 4	21	28	22	20	18		

13.180 During a normal 8 hours shift, the production manager experiments with the speed of the conveyor belt for assembly operations and he finds that number of defectives produced are as under

Defectives Produced Per Shift			
Speed A	*Speed B*	*Speed C*	*Speed D*
27	37	33	35
25	35	30	39
29	38	29	28
31	36	27	31
25	34	35	29

(a) Calculate the mean number of defectives for each speed and then the average number of defectives during a shift

(b) Estimate population variance *i.e.* between - speed variance

(c) Estimate variance within the sample, *i.e.* within - speed variance

(d) Calculate F-ratio and establish any significant variation in defectives for various speeds at a significance level of 0.05.

13.181 A fast food restaurant system was studied by you to determine the level of customer satisfaction in terms of time taken to serve. The recorded time of service for 5 random customers restaurants are as under

Restaurant	1	3	4	6	7	5

Restaurant	2	3	2	5	3	4
Restaurant	3	2	3	5	3	6
Restaurant	4	3	4	6	3	3

(a) Using a 0.05 level of significance, do all the restaurants have the same mean service time.

(b) What recommendations would you make to the system association (is restaurant managers) whether all restaurants operate at the same level of customer satisfaction in service time

13.182 It is a matter of concern to a real estate manager that rising interest rates for loans may be affecting the sales of houses in a particular geographical area. He collects the following data on new housing colonies starting during the past 3 quarters at 5 nearby locations. The information is recorded in the following table

Quarter	1	144	151	154	160	143
Quarter	2	145	148	149	148	149
Quarter	3	134	172	146	145	151

At the level of significance of 0.05, establish whether there is any difference in the number of housing colony starts during the three quarter.

13.183 A manufacturer claims that through the use of a fuel additive, the KPL (Kilometer per litre) efficiency of the automobile should increase by 2 kilometre per litre. A random sample of 100 automobiles was taken to evaluate the result. The sample mean was found to have an increase of 1.6 km per litre and standard deviation of the sample was 0.3 km per litre. Test the null hypothesis that the population mean is at least 2 km per litre.

13.184 An advertising result survey was conducted for sales of PCs (personal computers). A total of 120 persons were randomly split into 3 groups of 40 each and the advertising material was shown to them. The result showed that the average livelihood of purchase was

Advertisement A	5.5
Advertisement B	5.8
Advertisement C	5.2

The ANOVA table was prepared as under

Source of variation	*Sum of squares*	*df*	*MSS*	*F-ratio*
Due to advertisement	12	2	6.0	
Unexplained	23.4	117	2.0	
Total	246	119		

(a) What is the null and the alternative hypothesis

(b) What is the *F*-ratio

(c) Is the result significant at a level of 0.05 ?

13.185 For the same class of statistics, the division of class was necessitated due to large strength of students. Each class was allotted a different teacher. The final grades obtained by students were as under :

Section A	*Section B*	*Section C*
98.4	97.5	62.6
97.6	98.3	68.7
84.7	92.4	92.7
84.9	95.3	82.3

87.3	96.5	91.6
88.3	82.5	93.3
91.4	85.6	92.6
92.3	68.6	62.3
97.3	69.7	93.7
90.7	75.6	94.3
88.5	69.3	68.7
89.6	77.6	75.7
84.5	88.3	78.7
84.3	91.7	77.7
95.1	93.3	80.5
92.7		
65.6		
68.7		
83.4		
98.0		

In there any significant difference in the average grades of three sections, allocated by 3 teachers. Select 0.05 as level of significance.

13.186 A research study was conducted for 4 departments of a larger organization. From the following data of expenses by these departments, establish whether the average expenses for all the departments are the same. Use 0.01 level of significance

Department	*Monthly Expenditure for last one year (Rs. thousand)*											
	I	*II*	*III*	*IV*	*V*	*VI*	*VII*	*VIII*	*IX*	*X*	*XI*	*XII*
A	10	11	8	5	7	12	11	10	9	10	11	12
B	15	9	8	10	12	12	11	13	15	8	9	10
C	8	16	12	12	8	9	10	12	12	9	9	11
D	12	13	14	15	15	15	10	11	12	10	10	12

CHAPTER 14

STATISTICAL QUALITY CONTROL TECHNIQUES

14.1 INTRODUCTION

Quality of product and process is something that everyone talks about, but when it comes to doing something about it, we may be complacent about it, thinking, that we possibly can do nothing much about it, because produce and process are handled at the manufacturers end or at the service point. It is very wrong notion because quality starts at home. The quality description starts from the customer and not from producer.

Let us take a case of asking for a cup of tea and if we accept a dirty cup, thinking this is how it is normally offered, the quality level of the canteen man will never improve, if not go down. If we refuse this cup, (set your quality level at a neat cup), the next cup offered will be clean and no spilled over cup. This is where customer becomes the king or the starter of the quality.

As Juran says "Quality implies FITNESS FOR USE", the usage value has to indicate the quality of work, be it a product or a process.

Quality is also described as "Conformance to requirements". Thus the customers requirements have to be understood in details in order to make product suitable for the use, conforming to all his requirements. It also implies that requirements of one set of customers may not be the same that for another set of customers. A product may be of very good quality for an Asian customer, but for American or European customers, it may be totally different, depending on customer culture and behaviour at any point of time.

Quality of product/service is the demand and perception of the customer. Conformance to the customer's requirement, therefore, has to be the watchword of the manufacturer and the service provider. Changing customer perception and behaviour keeps the quality dynamic.

Also we have to differentiate between luxury and quality. Expensive leather seats on a sofa in the house may be luxurious, but if not comfortable to sit, the quality of comfort is not good. Similarly, poor start up of an automobile engine will amount to poor quality car even if seats are very comfortable. Thus even very cheap products may be of very high quality and very costly item may be poor in quality.

14.2 VARIABILITY IN THE QUALITY

Another concept of quality as "Things that work the way we expect them to" indicates that quality, though specified by the customer, has to be understood and translated into action by the producer.

Yes Another aspect of quality is reflected in the definition given by Dr. Edward Deming. It says that quality implies **"Do it right the first time and every time."** This indicates that the quality of specifications and performance must be maintained at the same level (as best as could) within the frame work of available facilities. Thus variability is the biggest enemy of quality. Certain amount of variation is inevitable due to probabilities state of nature, but this variation should not be beyond the limit of acceptance as per the nature of fit or usage. This variation permissble is called "Limits of Tolerance".

Quality control can apply the theory of probability and statistics. The concept of quality control has many facets and is the concern of most of the function areas of Business organisation. Normally, the quality control techniques associate themselves with the production lines, where the quality of the manufactured product is checked and to ascertain, whether the product is acceptable in the market or not, the quality control techniques are used. The other areas where quality control is effectively used is the control of the supplied items by the outside vendors. In this area, some techniques of sampling (Acceptable limits as per Acceptance Sampling) associated with limit or control charts are found useful. During our disscussion, both these areas will be highlighted and application of techniques will be amplifed.

Variability is the way of life. Change in the basic or perceived specification of the product/service dictates constant upgradation and innovation at the level of all business managers.

Let us first discuss the quality control aspects of the manufactured region. Any manufacturing unit will have the following areas of concern :

1. The Input — *i.e.*, materials, machines and time.
2. The Process — *i.e.*, the method of manufacture and conversion process.
3. The Output — *i.e.*, the product needing quality control at the market acceptability level.

This can be shown in the following figure.

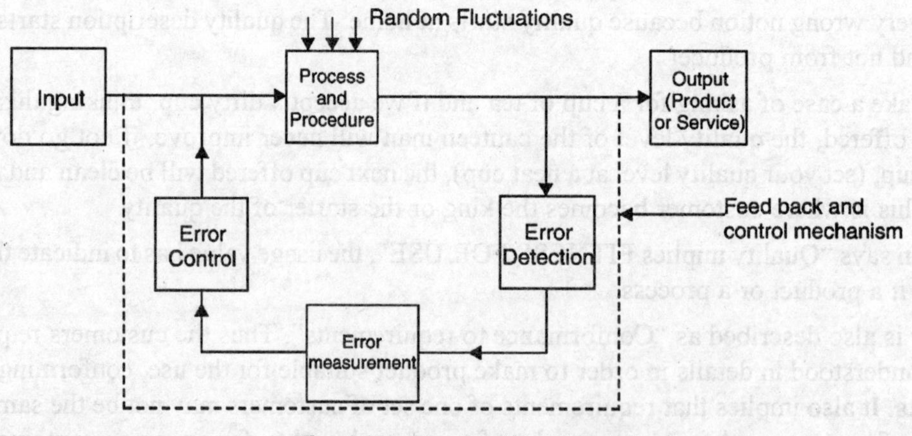

Fig. 14.1. Production Model

As can be seen from figure 14.1, the random fluctuations in terms of change in the efficiency of manpower, quality of machine and other inputs such as non-availability of quality material, can disturb the balance of quality in product/service as the output of the production system, there is a definite necessity of feedback, inspection and control system for removing these variations.

More than the quality control at the output end, we need paying attention on the input side *i.e.*, quality of men, machines and materials so that the efforts during production are not wasted out.

The working principle should be "prevention of defects rather than detecting and controlling these". This helps in better control of quality right from the input stage and improved quality of products results in better customer satisfaction and good will and savings in costs in the form of rejects/defectives as well as warranty costs.

The decrease in the defectives and ensuring production within the limits of tolerance was conceptualised as ZERO defect products. For this purpose, a rigid process control is necessary.

14.3. STATISTICAL QUALITY CONTROL

It can be seen that while the input levels needs quality check, be it the quality of materials or the machine performance, or the proficiency and attitude level of the human beings (the workers), there is bound to be variations in the quality of product and hence the necessity of the control mechanism at input/process stage. In addition, the random fluctuations in temperature, humidity, union atmosphere or absentism etc. also cause variation in the quality of product. Whatever care is taken by the persons responsible for the production, there are bound to be some inherent variations. These variations can be termed as variability due to chance factors, while some other factors become responsible for variations due to mistakes at different levels such as wrong setting of the machine, old aged machine going out of alignment, defective raw materials etc. This variation or shift from the desired level is called variability due to assignable causes. And it is assignable causes that need be controlled rigidly for which a strict quantity control becomes necessary. Statistical Quality Control (SQC) techniques help in achieving the objective of removal of assignable causes.

A typical control Chart is shown below

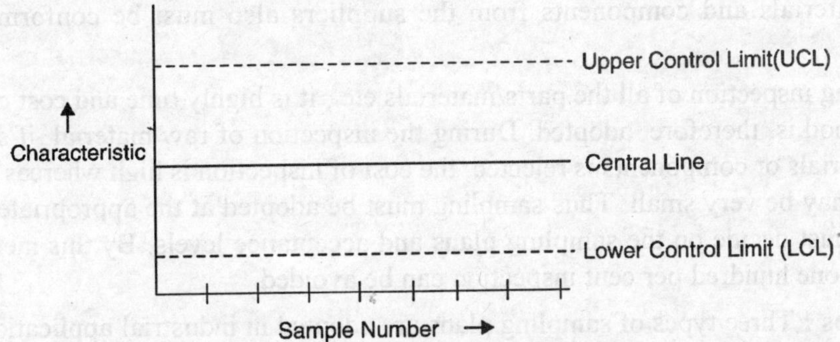

Fig. 14.2. Control Chart

Providing the quality product/service is the datum line of working for any provider. Segmentation of the customers as per the general standard of quality ensures listing out of the requirements. To ensure customer retention, quality control becomes a necessity.

The Central line indicates desired average quality level of the outcome. UCL and LCL are upper and lower limits of accepted variations. These upper and lower limits can be established based on the product quality acceptability and hence help in finding out, when the quality is out of the control limits. These control limits, thus, will be useful in examining the variations of quality of product from one sample to the other. If the observations of quality parameter value lie within these upper and lower limits, then the quality is said to be satisfactory or acceptable. It is generally followed that a large number of observations, say about 60 to 70per cent, should remain near the centre line (average acceptable level) and few points around the centre line and the variation values should be generally balanced on both the sides on the centre line. The problem on the quality arises, when the values fall above or below the UCL and LCL because it will indicate an out-of-control situation. The use of this chart can be explained as follows.

Out of control situation are noticed on the chart in the following manner —

(*a*) Point(s) on side	–	indicates external influences *i.e.*, presence of an assignable cause.
(*b*) Change or Jump in level	–	There can be a change in level even when all points are within limit *i.e.*, all points can be on one side of central line.
(*c*) Trend or steady change in level	–	A steady progressive change in the plotted point may

		be observed. This is called a trend and may be caused by machine deterioration or tool wear.
(*d*) Recurring Cycle	–	Due to some Psychological chemical or mechanical reason or by daily, weekly or season effects, a cyclic patterns may be observed (up and down pattern).

14.4 TECHNIQUES FOR STATISTICAL QUALITY CONTROL

There are two techniques for statistical quality control

1. Acceptance Sampling (AS)

2. Statistical Process Control (SPC)

Acceptance Sampling

It is an important statistical technique used for quality control. As the name suggests, the concept is based on sampling the input or output and comparing the results of samples based on acceptable quality laid down as per limit of tolerance for a product. This technique is adopted to decide whether to accept or reject a shipment of input of output. Generally it is perceived to be an "after-the-fact" procedure *i.e.* quality control applied after the production has ended. But the technique is equally applicable and must be applied even to be the input-level quality control. Quality control applies to each stage of operation so as to ensure defect free product, by ensuring all preceeding stage operations under control. In order to make products/services defect free, the operations of receipt of raw materials and components from the suppliers also must be conforming to the specifications.

Since variability or change is totally dynamic in nature at all times, the general range of specifications for a target segment of the customers has to be ensured. This concept is important in quality control. The control has to be through sample testing procedure, most of the time. In this regard, concept of Acceptance Sampling needs careful understanding.

If we start doing inspection of all the parts/materials etc., it is highly time and cost consuming. The sampling method is, therefore, adopted. During the inspection of raw material. if some small percentage of materials or components is rejected, the cost of inspection is high whereas the cost of replacement of it may be very small. Thus sampling must be adopted at the appropriate level. For this purpose, we must decide on the sampling plans and acceptance levels. By this method, time, efforts and cost of one hundred per cent inspection can be avoided.

Sampling plans : Three types of sampling plans are adopted in industrial applications.

1. ***Single sampling plans*** **:** A randomly selected sample of size n is taken from the total supplies and the quality of each unit of the sample is determined based on specified parameter for testing. For acceptance of the lot, from which this sample is taken, a value of c, (number of defects/defectives) is specified and if actual testing observations show the level of defects higher than c the entire lot is rejected, otherwise the lot is accepted based on sample result (if defects are fewer than c), c is called acceptance number.

2. ***Double sampling plan*** **:** It is a two stage plan. We take first sample of small size and check if there is clear decision to accept or reject the entire lot as done in single sampling plan. If this result is not conclusive, a larger size sample is chosen and results weighted against the acceptance number proportion. The final decision is taken based on cumulative results of both the samples *i.e.* $n = n_1 + n_2$ $(n_2 > n_1)$ and $c = c_1 + c_2$.

3. ***Multiple sampling plan*** **:** As an extension of the double sampling plan, we use number of small size samples and cumulative evidence decides the acceptance or otherwise of the lot on $n = n_1 + n_2 + n_3 + \ldots\ldots$ and $c = c_1 + c_2 + c_3 + \ldots\ldots$

Operating characteristic curve

When the shipment of product is large, then appropriate sample size is selected based on statistical relationship.

$$z = \frac{x - \bar{x}}{\sigma/\sqrt{n}}$$

Where z = normal variate *i.e.,* value of acceptable level of deviation from the mean value
x = value of the parameter tested
$\bar{x}$ = mean value of the specification
σ = standard deviation of the population
n = size of the sample.

Similarly choice of 'c' also must be done judiciously, so to use correct sampling plan For a selected or given value of n and c, we then draw a curve. (shown in Fig. 14.3.)

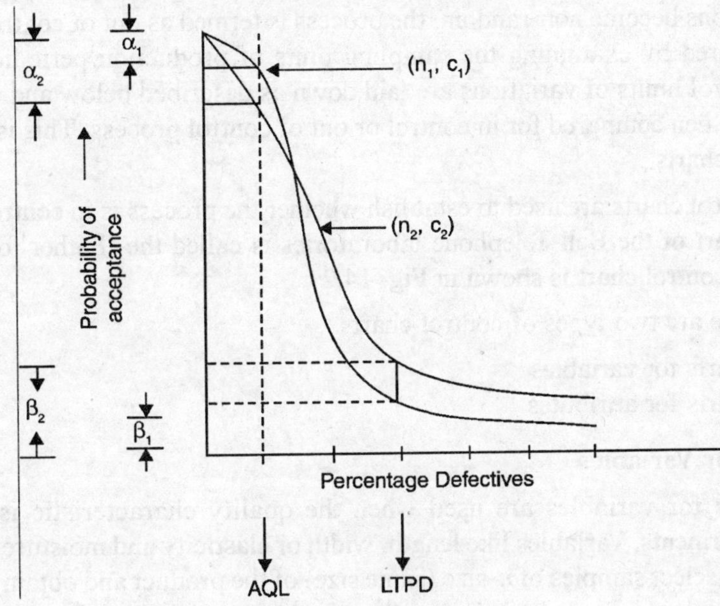

Fig. 14.3. OC Curve

From the above curve, we obtain the following information.

AQL = Acceptance quality level
LTPD = lot tolerance per cent defective
α = Producer's risk
β = consumer's risk.

A sampling plan for a particular value of n and c will have a unique OC curve as can be seen above (one curve for n_1, c_1 and the other for n_2, c_2) though the ratio of n and c may be same. For plans of larger n, the probability of acceptance of good quality lot is high than the plan with lower n. If we increase the sample size n, the probability of accepting a shipment for all levels of per cent defectives other than zero is higher.

To illustrate the concept, let us have 1 per cent as AQL with sample size $n = 100$.

$$P(r = \text{zero defect}) = \frac{n!}{r!(n-r)!}p^r q^{n-r}$$

$$= \frac{100!}{0!100!}(0.01)^0\,(0.99)^{100}$$

$$= 0.3660$$

and $$p(r = 1\text{defect}) = \frac{100!}{01!99!}(0.01)^1(0.99)^{99} = 0.2697$$

Since a hundred per cent defect-free product/service is neither necessary, not desirable under general conditions, the Acceptance Quality Level (certain minimum defect level to be accepted by the customer as good products) describes the effort to be put in for production and control purposes.

Thus, the probability of a lot being rejected will be 1 – 0.3660 – 0.2697 = 0.2643. This is called producer's risk corresonding to type 1 error (α).

On the other hand, if we select 3 per cent as the LTPD level, the similar calculation can establish the type II error or the customer's risk for lot acceptance.

Since the sampling in this case is without replacement, the application of binomial distribution is not correct. We use hyper-geometric distribution, described in this book earlier in chapter 11.

Statistical Process Control

This is quality control technique for detecting and eliminating non-random variations, arising during production process. When the variations are random, the process is said to be in control and when these variations become non-random, the process is termed as out of control. The process will have to be monitored by examining the sampling units of production periodically. The limits of tolerance *i.e.*, control limits of variations are laid down as described below and actual sample units measurements are then compared for in control or out of control process. This is done with the help of quality control charts.

Once the Acceptance Quality Level for a particular target customer segment is established, it denotes the limit of Quality tolerance by the customer. Thus, we use control limit for quality of process, through which the product/service is made available to the end user.

Shewhart control charts are used to establish whether the process is in control or out of control. Dr. Walter Shewhart of the Bell Telephone laboratories is called the 'Father' of statistical quality control. A typical control chart is shown in Fig. 14.2.

Generally there are two types of control charts

1. Control Charts for variables
2. Control Charts for attributes

Control Charts for Variables

Control charts for variables are used when the quality characteristic is capable of direct quantitative measurments. Variables like length, width or elasticity and moisture content are studied on such charts. We select samples of n-size (same size) of the product and obtain mean and standard deviation of the measurement desired. Generally two charts are prepared :-

1. Mean chart (called $\overline{X}$ -chart)— Variations from the mean value of the observations are marked and compared.
2. Range chart (called R-chart) — Here variations in range (difference between highest and lowest observation) are studied.

The results from these charts can show that,

(*i*) both the Mean and deviation are within permissible acceptable limits and hence process is under control,
(*ii*) or, average is out of control, whereas deviation is not,
(*iii*) or, deviation is out of control, while the average is within limits,
(*iv*) or, both, the mean and variability are out of control.

When Mean-chart is out of limit and R-chart within limit, it indicates that the process has moved to a new average. Sudden change in purity level of material, change in setting of temperature controller, start of operation by a new operator, may be possible causes.

When R-chart is out of limit, it indicates variability in the quality change in bearing condition or change in raw material.

Construction of Control Chart – When standards are given

Control Charts for Mean ($\overline{X}$ chart)

If μ and σ, are the mean and standard deviation of the population of the random samples of size n, then

Control line, CL denotes μ value and

$$UCL(\bar{x}) = \mu + \frac{3\sigma}{\sqrt{n}}$$

$$LCL(\bar{x}) = \mu - \frac{3\sigma}{\sqrt{n}}$$

we generally adopt 1.96 σ distance on either side of CL, as warning limits, (It is 95% confidence level)

$$UWL = \text{upper warning limit } (\bar{x}) = \mu + \frac{1.96\sigma}{\sqrt{n}}$$

$$LWL = \text{lower warning limit } (\bar{x}) = \mu - \frac{1.96\sigma}{\sqrt{n}}$$

where the limits indicate that the process might have gone out of limits.

Thus the limits are dependent on the sample size *n*, if , μ and σ are given.

When we use 3σ limits, we understand that no matter what the underlying distribution at least 99% of all observations fall within ±3 standard deviations from the mean. This is as per Chabyshev's theorem. For normal distribution, 99.7 per cent observations fall within this interval. Hence, if some observation process is out of control, it can be seen by the following chart.

The upper control limit describes the maximum positive variation acceptable with reference to the desired level of quality (average specification). The lower control limit, similarly, is the maximum negative variation acceptable from the mean value of the measurable parameter.

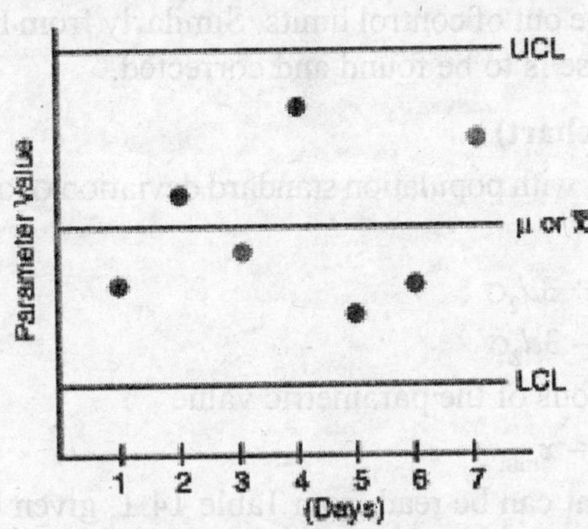

Figure 14.4. Process in control

All daily observations are well within the UCL and LCL as denoted by the chart, the process is said to be in control.

Now consider the observations placed on the chart below.

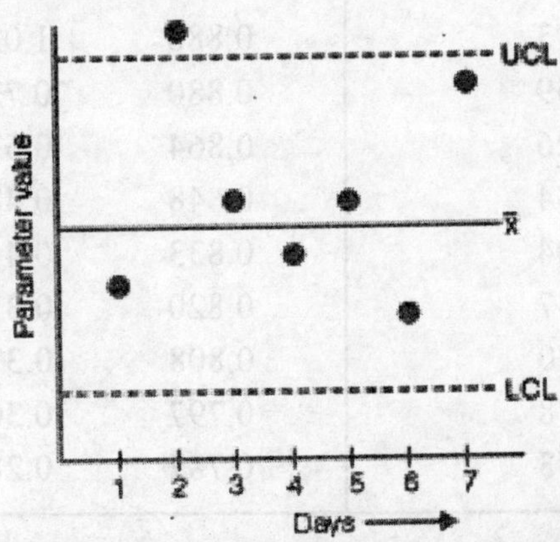

Figure 14.5. Process out of control

Process is out of control, as obervation falls outside the control limits.

Let us examine one more trend given in figure 14.6. below.

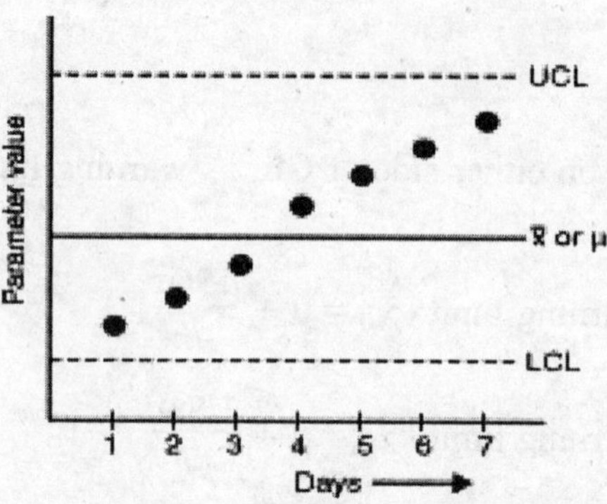

Figure 14.6. Process needing control

Mean chart and Range Chart are two methods available to control the specification variation with reference to either the mean value or the spread in a given sample.

In this case, though all the observation are within the control limits, there is definite pattern of regular increase. Thus the variation is not random and hence we should analyse the cause for such a variation.

From figure 14.5, we can conclude that possibly machine was not working well on a particular day or the acual operator might be sick and some standby has operated the machine on that day, the observation has been found to be out of control limits. Similarly from fig. 14.6., a pattern of increase emerges and an assignable cause is to be found and corrected.

Control Chart for Range (*R*-chart)

For construction of R-chart, with population standard deviation σ known, we use the relationships

$$\text{CL} = d_1\sigma$$
$$\text{UCL}(R) = d_1\sigma + 3d_2\sigma$$
$$\text{LCL}(R) = d_1\sigma - 3d_2\sigma$$

where R is the range of variations of the parametric value

i.e. $R = x_{\max} - x_{\min}$

and d_1, d_2 are control values that can be read from Table 14.1. given below.

TABLE 14.1. Factors for Control Limits

Sample size	*Factors for central line*	*Factors for central limits*			
(n)	d_1	d_2	A_2	D_3	D_4
2	1.128	0.893	1.881	0	3.269
3	1.693	0.888	1.023	0	2.574
4	2.059	0.880	0.729	0	2.282
5	2.326	0.864	0.577	0	2.114
6	2.534	0.848	0.483	0	2.004
7	2.704	0.833	0.419	0.079	1.924
8	2.847	0.820	0.373	0.136	1.864
9	2.970	0.808	0.373	0.136	1.864
10	3.078	0.797	0.308	0.223	1.777
11	3.173	0.787	0.285	0.256	1.747

TABLE 14.1. (Contd...)

(n)	d_1	d_2	A_2	D_3	D_4
12	3.258	0.779	0.266	0.283	1.717
13	3.336	0.770	0.249	0.308	1.692
14	3.407	0.763	0.235	0.328	1.672
15	3.472	0.756	0.223	0.348	1.653
16	3.532	0.750	0.212	0.363	1.637
17	3.588	0.744	0.203	0.378	1.622
18	3.640	0.739	0.194	0.391	1.609
19	3.689	0.734	0.187	0.403	1.597
20	3.735	0.729	0.180	0.414	1.586
25	3.931	0.708	0.153	0.460	1.540

The other values can be computed relatively for approximation

Construction of Control Charts – *When standards are not given*

Control Chart for mean ($\bar{x}$–chart)

When specification or standards are not given, then μ is estimated as $\bar{x}$, *i.e.*, the mean of the sample means, and is used for determination of centre linee and control limits as follows :

$$CL = \bar{\bar{X}} = \frac{\Sigma.\overline{Xi}}{k} \quad \text{where } \overline{Xi} \text{ is the mean of the } ith \text{ sample}$$

and *k* is the number of samples.

when σ is not given, we determine its value as $\sigma = \dfrac{\bar{R}}{d_1}$

when $\bar{R} = \dfrac{\Sigma Ri}{k}$, *Ri* being the Range of *i*th sample

Thus, we can write the control limits as follows :

$$UCL(\bar{x}) = \bar{\bar{X}} + \frac{3\bar{R}}{d_1\sqrt{n}}$$

$$LCL(\bar{x}) = \bar{\bar{X}} - \frac{3\bar{R}}{d_1\sqrt{n}}$$

Values of d_1 can be used from Table 14.1.

We can also write the control limits as

$$UCL = \bar{\bar{X}} + A_2\bar{R}$$

and $$LCL = \bar{\bar{X}} - A_2\bar{R}$$

where values of A_2 can be read from table 14.1.

Control Chart for Range (*R*-chart)

When σ is not known, we can use the following relationship for various parameters.

$$CL \text{ or } \bar{R} = \frac{\Sigma Ri}{k}$$

and $$UCL(R) = \bar{R}\,D_4$$

and $$LCL(R) = \bar{R}\,D_3$$

The values of D_3 and D_4 can be obtained from Table 14.1. for a given value of *n*.

In order to control parameter variation when the given (desired) standards are not available, (i.e., mean and the standard deviation of the population not known), different relationships can be used to draw mean and range chart for process control.

we know that $\sigma_x = \frac{\sigma}{\sqrt{n}}$

Here in case of range,

$$\sigma_R = d_2\sigma$$

Hence the values of control limits can be written as

$$CL = \overline{R}$$

$$ULC\ (R) = D_4 . \overline{R}$$

$$= \overline{R} + 3\left(\frac{d_2}{d_1}\right)\overline{R}$$

$$= \overline{R}\left(1+\frac{3d_2}{d_1}\right)$$

and $LCL(R) = D_3\overline{R}$

$$= \overline{R}\left(1-\frac{3d_2}{d_1}\right)$$

Hence we can calculate the control limits even by using the values of d_1 and d_2 from table 14.1.

There are some methods available to control a process based on the production attributes, such as defect levels or proportion of defects in various samples. Such relationships can be used to draw control charts for process control.

Control Chart for Attributes

We can draw two types of charts for attributes, one based on defectives and the second on defects. The deffective is a product which fails on quality characteristics within the tolerance given. This could be due to one or more defects making it defective. Hence, we can draw three types of charts.

1. *p–chart (proportion defectives)* — It is drawn based on the proportion of defectives in a lot or sample tested. The central limit in this case is determined by the proportion of the defectives found in the test sample. If p is the defective proportion, the average proportion of defectives can be calculated as $\overline{p}$ (which is the measure of central limit) and the control limits based on 3-sigma concept are given by

$$\text{control limits} = \overline{p} \pm 3\sqrt{\frac{\overline{p}(1-\overline{p})}{n}}$$

2. *np-chart* — It is similar to *p*-chart, but it is based on the number of defectives in different samples. With sample size n, with proportion of defectives p, the average number of defectives will be np. Hence, the control limits for *np*-chart undergoes the change as :

$$\text{control limits} = n\,\overline{p} \pm 3\sqrt{n\overline{p}(1-\overline{p})}$$

3. *c-chart* — In this case, we draw the control charts based of number of defects in different product items, We first, find the average number of defects denoted by $\overline{c}$ and then obtain the control limits as:

$$\text{control limits} = \overline{c} \pm 3\sqrt{\overline{c}}$$

In case any LCL is calculated to be negative, it is to be limited to zero i.e.upto X-axis.

To illustrate these charts for attributes, we solve problems related to the concept and the control limits can be marked on the chart as follows :

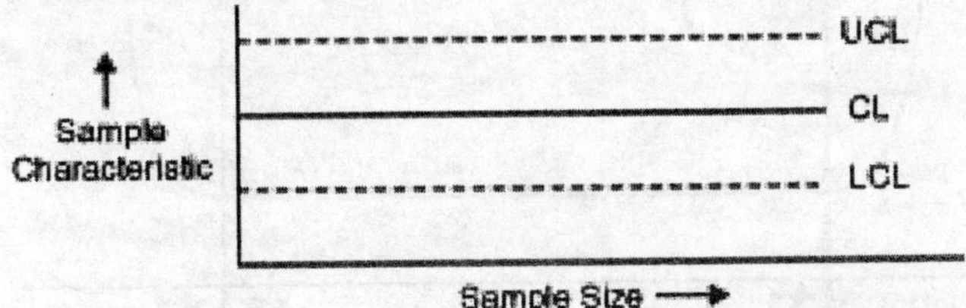

Fig. 14.7. Control Chart for Attributes

14.5. CAUSES OF VARIATION

From the above discussion,we can deduce that for the utility control, the product quality parameter has to be measured and then only improvement / control can be exercised. There may be large number of parameters or characteristics used for measurement such as diameter of a bolt, length of a screw, tensile strength of a vise, hardness of a cutting tool etc. While measuring such dimensions, with whatever method or precision the product is manufactured, there is bound to be variation either due to known or unknown reasons, natural or man-made. These causes of variation can be described under two main headings.

1. Chance or unassignable reasons.
2. Assignable causes

For quality control to be effective, it is essential to know the level and cause of variation, so that corrective action (proactive or reactive, i.e., prevention or detection) can be taken to ensure conformance to the customers specifications.

Unassignable causes

These are some causes which occur randomly and may or may not be known. These may affect the quality marginally, but are difficult to control because identification and root cause of such variations are difficult to obtain. There may be inherent defects in the machines, materials or in the way of working of the workmen. It also could be caused due to the method or the manufacturing technique itself.

For controlling or removal of any such variation, we have to go into the details of processes themselves and modification of method may be largely required. Some small variations in the quality of raw materials or atmospheric condition can be controlled by proper inspections of incoming material or substitution of materials. Skill of the workmen can be improved by proper training for the specific area of deficiency. Such variations are generally large in number, random in nature and cannot be easily eliminated.

Assignable causes

There are some reasons of variations which occur due to causes that can be identified and easily located, measured and controlled.These variations are due to changes in production process itself. The effect may be detrimental to the efficient functioning of the plant and machinery. Since these are identifiable, the removal is easy. Mechanical faults, poor workmanship due to inexperienced worker or defective raw material etc are reasons for defects. Resetting or readjustment of machines are some of the methods adopted to improve the variations resulting in quality improvement.

14.6. DISTRIBUTION CURVE

Various limits with reference to expected standards in quality can be drawn taking available test result data into consideration. These limits need to be analysed for the failure pattern to establish reliability of the system.

Normally the methods used are the distribution curves. Failure rate is calculated for equal time intervals. It can be a familier pattern as "Bath Tub Curve". Analysis of the curve indicates the following.

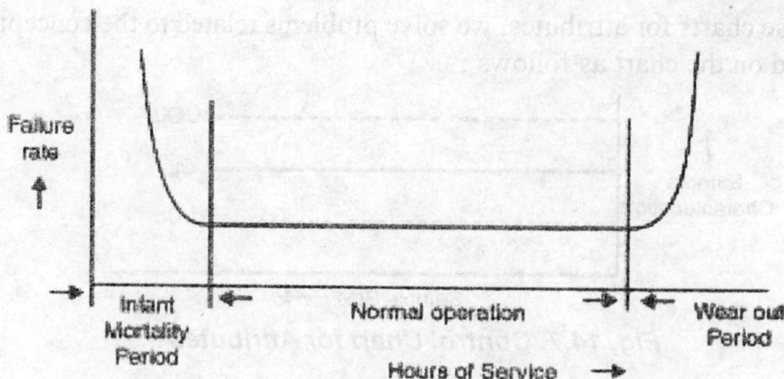

Fig. 14.8. Bath Tub Curve (Failure pattern)

1. **Infant-Mortality period** — Early high failure rate as a result of blunder in design, manufacture, misuse or mis application. Once corrected, failure should not occur again.

2. **Constant failure rate period** — Failures result from limitations inherent in design, changes in environment, and accidents caused by use or poor maintenance. Good control on operating and maintenance procedures can hold down the accident level.

3. **Wear-out period** — Failures occur due to old age; *i.e.*, metal becomes embrittled or insulation dries out. Preventive maintenance by periodical inspections will help.

Through the bath-tub curve, we understand the dynamic nature of operations from the point of view of defects. This concept is useful to work out the maintenance schedules of the resources depending on the stage of operation.

14.7. USE OF PROBABILITY DISTRIBUTION

While using the theory of probability, an idea the dispersion levels of various outcomes need to be obtained and hence the study of distribution concepts. Dispersion or distribution indicates the extent to which the individual values scatter around the average or Central Value in a group of data.

In order to cover all possible outcome in a situation, a generalised probability formula may be obtained. This is called Probability Distribution Function. This is obtained on the basis of historical data and are being briefly discussed in the next paragraph.

14.8. TYPES OF DISTRIBUTIONS

Various type of distribution can be described as follows :

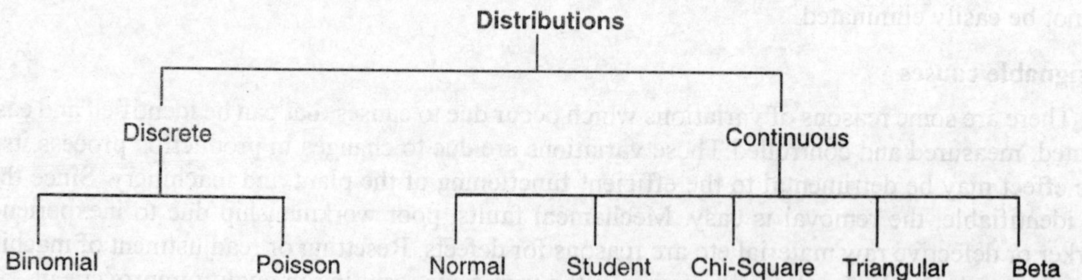

These are the methods used for Quality Control denoting the limits of the control parameter.

Binomial (Bernoullis) Distribution

Consider the situation of a production process, where the units of outputs may be classified as either being defective or non-defective. So two mutually exclusive outcomes can be termed as Success and Failure. Say, in n trials, probability of getting x number of successes is given as follows :

$$p(x) = {}^nC_x q^{n-x} p^x = \frac{n!\, p^x q^{n-x}}{x!(n-x)!}$$

Where p is the probability of success and q that of faillure.

Few important characteristics of Binomial distribution are given below :

1. A binomial distribution is applicable where an experiment involves n trials, each trials can result in success or failure, all trials are independent and outcomes are mutually exclusive.
2. Probability of occurence of 0, 1, 2,.........n successes are given by the relationship.
   $p(x) = {}^nC_x p^x q^{n-x}$
3. The distribution has two variables n and x.
4. The mean of the distribution = np and standard deviation = npq.
5. The distribution can be symmterical if $p = q = 0.5$ or skew if $p > q$.

Poission Distribution

When the number involved becomes infinite, the Poission Distribution will be a better representation of the situation. As per this model,

$$p(x) = e^{-\lambda} \frac{\lambda^x}{x!}$$

where
e = exponential = 2.7183
λ = mean value
x = number of occurences $0 < x < \infty$

This distribution deals with the situations where the chances of occurences of an event are very low and where event happens at random *i.e.*, one cannot predict precisely when each would occur or how many would occur together. This is widely used in simulation models, where arrival pattern is generally random and hence presumed to be following Poisson Distribution.

Some of the main features of the Poission Distribution are listed out as follows :

1. There is no theorical maximum number of events that can occur.
   Total probability $= p(0) + p(2) + \ldots p(n)$
   $$= e^{-\lambda}\left(1 + \lambda + \frac{\lambda^2}{2!} + \frac{\lambda^3}{3!} + \ldots\ldots\right) = e^{-\lambda}.e^{\lambda} = 1.$$
2. This distribution is positively skewed and the skewness is less pronounced with mean value increasing.
3. It has only one parameter λ.
4. Mean and Variance are each equal to 1.

To ensure quality control under uncertain situations (much nearer to the actual life events), the use of some theoretical probability distributions is made to cater for dynamic production.

Normal (Gaussian) Distribution

Normal distribution is very important and useful for any manager because many phenomena follow such a distribution or are close to it. A characteristic or variable is said to be distributed normally if its curve appears as follows :

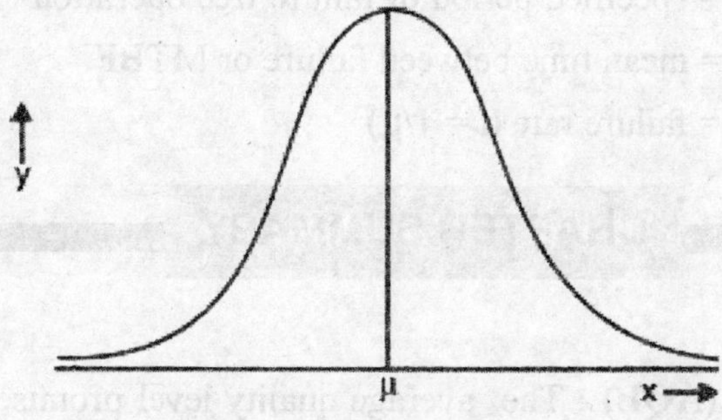

Fig. 14.9 Normal Distribution Curve

Curve can be expressed as $y(x) = \frac{1}{\sigma\sqrt{2\pi}} e^{-(x-\mu)^2/2\sigma^2}$

Here μ = mean = $\frac{\Sigma xi}{n}$ and σ = std deviation = $\sqrt{\Sigma(xi-\mu)^2 / n}$

Properties of Normal Curve

1. The normal curve is uninodal, bell shaped and symmetrical about its mean. The mean, median and mode coincide at the central value.
2. The curve never touches the *x*-axis and extends to infinity on left and right of central value.
3. The total area under the curve is divided evenly due to symmetry and can take value between $-\infty$ to ∞. The normal distribution is a function of Z, the standard normal variate and can be defined as

$$f(z) = \frac{1}{\sqrt{2\pi}} e^{-z^2/2}$$

where $$z = \frac{(X-\mu)}{\sigma}$$

Normal, poisson and exponential distribution are generally used in case of quality control operations.

Exponential Distribution

The Exponential distribution is a useful tool to predict occurrance. The events occur at random and hence cannot be predicted. The time interval in between events is also not the same. The variability can be formulated into Exponential distribution, when events, occurring in a specified time happen as per Poisson Distribution with mean λ, the first occurance waiting time will follow exponential distribution with mean $\frac{1}{\lambda}$ and variance $\frac{1}{\lambda^2}$.

The relationship of probability of *x* number of occurrences in time *t* units and *x* following Poisson Distribution will be

$$p(x=0) = \frac{e^{-\lambda t}(\lambda t)^0}{0!} = e^{-\lambda t}$$

This concept can be effectively used to predict failures of machines or its subparts.The relationship remains

$$p(s) = e^{-\lambda t} \text{ or } e^{-t/\mu} \text{ with usual notations.}$$

where $p(s)$ = Probability of failure free operation

e = 2.7183

t = specified period of failure free operation

μ = mean time between failure or MTBF

λ = failure rate (l = $1/\mu$)

CHAPTER SUMMARY

Important Terms used

- **Acceptance quality level (AQL) :** The average quality level promised by the producer *i.e.*, maximum percentage of defectives in a good lot acceptable to customer.

- **Acceptance number :** The maximum number of defective parts in a lot for it to be acceptable as good.
- **Acceptance sampling :** A statistical quality control technique to determine whether to accept or reject a lot of products on the basis of sample taken from the lot.
- **Assignable variation :** Non-random systematic variability in a process.
- **Attributes :** Qualitative variables.
- **Consumer's Risk :** A chance or probability that a bad lot will be accepted. It is called type II error (β).
- **Control charts :** A graphical representation of some parameter of interest, indicating the quality level of the product, to identify assignable variations.
- **Control limits :** Upper and lower bounds on control charts based on customers limit of tolerance on the quality of product.
- **Inherent variation :** Variation due to natural or common reasons.
- **Lot tolerance per cent defective (LTPD) :** The minimum number of defects in a bad lot.
- **Operating characteristic (OC) curve :** A graphical representation indicating the probability of acceptance of a product with given number or defectives for a given sample size and acceptance number.
- **Out of control :** Observations falling outside the control limits or showing an unexplained trend even though observations within limits.
- **Producers risk :** The probability of a good lot being rejected. It is also called type I error (α).
- **Quality :** "Fitness for use" or "conformance to the requirements"
- **Quantitative Variables :** Variables with numericals values.
- **Statistical Process Control (SPC) :** A statistical quality control technique using Shewart control charts to establish whether a process is in control with reference to quality standards.

Relationships used

- Mean $\bar{x}$-chart

$$UCL_{(\bar{x})} = \bar{x} + \frac{3\sigma}{\sqrt{n}}$$

$$LCL_{(\bar{x})} = \bar{x} - 3\frac{\sigma}{\sqrt{n}}$$

- Mean $\bar{x}$-chart

$$UCL_{(\bar{x})} = \bar{\bar{x}} + \frac{3\bar{R}}{d_1\sqrt{n}}$$

$$LCL_{(\bar{x})} = \bar{\bar{x}} - \frac{3\bar{R}}{d_1\sqrt{n}}$$

- Mean $\bar{x}$-chart

$$UCL_{(\bar{x})} = \bar{\bar{x}} + A_2\bar{R}$$

$$LCL_{(\bar{x})} = \bar{\bar{x}} - A_2\bar{R}$$

- Range chart

$$UCL_{(R)} = D_4\bar{R}$$

$$LCL_{(R)} = D_3\bar{R}$$

- Range chart

$$UCL_{(R)} = \bar{R} + \frac{3d_2\bar{R}}{d_1}$$

$$\text{LCL}_{(R)} = \bar{R} - \frac{3d_2\bar{R}}{d_1}$$

- c-chart $\quad \text{UCL}_{(\bar{c})} = \bar{c} + 3\sqrt{\bar{c}}$

$$\text{LCL}_{(\bar{c})} = (\bar{c}) - 3\sqrt{\bar{c}}$$

- p-chart $\quad \text{UCL}_{(\bar{p})} = \bar{p} + 3\sqrt{\frac{\bar{p}(1-\bar{p})}{n}}$

$$\text{LCL}_{(\bar{p})} = \bar{p} - 3\sqrt{\frac{\bar{p}(1-\bar{p})}{n}}$$

- np - chart $\quad \text{UCL}_{(n\bar{p})} = n\bar{p} + 3\sqrt{n\bar{p}(1-\bar{p})}$

$$\text{LCL}_{(n\bar{p})} = n\bar{p} - 3\sqrt{n\bar{p}(1-\bar{p})}$$

- Bernoulli's distribution $\quad p(x) = {}^nC_x\, p^x q^{(n-x)}$
- Poisson Distribution $\quad p(x) = \frac{e^{-\lambda}\lambda^x}{x!}$
- Normal Distribution $\quad Z = \frac{x-\mu}{\sigma}$

SOLVED PROBLEMS

Problem 14.1.

For a production process, the given parameters are mean diameter of the work piece as 10 cm and standard deviation as 0.7 cm. While checking the quality of the outgoing workpiece, the inspector draws the mean sample of size 16 and 25. Show the warning and control limits on the control chart.

Solution

Data given,

$$\mu = 10 \text{ cm}$$

$$\sigma = 0.7 \text{ cm}$$

$$n_1 = 16 \quad \text{and } n_2 = 25$$

Hence the central line will be marked at average value of the diameter of the work piece *i.e.*,

$$\text{CL} = 10 \text{ cm.}$$

(*a*) for $n_1 = 16$,

$$\text{UCL}_{(\bar{x})} = \mu + \frac{3\sigma}{\sqrt{n}}$$

$$= 10 + \frac{3 \times 0.7}{\sqrt{16}}$$

$$= 10 + \frac{2.1}{4} = 10.52 \text{ cm}$$

$$\text{LCL}_{(\bar{x})} = \mu - \frac{3\sigma}{\sqrt{n}}$$

$$= 10 - \frac{3 \times 0.7}{\sqrt{16}} = 9.48 \text{ cm}$$

$$\text{UWL}_{(\bar{x})} = \mu + \frac{1.96\sigma}{\sqrt{n}}$$

$$= 10 + \frac{1.96 \times 0.7}{\sqrt{16}}$$

$$= 10 + \frac{1.372}{4} = 10.343 \text{ cm}$$

and $$\text{LWL}_{(\bar{x})} = \mu - \frac{1.96\sigma}{\sqrt{n}}$$

$$= 10 - \frac{1.96 \times 0.7}{\sqrt{16}} = 9.657 \text{ cm}$$

The control chart for mean ($\bar{x}$) is thus drawn as follows (Fig. 14.11.)

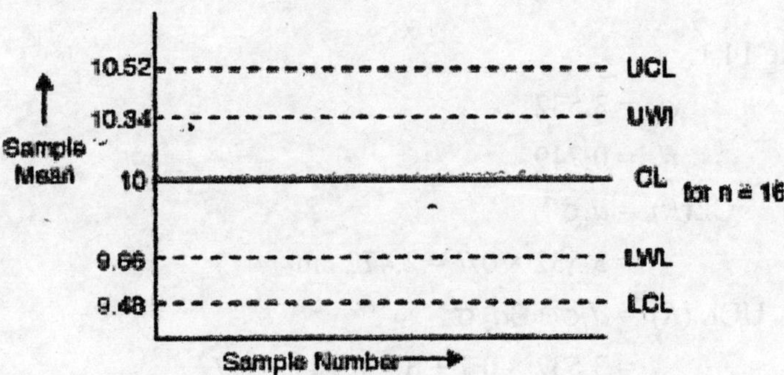

Fig. 14.11. Mean Chart (n = 16)

(*b*) for $n_2 = 25$.

$$\text{UCL}(\bar{x}) = 10 + \frac{3 \times 0.7}{\sqrt{25}}$$

$$= 10 + \frac{2.1}{5} = 10.42 \text{ cm}$$

$$\text{LCL}(\bar{x}) = 10 - \frac{2.1}{5} = 9.58 \text{ cm}$$

$$\text{UWL}(\bar{x}) = 10 + \frac{1.96 \times 0.7}{\sqrt{25}}$$

$$= 10 + \frac{1.372}{5} = 10.364 \text{ cm}$$

$$\text{LWL}(\bar{x}) = 10 - \frac{1.372}{5} = 9.636 \text{ cm}$$

The control and warning limits can thus be drawn on the control chart as follows : (Fig. 14.12.)

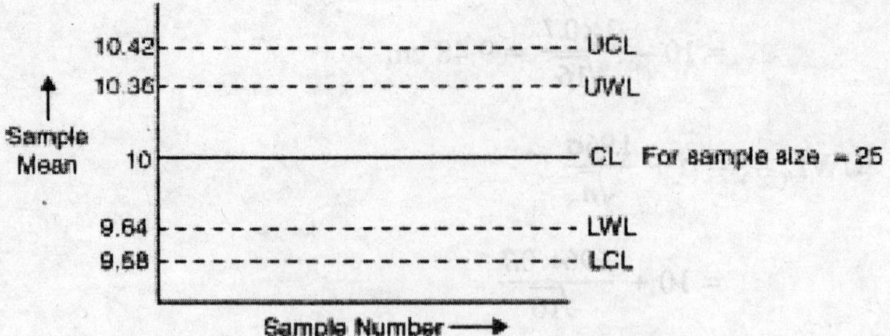

Fig.14.12 Mean Chart (n = 25)

Problem 14.2

Draw *R*-chart for the data given in problem 14.1.

Solution

Taking the data from problem 14.1., we obtain various values from the table 14.1. and establish control limits.

(*a*) Given $n = 16$,

from the Table 14.1.

Values of $d_1 = 3.532$

and $d_2 = 0.749$

$$CL(R) = d_1\sigma$$

$$= 3.532 \times 0.7 = 2.472 \text{ cm}$$

$$UCL\ (R) = d_1\sigma + 3d_2\sigma$$

$$= 3.532 \times 0.7 + 3 \times 0.749 \times 0.7$$

$$= 2.472 + 1.572 = 4.044 \text{ cm}$$

$$LCR(R) = d_1\sigma - 3d_2\sigma$$

$$= 2.472 - 1.572 = 0.9 \text{ cm}$$

Control chart based on these values is drawn as Fig. 14.13.

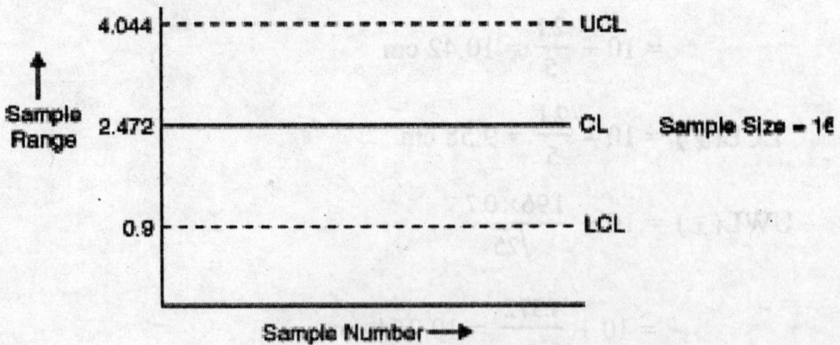

Fig. 14.13. Range Chart (n = 16)

(*b*) When $n = 25$,

Then $d_1 = 3.931$

and $d_2 = 0.709$

Hence $\quad CL(R) = d_1\sigma$

$= 3.931 \times 0.7 = 2.752$ cm

$UCL(R) = d_1\sigma + 3d_2\sigma$

$= 3.931 \times 0.7 + 3 \times 0.709 \times 0.7$

$= 4.241$ cm

$LCL(R) = d_1\sigma - 3d_2\sigma$

$= 2.752 - 1.489$

$= 1.263$ cm

The control chart for Range for sample size 25 can be drawn as follows : (Fig. 14.14)

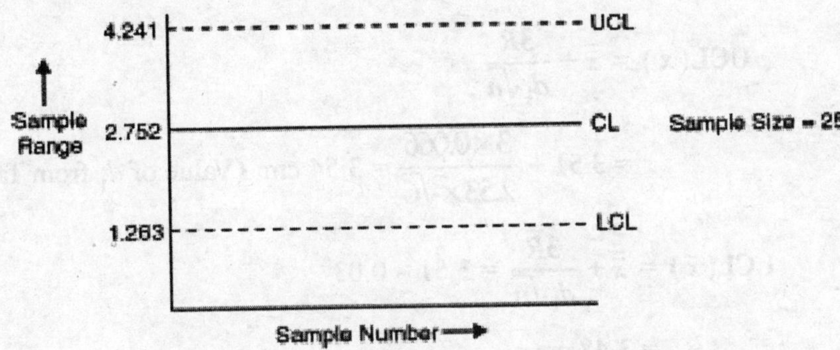

Fig. 14.14. Range Chart (n = 25)

Problem 14.3

An inspection team has collected the following data during the quality control exercise in a computer cabinet manufacturing unit.

Samples	*Observed Dimensions (in cms)*					
	1	*2*	*3*	*4*	*5*	*6*
1	3.56	3.49	3.48	3.51	3.50	3.53
2	3.50	3.50	3.52	3.53	3.49	3.47
3	3.49	3.54	3.55	3.54	3.49	3.48
4	3.55	3.52	3.52	3.50	3.51	3.52
5	3.49	3.48	3.49	3.49	3.53	3.54
6	3.48	3.47	3.53	3.54	3.55	3.53

Work out the control chart for the observations so obtained.

Solution :

From the data given in the table,

(*a*) $\overline{X}_1$ = average/mean dimension of sample 1 = 3.51 cm.

Similarly $\overline{X}_2 = 3.50$ cm, $\overline{X}_3 = 3.51$ cm, $\overline{X}_4 = 3.52$ cm, $\overline{X}_5 = 3.5$ cm, $\overline{X}_6 = 3.52$ cm

$\therefore$ Hence $\overline{\overline{X}} = \dfrac{\Sigma\overline{X}i}{k} = 3.51$ cm

(b) R_1 = Range for sample 1 $= 3.56 - 3.48 = 0.08$ cm

$R_2 = 3.53 - 3.47 = 0.06$ cm

$R_3 = 3.55 - 3.48 = 0.07$ cm

$R_4 = 3.55 - 3.50 = 0.05$ cm

$R_5 = 3.54 - 3.48 = 0.06$ cm

$R_6 = 3.55 - 3.47 = 0.08$ cm

$$\overline{R} = \frac{\Sigma Ri}{k} = \frac{0.40}{6} = 0.066$$

Hence for $\overline{X}$-chart

$$CL(\bar{x}) = 3.51 \text{ cm}$$

$$UCL(\bar{x}) = \bar{\bar{x}} + \frac{3\overline{R}}{d_1\sqrt{n}}$$

$$= 3.51 + \frac{3\times0.066}{2.53\times\sqrt{6}} = 3.54 \text{ cm}$$ (Value of d_1 from Table 14.1)

and $$LCL(\bar{x}) = \bar{\bar{x}} + \frac{3\overline{R}}{d_1\sqrt{n}} = 3.51 - 0.03$$

$$= 3.48 \text{ cm}$$

For *R*-chart

We have $\quad CL = \overline{R} = 0.066$ cm

for $\quad n = 6, d_2 = 0.848$ (Value of d_2 from Table 14.1)

$\therefore$ $$UCL(R) = \overline{R} + \frac{3d_2\overline{R}}{d_1}$$

$$= 0.066 + \frac{3\times0.848\times0.066}{2.53}$$

$$= 0.066 + 0.066 = 0.132 \text{ cm}$$

and $LCL(R) = 0.066 - 0.066 = 0$ $\quad D_4 = 2.004$ from Table 14.1.

or $$UCL(R) = \overline{R}\, D_4$$

$$= 0.066 \times 2.044 = 0.1322 \text{ cm}$$

and $$LCL(R) = \overline{R}\, D_3$$

$$= 0.066 \times 0 = 0$$ (Value of D_3 from Table 14.1)

Hence both ways the values of UCL and LCL are the same.

Problem 14.4

The following table indicates the results obtained from an inspection of equipment (product line).

Product Number	*Product defects (Number)*
1	5
2	3

3	6
4	3
5	3
6	4
7	3
8	5
9	4
10	4

Work out the control limits and draw the *c*-chart for the same.

Solution

Total number of defects = 40

number of products = 10

$\therefore$ Average number of defectives $(\bar{c}) = \frac{40}{10} = 4.$

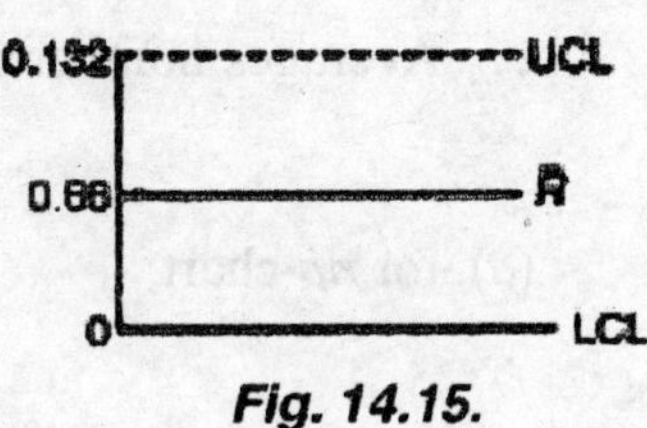

Fig. 14.15.

Hence, $\text{CL} = \bar{c} = 4$

$$\text{UCL}(c) = \bar{c} + 3\sqrt{\bar{c}}$$

$$= 4 + 3\sqrt{4} = 10$$

$$\text{LCL}(c) = 4 - 3\sqrt{4} = -2$$

Since there is negative lower limits, it is considered as zero. The *c*-chart is drawn as Fig. 14.16.

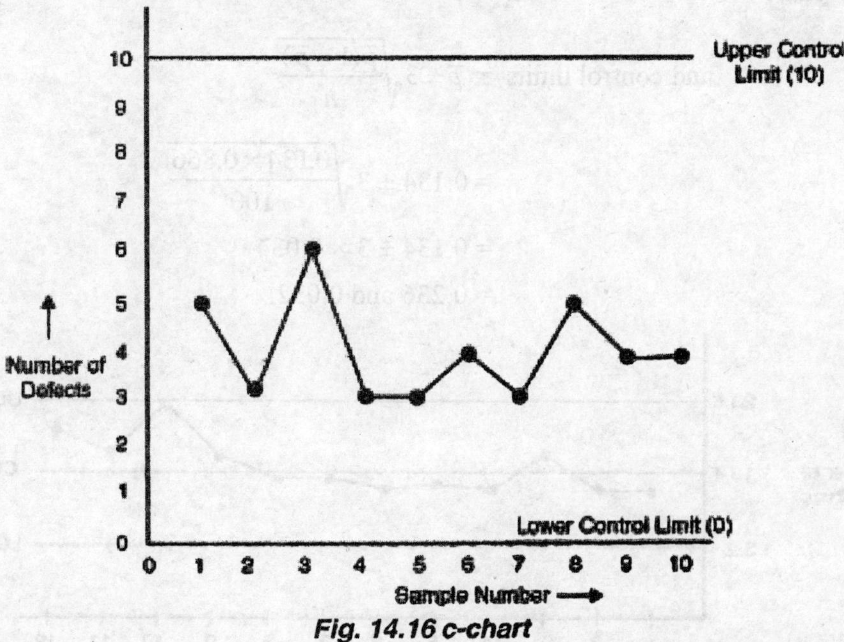

Fig. 14.16 c-chart

Here all the observation values fall within the upper and lower limits. Hence, the process is said to be "in control".

Problem 14.5

A consignment is inspected by the Quality Control team, as the material is brought in by the vendor to the warehouse. The results are given in the table below (there are samples of 100 items chosen very time the inspection is carried out).

Lot Number :	1	2	3	4	5	6	7	8	9	10	11	12
No. of defectives :	10	12	15	10	12	11	12	13	14	20	15	17

Draw an *np-chart* and *p*-chart, with identification of any out of control lot (beyond the acceptable limit).

Solution

Total number of items inspected $= 12 \times 100 = 1200$

Total number of defectives $= 161$

$\therefore$ Averages number of defectives $= \bar{p} = \dfrac{161}{1200}$

$= 0.134$

(*a*) for *np*-chart, $n = 100$

$\therefore$ $CL = n\bar{p} = 100 \times 0.134$

$= 13.4$

$UCL(p) = n\bar{p} + 3\sqrt{n\bar{p}(1-\bar{p})}$

$= 100 \times 0.134 + 3\sqrt{100 \times 0.134 \times 0.866}$

$= 13.4 + 3 \times 3.4 = 23.6$

$LCL(p) = 13.4 - 10.2 = 3.2$

(*b*) for *p*-chart $CL = \bar{p} = 0.134$

and control limits $= \bar{p} \pm 3\sqrt{\dfrac{\bar{p}(1-\bar{p})}{n}}$

$= 0.134 \pm 3\sqrt{\dfrac{0.134 \times 0.866}{100}}$

$= 0.134 \pm 3 \times 0.034$

$= 0.236$ and 0.032.

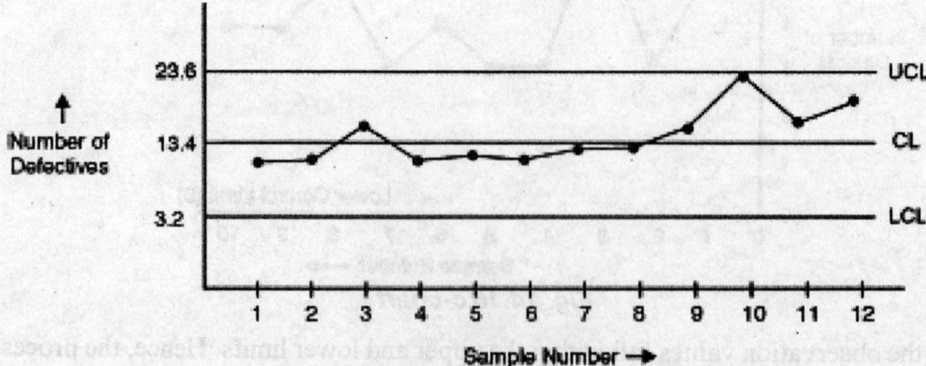

Fig. 14.17. np-chart

Proportion of defectives calculated from the above has been planted on the control chart and the values are found to be within limits of acceptance.

All values are within control limits, hence lots are acceptable.

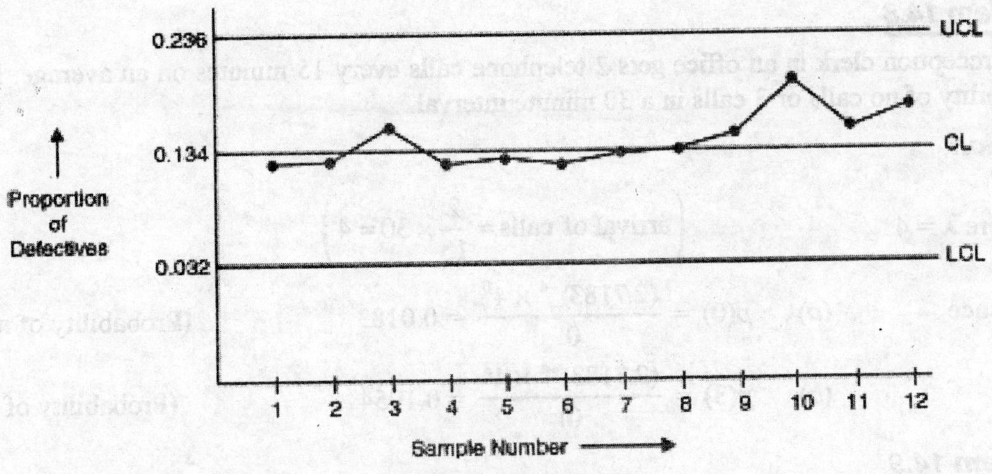

Fig. 14.18. p-chart

Problem 14.6

The following table indicates attendance of students over a period of 60 days.

No. of students present	25	26	27	28	29	30	
No. of days	4	9	10	20	12	5	Total 60 days

Work out the distribution pattern of class strength.

Solution

On the basis of this information, the probability distribution is given as follows :

No. of students	25	26	27	28	29	30	
Probabilities	0.06	0.15	0.17	0.34	0.20	0.08	Total 1.00

These types of distributions are special, In actual practice, some generalised distribution based on theoratical assumptions resembling real life situations are obtained and analysed.

Problem 14.7

The items out of various lots received from a vendor are found to be 30% defective. What is the probability that a sample of 5 items would contain 0, 1, 2, 3, 4, 5 defectives, if the lot follows Binomial distribution pattern.

Solution

Probability of defective items $p = 0.3$ and have $q = 1 - 0.3 = 0.7$

We are given $n = 5$

Hence, we tabulate the results as follows :

No. of Defectives	*Probability* $p(x)$
0	0.169
1	0.360
2	0.309
3	0.133
4	0.028
5	0.002

Problem 14.8

A reception clerk in an office gets 2 telephone calls every 15 minutes on an average. Find the probability of no calls or 3 calls in a 30 minute interval.

Solution

Here $\lambda = 4$. $\left(\text{arrival of calls} = \frac{2}{15} \times 30 = 4\right)$

Hence (*a*) $p(0) = \frac{(2.7183)^{-4} \times 4^0}{0!} = 0.0183$ (Probability of no calls)

(*b*) $p(3) = \frac{(2.7183)^{-4} \times 4^3}{0!} = 0.1954$ (Probability of 3 calls)

Problem 14.9

If the pay packets of employees are normally distributed with means pay Rs. 5,000 and standard deviation as Rs. 1,000, calculate the probability that an individual at random will draw more than Rs. 7,000.

Solution

$$z = \frac{(x-\mu)}{\sigma} = \frac{7{,}000 - 5{,}000}{1{,}000} = 2$$

From table 2 of normal distribution, the probability against the value of $z = 2$, will be the area under the curve as 0.97725.

Hence the probability that an individual will draw more than Rs. 7,000 will be 1 – 0.97725 as 0.02275.

Problem 14.10

A battery manufacturer is contemplating a waranty clause in his agreement to the customers that if the battery fails during the waranty period, he would replace it. Due to his confidence in his manufacturing capability, he feels he does not have to replace more than 5% of the batteries, when found defective. The average life of the battery is expected to be 1,500 hrs. Following normal distribution and the standard deviation as 100 hrs, work out whether the manufacturer is correct in his assumption and confidence.

Solution

Given here, we have $\mu = 1{,}500$ hrs.

$\sigma = 100$ hrs.

If he has decided to replace defective batteries for no more than 5% cases, the normal curve can depict it as follows :

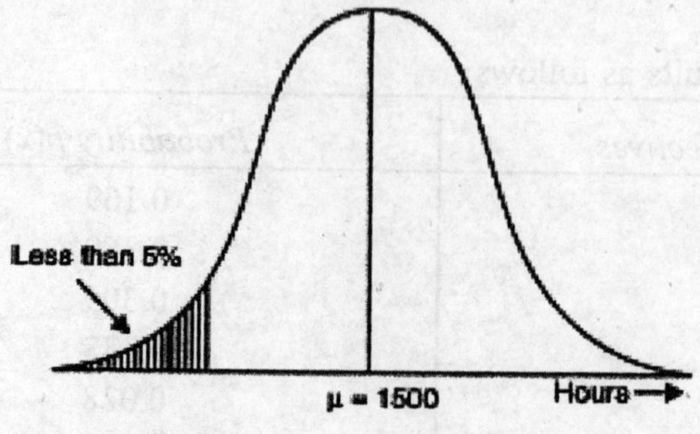

Fig. 14.19.

From the table of Z for normal distribution, (for less than 5% cases *i.e.*, area marked)

$$Z = -1.645 = \frac{X - 1{,}500}{100} \quad \text{(Value from table 2)}$$

or $$X = 1{,}500 - 100 \times 1.645 = 1.335 \text{ hours.}$$

Hence he is quite safe in his warranty clause, if waranty stands upto 1,335 hrs. only.

Problem 14.11

A concrete mixer takes 15 minutes to prepare and transfer a concrete batch. The Mean time between failure of the machine in 100 hrs. Assuming constant failure rate, what is the chance of the machine (mixer) completing a cycle without failure.

Solution

$$p(s) = e^{-t/u} = e^{-0.25/100} = 99.5\%$$

It is very good probability of operation reliability. This is also confidence level of failure free operation.

Problem 14.12

For a machine, operating temp. is a critical parameter and max expected temp. of 165°F. Futher, capability has been idicated by a strength distribution having a mean temp of 145°F. Standard deviation for the distribution is 130°F. Is the machine reliable under given conditions ?

Solution

$$\text{Safety margin} = \frac{165 - 145}{130} = 1.54$$

i.e., average strength is 1.54 times the standard deviation above max, expected temp. of 145°F. The reliability can be calculated as area beyond 145°F and it is 93.8%. Hence, safety factor is as average strength to worst stress expected and is high. Hence the machine is reliable under given conditions.

PRACTICE PROBLEMS

14.13 From the following data, comment whether prices have kept with the rising costs.

	1992	1993	1994	1995	1996	1997
Cost per unit	305	311	326	330	335	341
Price of output	325	340	345	352	361	370

14.14 The weekly demand of eggs is normally distributed with an average of 100 and standard deviation 10. The lead time is one week. At what level the stock be kept to ensure 95% chance of no shortage?

14.15 Following table indicates the production level of a factory having 5 machines.

Machine	1	2	3	4	5
Production	200	250	150	200	160

For a production of 1,500 units next year, how many units are likely to be produced by each machine ?

14.16 The weekly demand for a product, which is presented to be normally distributed, has an average level at 100 and standard deviation 10. How low the stock level be accepted so that we can be sure 95% of the time that product will be supplied to the market well before the stock out situation?

14.17 Mean dimension of a machine having been adjusted at 0.3 mm with standard deviations as 0.01, twenty five sample measurements indicate mean dimension as 0.295. At 5% significance level, work out whether the machine would need the readjustment at this stage ?

14.18 Following table indicates various samples position of 15 lots of 100 items each

Lot No. :	1	2	3	4	5	6	7	8	9	10	11	12	13	14	15
No. of defectives :	5	3	2	7	8	10	5	6	2	3	4	9	8	10	7

Draw a suitable chart and find out if the process is in control.

14.19 In a manufacturing unit, a sample of 5 sheets is taken every one hour. The data collected from the measurment of thickness of these sheets is tabulated below :

Sample No.	*Thickness in mm for 5 sheets* I	II	III	IV	V
1	25	31	22	26	24
2	32	31	30	34	33
3	35	34	33	32	32
4	26	25	29	30	25
5	33	34	30	29	33
6	34	32	31	28	27

Draw the control chart for mean and range and establish whether the process is under control.

14.20 The manufacturer has assured a mean life of the machine to be 8 years with standard deviation of 1 year. Work out the probability that machine will last 10 years. Also establish the life of the machine with 95% reliability.

14.21 Control charts for $\bar{x}$ and R are to be established. The data were collected in a sample size of 6 and are given below. Determine the central line value and the control limits for it. State, if the process is in control.

Sample Number	*Mean* $= \bar{x}$	*Range* $= R$
1	20.35	0.34
2	20.40	0.36
3	20.15	0.30
4	19.95	0.37
5	20.20	0.33
6	20.38	0.30
7	20.43	0.31
8	20.39	0.33

14.22 While exercising quality control, the inspectors produced the following data. Determine the centre line and control limits for the data.

Sample Number	*Observations*		
	1	*2*	*3*
1	6.0	5.8	6.1
2	5.2	6.4	6.9
3	5.5	5.8	5.2
4	5.0	5.7	6.5
5	6.7	6.5	5.5
6	5.8	5.2	5.0
7	5.6	5.1	5.2
8	6.0	5.8	6.0
9	5.5	4.9	5.7
10	4.3	6.4	6.3
11	6.2	6.9	5.0
12	6.7	7.1	6.2

14.23 Workout the lot centre line and control limits on a control chart. State if the process is stable (sample size = 300)

Sample Number	*No. not conforming*	*Sample Number*	*No. not coforming*
	1	2	3
1	3	13	5
2	6	14	6
3	4	15	7
4	6	16	4
5	20	17	5
6	2	18	7
7	6	19	5
8	7	20	0
9	3	21	2
10	0	23	6
11	6	24	1
12	9	25	8

14.24 Draw an *np*-chart for a process to establish its statistical control, for sample of 30 products inspected every 4 hours and the fraction non-conforming is 0.06. Determine centre line and control limits.

14.25 For the given data, work out the centre value and control limits to establish if the process is in control

Sample Number	*Sample size*	*Number not conforming*
1	10	32
2	10	38
3	9	40
4	10	42
5	10	38
6	10	5
7	9	22
8	10	22
9	8	23
10	8	25
11	10	15
12	10	43
13	13	30
14	12	32
15	12	27

❀❀❀

TABLES

TABLE 1. RANDOM DIGITS

Row	Random Numbers of 4-digits								
1	0695	7741	8254	4297	0000	5277	6563	9265	1023	5925
2	0437	5434	8503	3928	6979	9393	8936	9088	5744	4790
3	6242	2998	0205	5469	3365	7950	7256	3716	8385	0253
4	7090	4074	1257	7175	3310-	0712	4748	4226	0604	3804
5	0683	6999	4828	7888	0087	9288	7855	2678	3315	6718
6	7013	4300	3768	2572	6473	2411	6285	0069	5422	6175
7	8808	2786	5369	9571	3412	2465	6419	3990	0294	0896
8	9876	3602	5812	0124	1997	6445	3176	2682	1259	1728
9	1873	1065	8976	1295	9434	3178	0602	0732	6616	7972
10	2581	3075	4622	2974	7069	5605	0420	2949	4387	7679
11	3785	6401	0540	5077	7132	4135	4646	3834	6753	1593
12	8626	4017	1544	4202	8986	1432	2810	2418	8052	2710
13	6253	0726	9483	6753	4732	2284	0421	3010	7885	8436
14	0113	4546	2212	9829	2351	1370	2707	3329	6574	7002
15	4646	6474	9983	8738	1603	8671	0489	9588	3309	5860
16	7873	7343	4432	2866	7973	3765	2888.	5154	2250	4339
17	3756	9204	2590	6577	2409	8234	8656	2336	7948	7478
18	2673	7115	5526	0747	3952	6804	3671	7486	3024	9858
19	0187	7045	2711	0349	7734	4396	0988	4887	7682	8990
20	7976	3862	8323	5997	6904	4977	1056	6638	6398	4552
21	5605	1819	8926	9557	2905	0802	7749	0845	1710	4125
22	2225	5556	2545	7480	8804	4161	0084	0787	2561	5113
23	2549	4166	1609	7570	4223	0032	4236	0169	4673	8034
24	6113	1312	5777	7058	2413	3932	5144	5998	7183	5210
25	2028	2537	9819	9215	9327	6640	5986	7935	2750	2981
26	7818	3655	5771	4026	5757	3171	6435	2990	I860	1796
27	9629	3383	1931	2631	5903	9372	1307	4061	5443	8663
28	6657	5967	3277	7141	3628	2588	9320	1972	7683	7544
29	4344	7388	2978	3945	0471	4882	1619	0093	2282	7024
30	3145	8720	2131	1614	1575	5239	0766	0404	4873	7986
31	1848	4094	9168	0903	6451	2823	7566	6644	1157	8889
32	0915	5578	0822	5887	5354	3632	4617	6016	8989	9482
33	1430	4755	7551	9019	8233	9625	6361	2589	2496	7268
34	3473	7966	7249	0555	6307	9524	4888	4939	1641	1573
35	3312	0773	6296	1348	5483	5824	3353	4587	1019	9677
36	6255	4204	5890	9273	0634	9992	3834	2283	1202	4849
37	0562	2546	8559	0480	9379	9282	8257	3054	4272	9311
38	1957	6783	4105	8976	8035	0883	8971	0017	6476	2895
39	7333	1083	0398	8841	0017	4135	4043	8157	4672	2424
40	4601	8908	1781	4287	2681	6223	0814	4477	3798	4437

TABLE 1. Continued

Row	Random Numbers of 4-digits									
41	2628	2233	0708	0900	1698	2818	3931	6930	9273	6749
42	5318	8865	6057	8422	6992	9697	0508	3370	5522	9250
43	6335	0852	8657	8374	0311	6012	9477	0112	8976	3312
44	0301	8333	0327	0467	6186	1770	4099	9588	5382	8958
45	1719	9775	1566	7020	4535	2850	0207	4792	6405	1472
46	8907	8226	4249	6340	9062	3572	7655	6707	3685	1282
47	6129	5927	3731	1125	0081	1241	2772	6458	9157	4543
48	7376	3150	8985	8318	8003	6106	4952	8492	2804	3867
49	9093	3407	4127	9258	3687	5631	5102	1546	2659	0831
50	1133	3086	9380	5431	8647	0910	6948	2257	0946	1245
51	4567	0910	8495	2410	1088	7067	8505	9083	4339	2440
52	6141	8380	2302	4608	7209	5738	9765	3435	9657	6061
53	1514	8309	8743	3096	0682	7902	8204	7508	8330	1681
54	7277	1634	7866	9883	0916	6363	5391	6184	8040	3135
55	4568	4758	0166	1509	2105	0976	0269	0278	7443	2431
56	9200	7599	7754	4534	4532	3102	6831	2387	4147	2455
57	3971	8149	4431	2345	6436	0627	0410	1348	6599	1296
58	2672	9661	2359	8477	3425	8150	6918	8883	1518	4708
59	1524	3268	3798	3360	2255	0371	7610	9114	9466	0901
60	6817	9007	5959	0767	1166	7317	7502	0274	6340	0427
61	6762	3502	9559	4279'	9271	9595	3053	4918	7503	5169
62	5264	0075	6655	4563	7112	7264	3240	2150	8180	1361
63	5070	8428	5149	2137	8728	9110	2334	9709	8134	3925
64	1664	3379	5273	9367	6950	6828	1711	7082	4783	0147
65	6962	7141	1904	6648	7328	2901	6396	9949	6274	1672
66	7541	4289	4970	2922	6670	8540	9053	3219	8881	1897
67	5244	4651	2934	6700	8869	0926	4191	1364	0926	2874
68	2939	3890	0745	2577	7931	3913	7877	2837	2500	8774
69	4266	6207	8083	6564	5336	5303	7503;	6627	6055	3606
70	7848	5477	5588	3490	0294	3609	1632	5684	1719	6162
71	3009	1879	0440	7916	6643	9723'	5933	0574	2480	6893
72	9865	7813	7468	8493	3293	1071	7183	9462	2363	6529
73	1196	1251	2368	1262	5769	9450	7485	4039	4985	6612
74	1067	3716	8897	1970	8799	5718	4792	7292	4589	4554
75	5160	5563	6527	7861	3477	6735	7748	4913	6370	2258
76	4560	0094	8284	7604	1667	9286	2228	9507	1838	4646
77	7697	2151	4860	0739	4370	3992	8121	2502	7670	4470
78	8675	2997	9783	7306	4116	6432	7233	4611	7121	9412
79	3597	3520	5995	0892	3470	4581	1068	8801	1254	8607
80	4281	8802	5880	6212	6818	8162	0052	1755	7107	5197

TABLE 2. AREAS UNDER THE NORMAL CURVE

(For positive values of Z)

An entry in the table is the proportion under the entire curve which is between z = 0 and a positive value of Z.

Example Z = 1.96, Area = Prob. = 0.4750

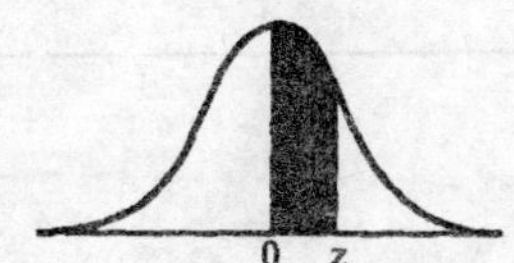

z	.00	.01	.02	.03	.04	.05	.06	.07	.08	.09
.0	.5000	.5040	.5080	.5120	.5160	.5199	.5239	.5279	.5319	.5359
.1	.5398	.5438	.5478	.5517	.5557	.5596	.5636	.5675	.5714	.5753
.2	.5793	.5832	.58711	.5910	.5948	.5987	.6026	.6064	.6103	.6141
.3	.6179	.6217	.6255	.6331	.6331	.6368	.6406	.6443	.6480	.6517
.4	.6554	.6591	.6628	.6664	.6700	.6736	.6772	.6808	.6844	.6879
.5	.6915	.6950	.6985	.7019	.7054	.7088	.7123	.7157	.7190	.7224
.6	.7257	.7291	.7324	.7357	.7389	.7422	.7454	.7486	.7517	.7549
.7	.7580	.7611	.7642	.7673	.7703	.7734	.7764	.7794	.7823	.7852
.8	.7881	.7910	.7939	.7967	.7995	.8023	.8051	.8078	.8106	.8133
.9	.8159	.8186	.8212	.8238	.8264	.8315	.8315	.8340	.8365	.8389
1.0	.8413	.8438	.8461	.8485	.8508	.8531	.8554	.8577	.8621	.8621
1.1	.8643	.8665	.8686	.8708	.8729	.8749	.8770	.8790	.8810	.8830
1.2	.8849	.8869	.8888	.8907	.8925	.8944	.8962	.8980	.8997	.9015
1.3	.9032	.9049	.9066	.9082	.9099	.9115	.9131	.9147	.9162	.9177
1.4	.9192	.9207	.9222	.9236	.9251	.9265	.9279	.9292	.9306	.9319
1.5	.9332	.9345	.9357	.9370	.9382	.9394	.9406	.9418	.9429	.9441
1.6	.9452	.9463	.9474	.9484	.9495	.9505	.9515	.9525	.9535	.9545
1.7	.9554	.9564	.9573	..9582	.9591	.9599	.9618	.9616	.9625	.9633
1.8	.9641	.9649	.9656	.9664	.9671	.9678	.9686	.9693	.9699	.9706
1.9	.9713	.9719	.9726	.9732	.9738	.9744	.9750	.9756	.9761	.9767
2.0	.9772	.9778	.9783	.9788	.9793	.9798	.9803	.9808	.9812	.9817
2.1	.9821	.9826	.9830	.9834	.9838	.9842	.9840	.9850	.9854	.9857
2.2	.9861	.9864	.9868	.9871	.9875	.9878	.9881	.9884	.9887	.9890
2.3	.9893	.9896	.9898	.9901	.9904	.9906	.9909	.9911	.9913	.9916
2.4	.9918	.9920	.9927	.9925	.9927	.9929	.9931	.9932	.9934	.9936
2.5	.9938	.9940	.9941	.9943	.9945	.9946	.9948	.9949	.9951	.9952
2.6	.9953	.9955	.9956	.9957	.9959	.9960	.9961	.9962	.9963	.9964
2.7	.9965	.9966	.9967	.9968	.9969	.9970	.9971	.9972	.9973	.9974
2.8	.9974	.9975	.9976	.9977	.9977	.9978	.9979	.9979	.9980	.9981
2.9	.9981	.9982	.9982	.9983	.9984	.9984	.9985	.9985	.9986	.9986
3.0	.9987	.9987	.9987	.9988	.9988	.9989	.9989	.9989	.9990	.9990
3.1	.9990	.9991	.9991	.9991	.9992	.9992	.9992	.9992	.9993	.9993
3.2	.9993	.9993	.9994	.9994	.9994	.9994	.9994	.9995	.9995	.9995
3.3	.9995	.9995	.9995	.9996	.9996	.9996	.9996	.9996	.9996	.9997
3.4	.9997	.9997	.9997	.9997	.9997	.9997	.9997	.9997	.9997	.9998
3.5	.9998	.9998	.9998	.9998	.9998	.9998	.9998	.9998	.9998	.9998

TABLE 3 : VALUES OF EXPONENTIAL FUNCTIONS

x	e^x	e^{-x}	x	e^x	e^{-x}
0.0	1.000	1.000	5.0	1.48.4	0.0067
0.1	1.105	0.905	5.1	164.0	0.0061
0.2	1.221	0.819	5.2	181.3	0.0055
0.3	1.350	0.741	5.3	200. 3	0.0050
0.4	1.492	0.670	5.4	221.4	0.0045
0.5	1.649	0.607	5.5	244.7	0.0041
0.6	1.822	0.549	5.6	270.4	0.0037
0.7	2.014	0.497	5.7	298.9	0.0033
0.8	2.226	0.449	5.8	330.3	0.0030
0.9	2.460	0.407	5.9	365.0	0.0027
1.0	2.718	0.368	6.0	403.4	0.0025
1.1	3.004	0.333	6.1	445.9	0.0022
1.2	3.320	0.301	6.2	492.8	0.0020
1.3	3.669	0.273	6.3	544.6	0.0018
1.4	4.055	0.247	6.4	601.8	0.0017
1.5	4.482	0.223	6.5	665.1	0.0015
1.6	4.953	0.202	6.6	735.1	0.0014
1.7	5.474	0.183	6.7	812.4	0.0012
1.8	6.050	0.165	6.8	897.8	0.0011
1.9	6.686	0.150	6.9	992.3	0.0010
2.0	7.389	0.135	7.0	1,096.6	0.0009
2.1	8.166	0.122	7.1	1,212.0	0.0008
2.2	9.025	0.111	7.2	1,339.4	0.0007
2.3	9.974	0.100	7.3	1,480.3	0.0007
2.4	11.023	0.091	7.4	1,636.0	0.0006
2.5	12.18	0.082	7.5	1,808.0	0.00055
2.6	13.46	0.074	7.6	1,998.2	0.00050
2.7	14.88	0.067	7.7	2,208.3	0.00045
2.8	16.44	0.061	7.8	2,440.6	0.00041
2.9	18.17	0.055	7.9	2,697.3	0.00037
3.0	20.09	0.050	8.0	2,981.0	0.00034
3.1	22.20	0.045	8.1	3,294.5	0.00030
3.2	24.53	0.041	8.2	3,641.0	0.00027
3.3	27.11	0.037	8.3	4,023.9	0.00025
3.4	29.69	0.033	8.4	4,447.1	0.00022
3.5	33.12	0.030	8.5	4,914.8	0.00020
3.6	36.60	0.027	8.6	5,431.7	0.00018
3.7	40.45	0.025	8.7	6,002.9	0.00017
3.8	44.70	0.022	8.8	6,634.2	0.00015
3.9	49.40	0.020	8.9	7,332.0	0.00014
4.0	54.60	0.018	9.0	8,103.1	0.00012
4.1	60.34	0.017	9.1	8,955.3	0.00011
4.2	66.69	0.015	9.2	9,897.1	0.00010
4.3	73.70	0.014	9.3	10,938	0.00009
4.4	81.45	0.012	9.4	12,088	0.00008
4.5	90.02	0.011	9.5	13,360	0.00007
4.6	99.48	0.010	9.6	14,765	0.00007
4.7	109.95	0.009	9.7	16,318	0.00006
4.8	121.51	0.008	9.8	18,034	0.00006
4.9	134.29	0.007	9.9	19,930	0.00005

TABLE 4. BINOMIAL COEFFICIENTS

$$P(X < c) = \sum_{x=0}^{c} \binom{n}{x} p^x (1-p)^{n-x}$$

		P										
		.05	.10	.20	.30	.40	.50	.60	.70	.80	.90	.95
	c											
n - 1	0	.950	.900	.800	.700	.600	.500	.400	.300	.200	.100	.050
	1	1.000	1.000	1.000	1.000	1.000	1.000	1.000	1.000	1.000	1.000	1.000
n = 2	0	.902	.810	.640	.490	.360	.250	.160	.090	.040	.010	.002
	1	.997	.990	.960	.910	.840	.750	.640	.510	.360	.190	.097
	2	1.000	1.000	1.000	1.000	1.000	1.000	1.000	1.000	1.000	1.000	1.000
n = 3	0	.857	.729	.512	.343	.216	.125	.064	.027	.008	,.001	.000
	1	.993	.972	.896	.784	.648	.500	.352	.216	.104	.028	.007
	2	1.000	.999	.992.	.973	.936	.875	.784	.657	,488	.271	.143
	3	1.000	1.000	1.000	1.000	1.000	1.000	1.000	1.000	1.000	1.000	1.000
n - 4	0	.815	.656	.410	.240	.130	.063	.026	.008	.002	.000	.000
	1	.986	.948	.819	.652	.475	.313	.179	.064	.027	.004	.000
	2	1.000	.996	.973	.916	.821	.688	.525	.348	.181	.052	.014
	3	1.000	1.000	.998	.992	.974	.938	.870	.760	.590	.344	.185
	4	1.000	1.000	1.000	1.000	1.000	1.000	1.000	1.000	1.000	1.000	1.000
n- 5	0	.774	.590	.328	.168	.078	.031	.010	.002	.000	.000	.000
	1	.977	.919	.737	.528	.337	.188	.087	.031	.007	.000	.000
	2	999	.991	.942	.837	.683	.500	.317	.163	.058	.009	.001
	3	1.000	1.000	993	.969	.913	.813	.663	.472	.263	.081	.023
	4	1.000	1.000	1.000	.998	.990	.969	.922	.832	.672	.410	.226
	5	1.000	1.000	1.000	1.000	1.000	1.000	1.000	1.000	1.000	1.000	1.000
n = 6	0	.735	.531	.262	.118	.047	.016	.004	.001	.000	.000	.000
	1	.967	.886	.655	.420	.233	.109	.041	.011	.002	.000	.000
	2	.998	.984	.901	.744	.544	.344	.179	.070	.017	.001	.000
	3	1.000	.999	.983	.930	.821	.656 .	.456	.256	.099	.016	.002
	4	1.000	1.000	.998	.989	.959	.891	.767	.580	.345	.114	.033
	5	1.000	1.000	1.000	.999	.996	.984	.953	.882	.738	.469	.265
	6	1.000	1.000	1.000	1.000	1.000	1.000	1.000	1.000	1.000	1.000	1.000
n = 7	0	.698	.478	.210	.082	.028	.008	.002	.000	.000	.000	.000
	1	.956	.850	.577	.329	.159	.063	.019	.004	.000	.000	.000
	2	.996	.974	.852	.647	.420	.227	.096	.029	.005	.000	.000
	3	1.000	.997	.967	.874	.710	.500	.290	.126	.033	.003	.000
	4	1.000	1.000	.995	.971	.904	.773	.580	.353	.148	.026	.004
	5	1.000	1.000	1.000	.996	.981	.938	.841	.671	.423	.150	.044
	6	1.000	1.000	1.000	1.000	.998	.992	.972	.918	.790	.522	.302
	7	1.000	1.000	1.000	1.000	1.000	1.000	1.000	1.000	1.000	1.000	1.000

TABLE 4. (Continued)

		P										
		.05	.10	.20	.30	.40	.50	.60	.70	.80	.90	.95
	c											
$n = 8$	0	.663	.430	.168	.058	.017	.004	.001	.000	.000	.000	.000
	1	.943	.813	.503	.255	.106	.035	.009	.001	.000	.000	.000
	2	.994	.962	.797	.552	.315	.145	.050	.011	.001	.000	.000
	3	1.000	.995	.944	.806	.594	.363	.174	.058	.010	.000	.000
	4	1.000	1.000	.990	.942	.826	.637	.406	.194	.056	.005	.000
	5	1.000	1.000	.999	.989	.950	.855	.685	.448	.203	.038	.006
	6	1.000	1.000	1.000	.999	.991	.965	.894	.745	.497	.187	.057
	7	1.000	1.000	1.000	1.000	.999	.996	.983	.942	.832	.570	.337
	8	1.000	1.000	1.000	1.000	1.000	1.000	1.000	1.000	1.000	1.000	1.000
$n = 9$	0	.630	.387	.134	.040	.010.	.002	.000	.000	.000	.000	.000
	1	.929	.775	.436	.196	.071	.020	.004	.000	.000	.000	.000
	2	.992	.947	.738	.463	.232	.090	.025	.004	.000	.000	.000
	3	.999	.992	.914	.730	.483	.254	.099	.025	.003	.000	.000
	4	1.000	.999	.980	.901	.733	.500	.267	.099	.020	.001	.000
	5	1.000	1.000	.997	.975	.901	.746	.517	.270	.086	.008	.001
	6	1.000	1.000	1.000	.996	.975	.910	.768	.537	.262	.053	.008
	7	1.000	1.000	1.000	1.000	.996	.980	.929	.804	564	.225	.071
	8	1.000	1.000	1.000	1.000	1.000	.998	.990	.960	.866	.613	.370
	9	1.000	1.000	1.000	1.000	1.000	1.000	1.000	1.000	1.000	1.000	1.000
$n = 10$	0	.599	.349	.107	.028	.006	.001	.000	.000	.000	.000	.000
	1	.914	.736	.376	.149	.046	.011	.002	.000	.000	.000	.000
	2	.988	.930	.678	.383	.167	.055	.0.12	.002	.000	.000	.000
	3	.999	.987	.879	.650	.382	.172	.055	.011	.001	.000	.000
	4	1.000	.998	.967	.850	.633	.377	.166	.047	.006	.000	.000
	5	1.000	1.000	.994	.953	.834	.623	.367	.150	.033	.002	.000
	6	1.000	1.000	.999	.989	.945	.828	.618	.350	.121	.013	.001
	7	1.000	1.000	1.000	.998	.988	.945	.833	.617	.322	.070	.012
	8	1.000	1.000	1.000	1.000	.998	.989	.954	.851	.624	.264	.086
	9	1.000	1.000	1.000	1.000	1.000	.999	.994	.972	.893	.651	.401
	10	1.000	1.000	1.000	1.000	1.000	1.000	1.000	1.000	1.000	1.000	1.000
$n = 11$	0	.569	.314	.086	.020	.004	.000	.000	.000	.000	.000	.000
	1	.898	.697	.322	.113	.030	.006	.001	.000	.000	.000	.000
	2	.985	.910	.617	.313	.119	.033	.006	.001	.000	.000	.000
	3	.998	.981	.839	.570	.296	.113	.029	.004	.000	.000	.000
	4	1.000	.997	.950	.790	.533	.274	.099	.022	.002	.000	.000
	5	1.000	1.000	.988	.922	.753	.500	.247	.078	.012	.000	.000
	6	1.000	1.000	.998	.978	.901	.726	.467	.210	.050	.003	.000
	7	1.000	1.000	1.000	.996	.971	.887	.704	.430	.161	.019	.002
	8	1.000	1.000	1.000	.999	.994	.967	.881	.687	.383	.090	.015
	9	1.000	1.000	1.000	1.000	.999	994	.970	.887	.678	.303	.102
	10	1.000	1.000	1.000	1.000	1.000	1.000	.996	.980	.914	.686	.431
	11	1.000	1.000	1.000	1.000	1.000	1.000	1.000	1.000	1.000	1.000	1.000

TABLE 4. (Continued)

		P										
	c	.05	.10	.20	.30	.40	.50	.60	.70	.80	.90	.95
$n = 12$	0	.540	.282	.069	.014	.002	.000	.000	.000	.000	.000	.000
	1	.882	.659	.275	.085	.020	.003	.000	.000	.000	.000	.000
	2	.980	.889	.558	.253	.083	.019	.003	.000	.000	.000	.000
	3	.998	.974	.795	.493	.225	.073	.015	.002	.000	.000	.000
	4	1.000	.996	.927	.724	.438	.194	.057	.009	.001	.000	.000
	5	1.000	.999	.981	.882	.665	.387	.158	.039	.004	.000	.000
	6	.000	1.000	.996	.961	.842	.613	.335	.118	.019	.001	.000
	7	.000	1.000	.999	.991	.943	.806	.562	.276	.073	.004	.000
	8	.000	1.000	1.000	.998	.985	.927	.775	.507	.205	.026	.002
	9	.000	1.000	1.000	1.000	.997	.981	.917	.747	.442	.111	.020
	10	.000	1.000	1.000	1.000	1.000	.997	.980	.915	.725	.341	.118
	11	.000	1.000	1.000	1.000	1.000	1.000	.998	.986	.931	.718	.460
	12	1.000	1.000	1.000	1.000	1.000	1.000	1.000	1.000	1.000	1.000	1.000
$n = 13$	0	.513	.254	.055	.010	.001	.000	.000	.000	.000	.000	.000
	1	.865	.621	.234	.064	.013	.002	.000	.000	.000	.000	.000
	2	.975	.866	.502	.202	.058	.011	.001	.000	.000	.000	.000
	3	.997	.966	.747	.421	.169	.046	.008	.001	.000	.000	.000
	4	1.000	.994	.901	.654	.353	.133	.032	.004	.000	.000	.000
	5	1.000	.999	.970	.835	.574	.291	.098	.018	.001	.000	.000
	6	1.000	1.000	.993	.938	.771	.500	.229	.062	.007	.000	.000
	7	1.000	1.000	.999	.982	.902	.709	.426	.165	.030	.001	.000
	8	1.000	1.000	1.000	.996	.968	.867	.647	.346	.099	.006	.000
	9	1.000	1.000	1.000	.999	.992	.954	.831	.579	.253	.034	.003
	10	1.000	1.000	1.000	1.000	.999	.989	.942	.798	.498	.134	.025
	11	1.000	1.000	1.000	1.000	1.000	.998	.987	.936	.766	.379	.135
	12	1.000	1.000	1.000	1.000	1.000	1.000	.999	.990	.945	.746	.487
	13	1.000	1.000	1.000	1.000	1.000	1.000	1.000	1.000	1.000	1.000	1.000
$n = 14$	0	.488	.229	.044	.007	.001	.000	.000	.000	.000	.000	.000
	1	.847	.585	.198	.047	.008	.001	.000	.000	.000	.000	.000
	2	.970	.842	.448	.161	.040	.006	.001	.000	.000	.000	.000
	3	.996	.956	.698	.355	.124	.029	.004	.000	.000	.000	.000
	4	1.000	.991	.870	.584	.279	.090	.018	.002	.000	.000	.000
	5	1.000	.999	.956	.781	.486	.212	.058	.008	.000	.000	.000
	6	1.000	1.000	.988	.907	.692	.395	.150	.031	.002	.000	.000
	7	1.000	1.000	.998	.969	.850	.605	.308	.093	.012	.000	.000
	8	1.000	1.000	1.000	.992	.942	.788	.514	.219	.044	.001	.000
	9	1.000	1.000	1.000	.998	.982	.910	.721	.416	.130	.009	.000
	10	1.000	1.000	1.000	1.000	.996	.971	.876	.645	.302	.044	.004
	11	1.000	1.000	1.000	1.000	.999	.994	.960	.839	.552	.158	.030
	12	1.000	1.000	1.000	1.000	1.000	.999	.992	.953	.802	.415	.153
	13	1.000	1.000	1.000	1.000	1.000	1.000	.999	.993	.956	.771	.512
	14	1.000	1.000	1.000	1.000	1.000	1.000	1.000	1.000	1.000	1.000	1.000

TABLE 4. (Continued)

		P										
		.05	.10	.20	.30	.40	.50	.60	.70	.80	.90	.95
	c											
n = 15	0	.463	.206	.035	.005	.000	.000	.000	.000	.000	.000	.000
	1	.829	.549	.167	.035	.005	.000	.000	.000	.000	.000	.000
	2	.964	.816	.398	.127	.027	.004	.000	.000	.000	.000	.000
	3	.995	.944	.648	.297	.091	.018	.002	.000	.000	.000	.000
	4	.999	.987	.836	.515	.217	.059	.009	.001	.000	.000	.000
	5	1.000	.998	.939	.722	.403	.151	.034	.004	.000	.000	.000
	6	1.000	1.000	.982	.869	.610	.304	.095	.015	.001	.000	.000
	7	1.000	1.000	.996	.850	.787	.500	.213	.050	.004	.000	.000
	8	1.000	1.000	.999	.985	.905	.696	.390	.131	.018	.000	.000
	9	1.000	1.000	1.000	.996	.966	.849	.597	.278	.061	.002	.000
	10	1.000	1.000	1.000	.999	.991	.941	.783	.485	.164	.013	.001
	11	1.000	1.000	1.000	1.000	.998	.982	.909	.703	.352	.056	.005
	12	1.000	1.000	1.000	1.000	1.000	.996	.973	.873	.602	.184	.036
	13	1.000	1.000	1.000	1.000	1.000	1.000	.995	.965	.833	.451	.171
	14	1.000	1.000	1.000	1.000	1.000	1.000	1.000	.995	.965	.794	.537
	15	1.000	1.000	1.000	1.000	1.000	1.000	1.000	1.000	1.000	1.000	1.000
n = 16	0	.440	.185	.028	.003	.000	.000	.000	.000	.000	.000	.000
	1	.811	.515	.141	.026	.003	.000	.000	.000	.000	.000	.000
	2	.957	.789	.352	.099	.018	.002	.000	.000	.000	.000	.000
	3	.993	.932	.598	.246	.065	.011	.001	.000	.000	.000	.000
	4	.999	.983	.798	.450	.167	.038	.005	.000	.000	.000	.000
	5	1.000	.997	.918	.660	.329	.105	.019	.002	.000	.000	.000
	6	1.000	999	.973	.825	.527	.227	.058	.007	.000	.000	.000
	7	1.000	1.000	.993	.926	.716	.402	.142	.026	.001	.000	.000
	8	1.000	1.000	.999	.974	.858	.598	.284	.074	.007	.000	.000
	9	1.000	1.000	1.000	.993	.942	.773.	.473	.175	.027	.001	.000
	10	1.000	1.000	1.000	.998	.981	.895	.671	.340	.082	.003	.000
	11	1.000	1.000	1.000	1.000	.995	.962	.833	.550	.202	.017	.001
	12	1.000	1.000	1.000	1.000	.999	.989	.935	.754	.402	.068	.007
	13	1.000	1.000	1.000	1.000	1.000.	.998	.982	.901	.648	.211	.043
	14	1.000	1.000	1.000	1.000	1.000	1.000	.997	.974	.859	.485	.189
	15	1.000	1.000	1.000	1.000	1.000	1.000	1.000	.997	.972	.815	.560
	16	1.000	1.000	1.000	1.000	1.000	1.000	1.000	1.000	1.000	1.000	1.000

TABLE 4. (Continued)

	c	P .05	.10	.20	.30	.40	.50	.60	.70	.80	.90	.95
$n = 17$	0	.418	.167	.023	.002	.000	.000	.000	.000	.000	.000	.000
	1	.792	.482	.118	.019	.002	.000	.000	.000	.000	.000	.000
	2	.950	.762	.310	.077	.012	.001	.000	.000	.000	.000	.000
	3	.991	.917	.549	.202	.046	.006	.000	.000	.000	.000	.000
	4	.999	.978	.758	.389	.126	.025	.003	.000	.000	.000	.000
	5	1.000	.995	.894	.597	.264	.072	.011	.001	.000	.000	.000
	6	1.000	.999	.962	.775	.448	.166	.035	.003	.000	.000	.000
	7	1.000	1.000	.989	.895	.641	.315	.092	.013	.000	.000	.000
	8	1.000	1.000	.997	.960	.801	.500	.199	.040	.003	.000	.000
	9	1.000	1.000	1.000	.987	.908	.685	.359	.105	.011	.000	.000
	10	1.000	1.000	1.000	.997	.965	.834	.552	.225	.038	.001	.000
	11	1.000	1.000	1.000	.999	.989	.928	.736	.403	.106	.005	.000
	12	1.000	1.000	1.000	1.000	.997	.975	.874	.611	.242	.022	.001
	13	1.000	1.000	1.000	1.000	1.000	.994	954	.798	.451	.083	.009
	14	1.000	1.000	1.000	1.000	1.000	.999	.988	.923	.690	.238	.050
	15	1.000	1.000	1.000	1.000	1.000	1.000	.998	.981	.882	.518	.208
	16	1.000	1.000	1.000	1.000	1.000	1.000	1.000	.998	.977	.833	.582
	17	1.000	1.000	1.000	1.000	1.000	1.000	1.000	1.000	1.000	1.000	1.000
$n = 18$	0	.397	.150	.018	.002	.000	.000	.000	.000	.000	.000	.000
	1	.774	.450	.099	.014	.001	.000	.000	.000	.000	.000	.000
	2	.942	.734	.271	.060	.008	.001	.000	.000	.000	.000	.000
	3	.989	.902	.501	.165	.033	.004	.000	.000	.000	.000	.000
	4	.998	.972	.716	.333	.094	.015	.001	.000	.000	.000	.000
	5	1.000	.994	.867	.534	.209	.048	.006	.000	.000	.000	.000
	6	1.000	.999	.949	.722	.374	.119	.020	.001	.000	.000	.000
	7	1.000	1.000	.984	.859	.563	.240	.058	.006	.000	.000	.000
	8	1.000	1.000	.996	.940	.737	.407	.135	.021	.001	.000	.000
	9	1.000	1.000	.999	.979	.865	.593	.263	.060	.004	.000	.000
	10	1.000	1.000	1.000	.994	.942	.760	.437	.141	.016	.000	.000
	11	1.000	1.000	1.000	.999	.980	.881	.626	.278	.051	.001	.000
	12	1.000	1.000	1.000	1.000	.994	.952	.791	.466	.133	.006	.000
	13	1.000	1.000	1.000	1.000	.999	.985	.906	.667	.284	.028	.002
	14	1.000	1.000	1.000	1.000	1.000	.996	.967	.835	.499	.098	.011
	15	1.000	1.000	1.000	1.000	1.000	.999	.992	.940	.729	.266	.058
	16	1.000	1.000	1.000	1.000	1.000	1.000	.999	.986	.901	.550	.226
	17	1.000	1.000	1.000	1.000	1.000	1.000	1.000	.998	.982	.850	.603
	18	1.000	1.000	1.000	1.000	1.000	1.000	1.000	1.000	1.000	1.000	1.000

TABLE 4. (Continued)

		P										
		.05	.10	.20	.30	.40	.50	.60	.70	.80	.90	.95
	c											
n = 19	0	.377	.135	.014	.001	.000	.000	.000	.000	.000	.090	.000
	1	.755	.420	.083	.010	.001	.000	.000	.000	.000	.000	.000
	2	.933	.705	.237	.046	.005	.000	.000	.000	.000	.000	.000
	3	.987	.885	.455	.133	.023	.002	.000	.000	.000	.000	.000
	4	.998	.965	.673	.282	.070	.010	.001	.000	.000	.000	.000
	5	1.000	.991	.837	.474	.163	.032	.003	.000	.000	.000	.000
	6	1.000	.998	.932	.666	.308	.084	.012	.001	.000	.000	.000
	7	1.000	1.000	.977	.818	.488	.180	.035	.003	.000	.000	.000
	8	1.000	1.000	.993	.916	.667	.324	.088	.011	.000	.000	.000
	9	1.000	1.000	.998	.967	.814	.500	.186	.033	.002	.000	.000
	10	1.000	1.000	1.000	.989	.912	.676	.333	.084	.007	.000	.000
	11	1.000	1.000	1.000	.997	.965	.820	.512	.182	.023	.000	.000
	12	1.000	1.000	1.000	.999	.988	.916	.692	.334	.068	.002	.000
	13	1.000	1.000	1.000	1.000	.997	.968	.837	.526	.163	.009	.000
	14	1.000	1.000	1.000	1.000	.999	.990	.930	.718	.327	.035	.002
	15	1.000	1.000	1.000	1.000	1.000	.998	.977	.867	.545	.115	.013
	16	1.000	1.000	1.000	1.000	1.000	1.000	.995	.954	.763	.295	.067
	17	1.000	1.000	1.000	1.000	1.000	1.000	.999	.990	.917	.580	.245
	18	1.000	1.000	1.000	1.000	1.000	1.000	1.000	.999	.986	.865	.623
	19	1.000	1.000	1.000	1.000	1.000	1:000	1.000	1.000	1.000	1.000	1.000
n = 20	0	.358	.122	.012	.001	.000	.000	.000	.000	.000	.000	.000
	1	.736	.392	.069	.008	.001	.000	.000	.000	.000	.000	.000
	2	.925	.677	.206	.035	.004	.004	.000	.000	.000	.000	.000
	3	.984	.867	.411	.107	.016	.001	.000	.000	.000	.000	.000
	4	.997	.957	.630	.238	.051	.006	.000	.000	.000	.000	.000
	5	1.000	.989	.804	.416	.126	.021	.002	.000	.000	.000	.000
	6	1.000	.998	.913	.608	.250	.058	.006	.000	.000	.000	.000
	7	1.000	1.000	.968	.772	.416	.132	.021	.001	.000	.000	.000
	8	1.000	1.000	.990	.887	.596	.252	.057	.005	.000	.000	.000
	9	1.000	1.000	.997	.952	.755	.412	.128	.017	.001	.000	.000
	10	1.000	1.000	.999	.983	.872	.588	.245	.048	.003	.000	.000
	11	1.000	1.000	1.000	.995	.943	.748	.404	.113	.010	.000	.000
	12	1.000	1.000	1.000	.999	.979	.868	.584	.228	.032	.000	.000
	13	1.000	1.000	1.000	1.000	.994	.942	.750	.392	.087	.002	.000
	14	1.000	1.000	1.000	1.000	.998	.979	.874	.584	.196	.011	.000
	15	1.000	1.000	1.000	1.000	1.000	.994	.949	.762	.370	.043	.003
	16	1.000	1.000	1.000	1.000	1.000	.999	.984	.893	.589	.133	.016
	17	1.000	1.000	1.000	1.000	1.000	1.000	.996	.965	.794	.323	.075
	18	1.000	1.000	1.000	1.000	1.000	1.000	.999	.992	.931	.608	.264
	19	1.000	1.000	1.000	1.000	1.000	1.000	1.000	.999	.988	.878	.642
	20	1.000	1.000	1.000	1.000	1.000	1.000	1.000	1.000	1.000	1.000	1.000

TABLE 4. (Continued)

		p										
		.05	.10	.20	.30	.40	.50	.60	.70	.80	.90	.95
	c											
n = 25	0	.277	.072	.004	.000	.000	.000	.000	.000	.000	.000	.000
	1	.642	.271	.027	.002	.000	.000	.000	.000	.000	.000	.000
	2	.873	.537	.098	.009	.000	.000	.000	.000	.000	.000	.000
	3	.966	.764	.234	.033	.002	.000	.000	.000	.000	.000	.000
	4	.993	.902	.421	.090	.009	.000	.000	.000	.000	.000	.000
	5	.999	.967	.617	.193	.029	.002	.000	.000	.000	.000	.000
	6	1.000	.991	.780	.341	.074	.007	.000	.000	.000	.000	.000
	7	1.000	.998	.891	.512	.154	.022	.001	.000	.000	.000	.000
	8	1.000	1.000	.953	.677	.274	.054	.004	.000	.000	.000	.000
	9	1.000	1.000	.983	.811	.425	115	.013	.000	.000	.000	.000
	10	1.000	1.000	.994	.902	.586	.212	.034	.002	.000	.000	.000
	11	1.000	1.000	.998	.956	.732	.345	.078	.006	.000	.000	.000
	12	1.000	1.000	1.000	.983	.846	.500	.154	.017	.000	.000	.000
	13	1.000	1.000	1.000	.994	.922	.655	.268	.044	.002	.000	.000
	14	1.000	1.000	1.006	.998	.966	.788	.414	.096	.006	.000	.000
	15	1.000	1.000	1.000	1.000	.987	.885	.575	.189	.017	.000	.000
	16	1.000	1.000	1.000	1.000	.996	.946	.726	.323	.047	.000	.000
	17	1.000	1.000	1.000	1.000	.999	.978	.846	.488	.109	.002	.000
	18	1.000	1.000	1.000	1.000	1.000	.993	.926	.659	.220	.009	.000
	19	1.000	1.000	1.000	1.000	1,000	.998	.971	.807	.383	.033	.001
	20	1.000	1.000	1.000	1.000	1.000	1.000	.991	.910	.579	.098	.007
	21	1.000	1.000	1.000	1.000	1.000	1.000	.998	.967	.766	.236	.034
	22	1.000	1.000	1.000	1.000	1.000	1.000	1.000	.991	.902	.463	.127
	23	1.000	1.000	1.000	1.000	1.000	1.000	1.000	.998	.973	.729	.358
	24	1.000	1.000	1.000	1.000	1.000	1.000	1.000	1.000	.996	.928	.723
	25	1.000	1.000	1.000	1.000	1.000	1.000	1.000	1.000	1.000	1.000	1.000

TABLE 5. VALUES FOR POISSON DISTRIBUTION

x\λ	0.1	0.2	0.3	0.4	0.5	0.6	0.7	0.8	0.9	1.0
0	0.9048	0.8187	0.7408	0.6703	0.6065	0.5488	0.4966	0.4493	0.4066	0.3679
1	0.0905	0.1637	0.2222	0.2681	0.3033	0.3293	0.3476	0.3595	0.3639	0.3679
2	0.0045	0.0164	0.0333	0.0536	0.0758	0.0988	0.1217	0.1438	0.1647	0.1839
3	0.0002	0.0011	0.0033	0.0072	0.0126	0.0198	0.0284	0.0383	0.0494	0.0613
4	0.0000	0.0001	0.0003	0.0007	0.0016	0.0030	0.0050	0.0077	0.0111	0.0153
5	0.0000	0.0000	0.0000	0.0001	0.0002	0.0004	0.0007	0.0012	0.0020	0.0031
6	0.0000	0.0000	0.0000	0.0000	0.0000	0.0000	0.0001	0.0002	0.0003	0.0005
7	0.0000	0.0000	0.0000	0.0000	0.0000	0.0000	0.0000	0.0000	0.0000	0.0001

x\λ	1.1	1.2	1.3	1.4	1.5	1.6	1.7	1.8	1.9	2.0
0	0.3329	0.3012	0.2725	0.2466	0.2231	0.2019	0.1827	0.1653	0.1496	0.1353
1	0.3662	0.3614	0.3543	0.3452	0.3347	0.3230	0.3106	0.2975	0.2842	0.2707
2	0.2014	0.2169	0.2303	0.2417	0.2510	0.2584	0.2640	0.2678	0.2700	0.2707
3	0.0738	0.0867	0.0998	0.1128	0.1255	0.1378	0.1496	0.1607	0.1710	0.1804
4	0.0203	0.0260	0.0324	0.0395	0.0471	0.0551	0.0636	0.0723	0.0812	0.0902
5	0.0045	0.0062	0.0084	0.0111	0.0141	0.0176	0.0216	0.0260	0.0309	0.0361
6	0.0008	0.0012	0.0018	0.0026	0.0035	0.0047	0.0061	0.0078	0.0098	0.0120
7	0.0001	0.0002	0.0003	0.0005	0.0008	0.0011	0.0015	0.0020	0.0027	0.0034
8	0.0000	0.0000	0.0001	0.0001	0.0001	0.0002	0.0003	0.0005	0.0006	0.0009
9	0.0000	0.0000	0.0000	0.0000	0.0000	0.0000	0.0001	0.0001	0.0001	0.0002

x\λ	2.1	2.2	2.3	2.4	2.5	2.6	2.7	2.8	2.9	3.0
0	0.1225	0.1108	0.1003	0.0907	0.0821	0.0743	0.0672	0.0608	0.0550	0.0498
1	0.2572	0.2438	0.2306	0.2177	0.2052	0.1931	0.1815	0.1703	0.1596	0.1494
2	0.2700	0.2681	0.2652	0.2613	0.2565	0.2510	0.2450	0.2384	0.2314	0.2240
3	0.1890	0.1966	0.2033	0.2090	0.2138	0.2176	0.2205	0.2225	0.2237	0.2240
4	0.0992	0.1082	0.1169	0.1254	0.1336	0.1414	0.1488	0.1557	0.1622	0.1680
5	0.0417	0.0476	0.0538	0.0602	0.0668	0.0735	0.0804	0.0872	0.0940	0.1008
6	0.0146	0.0174	0.0206	0.0241	0.0278	0.0319	0.0362	0.0407	0.0455	0.0504
7	0.0044	0.0055	0.0068	0.0083	0.0099	0.0118	0.0139	0.0163	0.0088	0.0216
8	0.0011	0.0015	0.0019	0.0025	0.0031	0.0038	0.0047	0.0057	0.0068	0.0081
9	0.0003	0.0004	0.0005	0.0007	0.0009	0.0010	0.0014	0.0018	0.0022	0.0027
10	0.0001	0.0001	0.0001	0.0002	0.0002	0.0003	0.0004	0.0005	0.0006	0.0008
11	0.0000	0.0000	0.0000	0.0000	0.0000	0.0001	0.0001	0.0001	0.0002	0.0002
12	0.0000	0.0000	0.0000	0.0000	0.0000	0.0000	0.0000	0.0000	0.0000	0.0001

TABLE 5. CONTINUED

x \ λ	3.1	3.2	3.3	3.4	3.5	3.6	3.7	3.8	3.9	4.0
0	0.0450	0.0408	0.0379	0.0334	0.0302	0.0273	0.0247	0.0224	0.0202	0.0183
1	0.1397	0.1304	0.1217	0.1135	0.1057	0.0984	0.0915	0.0850	0.0789	0.0733
2	0.2165	0.2087	0.2008	0.1929	0.1850	0.1771	0.1692	0.1615	0.1539	0.1465
3	0.2237	0.2226	0.2209	0.2186	0.2158	0.2125	0.2087	0.2046	0.2001	0.1954
4	0.1734	0.1781	0.1823	0.1858	0.1888	0.1912	0.1931	0.1944	0.1951	0.1954
5	0.1075	0.1140	0.1203	0.1264	0.1322	0.1377	0.1429	0.1477	0.1522	0.1563
6	0.0555	0.0608	0.0662	0.0716	0.0771	0.0826	0.0881	0.0936	0.0989	0.1042
7	0.0246	0.0278	0.0312	0.0348	0.0385	0.0425	0.0466	0.0508	0.0551	0.0595
8	0.0095	0.0111	0.0129	0.0148	0.0169	0.0191	0.0215	0.0241	0.0269	0.0298
9	0.0033	0.0040	0.0047	0.0056	0.0066	0.0076	0.0089	0.0102	0.0116	0.0132
10	0.0010	0.0013	0.0016	0.0019	0.0023	0.0028	0.0033	0.0039	0.0045	0.0053
11	0.0003	0.0004	0.0005	0.0006	0.0007	0.0009	0.0011	0.0013	0.0016	0.0019
12	0.0001	0.0001	0.0001	0.0002	0.0002	0.0003	0.0003	0.0004	0.0005	0.0006
13	0.0000	0.0000	0.0000	0.0000	0.0001	0.0001	0.0001	0.0001	0.0002	0.0002
14	0.0000	0.0000	0.0000	0.0000	0.0000	0.0000	0.0000	0.0000	0.0000	0.0001

For a given value of λ, entry indicates the proability of obtaining a specified value of x.

TABLE 6. VALUES FOR SPEARMAN'S RANK CORRELATION

n	0.20	0.10	0.05	0.02	0.01	0.002
4	0.8000	0.8000				
5	0.7000	0.8000	0.9000	0.9000		
6	0.6000	0.7714	0.8286	0.8857	0.9429	
7	0.5357	0.6786	0.7450	0.8571	0.8929	0.9643
8	0.5000	0.6190	0.7143	0.8095	0.8571	0.9286
9	0.4667	0.5833	0.6833	0.7667	0.8167	0.9000
10	0.4424	0.5515	0.6364	0.7333	0.7818	0.8667
11	0.4182	0.5273	0.6091	0.7000	0.7455	0.8364
12	0.3986	0.4965	0.5804	0.6713	0.7273	0.8182
13	0.3791	0.4780	0.5549	0.6429	0.6978	0.7912
14	0.3626	0.4593	0.5341	0.6220	0.6747	0.7670
15	0.3500	0.4429	0.5179	0.6000	0.6536	0.7464
16	0.3382	0.4265	0.5000	0.5824	0.6324	0.7265
17	0.3260	0.4118	0.4853	0.5637	0.6152	0.7083
18	0.3148	0.3994	0.4716	0.5480	0.5975	0.6904
19	0.3070	0.3895	0.4579	0.5333	0.5825	0.6737
20	0.2977	0.3789	0.4451	0.5203	0.5684	0.6586
21	0.2909	0.3688	0.4351	0.5078	0.5545	0.6455
22	0.2829	0.3597	0.4241	0.4963	0.5426	0.6318
23	0.2767	0.3518	0.4150	0.4852	0.5306	0.6186
24	0.2704	0.3435	0.4061	0.4748	0.5200	0.6070
25	0.2646	0.3362	0.3977	0.4654	0.5100	0.5962
26	0.2588	0.3299	0.3894	0.4564	0.5002	0.5856
27	0.2540	0.3236	0.3822	0.4481	0.4915	0.5757
28	0.2490	0.3175	0.3749	0.4401	0.4828	0.5660
29	0.2443	0.3113	0.3685	0.4320	0.4744	0.5567
30	0.2400	0.3059	0.3620	0.4251	0.4665	0.5479

For a two-tailed significance test at the 0.20 level with n = 15, the appropriate value of Rs. can be found by looking under the 0.20 column and n = 15 row. The value at the intersection is 0.3500.

TABLE 7. χ^2 DISTRIBUTION VALUES

Degree of freedom	Area in right tail for confidence level 0.99	0.975	0.95	0.90	0.10	0.05	0.25	0.01
1	0.00016	0.00098	0.00398	0.0158	2.706	3.841	5.024	6.635
2	0.0201	0.0506	0.103	0.211	4.605	5.991	7.378	9.210
3	0.115	0.216	0.352	0.584	6.251	7.815	9.348	11.345
4	0.297	0.484	0.711	1.064	7.779	9.488	11.143	13.277
5	0.554	0.831	1.145	1.610	9.236	11.070	12.833	15.086
6	0.872	1.237	1.635	2.204	10.645	12.02	14.449	16.812
7	1.239	1.690	2.167	2.833	12.017	14.067	16.013	18.475
8	1.646	2.180	2.733	3.490	13.362	15.507	17.535	20.090
9	2.088	2.700	3.325	4.168	14.684	16.919	19.023	21.666
10	2.558	3.247	3.940	4.865	15.987	18.307	20.483	23.209
11	3.053	3.816	4.575	5.578	17.275	19.675	21.920	24.725
12	3.571	4.404	5.226	6.304	18.549	21.026	23.337	26.217
13	4.107	5.009	5.892	7.042	19.812	22.362	24.736	27.688
14	4.660	5.629	6.571	7.790	21.064	23.685	26.119	29.141
15	5.229	6.262	7.261	8.547	22.307	24.996	27.488	30.578
16	5.812	6.908	7.962	9.312	23.542	26.296	28.845	32.000
17	6.408	7.564	8.672	10.085	24.769	27.587	30.191	33.409
18	7.015	8.231	9.390	10.865	25.989	28.869	31.526	34.805
19	7.633	8.907	10.117	11.651	27.204	30.144	32.852	36.191
20	8.260	9.591	10.851	12.443	28.412	31.410	34.170	37.566
21	8.897	10.283	11.591	13.240	29.615	32.671	35.479	38.932
22	9.542	10.982	12.338	14.041	30.813	33.924	36.781	40.289
23	10.196	11.689	13.091	14.848	32.007	35.172	38.076	41.638
24	10.856	12.401	13.848	15.658	33.196	36.415	39.364	42.980
25	11.524	13.120	14.611	16.473	34.328	37.652	40.647	44.314
26	12.198	13.844	15.379	17.292	35.563	38.885	41.923	45.642
27	12.879	14.573	16.151	18.114	36.741	40.113	43.194	46.963
28	13.565	15.308	16.928	18.939	37.916	41.337	44.461	48.278
29	14.256	16.047	17.708	19.768	39.087	42.557	45.722	49.588
30	14.953	16.791	18.493	20.599	40.256	43.773	46.979	50.892

In a Chi-square (χ^2) Distribution with 10 degrees of freedom, to find the value under 0.05 of area on the right, look for cross-section of values of 10 degrees of freedom row and 0.05 column to find the value 18.307.

TABLE 8. t-DISTRIBUTION VALUES

Degree of freedom	Area in both tails combined			
	0.10	0.05	0.02	0.01
1	6.314	12.706	31.821	63.657
2	2.920	4.303	6.965	9.925
3	2.353	3.182	4.541	5.841
4	2.132	2.776	3.747	4.604
5	2.015	2.571	3.365	4.032
6	1.943	2.447	3.143	3.707
7	1.895	2.365	2.998	3.499
8	1.860	2.306	2.896	3.355
9	1.833	2.262	2.821	3.250
10	1.812	2.228	2.764	3.169
11	1.796	2.201	2.718	3.106
12	1.782	2.179	2.681	3.055
13	1.771	2.160	2.650	3.012
14	1.761	2.145	2.624	2.977
15	1.753	2.131	2.602	2.947
16	1.746	2.120	2.583	2.921
17	1.740	2.110	2.567	2.898
18	1.734	2.101	2.552	2.878
19	1.729	2.093	2.539	2.861
20	1.725	2.086	2.528	2.845
21	1.721	2.080	2.518	2.831
22	1.717	2.074	2.508	2.819
23	1.714	2.069	2.500	2.807
24	1.711	2.064	2.492	2.797
25	1.708	2.060	2.485	2.787
26	1.706	2.056	2.479	2.779
27	1.703	2.052	2.473	2.771
28	1.701	2.048	2.467	2.763
29	1.699	2.045	2.462	2.756
30	1.697	2.042	2.457	2.750
40	1.684	2.021	2.423	2.704
60	1.671	2.000	2.390	2.660
120	1.658	1.980	2.358	2.617
Normal Distribution	1.645	1.960	2.326	2.576

To find the value of t that corresponds to an area of 0.10 in both the tails combined when there are 12 degrees of freedom, look under 0.10 column and stop where degess of freedom is equal to 12. The value is 1.782.

TABLE 9. F - DISTRIBUTION VALUE ($\alpha = 0.01$)

Degress of freedom for denominator	Degrees of freedom for numerator																		
	1	2	3	4	5	6	7	8	9	10	12	15	20	24	30	40	60	120	∞
1	4,052	5,000	5,403	5,625	5,764	5,859	5,928	5,982	6,023	6,056	6,106	6,157	6,209	6,235	6,261	6,287	6,313	6,339	6,366
2	98.5	99.0	99.2	99.2	99.3	99.3	99.4	99.4	99.4	99.4	99.4	99.4	99.24	99.5	99.5	99.5	99.5	99.5	99.5
3	34.1	30.8	29.5	28.7	28.2	27.9	27.7	27.5	27.3	27.2	27.1	26.9	26.7	26.6	26.5	26.4	26.3	26.2	26.1
4	21.2	18.0	16.7	16.0	15.5	15.2	15.0	14.8	14.7	14.5	14.4	14.2	14.0	13.9	13.8	13.7	13.7	13.6	13.5
5	16.3	13.3	12.1	11.4	11.0	10.7	10.5	10.3	10.2	10.1	9.89	9.72	9.55	9.47	9.38	9.29	9.20	9.11	9.02
6	13.7	10.9	9.78	9.15	8.75	8.47	8.26	8.10	7.98	7.87	7.72	7.56	7.40	7.31	7.23	7.14	7.06	6.97	6.88
7	12.2	9.55	8.45	7.85	7.46	7.19	6.99	6.84	6.72	6.62	6.47	6.31	6.16	6.07	5.99	5.91	5.82	5.74	5.65
8	11.3	8.65	7.59	7.01	6.63	6.37	6.18	6.03	5.91	5.81	5.67	5.52	5.36	5.28	5.20	5.12	5.03	4.95	4.86
9	10.6	8.02	6.99	6.42	6.06	5.80	5.61	5.47	5.35	5.26	5.11	4.96	4.81	4.73	4.65	4.57	4.48	4.40	4.31
10	10.0	7.56	6.55	5.99	5.64	5.39	5.20	5.06	4.94	4.85	4.71	4.56	4.41	4.33	4.25	4.17	4.08	4.00	3.91
11	9.65	7.21	6.22	5.67	5.32	5.07	4.89	4.74	4.63	4.54	4.40	4.25	4.10	4.02	3.94	3.86	3.78	3.69	3.60
12	9.33	6.93	5.95	5.41	5.06	4.82	4.64	4.50	4.39	4.30	4.16	4.01	3.86	3.78	3.70	3.62	3.54	3.45	3.36
13	9.07	6.70	5.74	5.21	4.86	4.62	4.44	4.30	4.19	4.10	3.96	3.82	3.66	3.59	3.51	3.43	3.34	3.25	3.17
14	8.86	6.51	5.56	5.04	4.70	4.46	4.28	4.14	4.03	3.94	3.80	3.66	3.51	3.43	3.35	3.27	3.18	3.09	3.00
15	8.68	6.36	5.42	4.89	4.56	4.32	4.14	4.00	3.89	3.80	3.67	3.52	3.37	3.29	3.21	3.13	3.05	2.96	2.87
16	8.53	6.23	5.29	4.77	4.44	4.20	4.03	3.89	3.78	3.69	3.55	3.41	3.26	3.18	3.10	3.02	2.93	2.84	2.75
17	8.40	6.11	5.19	4.67	4.34	4.10	3.93	3.79	3.68	3.59	3.46	3.31	3.16	3.08	3.00	2.92	2.83	2.75	2.65
18	8.29	6.01	5.09	4.58	4.25	4.01	3.84	3.71	3.60	3.51	3.37	3.23	3.08	3.00	2.92	2.84	2.75	2.66	2.57
19	8.19	5.93	5.01	4.50	4.17	3.94	3.77	3.63	3.52	3.43	3.30	3.15	3.00	2.92	2.84	2.76	2.67	2.58	2.49
20	8.10	5.85	4.94	4.43	4.10	3.87	3.70	3.56	3.46	3.37	3.23	3.09	2.94	2.86	2.78	2.69	2.61	2.52	2.42
21	8.02	5.78	4.87	4.37	4.04	3.81	3.64	3.51	3.40	3.31	3.17	3.03	2.88	2.80	2.72	2.64	2.55	2.46	2.36
22	7.95	5.72	4.82	4.31	3.99	3.76	3.59	3.45	3.35	3.26	3.12	2.98	2.83	2.75	2.67	2.58	2.50	2.40	2.31
23	7.88	5.66	4.76	4.26	3.94	3.71	3.54	3.41	3.30	3.21	3.07	2.93	2.78	2.70	2.62	2.54	2.45	2.35	2.26
24	7.82	5.61	4.72	4.22	3.90	3.67	3.50	3.36	3.26	3.17	3.03	2.89	2.74	2.66	2.58	2.49	2.40	2.31	2.21
25	7.77	5.57	4.68	4.18	3.86	3.63	3.46	3.32	3.22	3.13	2.99	2.85	2.70	2.62	2.53	2.45	2.36	2.27	2.17
30	7.56	5.39	4.51	4.02	3.70	3.47	3.30	3.17	3.07	2.98	2.84	2.70	2.55	2.47	2.39	2.30	2.21	2.11	2.01
40	7.31	5.18	4.31	3.83	3.51	3.29	3.12	2.99	2.89	2.80	2.66	2.52	2.37	2.29	2.20	2.11	2.02	1.92	1.80
60	7.08	4.98	4.13	3.65	3.34	3.12	2.95	2.82	2.72	2.63	2.50	2.35	2.20	2.12	2.03	1.94	1.84	1.73	1.60
120	6.85	4.79	3.95	3.48	3.17	2.96	2.79	2.66	2.56	2.47	2.34	2.19	2.03	1.95	1.86	1.76	1.66	1.53	1.38
∞	6.63	4.61	3.78	3.32	3.02	2.80	2.64	2.51	2.41	2.32	2.18	2.04	1.88	1.79	1.70	1.59	1.47	1.32	1.00

TABLE 10. F - DISTRIBUTION VALUE ($\alpha = 0.05$)

Degress of freedom for denominator

	1	2	3	4	5	6	7	8	9	10	12	15	20	24	30	40	60	120	∞
1	161	200	216	225	230	234	237	239	241	242	244	246	248	249	250	251	252	253	254
2	18.5	19.0	19.2	19.2	19.3	19.3	19.4	19.4	19.4	19.4	19.4	19.4	19.4	19.5	19.5	19.5	19.5	19.5	19.5
3	10.1	9.55	9.28	9.12	9.01	8.94	8.89	8.85	8.81	8.79	8.74	8.70	8.66	8.64	8.62	8.59	8.57	8.55	8.53
4	7.71	6.94	6.59	6.39	6.26	6.16	6.09	6.04	6.00	5.96	5.91	5.86	5.80	5.77	5.75	5.72	5.69	5.66	5.63
5	6.61	5.79	5.41	5.19	5.05	4.95	4.88	4.82	4.77	4.74	4.68	4.62	4.56	4.53	4.50	4.46	4.43	4.40	4.37
6	5.99	5.14	4.76	4.53	4.39	4.28	4.21	4.15	4.10	4.06	4.00	3.94	3.87	3.84	3.81	3.77	3.74	3.70	3.67
7	5.59	4.74	4.35	4.12	3.97	3.87	3.79	3.73	3.68	3.64	3.57	3.51	3.44	3.41	3.38	3.34	3.30	3.27	3.23
8	5.32	4.46	4.07	3.84	3.69	3.58	3.50	3.44	3.39	3.35	3.28	3.22	3.15	3.12	3.08	3.04	3.01	2.97	2.93
9	5.12	4.26	3.86	3.63	3.48	3.37	3.29	3.23	3.18	3.14	3.07	3.01	2.94	2.90	2.86	2.83	2.79	2.75	2.71
10	4.96	4.10	3.71	3.48	3.33	3.22	3.14	3.07	3.02	2.98	2.91	2.85	2.77	2.74	2.70	2.66	2.62	2.58	2.54
11	4.84	3.98	3.59	3.36	3.20	3.09	3.01	2.95	2.90	2.85	2.79	2.72	2.65	2.61	2.57	2.53	2.49	2.45	2.40
12	4.75	3.89	3.49	3.26	3.11	3.00	2.91	2.85	2.80	2.75	2.69	2.62	2.54	2.51	2.47	2.43	2.38	2.34	2.30
13	4.67	3.81	3.41	3.18	3.03	2.92	2.83	2.77	2.71	2.67	2.60	2.53	2.46	2.42	2.38	2.34	2.30	2.25	2.21
14	4.60	3.74	3.34	3.11	2.96	2.85	2.76	2.70	2.65	2.60	2.53	2.46	2.39	2.35	2.31	2.27	2.22	2.18	1.13
15	4.45	3.68	3.29	3.06	2.90	2.79	2.71	2.64	2.59	2.54	2.48	2.40	2.33	2.29	2.25	2.20	2.16	2.11	2.07
16	4.49	3.63	3.24	3.01	2.85	2.74	2.66	2.59	2.54	2.49	2.42	2.35	2.28	2.24	2.19	2.15	2.11	2.06	2.01
17	4.45	3.59	3.20	2,96	2.81	2.70	2.61	2.55	2.49	2.45	2.38	2.31	2.23	2.19	2.15	2.10	2.06	2.01	1.96
18	4.41	3.55	3.16	2.93	2.77	2.66	2.58	2.51	2.46	2.41	2.34	2.27	2.19	2.15	2.11	2.06	2.02	1.97	1.92
19	4.38	3.52	3.13	2.90	2.74	2.63	2.54	2.48	2.42	2.38	2.31	2.23	2.16	2.11	2.07	2.03	1.98	1.93	1.88
20	4.35	3.39	3.10	2.87	2.71	2.60	2.51	2.45	2.39	2.35	2.28	2.20	2.12	2.08	2.04	1.99	1.95	1.90	184
21	4.32	3.47	3.07	2.84	2.68	2.57	2.49	2.42	2.37	2.32	2.25	2.18	2.10	2.05	2.01	1.96	1.92	1.87	1.81
22	4.30	3.44	3.05	2.82	2.66	2.55	2.46	2.40	2.34	2.30	2.23	2.15	2.07	2.03	1.98	1.94	1.89	1.84	1.78
23	4.28	3.42	3.03	2.80	2.64	2.53	2.44	2.37	2.32	2.27	2.20	2.13	2.05	2.01	1 96	1.91	1.86	1.81	1.76
24	4,26	3.40	3.01	2.78	2.62	2.51	2.42	2.36	2.30	2.25	2.18	2 11	2.03	1.98	1.94	1.89	1.84	1.79	1.73
25	4.24	3.39	2.99	2.76	2.60	2.49	2.40	2.34	2.28	2.24	2.16	2.09	2.01	1.96	1.92	1.87	1.82	1.77	1.71
30	4.17	3.32	2.92	2.69	2.53	2.42	2.33	2.27	2.21	2.16	2.09	2.01	1.93	1.89	1.84	1.79	1.74	1.68	1.62
40	4.08	3.23	2.84	2.61	2.45	2.34	2.25	2.18	2 12	2.08	2.00	1 92	1.84	1.79	1.74	1.69	1.64	1.58	1.51
60	4.00	3.15	2.76	2.53	2.37	2.25	217	2.10	2.04	1.99	1.92	1 84	1.75	1.70	1.65	1.59	1.53	1.47	1.39
120	3.92	3.07	2.68	2.45	2.29	2.18	2.09	2.02	1.96	1.91	1.83	1.75	1.66	1.61	1.55	1.50	1.43	1.35	1.25
∞	3.84	3.00	2.60	2.37	2.20	2.10	2.01	1.94	1.88	1.83	1.75	1.67	1.57	1.52	1.46	1.39	1.32	1.22	1.00

TABLE 11 : Values for D in the Kolmogorov goodness of fit test

Sample Size (n)	Level of Significance for D = Maximum $f_e - f_o$ 0.20	0.15	0.10	0.05	0.01
1	0.900	0.925	0.950	0.975	0.995
2	0.684	0.726	0.776	0.842	0.929
3	0.565	0.597	0.642	0.708	0.828
4	0.494	0.525	0.564	0.624	0.733
5	0.446	0.474	0.510	0.565	0.669
6	0.410	0.436	0.470	0.521	0.618
7	0.381	0.405	0.438	0.486	0.577
8	0.358	0.381	0.411	0.457	0.543
9	0.339	0.360	0.388	0.432	0.514
10	0.322	0.342	0.368	0.410	0.490
11	0.307	0.326	0.352	0.391	0.468
12	0.295	0.313	0.338	0.375	0.450
13	0.284	0.302	0.325	0.361	0.433
14	0.274	0.292	0.314	0.349	0.418
15	0.266	0.283	0.304	0.338	0.404
16	0.258	0.274	0.295	0.328	0.392
17	0.250	0.266	0.286	0.318	0.381
18	0.244	0.259	0.278	0.309	0.371
19	0.237	0.252	0.272	0.301	0.363
20	0.231	0.246	0.264	0.294	0.356
25	0.21	0.22	0.24	0.27	0.32
30	0.19	0.20	0.22	0.24	0.29
35	0.18	0.19	0.21	0.23	0.27
Over 35	$\frac{1.07}{\sqrt{n}}$	$\frac{1.14}{\sqrt{n}}$	$\frac{1.22}{\sqrt{n}}$	$\frac{1.36}{\sqrt{n}}$	$\frac{1.63}{\sqrt{n}}$

Note : The values of *D* given in the table are critical values associated with selected values of *n*. Any value of D that is greater than or equal to the tabulated values is significant at the indicated level of significance.

Table 12 : Control Chart Factors

Sample Size, n	Factors for $\bar{x}$ Charts: $d_2 = \frac{R}{\sigma}$	$A_2 = \frac{3}{d_2\sqrt{n}}$	$d_3 = \frac{\sigma_R}{\sigma}$	Factors for R Charts: $D_3 = 1 - \frac{3d_3}{d_2}$	$D_4 = 1 + \frac{3d_3}{d_2}$
2	1.128	1.881	0.853	0	3.269
3	1.693	1.023	0.883	0	2.574
4	2.059	0.729	0.880	0	2.282
5	2.326	0.577	0.864	0	2.114
6	2.534	0.483	0.848	0	2.004
7	2.704	0.419	0.833	0.076	1.924
8	2.847	0.373	0.820	0.136	1.864
9	2.970	0.337	0.808	0.184	1.816
10	3.078	0.308	0.797	0.223	1.777
11	3.173	0.285	0.787	0.256	1.744
12	3.258	0.266	0.779	0.283	1.717
13	3.336	0.249	0.770	0.308	1.692
14	3.407	0.235	0.763	0.328	1.672
15	3.472	0.223	0.756	0.347	1.653
16	3.532	0.212	0.750	0.363	1.637
17	3.588	0.203	0.744	0.378	1.622
18	3.640	0.194	0.739	0.391	1.609
19	3.689	0.187	0.734	0.403	1.597
20	3.735	0.180	0.729	0.414	1.586
21	3.778	0.173	0.724	0.425	1.575
22	3.819	0.167	0.720	0.434	1.566
23	3.858	0.162	0.716	0.443	1.567
24	3.895	0.157	0.712	0.452	1.548
25	3.931	0.153	0.708	0.460	1.540

Note : If $1 - 3d_3/d_2 < 0$, then $D_3 = 0$

Table 13 : Logarithms

	0	1	2	3	4	5	6	7	8	9	Mean Differences								
											1	2	3	4	5	6	7	8	9
10	0000	0043	0086	0128	0170	0212	0253	0294	0334	0374	4	8	12	17	21	25	29	33	34
11	0414	0453	0492	0531	0569	0607	0645	0682	0719	0755	4	8	11	15	19	23	26	30	31
12	0792	0828	0864	0899	0934	0969	1004	1038	1072	1106	3	7	10	14	17	21	24	28	29
13	1139	1173	1206	1239	1271	1303	1335	1367	1399	1430	3	6	10	13	16	19	23	26	27
14	1461	1492	1523	1553	1584	1614	1644	1673	1703	1732	3	6	9	12	15	18	21	24	25
15	1761	1790	1818	1847	1875	1903	1931	1959	1987	2014	3	6	8	11	14	17	20	22	24
16	2041	2068	2095	2122	2148	2175	2201	2227	2253	2279	3	5	8	11	13	16	18	21	22
17	2304	2330	2355	2380	2405	2430	2455	2480	2504	2529	2	5	7	10	12	15	17	20	21
18	2553	2577	2601	2625	2648	2672	2695	2718	2742	2765	2	5	7	9	12	14	16	19	20
19	2788	2810	2833	2856	2878	2900	2923	2945	2967	2989	2	4	7	9	11	13	16	18	19
20	3010	3032	3054	3075	3096	3118	3139	3160	3181	3201	2	4	6	8	11	13	15	17	18
21	3222	3243	3263	3284	3304	3324	3345	3365	3385	3404	2	4	6	8	10	12	14	16	17
22	3424	3444	3464	3483	3502	3522	3541	3560	3579	3598	2	4	6	8	10	12	14	15	17
23	3617	3636	3655	3674	3692	3711	3729	3747	3766	3784	2	4	6	7	9	11	13	15	16
24	3802	3820	3838	3856	3874	3892	3909	3927	3945	3962	2	4	5	7	9	11	12	14	15
25	3979	3997	4014	4031	4048	4065	4082	4099	4116	4133	2	3	5	7	9	10	12	14	15
26	4150	4166	4183	4200	4216	4232	4249	4265	4281	4298	2	3	5	7	8	10	11	13	14
27	4314	4330	4346	4362	4378	4393	4409	4425	4440	4456	2	3	5	6	8	9	11	13	14
28	4472	4487	4502	4518	4533	4548	4564	4579	4594	4609	2	3	5	6	8	9	11	12	13
29	4624	4639	4654	4669	4683	4698	4713	4728	4742	4757	1	3	4	6	7	9	10	12	13
30	4771	4786	4800	4814	4829	4843	4857	4871	4886	4900	1	3	4	6	7	9	10	11	12
31	4914	4928	4942	4955	4969	4983	4997	5011	5024	5038	1	3	4	6	7	8	10	11	12
32	5051	5065	5079	5092	5105	5119	5132	5145	5159	5172	1	3	4	5	7	8	9	11	12
33	5185	5198	5211	5224	5237	5250	5263	5276	5289	5302	1	3	4	5	6	8	9	10	11
34	5315	5328	5340	5353	5366	5378	5391	5403	5416	5428	1	3	4	5	6	8	9	10	11
35	5441	5453	5465	5478	5490	5502	5514	5527	5539	5551	1	2	4	5	6	7	9	10	11
36	5563	5575	5587	5599	5611	5623	5635	5647	5658	5670	1	2	4	5	6	7	8	10	11
37	5682	5694	5705	5717	5729	5740	5752	5763	5775	5786	1	2	3	5	6	7	8	9	10
38	5798	5809	5821	5832	5843	5855	5866	5877	5888	5899	1	2	3	5	6	7	8	9	10
39	5911	5922	5933	5944	5955	5966	5977	5988	5999	6010	1	2	3	4	5	7	8	9	10
40	6021	6031	6042	6053	6064	6075	6085	6096	6107	6117	1	2	3	4	6	6	8	9	10
41	6128	6138	6149	6160	6170	6180	6191	6201	6212	6222	1	2	3	4	5	6	7	8	9
42	6232	6243	6253	6263	6274	6284	6294	6304	6314	6325	1	2	3	4	5	6	7	8	9
43	6335	6345	6355	6365	6375	6385	6395	6405	6415	6425	1	2	3	4	5	6	7	8	9
44	6435	6444	6454	6464	6474	6484	6493	6503	6513	6522	1	2	3	4	5	6	7	8	9
45	6532	6542	6551	6561	6571	6580	6590	6599	6609	6618	1	2	3	4	5	6	7	8	9
46	6628	6637	6646	6656	6665	6675	6684	6693	6702	6712	1	2	3	4	5	6	7	7	8
47	6721	6730	6739	6749	6758	6767	6776	6785	6794	6803	1	2	3	4	5	5	6	7	8
48	6812	6821	6830	6839	6848	6857	6866	6875	6884	6893	1	2	3	4	4	5	6	7	8
49	6902	6911	6920	6928	6937	6946	6955	6964	6972	6981	1	2	3	4	4	5	6	7	8
50	6990	6998	7007	7016	7024	7033	7042	7050	7059	7067	1	2	3	3	4	5	6	7	8
51	7076	7084	7093	7101	7110	7118	7126	7135	7143	7152	1	2	3	3	4	5	6	7	8
52	7160	7168	7177	7185	7193	7202	7210	7218	7226	7235	1	2	2	3	4	5	6	7	7
53	7243	7251	7259	7267	7275	7284	7292	7300	7308	7316	1	2	2	3	4	5	6	6	7
54	7324	7332	7340	7348	7356	7364	7372	7380	7388	7396	1	2	2	3	4	5	6	6	7

Table 13 : (Continued)

	0	1	2	3	4	5	6	7	8	9	Mean Differences								
											1	2	3	4	5	6	7	8	9
55	7404	7412	7419	7427	7435	7443	7451	7459	7466	7474	1	2	2	3	4	5	5	6	7
56	7482	7490	7497	7505	7513	7520	7528	7536	7543	7551	1	2	2	3	4	5	5	6	7
57	7559	7566	7574	7582	7589	7597	7604	7612	7619	7627	1	2	2	3	4	5	5	6	7
58	7634	7642	7649	7657	7664	7672	7679	7686	7694	7701	1	1	2	3	4	4	5	6	7
59	7709	7716	7723	7731	7738	7745	7752	7760	7767	7774	1	1	2	3	4	4	5	6	7
60	7782	7789	7796	7803	7810	7818	7825	7632	7839	7846	1	1	2	3	4	4	5	6	6
61	7853	7860	7868	7875	7882	7889	7896	7903	7910	7917	1	1	2	3	4	4	5	6	6
62	7924	7931	7938	7945	7952	7959	7966	7973	7980	7987	1	1	2	3	3	4	5	6	6
63	7993	8000	8007	8014	8021	8028	8035	8041	8048	8055	1	1	2	3	3	4	5	5	6
64	8062	8069	8075	8082	8089	8096	8102	8109	8116	8122	1	1	2	3	3	4	5	5	6
65	8129	8136	8142	8149	8156	8162	8169	8176	8182	8189	1	1	2	3	3	4	5	5	6
66	8195	8202	8209	8215	8222	8228	8235	8241	8248	8254	1	1	2	3	3	4	5	5	6
67	8261	8267	8274	8280	8287	8293	8299	8306	8312	8319	1	1	2	3	3	4	5	5	6
68	8325	8331	8338	8344	8351	8357	8363	8370	8376	8382	1	1	2	3	3	4	4	5	6
69	8388	8395	8401	8407	8414	8420	8426	8432	8439	8445	1	1	2	2	3	4	4	5	6
70	8451	8457	8463	8470	8476	9482	8488	8494	8500	8506	1	1	2	2	3	4	4	5	6
71	8513	8519	8525	8531	8537	8543	8549	8555	8561	8567	1	1	2	2	3	4	4	5	5
72	8573	8579	8585	8591	8597	8603	8609	8615	8621	8627	1	1	2	2	3	4	4	5	5
73	8633	8639	8645	8651	8657	8663	8669	8675	8681	8686	1	1	2	2	3	4	4	5	5
74	8692	8698	8704	8710	8716	8722	8727	8733	8739	8745	1	1	2	2	3	4	4	5	5
75	8751	8756	8762	8768	8774	8779	8785	8791	8797	8802	1	1	2	2	3	3	4	5	5
76	8808	8814	8820	8825	8831	8837	8842	8848	8854	8859	1	1	2	2	3	3	4	5	5
77	8865	8871	8876	8882	8887	8893	8899	8904	8910	8915	1	1	2	2	3	3	4	4	5
78	8921	8927	8932	8938	8943	8949	8954	8960	8965	8971	1	1	2	2	3	3	4	4	5
79	8976	8982	8987	8993	8998	9004	9009	9015	9020	9025	1	1	2	2	3	3	4	4	5
80	9031	9036	9042	9047	9053	9068	9063	9069	9074	9079	1	1	2	2	3	3	4	4	5
81	9085	9090	9096	9101	9106	9112	9117	9122	9128	9133	1	1	2	2	3	3	4	4	5
82	9138	9143	9149	9154	9159	9165	9170	9175.	9180	9186	1	1	2	2	3	3	4	4	5
83	9191	9196	9201	9206	9212	9217	9222	9227	9232	9238	1	1	2	2	3	3	4	4	5
84	9243	9248	9253	9258	9263	9269	9274	9279	9284	9289	1	1	2	2	3	3	4	4	5
85	9294	9299	9304	9309	9315	9320	9325	9330	9335	9340	1	1	2	2	3	3	4	4	5
86	9345	9350	9355	9360	9365	9370	9375	9380	9385	9390	1	1	2	2	3	3	4	4	5
87	9395	9400	9405	9410	9415	9420	9425	9430	9435	9440	0	1	1	2	2	3	3	4	4
88	9445	9450	9455	9460	9465	9469	9474	9479	9484	9489	0	1	1	2	2	3	3	4	4
89	9494	9499	9504	9509	9513	9518	9523	9528	9533	9538	0	1	1	2	2	3	3	4	4
90	9542	9547	9552	9557	9562	9566	9571	9576	9581	9586	0	1	1	2	2	3	3	4	4
91	9590	9595	9600	9605	9609	9614	9619	9624	9628	9633	0	1	1	2	2	3	3	4	4
92	9638	9643	9647	9652	9657	9661	9666	9671	9675	9680	0	1	1	2	2	3	3	4	4
93	9685	9689	9694	9699	9703	9708	9713	9717	9722	9727	0	1	1	2	2	3	3	4	4
94	9731	9736	9741	9745	9750	9754	9759	9763	9768	9773	0	1	1	2	2	3	3	4	4
95	9777	9782	9786	9791	9795	9800	9805	9809	9814	9878	0	1	1	2	2	3	3	4	4
96	9823	9827	9832	9836	9841	9845	9850	9854	9859	9863	0	1	1	2	2	3	3	4	4
97	9868	9872	9877	9881	9886	9890	9894	9899	9903	9908	0	1	1	2	2	3	3	4	4
98	9912	9917	9921	9926	9930	9934	9939	9943	.9948	9952	0	1	1	2	2	3	3	4	4
99	9956	9961	9965	9969	9974	9978	9983	9987	9991	9996	0	1	1	2	2	3	3	3	4

Table 14 : Anti-logarithms

	0	1	2	3	4	5	6	7	8	9	Mean Differences								
											1	2	3	4	5	6	7	8	9
.00	1000	1002	1005	1007	1009	1012	1014	1016	1019	1021	0	0	1	1	1	1	2	2	2
.01	1023	1026	1028	1030	1033	1035	1038	1040	1042	1045	0	0	1	1	1	1	2	2	2
.02	1047	1050	1052	1054	1057	1059	1062	1064	1067	1069	0	0	1	1	1	1	2	2	2
.03	1072	1074	1076	1079	1081	1084	1086	1089	1091	1094	0	0	1	1	1	1	2	2	2
.04	1096	1099	1102	1104	,1107	1109	1112	1114	1117	1119	0	1	1	1	1	2	2	2	2
.05	1122	1125	1127	1130	1132	1135	1138	1140	1143	1146	0	1	1	1	1	2	2	2	2
.06	1148	1151	1153	1156	1159	1161	1164	1167	1169	1172	0	1	1	1	1	2	2	2	2
.07	1175	1178	1180	1163	1186	1189	1191	1194	1197	1199	0	1	1	1	1	2	2	2	2
.08	1202	1205	1208	1211	1213	1216	1219	1222	12?.5	1227	0	1	1	1	1	2	2	2	3
.09	1230	1233	1236	1239	1242	1245	1247	1250	1253	1256	0	1	1	1	1	2	2	2	3
.10	1259	1262	1265	1268	1271	1274	1276	1279	1282	1285	0	1	1	1	1	2	2	2	3
.11	1288	1291	1294	1297	1300	1303	1306	1309	1312	1315	0	1	1	1	2	2	2	2	3
.12	1318	1321	1324	1327	1330	1334	1337	1340	1343	1346	0	1	1	1	2	2	2	2	3
.13	1349	1352	1355	1358	1361	1365	1368	1371	1374	1377	0	1	1	1	2	2	2	3	3
.14	1380	1384	1387	1390	1393	1396	1400	1403	1406	1409	0	1	1	1	2	2	2	3	3
.15	1413	1416	1419	1422	1426	1429	1432	1435	1439	1442	0	1	1	1	2	2	2	3	3
.16	1445	1449	1452	1455	1459	1462	1466	1469	1472	1476	0	1	1	1	2	2	2	3	3
.17	1479	1483	1486	1489	1493	1496	1500	1503	1507	1510	0	1	1	1	2	2	2	3	3
.18	1514	1517	1521	1524	1528	1531	1535	1538	1542	1545	0	1	1	1	2	2	2	3	3
.19	1549	1552	1556	1560	1563	1567	1570	1574	1578	1581	0	1	1	1	2	2	3	3	3
.20	1585	1589	1592	1596	1600	1603	1607	1611	1614	1618	0	1	1	1	2	2	3	3	3
.21	1622	1626	1629	1633	1637	1641	1644	1648	1652	1656	0	1	1	2	2	2	3	3	3
.22	1660	1663	1667	1671	1675	1679	1683	1687	1690	1694	0	1	1	2	2	2	3	3	3
.23	1698	1702	1706	1710	1714	1718	1722	1726	1730	1734	0	1	1	2	2	2	3	3	4
.24	1738	1742	1746	1750	1754	1758	1762	1766	1770	1774	0	1	1	2	2	2	3	3	4
.25	1778	1782	1786	1791	1795	1799	1803	1807	1811	1816	0	1	1	2	2	2	3	3	4
.26	1820	1824	1828	1832	1837	1841	1845	1849	1854	1858	0	1	1	2	2	3	3	3	4
.27	1862	1866	1871	1875	1879	1884	1888	1892	1897	1901	0	1	1	2	2	3	3	3	4
.28	1905	1910	1914	1919	1923	1928	1932	1936	1941	1945	0	1	1	2	2	3	3	4	4
.29	1950	1954	1959	1963	1968	1972	1977	1982	1986	1991	0	1	1	2	2	3	3	4	4
.30	1995	2000	2004	2009	2014	2018	2023	2028	2032	2037	0	1	1	2	2	3	3	4	4
.31	2042	2046	2051	2056	2061	2065	2070	2075	2080	2084	0	1	1	2	2	3	3	4	4
.32	2089	2094	2099	2104	2109	2113	2118	2123	2128	2133	0	1	1	2	2	3	3	4	4
.33	2138	2143	2148	2153	2158	2163	2168	2173	2178	2183	0	1	1	2	2	3	3	4	4
.34	2188	2193	2198	2203	2208	2213	2218	2223	2228	2234	1	1	2	2	3	3	4	4	5
.35	2239	2244	2249	2254	2259	2265	2270	2275	2280	2286	1	1	2	2	3	3	4	4	5
.36	2291	2296	2301	2307	2312	2317	2323	2328	2333	2339	1	1	2	2	3	3	4	4	5
.37	2344	2350	2355	2360	2366	2371	2377	2382	2388	2393	1	1	2	2	3	3	4	4	5
.38	2399	2404	2410	2415	2421	2427	2432	2438	2443	2449	1	1	2	2	3	3	4	4	5
.39	2455	2460	2466	2472	2477	2483	2489	2495	2500	2506	1	1	2	2	3	3	4	5	5
.40	2512	2518	2523	2529	2535	2541	2547	2553	2559	2564	1	1	2	2	3	4	4	5	5
.41	2570	2576	2582	2588	2594	2600	2606	2612	2618	2624	1	1	2	2	3	4	4	5	5
.42	2630	2636	2642	2649	2655	2661	2667	2673	2679	2685	1	1	2	2	3	4	4	5	6
.43	2692	2698	2704	2710	2716	2723	2729	2735	2742	2748	1	1	2	3	3	4	4	5	6
.44	2754	2761	2767	2773	2780	2786	2793	2799	2805	2812	1	1	2	3	3	4	4	5	6
.45	2818	2825	2831	2838	2844	2851	2858	2864	2871	2877	1	1	2	3	3	4	5	5	6
.46	2884	2891	2897	2904	2911	2917	2924	2931	2938	2944	1	1	2	3	3	4	5	5	6
.47	2951	2958	2965	2972	2979	2985	2992	2999	3006	3013	1	1	2	3	3	4	5	5	6
.48	3020	3027	3034	3041	3048	3055	3062	3069	3076	3083	1	1	2	3	4	4	5	6	6
.49	3090	3097	3105	3112	3119	3126	3133	3141	3148	3155	1	1	2	3	4	4	5	6	6

Table 14 : (Continued)

	0	1	2	3	4	5	6	7	8	9	Mean Differences 1	2	3	4	5	6	7	8	9
.50	3162	3170	3177	3184	3192	3199	3206	3214	3221	3228	1	1	2	3	4	4	5	6	7
.51	3236	3243	3251	3258	3266	3273	3281	3289	3296	3304	1	2	2	3	4	5	5	6	7
.52	3311	3319	3327	3334	3342	3350	3357	3365	3373	3381	1	2	2	3	4	5	5	6	7
.53	3388	3396	3404	3412	3420	3428	3436	3443	3451	3459	1	2	2	3	4	5	6	6	7
.54	3467	3475	3483	3491	3499	3508	3516	3524	3532	3540	1	2	2	3	4	5	6	6	7
.55	3548	3556	3565	3573	3581	3589	3597	3606	3614	3622	1	2	2	3	4	5	6	7	7
.56	3631	3639	3648	3656	3664	3673	3681	3690	3698	3707	1	2	3	3	4	5	6	7	8
.57	3715	3724	3733	3741	3750	3758	3767	3776	3784	3793	1	2	3	3	4	5	6	7	8
.58	3802	3811	3819	3828	3837	3846	3855	3864	3873	3882	1	2	3	4	4	5	6	7	8
.59	3890	3899	3908	3917	3926	3936	3945	3954	3963	3972	1	2	3	4	5	5	6	7	8
.60	3981	3990	3999	4009	4018	4027	4036	4046	4055	4064	1	2	3	4	5	6	6	7	8
.61	4074	4083	4093	4102	4111	4121	4130	4140	4150	4159	1	2	3	4	5	6	7	8	9
.62	4169	4178	4188	4198	4207	4217	4227	4236	4246	4256	1	2	3	4	5	6	7	8	9
.63	4266	4276	4285	4295	4305	4315	4325	4335	4345	4355	1	2	3	4	5	6	7	8	9
.64	4365	4375	4385	4395	4406	4416	4426	4436	4446	4457	1	2	3	4	5	6	7	8	9
.65	4467	4477	4487	4498	4508	4519	4529	4539	4550	4560	1	2	3	4	5	6	7	8	9
.66	4571	4581	4592	4603	4613	4624	4634	4645	4656	4667	1	2	3	4	5	6	7	9	10
.67	4677	4688	4699	4710	4721	4732	4742	4753	4764	4775	1	2	3	4	5	7	8	9	10
.68	4786	4797	4808	4819	4831	4842	4853	4864	4875	4887	1	2	3	4	6	7	8	9	10
.69	4898	4909	4920	4932	4943	4955	4966	4977	4989	5000	1	2	3	5	6	7	8	9	10
.70	5012	5023	5035	5047	5058	5070	5082	5093	5105	5117	1	2	4	5	6	7	8	9	11
.71	5129	5140	5152	5164	5176	5188	5200	5212	5224	5236	1	2	4	5	6	7	8	10	11
.72	5248	5260	5272	5284	5297	5309	5321	5333	5346	5358	1	2	4	5	6	7	9	10	11
.73	5370	5383	5395	5408	5420	5433	5445	5458	5470	5483	1	3	4	5	6	8	9	10	11
.74	5495	5508	5521	5534	5546	5559	5572	5585	5598	5610	1	3	4	5	6	8	9	10	12
.75	5623	5636	5649	5662	5675	5689	5702	5715	5728	5741	1	3	4	5	7	8	9	10	12
.76	5754	5768	5781	5794	5808	5821	5834	5848	5861	5875	1	3	4	5	7	8	9	11	12
.77	5888	5902	5916	5929	5943	5957	5970	5984	5998	6012	1	3	4	5	7	8	10	11	12
.78	6026	6039	6053	6067	6081	6095	6109	6124	6138	6152	1	3	4	6	7	8	10	11	13
.79	6160	6180	6194	6209	6223	6237	6252	6266	6281	6295	1	3	4	6	7	9	10	11	13
.80	6310	6324	6339	6353	6368	6383	6397	6412	6427	6442	1	3	4	6	7	9	10	12	13
.81	6457	6471	6486	6501	6516	6531	6546	6561	6577	6592	2	3	5	6	8	9	11	12	14
.82	6607	6622	6637	6653	6668	6683	6699	6714	6730	6745	2	3	5	6	8	9	11	12	14
.83	6761	6776	6792	6808	6823	6839	6855	6871	6887	6902	2	3	5	6	8	9	11	13	14
.84	6918	6934	6950	6966	6982	6998	7015	7031	7047	7063	2	3	5	6	8	10	11	13	15
.85	7079	7096	7112	7129	7145	7161	7178	7194	7211	7228	2	3	5	7	8	10	12	13	15
.86	7244	7261	7278	7295	7311	7328	7345	7362	7379	7396	2	3	5	7	8	10	12	13	15
.87	7413	7430	7447	7464	7482	7499	7516	7534	7551	7568	2	3	5	7	9	10	12	14	16
.88	7586	7603	7621	7638	7656	7674	7691	7709	7727	7745	2	4	5	7	9	11	12	14	16
.89	7762	7780	7798	7816	7834	7852	7870	7889	7907	7925	2	4	5	7	9	11	13	14	16
.90	7943	7962	7980	7998	8017	8035	8054	8072	8091	8110	2	4	6	7	9	11	13	15	17
.91	8128	8147	8166	8185	8204	8222	8241	8260	8279	8299	2	4	6	8	9	11	13	15	17
.92	8318	8337	8356	8375	8395	8414	8433	8453	8472	8492	2	4	6	8	10	12	14	15	17
.93	8511	8531	8551	8570	8590	8610	8630	8650	8670	8690	2	4	6	8	10	12	14	16	18
.94	8710	8730	8750	8770	8790	8810	8831	8851	8872	8892	2	4	6	8	10	12	14	16	18
.95	8913	8933	8954	8974	8995	9016	9036	9057	9078	9099	2	4	6	8	10	12	15	17	19
.96	9120	9141	9162	9183	9204	9226	9247	9268	9290	9311	2	4	6	8	11	13	15	17	19
.97	9333	9354	9376	9397	9419	9441	9462	9484	9506	9528	2	4	7	9	11	13	15	17	20
.98	9550	9572	9594	9616	9638	9651	9683	9705	9727	9750	2	4	7	9	11	13	16	18	20
.99	9772	9795	9817	9840	9863	9886	9908	9931	9954	9977	2	5	7	9	11	14	16	18	20

ANNEXURE 'A'

List of Computer Programmes Recommended

1. Lotfit and Pagel's Software Package
2. IFPS/Optimum [Comshare Inc. (LP Integer)]
3. MPI–MP8 [SCI Computing, Wilmette II]
4. LINDO, LINDO/PC, GINO, VINO [LINDO System Inc.]
5. MPS III [Ketron Inc. Arlington, Va]
7. GAMS/MINOS [IBM, Armonk, NY]
8. LP83, MIP 83, XA [Stanford University, California]
9. XPRESS MP [Sunset Software, San Marino]
10. CPLEX [Data Assoc. Ltd./Math PRO, Washington]
11. SAS/OR [CPLEX Optimisation Inc. Houston]
12. Criterium [SAS Institute, Cary, NC]
13. Decision Master [Sygenex, Redmond, Washington]
14. Decision AID [Generic Software Construction Inc. NY]
15. Decision AID II [Kepner – Tregue Inc. Princeton]
16. Decision PAD [Apian Software, Menlon Parkm, Calif]
17. Logical Decision [Logical Decision Inc. Point Richmond, VA]
18. Light Year [Light Year Inc. Point Richmond, VA]
19. Orion [Comshare Inc. Ann Arbov, Mich]
20. SMART Edge [Hariland – Lee Inc. Pasadena Calif]
21. SUPER TREE [SDG Decision System, Menlo Partk Calif]
22. Arborist [Texas Instruments, Dallas, Texas]
23. Decision 1-2-Tree [Fast Division System, Cambridge]
24. MSS Package [Nelson S.T. Homewood]
25. Autobox, Boxx [Automatic Forecasting System, Inc.]
26. EXEC $^{x}U^{x}$ STAT [EXEC $^{x}U^{x}$ STAT, Inc. Princeton]
27. Fore Cale, Forecast Pro [Business Forecast Systems]
28. Forecast GFX [Index Solutions, Needham]
29. Forecast Master [Scientific Systems Inc. Cambridge]
30. Forecast Plus [Walonick Assoc Inc. Pittsberg]
31. Smart Forecast [Smart Software Inc.]
32. 1-2-3 Forecast [1-2-3 Forecast, Salem]

33. MS Project [Microsoft Corp. Northup way]
34. Primavera R-3
35. The Project Manager [Wiley Professional Software]
36. Project Manager IBM [IIE, Norcross]
37. Project Scheduler Network [Scitor Crop. Foster City]
38. Harvard Project Manager (HMP) [Software Publishing Co. Mountain View]
39. Mac Project [Apple Computer Inc. Cupertino, Calif]
40. PC MIS [Davis and Associates, Atlanta]
41. Scheduling and Control [Softext Publishing Co. New York]
42. MRP Packages by IMB, Xexor, Mirco MRP, CINCOH and UNISYS etc.
43. SAS/OR [SAS Institute, Carry NC]
44. M^x/D/C [A and A Publications, Kindgston, Ontario]
45. FACTOR [Prisker Co. Indianpolis. IN]
46. GPSS/H [Wolverine Software Annadale, VA]
47. GPSS/PC [Wolverin Software, Stow]
48. GPSS [IBM]
49. SIGMA [Scientific Press, San Francisco]
50. SIM Factory [CACI, La Jolla, LA]

INDEX

E

F

G

H

I

J

K

L

M

N

O

P

Q

R

S

T

U

V

W

X

Y

Z

BIBLIOGRAPHY

1. The History of Statistics by Stigler, Cambidge MA, Belknap Press, 1986
2. Statistical Quality Control by Grant LE and RC Leavenworth, McGraw-Hill Book Co., 1996
3. The Visual Display of Quantitative Information by Tufte, E.R. Graphics Press, 1983
4. Probability by Rowntree, D. Charles Scribner's Sons, 1984
5. Statistics for Management, by Levin RI and DS Rubin, Prentice Hall (India), 1997
6. Business Statistics – "Decision Making with Data", by Johnson, R.A. and DW Wichern, John Wiley and sons, Inc. 2003.
7. Theory of Sampling by Deming, W.E. John Wiley and Sons.
8. Economic Control of Quality of Manufactured Products; by Schewhart W.A, Van Nostrand, 1931
9. Statitics for Applied Economics and Business by Mills, R.L. McGraw Hill Book Co.
10. Quantitative Methods of Decision Making in Business by Trueman, R.E. Half Saundss, NewYork, 1981.